MODELS OF MANAGEMENT

MODELS OF MANAGEMENT

Work, Authority, and Organization in a Comparative Perspective

MAURO F. GUILLÉN

The University of Chicago Press • Chicago and London

MAURO F. GUILLÉN is assistant professor of international
management and sociology in the Sloan School of
Management at the Massachusetts Institute of Technology.

The University of Chicago Press, Chicago 60637
The University of Chicago Press, Ltd., London
© 1994 by The University of Chicago
All rights reserved. Published 1994
Printed in the United States of America
03 02 01 00 99 98 97 96 95 94   1 2 3 4 5

ISBN: 0-226-31035-3 (cloth)
       0-226-31036-1 (paper)

Library of Congress Cataloging-in-Publication Data

Guillén, Mauro F.
    Models of management : work, authority, and
organization in a comparative perspective / Mauro F.
Guillén.
        p.   cm.
    Includes bibliographical references and index.
    1. Comparative management.   2. Organizational
sociology.   I. Title.
    HD30.55.G85   1994
    658—dc20   94-3887
                                                 CIP

Contents

v

FIVE

Great Britain / 205
Industrial Retardation, Religious-Humanist Ideals, and the Rise of Social Science

SIX

Comparing Patterns of Adoption / 266

SEVEN

A Historical and Comparative Perspective on *Homo Hierarchicus* / 281

FIGURES AND TABLES

PREFACE AND ACKNOWLEDGMENTS

Authority and organization seem to be indispensable features of modern, bureaucratized economic activity. Historically, varying structural and institutional conditions by country have produced different models of organizational management. This book is a comparative sociological study of the adoption of scientific management, human relations, and structural analysis as paradigms of organization in the United States, Germany, Spain, and Great Britain over the last century. It explores how managers and employers perceive and solve organizational problems related to the maintenance of authority in the workplace and the management of organizations.

This book both presents fresh evidence and makes arguments that invite the reader to see old problems in a new light. The major thesis is that the adoption of models of organizational management during the twentieth century cannot be explained solely by reference to the scientific value of the theories supporting them or to purely economic or technological factors. Institutional factors play a key role in their adoption. In the last chapter, current paradigms of organization, such as organizational culture, lean production, and total quality management are discussed to ascertain whether the evolution of organizational paradigms exhibits a cyclical pattern. The book concludes with an analysis of the relationship between managerial ideologies and the political order. The evidence presented shows that the dominant pattern of politics sets limits to the repertoire of organizational approaches that are either possible or necessary, while the characteristic mode of thought affects the choice of alternatives by managers and firms.

I started working on this project in January of 1990 as a graduate student in Sociology at Yale University. I have been fortunate to receive support and encouragement from a huge number of people and institutions in the United States, Germany, Britain, and Spain. None of them is responsible for the imperfections of this book. I have received helpful information, suggestions, and comments on different parts of the project from a large number of colleagues: Rikki Abzug,

Nicola Beisel, Daniel Bell, Neil Bennett, Steve Brint, José Manuel Campa, Alvaro Cuervo, Juan Díez Medrano, Kai Erikson, Robert Fishman, Julio García Cobos, Bradford Gray, Ana Guillén, Rodolfo Gutiérrez, Robert Jenkins, Charles Kadushin, Bruce Kogut, Emmanuel Lazega, Donald Lessard, Richard Locke, Lee Miller, John Mohr, William Ocasio, Jeffrey Olick, Víctor Pérez Díaz, Michael Piore, William Pounds, Walter Powell, Josep Rodríguez, Edgar Schein, Dimitrios Sotiropoulos, Robert Thomas, John Van Maanen, Eleanor Westney, JoAnne Yates, and Nicholas Ziegler. Edward Bowman of the University of Pennsylvania, Alfred Kieser of Universität Mannheim, John Meyer of Stanford University, Neil Smelser of the University of California at Berkeley (as a referee), and Mayer Zald of the University of Michigan (as a referee) provided detailed comments and suggestions on the entire manuscript. Thanks are also due to Allan Bogue of the University of Wisconsin–Madison, the chair of the jury that honored this book with the President's Book Award for 1993 of the Social Science History Association, and to Carol Heimer of Northwestern University, the chair of the American Sociological Association committee that voted this study a finalist in the Best Dissertation Award 1993. I am grateful as well to Yale's Sociology Department for awarding my thesis the Marvin B. Sussman Prize. Finally, my friends and colleagues Ruth Aguilera, María Eugenia Arias, Mayder Dravasa, and Herminia Ibarra have given me great professional advice, comments, and support.

I tested parts of this study in front of demanding faculty and graduate-student audiences in the Sociology Departments at the universities of Arizona, California at Irvine, California at San Diego, Minnesota, and Northwestern, as well as at The Minda de Gunzburg Center for European Studies at Harvard, the Center for Advanced Study in the Social Sciences at the Juan March Foundation in Madrid, the European Institute of Business Administration (INSEAD) in Fontainebleau, the Harris School of Public Policy Studies at The University of Chicago, The Alfred P. Sloan School of Management at Massachusetts Institute of Technology, and the European Group of Organization Studies in Paris. While at Yale, I made several presentations at the Complex Organizations Seminar (COSI).

This study would have been impossible without the assistance of the reference and interlibrary loan librarians at Yale's Sterling Memorial, Mudd, Medical, Law, Divinity, and Social Science libraries. I have also made extensive use of the collections at the New York Public Library, the Engineering Societies Library in New York City, the Baker Library at the Harvard Business School, the library at the Tavistock Institute of Human Relations in London, the London Business School Library, the Stadts- und Universitätsbibliothek Köln, and the Bauhaus-Archiv in Berlin. In Spain I found bibliographical assistance at the following institutions: Real Academia de Ciencias Morales y Políticas, Ministerio de Trabajo y Seguridad Social, Instituto de Estudios Políticos, Fundación José Ortega y Gasset, Fundación Pablo Iglesias, Fundación Fondo para la Investigación Económica y Social, Escuela de Organizatión Industrial, and of course the Biblioteca Nacional, Madrid.

Several institutions have provided me with much-needed financial support: Banco de España, Spain's Ministerio de Educación y Ciencia, Centro de Investigaciones Sociológicas, the Fulbright Commission, the John D. Rockefeller 3rd Fellowship of Yale's Program on Nonprofit Organizations (PONPO), the Mellon-West European Project at Yale, and the Marion and Jasper Whiting Foundation. The Alfred P. Sloan School of Management at MIT funded the phase of manuscript revision and publication with generous summer research support. Michelle Fiorenza handled a myriad of administrative tasks effectively. My affiliation with The Minda de Gunzburg Center for European Studies at Harvard has been most helpful in establishing links with other scholars.

My foremost intellectual debt is to my early mentor and friend Jesús M. de Miguel for converting me to Sociology while I was an undergraduate student majoring in political economy and business management at the University of Oviedo in Spain, as well as to my Yale advisors—Paul DiMaggio, Juan Linz, and Charles Perrow. Douglas Mitchell, Lila Weinberg, and my copy editor, Nicholas Murray, have made publishing a book with Chicago a most enjoyable, albeit demanding experience. I would like to dedicate the book to my parents María Flor and Julián.

Cambridge, Massachusetts
Spring, 1994

ONE

The Comparative Study of Organizational Paradigms

> Ideas, unless outward circumstances conspire with them, have in general no very rapid or immediate efficacy in human affairs.[1]

Managers use new organizational models to address the ideological and technical problems that appear whenever changes in the scale and complexity of the firm, the international competitive environment, or working-class unrest challenge current practices. This book analyzes the adoption of the three major models or paradigms of organizational management: scientific management, human relations, and structural analysis. One might have the impression that there was a single evolutionary sequence in all countries from one managerial model to another as organizations sought the most efficient means to produce and distribute goods and services. In this view, national variations in degree and timing of adoption typically resulted in relative disadvantages or inefficiencies. It would seem that since industry imposed its own logic of heavy capital investment, mass production, and large establishments, the organization of economic enterprises should have followed a path that was relatively independent of national cultures, politics, or intellectual heritages. In particular, one might assume that the rationale of employers and managers ruled without interference and that the workforce everywhere was similarly subservient and powerless. This was certainly not true. The adoption of the three paradigms varied among countries, and they were variously adapted to national circumstances, including the characteristics of the workforce.

The main thesis of this book is that the adoption of models or paradigms of organizational management does not necessarily follow from their scientific credibility and is not solely determined by economic and technological factors. For ideas to be adopted in practice, *institutional* circumstances have to be conducive. Managers in differ-

---

1. J. S. Mill, "The claims of labour" (1845, p. 503).

ent countries adopted the three paradigms in selective ways during the twentieth century, depending on the problems they were facing and such institutional factors as their mentalities and training, the activities of professional groups, the role of the state, and the attitude of the workers. A related thesis is that organizational paradigms that are relevant to employers and managers include both an ideology of organizational management and a set of techniques. Finally, this study puts forth a framework for the cross-national, comparative analysis of organizational change, and then applies it to the cases of two liberal-democratic countries, the United States and Great Britain, and two corporatist societies, Germany and Spain.

The book studies organizational change in the historical context of the rise of wage dependency, factory bureaucracy, and international competition. It explores the configurations of institutional factors that account for the adoption of the paradigms by management intellectuals and practitioners. The intention is in part to extend the decades-old classic book by Reinhard Bendix, *Work and Authority in Industry*.[2] Considerable attention, however, will be given to aspects not systematically covered by Bendix, such as the processes of competition and imitation among nation-states, the actions of professional groups, the effects of elite mentalities and of religion, the interplay between ideologies and techniques, the correlation between theoretical discussion and managerial practice, and the contrast between liberal-democratic and corporatist societies.

Current developments enhance the importance of doing comparative and historical research on the adoption of organizational ideologies and techniques. On the one hand, there is a renewed interest in the phenomenon of cross-national emulation. On the other, the history of organizational ideologies and techniques seems to be repeating itself in that old ideas are being refurbished and reintroduced, as in the case of some recent "Japanese" management techniques which combine elements drawn from the three paradigms considered in this study. Also, the finding that American top CEOs earn more than those from other countries, including Germany and Japan, has stirred a controversy over the relationship between executive pay and firm performance, thus reopening the old ideological debates over getting rich, shareholders' control, entrepreneurship, and the legitimacy of bureaucratic bosses in business.

2. Bendix, *Work and Authority in Industry* (1974). The original edition dates back to 1956.

THE NEED FOR ORGANIZATIONAL IDEOLOGIES
AND TECHNIQUES

The terms *management* and *management model* may be invoked to convey at least two different concepts. First, *management* may refer to the *technical task* of organization. In this context, models of management become a body of technical knowledge applicable to practical situations. Second, the term *management* may be used to denote the concept of a *system of hierarchical authority*. While the few who rule no longer own the modern firm, they arrange working conditions for the many (who must obey) and make decisions about the distribution of the income generated in the process of producing and selling goods and services. As Bendix noted, "The few, however, have seldom been satisfied to command without a higher justification even when they abjured all interest in ideas, and the many have seldom been docile enough not to provoke such justifications." In this second context a model of management is in fact an ideology aimed at establishing legitimacy and reinforcing credibility.[3] This study is concerned both with the technical task of organization and with *organizational ideologies,* i.e. rationalizations of the system of hierarchical authority in the firm.[4] Ultimately, in our "societies of organizations" most people (including managers, employees, and wage laborers) work under the influence of some organizational model or paradigm, i.e. a particular ideological and technical approach to organization.[5]

Ideologies can be conceptualized in a variety of ways. Karl Marx argued that ideologies are a class-based, interested distortion or inversion of reality (a *camera obscura*). Max Weber proposed that ideologies can be used as a "mask and a weapon" in the pursuit of power and the maintenance of authority. Talcott Parsons suggested that ideolo-

3. Bendix (1974, p. 1); Child, *British Management Thought* (1969, pp. 13, 23); Whitley, *Business Systems in East Asia* (1992, pp. 1–21). See also the discussion by Carruthers and Espeland, "Accounting for rationality" (1991).

4. As opposed to organizational ideologies, *managerial* ideologies also include justifications of capitalism, ownership, profits, free trade, and class inequalities, which will not be explored in this book. For an analysis of these issues, see Sutton et al., *The American Business Creed* (1962), and Bendix (1974).

5. Perrow, "A society of organizations" (1991). Ideological views and organizational techniques emerge as the result of developmental processes of "rationalization" in the Weberian sense of "systematization of ideas." See Swidler, "The concept of rationality in the work of Max Weber" (1973); Schluchter, *The Rise of Western Rationalism* (1981, p. 5); Habermas, *The Theory of Communicative Action* (1984, 1:143–185). See also Alexander and Giesen, "From reduction to linkage: The long view of the micro-macro debate" (1987, p. 16).

gies help to "knit" or "integrate" the social group or class together so as to relieve anxiety. Clifford Geertz emphasized cognitive aspects when he argued that ideologies are "systems of interacting symbols" that help to "render incomprehensible social situations meaningful" and facilitate purposeful action. As Geertz concluded, "whatever else ideologies may be—projections of unacknowledged fears, disguises for ulterior motives, phatic expressions of group solidarity—they are, most distinctively, maps of problematic social reality and matrices for the creation of collective conscience."[6] The concept of organizational ideology includes, but is not limited to, a discourse, demagoguery, rhetoric, language, public-relations effort, or sheer talk. Similarly, an organizational ideology is more than a mere creed, philosophy, style, or fad. Managers use organizational ideologies to inform perception and action as well as to justify their authority. Organizational ideologies can serve as cognitive tools that managers use to sort out the complexities of reality, frame the relevant issues, and choose among alternative paths of action.

The goal of the present study is to evaluate, understand, and explain the success or failure of organizational ideologies and techniques among two distinct groups of managers, namely, management intellectuals and management practitioners. Management *intellectuals* form a restricted group, an elite. They are a self-selected group of spokespeople, opinion leaders, philosophers, or apologists of the managerial class. They typically work for the largest or most prominent companies, consulting firms, government agencies related to the economy, employer associations, research institutions, think tanks, or business schools. Their thought is expressed at the theoretical level in speeches, pamphlets, books, and articles published in the press, in specialized journals, or in the publications of the major firms. Management intellectuals create, receive, interpret, and diffuse knowledge about management and organization. They are primarily concerned with the ideological component of organizational paradigms, but they also pay attention to techniques, suggesting which are consistent with the ideology of the paradigm. Management intellectuals are not only to be

6. Geertz, "Ideology as a cultural system," in *The Interpretation of Cultures* (1973, pp. 201, 205, 207, 220); Ricoeur, *Lectures on Ideology and Utopia* (1986, pp. 1–18); Tafuri, *Architecture and Utopia* (1976, pp. 1–2); Weber, *Economy and Society* (1978, pp. 212–254); Parsons, *The Social System* (1964, pp. 348–359). On the history of the concept of ideology, see Mannheim, *Ideology and Utopia* (1936, pp. 55–108); Bell, *The End of Ideology* (1988, pp. 394–401). See also the idea of "conceptions of control" in Fligstein, *The Transformation of Corporate Control* (1990, pp. 10, 12).

identified by their structural position within the network of top managers and directors, as in Michael Useem's "inner circle" theory of business political activity, but also by their mentality, intellectual orientation, and willingness to become opinion leaders.[7]

As opposed to management intellectuals, management *practitioners* number in the tens of thousands, and work for firms, banks, government agencies, hospitals and many other types of organizations, both large and small, prominent and ordinary. They express their ideas by acting, by implementing policies; they apply knowledge to practical situations. Their overriding concern lies with the technical component of management thought, although they also pay attention to the ideological one, especially when confronting a problem of worker unrest. It should be carefully noted that "ideologies affect and reflect action without necessarily involving the personal convictions of the actors or their spokesmen." Obviously, one can find only a few "true believers" in the dominant managerial and organizational ideology (the management intellectuals), and a few cynics. Most practicing managers will subscribe to an ideology as a matter of course in order to promote their own interests and facilitate cognition.[8]

This study considers two broad kinds of empirical evidence of organizational change resulting from the adoption of the three major paradigms of organization. First we consider evidence of the theoretical discussion and degree of acceptance by management intellectuals of the ideology and techniques associated with each of the paradigms. Books, articles, and speeches by the relevant actors (employers, managers, management intellectuals, labor unionists, government officials) are used to assess theoretical change over time. The second kind of evidence has to do with the extent to which management practitioners in firms actually used the techniques associated with each of the paradigms. A variety of surveys, reports, case studies at the firm level, and other secondary sources are used to ascertain the degree to which firms implemented the organizational techniques proposed by the management intellectuals. It will become apparent that in some countries both the ideology and the techniques of organizational paradigms were accepted in theory or in practice, in others either the ideology or the techniques were adopted after a period of in-depth discussion, and yet in other cases both were rejected.

7. Useem, *The Inner Circle* (1984).
8. Bendix (1974, pp. 341–343).

WHY A CROSS-NATIONAL, COMPARATIVE APPROACH?

Cross-national patterns of adoption and change are the focus of this book. The country or the nation-state is the most adequate level of analysis for the study of how management intellectuals generate or receive managerial models. Management intellectuals happen to be a national group. When they theorize about management and organization, they speak not only for themselves but for the national business community as a whole. Management practitioners behave quite differently. It may be argued that the behavior of practitioners depends more on variables operating at lower levels of analysis like the particular geographical region, the industry, the organization, or even individual characteristics like education, family background, or religion. This book also takes into consideration differences within countries at the regional and industry levels of analysis that had an effect on the adoption of the three paradigms. Case studies of firms that adopted or attempted to adopt the paradigms exemplify how macroinstitutional factors affected the behavior of particular managers and firms. Thus, the cases of Ford and IBM will help us to understand developments in the United States; the case of AEG will illustrate the interplay of institutional factors in Germany; the cases of Duro-Felguera and Standard Eléctrica will be analyzed in the chapter on Spain; and the cases of Rover, Rowntree, Shell, and ICI will illustrate the patterns of organizational change observed in Great Britain.

This book does not belong to the branch of cross-national research on organizations that focuses on testing whether general propositions hold cross-culturally in spite of national characteristics.[9] Rather, it puts cross-national differences and similarities in their historical and world-systemic context with the intention of understanding the configurations of institutional factors that account for observed patterns of change.[10] Nation-states are considered as the *structured* setting in

---

9. See, among others, Chandler, *Scale and Scope* (1990); Hickson et al., "The culture-free context of organization structure" (1974); Nath, "A methodological review of cross-cultural management research" (1968); Glaser, "Cross-national comparisons of the factory" (1971).

10. Thus, this book attempts to follow in the tradition of Bendix (1974); Dore, *British Factory, Japanese Factory* (1973); Sabel, *Work and Politics* (1982); Piore and Sabel, *The Second Industrial Divide* (1984); Burawoy, *The Politics of Production* (1985); Westney, *Imitation and Innovation* (1987); and Cole, *Strategies for Learning* (1989). See also Whitley (1992); Brossard and Maurice, "Is there a universal model of organization structure?" (1976); Maurice et al., "Societal differences in organizing manufacturing units" (1980); Child, "Culture, contingency and capitalism in the cross-national study

which a variety of institutional patterns, as well as economic and technological factors, affect the adoption of different models of management.[11]

The choice of the United States, Germany, Spain, and Great Britain as cases for intensive comparative study was based on several important criteria. First, Germany and Spain went through periods of authoritarian rule and had important corporatist traditions, while Britain and the United States did not. Different political traditions set limits to the ways in which employers and managers address issues of order, authority, and organization.[12] Second, these are four countries with different degrees and timings of economic development. Great Britain was an early industrializer that during this century became an economic laggard. The United States and Germany were two second-wave industrializers that became the leading economic powers of the twentieth century. Unlike the United States, however, Germany underwent several crises as a result of international isolation and war. Spain became a fully industrialized country only after mid-century. Third, patterns of professionalization, governmental intervention, and labor-union behavior exhibited fundamental differences. Fourth, the United States and Britain can be contrasted with a predominantly Catholic Spain and a mixed Protestant-Catholic Germany. Last, but not least, the timing and degree of adoption of the three organizational paradigms also differed by country. Each of these differences will be used to put national peculiarities in their larger context and to understand cross-national patterns of organizational change.

The Paradigmatic Development of Organizational Models

Paradigms are systems of interrelated ideas and techniques that offer a distinctive diagnosis and solution to a set of problems. A model

---

of organizations" (1981); Negandhi, "Cross-cultural management research" (1983); Skocpol, *States and Social Revolutions* (1979, pp. 19–24); and "Bringing the state back in," in Evans, Rueschemeyer, and Skocpol, eds., *Bringing the State Back In* (1985).

11. For a definition of the concepts of structure and structuration, see Giddens, *Central Problems in Social Theory* (1979), and *Profiles and Critiques in Social Theory* (1982, pp. 8–16, 28–39). See also DiMaggio and Powell, "The Iron Cage revisited" (1983, p. 147); DiMaggio, "State expansion and organizational fields" (1983, pp. 149–150).

12. Jepperson and Meyer, "The public order and formal institutions" (1991, pp. 214–225); Schmitter, "Still the Century of Corporatism?" (1974, pp. 87, 93–94, 96); Schmitter and Lehmbruch, eds., *Trends Toward Corporatist Intermediation* (1979, pp. 160–164, 213–230).

or paradigm of organizational management is a system of ideas and techniques about the management of workers and the administration of economic or non-economic enterprises. Organizational paradigms usually present an ideological view of organizations, workers, management, and the hierarchical system in the firm. Not all theoretical organizational paradigms with an academic reputation have had a practical impact on actual organizations. This study only takes into account organizational paradigms that (1) used a "normative" rather than a disinterestedly scholarly approach, (2) offered complete arguments, and (3) achieved a broad appeal among managers and entrepreneurs in more than one country.[13]

Of all organizational theories proposed before 1975, only the scientific management, human relations, and structural analysis paradigms offered complete arguments of the normative kind and gained widespread acceptance among entrepreneurs and managers in more than one country. The general characteristics, ideological features, and techniques associated with each of the three paradigms are summarized in Table 1.1. This classification of organizational paradigms is similar to the ones proposed by Richard Scott in *Organizations: Rational, Natural, and Open Systems,* Charles Perrow in *Complex Organizations,* Amitai Etzioni in *Modern Organizations,* Edgar Schein in *Organizational Psychology,* and Michael Burawoy in his review article, "The Anthropology of Industrial Work."[14]

The first paradigm—scientific management—is defined here as an organizational ideology and a set of techniques conceived to address problems such as workers' soldiering, waste (i.e. lack of efficiency), and disorder, as well as management's arbitrariness, greed, and lack of control. Taylorism and the Taylor System are no more than specific versions of scientific management among many others (e.g., Fordism, the Bedaux System, German industrial rationalization, and so on). The initial formulation of the scientific-management paradigm dates back to the years before World War I. It proposed to study individuals and tasks from the perspective of engineering, industrial psychology,

---

13. The criteria are similar to Bendix's (1974, pp. 1–21).

14. Scott, *Organizations* (1987, pp. 31–116); Burawoy, "The anthropology of industrial work" (1979b); Perrow, *Complex Organizations* (1986); Schein, *Organizational Psychology* (1988, pp. 50–72, 93–101); Etzioni, *Modern Organizations* (1964). See also Burrell and Morgan, *Sociological Paradigms and Organisational Analysis* (1985, pp. 126–184); Huczynski, *Management Gurus* (1993, pp. 1–58). On the concept of paradigm, see Blaug, "Kuhn versus Lakatos" (1975); Kuhn, *The Structure of Scientific Revolutions* (1970); Martins, "The Kuhnian 'Revolution' and Its Implications for Sociology" (1972).

ergonomics, and physiology in order to improve efficiency. As an ideology, scientific management assumed that all actors (workers, managers, entrepreneurs, owners) could behave rationally. Industrial conflict could be avoided because an increased surplus was supposed to benefit all groups involved, thus eliminating the need for labor unions. Management ought to tell workers exactly what to do and how to do it, and supervise them closely. Intellectuals supporting scientific management views were frequently fascinated with machinery, technology, the factory aesthetic, and mass production. They tended to be technocratic modernists, i.e. they identified human progress with material and technological advance, and thought of themselves as visionaries.

As an organizational technique, scientific management aimed at discovering the "one best way" of managing workers and organizing tasks. The methodology consisted of various experimental job-analysis techniques, of which time-and-motion study was the most important. The stopwatch, the motion-picture camera, the slide rule, and the psycho-physiological test formed its paraphernalia of field instruments. Efficiency was to be increased by maximizing the advantages deriving from the separation of task conception from task execution, division of labor, and specialization. Authority was to be centralized, following the principle of unity of command. Supervisory autonomy needed to be reduced.[15] The process of work was to be simplified, mechanized, and, whenever possible, arranged in assembly-line fashion. Workers were assumed to be motivated solely by monetary incentives, and the preferred form of incentive was piecework wages, except for workers on the powered assembly line.

The human relations paradigm offered a fundamentally different view of management and organization from that presented by scientific management. Some previous studies have challenged the argument that the formulation of the human relations paradigm in the 1930s represented a break with previous organizational theories such as scientific management.[16] It is true that scientific management and human relations shared the goals of improving cooperation in the workplace, increasing productivity, and justifying managerial author-

15. Note here that "functional foremanship" (i.e. the division and specialization of foremanship so that its various functions are performed by different supervisors) is a feature of Taylor's system of management, but most other scientific management experts advocated unity of command.

16. Braverman, *Labor and Monopoly Capital* (1974, pp. 86–87); Waring, *Taylorism Transformed* (1991).

TABLE 1.1 Ideological features and techniques of the three organizational paradigms

	Scientific Management	Human Relations	Structural Analysis
General Features			
Perceived problem	Soldiering, waste, disorder; management's arbitrariness and greed, lack of control	Monotony of work, absenteeism, turnover, conflict, unrest, wrong attitudes, low morale	Organizational structure-technology-environment mismatch
Organization *vis-à-vis* its environment	Closed	Closed	Open
Basic unit(s) of analysis	Individuals and tasks	Small groups	Organizations
Predominant social relationships	Authority (formal)	Leadership and participation (informal)	Both formal and informal
Formal knowledge bases	Engineering, industrial psychology, ergonomics, physiology	Paretian and Durkheimian sociology, sociol psychology, social anthropology	Weberian and structural-functional sociology, modern behavioral management theory
Ideological Features			
Rationality assumptions	All actors can behave rationally.	All actors are emotionally dependent, but managers have superior skills.	All actors are rationally bounded.
Predominant conditions	Technical	Psychological and social	Technical and social
View of industrial conflict	Avoidable: Increased surplus benefits both workers and management; need to eliminate unions	Avoidable and aberrant: natural instinct for cooperation; the firm as a social system; need to undermine unions	Conflict in the firm is not necessarily bad; it generates change, and may help resolve disputes; industrial conflict not a central concern.
View of workers	Blindly driven by self-interest	Driven by psychosocial norms, needs, emotions	Adaptable; behave according to their structural situation
How to manage workers	Tell them what to do, and supervise them closely.	Lead them, gain their confidence.	Detached, structural approach to workers: decentralization helps develop their initiative and responsibility while unobtrusively controlling them.

(Continued)

Fascination with	Machinery, technology, factory aesthetic, mass production	Communal life, human interaction in social groups	Ubiquity and complexity of organizations in modern society
Social and intellectual agenda	Modernism, human mastering of nature	Nostalgia, romanticism, social harmony	Disciplinary; defense of the free enterprise system
Particular Techniques			
General form of solution	Normative: one best way	Normative: one best way	Contingency approach
Methodology	Experimentation, time-and-motion studies, job analysis	Surveys, interviews, discussion groups, clinical counseling	Comparative study of cases, typologies of organizations
Selection of workers	On-site, scientific psycho-physiological testing and evaluation	On-site selection based on social affinity, attitudes, personality	Formal educational credentials
Distribution of tasks	Task conception and execution separated, division of labor among individual workers, specialization	Job enlargement, enrichment, rotation	Differentiation and integration of functions
Authority structures	Simple managerial hierarchy	Downplays hierarchy, emphasizes leadership and communication	Complex hierarchy, line-and-staff structures, ambiguity of hierarchy
Optimal degree of concentration of authority	Unity of command, control of supervisory authority	Managers lead, limited participation in lower decisions	Centralization and decentralization as policy variables
Organization of the process of work	Work simplification, mechanization, assembly-line work	Small-group activities, teamwork	Departmentalization, divisionalization, matrix structures, profit centers
Preferred rewards	Wages, bonuses	Stability, security, work satisfaction, recognition	Prestige, status, power, promotion, salary
Preferred economic incentives	Piecework wages	Group wage incentives	Seniority-based salaries

Sources: Baron et al., "Mission control? The development of personnel systems in U.S. industry" (1988); Braverman, *Labor and Monopoly Capital* (1974); Burawoy, "The Anthropology of Industrial Work" (1979); Edwards, *Contested Terrain* (1979); Etzioni, *Modern Organizations* (1964); Henderson, L. J. *Henderson on the Social System* (1970); Perrow, *Complex Organizations* (1986); Pugh and Hickson, *Writers on Organizations* (1989); Scott, *Organizations* (1987).

ity. Also, both paradigms claimed scientific objectivity and neglected the environment of the organization. But a comparison of the corresponding columns in Table 1.1 will suffice to realize the many ways in which they diverged as paradigms of organization. The typical human relations analysis focused on such problems as the monotony of work, absenteeism, turnover, conflict, unrest, wrong attitudes, and low morale, all of which lead to restricted productivity. Human relations proponents argued that those problems generally resulted from excessive mechanization and industrial rationalization.[17] This kind of analysis was based on Paretian and Durkheimian sociology as well as on social psychology and social anthropology. Workers were not seen as individuals, as mere sellers of labor power. They were people with group identifications and emotional dependencies, driven by psychosocial norms and needs. Managers shared the same qualities of workers, but their superior ability and skill in human relations should allow them to exercise self-control and to arrange the conditions necessary for continued cooperation in the factory. People had an instinct for cooperation, so industrial conflict was not only avoidable but aberrant. The manager's role was to balance the social system of the factory, harmonize relationships, and lead and integrate the work force to achieve maximum productivity through increased cooperation. Obviously, this approach undermined the need for labor unions. Management intellectuals using a human relations approach were typically fascinated with communal life and the interaction of people in social groups. Their agenda was nostalgic, romantic, and, in Albert Hirschman's sense of the term, *reactionary*. They sought to reestablish the social harmony of the preindustrial past, and avoid the "social diseases" of industrialism that "jeopardized" such previous achievements of mankind as inter-personal cooperation (teamwork) and orderly community life.[18] The ideological contrast with scientific management could not be sharper; in fact the human relations paradigm represented a reaction against scientific management.

The supporters of both scientific management and human relations hoped to find the "one best way" of organizing, but the organizational techniques proposed differed greatly, another sign of their paradigmatic opposition. Human relations experts recommended a variety of diagnosis and intervention techniques to find out about the social

17. The best book on this topic is Giedion, *Mechanization Takes Command* (1969). See also Erikson, "On Work and Alienation," in Erikson and Vallas, eds., *The Nature of Work* (1990, pp. 19–35).

18. For an analysis of reactionary arguments based on the "jeopardy" thesis, see Hirschman, *The Rhetoric of Reaction* (1991, pp. 81–132).

situation in the workplace and to improve social relationships by allowing workers to express their feelings and concerns: interviews, surveys, T-groups, discussion groups, sensitivity training, clinical counseling, psychodrama, role-playing, and so on. Workers were to be selected not on the basis of their physical aptitudes or dexterity but according to their social characteristics, personalities, attitudes, and potential for integration and adaptation. Excessive division of labor and specialization were criticized for provoking unnecessary monotony, absenteeism, turnover, and low morale. Job enlargement, enrichment, and rotation were presented as suitable alternatives to avoid the "perverse effects" of scientifically engineered jobs.[19] Similarly, small-group activities and teamwork were to be substituted for assembly-line work. Hierarchy was downplayed in favor of leadership, participation, and communication. Human relations proponents argued that workers were not only motivated by money but also sought security, stability, satisfaction, and recognition at work. If economic incentives had to be used, they should be based on the performance of the group, not of the individual worker.

Structural analysis approached the world of organizations from a radically different angle. It emerged during the late 1950s and 1960s at a time when the organizational landscape was becoming dominated by large, bureaucratized firms engaged in the production and distribution of a variety of products and services, and frequently operating on several continents. Simultaneously, the welfare state expanded, creating new organizational fields and a greater variety of organizational forms, in part to cope with the externalities brought about by large-scale industry. Modern structural thinkers argued that the analysis of the technology and the competitive environment of the organization could help to find the adequate organizational structure within the frameworks of Weberian and structural-functional sociology as well as modern behavioral management theory.

As an organizational ideology, structural analysis departed from both scientific management and human relations in several respects. Industrial strife and class warfare no longer occupied such a central position. The late 1950s and 1960s were years of relative industrial peace in most capitalist countries. All organizational actors were believed to be rationally bounded. Professional, salaried managers were assigned the authority over long-range planning, goal setting, problem definition, alternative-listing, and decision making because of their superior technical knowledge. Workers were assumed to be

19. Reactionary arguments based on the "perversity" thesis are also discussed by Hirschman (1991, pp. 11–42).

adaptable to their structural situation, and decentralization was supposed to help develop their initiative, responsibility, and professional growth. Unobtrusive control devices such as job specifications, internal career ladders, programs, procedures, guidelines, classifications, routines, scripts, and schema were to be used to monitor the performance of both workers and managers. Paternalism was fiercely attacked as a managerial strategy, while conflict within the firm was seen in a favorable light because it could help resolve disputes, improve decisions, and generate change. Another major departure from previous approaches was the view of labor unions as partners in the industrial endeavor. Management was advised to develop a long-term working relationship with them, the strategy being to provide stable employment and incomes so as to upgrade workers to the middle class.

Management intellectuals using a structural approach were generally fascinated with the complexity and ubiquity of organizations in modern society, and they hoped to understand modern society precisely through the study of its complex organizations. The agenda of top management intellectuals favoring a structural approach (e.g. Sloan, Drucker, Dale, Chandler) had a dominant implicit theme: defending the system of free enterprise, including a justification of the role of the large business firm. By contrast, most structural sociologists and behavioral scientists tended to limit themselves to a disciplinary, purely scholarly agenda. Both the structural management intellectuals and the discipline-based structural theorists, however, accepted the rationality, technical superiority, and legitimacy of bureaucratic organization under stable conditions.[20] Finally, one important difference that set structural analysis apart from both scientific management and human relations was that these two other paradigms forcefully promised a better world and tended to be utopian, while structural analysis was rather vague about the future.

As a set of organizational techniques, structural analysis was far more powerful than as an ideology. The centerpiece was the "contingency approach," i.e. organizing differently for different products, production processes, and external environments. Typologies of organizations were designed to see how to differentiate and integrate functions (e.g. production, sales, R&D), build the organization's complex

20. On the ideology of structural analysis, see Sloan, *My Years with General Motors* (1972, pp. 505–512); Drucker, *The Practice of Management* (1954, pp. 341–392); Dale, *The Great Organizers* (1960, pp. 181–201); Chandler, *Strategy and Structure* (1962, pp. 394–396); Lawrence and Lorsch, *Organization and Environment* (1969, pp. 211–245).

hierarchy, decentralize decision making, centralize control, and decide whether to create divisions, matrix structures, and profit centers.[21] Thus, structural thinking shifted the level of analysis upwards while claiming that problems at lower levels could still be handled according to scientific management, human relations, or some other approach, depending on the circumstances. In that sense, structural analysis represented a subsumption of older paradigms as special cases of a more comprehensive scheme. Less developed in the structural analysis paradigm were the techniques for worker selection (formal educational credentials were preferred), rewards (combinations of prestige, status, power, promotion, and salary were preferred), and economic incentives (seniority-based salaries were preferred).

PARADIGMS AND GENERATIONS

Organizational paradigms have frequently been the result of the theoretical and practical work of a generation of leading managers, consultants, researchers, and theorists. Thus, a group of efficiency experts published the major works of scientific management between 1880 and 1920. In the cases of human relations (circa 1930–1970) and structural analysis (circa 1950–1975), there was a certain overlap in the timing of publications. A graphical representation of the generational development of organizational thought in the century after 1880 appears in Figure 1.1, showing the life spans of the leading thinkers and their major publications. Table 1.2 lists the dates for the original editions and the translations into German and Spanish of each of the works indicated in Figure 1.1.

The concept of a generation is a crucial element in an institutional analysis of the adoption of models of management. Members of a generation experience similar circumstances regardless of whether they know or have knowledge of each other. They share a "common location in the social and historical process," a "specific range of potential experience" that predisposes them "for a certain characteristic mode of thought and experience, and a characteristic type of historically relevant action."[22] The scientific management thinkers included in Figure 1.1 shared a social location. Most of them were self-made mechanical engineers impregnated by the so-called shopfloor culture. Except for Hugo Münsterberg and Lillian Gilbreth, none of them

---

21. Scott (1987, pp. 102–105); Perrow (1986, pp. 119–192); Burawoy (1979b; pp. 248–256). On the use of type-concepts or typologies in social research, see Stinchcombe, *Constructing Social Theories* (1987, pp. 43–47).

22. Mannheim, "The problem of generations" (1952, pp. 291–292). See also Crane, *Invisible Colleges* (1972, p. 35).

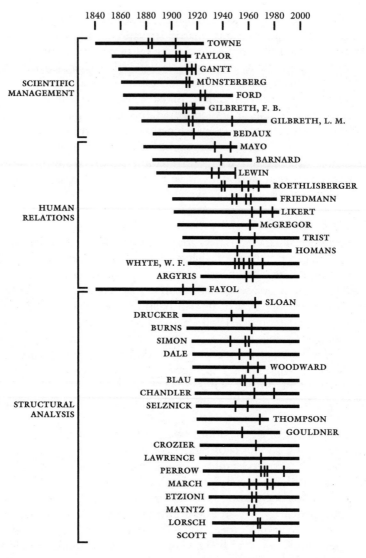

Figure 1.1. Three generations of organizational thinkers. (First edition of major published work[s] indicated by thin vertical lines. Living authors as of 1994 are indicated with their name to the left of the bar.)

TABLE 1.2   Original editions and translations of the major works on organization

SCIENTIFIC MANAGEMENT				
Author and Works	English	German	Spanish	French
Henry Robinson Towne				
Towne on Cranes	1883*	—	—	
"The Engineer as an Economist"	1886*	—	—	
Locks and Builders' Hardware	1904*	—	—	
Frederick Winslow Taylor				
"A Piece-Rate System"	1895*	. . .	—	
Shop Management	1903*	1909	1914	
Art of Cutting Metals	1907*	1908	1912	
Principles of Scientific Management	1911*	1913	1944#	
Henry Lawrence Gantt				
Work, Wages, and Profits	1913*	—	—	
Industrial Leadership	1916*	—	—	
Organizing for Work	1919*	1922	—	
Hugo Münsterberg				
Psychology and Industrial Efficiency	1913*[a]	1912*[a]	1914	
Grundzüge der Psychotechnik	—	1914*	—	
Henry Ford				
My Life and Work	1923*	1923	1924	
Today and Tomorrow	1926*	—	—	
Frank Bunker Gilbreth				
Bricklaying System	1909*	—	—	
Primer of Scientific Management	1912*	1920	—	
Fatigue Study (with L. E. M. Gilbreth)	1916*	1921	—	
Applied Motion Study	1917*	1920	—	
Lillian Evelyn Moller Gilbreth				
Psychology of Management	1914*	1922	—	
Foreman and Manpower	1947*	—	—	
Charles Eugène Bedaux				
Bedaux Efficiency Course	1917*	—	—	

HUMAN RELATIONS				
Author and Works	English	German	Spanish	French
Elton Mayo				
Human Problems of an Industrial Civilization	1933*	1950	1959#	
Social Problems of an Industrial Civilizaton	1945*	1949	. . .	
Chester Irving Barnard				
Functions of the Executive	1938*	1970	1959	
Kurt Lewin				
Die psychologische Situation bei Lohn und Strafe	. . .	1931*	—	
Resolving Social Conflicts	1948*	1953	—	
Fritz Jules Roethlisberger				
Management and the Worker	1939*	—	. . .	
Management and Morale	1941*	1954	—	
Training for Human Relations	1954*	—	—	
Motivation, Productivity, and Satisfaction of Workers	1958*	—	—	
Counseling in an Organization	1966*	—	—	

(Continued)

TABLE 1.2 *(Continued)*

HUMAN RELATIONS *(Continued)*				
Author and Works	English	German	Spanish	French
Georges Friedmann				
Problèmes humains du machinisme industriel	1955	1952	1956#	1946*
Où va le travail humain?	. . .	1953	1961#	1950*
Le travail en miettes	1961	1959	1958#	1956*
Traité de sociologie du travail	. . .	. . .	. . .	1961*
Rensis Likert				
New Patterns of Management	1961*	1972	1965	
Human Organization	1967*	—	—	
New Ways of Managing Conflict	1976*	—	1986	
Douglas McGregor				
The Human Side of Enterprise	1960*	1970	1975#	
George Caspar Homans				
The Human Group	1950*	1960	1964#	
Social Behavior	1961*	—	—	
William Foote Whyte				
Human Relations in the Restaurant Industry	1948*	—	—	
Pattern for Industrial Peace	1951*	1956	—	
Money and Motivation	1955*	1958	1961	
Man and Organization	1959*	—	—	
Men at Work	1961*	—	—	
Organizational Behavior	1969*	—	—	
Eric Landsowne Trist				
Organizational Choice	1963*	—	—	
Chris Argyris				
Personality and Organization	1957*	—	1964	
Interpersonal Competence	1962*	—	—	

STRUCTURAL ANALYSIS				
Author and Works	English	German	Spanish	French
Henri Fayol				
"L'exposé des principes généreux d'administration"	—	—	—	1908*
Administration industrielle et générale	1930	1929	1942#	1916*
Alfred Pritchard Sloan, Jr.				
My Years with General Motors	1963*	1965	. . .	
Peter Ferdinand Drucker				
Concept of the Corporation	1946*	. . .	. . .	
Practice of Management	1954*	1956	. . .	
Tom Burns				
Management of Innovation (with G. M. Stalker)	1961*	. . .	. . .	
Herbert Alexander Simon				
Administrative Behavior	1945*	1955	1962	
Models of Man	1956*	—	—	
Organizations (with J. G. March)	1958*	1977	1961	
Ernest Dale				
Planning and Developing the Company Organization Structure	1952*	. . .	—	
The Great Organizers	1960*	1962	—	

TABLE 1.2 *(Continued)*

STRUCTURAL ANALYSIS *(Continued)*				
Author and Works	*English*	*German*	*Spanish*	*French*
Joan Woodward				
Management and Technology	1958*	—	—	
Industrial Organization	1965*	—	—	
Peter Michael Blau				
The Dynamics of Bureaucracy	1955*	—	—	
Bureaucracy in Modern Society	1956*	—	1962#	
Formal Organizations (with W. R. Scott)	1962*	—	—	
The Structure of Organizations	1971*	—	—	
Alfred DuPont Chandler, Jr.				
Strategy and Structure	1962*	—	—	
The Visible Hand	1977*	—	1987	
Philip Selznick				
TVA and the Grass Roots	1949*	—	—	
Leadership in Administration	1957*	—	—	
James D. Thompson				
Organizations in Action	1967*	—	—	
Alvin Ward Gouldner				
Patterns of Industrial Bureaucracy	1954*	—	—	
Michel Crozier				
Le phénomène bureaucratique	1964	—	1969#	1963*
Paul Roger Lawrence				
Organization and Environment (with J. Lorsch)	1967*	—	1976	
Charles Perrow				
"Framework for the Comparative Analysis of Organizations"	1967*	. . .	—	
Organizational Analysis	1970*	—	1972#	
Complex Organizations	1972*	—	1990	
Normal Accidents	1984*	1987	—	
James Gardner March				
Behavioral Theory of the Firm	1963*	—	—	
"A Garbage Can Model of Organizational Choice"	1972*	—	—	
Ambiguity and Choice in Organizations	1976*	—	—	
Amitai Werner Etzioni				
Comparative Analysis of Complex Organizations	1961*	1969	—	
Modern Organizations	1964*	—	1965#	
Renate Mayntz				
Die soziale Organisation des Industriebetriebes	. . .	1958*	—	
Soziologie der Organisation	. . .	1963*	1967	
Jay William Lorsch				
Product Innovation and Organization	1965*	—	—	
William Richard Scott				
Organizations	1981*	—	—	

Notes: Authors are arranged by birth date within each of the paradigms. Books by more than one author are only entered once. Ellipsis points (. . .) indicate missing data. Dash (—) indicates translation not available in that language. Asterisk (*) indicates the original edition. The number sign (#) indicates that the book is available in the corresponding language but published in a country other than those included in this study, e.g. books in Spanish published in Mexico.

  [a]The German and American editions of Münsterberg's *Psychology and Industrial Efficiency* were somewhat different.

held a doctoral degree. They all had extensive management or con-sulting experience and witnessed the transition phase leading to the consolidation of mass production during the 1920s. In contrast to the scientific managers, most of the leading human relations and struc-tural analysis thinkers were academics or had links to universities. They all held doctoral degrees (except for Chester Barnard and Profes-sor Homans) and witnessed the rise of the giant bureaucratized indus-trial and service company. The chronological overlap shown in Figure 1.1 between human relations and structural analysis publications re-fers only to the "second wave" of human relations thinkers, i.e. the one after Mayo, Barnard, Lewin, and Roethlisberger. The problem of overlap can be addressed with the idea of a "generation unit." Different generation units may coexist within the same chronological generation if members of the different units interpret and react to the common experiences of the entire generation in different ways. In the extreme case, antagonistic "generation units" constitute one "actual generation" because they "are oriented toward each other, even though only in the sense of fighting one another."[23]

National generations of less renowned theorists and practitioners were involved in the adoption of organizational paradigms, and in their adaptation to country-specific conditions. Therefore, it is impor-tant to analyze the educational backgrounds, work experiences, men-talities, and religious affiliations common to national generations of organizational thinkers. The adoption of organizational ideas will de-pend on the mobilization by national managerial elites of all sorts of capital, i.e. economic, social, cultural, symbolic, and political.[24] How those elites mobilize social and economic influence, prestige, and in-stitutional resources such as state agencies, professional associations, employers' associations, and educational institutions is crucial to an understanding of cross-national patterns of adoption.[25]

An Institutional and Comparative Framework of Analysis

Most previous organizational research grounded in anthropology, economics, political economy, political science, psychology, and even

23. Mannheim (1952, pp. 304, 306–307).
24. For a conceptualization of the different forms of capital, see: Bourdieu, *Homo Academicus* (1988, pp. 36–39, 43–47, 227–242), and *Outline of a Theory of Practice* (1977, pp. 171–197).
25. On the social and cultural bases underlying the production of knowledge, see Merton, "Paradigm for the sociology of knowledge," in *The Sociology of Science* (1973, p. 12).

sociology assumes that models or paradigms of management originate and can be implemented in an institutional vacuum. Real-life managers, however, operate within the constraints of economic competition, state regulation, the collective power of workers, the position of the country in the international system of nation-states, and their own mentalities. A cloud of uncertainty frequently envelops the kinds of complicated problems that preoccupy management intellectuals. Practicing managers frequently listen to professionals or use the knowledge generated by them. In a world of unclear cause-effect relationships, managers often resort to imitating the behavior of other domestic or foreign organizations perceived as successful. As a result, their behavior tends to follow a combination of normative, coercive, and mimetic patterns.[26]

Organizational ideologies and techniques are aimed at solving perceived organizational problems, although in some instances ideologies and techniques themselves may create new problems as they attempt to solve older ones. Management intellectuals and practitioners embedded in the institutional contexts of their countries and time periods conceive of and solve organizational problems in varying ways. For the purposes of the present study, an *organizational problem* is defined as resulting from the *perceived* presence of at least one of the three following conditions: (1) structural-economic changes, including bureaucratization, separation of management from ownership, increases in size and complexity, and within-firm diversification of product lines; (2) international pressures or opportunities, i.e. those resulting from international economic, political, and military competition or cooperation among nation-states; and (3) labor unrest, i.e. challenges to managerial authority. Management intellectuals and practitioners in dissimilar countries may face a diversity of organizational problems in different time periods. Their choice of *organizational solutions* may be affected by the following institutional factors: (1) business-elite mentalities, i.e. intellectual dispositions favoring particular solutions; (2) professional groups that elaborate organizational theories and offer employers and managers solutions to their organizational problems; (3) state actions supporting employers or particular solutions; and (4) workers' responses (collaboration, resistance, indifference) to the implementation of a particular organiza-

---

26. DiMaggio and Powell (1983); DiMaggio and Powell, "Introduction," in Powell and DiMaggio, eds., *The New Institutionalism in Organizational Analysis* (1991). On the role of power, interest, and agency in neo-institutional theory, see DiMaggio, "Interest and agency in institutional theory" (1988, p. 11).

tional solution. This analytic framework combines material circumstances, coercive factors, preexisting elite mentalities, and opposition forces to account for the adoption of organizational ideas in comparative perspective.[27] One crucial advantage of this framework is that it can accommodate two special situations: the appearance of organizational problems with no solution emerging and the adoption of a solution not because it is the one best suited to address the problem at hand or because it addresses it at all, but just because it happens to be available at the time, as in "garbage can" models of organizational choice.[28]

INITIAL PROPOSITIONS

Structural Change. Changes in the internal organizational structure of firms have an impact on the kinds of theories that can be useful and practical. In particular, increases in size and complexity often result in reorganization along, among others, scientific management or human relations lines so as to reduce chaos and motivate workers to exert themselves. The diversification of the products manufactured or of the services rendered by the firm opens up the opportunity for applying structural analysis ideas such as contingent organization or multidivisionalization.

Industrial bureaucratization is another structural change with important implications, although its concrete effects on management have always been a controversial matter.[29] The bureaucratization of economic enterprises has important consequences for the relevance and applicability of scientific management, human relations, and structural analysis. First, the bureaucratization of management brings into the firm great numbers of experts in the technical, social-

27. A similar rationale is used by Hirschman, "How the Keynesian revolution was exported from the United States" (1989); and by P. Hall, "Conclusion: The politics of Keynesian ideas" (1989).

28. Cohen, March, and Olsen, "A garbage can model of organizational choice" (1972).

29. On the historical significance of industrial bureaucratization, see Weber, *Economy and Society* (1978, p. 987); Marx, *Capital* (1967, vol. 3, p. 438); Smith, *An Inquiry into the Nature and Causes of the Wealth of Nations* (1976, vol. 2, p. 741); Schumpeter, *Capitalism, Socialism and Democracy* (1976, p. 134), and *The Theory of Economic Development* (1949, pp. 57–94, 128–156). See also Avineri, *The Social & Political Thought of Karl Marx* (1968, pp. 177–179); Pérez-Díaz, *State, Bureaucracy and Civil Society* (1978); Clawson, *Bureaucracy and the Labor Process* (1980, pp. 18–24); Goldman and Van Houten, "Managerial strategies and the worker." (1977, p. 115); Burnham, *The Managerial Revolution* (1941, pp. 82–85); Hirschman, "Rival interpretations of market society" (1982).

psychological, and structural-organizational aspects of managing an enterprise.[30] Here the bureaucratization of the enterprise is assumed to be a precondition for the application of each of the three organizational paradigms. Thus, managers in countries with comparatively high indexes of industrial bureaucratization are expected to be more likely to accept and implement the ideas contained in each of the three paradigms (depending on the time period when comparisons are made). Second, chances of individual success appear greatly diminished in the eyes of the worker, the employee, or even the manager of the large, bureaucratized organization. The way to the top is far longer in bureaucratized firms than in the old world of smaller and traditionally ruled industrial firms. Therefore, the motivation to produce will be maximized if satisfactions in the work itself are emphasized over satisfactions derived from success in getting to the top, as in the human relations approach. In addition, ability and skill in handling human relationships become increasingly useful in pursuing a bureaucratic career. But bureaucratization, large size, or complexity alone do not help to explain why human relations did not appear until the 1940s and 1950s, and structural analysis until the 1960s. At best, structural factors are preconditions for the emergence and application of organizational paradigms, not causes.

The nature of authority or domination (*Herrschaft*) in the business firm and its evolution over time also has implications for the adoption of the various organizational paradigms.[31] Historically, entrepreneurs and heirs of entrepreneurs have been much less likely to implement scientific management and structural analysis than salaried managers. Entrepreneurs and heirs characteristically eschew detached, analytical approaches, preferring to rely instead on their intuition and experience. The paternalism intrinsic in the human relations approach, by contrast, has frequently appealed to entrepreneurs and heirs.

International Pressures or Opportunities. A second relevant condition affecting the cross-national adoption of organizational paradigms is the position of the country in the international arena, or "world-system," of nation-states. Nation-states may compete or cooperate with each other. When a nation-state comes under pressure or international isolation, or when economic lags or backwardness become an issue, a characteristic response is to imitate the organizational models of successful countries with or without the support of the state. Japan,

30. Bendix (1974, pp. 281–308).
31. Bendix (1974, pp. xxv–xxvi); Weber (1978, pp. 212–254).

Germany, and the Soviet Union followed this pattern during critical periods of their respective national histories. It is important to understand the comparative timing of economic development, geopolitical relations, patterns of trade, international division of production activities, and emergence of organizational models that may be transferred across national boundaries.[32] International isolation and pressure are hypothesized to lead to the application of scientific management, especially when management elites perceive their country as being backward, isolated, or otherwise threatened. Such international threats decrease the economic and political "slack" of the country, making it very important to achieve technical improvements (including those related to the management of labor) while relegating social-psychological concerns to the background. Therefore, it is expected that international threats will not facilitate the adoption of human relations ideas unless the threatening country uses human relations and that is perceived by threatened countries as a source of competitive advantage. Finally, it is expected that structural analysis theories are more likely to gain acceptance in countries with access to free-trade areas that facilitate the geographical expansion of large companies. The management of R&D, production, and marketing on a world scale requires new structures of coordination, and frequently leads to structural reorganizations resulting in the multidivisional or matrix forms of organization.[33]

Labor Unrest.   The challenge to entrepreneurial and managerial authority in the workplace has frequently prompted the use of innovative organizational models either as ideological weapons or as practical techniques, or both. Industrial conflict is a pervasive engine of organizational change, perhaps one of the most important factors behind the refinement of capitalism as a viable economic system. Employers and engineers attempted to use scientific management to justify their authority by reference to a neutral, scientific knowledge, as well as to "rationalize" the labor market through a methodical analysis of worker aptitudes and performance. Human relations ideas also served a legitimatory purpose, having been frequently used to reach

32. Skocpol (1979, p. 19), and "Bringing the state back in," in Evans, Rueschemeyer, and Skocpol, eds. (1985, p. 9); Wallerstein, *The Modern World-System* (1974, 1980, 1988); Westney (1987, p. 9); Gerschenkron, *Economic Backwardness in Historical Perspective* (1962, pp. 7–10, 52–71); Olson, *The Rise and Decline of Nations* (1982), and *The Logic of Collective Action* (1965); Dore (1973, pp. 404–420).

33. Franko, *The European Multinationals* (1976, pp. 186–212).

workers directly in the hope of circumventing labor unions and eliminating their reason for existence. Unlike scientific management and human relations, structural analysis does not deal with problems of industrial conflict directly. In fact, it is hypothesized that structural analysis will only become a prominent organizational technique when industrial relations are stable enough to allow managers to collaborate with the unions and focus their attention on the larger picture of the organizational structure and the competitive environment.

Elite Mentalities. Mentalities are enduring modes of thought characteristic of a group or class. The concept of mentality has its roots in several European social science traditions, including German sociology and French *Annales* history. A mentality is based upon implicit, non-reflective, and subjective assumptions as to how the world works. A mentality may dispose members of the group or class to accept one particular organizational solution over others. As noted above, organizational paradigms incorporate an ideological and a technical element, but never a mentality. The distinction between ideology and mentality is analytically important. A mentality is a "spiritual disposition," while an ideology is "persuasive content."[34] For example, managerial modernism, authoritarianism, or paternalism are mentalities, while scientific management, human relations, and structural analysis are ideologies or paradigms of ideas (i.e. rationalized systems of thought including a worldview).

Although the correlation between mentalities and organizational ideologies is seldom perfect, the mentality dominant among a country's managerial elite affects the chances of an organizational paradigm being accepted and implemented. The elite mentality created by machine-age modernism in Weimar Germany, by Futurism in Fascist Italy, or by the various avant-garde movements in the early Soviet Union was one of the factors inducing the German, Italian, and Soviet managerial elites of the time to embrace scientific management. In other countries prevailing mentalities proved negative for the adoption of scientific management. The best examples are Fabianism, Quakerism, and the industrial betterment movement in Great Britain, and *Regeneracionismo* in Spain. All of these movements shared an interest in vocational guidance, worker training, and human relationships at work.

The elite mentality created by the social doctrine of the Catholic

34. See the discussion by Geiger, "Ideologie und Mentalität," in *Die soziale Schichtung des deutschen Volkes* (1932, pp. 77–79).

Church or by Christian humanism in certain countries was extremely consequential for the success of the human relations paradigm. Most of the German and Spanish academics and managers proposing human relations approaches to organization during the 1950s and 1960s in part owed their interest in that paradigm to the influence of social Catholicism. In contrast, the leading German supporters of scientific management in the 1920s were Protestants. Thus, this book advances an important connection between religion and the organizational behavior of managers, reminiscent of Weber's thesis on the link between Calvin's morals and the entrepreneurial spirit in early capitalist development.[35]

Professional Groups. Employers and top managers frequently make decisions based on the judgment of professionals working for the organization, or they have professional training themselves. Professions "are exclusive occupational groups applying somewhat abstract knowledge."[36] The different professional groups performing managerial functions in line or staff positions (engineers, managers with formal management training, sociologists, psychologists, social workers) have competing worldviews and value-orientations. As a result, the management of organizations often becomes an arena for inter-professional struggle. A profession's claim over turf provokes continuous disputes with other interests (e.g. other professions, occupations, or groups in society), although the claim is often presented to public opinion as a contribution to society's welfare. It is useful to conceptualize the actions of professionals in business as aimed at gaining influence and power in the firm.[37] The development of engineering as a profession was a direct cause of the rise of scientific management, much as the development of social-psychological science accounted in part for the appearance of the human relations paradigm. Sociology and the behavioral science of management lie at the roots of the formulation of the structural analysis paradigm. The strategy becomes then to study the relative strength and influence of different profes-

35. Weber, *The Protestant Ethic and the Spirit of Capitalism* (1958); see also Swidler, "Culture in action" (1986, p. 273).

36. Abbott, *The System of Professions* (1988, p. 8). Freidson, in *Professional Powers* (1986, pp. 1–19), also defines professions around bodies of knowledge. A more restricted definition is that of Wilensky, "The professionalization of everyone?" (1964, p. 138).

37. Abbott (1988, pp. 125–142, 177–211); Brint, "Rethinking the policy influence of experts." (1990).

sional groups in each country and their contribution to the adoption and implementation of organizational paradigms.

State Involvement. States can become major actors in the generation, reception, and application of organizational paradigms. They can put all sorts of resources (political, economic, legitimatory, symbolic) at the disposal of employers and managers. Under some circumstances state-sponsored organizational innovations may be initiated autonomously as part of a wider program of national modernization. Radical nationalist critiques may produce a state-led industrialization process. These nationalist drives for industrialization have tended to facilitate the adoption of foreign systems of work organization, as in Brazil during the 1930s and in Spain during the 1940s and early 1950s. Whoever is to be credited for the initiative, the comparative study of state involvement in the adoption of organizational ideologies and techniques will be systematically pursued in this book. The state has tended to play a lesser role in the Anglo-Saxon countries than in continental European countries or economically backward ones like Spain or Brazil. In some cases, as in Germany, the state created powerful research and advisory organizations that promoted the adoption of new organizational ideas.

Workers' Responses. Previous studies of the practical implementation of organizational ideas have minimized or entirely neglected the role played by workers and their collective organizations. Workers and labor unions must be seen as relevant discretionary actors whose ideological position and practice cannot be taken for granted, or else accounting for the historical record becomes quite difficult indeed. Thus, it is crucial to avoid Chandler's complete negligence of labor unions and of the industrial relations system, Braverman's or Edwards's extreme assumptions about ultimate managerial omniscience and worker powerlessness, and Burawoy's or Hechter's premise that workers and labor unions invariably reject management's organizational proposals.[38] Part of the problem lies in assuming that members of a class become "oversocialized," even totally socialized, into its

38. Chandler, *The Visible Hand* (1977); Braverman (1974); Edwards, *Contested Terrain* (1979); Burawoy (1985, pp. 40–47); Hechter, *Principles of Group Solidarity* (1987, pp. 138–141). The best critique of Braverman's work is that by Stark, "Class struggle and the transformation of the labor process" (1980). For a criticism of Chandler's approach, see DuBoff and Herman, "Alfred Chandler's new business history" (1980).

norms and cultural traditions. This study will show that corporatist solutions to politics frequently achieved a collaboration between managers and workers that facilitated the adoption of new organizational paradigms. Instead of using an "integral" concept of power, one needs to use an "intercursive" one that allows for countervailing actions and division of scopes of action by workers and employers.[39] In this book, labor-union policy regarding working conditions and organization (as revealed by union publications, statements by union leaders, and actual behavior in the factory) will be examined as a variable in order to determine whether unions actually opposed, supported, or ignored attempts by management to introduce new organizational ideologies and techniques. Work cultures and informal patterns of workplace resistance, indifference, or support will also be considered carefully, given that official union policy may not be accepted by the rank-and-file.[40]

THE COMPARATIVE STUDY

The institutional framework outlined above will be used in conjunction with a comparative-historical research approach. This study is comparative because of its methodology, rather than because it takes into account empirical evidence from more than one country.[41] Two steps will be followed as part of a unified comparative scheme. First, the seven factors outlined above will be used to develop a meaningful historical interpretation of each case (country). Second, causal regularities over time in a multiplicity of cases will be analyzed, following a "variation-finding" approach. The comparative strategy follows what has been termed "standardized case comparison" based on a systematic analysis of differences and similitudes across cases.[42] Thus, the degree of acceptance and implementation of scientific manage-

---

39. Wrong, "The oversocialized conception of man in modern sociology" (1961); *Power* (1988, p. 11).

40. See DiMaggio, "Review essay: On Pierre Bourdieu" (1979, p. 1461); Bourdieu (1977, pp. 79, 81–83). Bendix (1974, pp. 443–444, 446, 449–450) refers to "work cultures" with the term *historical legacies*. Also, Burawoy, *Manufacturing Consent* (1979a, pp. 63–65), writes about "shop-floor cultures" from a quite different perspective (a Marxist one).

41. Kalleberg, "The logic of comparison" (1966, p. 72).

42. Walton, "Standardized case comparison" (1973, pp. 179–180). On the methods of agreement and difference, see Skocpol, "Emerging agendas and recurrent strategies in historical sociology," in Skocpol, ed. (1984, pp. 363, 368–380); Tilly, *Big Structures, Large Processes, Huge Comparisons* (1984, pp. 81–82); Smelser, *Comparative Methods in the Social Sciences* (1976, pp. 198–202). See also the classic exposition by J. S. Mill, "Of the four methods of experimental inquiry" (1950).

ment will be compared for the countries included in the study and evaluated during the 1910–1940 period. Similarly, the human relations paradigm will be studied during the 1945–1960 period, and structural analysis will be analyzed between 1960 and 1975. Attention will be focused on studying *configurations* of factors producing different or similar outcomes of adoption rather than on testing the relative importance of each individual factor. This study will show that the adoption of organizational paradigms has followed different paths and sequences by country, that sequences of events are relevant to explaining outcomes, and that the same outcome of adoption can result from different configurations of factors.[43]

The following four chapters analyze in depth the patterns of organizational change in the United States, Germany, Spain, and Great Britain during the twentieth century, using a logic of historical interpretation with specific reference to each of the seven explanatory conditions outlined above. The sixth chapter summarizes and compares the experiences of the four countries. Finally, the seventh chapter follows up on the general theme of managerial approaches to the problem of hierarchical organization and discusses the implications and contributions of this book.

43. See Sabel (1982, pp. 4–10); Habermas, "Technology and science as 'ideology'" (1971). On the sociological relevance of the timing of events, see Erikson, "Sociology and the historical perspective" (1970); Hannan and Freeman, *Organizational Ecology* (1989, pp. 66–80); Abbott, "Event sequence and event duration" (1984), and "Sequences of social events" (1983).

Two

The United States

Economic Transformations, Labor Problems, and Organizational Innovations

Countless shelves could be filled with studies about the origins and adoption of organizational ideas in the United States. The reason for attempting yet another study is that little previous research uses a cross-national comparative perspective to single out the distinctive aspects of the American experience. The case of the United States is important both in itself and because American developments influenced organizational thought and practice in many other countries throughout the twentieth century. Clearly unique about the United States was the need of managers to tackle the problems deriving from labor unrest in combination with the increasing size and complexity of the business enterprise, but in the absence of sustained international pressures. Most interesting was the historical process by which the ideological justification of managerial and organizational practices shifted from religious and paternalistic grounds to scientific ones, including the extensive influence of engineering science between the world wars and of social and behavioral science after 1945. When compared to continental European countries, the United States stands out for the pervasive influence of the science-based professions and the opposition of organized labor to many organizational innovations. This chapter includes few comparative materials, for one of its purposes is to set the stage for the study of the adoption of organizational ideas and techniques in Germany, Spain, and Great Britain.

From Religious Ethics to the Rise of Scientific Management

Until World War I the impact of religion on American business thought was far-reaching. Yet religion did not provide the basis for organizational ideas like human relations, as was the case in Germany, Spain, and Britain; rather, science did. This is paradoxical given that the United States is among the most religious societies in the world. The triumph of science-based management and organization in the United States represents such a discontinuity with the religious basis

30

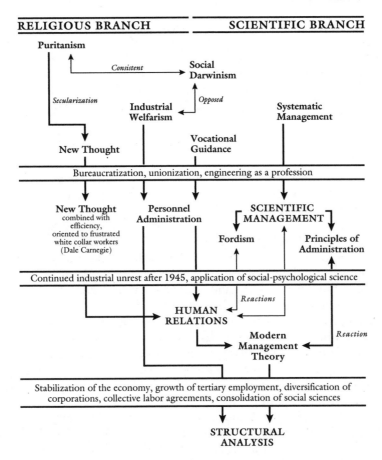

Figure 2.1. American managerial ideologies and organizational paradigms.

of previous organizational ideologies that it becomes essential to review the early ideas. Figure 2.1 summarizes the evolution of American managerial ideologies and organizational paradigms, and serves as an outline of the present chapter. First, the shift from religious to scientific justifications of organizational ideas will be related to the general process of industrialization in the United States, a change that differed from that in Germany and Spain. Second, bureaucratization, unionization, and the rise of the engineering profession will help to explain the emergence of scientific management. Third, the human relations school will be traced back to the rise of welfare capitalism, vocational guidance, and personnel administration, as well as to the growing importance of social-psychological science and consulting. Finally, the stabilization of the economy, the growth in service employment, the international expansion of American corporations, the diversification of their product lines, the increase in collective labor agreements, and the consolidation of the academic social sciences will be used to understand the appearance of structural theories of organization.

INDUSTRIALIZATION AND THE BREAKDOWN OF EARLY
ENTREPRENEURIAL IDEOLOGIES

Religious ethics provided the foundation of early entrepreneurial thought in the United States. The rationalization of the Puritan ethic of success was a slow but steady process dating back to the first settlers of Massachusetts. The major early figures included Cotton Mather and Benjamin Franklin, while Timothy Dwight continued the systematization of the ideology after 1812 with the addition of a patriotic component to the religious one.[1] American Puritans, Franklin in particular, promoted rational and systematic profit seeking as opposed to more "traditionalistic" ethics like that of Luther. This amounted to a continuation of the systematic innerworldliness of Calvinism.[2] Puritans held that earthly success represented proof of God's choice for predestination, the *calling*. Such an ideology of success and failure was compatible with the political values of the new nation, such as liberty, equality of opportunity, and individualism.[3] Becoming rich represented the stated patriotic goal in life, as was taught by Methodist, Baptist, and Congregational preachers. "From the pulpit you were told to get rich, and from the counting house to go to church."[4]

In addition to the calling, American Puritanism presented the frontiersman, the self-made man, as the role model. The message contained a critique of wage labor as a waste of time, and an explicit celebration of self-employment.[5] This should not be surprising given the geographical extension of the young republic, its endowment with natural resources, the predominantly agricultural basis of the work force, and the high proportion of family farms. "Go West, young man," exhorted journalist and politician Horace Greeley. Until shortly

1. Griswold, "Three puritans on prosperity" (1934a, p. 490).
2. For Weber, Benjamin Franklin was the best example of this rational attitude. See *The Protestant Ethic and the Spirit of Capitalism* (1958, pp. 65, 79–92, 117–118).
3. On the persistence of these values, see Lane, *Political Ideology* (1962).
4. Griswold, *The American Gospel of Success* (1933, p. 38).
5. Griswold (1933, pp. 2, 61–77).

before 1880 more than half of the gainfully employed population in the United States worked on the land.

The unique blend of religious asceticism, political ideas, and patriotic pursuit of wealth opened the way for a celebration of entrepreneurial success and an explanation of failure.[6] Most of these features were also present under scientific guise in the tracts of the social Darwinists beginning in the 1880s. In the eyes of William Graham Sumner, the founder of American sociology, people "struggled for existence" with the "subjugation of raw land." The accumulation of a business fortune "proved" one's ability to survive and thrive. The "doctrine of liberty" occupied a central position in his framework. But the victory of industry (and protectionism) in the Civil War, with the associated growth of the cities and of the wage-dependent population, demanded a change in the traditional explanations of economic success in life. In the Gilded Age the frontiersman and the self-employed became less and less common. Employers organized industrial activities and exercised authority over employees who sold their labor power for a wage. Due to their popularity during this transition period, the social Darwinists had the first chance to meet the ideological challenge of explaining the new realities. A first step was to recognize not just one way of earning one's living (i.e. self-employment on the land or as a businessman), but a variety of economic roles, including the investor of capital, the organizer of complex business activities, and the free seller of labor power. The scientific reasoning of the social Darwinists, however, pushed them in a direction incompatible with business interests, although they remained quite influential in government and reform circles. For Sumner, employer and employee "as parties to a [labor] contract are antagonistic," and to say that they "are partners in an enterprise is only a delusive figure of speech." Furthermore, Sumner justified the existence of labor unions because they were a weapon for workers in their struggle for existence, needing perhaps "development, correction, and perfection."[7] Given Sumner's logic, the impact of social Darwinism as an ideology of management could only be ephemeral.

But scientific social Darwinism was by no means the only way out of the breakdown of the traditional explanations caused by urbanization and wage-dependency. Posing no challenge to the assumptions of social Darwinism, the New Thought movement of 1890–1915

6. Bendix, *Work and Authority in Industry* (1974, pp. 257–258).
7. Sumner, *What Social Classes Owe to Each Other* (1974, pp. 44–48, 54, 67, 71–75, 82, 104).

presented the idea that "business success is due to certain qualities of the mind, character or temperament. Of these three qualities, the first is the only *real* one, as the last two are but the results of the first." New Thought was directed towards wage-dependent employees, who were exhorted to liberate themselves from their dull predicament: "Anything is yours if you only want it hard enough. Just think of that. *Anything*. Try it. Try it in earnest and you will succeed. It is the operation of a mighty law."[8] The crucial contribution of the New Thought movement was to relegate the individualism of the frontiersman or the self-employed to the background, emphasizing instead the qualities of the mind. Thus, the numerous New Thought tracts published at the turn of the century provided those urban workers who read them with a reason not to despair. It was not that one was biologically unfit, but that one had not tried hard enough.[9] The authority of the employer or the manager could be justified by reference to entrepreneurial success now being based on the power of the mind. But further changes in industry and trade would undermine the foundations of these new ideologies.

ECONOMIC TRANSFORMATIONS AND THE RISE OF LARGE FIRMS

After 1880 industrialization achieved a momentum of its own in the United States. Some traditional entrepreneurs prospered and concentrated production to such an extent that it was not unusual for them to employ thousands, even tens of thousands, of workers under one roof.[10] Gradually, craft-based production, whether organized as an internal contracting scheme or not, gave way to the factory system. In these medium and large-scale establishments, work proceeded in a fairly unstructured fashion due to the discretion that craftsmen and unskilled workers alike could exercise. In smaller establishments in semi-rural areas, workers maintained close ties with the surrounding community, foremen made decisions on particularistic grounds, and kinship relationships among workers remained dominant. Regardless of establishment size and location, however, deliveries of products to customers were irregular in terms of both quality and scheduling. In the old industries (textiles, iron, steel, machinery) the transition to the factory system was in part achieved by means of mechanization.

8. Both quotes from Griswold, "New Thought: A cult of success" (1934b, p. 313).
9. For an overview of the movement, see Dresser, *A History of the New Thought Movement* (1919).
10. Nelson, *Managers and Workers* (1975, pp. 7–8, 48–54).

The new electromechanical and chemical industries, however, could do without the craft-based model and proceed directly to implement the mass-production or continuous-flow techniques known at the time.[11]

The average size of industrial establishments increased steadily as a result of different actions aimed at various goals such as enhancing control over workers, attaining economies of scale, and reducing competition. According to business historian Alfred Chandler, the rise of the modern industrial enterprise rested upon the mass-consumption markets that emerged in the 1880s. In his view, the railroads and the telegraph not only unified the market but also pioneered modern management techniques later imitated by organizations in other sectors of the economy. By substituting managerial decision making for market allocation, firms could take advantage of the economies of scale (reduction of unit costs by increased throughput given fixed investments) and, albeit limitedly, of the economies of scope (gains from the integration of volume production with volume distribution) that could be realized in the world's largest, fastest-growing, and most homogeneous market. Chandler further explains that, as in Germany, but not in Britain, the largest industrial firms concentrated in capital-intensive and technologically advanced sectors such as food processing, chemicals, petroleum, primary metals, electrotechnical, machinery, and transportation equipment. Although improved throughput, horizontal mergers, and vertical integration generally resulted in increased market power that could be misused in "predatory" or "antisocial" ways, Chandler warns that "such power required a sound economic base."[12]

As sociologist Neil Fligstein has convincingly argued, with the support of systematic empirical evidence, between the late 1870s and the Great Depression industrialists and government actively engaged in a series of strategic moves and counter-moves. In the process, American capitalism adopted its present configuration for reasons quite different from the ones proposed by Chandler. When cartels were outlawed in the 1880s, groups of industrial leaders created trusts in order to "coordinate" their mutual economic interests. As a reaction to the enforcement of the 1890 Sherman antitrust legislation, employers devised holding companies and initiated an intense period of horizontal mergers, peaking in the four years following the

---

11. Jacoby, *Employing Bureaucracy* (1985, pp. 13–21).

12. Chandler, *The Visible Hand* (1977, pp. 209–239), and *Scale and Scope* (1990, pp. 52–53, 90–91, 224–233, 227).

Spanish-American War of 1898. Finally, further antitrust enforcement and the "preventive" Clayton Act of 1914 paved the way for the vertical mergers of the 1920s and the generalization of unitary or functional structures that signaled the triumph of the "manufacturing conception" of business management. According to Fligstein, then, economic efficiency operated only as a restriction, while most of the process was accounted for by coercive actions (state legislation enforcement) and mimetic behaviors.[13]

The transition from an entrepreneurial to a bureaucratic model had direct consequences for the separation of management from control (ownership), as both Chandler and Fligstein point out. While 56 percent of the American business elite born between 1831 and 1860 were "entrepreneurs," this was true of only 18 percent of those born between 1891 and 1920. Twenty-three percent of those born in 1831–1860 and 34 percent of those born in 1891–1920 inherited their position as business leaders ("heirs") or received enough wealth to purchase an enterprise. The proportion of elite members that followed a "bureaucratic" career to top management without inheriting wealth jumped from 21 percent among those born in 1831–1860 to 48 percent among the ones born in 1891–1920.[14] The critical consequence of these changes was that while three-fifths of those born in 1831–1860 could truly justify their authority by reference to their own entrepreneurial success, only one-fifth of the 1891–1920 birth group could do so. In addition, the number of administrative employees relative to those directly engaged in industrial production increased rapidly in the United States and remained higher than in any other major capitalist country until 1950. In 1900 manufacturing firms employed about 8 administrative workers for each 100 production workers. The ratio rose to 13 in 1913, 16 in 1920, and 18 in 1929. The increasing numbers of white-collar workers were an indication that the necessary knowledge and support staff to study and improve production methods was becoming available.

UNCONTROLLED GROWTH AND LABOR UNREST

Wage dependency, increased competition in factor and consumer markets, changes in the composition of the business elite, and the rise

---

13. Fligstein, *The Transformation of Corporate Control* (1990, pp. 1–115). A legal, ideological, and political analysis of this process throughout the Progressive Era is provided by Sklar, *The Corporate Reconstruction of American Capitalism* (1988).

14. Bendix (1974, p. 229). The data come from a sample of over 1,000 leading businessmen whose biographies appear in the *National Cyclopedia of American Biography*.

of factory bureaucracy—these cardinal changes evoked not only desires and actions to avoid "ruinous" competition. It is striking to note how Fligstein overstates the role of exogenous growth by horizontal or vertical mergers as a response to competitive pressures at the expense of neglecting changes and adaptations to competition taking place *within* the firm, regardless of its size or growth. Beneath the turbulent surface of merger movements and the enforcement of antitrust legislation lay the mundane reality of the shops, where momentous changes were happening perhaps even more rapidly. Industrialists were introducing labor-saving machinery, and dividing and simplifying tasks in an attempt to reserve the more skilled (and expensive) workers for the most difficult tasks.[15] Leading employers, engineers, and consultants of the time, however, complained that this specialization of machinery and division of labor by skill and task resulted in "a loss of direction, a decrease in efficiency, and a basic need for much greater coordination of activities and operations." Coordination among subordinates and relationships between top and lower management levels were breaking down. Clearly, the uncontrolled growth of industry as a result of market stimuli created confusion, duplication of efforts, and an unmanageable multiplicity of products, parts, and designs.[16]

Furthermore, the rush to take advantage of new economic and technological opportunities resulted in a growing labor problem that could ultimately offset and even totally wipe out the expected gains. The new organizational practices seemed to erode rather than strengthen worker discipline and motivation to produce. The advantages of mechanization, first-entry, and increased economies of scale were only realized at the cost of rapid urbanization, massive immigration, and considerable social dislocation. Over half of the work force in many areas during 1890–1910 had migrated directly from Europe. Workplace discipline became hard to enforce because the bases of traditional authority had thereby been undermined. Labor costs soared as employers were forced to compete for scarce skilled labor. The very concentration of a greater number of workers under the same roof prompted the development of a working-class consciousness and encouraged the organization of the first trade unions after

15. Litterer, "Systematic management: The search for order and integration" (1961, pp. 464–466).
16. Litterer (1961, pp. 372–373). See also Nelson, "Scientific management, systematic management, and labor, 1880–1915" (1974, p. 480); Noble, *America by Design* (1977, p. 69).

socialist principles, which later were to be abandoned. Given that most workers were paid on a day-rate basis, they engaged in output restriction. This was a quite rational response, for they feared that productivity increases could lead to dismissals. Employers and foremen too were responsible in part for the allegedly "chaotic" situation in the shops because they saw no good reason to avoid the "waste" of resources like raw materials, capital, or unskilled labor so long as profit margins remained high.[17]

What started as isolated individual unrest quickly turned into organized protest. Many employers responded by fortifying their factories and mines with walls and barbed wire. During strikes and lockouts, workers fought state militias and federal troops with rifles, pistols, dynamite, and even artillery pieces. Labor turmoil looked so alarming in the eyes of industrial and government elites that the U.S. Senate initiated an investigation in 1885, followed by a series of others during the 1890s by both houses of Congress. Bloody railway stoppages and the famous 1892 steel strike in Homestead, Pennsylvania, against Andrew Carnegie and Henry Clay Frick made it clear that an important cleavage had emerged as a result of rapid industrialization and social change, with state and local governments frequently taking sides with the robber barons. Labor unrest ceased being a mere lack of internalization of "machine-age conditions" or of the "industrial sense of time." Rather, the problem became that American workers rejected both docile obedience and individualism in favor of "collective, deliberate, and aggressive" behaviors. Employers showed dismay at the craftsmen's exercise of autonomy, the establishment of union work rules, including output quotas, and the widespread occurrence of stoppages and sympathetic strikes. Worker power soared during the expansion years of 1897–1903 as union membership quadrupled. The American Federation of Labor (AFL) became the largest union, with the Knights of Labor also gaining in membership. A radical competitor, the Industrial Workers of the World (IWW), was founded in 1905. The presence of foreign-born workers was proportionally growing, and they too organized into unions, except in the new industries such as autos and electricals. Industrial conflict remained rampant during the early twentieth century, reaching levels higher than in other comparable countries. The numbers of strikes and of workers involved in the United States between 1900 and 1920 were much higher than in Germany, Britain, or France. Strikes in

17. Nelson (1974, p. 481); Litterer (1961, pp. 462–463); Merkle, *Management and Ideology* (1980, pp. 16–20).

America were, according to historian Robert Zieger, "more savage and bloody" than anywhere else in the industrial world. Private and public police forces had to intervene frequently to break up meetings, threaten labor leaders, and destroy their organizations. After 1903, blacklisting, parallel unionization, strikebreaking, arbitrary firings, spying, coercion, and physical violence became common employer practices under the banner of the "open shop" movement.[18]

The diagnosis of the situation was quite simple: A comprehensive framework to handle the managerial and organizational problems deriving from factory bureaucratization, increased organizational complexity, and labor unrest was clearly lacking. Horizontal and vertical mergers to limit competition were of course important parts of the solution, as Fligstein has shown, but employers also had to cope with increased bureaucracy deriving from the scope and scale of effort in the larger firms, with the complexity of serving vast markets and utilizing the endless stream of technological innovations, and above all with the problem of organized labor protest. It is important to underscore that international competitive pressures were not relevant in the case of the United States. Unlike those in Germany, Spain or Britain, American businesses were not dependent on world trade because of the availability of a mass domestic market. American exports and imports represented only 12 percent of the national product in 1900, versus 32 percent for Germany and 39 percent for Britain, and while the proportions for Germany and Britain grew steadily to reach 34 and 48 percent, respectively, in 1929, the one for the United States actually decreased to 9 percent. For American firms, growth opportunities were domestic rather than international. Even in backward and relatively isolated Spain, exports and imports represented a proportion of the national product twice as large as in the United States.[19]

Structural, economic, and labor changes demanded new organizational and ideological approaches. Social Darwinism and New Thought could justify the subordination of the employee to the employer in ways that bore little relationship to the economic and social realities of huge, complex, bureaucratized firms manned by foreign-

18. Montgomery, *Workers' Control in America* (1979, pp. 9–27, 40–41, 91), *The Fall of the House of Labor* (1987, pp. 5–6, 13, 311); Jacoby (1985, pp. 23–30); Zieger, *American Workers, American Unions* (1986, pp. 5–6); Brody, *Workers in Industrial America* (1980, pp. 14–47); Rodgers, *The Work Ethic in Industrial America* (1978); Bendix (1974, pp. 267–274).

19. See the comparative statistics in Appendix B.

born labor that was organizing after the turn of the century. They were secularized rationalizations of economic success sharing a common origin in the Puritan ethic and the ideal of equality of opportunity. The tasks of justifying authority in the workplace and of securing orderly production became more complicated as industrial establishments grew larger, management became separated from ownership, and workers organized unions. None of these challenges could adequately be dealt with by self-explanatory references to economic or entrepreneurial success based on the survival of the fittest or on the power of the mind. It was no longer a question of randomness or of trying hard. Social Darwinism and New Thought remained very popular throughout the Progressive Era, but new solutions based on order, organization, method, system, and science replaced them as the dominant sources of organizational and managerial thought.

ENTER THE ENGINEERS

Ideas are not developed, let alone adopted, without prophets and apostles. It was precisely at the time when labor unrest and the complexity of the industrial enterprise became pressing problems that the new professional group of engineers started to gain power and influence in managerial spheres. At first, these two parallel phenomena appeared to be unrelated to each other, but their historical coincidence had momentous consequences for organizational debates and change. Modern engineering education and practice developed shortly after the Civil War, based on the so-called shop culture, on practical empiricism. Only the land-grant colleges and a few scientific schools (like Sheffield at Yale) included technical subjects in their curricula. It was not until the 1880s that science-based engineering combining elements from the French and German models emerged. The American Society of Mechanical Engineers (ASME), founded in 1880, relied on the shop culture, but it was an elitist and dynamic organization that proved both adaptive and conducive to the transformation of American industry. By 1900 the United States led the world in number of engineers relative to industrial employment, and its advantage over the closest competitor, Germany, widened during the 1910s and 1920s.[20]

Moreover, American mechanical engineers were the first to become interested in economic variables, not just technical ones. They had direct experience in the shops, and had to face the constraints of

20. Calvert, *The Mechanical Engineer in America* (1967); Abbott, *The System of Professions* (1988, pp. 105, 230).

economic cost on a daily basis. Henry R. Towne, of the Yale & Towne Manufacturing Co. in Stamford, Connecticut, was the first to discuss this need for economic knowledge in a paper presented at the ASME: "There are many good mechanical engineers—there are also many good 'business men'—but the two are rarely combined in one person."[21] Among many other conscientious management thinkers, John Tregoing, author of an 1891 *Treatise on Factory Management,* argued that the solution did not lie in "involving the company in a large outlay of money—it is simply a question of *method,* the application of a few simple rules."[22] Thus, cost accounting, production and inventory controls, and piecework rates were introduced not only to ease the "labor problem" but also to improve on the wasteful use of raw materials and capital equipment. Various piecework systems were tried, including the famous Halsey, Gantt, and Taylor schemes. The effective application of productivity-based wage schedules reinforced the unfolding of cost accounting, which had been neglected for decades despite rapid industrial growth. The simultaneous development of cost accounting, production-control procedures, inventory controls, and piecework schemes was the most important aspect of the movement towards more *systematic* management practices in industry.[23]

SCIENTIFIC MANAGEMENT AS A SOLUTION TO COMPLEXITY AND UNREST

It was in this context of evolving bureaucratic capitalism, mounting industrial turmoil, proliferation of engineers, and emerging systematic management practices that scientific management came to dominate the debate over the organization of work.[24] The early Frederick Winslow Taylor, a self-made engineer, devoted much effort to the experi-

---

21. Towne, "The engineer as an economist" (1886, p. 428).

22. Quoted in Litterer (1961, p. 473).

23. Yates, *Control through Communication* (1989); Diemer, "A bibliography of works management" (1904); Nelson (1974, pp. 480–482, 484); Dobb, *Wages* (1959, pp. 60–63); Garner, "Highlights in the development of cost accounting" (1968, p. 216); Jenks, "Early phases of the management movement" (1960, pp. 433–434); Chandler (1977, pp. 109–120, 272); Litterer (1963, pp. 380–387); Jelinek, "Toward systematic management" (1980). See also Haber, *Efficiency and Uplift* (1964, pp. 18–19), and Jacoby (1985, pp. 40–46), for the rise of the systematic managers as a group.

24. I will use the term *Taylorism* to refer to the "Taylor system." *Scientific management* is a much broader term that, of course, includes Taylorism. Taylor himself preferred the term *scientific management.* See *Taylor's Testimony Before the Special House Committee* (1972b, p. 6).

mental study of work. He rejected outright any kind of paternalism and cooperative experiments, including profit sharing, which he believed were "destined to fail" because they tended to constrain "personal ambition" and because of the "remoteness of the reward."[25] After having discovered high-speed steel, Taylor envisaged the gains that could be derived from the speedup of the work process if tools and machinery were standardized, machine times estimated, and the human factor adapted to ever higher speeds.[26] Manual tasks could now be studied, divided, and, when necessary and economical, performed by different people.[27] Taylor proposed a paradigm of organization that was in fact a combination of four principles, or elements: first, time-and-motion studies to standardize work tools and working conditions, and to divide the process into its simplest constituent tasks; second, selection of the cheapest adequate worker to perform each of the divided tasks; third, the "bringing together" of the scientifically determined task and the scientifically selected worker by means of functional foremanship, and an incentive system based on differential rates; and fourth, separation of the execution of work by the workers from its conception, which belonged to a "planning department."[28]

Taylor's ideas were not readily accepted by engineers outside his inner circle or by the ASME. In fact, the ASME avoided endorsing the arguments of the scientific managers in public controversies like the Eastern Railway rate case, and refused to publish Taylor's most popular book, *Principles of Scientific Management*. Many engineers thought that the Taylor System entailed dangers and pitfalls, and that

---

25. Taylor, "A piece-rate system" (1895, p. 866).

26. Nelson, *Frederick W. Taylor and the Rise of Scientific Management* (1980, pp. 80–103).

27. In this sense Taylor followed the line of reasoning pursued by political economists such as Smith and Babbage, as Etzioni has pointed out in his *Modern Organizations* (1964, p. 22). For the classic statements, see Smith, *Wealth of Nations* (1976, pp. 13–36), and Babbage, *On the Economy of Machinery and Manufactures* (1835, pp. 169–190). Haber (1964, p. 25) argues that neither the extreme division of labor nor the availability of mass-production techniques were essential to the application of the Taylor System. The reason he mentions is that Taylorism succeeded in many small workshops in which the possibilities for the division of labor were limited.

28. A concise statement of the principles as applied to bricklaying appears in Taylor, *The Principles of Scientific Management* (1967, p. 85). Taylor explained again the four principles on the occasion of his *Testimony* (1972b, pp. 40–45). A detailed exposition of the functions of the planning department can be found in Taylor, *Shop Management* (1972a, pp. 110–120).

much truly scientific refinement of the system was needed. That was precisely what Taylor's followers did. Frank and Lillian Gilbreth improved the methodology of time-and-motion study, introducing the cyclograph and the chronocyclograph. (Motion study using motion-picture cameras also became much easier and cheaper to implement with the introduction of 16mm film in 1921.) Henry Gantt developed progress charts to optimize the use of resources over time, and Harrington Emerson contributed to the clarification of the concept of efficiency.[29] Thanks to these improvements and to the rising tide of technocratic social reform, more and more engineers began to accept scientific management principles.[30]

Taylor's scientific management was not only a set of organizational techniques but also a managerial ideology, including a particular view of industry and society that emphasized individualism and "exact scientific knowledge" in order to determine what was "a fair day's work." Taylor provided the synthesis of most of the existing ideas about the replacement of industrial chaos and conflict with order and joint effort. In so doing, he challenged the "old" practices of both workers and managers on two counts: their unmethodic arbitrariness and their antagonistic attitudes. As for labor unions, Taylor argued that he favored shorter hours and "even higher wages than the unions do," but that he could not accept output restriction. Under scientific management, he thought, labor unions and collective bargaining would be "of trifling importance"; given the new collaborative spirit, one or more workers could bring to the attention of management anything they found wrong. If management failed to meet the complaint, the worker could simply stop collaborating and revert to the old ways. Scientific management also provided a direct answer to the question of the "one best way" to organize, and promised social harmony and economic affluence, once a "mental revolution" was firmly established in the minds of both employer and employee, so that their attention was focused on the "increasing size of the surplus," making it "unnecessary to quarrel over how it shall be divided." Thus, Taylor was unique among the scientific managers in that he continued the line

29. F. B. Gilbreth, *Bricklaying System* (1909), *Motion Study* (1911), *Primer of Scientific Management* (1912); F. B. Gilbreth and L. M. Gilbreth, *Applied Motion Study* (1917), *Fatigue Study* (1918); L. M. Gilbreth, *The Psychology of Management* (1914); Gantt, *Work, Wages, and Profits* (1911), *Industrial Leadership* (1916), *Organizing for Work* (1919); Emerson, *The Twelve Principles of Efficiency* (1912). On Gilbreth, see Giedion, *Mechanization Takes Command* (1969, pp. 17–30, 101–113).

30. Layton, *The Revolt of the Engineers* (1971, pp. 140–141, 154–172).

of reasoning initiated by the New Thought movement at the turn of the century. Mental attitudes mattered now as much as then, the big difference being the substitution of "scientific investigation and knowledge" for "individual judgment or opinion."[31] The string of events includes, then, a first shift from religious revival in the nineteenth century to a more analytical New Thought movement, and a second shift from New Thought to scientific management's claim to neutral science.

Psychologist Hugo Münsterberg was the other great early contributor to the translation of New Thought narrative into scientific discourse. In his 1913 book, *Psychology and Industrial Efficiency*, he observed, "The inner labor, the inner values, and the inner difficulties are too often unknown to those who decide for a vocation." Before moving to the United States, Münsterberg had been a student of Wilhelm Wundt at Leipzig, where a new conception of psychology took shape in the two decades after German unification in 1870. The old pursuit of general laws applicable to the human species was giving way to an individual psychology that searched for individual differences. Methodologically, laboratory experimentation and measurement were emphasized over introspection. Münsterberg refined New Thought ideas in a distinctive way, arguing that human beings concealed "an unlimited manifoldness of talents and abilities." It was the task of the industrial psychologist to discern and measure each of those, to develop laboratory tests for use instead of arbitrary on-the-job selection, and to suggest which job fit each individual best. Münsterberg's psychology would have effects on society as a whole: "Still more important than the naked commercial profit on both sides, is the cultural gain which will come to the total economic life of the nation." The application of industrial psychology would achieve an "adjustment of work and psyche by which mental dissatisfaction in the work, mental depression and discouragement may be replaced in our social community by overflowing joy and perfect inner harmony."[32]

Münsterberg clearly conceived of his book as a complement to scientific management ideas. He was very much impressed by the achievements of motion study but pointed out that the Achilles' heel

---

31. Taylor (1972b, pp. 29–31, 150–151, 182–183).
32. Münsterberg, *Psychology and Industrial Efficiency* (1913, pp. 28, 33, 38, 39, 50, 51–53, 158–159, 198–220, 308–309). The book was first published in German in late 1912, and then in English in early 1913. The two versions are similar but not identical. See Münsterberg (1913, p. v). See also Baritz, *The Servants of Power* (1960, pp. 21–30).

of scientific management was the selection of workers. In responding to critics of scientific management, he proposed to eliminate the problems of monotony and fatigue by psychological selection of the workers who were mentally fit to endure scientifically engineered tasks. As in the case of *The Principles of Scientific Management*, Münsterberg's book was less a scientific work than a manifesto that initiated a movement of much importance. His constant contacts with American managers from his position as professor of psychology and director of the psychological laboratory at Harvard made him aware of the possibilities of applied industrial psychology. His sudden death in 1916 prevented him from witnessing the boom in psychological testing that started during World War I.

PROGRESSIVISM, THE STATE, AND MASS CULTURE

The early adoption of scientific management owed much to certain cultural factors that contributed to an increasingly modernistic mentality among both the business elite and the general public. Taylorism became the center of a national controversy during the famous Eastern Rate Case of 1910–1911. Lawyer and Democratic reformer Louis D. Brandeis, representing business associations from all over the East Coast, argued that wages could be raised, even leaving railroad rates unchanged, if scientific management techniques were implemented. The publicity given to this attractive idea marked the start of America's "efficiency craze," which was to last until the entry of the United States into World War I.[33] In 1912 the Congress held hearings on scientific management after the start of a much-publicized strike at Watertown Arsenal over the implementation of the Taylor system, adding publicity to Taylorism, but also providing its critics with arguments.[34]

Scientific management also profited from certain reform movements. Taylorism captured the imagination of the Progressives because of the possibility of using neutral, science-based expertise to "reform social reform." As historian Samuel Haber has documented, there was a mutual influence between both movements. Government reform was to be inspired by scientific management principles, and scientific management would be modified to allow for its implementation in non-industrial settings, including public schools, operating

33. Haber (1964, pp. 52–54); Sullivan, *Our Times* (1932, pp. 74–75); Bell, *The End of Ideology* (1988, pp. 231–235).
34. Hoxie, *Scientific Management and Labor* (1915).

theaters in hospitals, and outpatient clinics.[35] But this is not to say that the state formally and directly promoted the application of scientific management to industry as in Germany and the Soviet Union during the 1920s or in Spain during the 1940s. Quite on the contrary, in what amounted to a symbolic gesture, the stopwatch was banned from government arsenals. The promotion of scientific management was left to private initiative (the engineering societies, the Taylor Society, and the activities of the Boston philanthropists, e.g., Edward Filene and his Twentieth Century Fund). The only exception were the efforts at industrial standardization and simplification through the Bureau of Standards.[36] What Progressivism achieved was the acceptance by the elite and by large segments of the population of the modernistic equation of human progress with material and technological advance, an idea central to scientific management.[37]

Both the "efficiency craze" and Progressive reformism lost momentum after World War I, although engineer-politicians like Republican President Herbert Hoover (who had been the first president of the Federated American Engineering Societies) successfully combined Progressive ideals with scientific management principles in the quest for higher efficiency and reduced waste.[38] But if efficiency and reform subsided, the cultural climate favoring the scientific management of both mass production and distribution continued with the consolidation of the mass-consumption culture during the 1920s. The twenties were characterized by the end of mass immigration, the electrification of industry, and an accelerated urbanization process. Mass culture justified the adaptation of the worker to stringent factory conditions in exchange for higher wages and consumption. It emphasized that citizens were "consumers" rather than "producers" or "workers." The American system of high production, high wages, high consumption, and high profits became firmly established in the consciousness of the business elite and huge segments of the general public, as John Dos Passos sagaciously showed in *The Big Money* (1933). The late 1920s and 1930s were also the heyday of machine-age industrial design in America, with its emphasis on standardized goods and large produc-

35. Haber (1964, pp. 75–159); Bell, *The Coming of Post-Industrial Society* (1973, pp. 352–353); Callahan, *Education and the Cult of Efficiency* (1962); Morman, ed., *Efficiency, Scientific Management, and Hospital Standardization* (1989).

36. Noble (1977, pp. 71–83).

37. Akin, *Technocracy and the American Dream* (1977, pp. 1–26).

38. Hoover promoted a controversial study that blamed mostly management, but also labor, for the wasteful use of resources. See Committee on Elimination of Waste in Industry, *Waste in Industry* (1921).

tion batches. The implementation of scientific management techniques as applied to mass production could not find a more munificent cultural environment.[39]

THE OPPOSITION OF THE UNIONS TO SCIENTIFIC MANAGEMENT

Organized labor became involved in discussions about organizational theory and practice quite early. Before 1911 no strikes were reported in plants where scientific management was being introduced. A 1908 survey found that three-fourths of local unions defending the interests of workers affected by piecework accepted performance-based schemes. But the publicity given to scientific management by the Eastern Rate Case and Taylor's *Principles* in 1911 did not please the leadership of the AFL. A major concern was the constant attacks on unions by the scientific managers. During the railroad controversy, the unions took sides with management, not with the apologist of scientific management, Brandeis. The executive council of the AFL declared war on Taylorism, for it saw in its implementation a naked attack on workers and their unions. Opposition and strikes mounted. It was among unskilled workers in the mass-assembly industries that the major battles were fought, including the strikes and sabotage organized by the Industrial Workers of the World.[40]

World War I and its aftermath changed the ideological position of American unions but *not* their practical stand or the patterns of workplace resistance. The AFL had gained much respect among government officials and the public as a result of its policy of cooperation during the war, but the armistice, the economic downturn, and the loss in membership initiated a deep crisis in union goals and strategy. Inflation, strikes, and the "Red scare" ostracized the AFL. Unemployment and stagnant real wages remained the rule throughout the 1920s

39. Layton (1971, pp. 190–195); Merkle (1980, pp. 58–71); Ewen, *Captains of Consciousness* (1976); Hounshell, *From the American System to Mass Production* (1984, pp. 303–330); Dos Passos, *The Big Money* (1979, pp. 44–48, 70–77); Meikle, *Twentieth Century Limited* (1979); Wilson, Pilgrim, and Tashjian, *The Machine Age in America* (1986); Jordy, *The Impact of European Modernism in the Mid-Twentieth Century* (1986); Banham, *A Concrete Atlantis* (1986); Smith, *Making the Modern* (1993, pp. 16–92); Banta, *Taylored Lives* (1993).

40. Nadworny, *Scientific Management and the Unions* (1955, pp. 23, 38, 43, 48–67); Jacoby, "Union-management cooperation in the United States" (1983, p. 19); MacKelvey, *AFL Attitudes toward Production* (1952, pp. 1–26); Davis, "The stopwatch and the wooden shoe" (1975, pp. 74–75, 86–87); Licht, "Studying Work," in Jacoby, ed., *Masters to Managers* (1991, pp. 71–72).

despite the boom starting at the middle of the decade. As part of a complex reaction to changing circumstances, the AFL began to collaborate with the engineering profession and the Taylor Society in an attempt to break its isolation and gain influence. Management-union cooperation was encouraged by government officials, union leaders, and Taylor Society members, but individual employers and the National Association of Manufacturers (NAM) remained faithful to the open-shop creed and refused to cooperate. In fact, the open-shop drive of 1920–23 was tremendously successful. Unlike employers in the continental countries of Europe, American employers followed a confrontational, union-busting strategy because of the very conservatism of American labor unions, which were averse to socialism, and thus "ineligible" to be bought out through collective bargaining.[41] The new mass-production industries remained largely non-unionized, so the little cooperation that took place was limited to some small plants in mature industries like textiles, where the unions were more militant. Moreover, these cooperative experiments were not the result of a belief in the convenience of joint management-union implementation of scientific management, but a necessity in the face of declining profits and competition from other non-unionized firms. In other words, the alliance among Progressive social reformers, labor leaders, and the Taylor Society threatened the power of employers.

The employers, for their part, still saw in scientific management a way to rationalize their enterprises and hold the unions in check, especially be preventing the unionization of unskilled immigrant workers. In brief, the implementation of scientific management in American industry during the 1920s did not owe anything to the attitude of the AFL or any other labor union, despite the occasional collaboration with the Taylor Society. Quite on the contrary, most local unions, even those affiliated with the AFL, continued their practice of opposing the use of the stopwatch, and many remained wary of bonuses and incentive-wage schemes. The AFL also fought new forms of scientific management such as Fordism and the Bedaux System.[42]

THE THEORETICAL IMPACT OF SCIENTIFIC MANAGEMENT

After Taylor's death in 1915, scientific management became more useful as a set of techniques than as an ideology to justify the absolute

41. Jacoby, "American exceptionalism revisited," in Jacoby, ed. (1991, pp. 174–176).
42. Zieger (1986, pp. 1–10); Nadworny (1955, pp. 73–74, 114–117, 119–121, 134–143); Jacoby (1983); McKelvey (1952, pp. 78, 114–126); *American Federationist,* "A. F. L. report on the Bedaux system" (1935).

authority of the employer or manager. The NAM initially backed Taylorism mainly because of its justification of a union-free workplace, but its criticism of the employers' arbitrariness and "unscientific" discretion was not met with enthusiasm.[43] The influence of scientific management ideas among those managers who expressed themselves during the 1920s and 1930s in the leading management journals is clear and dominates that of other theories of organization, but the emphasis was placed on the need to eliminate waste and to implement practical techniques, not on the potential of the paradigm as an ideology to address the union challenge. The technical component of scientific management ultimately appealed to American employers and managers.[44] Tables 2.1 and 2.2 show the results of a content analysis of the articles published in the *Harvard Business Review*, the most important journal of general management, and *Industrial Management* (later, *Factory and Industrial Management* and *Factory Management and Maintenance*), the leading American magazine for shop management. (Journal articles were coded according to the rules explained in Appendix A.) The results in panel A of Tables 2.1 and 2.2 confirm the failure of scientific management as an ideology and its success as a set of techniques. Scientific management articles outnumbered those using a human relations or structural approach during the first five years of the *Harvard Business Review* (1923–28), as documented in panel B of Table 2.1. The same dominance was found in *Industrial Management* between 1918 and 1927 (see panel B of Table 2.2), a journal far more committed to scientific management because of its focus on shop management and production methods as opposed to *Harvard Business Review's* broader coverage of the general field of business management. The management theorists and practicing managers who contributed to these two journals almost always recommended the use of the most popular scientific management techniques (time-and-motion study, job analysis, and simplification and standardization). Topics such as plant layout, motion study, and incentives figured prominently in management guides such as the *Handbook of Business Administration,* published in 1931 by the

43. Haber (1964, p. 71); Bendix (1974, pp. 280–281).
44. In this respect, Bendix (1974, pp. 280–281) offers no evidence to conclude that "the social philosophy rather than the techniques of scientific management became a part of the prevailing managerial ideology." Bendix focuses too narrowly on the Taylor system, which of course was not accepted as such. Scientific management techniques did spread, as will be documented in the following pages, but many of its ideological themes were not widely accepted.

American Management Association, although chapters on leadership, group incentives, and suggestion systems were also included.[45] Lastly, scientific management techniques became a part of the curriculum at leading business schools like Wharton, Harvard, and Dartmouth. Scientific management clearly contributed to the trend toward the professionalization of management because it assigned the manager a technical function based on science and not on guesswork, intuition, or personal discretion.[46]

THE PRACTICAL IMPACT OF SCIENTIFIC MANAGEMENT, FORDISM, AND THE BEDAUX SYSTEM

American employers generally agreed with the basic scientific management goals of eliminating waste and cooperating with labor to increase production, but they felt uneasy about the proposal of reducing the traditional sphere of managerial discretion. They also disliked the costs and uncertainties associated with the full implementation of specific versions of scientific management like the one proposed by Taylor. The Taylor System of scientific management never achieved widespread adoption in practice. By 1915 Taylorism had been intro-

TABLE 2.1 Results of the content analysis of the articles and lengthy book reviews published in the *Harvard Business Review*, 1923–1970, by paradigm (SM: scientific management; HR: human relations; SA: structural analysis; NC: not classifiable)

A. Number of articles mentioning each of the content categories (see Appendix A) and themes (155 articles examined)

Content Categories	SM	HR	SA
Perceived problem	15	79	31
Form of solution	2	2	18
View of conflict	2	19	18
View of workers	2	50	4
Fascination with	3	49	2
Methodology	4	33	7
Selection of workers	5	6	2
Distribution of tasks	5	9	20
Authority structures	3	67	25
Process of work	9	15	26
Preferred rewards	4	27	3
Economic incentives	3	6	1

45. Donald, ed., *Handbook of Business Administration* (1931).
46. Nelson (1980, pp. 188–189); Jacoby (1985, pp. 128–129).

TABLE 2.1 *(Continued)*

B. Number of articles (N) and themes classified by paradigm

Year Period	SM				HR				SA				NC
	N	Mean	Min	Max	N	Mean	Min	Max	N	Mean	Min	Max	N
1923–25	5	3.0	1	6	1	3.0	3	3	3	4.7	3	6	2
1926–28	3	4.0	4	4	0	—	—	—	1	3.0	3	3	0
1929–31	1	2.0	2	2	1	2.0	2	2	0	—	—	—	0
1932–34	1	2.0	2	2	4	4.0	3	6	2	4.0	3	5	1
1935–37	0	—	—	—	3	4.3	3	5	0	—	—	—	0
1938–40	0	—	—	—	3	3.0	2	4	0	—	—	—	0
1941–43	.0	—	—	—	2	4.5	3	6	0	—	—	—	0
1944–46	0	—	—	—	6	4.7	3	7	2	4.5	4	5	4
1947–49	0	—	—	—	6	4.3	3	6	2	5.0	4	6	1
1950–52	1	5.0	5	5	8	3.6	2	6	0	—	—	—	4
1953–55	0	—	—	—	14	4.2	2	7	2	4.0	4	4	2
1956–58	0	—	—	—	11	4.3	3	6	2	4.5	4	5	4
1959–61	0	—	—	—	5	4.0	2	6	2	6.0	6	6	3
1962–64	0	—	—	—	9	3.9	2	6	7	4.3	3	5	4
1965–67	1	2.0	2	2	6	4.0	3	5	5	3.8	1	5	3
1968–70	1	4.0	4	4	5	3.4	3	4	2	4.0	3	5	0
All years	13	3.2	1	6	84	4.0	2	7	30	4.3	1	6	28
Pages	134	10.3	4	20	891	10.6	4	26	303	10.1	5	17	262

Note: For volumes 1 (1922–23) through 25 (1946–47) all articles were allocated to the second year (e.g. all articles in volume 1 to year 1923).

Sources: The articles included in the analysis are the following:

SM: *HBR* 1:71–80, 331–341, 342–354, 417–427; 2:13–22; 5:11–20, 269–280; 6:264–269; 7:170–174; 10:399–410; 28(3):33–53.

HR: *HBR* 1:438–450; 7:143–155; 10:40–53; 11:57–66; 12:106–115, 458–471; 14:1–13, 161–171, 405–413; 16:424–435; 18:275–284, 285–294; 20:21–53; 21:415–424; 23:283–298, 469–483, 484–492; 24:119–132, 197–214, 228–244; 25:145–157, 318–338, 339–347; 26:267–281; 27:521–541, 542–558; 28(1):61–73; 28(3):54–58; 28(5):42–48; 29(1):29–55; 29(5):47–57; 30(2):33–45, 73–80; 30(3):71–83; 31(1):29–38, 97–110; 31(6):55–62, 72–78; 32(1):63–75, 76–86; 32(3):49–57; 32(5):63–72; 33(1):33–42; 33(2):90–100; 33(5):40–48; 59–67; 33(6):48–60, 91–99; 34(1):41–48; 34(4):61–72; 34(5):55–62; 35(5):85–92; 35(6):41–47; 36(1):111–119; 36(2):41–50, 95–101; 36(3):69–75; 36(4):123–135; 36(6):107–116; 37(1):79–86; 37(4):75–82; 37(5):81–92; 38(3):137–146; 38(5):80–102; 40(1):133–138; 41(3):130–145; 41(4):49–55; 41(6):53–61; 42(1):73–88, 89–94; 42(2):60–74; 42(3):133–143; 42(6):133–155; 43(4):148–163; 44(4):154–162; 44(5):111–116, 117–128; 45(2):22–40 and 172–178; 46(1):53–62, 118–126; 47(1):4–12 and 166–176; 47(2):61–78; 47(5):109–118; 48(3):97–110.

SA: *HBR* 1:368–374; 3:287–296, 321–338; 4:106–111; 10:269–279; 11:244–252; 22:477–494; 23:360–371; 26:313–328; 27:107–122; 31(5):43–49; 32(2):89–96; 34(3):39–47; 35(3):49–62; 37(6):77–89; 39(5):67–79; 40(4):81–89; 40(5):121–129; 40(6):111–118, 140–154; 41(1):73–81; 41(5):121–132; 42(3):158–178; 42(6):55–67; 43(1):109–122; 43(3):93–102; 44(6):96–104; 45(2):73–82; 45(5):84–90; 45(6):142–151; 46(6):129–138; 48(3):61–68.

NC: *HBR* 2:373–376; 3:99–103; 12:47–58; 22:239–248; 24:405–426; 427–437, 466–497; 27:480–497; 28(1):80–86, 127–144; 30(4):64–74; 30(5):72–82; 31(2):116–126; 32(6):103–112; 34(2):49–56; 34(4):105–112; 34(5):125–132; 36(1):69–76; 37(2):79–86; 37(3):121–125; 38(3):123–125; 40(2):113–116; 40(4):90–98; 42(4):62–68; 43(2):74–82; 44(3):106–114; 45(3):119–130; 48(3):47–60.

duced in 140 establishments totalling 63,000 workers, but only a handful of plants implemented it in full for an extended period of time. The leading scientific managers themselves (Taylor, Emerson, Gantt, Gilbreth) disagreed about the relative importance of each of the elements of the system and the order in which they should be implemented. In an attempt to reduce its complexity and cost, employers often identified scientific management with time study plus a performance-based economic incentive system.[47]

Employers soon realized that the labor problems of the 1920s required bolder initiatives, and introduced industrial betterment and participation programs with mixed results as part of the welfare capitalism movement ("the American Plan"). But scientific management techniques were useful to cope with specific problems associated with the increasing scale and complexity of production operations. There is a wealth of historical case studies documenting the use of scientific management techniques by American firms during the 1920s and early 1930s, with engineers playing a key role, and labor unions in the traditional industrial sectors delaying and partially deflecting the

47. Littler, *The Development of the Labour Process in Capitalist Societies* (1982, p. 179); Nelson (1980, pp. 149–167); Nelson (1975, pp. 61–72); Merkle (1980, pp. 37–100).

TABLE 2.2   Results of the content analysis of the articles and lengthy book reviews published in *Industrial Management/Factory*, 1918–1958, by paradigm (SM: scientific management; HR: human relations; SA: structural analysis; NC: not classifiable)

A. Number of articles mentioning each of the content categories (see Appendix A) and themes (177 articles examined)

Content Categories	SM	HR	SA
Perceived problem	64	46	0
Form of solution	13	1	2
View of conflict	9	6	0
View of workers	3	15	0
Fascination with	1	10	0
Methodology	95	16	0
Selection of workers	11	4	0
Distribution of tasks	23	3	0
Authority structures	4	35	0
Process of work	55	3	0
Preferred rewards	23	14	0
Economic incentives	41	6	0

TABLE 2.2 *(Continued)*

B. Number of articles (*N*) and themes classified by paradigm

Year Period	SM				HR				SA				NC
	N	Themes Mean	Min	Max	*N*	Themes Mean	Min	Max	*N*	Themes Mean	Min	Max	*N*
1918–19	10	4.3	2	9	3	3.0	3	3	0	—	—	—	5
1920–22	20	3.4	1	5	7	2.3	1	3	0	—	—	—	5
1923–25	10	3.2	1	5	3	3.7	2	5	0	—	—	—	1
1926–28	5	3.4	2	4	4	3.2	2	4	0	—	—	—	3
1929–31	8	2.6	1	4	1	3.0	3	3	0	—	—	—	2
1932–34	6	2.8	1	4	1	3.0	3	3	0	—	—	—	0
1935–37	6	2.8	1	4	3	3.3	3	4	0	—	—	—	1
1938–40	4	2.0	1	3	2	2.5	2	3	0	—	—	—	1
1941–43	10	2.1	1	4	1	3.0	3	3	0	—	—	—	0
1944–46	11	3.0	1	6	10	2.6	2	3	0	—	—	—	0
1947–49	9	2.6	1	4	4	1.8	1	3	0	—	—	—	3
1950–52	9	2.6	1	4	5	2.2	1	3	0	—	—	—	0
1953–55	0	—	—	—	1	4.0	4	4	0	—	—	—	1
1956–58	0	—	—	—	4	3.8	3	4	0	—	—	—	0
All years	106	3.0	1	9	49	2.8	1	5	0	—	—	—	22
Pages	425	4.0	1	10	179	3.7	1	8	0	—	—	—	82

Notes: The title of the journal varies: *Industrial Management* (1918–1927); *Factory and Industrial Management* (1928–1933); and *Factory Management and Maintenance* (1934–1958, vols. 92–116). For even years only the articles published in the January through June monthly issues were considered. For odd years only the articles published in the July through December issues were considered.

Sources: The articles included in the analysis are the following:

SM: 55(1918):108–109, 380–384, 441–446, 480–483, 485–490; 58(1919):1–8, 54–61, 134–138, 140–145, 325–327; 59(1920):41–42, 120–122, 143–145, 145–148, 301–306, 306–310, 311–313, 323–324, 361–366, 367–371, 409–411, 487–491; 62(1921):16–17, 76–82, 141–144, 182–187, 244–250, 292–297; 63(1922):7–11, 143–145, 341–346; 66(1923):196–200, 228–229, 368–372; 67(1924):105–106, 145–149, 231–234, 280–283, 375–382; 70(1925):38–39, 141–149; 74(1927):224–229, 289–296; 330–333; 75(1928):1183–1185; 78(1929):831–833, 1066–1068, 1335; 79(1930):296–298, 1081–1082, 1360–1362; 82(1931):52–54, 334–336; 83(1932):115–117, 164–165; 91(1933):265–267, 394–396, 482–484; 92:19–21; 93:328–330, 510–511; 94(5):177–178, (6):209–210; 95(8):60–62, (10):80–81; 96(6):56–57, 132, 134; 100(6):88–89, 216, 218, 220; 101(7):117–118, (8):96–105, 154–163, (10): 90–92, 97–101, (11):116–118, 122–123; 102(2):93–95, (3):119–121, (4):96–97, (5):89–91, (6):122–123; 103(8):120–127, 117–124, 118–122; 104(1):113–116, (2):92–96, (3):126–130; 105(8):78–80, (10):74–75; 106(1):86–87, 117, 118–119, (2):86–87, 132, 134, (5):126–128; 107(7):66–69; 108(5):100–103, 104–105, 106–108, 112–113; 110(1):124–125, (2):138–139,(6):94–95.

HR: 55(1918):210–217, 303–306, 312–314; 59(1920):18–20; 62(1921):48–51, 59–60, 223–227, 273–274, 341–344, 363–369; 66(1923):307–310; 70(1925):282–283, 287–288; 71(1926):19–25, 93–98, 366–372; 74(1927):286–296; 75(1928):72–75; 78(1929):41–43; 83(1932):15–16; 94(3):117–118, (6): 206–207; 95(11):63; 96(5):62–63, 130, 132, 134, (6):45; 101(10):122–126; 102(2):96–98, (5):101–104; 103(7):108–110, 121–124; 104(1):117–120, 131–132, (2):113–120, (3):90–94, 120–124, (5):108–112; 106(4):94–96, (5):78–79, (5):82–83, 126–128; 108(1):109–110; 109(8):104–106, (9):104–106, (10): 126–129; 110(1):122–123; 111(9):148–150; 114(2):130–136; 115(7):94–97, (9):98–100.

NC: 55(1918):225–227, 408–410, 457–460; 58(1919):17–20, 89–94, 265–268; 59(1920):43–47, 199–202; 62(1921):195–198; 63(1922):143–145, 371–374; 67(1924):47–51; 74(1927):129–135, 270–275; 75(1928):83–84; 78(1929):43–46; 79(1930):527–529; 95(12):82–83; 106(2):118–119, (3):65, (5): 131, 111(9):104–106.

process.[48] Techniques of worker selection, plant layout, job analysis, time study, division of labor, and piecework compensation were introduced in piecemeal fashion or in combination with single-purpose machinery, allowing for the mass production of goods.[49]

It is hard to find representative empirical evidence about the prevalence of isolated scientific management practices. The best indicator is the number of firms using time-and-motion study. The surveys conducted by the National Industrial Conference Board (NICB) starting in the 1930s are the best sources available. Table 2.3 summarizes the available prevalence data on time study, motion study, and piecework in 1935, 1939, and 1946. Although the 1935 levels of prevalence may seem low for the world's scientific management pioneer (27 percent for all firms, 31 percent among manufacturing firms, and about 40 percent among firms with 1,000 or more employees), the upward trend between 1935 and 1946 clearly indicates that the use of scientific management techniques was gaining acceptance. The highest proportions (sometimes over 80 percent) of firms implementing time-and-motion study were to be found in sectors such as automobiles and parts, electrical, and machines and machine tools. Scientific management techniques were not as quickly adopted in older industries such as lumber, printing and publishing, and stone, clay, and glass, because of their more traditionalistic managers, stronger unions, and higher proportions of skilled workers. Service-sector firms only applied scientific management techniques in rare cases.[50]

Scientific management techniques were fundamental to the development of what became to be known as Fordism. Like Taylor, Henry Ford was a self-made mechanic.[51] Ford made extensive use of scientific management techniques at his new factory at Highland Park in Detroit. He hired the best mechanics and scientific management experts in the area, among them Charles Sorensen. Ford's plant managers improved the production process on a trial-and-error basis, making

48. See Littler (1982, pp. 179–185); Nadworny (1955); Nelson (1980); Jacoby (1985).

49. Bendix (1974, pp. 280–281); Chandler (1977, pp. 209–283); Edwards (1979, pp. 97–104).

50. Baron et al., "Mission control?" (1988), and "War and peace" (1986). Appendix C explores industry-level differences in the adoption of time study with the aid of multivariate statistical techniques.

51. Unless otherwise noted, the source for all that follows on Ford is Sward, *The Legend of Henry Ford* (1972, pp. 3–80). See also his autobiography, *My Life and Work* (1923), and Sullivan, *Our Times: The United States 1900–1925, vol. 4, The War Begins* (1932, pp. 50–72).

TABLE 2.3 Indicators of the practical implementation of scientific management techniques in American firms, by sector (manufacturing and non-manufacturing) and firm size, in 1935–1946 (in percentages)

Practice	1935	1939	1946
Time study			
All firms	27%	41%	45%
Manufacturing	31	48	51
Non-manufacturing	5	9	8
1–249 workers	13	23	27
250–999 workers	31	47	47
1,000–4,999 workers	41	51	56
5,000 or more workers	40	53	59
Motion study			
All firms	—	14	18
Manufacturing	—	16	20
Non-manufacturing	—	4	5
1–249 workers	—	5	8
250–999 workers	—	14	16
1,000–4,999 workers	—	23	28
5,000 or more workers	—	27	35
Piecework			
All firms	47	. . .	. . .
Manufacturing	53	. . .	. . .
Non-manufacturing	13	. . .	. . .
1–249 workers	37	. . .	. . .
250–999 workers	50	. . .	. . .
1,000–4,999 workers	56	. . .	. . .
5,000 or more workers	42	. . .	. . .
Total sample	2,452	2,700	3,498
Manufacturing sample	2,075	2,216	3,039
Non-manufacturing sample	377	484	459

Notes: For 1935, Time study includes both time and motion study. Dashes indicate not applicable; ellipsis points indicate data not available.

Sources: *What Employers Are Doing for Employees,* NICB Studies No. 221 (New York: NICB, 1936), pp. 36, 62–63. *Personnel Activities in American Business,* Studies in Personnel Policy No. 20 (New York: NICB, 1940), p. 20; *Personnel Activities in American Business,* Studies in Personnel Policy No. 86 (New York: NICB, 1947), p. 29.

use of standardization, time study, and systematic planning techniques. Gravity-slides, automatic conveyors, overhead conveyors, and the endless-chain conveyor for final assembly (1914) were the major technological innovations that resulted from their attempts to optimize the production of Model T cars. Other strategic moves like the "Five-Dollar Day," initially presented as a "humanitarian" or "social justice" measure, actually created a reserve army of several thousands of job applicants ready to work for Ford. Each increase in pay, while not always applicable to all employees, invariably entailed a speedup of the production line. The final result of such an "economy-by-largesse" move was that workers were paid less *per unit of work* performed.[52]

Fordism exemplifies how scientific management principles can be *selectively* implemented while worker resistance is kept to a minimum. Time-and-motion studies, standardization of tools, machinery and working conditions, division of labor, and separation of conception from execution were carried to their last consequences in the Ford plants. For Ford, mass production was "power, accuracy, economy, system, continuity and speed."[53] The only Taylorite principles that Ford did not implement were functional foremanship and the differential wage rate. Because the speed of the assembly line and the feeder routes dictated the pace of work, the need for incentives and continuous supervising was greatly reduced or even eliminated.[54] But the technological conditions created by Ford to mass-produce automobiles and control the work process were not transferable to all industries. For one thing, Ford was not forced to sign a union contract until 1937. Where scientific management encountered the resistance of unionized workers or traditional managers, and assembly-line control was not technologically possible, the efficiency engineers introduced other disguised forms of scientific management. The Bedaux system was arguably the most important of them.

The activities of Charles Eugène Bedaux and his consulting companies have not been studied thoroughly. His impact in the United States as well as worldwide justifies retrieving him from the dustbin of history.[55] While avoiding the negative stigma attached to anything

52. Ford (1923, p. 147); Raff, "Wage determination theory and the Five-Dollar Day at Ford" (1988), "Ford welfare capitalism in its economic context," in Jacoby, ed. (1991, pp. 90–105).

53. Ford, "Henry Ford expounds mass production." (1926). This article, prepared for the 1926 edition of the *Encyclopaedia Britannica* and later published in the *New York Times,* was in fact written by a collaborator of Ford's, William J. Cameron. See Hounshell (1984, p. 304).

54. Edwards, *Contested Terrain* (1979, pp. 113–115); Hill, *Competition and Control at Work* (1981, pp. 24–31); Layton, "The diffusion of scientific management and mass production from the U.S. in the twentieth century" (1975).

55. Bendix (1974), Haber (1964), and Merkle (1980) fail to make any reference to the activities of Bedaux or his companies. The only available biography of Bedaux is Christy, *The Price of Power* (1984), which describes his links to the Nazis and to French fascists during World War II as well as his capture by the U.S. army in North Africa, and his suicide in the United States before standing trial for treason.

presented under the name of Taylorism, many employers and managers used the Bedaux System to introduce scientific management through the back door. Unlike Taylor's the Bedaux System could be implemented without revamping the entire management practices of the firm, a feature that employers welcomed. Also, Bedaux argued that his system rewarded labor for the effort expended and not for actual output. Above all, the Bedaux System was a confusing scheme, and precisely for this reason it pleased employers and annoyed workers and union leaders. It was first laid out formally in his book, *The Bedaux Efficiency Course for Industrial Application* (1917).[56] Bedaux drew on Gilbreth's and Taylor's ideas about time-and-motion study and incentives but dismissed them for being too mechanistic. Like the Taylorite engineers, Bedaux observed that negligence and lack of common sense were so widespread among workers and foremen alike that output could only be severely restricted. In brief, the Bedaux System was no more than a method to standardize the time spent on a task, factoring fatigue and rest separately. Thus, the Bedaux unit was to be calculated by adding a "rest allowance" to the "element of work itself" to become "the standard amount of work that can be done in one man-minute or one man-hour." The finesse consisted in making it difficult for the worker, but not for the supervisor, to understand how to convert actual work into Bedaux units, these into a measure of performance, and, finally, performance into pay. Over 700 American businesses, including General Electric and other large firms, employing about 675,000 workers were advised by the Bedaux Company between 1918 and 1942.[57]

Over the years, scientific management provided American business with extremely useful techniques to improve the organization of production activities. The contribution to managerial ideology was much more limited, despite the fact that the initial appeal of Taylorism to the business elite was based on its anti-union potential. Most of that potential, however, derived indirectly from its technical propositions,

56. There are two editions, one published in Grand Rapids, Michigan, the other in Cleveland, Ohio. As far as I have been able to determine, both editions are identical except that the Grand Rapids one includes a section with exercises at the end of each chapter. See also, Morrow, "The Bedaux principle of human power measurement" (1922).

57. Bedaux Company, *More Production, Better Morale* (1942, pp. 5, 15); Montgomery (1987, pp. 440–441); *Time*, "Bedaux reformed." (1942); Person, "The Bedaux system" (1937). See also Bell (1988, p. 234 n. 55). In Chaplin's *Modern Times* (1936) there is a scene in which a Mr. Beddoes tries to convince the factory owner of buying an automatic machine to feed workers while performing tasks on the assembly line.

not from its ideology. By expanding the universe of tasks and jobs suitable for unskilled workers, scientific management could be used to avoid the employment of unionized skilled workers and craftsmen. But even this "second-order" antiunion effect disappeared with the increasing unionization of unskilled workers in the mass-production industries. The durable use of scientific management came in the form of isolated techniques implemented in connection with the introduction of mass-production technologies. Such a process was greatly facilitated by the rise of the engineering profession and of the mass-production/consumption culture. In brief, the evidence presented so far confirms Littler's conclusion that on the one hand Taylorism (and, in general, scientific management) "is a failed ideology, and on the other, it represents the basic principles of the structuring of work down to the present."[58]

The Human Relations Revolution

As argued in the previous section, scientific management provided solutions to many technical problems associated with the rise of large-scale industry. American employers and managers, however, confronted not only technical problems but also ideological ones. Scientific management tried to solve the problem of labor unrest by increasing the size of the pie. Such a typically technocratic solution ignored a great number of variables central to the nature of industrial production. The rise of the human relations school produced a paradigmatic revolution in organizational thought and practice because it shifted attention from the technical to the social-psychological aspects of work. To be sure, productivity and profits were still thought to be relevant and certainly related to the technical factors of production, but it was increasingly understood that neglecting the morale, sentiments, and emotions of both the worker and the manager would set limits to the firm's productivity and profitability. As in the case of scientific management, human relations could make contributions both as a managerial ideology and a set of organizational techniques. Unlike scientific management, human relations actually served American business managers on both counts.

THE HUMAN PROBLEMS OF INDUSTRY AND THE INTEGRATION OF THE FIRM

Puritanism, Greeley's "frontier" ideology, social Darwinism, New Thought, and scientific management all shared an important feature:

58. Littler, "Understanding Taylorism" (1978, p. 186).

the conception of the manager and the worker as self-interested, individualistic, and materialistic beings. Industrial conflict, lack of cooperation, imperfect adaptation at work and other symptoms of "social disease" prompted a growing number of managers, social critics, and even workers to question the basic assumption of individualism in all previous theories of organizational management. Enlightened employers and professional managers began seeing in the worker a "cooperator" rather than a mere "wage-earner." During the 1920s and 1930s American industry witnessed a surge in industrial betterment programs and vocational guidance efforts conducted by both firms and nonprofit groups that prepared the ground for later developments. The National Association of Corporation Schools (a vocational guidance organization) was created in 1913. The conservative National Association of Manufacturers (NAM) also became involved in vocational guidance activities. Implicit was a paternalistic mentality, a sense of obligation (often of Christian origin) towards the worker that the employer had to fulfill in exchange for loyalty and obedience. Of course, that subservience included renouncing union activities. Welfare programs such as health and accident insurance, old-age provisions, leisure activities, and improved factory amenities were introduced and administered by joint labor-management committees starting at the turn of the century and continuing most intensively after 1919.

These programs were frequently aimed at eroding or preventing unionization. A whole new field of personnel administration emerged with the centralization and bureaucratization of employee-related matters, a development dictated by the growing complexity of the firm and tighter government controls, especially during World War I and the 1930s.[59]

With the growing interest in the human element in industry came the anticipation of many themes later central to the human relations paradigm. The idea that the technical had received too much attention at the expense of the social and psychological was floating in the air long before the first major human relations treatises were published in the 1930s. Similarly anticipated was the conviction that workers were not only motivated by economic incentives. Workers were no longer conceptualized as interchangeable or disposable productive elements but as part of the community of the firm. Therefore, there was a need to integrate them fully, to harmonize interests and behavior, to develop a sense of belonging. A major exponent of this early trend

59. Jacoby (1985, pp. 49–54, 65–97, 137–149, 193–205); Brandes, *American Welfare Capitalism 1880–1940* (1976); Bendix (1974, pp. 287–308).

was Mary Parker Follett, a political scientist involved in social work in Boston, management lecturer at the Bureau of Personnel Administration in New York, and consultant for several businessmen. She also became quite influential in Britain.[60] Other early "human relations" proponents (the term was already in use by the mid-1920s) emphasized the importance of leadership and top-down communication, thus attempting to enlarge the scope of managerial discretion that scientific management had hoped to constrain.[61]

CONDITIONS FAVORING A HUMAN RELATIONS APPROACH

Academic Social and Psychological Science. Practicing managers have frequently hit upon important organizational ideas well before academics and management intellectuals. In this respect human relations is no exception. But the distinctive contribution of American management intellectuals to the problem of human relations in industry was the use of social-psychological concepts and techniques. Academics provided human relations ideas with a credible scientific basis and with respectability. The first research leading to human relations postulates was conducted in England during and after World War I by the Industrial Fatigue Research Board and the National Institute of Industrial Psychology. But American academics soon took the lead and eventually made human relations the dominant paradigm of organizational thought, especially after the breakthrough of the Hawthorne investigations of the 1920s.[62]

The major center of human relations theorizing was Harvard and its Paretian circle nurtured by the medical doctor and biological chem-

---

60. Follett, *The New State* (1918), *Creative Experience* (1924), *Dynamic Administration* (1942). Follett relied heavily on psychological concepts. See also Viteles, *Industrial Psychology* (1932).

61. See *Harvard Business Review* (hereafter abbreviated as *HBR*) 1(1922–23):438–450; 1(1922–23):143–155; 12(1933–34):106–115; *Industrial Management* 55(1918):312–314; 62(1921):59–60; 66(1923):307–310; 70(1925):282–283; 71(1926):19–25; 71(1926):366–372. See also Shepard, *Human Nature at Work* (1938).

62. The original account of the experiments is Roethlisberger and Dickson, *Management and the Worker* (1967). The best available history is Gillespie, *Manufacturing Knowledge* (1991). On the scientific soundness of the Hawthorne findings, see Landsberger, *Hawthorne Revisited* (1958); Franke and Kaul, "The Hawthorne experiments" (1978); Franke, "The Hawthorne experiments" (1979), and "Worker productivity at Hawthorne" (1980); Schlaifer, "The relay assembly test room" (1980); Wardwell, "Critique of a recent professional 'put-down' of the Hawthorne research" (1979); Jones, "Worker interdependence and output" (1990); Jones, "Was there a Hawthorne effect?" (1992).

ist Lawrence J. Henderson. Henderson was convinced of the need for social scientists to observe the world around them and depart from a purely rationalistic model of human behavior. He thought that much of social life could not be understood without making room for values, emotions, sentiments, and other sorts of non-rational behavior. Henderson admired Pareto and his concepts of equilibrium, system, social system, and reequilibration. He also borrowed from his Harvard Medical School colleague W. B. Cannon the term *homeostasis*. In a time when social disorganization and lack of cooperation seemed to characterize the world, Paretian sociology could help find ways to understand the reigning disequilibrium and design paths to approach a new equilibrium. Henderson's intellectual influence is clear in the human relations group at the Harvard Business School (Mayo, Roethlisberger, Whitehead, Barnard). His influence is also noticeable in the writings of Homans and W. F. Whyte, who were appointed junior members of the Harvard Society of Fellows. His seminar on Pareto was attended by such leading figures as Joseph Schumpeter and Hans Zinsser.[63]

The most important theorist of the Harvard group was Elton Mayo, an Australian-born physician and psychopathologist who first arrived in Cambridge with a one-year grant from the Rockefeller Foundation. His role in the tremendous success of human relations worldwide has been only partially understood. For example, Bendix argues that Mayo's central contribution was the application of the same set of basic ideas to both managers and workers, i.e., "adaptability and skill in human relations."[64] If one is concerned, however, with the diffusion of organizational ideas across national boundaries, then the distinctive contribution of Elton Mayo becomes the way in which he linked a theory of human relations at work with the evils of industrialism.[65] In 1927, together with Henderson, Mayo created the Laboratory of Industrial Physiology at Harvard, the famous Fatigue Lab.

Mayo's thought included two crucial elements: hostility to the idea of progress understood as technological and material advance (i.e., against the Progressives), and nostalgia for a better (preindustrial) past. (Similar ideas prompted Catholic management intellectuals in countries such as Germany and Spain to accept the human relations

63. Barber, "L. J. Henderson: An introduction" (1970); Scott, *Chester I. Barnard and the Guardians of the Managerial State* (1992, pp. 40–60).

64. Bendix (1974, pp. 309–315).

65. In fact, Bendix and Fisher touched on this theme in their earlier article, "The perspectives of Elton Mayo" (1949).

paradigm.) As the titles of his major books remind us, Mayo was interested in the human and social problems of *industrial* civilization and their impact on productivity. He was not directly concerned with the justification of managerial authority. For Mayo, "the seamy side of progress" was a direct consequence of technical development itself. Therefore, technical improvements would not solve the rampant problems of "absenteeism, labor turnover, [and] 'wildcat' strikes." Mayo held that the situation of workers could be best understood with the help of Durkheim's concept of "anomie." Progress had brought about social dislocation, lack of cooperation, absence of teamwork, and the disappearance of "well-knit" social groups. In other words, Mayo mounted a classic *reactionary* argument against scientific management and mechanized production, using both a perversity thesis (overreliance on technical variables actually decreases production), and a jeopardy argument (technical progress endangers previous achievements of human society), to use Hirschman's framework.[66] Mayo thus echoed the old Jeffersonian anti-industrialist attitude. Mayo went beyond this critical position to propose some solutions. Because the "unbalance between the development of technical and of social skill has been disastrous," he argued that the solution lay in the manipulation of personal and social variables rather than of technical ones.[67] His fondness for a preindustrial past and disdain for technical progress parallels the mentality of many English contemporaries. In fact, Mayo believed that "in England to a much larger extent than in the United States the social code [was] still undamaged" by industrialization. In his view, that played to the advantage of England, his own "criterion of excellence."[68]

Mayo's ideas about industrial progress and human relations were not fully shared by the other Harvard theorists. Fritz Jules Roethlisberger, who wrote the classic account of the Hawthorne experiments, never entertained the idea that there was something intrinsically wrong with technical progress.[69] The thinking of Chester Barnard was similar, in that his conception of organizations as cooperative systems did not interfere with the desirability of technical and material progress. Barnard also exemplifies the typical American human rela-

66. Hirschman, *The Rhetoric of Reaction* (1991). Other human relations theorists and managers also used these theses.

67. Mayo, *The Human Problems of an Industrial Civilization* (1933), and *The Social Problems of an Industrial Civilization* (1945, pp. 10, 23).

68. Mayo (1933, p. 184); Trahair, *The Humanist Temper* (1984, pp. 143, 350).

69. See Roethlisberger and Dickson (1967), and Roethelisberger's autobiography, *The Elusive Phenomena* (1977, pp. 195–196).

tions theorist and practitioner who turns to social science and philosophy for answers that religion cannot provide. As president of the New Jersey Bell Telephone Company, Barnard displayed his anti-union convictions but failed to keep the company profitable.[70] George Homans did share with Mayo an interest in medieval English rural life, although there is no evidence that he subscribed to Mayo's ideas about industrialism.[71] Whitehead was the Harvard theorist who came closest to Mayo's position.[72] None of the members of the second wave of human relations theorists (Whyte, Argyris, McGregor, Likert) shared the original Mayoistic concerns either. As will be seen in subsequent chapters, Mayo's reactionary position stimulated the minds of Catholic and Christian management intellectuals in Britain, Germany, and Spain, who, unlike their American counterparts, found in religion the initial inspiration to study organizational issues from a human relations perspective.

Academic support for the human relations paradigm continued during the 1940s, 1950s and 1960s at other major universities and training institutions as well as at Harvard. Burleigh Gardner chaired the Committee on Human Relations in Industry at the University of Chicago (1943–1950). He had been a researcher at Hawthorne. Lloyd Warner, William Foote Whyte, and James C. Worthy worked for the committee on worker turnover and absenteeism. Worthy, a personnel manager at Sears, Roebuck, and formerly a personnel counselor at Hawthorne, conducted a survey study of worker attitudes. William Foote Whyte moved to Cornell in 1948 to become a professor of industrial relations.[73] Leland P. Bradford and Kenneth D. Benne set up the National Training Laboratory (1947) in Bethel, Maine, to train managers in human relations techniques such as sensitivity training. They were greatly influenced by emigré psychologist Jacob L. Moreno, the pioneer of sociometry as well as of group therapy techniques (psychodrama, sociodrama, and role-playing). Since the late 1940s a second group of human relations academic theorists had developed at Yale University's Labor and Management Center, Department of Industrial Administration, and Institute of Human

70. Barnard, *The Functions of the Executive* (1938); Scott (1992, pp. 61–87, 147–156).

71. Homans, *Coming to My Senses* (1984, p. 168), *The Human Group* (1950), *Social Behavior* (1974), and "Some corrections" (1949).

72. Whitehead, *The Industrial Worker* (1938), *Leadership in a Free Society* (1947).

73. Whyte, *Pattern for Industrial Peace* (1951), *Leadership and Group Participation* (1953); Whyte, ed., *Industry and Society* (1946).

Relations, including Chris Argyris, E. Wight Bakke, F. L. W. Richardson, Charles R. Walker, and Arthur N. Turner.[74] The Yale group
conducted a series of empirical studies about monotony, absenteeism,
and adaptation, and developed important ideas about job enlargement, enrichment, and rotation. Chris Argyris, formerly a student of
W. F. Whyte's at Cornell and the youngest member of the human
relations school, became a major figure in the movement for his theory of individual self-actualization in different group and organizational situations. Related to both Harvard and the Yale group was
Stuart Chase, whose articles in *Reader's Digest* and books helped to
popularize the human relations approach.[75] In 1947 Rensis Likert
started his research on group relations at the Survey Research Center
and at the Research Center for Group Dynamics, both within the
Institute for Social Research (ISR) of the University of Michigan.
The Research Center for Group Dynamics had just moved from the
Massachusetts Institute of Technology (MIT), where it had been created two years before by Kurt Lewin, the pioneer of topological
psychology and of theories about small-group climate and leadership.
Another psychologist who contributed to the growing literature on
motivation at work was Abraham Maslow, with his needs hierarchy
theory.[76] Likert's long tenure as director of the ISR, as well as his
activities with the consulting firm Rensis Likert and Associates, made
him one of the most influential human relations theorists. His colleagues at ISR included social psychologists Daniel Katz, Robert
Kahn, Floyd Mann, Ronald Lippitt, and Stanley Seashore. Social
psychologist Douglas McGregor was the most influential member of
the MIT human relations faculty, and had been greatly influenced by
Joseph N. Scanlon's plan of teamwork and profit sharing dating back
to the 1930s. Likert's System 4 of participative group management
and McGregor's Theory Y of individual self-control, self-direction,
group integration, and creative participation, and the "managerial
grid" leadership model of Robert R. Blake and Jane S. Mouton (de-

74. See *HBR* 27(1949):107–122; 28(3) (1950):54–58; 30(3) (1952):71–83;
32(5) (1954):63–72; 33(5) (1955):40–48; 36(1) (1958):111–119; 36(6) (1958):
107–116.

75. Chase, *The Proper Study of Mankind* (1948); Gillespie (1991, p. 235). On the
Argyris group at Yale, see Berg, ed., *Keeping the Faith* (1992).

76. See Marrow, *The Practical Theorist* (1969), a biography of Lewin; Kornhauser,
"The contribution of psychology to industrial relations research" (1949); Mandler and
Mandler, "The diaspora of experimental psychology," in Fleming and Bailyn, *The
Intellectual Migration* (1969, pp. 399–405); Maslow, *Motivation and Personality*
(1954).

veloped at Humble Oil, currently part of Exxon) became the best known human relations models of the 1960s. Alex F. Osborn (inventor of the "brainstorm sessions") was a major popularizer of group dynamics and cooperation techniques during those years. Psychologist and consultant Frederick Herzberg refined the theory of satisfaction at work, distinguishing between hygienic and motivating factors, and developing techniques of job enrichment.[77] From Mayo to Argyris, academic human relations theorists provided American management students and practitioners with a steady stream of models and ideas emphasizing the importance of the human element and the social group in industry.

Human Relations Presented as a Solution to Industrial Conflict. The human relations paradigm of organization was presented by many academic theorists of the 1940s and early 1950s as a solution to industrial conflict. In fact, the early Bell System personnel policies (including the Hawthorne investigations) had been prompted by "labor unrest inside the companies and external political and social pressures."[78] They argued not only that the technical rationalization of industry had proceeded at the expense of the social and psychological well-being of the worker but also that an improvement of human relations at work would reduce industrial conflict and raise productivity.[79] The timing was appropriate. American business had faced a continuing challenge from labor and government ever since the New Deal reforms—a challenge that had nothing to do with productivity, since American firms were the most efficient and profitable in the world. The entry of the United States into the war had increased government intervention in the labor arena to unprecedented levels, while unions pledged not to go on strike. According to one labor historian, however, "even the enormous patriotic pressures of global conflict could not reverse the fundamentally contentious and conflictual nature of labor relations in the United States." During the 1930s

77. Likert, *New Patterns of Management* (1961); McGregor, *The Human Side of Enterprise* (1960); Blake and Mouton, *The Managerial Grid* (1964); Osborn, *Applied Imagination* (1953); Herzberg et al., *The Motivation to Work* (1959), *Work and the Nature of Man* (1973). See also Back, *Beyond Words* (1972). On industrial consulting, see Amon et al., *Management Consulting* (1958). Waring, *Taylorism Transformed* (1991, pp. 104–159) provides an excellent summary of the ideas of the second-wave human relations theorists.

78. Gillespie (1991, p. 17).

79. See Mayo (1945, pp. 1–33); Roethlisberger and Dickson (1967), pp. 552–553); Whyte (1951); Selekman, *Labor Relations and Human Relations* (1947).

the average annual number of person-days lost due to industrial conflict was 14.2 million. In 1942 the figure was down to 4.2 million, but in 1943 it went up to 13.5 million. 1944 was a record year in number of strikes, though not in working-days lost. Clearly, unions were unable to discourage workers from going on strike to demand higher wages and better working conditions.[80]

By the end of the war, the unions had reached an all-time high in membership at over 35 percent of total civilian employment. Fears of recession, the end of the No-Strike Pledge, and dissatisfaction with wages and working conditions produced the great 1945–46 strike wave. Nineteen forty-six was the year with the most strikes in American history. In all, 116 million person-days were lost, almost as many as during the decade of the 1930s altogether. The unions were able to sign contracts with considerable wage increases and improved working conditions, but the price was the introduction of "company rights" provisions that sought to guarantee unimpeded managerial authority in the work place. Another victory for employers was the passage of the Taft-Hartley Labor-Management Relations Act of 1947 limiting union activity, expanding managerial rights, and placing boundaries on the right to strike. It represented the first serious legal backlash to labor unions since the Wagner Act of 1935.[81] Nonetheless, industrial conflict stayed well above the levels of the 1920s and 1930s until the early 1960s. During the 1950s the average American worker lost 0.55 working days annually compared to 0.13 days in Britain, and just 0.04 days in Germany. American employers were facing a problem, and human relations theory could provide concepts and techniques to deal with it.[82]

Structural Changes in Firms.   The bureaucratization of American industry accelerated during the 1930s and 1940s. By 1950 American manufacturing firms employed almost 24 administrative employees for each 100 production workers, up from 18 in 1929. The ratio climbed to 29 in 1960, much higher than in most other industrial countries and only followed closely by Britain (27 for each 100 pro-

---

80. Zieger (1986, p. 75); see also the statistics in Appendix B.

81. Zieger (1986, pp. 35–41, 74–75, 84–87, 100–136); Liesner, ed., *Economic Statistics 1900–1983* (1985, p. 56).

82. Social scientists with different approaches studied the problem of industrial unrest. See Kornhauser, Dubin, and Ross, eds., *Industrial Conflict* (1954), with contributions by, among others, George Homans, Daniel Katz, C. Wright Mills, Reinhard Bendix, Melville Dalton, Wilbert Moore, and Daniel Bell.

duction workers). Industrial and service corporations grew larger. The growth in size and bureaucratization of industrial firms has been linked to the relevance of the human relations paradigm. First, in bureaucratized organizations with many hierarchical levels, success in getting to the top appears to be remote, and under no circumstances can all employees be promoted. Therefore, the motivation to produce will be maximized if satisfactions in the work itself are emphasized over satisfactions derived from success in getting to the top. Second, ability and skill in human relations become increasingly useful in pursuing a bureaucratic career. Third, the bureaucratization of employment management brings into the firm a legion of personnel managers and vocational guidance experts who are generally more receptive to the social and human situation of workers than the scientific managers.[83]

The Position of Labor Unions. Between 1920 and 1960 labor unions pursued collective bargaining agreements to limit managerial discretion over wages and working conditions. Their efforts were crowned with considerable success in the 1950s in some ways but not in others. Collective contracts achieved wage increases for workers but only at the expense of surrendering control over production decisions to management. The unions took a rather ambiguous stand towards the human relations movement in contrast with their sharp opposition to scientific management. In the immediate postwar period, leaders and intellectuals of the CIO expressed their support for human relations, but as employers increasingly used human relations techniques such as morale surveys and counseling in an attempt to reach workers directly (thus circumventing the unions), labor leaders and intellectuals withdrew their support. Although some labor leaders were willing to collaborate with management in the conduct of attitude and morale surveys, many others remained neutral or opposed to such cooperation. In 1949 the United Auto Workers' magazine, *Ammunition,* mounted a devastating attack on human relations research, but the *American Federationist,* which after 1955 represented both the AFL and the CIO, remained silent about human relations. In general, the implementation of human relations techniques was neither facilitated nor bitterly opposed by the attitudes and actions of labor unions.[84]

83. Bendix (1974, pp. 281–308); see also the statistics in Appendix B.
84. Carew, *Labour Under the Marshall Plan* (1987, pp. 49–50, 52–56); Barkin in *HBR* 28(5) (1950):59–64; Jacoby (1985, pp. 269–271); Baritz (1960, pp. 114–115, 149–150, 157–158, 175); Gillespie (1991, p. 231); UAW, "Deep therapy on the assembly line" (1949).

THEORETICAL SUCCESS OF HUMAN RELATIONS AMONG THE
BUSINESS ELITE

American top business leaders found in the human relations paradigm
the ideology and the techniques necessary to address what they perceived as persistent problems of industrial conflict, worker unhappi-
ness, and increasing bureaucratization of their enterprises. The United
States was the dominant industrial power in a world economy recovering from destruction during World War II, and there was no productivity crisis, but American business leaders were eager to reduce
conflict. According to Harvey Stowers, assistant to the president of
the Aircraft Industries Assocation of America, industry in 1946 was
"faced with human problems that may hold greater danger than the
Second World War." Despite the hyperbole, Stowers was by no
means the only business leader calling attention to the problems of
"suspicion, resentment, and open conflict between employees and
employers."[85] The following statement by Clarence Francis, chairman
of General Foods, in his address at a convention of the National
Association of Manufacturers summarizes the emerging consensus
among American business leaders:

> You can buy a man's time, you can buy a man's physical presence at a
> given place; you can even buy a measured number of skilled muscular
> motions per hour or day. But you cannot buy enthusiasm; you cannot
> buy initiative; you cannot buy loyalty; you cannot buy the devotion
> of hearts, minds and souls. You have to earn these things. . . . It is
> ironic that Americans—the most advanced people technically, mechani-
> cally and industrially—should have waited until a comparatively recent
> period to inquire into the most promising single source of productivity:
> namely, the human will to work.[86]

The American Management Association (AMA), founded in 1923
to continue the activities of the National Association of Corporation
Training Schools, became after World War II a major disseminator
of human relations ideas. The AMA was a progressive, influential,
and resourceful organization, self-proclaimed as "a group of executives insured against obsolescence in management." Its primary concern was with labor warfare and achieving industrial peace. In fact,
its largest section was the personnel division. In 1946 the AMA could
boast 10,000 members (of which two-thirds were corporations), and

85. Stowers, *Management Can Be Human* (1946, p. v); Biggers et al., *Human
Relations in Modern Business* (1949, p. iii).
86. Quoted in *Time*, "Human relations" (1952, p. 97).

twice that number by 1955. A 1946 poll of top executives associated with the AMA showed "the development of human beings in the industrial organization" high in their list of priorities. The survey also asked about the "managerial attributes for industrial understanding." The respondents mentioned communication skills, knowledge of psychology and people's instincts (competition, socializing, team spirit, self-preservation, recognition), ability to influence, ability to build men, social wisdom, and being a good listener and recognizer of others' ideas. Another survey found executives convinced that "sticking together" in the firm would boost productivity.[87] Numerous reports appeared in the *New York Times* in 1946–47 reflecting the view of prominent business executives that portrayed human relations as the "industrial key." Some top executives even argued that increased attention to human relations at work would help preserve the system of free enterprise and democratic capitalism from the worldwide threat posed by the advance of Socialism and Communism. In 1948, while celebrating its twenty-fifth anniversary, the AMA recommended more attention to the "prime function of human relations." AMA president Alvin E. Dodd argued in favor of the selection of managers based not only on "technical proficiency and knowledge" but on "knowledge and understanding of purely human relationships." In 1949 Lawrence A. Appley, then president of the AMA, showed his interest in satisfying "individual desires for participating in constructive work in the factory and office," and in giving "employees at all levels a greater sense of dignity and recognition as individuals and respected members of the industrial community." He further argued that "with some companies reporting the failure of financial incentives to interest workers in increasing production, there will be increased emphasis on nonfinancial incentives based on a common understanding of the cooperative effort necessary for a full production for American and world needs today." Foreign competition was not even mentioned. American firms were enjoying years of uncontested economic supremacy in the world.[88]

---

87. Milton, *Ethics and Expediency in Personnel Management* (1970, p. 181).

88. *Iron Age*, "Executive poll shows human relations to be prime responsibility" (1946); Mills, "The contribution of sociology to studies of industrial relations" (1949); AMA, *Annual Report 1946* (1946, pp. 3–9), and *25 Years of Management Progress* (1948, p. 16); Sutton et al., *The American Business Creed* (1962, p. 134, 135); Appley, *The Management Evolution* (1963); Gillespie (1991, pp. 235–236); *New York Times* (April 21, 1946): Business Section, pp. 1 and 5, (May 20, 1946): p. 2, (July 22, 1946): p. 23, (September 22, 1946): Business Section, p. 1, (May 18, 1947): Business Section, pp. 1 and 9, (November 9, 1947): Business Section, p. 5.

Human relations ideas gained acceptance in both conservative and liberal business milieux. The often reactionary National Association of Manufacturers (NAM) welcomed human relations ideas and argued that "efficient production is directly related to employee satisfaction on the job." NAM president Wallace F. Bennett asked managers to pay attention to "the most important problem . . . of human relationships," and make an effort to explain to employees the facts about wages, costs, and prices. A resolution adopted at NAM's 1948 meeting (the Congress of American Industry) declared the "sincere desire of management to understand the hopes and ambitions of employees," and its commitment to industrial "understanding, cooperation, and harmony." The 1953 edition of NAM's credo, *Industry Believes,* declared the need for employers to promote a "full consideration of the human personality and the need for individual recognition, opportunity, and development."[89] The same acceptance of human relations could be found in the pages of the liberal-minded *Fortune* magazine, the showcase for successful American corporate executives. *Fortune*'s editors argued in the early 1950s that the top task of management was to maintain equilibrium in the firm and make things run smoothly to give "meaning and satisfaction to those within it." "Human relations is now the key," they concluded in a review of the managing styles of the most successful companies and executives. Similarly, a group of business executives assembled by the Boston-based Twentieth Century Fund readily accepted the premise that "the problem of the age is the relationship between people."[90] Of course, the liberal or conservative inclinations of business executives actually played a diminished role in this case because the intention was not to equalize wages or achieve economic justice but to make the worker more productive and reduce the influence of the unions.

The urgent need to tackle the labor unrest problem and restore

89. NAM, *Human Relations and Efficient Production* (1946, p. 1), and *Industry Believes* (1949, pp. 6, 9); Sutton et al. (1962, p. 136); Bendix (1974, p. 326).

90. Sutton et al. (1962, p. 134); *Fortune,* "The crown princes of business" (1953, p. 264); Twentieth Century Fund, *Partners in Production* (1949, p. 3). See also the writings of William B. Given, Jr., president of the American Brake Shoe Co.: *Bottom-Up Management* (1949, pp. 96–97), and "From the point of view of management," in Chase et al. (1950, pp. 69–83). See also the speeches on human relations by top executives in *Vital Speeches of the Day* 4(1937–38):264–267, 540–542, 690–694; 5(1938–39):77–83; 8(1941–42):566–568; 10(1943–44:372–375; 14(1947–48): 379–384, 562–565; 19(1952–53):406–409; 20(1953–54):684–688; 22(1955–56):141–147; 25(1958–59):134–137; 31(1964–65):509–511; 34(1967–68): 725–728.

the public's confidence in management became the overriding reason for General Robert Wood Johnson (chairman of the board of Johnson & Johnson) to become an outspoken defender of the human relations approach to management. His case is interesting, for he is one of the few American management intellectuals directly influenced by the Catholic encyclicals *Rerum Novarum* (1891) and *Quadragesimo Anno* (1931), dealing with the social conditions of industrial workers. In his widely read books, Johnson argued for more worker participation, for the consideration of workers' sentiments and emotions, and for the implementation of techniques such as job rotation, job enlargement, teamwork, and discussion groups.[91] Another executive presenting unique viewpoints about human relations was Thomas G. Spates, for many years vice-president of General Foods, and later a professor of personnel administration at Yale. Spates thought human relations ideas could help out not only in the quest for higher productivity but also in the fight against Socialism and Communism. He is one of the few American examples of how a humanist mentality (the belief in human dignity and in the self-realization of human beings through reason) matches well with the tenets of the human relations school. A similar blend of humanism, Christian values, and anti-Communism pervades the thought of Thomas J. Watson, Sr., the founder of the modern International Business Machines Corporation.[92] Overall, though, American managers liked the human relations approach because of its relevance to dealing with labor unrest and its seemingly credible scientific foundations, not because of the support it received from Christian ethics or from social Catholicism. A few American bishops and Catholic management intellectuals discussed the problems of labor unrest and productivity in terms of the basic human relations postulates, but these analyses were neither as sophisticated nor as influential as the ones by the Spanish and British management intellectuals.[93]

91. Johnson, *People Must Live and Work Together or Forfeit Freedom* (1947, pp. 14–20, 71, 102, 109–110, 139, 185), and *Robert Johnson Talks It Over* (1949). See also his article in *HBR* 27(1949):521–541, and *Time* (1952, p. 97). The references to the social doctrine of the Catholic Church in the writings of American businessmen are rare. See for example, *HBR* 11(1932–33):57–66; Milton (1970, pp. 200–201). See also Bursk, ed., *Business and Religion* (1949), *Human Relations for Management* (1950). Bursk was editor of the *Harvard Business Review*.

92. Sutton et al. (1962, p. 137); Spates, *Human Values Where People Work* (1960), and *Man and Management* (1965, p. 166); Watson, *As a Man Thinks* (1954, pp. 61, 69, 73, 79, 81, 105, 115, 125, 141, 152–155, 165, 183).

93. See, in particular, *Vital Speeches of the Day* 13(1946–47):17–19; 14(1947–48):498–499; 18(1951–52):400–402; 24(1957–58):303–310.

Some business leaders—including Johnson, Spates and Watson Sr.—recognized that human relations ideas were not only useful in addressing labor unrest but also in humanizing working conditions in the system of mass production. Harry A. Bullis, chairman of the board of General Mills, argued before the Congress of American Industry in 1948 that workers were "human beings, not cogs in a machine." (The metaphor was first used by Britain's Harold Macmillan in the 1930s.) Management ought to take on the "task of satisfying the complete wants of its personnel. . . . The monotonous nature of much work in the modern mass-production system puts it up to the employer to provide some recognition for his workers to give them real satisfaction in their jobs." A similar viewpoint was adopted by *Time* magazine's editors in a 1952 special feature article on the "new art" of human relations in industry.[94]

In a matter of years more and more top executives committed themselves to human relations practices and asked others to follow suit.[95] Human relations became a management movement that America's top social critics and intellectuals took note of in their writings. Daniel Bell, then labor editor of *Fortune,* criticized the manipulative aspect of human relations theory, which he classified not as "a science of man but [as] a cow-sociology." For C. Wright Mills, human relations served managers in their "hope of lowering production costs, of easing tensions inside their plants, of finding new symbols to justify the concentrated power they exercise in modern society." Like Bell, Mills believed in the essentially manipulative nature of human relations, which aimed at "countering [the workers'] informal solidarities against management and exploiting these solidarities for smoother and less troublesome managerial efficiency." Similar criticisms were expounded by psychoanalyst Erich Fromm and writer-journalist William H. Whyte, Jr.[96] That such leading intellectuals voiced their criticisms of the human relations paradigm is but one more indicator of its widespread impact.

94. Sutton et al. (1962, p. 134); Johnson (1947, pp. 109–110, 131–144); Spates (1965); *Time* (1952); Milton (1970, pp. 171–179, 199–223).

95. See Biggers et al. (1949); Hoslett, ed., *Human Factors in Management* (1946); Allen, ed., *Individual Initiative in Business* (1950, pp. 99–128); Baritz, *The Servants of Power* (1960, pp. 167–190).

96. Bell, "Work and its discontents," originally published in 1956, reprinted in *The End of Ideology* (1988, pp. 244–252); Bell as quoted in UAW (1949, p. 48); Mills (1949, p. 202), *White Collar* (1951, pp. 234–235), and *The Power Elite* (1956, pp. 144–145); Fromm, "Man is not a thing" (1957, p. 9); Whyte et al., *Is Anybody Listening?* (1952); Whyte, Jr., *The Organization Man* (1956, pp. 32–59, 400–401).

The articles on business organization published in the *Harvard Business Review* between 1944 and 1961 were dominated by the human relations approach (see panel B of Table 2.1). Although over half of the articles were written by academics with limited managerial experience, in the late 1940s the *Review* was reaching the desks of some 16,000 top executives and department heads across the country.[97] Plant and personnel managers also became interested in human relations techniques such as attitude surveys, leadership development, and participatory programs. Most significantly, *Factory Management and Maintenance* devoted a great deal of attention to human relations between 1944 and 1952, although scientific management articles appeared more frequently (see panel B of Table 2.2). Beginning in the 1940s, *Factory* included a regular section on human relations news and trends. Panel A in Tables 2.1 and 2.2 shows that the articles contained a well-balanced mixture of ideological and technical themes associated with the human relations paradigm, in contrast with the ideological failure of scientific management.

PRACTICAL IMPLEMENTATION OF HUMAN RELATIONS TECHNIQUES

Was the human relations paradigm more than an ideology and a language to address labor problems? Did American firms implement human relations programs and techniques in any serious and consistent way so as to reduce conflict, promote cooperation, and boost productivity? Contrary to previous studies, the answer to both questions is in the affirmative.[98] The nationwide surveys conducted by the National Industrial Conference Board (NICB) between 1927 and 1963, among other less reliable reports and a handful of case studies, provide ample information on the prevalence of different human relations techniques across American industrial and service sectors.[99] As noted above, the adoption of human relations techniques was often, but not always, associated with the creation of personnel departments. Table 2.4 documents the rapid increase in the proportion of both service and manufacturing firms with personnel departments during the second quarter of the century. By 1946 over 60 percent of all

97. Bursk and Clark, "Reading habits of business executives" (1949).
98. See, for example, the conclusion by Bendix (1974, pp. 319–331) that human relations gained limited acceptance in managerial practice.
99. Other less comprehensive surveys include *FMM,* "How management in 100 plants gets information to workers" (1946a), and "Wage incentive practices in 65 plants" (1946b); Wallace, "How are you doing personnel-wise?" (1952).

TABLE 2.4 The spread of personnel departments and implementation of human relations techniques in American firms, by sector (manufacturing and non-manufacturing) and firm size, 1927–1963 (in percentages)

Practice	1927	1935	1939	1946	1953a	1953b	1963
Personnel Departments							
All firms	12%	32%	34%	63%	. . .	. . .	. . .
Manufacturing	. . .	29	32	63	. . .	. . .	. . .
Non-manufacturing	. . .	52	47	64	. . .	. . .	. . .
1–249 workers	3	5	7	30	. . .	. . .	. . .
250–999 workers		34	35	65	. . .	. . .	. . .
1,000–4,999 workers	34	62	62	86	. . .	. . .	. . .
5,000 or more workers		81	75	91	. . .	. . .	. . .
HUMAN RELATIONS							
Suggestion Systems							
All firms	10	23	26	30	32%	34%	—
Manufacturing	. . .	22	26	31	. . .	. . .	29%
Non-manufacturing	. . .	29	29	26	. . .	. . .	—
1–249 workers	5	10	15	15	20	18	—
250–999 workers		25	26	28	26	32	28
1,000–4,999 workers	23	34	37	40	39	42	26
5,000 or more workers		54	48	54	70	61	44
Morale surveys							
All firms	. . .	. . .	. . .	7	15	20	—
Manufacturing	. . .	. . .	. . .	6	. . .	. . .	21
Non-manufacturing	. . .	. . .	. . .	11	. . .	. . .	—
1–249 workers	. . .	. . .	. . .	3	5	11	—
250–999 workers	. . .	. . .	. . .	4	14	15	17
1,000–4,999 workers	. . .	. . .	. . .	11	15	26	21
5,000 or more workers	. . .	. . .	. . .	19	38	56	37
Employee magazines							
All firms	6	14	17	24	29	32	—
Manufacturing	. . .	20	12	20	. . .	. . .	18
Non-manufacturing	. . .	36	37	46	. . .	. . .	—
1–249 workers	2	5	3	5	5	22	—
250–999 workers		11	13	20	22	34	9
1,000–4,999 workers	18	26	33	39	48	52	25
5,000 or more workers		53	58	56	66	56	47
Employee newspapers							
All firms	. . .	. . .	. . .	17	20	28	—
Manufacturing	. . .	. . .	. . .	17	. . .	. . .	35
Non-manufacturing	. . .	. . .	. . .	17	. . .	. . .	—
1–249 workers	. . .	. . .	. . .	6	10	15	—
250–999 workers	. . .	. . .	. . .	16	19	26	29
1,000–4,999 workers	. . .	. . .	. . .	22	27	37	38
5,000 or more workers	. . .	. . .	. . .	35	24	41	58
Total sample	6,085	2,452	2,700	3,498	(see notes)		—
Manufacturing sample	. . .	2,075	2,216	3,039			473
Non-manufacturing sample	. . .	377	484	459			—

(Continued)

firms, and over 90 percent of firms with 5,000 or more workers had created a personnel department.

Certain human relations techniques were adopted quickly and extensively. *Suggestion systems* were certainly in use well before human relations appeared on the scene, but the expansion of their application, especially among the larger firms, took place between the early 1930s and the mid-1950s, precisely when the human relations paradigm came to the fore. By the mid-1950s over half of all firms with 5,000 or more employees had suggestion systems in place (see Table 2.4). Equally impressive prevalence figures were reported by NICB for the practice of publishing company *magazines and newspapers* directed to employees as an attempt to improve communication, participation, and workplace climate as well as to reduce conflict (see Table 2.4). A multivariate analysis of industry-level differences in the diffusion of suggestion systems and employee magazines appears in Table C.3 in Appendix C. *Role-playing* techniques were being used to train supervisors at one of every five firms surveyed by *Factory Management and Maintenance* in 1953. Some companies introduced *group dynamics* techniques à la Lewin: Detroit Edison, Michigan Bell, Johnson & Johnson, Minneapolis-Honeywell Regulator, Procter & Gamble, General Foods, Harwood, American Steel and Wire, IBM, Chrysler, and Standard Oil. In 1964 two of every five firms surveyed by the Conference Board were using *sensitivity training* (a combination of group dynamics and role-playing). Four years later, the proportion nearly reached four out of every five firms. A representative survey of

---

Notes to Table 2.4: Dashes indicate not applicable; ellipsis points indicate data not available. Data by firm size in 1927 refer to two categories, 1–250, and over 250 workers. The 1963 sample includes only manufacturing firms with 250 or more employees. For 1953, several different samples were drawn for different questions. The estimates in Group 1953a come from two samples: the first of 519 firms for magazine and newspaper, of which only 4.6 percent are service firms; and the second of 495 firms for suggestion system and morale survey, of which only 5.6 percent are service firms. Firms were supposed to answer the questions about prevalence of the techniques as they applied to hourly workers. The estimates in Group 1953b come from samples of 421 firms (28.6 percent service), and 469 firms (39.0 percent service). Firms in these two samples were supposed to answer the questions about prevalence of the techniques as they applied to non-exempt salaried employees. In sum, sample 1953a grossly underrepresents service firms, while sample 1953b gives a more accurate, albeit still distorted, picture of the population of firms.

Sources to Table 2.4: National Industrial Conference Board, *Industrial Relations Programs in Small Plants* (New York: NICB, 1929), p. 20; *What Employers Are Doing for Employees*, NICB Studies No. 221 (New York: NICB, 1936), pp. 36–37, 42–43, 58–65. *Personnel Activities in American Business*, Studies in Personnel Policy No. 20 (New York: NICB, 1940), pp. 19–21, 31; *Personnel Activities in American Business*, Studies in Personnel Policy No. 86 (New York: NICB, 1947), pp. 16, 29–30, 32–33; *Personnel Practices in Factory and Office*, Studies in Personnel Policy No. 145 (New York: NICB, 1954), pp. 55, 108–109; *Personnel Practices in Factory and Office: Manufacturing*, Personnel Policy Study No. 194 (New York: NICB, 1964), pp. 52, 54, 55, 58.

over 2,000 U.S. managers conducted by the AMA as late as 1973 documented that executives generally saw management development and human relations techniques as effective tools. Between 34 and 56 percent of the managers had been exposed to McGregor's Theories X and Y, Maslow's needs hierarchy theory, Herzberg's satisfiers-motivators theory, and Blake and Mouton's Managerial Grid.[100] *Job enlargement* was pioneered by IBM, Detroit Edison, Colonial Insurance Co., Maytag, and Sears, Roebuck in the 1950s. *Job enrichment* was introduced at AT&T, IBM, Texas Instruments, and other firms by consultant Frederick Herzberg, and became widely used in the late 1960s. After the failed promises of the early 1920s, *psychological testing* became a popular technique again after World War II. One survey found that only 14 percent of the corporations in a 1939 sample used testing. In 1947 the proportion was 50 percent, and 75 percent in 1952. It is important to note that psychological tests were adapted to fit the human relations paradigm. Thus, instead of testing for aptitudes, physical fitness, or dexterity (the major concerns of scientific management), the new tests were designed to assess the social adaptability, temperament, emotional stability, and other personality traits of workers. The NAM was a strong supporter of psychological testing, as were large corporations like AT&T and Lockheed.[101] *Training Within Industry* (*TWI*), the program established by the National Defense Advisory Commission in 1940, was in part a human relations effort heavily reliant on the Hawthorne findings and methods.[102]

A fundamental human relations technique used by American firms was the *morale survey*.[103] Over half of the manufacturing and service firms with 5,000 or more workers included in one 1953 NICB sample had conducted morale surveys. Moreover, this sample underrepresented service firms, which were more likely to have implemented such a technique (see Table 2.4). Thirty-seven percent of the manufac-

---

100. *Factory Management and Maintenance* 112(1)(1954):102; Baritz (1960, pp. 184–187); Waring (1991, p. 122); Pearse, *Manager to Manager* (1974, pp. 18, 31–32), and *Manager to Manager II* (1977).

101. Blumberg, *Industrial Democracy* (1973, pp. 66–69); Baritz (1960, pp. 155–160).

102. Gillespie (1991, pp. 234–235).

103. Attitude and morale surveys were first conducted in the early 1930s at firms such as Kimberly-Clark Corp., Procter & Gamble, and General Motors. See Baritz (1960, pp. 125–127). On the central importance of worker morale and of survey and interviewing methods for human relations theorists, see Mayo (1933, pp. 77–121), and (1945, pp. 29–30, 73–86), and Roethlisberger and Dickson (1967, pp. 189–205, 270–291, 592–603). See also NICB, *Experience with Employee Attitude Surveys* (1951).

turing firms with 5,000 or more workers included in a 1963 study had done so. Over half of the firms in the 1953 sample had conducted morale surveys only once, 20 percent twice, and about 10 percent three or four times.[104] Less than 10 percent had conducted morale surveys five or more times in the past. In the 1963 survey of manufacturing firms, only 10 percent had conducted morale surveys five times or more. Two-thirds of the firms conducting surveys relied on outside specialists. Three-fourths used a written questionnaire exclusively, 12 percent used individual interviews exclusively, and the remaining 14 percent used a combination of questionnaires and interviews. The highest proportions of firms conducting morale surveys by industry in 1946 (the last year for which information is available) were in aircraft, wholesale and retail, glass, and communications and broadcasting. The evidence collected by the NICB makes it hard to conclude that human relations techniques had no practical influence, especially if one takes into account that techniques such as the morale survey were rather recent, and their effectiveness was uncertain. Morale surveys were periodically conducted by such major companies as International Harvester, Bethlehem Steel, Carnegie-Illinois Steel, IBM, Ford, General Motors, Chrysler, North American Aviation, Standard Oil, Continental Oil, Continental Pipe Line, Sears, and AT&T in an attempt to find ways to curb industrial conflict and increase productivity.[105] At the end of the 1960s, and even in the 1990s, studies conducted among industrial and service firms showed a continuing concern with and implementation of human relations techniques.[106]

The case of International Business Machines (IBM) illustrates how large U.S. corporations implemented human relations techniques after their CEOs had committed to its ideology. Company literature has always emphasized "The IBM Family," "tolerance," "understanding," "community," and the "problems, ambitions, abilities, frustrations, and goals" of employees, while warning against boring jobs, excessive turnover, and absenteeism. Top management has traditionally committed to the ideology of human relations in an explicit way.[107] Starting in the 1950s, IBM pioneered the use of suggestion

---

104. Few firms conducted morale surveys on a regular basis. In fact, workers and unions were generally weary of surveys, and management had to experiment with them very carefully before implementing a definitive program. See NICB (1951, pp. 7, 45–51); Mason, "Experiences with employee opinion surveys" (1949).

105. Baritz (1960, pp. 148–155, 169–170); Mason (1949).

106. NICB, *Behavioral Science* (1969); Fisher, "Morale crisis" (1991).

107. Watson (1954); Watson, Jr., *A Business and Its Beliefs* (1963, p. 19).

systems, "Speak Up!" programs, group dynamics, job enlargement, job enrichment, and morale surveys. In the 1950s and 1960s IBM hired some of the best academic consultants, including Frederick Herzberg. Geert Hofstede, a leading Dutch academic and organizational consultant, served as Director of Personnel Research at IBM Europe between 1965 and 1971. Hofstede's classic book, *Culture's Consequences* (1980), is based on the data collected by means of 117,000 questionnaires from 88,000 IBM employees in 66 countries. Interestingly, Hofstede defined himself as a "Protestant Christian," clearly in the tradition of the Watsons.[108] IBM has been conducting employee morale surveys in the United States since 1957, and worldwide since 1966. Morale surveys are staggered so that each employee is surveyed every two years.

Bendix's basic hypothesis that large, bureaucratic organizations motivate employees and managers by emphasizing the satisfactions intrinsic to the job itself is confirmed by IBM policies. Thomas J. Watson, Jr., the heir of the empire-builder, was the leading figure at IBM from the mid-1950s to the late 1970s. He was a staunch advocate of the human relations approach to organization problems in his 125,000-worker company. This is how he assessed and proposed to solve the problems derived from IBM's bureaucratic structure in his 1963 book, *A Business and Its Beliefs:*

> You cannot always make as many promotions in a plant as you can elsewhere, but we have found that there are other things you can do to keep morale high. One technique is job enlargement. . . . We try to rotate the very boring jobs to break monotony. This helps a person to keep his sense of dignity, accomplishment, and involvement. . . . I have always been convinced that without our attitude toward human relations we would have fallen short of our business goals.[109]

Although Watson believed in and strongly defended the system of free enterprise against threats from both within and outside the United States, he admitted that the spread of wage dependency and factory bureaucracy undermined the very ideal of entrepreneurship, and reduced career options for most people.[110]

Watson also confirmed Bendix's conclusion that the contribution of the human relations approach was to reinterpret the role of manag-

108. Hofstede, *Culture's Consequences* (1980, p. 424).
109. Watson, Jr. (1963, p. 24); Bendix (1974, pp. 281–308).
110. Watson, Jr. (1963, pp. 86–87).

ers and workers on the basis of their shared human qualities. In a statement typical of business founders or heirs, he argued that

> a business is a sort of dictatorship. . . . The head of a business ha[s] responsibilities almost like the head of a government, without a supreme court and without checks and balances, except those that the marketplace and the annual report impose on his operation. One of the worst mistakes he can make is to apply a double standard to managers and employees. If a manager does something unethical, he should be fired just as surely as a factory worker. This is the wholesome use of the boss's power.[111]

The case of IBM exemplifies how a large company has used human relations ideology to support its strong corporate culture, long-term commitment to employees, and non-unionization policy. Following the overall American pattern, IBM implemented a variety of human relations techniques that are still being used today in its extensive human resource development, leadership training, and quality-enhancement programs.[112]

The importance of the human relations paradigm in American organizational thought and practice during the late 1940s and most of the 1950s raises the basic question of why that paradigm was used and not some other. After the engineering approach to industrial efficiency had become assimilated in the 1920s, American managers became convinced that the human element in industry had been neglected and that much improvement could be accomplished in that area. Academic social-psychological research and teaching in industrial human relations reinforced that belief. The distinctiveness of American human relations thought was precisely the scientific sophistication resulting from the involvement of top social-science researchers in the theoretical development of the paradigm as well as in related consulting work. Ultimately, human relations ideas and techniques seem to have served American business well. A variety of human relations techniques were widely implemented in practice by firms

111. Watson, Jr., and Petre, *Father, Son & Co.* (1990, pp. 306–307); Watson, Jr., "Tom Watson looks at the past and future" (1986); Bendix (1974, p. 309). The discussion of human relations at IBM is also based on the author's experience at IBM's corporate training center at Palisades, New York, over a five-day period in the summer of 1992.

112. See, for example, the brochures *Employee Involvement* (IBM Corporation, 1991); *Taking It Personally* . . . (IBM Corporation, 1991); *Leadership Development* (IBM Corporation, 1992). See Bendix (1974, pp. 327–331) for an analysis of similar human relations policies at General Motors.

with the purpose of reducing industrial conflict and raising productivity. Business embraced the human relations paradigm not only as a weapon in its ideological fight with organized labor but also as a source of techniques capable of increasing productivity and improving the overall management of their organizations. The next section argues that the stabilization of industrial relations, the expansion of the large corporation internationally and into diversified product lines, and the emerging criticisms of the human relations school from within the social-science research community initiated a shift in attention towards the structural aspects of organization.

Structural Analysis and the Large Firm

For decades American management intellectuals and practitioners focused most of their attention on the organization of tasks, workers, and work groups. The scientific management and human relations approaches dominated the debates about organization because they addressed precisely those issues. The larger picture of the organizational structure, with its different functions, departments, and divisions seemed to be relegated to the background. To be sure, many managers (especially those in large firms) had to deal with structural-organizational problems, but most of the attention seemed to focus on lower levels of analysis. Starting in the late 1950s, however, American management intellectuals and practitioners began to discuss more frequently whether their organization as a whole and its structural design were adequate or not. This development raises the puzzling question of why structural-organizational analysis did not attract much enthusiasm before mid-century, given that many American business firms of the 1920s were already big, bureaucratized, and complex.

NEW ORGANIZATIONAL PROBLEMS AND OPPORTUNITIES IN
THE LATE 1950S AND 1960S

Stabilization of Industrial Relations.   Perhaps the single most important factor making for the prominence of structural theories of organization from the late 1950s until the early 1970s—but not before—was the stabilization of industrial relations and the reduction of industrial conflict. While structural-organizational aspects were surely a concern of business managers in the 1880–1955 period, problems related to the creation and handling of an industrial work force, and the organization of tasks and work groups had necessarily captured most of their attention because of rampant industrial conflict and disorderly production practices. Scientific management and human relations became popular among managers because those two paradigms addressed the most pressing issues of industrial conflict and shop-floor organization. Structural analysis, with its ideology of union-management collaboration, could not succeed until industrial strife receded.

Working days lost due to industrial conflict decreased slowly after the record year of 1946. During the early and mid-1960s, levels of days lost were approximately half as high as in the early 1950s. Industrial conflict became less of a problem, although the United States was still leading the richest countries of the world. The increasing coverage of collective bargaining was behind the reduction in industrial conflict, because labor unions preferred to resolve disputes using the grievance procedures stipulated in collective contracts rather than resort to strikes. Collective agreements began to spread after the 1935 National Labor Relations Act. By 1945 about 67 percent of manufacturing and 34 percent of non-manufacturing wage workers were covered by collective agreements, a combined proportion of perhaps 45 percent. In 1960–61 the proportion had reached 73 percent of all plant workers in metropolitan industrial and service firms. The relative increase in white-collar employment pushed the coverage of agreements down to 65 percent in 1971–72. The power of labor unions as organizations representative of the working class eroded during the 1960s and early 1970s. In brief, a more predictable and stable industrial relations system allowed employers and managers to shift their focus of attention from the shop floor to the larger picture of the organizational structure and to establishing long-term collaboration schemes with the unions.[113]

New International Opportunities. The late 1950s and 1960s brought about another important change with implications for the kind of organizational theory most relevant to business managers. Historically, the international environment had had a limited impact on the development of American capitalism, except for the occurrence of the two world wars. But when domestic markets became saturated in the 1950s, American businesses stepped up their investments abroad in search of growth and profits. Fortunately for American firms, incomes and purchasing powers in other countries were recovering

---

113. Lipset, ed., *Unions in Transition* (1986); Zieger (1986, pp. 147–167); Dunlop and Galenson, eds., *Labor in the Twentieth Century* (1978, pp. 40–45); see also the statistics in Appendix B.

from postwar lows. In 1950 American firms owned some 7,400 foreign affiliates, and 10,300 in 1957. In less than ten years the figure
more than doubled to 23,300 foreign affiliates in 1966. Net capital
outflows in dollars increased at approximately the same rate. By 1967
American businesses held 56.6 billion current dollars in direct investment abroad, or 7.1 percent of that year's GDP (compared to only
2.4 percent for Germany, but 15.6 percent for Britain). The United
States ran in 1971 a surplus in royalties and fees equal to 0.29 percent
of GDP, while Britain earned a modest 0.04 percent, and Germany
suffered from a deficit.[114] Structural analysis—certainly not scientific
management or human relations—could provide concepts and tools
for addressing the need to coordinate product development, manufacturing, and marketing on a world scale with adequate organizational
structures.

Economic and Structural Changes.   The stabilization of industrial relations and the internationalization of large firms coincided with other
changes internal to the firm that tended to make structural approaches
even more relevant. The trend towards higher bureaucratization of
industrial firms continued. In 1950 there were 23.6 administrative
employees for each 100 production workers, 28.9 in 1960, and 30.3
in 1970, the highest ratio of the large industrial countries second only
to Britain. Industrial firms were also diversifying their products, a
development that required the manipulation of structural variables in
order to achieve a better match between the organizational structure
and the different technologies and markets. In 1950 just 38 of the
100 largest industrial corporations were diversified, versus 60 in 1960
and 76 in 1970. After World War II another important economic
trend made the world of organizations more diverse and complex to
manage: the rise of the service sector (including the government).
While back in 1929 only 20 percent of the labor force was employed
in the service sector, 54 percent was in 1950, and 67 percent in
1970.[115] Banks, insurance companies, department stores, welfare
agencies, hospitals, prisons, schools, universities, and other informa-
tion- or people-processing organizations proliferated, and new organizational problems appeared. The relevance of a "contingent," struc-

114. Department of Commerce, *U.S. Direct Investments Abroad 1966. Part I: Bal-
ance of Payments Data* (1971, pp. 40, 177); UNCTC, *Salient Features and Trends in
Foreign Direct Investment* (1983, pp. 34–35); see also the comparative statistics in
Appendix B.
    115. See the comparative statistics in Appendix B.

tural theory of organization was based on the fact that organizations were different: they pursued a variety of goals, produced different goods and services with different technologies, and were evaluated according to different performance criteria.

INSTITUTIONAL FACTORS FAVORING A STRUCTURAL APPROACH

Structural thinking in organizational analysis did not originate in the conditions of the post–World War II period. Management intellectuals had long been worried about structural specialization, coordination, planning, the grouping of tasks into sections and departments, the establishment of communication channels, the differentiation and integration of units, and the issues of hierarchical levels and span of control. Two well-known examples are the "principles of administration" school and Barnard's insights into decision making in organizations. Among the proponents of universal and structural principles of organization was James D. Mooney (a vice-president at General Motors), who combined administrative (or bureaucratic) theory and structural principles with human relations concerns. Luther Gulick (a professor of Municipal Science and Administration at Columbia and a member of President Roosevelt's Committee on Administrative Management, with ample experience in governmental and educational posts) discussed the organization of business firms and government service agencies by major purpose, by major process, by clientele or matériel, and by place.[116] The most important early contributor to decision making in organizations was Chester Barnard, the president of New Jersey Bell. Barnard's writings included not only pioneering ideas about decision making but also notions about human relations and the institutional character of organizations. Thanks to his contacts and collaboration with Harvard organizational theorists, Barnard was acquainted with social-science trends.[117]

These early contributions to structural theory were not systematic, however, and contained many internal inconsistencies. Only with the growth in social-science theorizing and research after World War II did a paradigm emerge. The initial steps leading to the birth of a structural paradigm of organization were taken by economist Herbert Simon. In several landmark volumes, Simon and his colleague James

---

116. Mooney, "The principles of organization" (1937); Mooney and Reiley, *The Principles of Organization* (1939); Gulick, "Notes on the theory of organization" (1937).
117. Barnard, *The Functions of the Executive* (1938); Scott (1992, pp. 91–101).

March, a political scientist by training, criticized the classical principles of organization for being commonsensical, wrong-headed, and mutually incompatible. They followed Barnard's leads about decision making, and built bridges of understanding between administrative theory and structural-functional sociology.[118] The most outstanding American sociologists of the 1940s and 1950s made contributions to organizational analysis from a structural perspective, departing from the Weberian theory of bureaucracy in crucial and fruitful ways. This truly "invisible college" included Talcott Parsons, Robert Merton, Peter Blau, Philip Selznick, Alvin Gouldner, and Amitai Etzioni. (Merton had studied with Parsons at Harvard, and, in turn, Blau, Selznick and Gouldner wrote their dissertations at Columbia under the direction of Merton.)[119] Still, a structural paradigm of organizational analysis with clear implications for managerial practice was not proposed until the 1960s by Joan Woodward in England, and, in the United States, by business historian Alfred Chandler (whose writings also represent an attempt to justify top management's authority and the role of large corporations in the economy), management theorists Paul Lawrence and Jay Lorsch (who directed the Harvard Business School Program on Technology and Society with funding from IBM and the Ford Foundation), and sociologists James Thompson and Charles Perrow (with support from the National Science Foundation). A key historical fact is that, while a graduate student, Chandler attended Parsons's seminars at Harvard, and was introduced to Weberian and structural-functional sociology. Thompson was the founding editor of what would become the leading journal in the field, *Administrative Science Quarterly*. Perrow had studied under Selznick at Berkeley and established contacts with the Carnegie School while at the University of Pittsburgh.[120] All these authors agreed that the

118. Simon, *Administrative Behavior* ([1945] 1976); March and Simon, *Organizations* (1958); Cyert and March, *A Behavioral Theory of the Firm* (1963).

119. For the contribution of sociologists to organizational analysis, see Etzioni, ed., *Complex Organizations* (1961); Scott, *Organizations* (1987); Perrow, *Complex Organizations* (1986).

120. Chandler, *Strategy and Structure* (1962, pp. 394–396); Lawrence and Lorsch, *Organization and Environment* (1967); Lorsch and Allen, *Managing Diversity and Interdependence* (1973); Thompson, *Organizations in Action* (1967); Perrow, "A framework for the comparative analysis of organizations" (1967); McCraw, ed., *The Essential Alfred Chandler* (1988, pp. 1–21). On the impact of social science on business practice, see Dahl, Haire, and Lazarsfeld, *Social Science Research on Business: Product and Potential* (1959); Zaleznik and Jardim, "Management," in Lazarsfeld, Sewell, and Wilensky, eds., *The Uses of Sociology* (1967, pp. 193–233).

adequate way to organize was contingent upon certain strategic and/ or technological choices made by management. In that sense, their theories were distinctively functionalist. The emphasis was on the discriminating dimensions making for differences among organizations or organizational subunits. Prescriptions about organizational structure, goals, integration, and coordination followed from those differences, often expressed in the form of ideal types. In the field of industrial psychology the behavioral revolution produced a rejection of human relations. Writers and consultants like Victor Vroom developed a contingency theory of leadership.[121]

THE IMPACT OF STRUCTURAL THINKING IN MANAGEMENT CIRCLES

The first management intellectuals to use a structural approach to organizing were Peter Drucker and Ernest Dale, two of the most influential authors, teachers, and consultants. Drucker published a famous study about General Motors' decentralized divisional organization in 1946. In 1954 he published *The Practice of Management*, a book widely read both in the United States and in Europe. The publication in 1963 of Alfred P. Sloan's *My Years with General Motors* certainly helped to popularize the structural-organizational issues associated with large-scale corporate management. Sloan's most important contribution, though, is his ideological justification of the authority of top management and of a detached, structural approach to labor management based on the introduction of unobtrusive controls.[122] Drucker introduced the concept of technology (unique-product, mass, and process) in the mid-1950s, arguing that different technologies make "specific demands on management." He suggested that the analysis of the different activities and decisions taking place in the organization provided the basis for building the appropriate structure. Drucker criticized the human relations school, the reduction of managerial action to mere leadership, and managerial paternalism in general. For him, "a poor organization structure makes good

---

121. Vroom, *Work and Motivation* (1964). The influence of the concepts of contingency and environment (a clear departure from previous organization theories) even reached some theorists working within the human relations tradition. See, for example, Whyte, *Man and Organization* (1959), *Men at Work* (1961), and *Organizational Behavior* (1969); Dubin et al., *Leadership and Productivity* (1965).

122. Drucker, *Concept of the Corporation* (1972); Sloan, *My Years with General Motors* (1972, pp. 505–512). See also the speech by Sloan, "'Road to Serfdom' has been blocked," in *Vital Speeches of the Day* 19(1952–53):297–298. The title refers to Friedrich von Hayek's famous book on the consequences of socialism.

performance impossible, no matter how good the individual managers may be." As a structural theorist, Drucker may be considered an intellectual heir to Henri Fayol, James Mooney, Mary Parker Follett, and Chester Barnard. As an apologist of management, Drucker provided an ideological justification for union-management collaboration, for the role of the manager as the foremost decision maker in the firm, and for the system of free enterprise ("our way of life").[123] Ernest Dale wrote several books about organization and management in which he used a structural approach and cited the works of Barnard, Weber, Parsons, Blau/Scott, Chandler, March/Simon, Etzioni, Woodward, and Burns/Stalker. Dale collaborated assiduously with the American Management Association, and proposed a managerial ideology similar to Drucker's.[124] Other consultants working individually or for big firms like McKinsey published books proposing structural approaches to organizing.[125] Contingency theory was accepted and used not only by organizational consultants but also in other management areas (e.g., McKinsey's 7's, Delta's systems approach, and the Boston Consulting Group's market growth-share matrix). With their celebration of the virtues of the large industrial company and its contributions to the progress of the United States, Sloan, Drucker, and Dale (together with Chandler) backed up the famous statement, "What is good for General Motors is good for the United States," originally made by Charles E. Wilson, who served as president of General Motors and U.S. Secretary of Defense.

The National Industrial Conference Board started funding and publishing reports about the organizational structures of business firms in the 1940s. By the mid-1960s the Board had conducted several of those studies with the hope of improving organizational management methods across American industry, especially among those corporations with multinational operations.[126] The American Manage-

---

123. Drucker, *The Practice of Management* (1954, pp. 42, 96–107, 144–145, 193–226, 264–280, 341–392). On the European and American intellectual origins of Drucker's approach, see Waring (1991, pp. 78–88).

124. Dale, *Planning and Developing the Company Organization Structure* (1959), *The Great Organizers* (1960, pp. 22–23, 143–174, 181–201), *Management* (1965), *Organization* (1967). Dale and Michelon, *Modern Management Methods* (1966).

125. Allen, *Management and Organization* (1958); Mann, ed., *The Arts of Top Management: A McKinsey Anthology* (1971, pp. 53–65, 66–78, 79–93).

126. NICB, *Company Organization Charts* (1944), *Organization of Staff Functions* (1958), *Charting the Company Organization Structure* (1959), *Top Management Organization in Divisionalized Companies* (1965a), *Organization Structure of International Companies* (1965b).

ment Association also contributed to the diffusion of structural analysis with the publication of several of Dale's books. The 1970 volume, *AMA Management Handbook,* with contributions from a large group of top executives, included chapters on scientific management, human relations, and structural analysis. All three paradigms of organization had been accepted and incorporated into the body of knowledge available to managers. Other top management guides dating from the mid-1970s featured essays by chief executives from a variety of industrial and service corporations. Structural aspects of organizing figured prominently, while human relations and scientific management were relegated to the background.[127] The most influential management journal, the *Harvard Business Review,* devoted increasing attention to structural analysis during the 1960s, although human relations topics still predominated (see Panel B of Table 2.1). Panel A of Table 2.1 shows that structural analysis articles touched on technical themes more often than on ideological themes, although the idea that conflict in the firm is not necessarily bad was presented in over half of the articles.

The theoretical acceptance of structural analysis was also facilitated by the changes in business education taking place after the publication of the Carnegie and Ford foundations reports in 1959 calling for the introduction of more discipline-based, analytical skills in the curriculum. Disciplines such as mathematics, statistics, economics, psychology, and sociology (e.g., human relations and structural organizational analysis) started then to exert a widespread influence in the education of future managers. In fact, most of the major structural organizational theorists (including many of those with sociological backgrounds) professed at or collaborated with business schools.[128]

THE PRACTICAL IMPLEMENTATION OF STRUCTURAL IDEAS

It is hard to come up with empirical evidence about the practical implementation of structural theories in American organizations.

127. Moore, ed., *AMA Management Handbook* (1970); Glover and Simon, eds., *Chief Executive's Handbook* (1976, pp. 50–61, 145–272, 915–939). See also the chapters on organizational structure written by practicing managers in Maynard, ed., *Top Management Handbook* (1960, pp. 317–337, 904–938), and Haire, ed., *Organization Theory in Industiral Practice* (1962, pp. 13–27, 56–67, 68–75, 88–104, 153–170). The President of Westinghouse, Gwilym A. Price, and the Chairman and President of Ogden Corp. endorsed a structural approach to management based on behavioral science. See *Vital Speeches of the Day* 19(1952–53):294–296, 34(1967–68).

128. Pierson et al., *The Education of American Businessmen* (1959); Gordon and Howell, *Higher Education for Business* (1959); Koontz, "The management theory jungle

There are simply no representative surveys indicating to what extent managers take into account the environment or the technology of their organization in order to make changes in the structural design, operating procedures, or decision-making routines. One of the few quantitative indicators available is the frequency of structural reorganizations and the prevalence of certain types of structures such as the holding company, the unitary organization, and the multidivisional form among the largest industrial firms. Unfortunately, such an indicator leaves out the service and government sectors.

In particular, the adoption of the multidivisional form of organization, although limited as an overall indicator, unambiguously points to the growing importance of structural analysis in industry. The origins of the new structural thinking by practicing managers can be examined by looking at the cases of General Motors, DuPont, Standard Oil, Westinghouse, and Sears, Roebuck.[129] Research has shown that the increasing product diversification and multinationalization of American industrial firms produced a wave of structural reorganizations mostly conducive to the adoption of the multidivisional form during the 1950s and 1960s. The access to top management positions of directors with backgrounds in sales and finance or with MBA degrees from elite schools also favored the process, as did the structure of interlocking directors connecting the largest U.S. firms with one another. Among the 100 largest industrial firms, only 38 pursued diversified product strategies in 1948, and 20 had reorganized into multiple divisions. By 1959 the number of diversified firms had increased steeply to 60, and there were 52 multidivisional firms. At the end of the 1960s roughly three-fourths of the largest firms were diversified, and all except for three had adopted the multidivisional form. Consulting firms (McKinsey; Robert Heller & Associates; Cresap; McCormick and Paget; Booz, Allen and Hamilton; and A. T. Kearney) helped out many American firms with their structural reorganizations.[130] Similar reorganizations have been documented as resulting from international expansion. At first multinational firms orga-

---

revisited" (1980); Whitley, "The development of management studies as a fragmented adhocracy" (1984a).

129. Chandler (1962); Sloan (1972, pp. 113–169); Drucker (1972); Dale (1960); Fligstein (1990, pp. 226–294).

130. Fligstein, "The spread of the multidivisional form among large firms, 1919–1979" (1985), "The intraorganizational power struggle" (1987), and (1990, pp. 275–294, 336); Palmer, Jennings, and Zhou, "Late adoption of the multidivisional form by large U.S. corporations" (1993); Chandler (1962, pp. 381–382). See also the comparative statistics in Appendix B.

nized their foreign operations into "international departments." As they expanded, they multidivisionalized those departments or created either area divisions or worldwide product divisions. Of the 162 most important American industrial enterprises with foreign operations, 51 percent had developed multidivisional structures within their international departments by 1966, around 19 percent had created worldwide product divisions, and 10 percent had set up area divisions. These statistics suggest the spread of structural thinking about organization as a result of growing multinationalization.[131]

The multidivisional form was adopted by International Business Machines (IBM) only after the death of the empire-builder, Thomas Watson, Sr., in 1956. This pattern was typical of many organizational reforms in American business, as Chandler has observed. Thomas Watson, Jr., was the architect of both the strategy of diversification into computers and electronics, and of the subsequent structural reorganization. By 1959 the company had separate divisions for data processing, data systems, electric typewriters, supplies, government procurement, and the international market. IBM created a new general products division in 1969 to cater to the needs of small businesses.[132]

AMERICAN ORGANIZATIONAL IDEAS IN HISTORICAL PERSPECTIVE

Broadly speaking, the relevance of organizational theories for firms in a particular country depends on the degree of economic development and the organizational sophistication of the firms themselves. By the 1920s American business firms had become large, bureaucratic, and complex enough to suffer from the organizational problems amenable to techniques derived from scientific management, human relations, and structural analysis theories. What were the reasons, then, that human relations theory was not widely adopted until the 1940s and 1950s? Why did structural analysis only gain wide acceptance in management circles after 1955? The actions of the state, business-elite mentalities, or labor union policies provide no clues to answering those questions.[133] Certain changing environmental condi-

131. Chandler (1990, pp. 613–614).
132. Chandler (1962, pp. 47, 370, 381); Watson, Jr. (1986); Lewis, "Big changes at Big Blue" (1988).
133. The only exception is the impact of the mentality created by the efficiency craze, Progressivism, and mass-production/consumption culture on the adoption of scientific management.

tions help to understand the pattern of emergence of organizational paradigms in the United States. Industrial strife was clearly behind the appearance of scientific management and human relations, and the relative decrease in industrial conflict after 1955 was one of the factors allowing managers to concentrate on the larger picture of the organizational structure. The diversification and multinationalization of big American firms in the 1950s and 1960s also drew attention to structural-organizational issues. But the unequivocal factor that helps to fully understand the pattern and timing of the emergence of the different paradigms in the United States is the actors who were actually producing, diffusing, and implementing organizational knowledge: the professions. Scientific management as a paradigm and as a practical reality in business was the creation of efficiency experts and engineers. Human relations theory drew national attention only when a group of influential psychologists and sociologists pointed out its promises as a management tool. Structural analysis did not appeal to managers until leading sociologists and management consultants emphasized the limitations of previous organizational theories and showed how structural thinking could address the new problems facing business. In brief, the professions and their capacity to generate useful knowledge were the primary engine in the history of organizational paradigms in the United States. The unique importance of the professions in the American context will be qualified in the chapters to follow as the international environment, the state, and business-elite mentalities become more relevant for understanding the historical patterns observed in Germany, Spain, and Great Britain.

THREE

Germany
Modernism, Traditionalism, and Bureaucracy

The case of Germany is crucial to understanding the cross-national adoption of organizational paradigms because of a series of distinctive features. Unlike the Anglo-Saxon countries, the German state provided a role model for industry to imitate, allocated resources to facilitate the adoption of new organizational ideas, and promoted the belief that German national progress depended on the adoption of scientific management. Because of Germany's long and rich technical and scientific tradition, professional groups in applied fields like engineering and business administration formed comparatively early, but the social sciences such as psychology and sociology remained weakly institutionalized before 1929, suffered from political repression in 1933–45, and grew in acceptance only in the 1960s. Therefore, human relations had few advocates in the late 1940s and 1950s, but structural analysis received strong support in the 1960s. As a late-industrializing nation, Germany had to face industrial competition from more advanced countries but could learn to imitate their successes and avoid their failures. Germany's predominant labor unions embraced Marxism but adopted viewpoints favorable to scientific management. Germany is a test case to assess the impact of religion on the reception of organizational ideas. Protestantism and a modernist elite mentality tended to facilitate the reception of scientific management, while the Catholic tradition historically tended to favor human relations approaches. Finally, after 1950, Germany's pioneering of new industrial relations schemes and economic integration had direct consequences for the relevance of structural analysis.

Scientific Management in Germany: A Landslide

As in most other countries during the early stages of industrialization, German entrepreneurs based their authority and power to organize on demonstrated business success. The separation of management from ownership, the increase in average firm size, and labor unrest produced a legitimation crisis. The response was to introduce bureaucratic ideas about order and duty borrowed from the German army

91

and state administration. When international economic and political pressures tightened at the turn of the century, however, German management intellectuals turned to scientific management in an attempt to improve the country's international competitive position. During the late 1910s and throughout the 1920s, scientific management was rapidly adopted in Germany due to an unusual coalition of industrialists, labor unionists, engineers, and a state convinced of the importance of improving work organization methods to modernize the country.

EARLY ENTREPRENEURIAL AND BUREAUCRATIC SOLUTIONS TO LABOR UNREST

German managerial thought was at first aimed at providing solutions to the problem of labor turmoil. Historian Jürgen Kocka starts his account of German managerial thought in 1848 when the German states passed liberal legislation to foster competition among entrepreneurs after the consolidation of the 1834 customs union (*Zollverein*). In the midst of *Konkurrenzangst* (competition fright), early entrepreneurs believed in their personal fitness and ability to survive, not in science or theoretical-managerial principles. Entrepreneurs of this early period were personally involved in running the businesses they had founded themselves. They generally based their authority in the workplace on ownership and demonstrated business success, which enabled them to discipline workers with threats, fines, firings, and even corporal punishment. It is no surprise, then, that the first book to propose a "System of Rules for the Successful Operation of a Business" stated that "the best instruction is the verbal, the one given by the omnipresent, penetrating entrepreneur himself, whose good example appears constantly in front of the eyes of the employees." In such circumstances, Kocka argues, personalities and relationships among persons mattered more than organization.[1]

The internal development of German capitalism undermined the early managerial ideology after unification in 1870. The deflationary Great Depression of 1873–96 rendered Germany's liberal entrepreneurial model obsolete. The state promoted the development of economic resources internal to the Reich, now including the industrial

---

1. Kocka, "Industrielles management" (1969, pp. 334–336), "Entrepreneurs and managers in German industrialization" (1978, pp. 546–547); Stolper, Häuser, and Borchardt, *The German Economy 1870 to the Present* (1967, pp. 14–15); Lee, "Labour in German industrialization" (1978, p. 445, table 131). The book quoted is A. Emminghaus, *Allgemeine Gewerkslehre*, published in Berlin in 1868.

facilities and rich mineral deposits of Alsace and Lorraine. Heavy industry became the engine for industrialization, thanks to the demand generated by investments in railroads, shipbuilding, and the machinery industry. Firm size in these sectors started to grow. Labor militancy, especially in socialist organizations, became relevant for the first time.[2] All these events had direct implications for the maintenance of managerial authority and the improvement of organizational capabilities. More frequent labor conflicts and growing firm size were steadily undermining the effectiveness of the model of direct and personalized entrepreneurial controls. Besides, the rise of salaried managers meant that a smaller proportion of business executives could claim personal business success and justify their authority by reference to it.[3]

The breakdown of personalized entrepreneurial controls challenged industrialists the world over. In the search for new models and ideas, German entrepreneurs were original in that they *imitated* two successful German organizations of the time: the Prussian army and state.[4] It should be noted carefully that in Germany the bureaucratization of the state and the army *preceded* that of industry, in sharp contrast with the British and, above all, the American experience. The state and military influences were clear in the writings of the leading management experts. For example, E. Roesky argued in his 1878 book, *Administration and Management of Factories,* that during times of crisis and change it was necessary to introduce "military discipline," and that the "latest successes" of the Prussian army represented a "good model for our factories; rule them according to the model of our military administration and they will perform as well as our army."[5] Moreover, as the only truly "national" army in the world in which all strata of the population actually served as conscripts, the Prussian military contributed to the socialization of both the elite and the working class into bureaucratic habits.[6]

---

2. Moses, *Trade Unionism in Germany from Bismarck to Hitler* (1982, pp. 42–65).

3. Kocka, "The rise of the modern industrial enterprise in Germany," in Chandler and Daems, eds., *Managerial Hierarchies* (1980, pp. 92–94); Pross, *Manager und Aktionäre in Deutschland* (1965, pp 58–91).

4. Kocka (1969, pp. 352, 368), and (1978, p. 547); Jacoby, *The Bureaucratization of the World* (1973, pp. 28–35).

5. Quoted in Kocka (1969, p. 367).

6. See Holborn, "The Prusso-German school" (1986, p. 282). There has been some controversy over the issue of the effects of long periods of military conscription on worker discipline. See Helfer, "Über militärische Einflüsse auf die industrielle Entwicklung in Deutschland" (1963, pp. 599–603, 604, 608).

There is ample evidence about the introduction of rules, often in written form, specifying worker duties and rights, as well as the customary sanctions and rewards. In Kocka's words, "insurgency," "dishonesty," "discipline" and the "safeguard of control" became the themes in the discourse of German organizational writers after 1870.[7] These management thinkers believed that "order within the firm is the guarantee for its prosperity." As Thorstein Veblen observed in his 1915 book on German capitalism, bureaucratic rule became an effective ideology for maintaining order and discipline in the factory.[8]

Events at the turn of the century reinforced the reliance on bureaucratic ideology. Since the mid-1890s, the state and the banks had begun to orchestrate the process of economic expansion by promoting protectionist measures and cartelization.[9] By 1913 Germany's big banks had representatives on 751 boards of directors of industrial companies, the Deutsche Bank alone on 221 of them. Entrepreneurial families gradually lost control over the firms they had founded due to the rise of the corporate form of ownership. This process favored the applicability of bureaucratized controls and managerial practices. By the 1920s, German industrial firms had caught up with the British in terms of bureaucratization.[10] The ideological *and* practical bureaucratization of German industry continued hand in hand, with increasing average firm size resulting from endogenous growth, vertical integration, and horizontal merger. The proportion of manufacturing workers in units with more than 200 workers doubled from 11 percent in 1882 to 22 percent in 1907, and for firms with more than 1,000 workers, it rose from 1.9 to 4.9 percent.[11]

---

7. Kocka (1978, p. 547); Lee (1978, p. 460); McCreary, "Social welfare and business" (1968, p. 44).

8. J. J. Bourcart, *Die Grundsätze der Industrieverwaltung* (*Principles of Industrial Administration*) (Zürich, 1874), as quoted in Kocka (1969, p. 340; see also pp. 338–341, 368). Veblen, *Imperial Germany and the Industrial Revolution* (1939, pp. 231–235).

9. Stolper, Häuser, and Borchardt (1967, pp. 19, 24–29, 39–43, 46–49); Kocka, "The rise of the modern industrial enterprise in Germany," in Chandler and Daems, eds. (1980, pp. 88–90). It is important to emphasize that German law never prohibited inter-firm agreements on market allocation, output quotas, and prices. Quite on the contrary, the *Reichsgericht* (the German high court) ruled in 1897 that private contracts among firms on those matters were enforceable in court. See Chandler, *Scale and Scope* (1990, p. 423).

10. Locke, *The End of the Practical Man* (1984, p. 262); see also the comparative statistics in Appendix B.

11. Kocka, "The rise of the modern industrial enterprise in Germany," in Chandler and Daems, eds. (1980, p. 79). Manufacturing units with five or less workers still

Oddly enough, German labor unions contributed to the success of bureaucratic controls and, later, of scientific management itself. Trade unions were first legalized by the North German Federation in 1869, though they did not grow much during the repressive Bismarck years. In 1895, at the end of the Great Depression, unions could only count on 332,000 members or 3 percent of the non-agricultural labor force. Union-organized strikes were rare: 285 in 1873 and only 6 in 1877. Membership grew—albeit more slowly than in the United States—until the early 1900s (1 million members in 1900), and then jumped to around 3 million in 1914, or 15 percent of the non-agricultural labor force. Despite unionization and the occasional occurrence of conflictive situations, during 1905 the average number of days lost was only two per worker, and did not even reach an average of three during the record year of 1924.[12]

The dominant organization, the General Commission of the Labor Unions of Germany (*Generalkommission der Gewerkschaften Deutschlands*) was founded in 1890 by the Social Democratic Workers Party to defend class-wide interests. They were commonly referred to as the Free Unions. It was designed as a centralized umbrella organization to coordinate the actions of the large number of local and regional Marxist unions—a model diametrically opposed to the one followed by most anarcho-syndicalist unions the world over or by the English craft-based trades unions. An important characteristic of German social democratic politics and unionism since Marxism became the dominant doctrine in the 1880s was the combination of "radical theory and moderate practice," in sharp contrast with their French and Spanish counterparts. The "blood and iron" policies of Bismarck—simultaneously repressive and permissive—the strong Prussian state, and the long period of stability between German unification and World War I were the factors that created this peculiar situation, later referred to by a Weimar social democrat as "Bismarxism." Alienated and ignored by the established institutions and elite groups of Bismarck Germany, but steadily gaining in membership, the Free Unions were forced to pursue reformist policies in order to legitimize their existence.

---

accounted in 1907 for 31 percent of all manufacturing jobs, down from 60 percent in 1882. Max Weber was among the first to note the dualistic industrial structure that emerged in Germany at the turn of the century, to which neither Kocka (1980) nor Chandler (1990) pay much attention. The relevant figure in this respect is that in 1907 only 5 percent of the total number of firms employed more than five people.

12. Lee (1978, pp. 474–475).

The adoption of the Marxist doctrine represented an additional thrust towards reformism because of its increasingly "deterministic" character. The early "voluntaristic" Marx, who advocated the overthrowing of bourgeois society by a class-conscious proletariat as soon as a major crisis allowed, turned to more scientific endeavors during the 1850s, after the failure of the 1848 revolution. The first volume of *Capital,* published in 1867, was an attempt to "prove" that capitalism was doomed. In the minds of the unionists, Bismarck or Wilhelmine Germany was no place for a revolutionary takeover. Therefore, the idea that the impersonal "forces of history" would abolish the system was ideologically reassuring. While waiting for the "inevitable" end to arrive, the Free Unions devoted their efforts to improving the living standards, working conditions, and recreational activities of their membership.[13] Partly as a result of the reformist state of mind, the Free Unions underwent a rapid process of bureaucratization. In 1898 they had 0.2 administrative staff in central offices per 1,000 members, while in 1904 the ratio was 0.6, and by 1914 it had doubled to 1.2. Robert Michels's theory about bureaucratic oligarchy was in part based on the experience of the large German Federation of Metal Workers. In 1914 the Free Unions accounted for over four-fifths of all union membership in Germany, and were willing to cooperate with the industrialists and the government, the *Integrationspolitik*. In sum, the bureaucratization and reformist mood of the dominant labor unions helped to diminish the labor unrest problem.[14]

THE "AMERICAN PERIL" AND THE RISE OF THE ENGINEERS

Bureaucratic ideas could solve some of the problems brought about by the separation of management from ownership, increasing firm size, and working-class challenges to traditional entrepreneurial authority, but in the particular case of Germany, other factors tended to make bureaucratic solutions insufficient. First, compared to both Britain and the United States, Germany lagged behind in industrialization. Second, she lacked the huge internal market of the United States or the vast colonial markets of the British Empire, and so was

13. Preface to the first German edition in Marx, *Capital* (1967, vol. 1, p. 18); Roth, *The Social Democrats in Imperial Germany* (1963, pp. 159–232, 257–266); Schumpeter, *Capitalism, Socialism, and Democracy* (1976, pp. 345–347).

14. Schönhoven, *Expansion und Konzentration* (1980, pp. 229–230); Stollberg, *Die Rationalisierungsdebatte* (1981, pp. 67–79); Stolper, Häuser, and Bochardt (1967, pp. 107–109); Slomp, *Labor Relations in Europe* (1990, pp. 29–40); Michels, *Political Parties* (1962, p. 281).

dependent on world trade.[15] Third, she was a politically isolated power. Starting in the early 1900s, German politicians, business leaders, managers, engineers, and industrial designers became aware of the economic threats coming from other world powers, especially from the United States. This realization prompted the study of those aspects of American industry thought to underlie its phenomenal economic success. Scientific management and Fordism captured the imagination of German elites.

Although some prominent German industrialists started to pay attention to certain American systematic management techniques during the 1880s and 1890s,[16] engineers became most interested in American shop management. Throughout most of the nineteenth century, German engineers neglected the fields of management and administration, in sharp contrast with their American counterparts.[17] Early German engineering schools were modeled after the French example in the 1820s, emphasizing mathematics and science in their curricula. The model of *Technische Hochschulen* was introduced in the 1860s after the founding in 1859 of the elitist Association of German Engineers (*Verein Deutscher Ingenieure*, VDI). Under the German scheme—one combining the pure sciences and the humanities— engineering became a popular profession, attracting numerous middle-class youngsters.[18] The number of engineers per industrial worker increased steeply between 1870 and World War I. In 1910 Germany could boast 60,000 qualified engineers. Relative to the size of the industrial proletariat, the German figure was similar to the French, three times greater than the British, but somewhat lower than the American.[19]

At the turn of the century, German engineers shifted their focus of attention from France to the United States. In 1903 engineer Peter Möller reported in the journal of the VDI about his seven-month "study trip" to the United States. He borrowed from Austrian-Hungarian minister Agenor Goluchowski his 1897 term of *amerikanische Gefahr* (American Peril). The feeling of being at the mercy of foreign competition had been in the making since at least the years

15. See the comparative statistics in Appendix B.

16. See Buddensieg, ed. (1984, pp. 105, 107, 121 n. 40).

17. Kocka (1969, pp. 345–346).

18. On engineering education and associations, see Gispen, "Engineers in Wilhelmian Germany" (1990), and *New Profession, Old Order* (1989); McClelland, *The German Experience of Professionalization* (1991, pp. 91–94, 148–152, 186–188).

19. Ahlström, *Engineers and Industrial Growth* (1982, pp. 13–14, 54–57, 106–108).

before the end of the Great Depression in the mid-1890s, but a general consensus was not reached until the early 1900s. It is interesting that the Spanish-American war of 1898, which offered Taylor an opportunity to show his talents at the Bethlehem Steel Co. and led Spanish intellectuals to react against technology and engineering, represented for German engineers "a clear indication of America's strengthening." German engineers working in the steel industry were impressed by Bethlehem Steel's high-speed metal-cutting demonstrations at the 1900 Paris Exposition. They started then to travel to the United States with staggering frequency. The important point about Möller's and other reports was the prescription that the emphasis should be on workshop management techniques. Möller finished his report with optimism: "Of course, we must prepare ourselves for a harsh competition with the United States, for we'd better not underestimate the peril of the American invasion [of products]; but there is no reason to face this peril with hopelessness."[20]

In 1907 a new journal, *Werkstattstechnik* (*Workshop Techniques*), was founded to foster the adoption of better workshop management practices. In a typical statement, one engineer seized the spirit of the time:

> Just observe the reaction when you mention the word "American" in a technical context! "American conditions," "American work methods," "American manufacturing systems." *Watchwords* whose resonance suffices to intoxicate the majority of our minds.[21]

Even the Kaiser entered the debate to promote engineering schools and urge them to contribute to solving social problems. Slowly but steadily, grand bureaucratic designs, discipline, and conscientiousness were relegated to the background. The topics of "efficiency," "unpunctuality," "inaccuracy," and "imperfection," that is, ideas on the mundane topic of workshop management, became fashionable.[22]

Frederick Taylor's ideas were first discussed in Germany in the

---

20. Möller, "Eine Studienreise in den Vereinigten Staaten von Amerika" (1903, pp. 972, 974, 975, 1010, 1014); Kocka (1969, pp. 348–349, 357–358); Burchardt, "Technischer Fortschritt und sozialer Wandel" (1977, pp. 69–70); Taylor, *Principles of Scientific Management* (1967, p. 41); Merkle, *Management and Ideology* (1980, p. 178).

21. Quoted in Kocka (1969, p. 358). Many other journals on organization appeared in the years following the end of the Great Depression: *Organisation* (1898), *Zeitschrift für handelswissenschaftliche Forschung* (1906), *Zeitschrift für Handelswissenschaft und Handelspraxis* (1908), *Zeitschrift für moderne Geschäfts- und Betriebskunde* (1908), and *Technik und Wirtschaft* (1908). See Kocka (1969, pp. 351 n. 81, and 369).

22. Kocka (1969, pp. 368, 370); Locke (1984, pp. 103–104).

early years of the century. His writings aroused much interest in engineering circles, especially at the VDI engineering association. Translations of his major books appeared promptly, and by the early 1920s many engineering schools were teaching scientific management.[23] Industrial psychology research was also made available through the works of Hugo Münsterberg and others.[24] The only group that criticized scientific management in any sustained and comprehensive way came from the *Verein für Sozialpolitik* (Association for Social Policy).[25] Thus, the debate over Taylorism before World War I was not very rich and produced very little of note for the study of organizational change in Germany. There is one clear reason for this comparatively quiet prewar period. The appearance of Taylorism on the German scene is largely attributable to the diffusion role played by the engineers.[26] The debate over Taylorism lacked flavor and originality of ideas as long as no other major group like the unions or the industrialists became involved.

In the absence of debate, implementation started at the hands of pioneering engineers. Modern piecework schemes had been introduced in German firms as early as the 1870s. There is also evidence from the 1880s and 1900s showing that unions did not oppose piecework as such but wanted to see it regulated. A few pioneers tried to implement the Taylor system as a whole, as at Robert Bosch. In general, the first German pioneers of the practical implementation of Taylorism became as frustrated as the first American pioneers had, especially because of localized, plant-level worker opposition. In Germany workers and, to some extent, unions were initially predisposed against Taylorism due to the news about labor opposition coming from America. In other cases of failure, advocates of Taylorism pointed to the "incomplete" application of the system, which diminished its chances of success. In brief, until 1914 Taylorization in

23. Burchardt (1977, pp. 71–72); Hoffmann, *Wissenschaft und Arbeitskraft* (1985, pp. 175–179, 202). The reviewer of the German edition of *Shop Management* pointed out in the journal of the VDI that the introduction of the Taylor System would be quite costly. See Burchardt (1977, p. 70 n. 73, and p. 74).

24. According to American observers, German industrial psychology was well ahead of American achievements. See Viteles, "Psychology in business" (1923, pp. 208–209); Kornhauser, "Industrial psychology in England, Germany, and the United States" (1930, p. 425).

25. The most outspoken were Richard Woldt, Emil Lederer, and Wilhelm Kochmann. See Burchardt (1977, p. 74).

26. See the remarks in the daily *Frankfurter Zeitung* in 1913 in Burchardt (1977, p. 74).

Germany proceeded in fits and starts along the same lines and facing similar problems as in the United States up to 1911 (i.e., before the "efficiency craze").[27]

THE GERMAN WAY TO SCIENTIFIC MANAGEMENT: INDUSTRIAL RATIONALIZATION

The story of German scientific management would change dramatically during the war. Industrial rationalization (*Rationalisierung*) was the concept and the term that German management intellectuals invented after 1917. German industrial rationalization represented a synthesis of a series of ideas about technical progress, a corporatist version of capitalism, and the combination of mass-production techniques with mass-consumption markets. It embodied a corporatist response to economic and political liberalism. Industrial rationalization appealed to many groups in Weimar Germany: industrial, intellectual, and artistic elites as well as social democratic politicians and labor-union leaders. In practice, German rationalization included scientific management, Fordism, and the reorganization of distribution channels and entire economic sectors.

The origin of this rationalization movement lies in the miscalculation of the duration of the war. As the front stabilized and Britain initiated its blockade, Walther Rathenau of the *Allgemeine Elektricitätsgesellschaft* (AEG) warned Chancellor Theobald von Bethmann Hollweg about the long-term implications of the situation and offered his services. In particular, Rathenau insisted on the need to economize on raw materials. The Chancellor paid attention to Rathenau, appointing him as head of a newly created War Raw Materials Department (*Kriegsrohstoffabteilung*) within the Ministry of War.[28] During his six months in office (until March 1915), Rathenau improved the supply of raw materials considerably, and introduced a key institutional innovation: the War Raw Materials Corporations (*Kriegsrohstoffgesellschaften*). This model of corporations followed the

27. Kocka (1969, pp. 358–359); Stollberg (1981, pp. 31–42); Schmiede and Schudlich, *Die Entwicklung der Leistungsentlohnung in Deutschland* (1978, pp. 52–238); Homburg, "Anfänge des Taylorsystems in Deutschland vor dem Ersten Weltkrieg" (1978); Seubert, *Aus der Praxis des Taylor-Systems* (1914); Stollberg (1981, pp. 38–40, 82, 110–123); Ebbinghaus, *Arbeiter und Arbeitswissenchaft* (1984, pp. 182–183, 190–191); Merkle (1980, pp. 180–181); Kieser, ed., *Organisationstheorien* (1993, pp. 96–97).

28. Joll, "Walter Rathenau" (1960, p. 87); Urwick and Brech, *The Making of Scientific Management*, vol. 1, *Thirteen Pioneers* (1945, p. 86).

classic corporatist hybrid of state industrial initiative with private ownership.[29]

Walter Rathenau became president of the AEG in June, 1915, after the death of his father. During the remaining war years he published two books that marked the beginning of a new period in the history of German scientific management: *In Days to Come,* originally published in 1917, and *The New Economy* (1918). *In Days to Come* sold 24,000 copies of three editions in the first three months, altogether 65,000 in the first eight months. An English translation was published in London in 1921. *The New Economy* sold 30,000 copies in one month, and remained widely-read throughout the 1920s, long after Rathenau was assassinated by right-wing extremists in 1922. In these two books Rathenau showed his belief in efficiency, mechanization, and mass production, which should be promoted by the state through the institution of economic planning, although ownership should remain private. He also stressed the need to cooperate and secure workers' consent, although he suggested no particular role for organized labor. The contrast with the American experience of private, market-driven organizational innovation is apparent.[30]

A second major contributor to the rationalization literature was Wichard von Moellendorff, the leader of a technocratic and conservative movement dubbed "organizational Socialism." An engineer and long-time collaborator of Rathenau at AEG and at the War Raw Materials Department, Moellendorff made himself a name as a pro-Taylorite in the early 1910s with articles on topics such as "German Lessons from America," and "Taylorism and Anti-Taylorism." He also endorsed Münsterberg's industrial psychology. He railed against economic liberalism, egoistic profit-seeking, and the shortsightedness of those who opposed Taylorism. He emphasized scientific management's virtues—cheaper production, lower prices, harmonization of

29. Kessler, *Walther Rathenau* (1930); Urwick and Brech (1945, pp. 82–92); Braun, *Konservatismus und Gemeinwirtschaft* (1978, pp. 47–95). It should not be forgotten that Rathenau ordered the confiscation of Belgian stocks of raw materials and the deportation of Belgian workers to German factories. See Strandmann, "Introduction: Walter Rathenau, a biographical sketch" (1985, p. 86); Kessler (1930, p. 232). On Gustav Schmoller's intellectual influence over Rathenau, see Bowen, *German Theories of the Corporative State* (1947, n. 51, pp. 189–190). See also Schmoller, "Ueber die Entwicklung des Grossbetriebes und die soziale Klassenbildung" (1892).

30. Rathenau, "Massengüterbahnen" (1918), *Von kommenden Dingen* (1918), *Die neue Wirtschaft* (1918); Strandmann (1985, pp. 86–90); Merkle (1980, p. 186 n. 25); Urwick and Brech (1945, pp. 86–87); Joll (1960, pp. 94–105); Schulin, "Max Weber and Walter Rathenau" (1987).

interests—and assigned technology and rationalization higher missions like the emancipation of humans from wage dependency. Moellendorff was persuaded that Taylorism would "socialize Capitalism and give Socialism an aristocratic orientation." He urged the industrialists not to "leave Germany's fate to God, to the Entente and to Bolshevism." Moellendorff saw the United States as the successful role model to imitate. He warned that if things continued unchanged, "in twenty years Thyssen, Kirdorf, Rathenau, Stinnes, and Mannesmann would emigrate to America because it would be too late to help out," and he asked, "Who will prepare a German way for us?"[31]

In 1916, once again using efficiency arguments, Moellendorff introduced the concept of "communal economy" in his pamphlet, *Deutsche Gemeinwirtschaft* (The German Communal Economy). Moellendorff's *Gemeinwirtschaft* was conceived of as an "economy controlled by society," which should be modeled after the Spartan, disciplined war economy that he helped to create with Rathenau in 1914–15.[32] The model was essentially corporatist. Engineers were to play a major role as the "priests of efficiency, of the applied and objective causality."[33] Moellendorff and many other social democrats favoring rationalization were arguing for a state-led introduction of Taylorism, for otherwise the new economic order would be undermined by private interests.[34] In a later piece, "The New Economy," Moellendorff coined the term *Gleichschaltung* (later used by the Nazis), meaning the "streamlining of . . . the various parts of economic and political life."[35] The potential appeal of Moellendorff's and Rathenau's ideas was thought to be so great that the powerful neoconservative publisher Eugen Diederichs decided to edit a series of pamphlets on the idea of the German Communal Economy that sold over 44,000 copies in 1917–20.[36]

---

31. Moellendorff, "Psychologie und Wirtschaftsleben" (1913), "Taylorismus und Antitaylorismus" (1914b, p. 414), "Germanische Lehren aus Amerika" (1914a, p. 332), and "Der Ingenieur" (1912). See also Burchardt (1977, pp. 72, 82); Braun (1978, pp. 35–45); Bowen (1947, p. 200).

32. Merkle (1980, p. 189).

33. Quoted in Burchardt (1977, pp. 78). Burchardt (1977, pp. 81–85) cites and quotes many other relevant articles published throughout the 1910s. See also Braun (1978, pp. 143–154).

34. Burchardt (1977, p. 82). See also the comparison of Rathenau and Moellendorff by Maier, "Between Taylorism and technocracy" (1970, pp. 46–48).

35. Published in 1919. See Bowen (1947, p. 191); Merkle (1980, p. 190).

36. Stark, *Entrepreneurs of Ideology* (1981, pp. 143–144). See also the books by Gustav Winter, as discussed by Merkle (1980, pp. 172 n. 1, 181).

Apart from Taylorism, the other significant influence that came to Germany from America was Fordism. Due to his phenomenal success as a mass-producer of cars, Henry Ford became a popular hero in Germany of no less stature than in the United States. The first Ford car built in Cologne rolled off the assembly-line in 1924. His autobiography, *My Life and Work,* was first published in German in 1923. It sold twenty-two editions in the first two years, a popular edition was published in 1926, and it had reached the thirty-second edition by 1939. Fordist standardization, plant rationalization, and assembly-line work were embraced in Germany because they fit the ideal image of German character. Similar success heralded Ford's racist book, *The International Jew: A World Problem,* first published in Germany in 1921, and reprinted thirty-two times before the war.[37] Scientific management became an important topic for discussion in the 1920s thanks to the works of Rathenau and Moellendorff, and to the special impact of Fordism.[38] But the Rathenau-Moellendorff ideas about a centrally planned economy guided by "conservative socialist" principles outraged industrialists in the more traditional steel and metal sectors. Army officers also showed their concern.[39] In contrast, we will see in later sections that intellectuals, artists, and union leaders prepared the ground for the success of scientific management.

OTHER INSTITUTIONAL FACTORS FAVORING THE ADOPTION OF SCIENTIFIC MANAGEMENT

Elite Agendas: Modernism, Standardization, and Technology. The debate over industrial rationalization was by no means monopolized by engineers and industrialists. German intellectual and artistic elites also engaged in the debate, taking sides with those favoring the implementation of scientific management. Unlike English elites at the turn of the century, German intellectuals and artists saw the challenge of modernity as creating opportunities for combining traditional values

---

37. Merkle (1980, p. 193); Oberschelp, ed. (1976, vol. 37, pp. 437–438). For a racism-based interpretation of Ford's popularity in Germany, see Herf, *Reactionary Modernism* (1984, p. 41).

38. One of the country's most influential newspapers, the *Frankfurter Zeitung,* published a series of articles on scientific management: *Wege zur Rationalisierung* (1927). On the impact of Taylorism, Fordism, and industrial rationalization in German newspapers and magazines during the interwar period, see the quantitative analysis by Homburg, "Le Taylorisme et la rationalisation de l'organisation du travail en Allemagne, 1918–1939" (1984). See also Giesel, *Der soziale Gehalt des Taylor-Systems* (1963).

39. Burchardt (1977, pp. 78, 86); Bowen (1947, pp. 200–201).

with the wonders of mass production. Historically, German intellectuals had devoted much attention to a series of pairs of opposed concepts such as modernity-tradition, progress-reaction, society-community, and rationalization-charisma. All these oppositions were the product of a country that achieved industrial status relatively late, precisely when large-scale industrial corporations became the rule, as Veblen observed,[40] and that had no previous experience in liberal democracy; a nation in which traditional conservative groups (Junkers, civil service, military) provided the role models for emerging industrialists and even labor unionists. But Germany also developed her industry and technology to a degree that placed her among the leading nations of the world. The *Streit um die Technik* (debate about technology), or the question of *Technik und Kultur*, was to reach a climax in the Weimar period when "military defeat, failed revolutions, successful counterrevolution, a divided Left, an embittered Right, and Germany's famous illiberalism" coincided all at once.[41] Eventually, the "conservative revolutionaries" (a group that also included Rathenau and Moellendorff) imposed their views on government, industry, and art. The result was an elevation of the "idea of beauty over normative standards," and a "nihilist embrace of technology."[42] Intellectuals like Werner Sombart succumbed to the idea of rationalization as an "intellectualization" of industry.[43] In the background of all these developments was the concept of *Kulturnation* (a term used by Heidegger), suggesting that Germany should achieve a synthesis of idealism and technology in opposition to both American liberal technocratism and Soviet totalitarian materialism.[44]

The typically German blend of aesthetic-philosophical ideas and technology was implemented for the first time at Rathenau's AEG. In 1907 the 32,000-worker company appointed Peter Behrens as chief architect and designer. Behrens promised to work towards the

---

40. Veblen (1939, pp. 86–87).

41. Herf (1984, p. 19). Willy Hellpach (a politician and psychologist), and Hugo Borst (manager of the Bosch works in Stuttgart), for example, pointed out the need of Germans to combine two forces: Western machinism and Eastern primitiveness. See the review of his contribution to the volume *Das Problem der Industriearbeit* (Berlin, 1925) in *Zeitschrift für Betriebswirtschaft* (hereafter abbreviated as *ZfB*) 3(1926):240–241. See also Kieser, ed. (1993, pp. 98–100); Campbell, *The German Werkbund* (1978, pp. 194–195).

42. Herf (1984, p. 30).

43. Sombart, *Die Rationalisierung in der Wirtschaft* (1927), as quoted by Brady (1932, p. 534).

44. Herf (1984, p. 168).

"most intimate union possible between art and industry."[45] Behrens was a fan of engineers ("the engineer is the hero of our age"), and quite nationalist. In his widely publicized lecture at the 1910 annual meeting of the Association of German Electro-Technicians, he remarked that Germany depended on the world market and that she would have to compete on both technical and artistic terms. He finished by saying:

> We do not want an aesthetic system that looks for its rules in romantic dreaming, but one that is based on the full legitimacy of bustling life. Nor, however, do we want a technology that goes its own way, but one that is receptive to the artistic will of our age. In this way, German art and technology will work toward one goal: toward the power of the German nation, which reveals itself in a rich material life ennobled by intellectually refined design.[46]

At AEG Behrens made enormous contributions in several areas: product standardization and design (arc lamps, switchgear, heaters, electric fans, circuit breakers, etc.), publicity materials, and the design of factory buildings. His 1908 Turbine Hall became "a paradigm of modern industrial architecture," a place where "rational creativity and rational production join together."[47] Of particular importance were the workers' housing projects designed by Behrens before resigning from his position in 1914. He also worked for the steel giant Mannesmann. In 1918 Behrens co-authored a treatise, *Vom sparsamen Bauen* ("On Economical Housing"). Due to the difficult economic situation, he envisioned the "most intensive use of labor power," the rationalization of methods of construction, and the implementation of the Taylor System. Other leading architects and designers such as Max Mayer and Martin Wagner (both holders of doctoral degrees in engineering), as well as Walter Gropius and Ludwig Hilberseimer, also recommended the application of scientific management and lectured on or wrote about the different methods and techniques.[48]

45. See his article in the *Berliner Tageblatt* on August 29, 1907, reproduced in Buddensieg, ed. (1984, pp. 207–208). See also *Jahrbuch des Deutschen Werkbundes* (1913):33–54.

46. Behrens, "Art and technology," in Buddensieg, ed. (1984, pp. 213, 219).

47. Richard Hammann, as quoted by Wilhelm, "Fabrikenkunst," in Buddensieg, ed. (1984, p. 143).

48. Behrens and De Fries, *Vom sparsamen Bauen* (1918, p. 61); Neumeyer, "The workers' housing of Peter Behrens," in Buddensieg, ed. (1984, pp. 124–137); Nerdinger, "Walter Gropius—From Americanism to the New World" (1985); Hays, *Modernism and the Posthumanist Subject* (1992, pp. 249–251).

The marriage between art and modern mass production at AEG was by no means an isolated phenomenon. The *Deutsche Werkstätten* (German Artistic Workshops) had started to design furniture for mass production in 1906. In 1907, a group of twelve artists and twelve industrialists, including Hermann Muthesius and publisher Eugen Diederichs (who edited a series on scientific management in the 1920s) founded the *Deutscher Werkbund* (German Federation of Artistic Workshops). Its initial purpose was to encourage the investment of money in good industrial and non-industrial design work. The Werkbund brought together the best architects of the time—Behrens, Gropius and Muthesius—and collaborated with some of the most important German firms: Krupp, Daimler, Mannesmann, AEG, Robert Bosch, Norddeutsche Lloyd, and Hamburg-Amerika Linie. In 1911, the topic of the Werkbund's Berlin congress was the "Spiritualization of German Production." Throughout the 1910s, the most important contribution of the Werkbund was to "introduce the idea of standardization as a virtue, and of abstract form as the basis of the aesthetics of product design."[49] This idea of standardization—which Behrens pioneered at AEG—was to occupy a central position in German industrial rationalization. As noted by contemporary American students of German rationalization, "standardization represents the conserving elements of order, arrangement, and selection,"[50] and was thus consistent with the German philosophical background. But standardization of designs, components, weights, measurements, and equipment also fulfilled the role of facilitating the "component-based" mass production of a relatively large range of products in a country with, compared to America, limited demand levels.[51]

The *Bauhaus*, a school of design, continued the support for scientific management during the interwar years. It was founded in 1919

49. Banham, *Theory and Design in the First Machine Age* (1980, pp. 68–69); Whitford, *Bauhaus* (1984, pp. 20–21); Kirsch, *The Weissenhofsiedlung* (1989); Junghanns, *Der Deutsche Werkbund* (1982, pp. 24, 37); Nerdinger, ed., *Richard Riemerschmid, vom Jugendstil zum Werkbund* (1982); Banham (1980, p. 72); Campbell (1978, pp. 46, 51). See also the comments by Muthesius at the first great exhibition of the *Werkbund* (1914) in Conrads, ed., *Programs and Manifestoes on 20th-Century Architecture* (1970, p. 29).

50. Brady (1933, p. 21).

51. Dolivo-Dobrowolsky, "Modern mass production in the electrical appliance factory of the AEG." (1984). The text is a 1912 lecture at the AEG conference hall in Berlin. See also an article by Hanns Gelbsattel in *ZfB* 3(1926):631–633; *ZfB* 2(1925): 91–94; Buddensieg (1984, p. 46).

by architect Walter Gropius at Weimar.[52] Although at first a defender of craftsmanship, Gropius changed his mind and started to favor a "partnership between the artist, industrialist, and technician who, organized in keeping with the spirit of the times, might perhaps eventually be in a position to replace all the factors of the old 'individual work.'"[53] His Fagus Shoe Last Factory (1911–13), with the famous glazed corners, represented an early achievement of this program. Gropius wanted to arrive at "practical designs for present-day goods" that could be mass-produced.[54] He also gave new dimensions to the then-prevalent belief in the need to rationalize people's life at home. He was one of the leading architects of the Siemensstadt worker apartment complex in Berlin (begun in 1929).[55] Thus, aside from the rationalization of working life in the machine age so vividly and admiringly depicted by Bernard Kellermann in his best-selling novel, *The Tunnel* (1913), Bertolt Brecht in the poems of *The Impact of the Cities* (1925–28), and Fritz Lang in *Metropolis* (1927),[56] the Bauhaus started a revolution in home interior design that found its match in the preoccupation of efficiency engineers with improving housework methods.[57]

52. On the origins of the Bauhaus idea, see Wingler, ed., *The Bauhaus* (1969, pp. 1–2). See also Lane, *Architecture and Politics in Germany, 1918–1945* (1968); Bayer, Gropius, and Gropius, *Bauhaus 1919–1928* (1975); Bauhaus-Archiv Museum, *Bauhaus-Archiv Museum* (1981); Droste, *Bauhaus 1919–1933* (1990); Farmer and Weiss, *Concepts of the Bauhaus* (1971); Scheidig, *Weimar Crafts of the Bauhaus* (1967); Schmied, ed., *Neue Sachlichkeit and German Realism of the Twenties* (1978); Wingler, *The Bauhaus-Archiv Berlin* (1983).

53. Whitford (1984, p. 36). On his early position on craftsmanship, see Gropius, "Die Entwicklung moderner Industriebaukunst," in Junghanns (1982, pp. 171–172).

54. Quoted in Buddensieg, ed. (1984, p. 18). See also Nerdinger, "Walter Gropius." (1985); Gropius, "Principles of Bauhaus production [Dessau]," in Conrads, ed. (1970, p. 96); Gropius, *The New Architecture and the Bauhaus* (1956, pp. 30–51); Lane (1968, pp. 110–111); Isaacs, *Gropius* (1991); Giedion, *Walter Gropius* (1992); Nerdinger, ed., *The Walter Gropius Archive* (1990).

55. Whitford (1984, pp. 143–146); Lane (1985, pp. 87–124).

56. Kellermann, *The Tunnel* (1915). See, in particular, Brecht's poems 'Still, When the Automobile Manufacturer's Eighth Model," and "Song of the Machines," in *Bertolt Brecht Poems* (1976, pp. 109–110, 126–127). On Lang, see Whitford (1984, p. 143).

57. For example, see Reuter, ed., *Handbuch der Rationalisierung* (1930, pp. 1032–1053), in which "rational" methods of peeling potatoes or cleaning the floors are described. This monumental handbook summarizes German achievements in the area of rationalization throughout the 1920s. A section on "home economics" was created at the Fourth International Congress on Scientific Management, held in Prague in 1924. See Giedion, *Mechanization Takes Command* (1969, pp. 511–627) on the origins and development of household mechanization.

When the Thuringian regional government cut its support for the Bauhaus in 1924, the school moved to Dessau, the home of major coal-mining operations and of the Junkers aircraft works, for which several *Bauhäusler* did design work. The Bauhaus also collaborated with the giant chemical combine I-G Farben. It was at Dessau that the Bauhaus turned to architecture, especially after Hannes Meyer's arrival in 1927, who later became director.[58] Gropius also took part in the plans for new methods of "rationalized housing construction," including the standardization of components, time-and-motion study, work-flow charts, and other scientific-management principles. He was a vice-chairman of the National Society for Research into Economic Building and Housing, a part of the large state rationalization agency devoted to the promotion of scientific management in industry (RKW).[59] The most important commission of the Bauhaus was the housing project in Dessau (1926–28), where "standardization made for speed and economy of production, and on-site manufacture dramatically reduced transport costs." Under such a scheme, it took merely three days to build a dwelling unit.[60] Gropius and the Bauhaus collaborated with many industrial firms, including Junkers, Adler-Automobilwerke, Deutz, Waggonfabrik of the Prussian State Railways, Hannoversche Papierfabriken, B. Feder Furniture Company, Rasch, Mannesmann, Vereinigte Stahlwerke, and Siemens. Gropius even created a limited liability company, the Bauhaus GmbH, which did not meet expectations as to revenue. The Bauhaus had to move out of Dessau due to Nazi control of the city parliament, and then out of Berlin in 1933 shortly after Hitler's seizure of power.[61]

The organizational ideas of the German avant-garde modernist artists had an impact in management circles. Management theorists writing in management journals criticized books that railed against modern art or design, that believed rationalization decreased the pos-

58. See the Bauhaus magazine for 1928, and Whitford (1984, p. 179–181).

59. Gropius, "Systematic preparation for rationalized housing construction," in Wingler, ed., *The Bauhaus* (1969, pp. 126–127). Originally published in *Bauhaus* in 1927. See also Bauhaus-Archiv Berlin, Schrank 34, Inv.-Nr. 9153/1-12; RFGWBW, *Bericht über die Versuchssiedlung in Dessau* (1929, pp. 92–130).

60. Whitford (1984, p. 181); Herbert, *The Dream of the Factory-Made House* (1984).

61. On Hitler's campaign against modern art, see Barron et al., *Degenerate Art* (1991); Darnton, "The fall of the house of art" (1991); Lane (1968, pp. 125–145); Jordy, "The aftermath of the Bauhaus in America," in Fleming and Bailyn, eds., *The Intellectual Migration* (1969, pp. 485–543). On the Bauhaus GmbH, see Bauhaus-Archiv Berlin, Schrank 58, GS 9/6–7.

sibilities for artistic expression, or that denied the conceptualization of industrial rationalization as a "manifestation" of human reason, as a "desirable" and "noble" endeavor.[62] German traditional or reactionary modernism, in sum, rather than creating a "disjunction" between the techno-economic and cultural realms, fused them in the most fruitful fashion. This is at variance with Daniel Bell's thesis in the *Cultural Contradictions of Capitalism*.[63] The rapid adoption of scientific management in Germany was in part a result of the ideological collaboration between avant-garde artists and conservative industrialists.

Labor's Endorsement of Scientific Management. Worker opposition and union organization are factors often neglected in historical studies of management and of organizational change.[64] Informal, shop-floor opposition to Taylorism was important during the 1910s both in Germany and the United States. Before World War I, German workers used to cry that "*Akkord ist Mord*" (piecework is murder). The dominant German Free Unions remained indifferent to Taylorism until the 1920s, when they massively supported its application to industry. Leaving aside the special case of the Soviet Union, German unions were the only ones to accept the convenience of industrial rationalization and the implementation of scientific management to the degree that will be documented in this section.

Germany's dominant labor unions had special characteristics to begin with. The social democratic Free Unions were decisively reformist in program and highly bureaucratized in action. In addition, the social democrats represented the largest faction in the Reichstag by 1912. When the war broke out, they found themselves again isolated from the government and the masses, which were in a nationalistic mood. But the prolongation of the war ultimately facilitated the integration of the Social Democratic Party and the Free Unions into German political life, especially after the government asked for their collaboration in 1916–17. The Russian revolution split the German social democratic movement into Communist and reformist wings. Military defeat and the subsequent revolutionary situation prompted a coalition of interests between the reformist social democrats (including the Free Unions) and bourgeois groups that led the country to

62. See the review of Bruno Rauecker's book, *Rationalisierung als Kulturfaktor* (Berlin, n.d.), in *ZfB* 6(1929):396–398.

63. Bell, *The Cultural Contradictions of Capitalism* (1978, pp. 46–54).

64. This is particularly so of studies in which technological determinism plays a central role. See, for instance, Chandler, *The Visible Hand* (1977).

democratic parliamentarism.[65] The first governments of the Weimar Republic were dominated by the social democrats. Many union leaders held economic and labor-related offices in the government, and some of them served in the cabinet. The Free Unions gained momentous membership (a total of over 7 million in 1919–22).[66] The tendencies towards centralization in German trade-unionism resulted in the creation of the *Allgemeiner Deutscher Gewerkschafts-Bund* (ADGB, General German Federation of Unions), the *Allgemeiner freier Angestellten-Bund* (AfA, General Federation of Free Salaried Employees), both in the Free Union camp, and the *Deutscher Gewerkschafts-Bund* (DGB, German Federation of Unions), unifying the Christian unions.[67] It was against this historical background that socialist labor leaders began to praise the introduction of science into the workplace.

Many prominent union leaders, often occupying top governmental or even managerial positions, openly declared their approval of scientific management. For example, Georg Chaym wrote in a 1920 issue of the *Sozialistischen Monatshefte* (*Socialist Monthly*) about the "obligation" of the working class to increase production with the implementation of the Taylor system. One could read in *Der Arbeiter-Rat* (*Works Council*) the same year that "we need the Taylor System; we need it as much as our daily bread."[68] Gustav Bauer—a labor unionist, member of the Social Democratic Party, Reichsminister for Labor, and later Chancellor of the Reich—explained in early 1919 that, "in the capitalistic economic order," Taylorism

> stood in opposition of the worker. Labor feared that the capitalist, and not itself, would be the beneficiary of the new method of work. Now that the democratization of Germany has ensured an ample economic influence of labor, these objections are not only futile but also obscure the fact of the possibilities offered by rationalization.[69]

The Free Unions adopted an official position on the subject at their 1925 national congress in Berlin. After recognizing the successes of American industrial methods and criticizing attempts to erect protectionist trade barriers in Germany, the participants agreed that

65. Feldman, "German interest group alliances in war and inflation, 1914–1923" (1981, pp. 168–182); Rokkan, *Citizens, Elections, Parties* (1970, p. 135); Roth (1963, pp. 285–296).

66. Stollberg, *Die Rationalisierungsdebatte* (1981, p. 75).

67. Schumann, *Nationalsozialismus und Gewerkschaftsbewegung* (1958, p. 15).

68. Stollberg (1981, p. 83).

69. Quoted in Stollberg (1981, p. 85).

not lower wages and longer working times in connection with technical backwardness, but higher wages, shorter working times, rational production methods, and economic organization guarantee the economic rise and the competitiveness of Germany in the world market.[70]

Industrial psychology was also accepted uncritically. Some unions even proposed to introduce mandatory testing of all workers applying for union affiliation or for admission to apprenticeship programs.[71] Fordism received an even better evaluation. A group of union leaders traveled to the United States in 1926 to visit Ford's plants. Some of them were worried about the dehumanization of work, but most returned extremely enthusiastic.[72] In an essay entitled "Why Be Poor?", Fritz Tarnow, of the national board of the Free Unions, held that Ford's autobiography was "the most revolutionary book in the economic literature ever."[73]

One factor behind the endorsement of scientific management by union leaders was the belief that its implementation represented a preparation for Socialism. Most of the time this belief remained implicit, but there are some texts which made it explicit. The first time such an idea was set in type dates back to as early as 1914, when unionist Wilhelm Eggert wrote in the official journal of the Free Unions that "humanity has based many achievements, as well as the whole culture, on the principle of division of labor. . . . Taylorite work methods may bring about struggles, and may represent a further stage in the way towards Socialism."[74]

In 1926, the Federation of Metal Workers declared that rationalization and centralization were "preparatory stages for the coming socialist communal economy."[75] Accordingly, ideas about vocational-

---

70. From the Proceedings of the 12th Congress of the Unions of Germany (1925), as reproduced in Stollberg (1981, p. 181). Similar viewpoints were adopted at the 13th Congress in 1928, and in the Free Unions' report, "Gegenwartsaufgaben deutscher Wirtschaftspolitik," addressed to the national government. See Hoff, "Gewerkschaften und Rationalisierung" (1978, p. 182); Hinrichs and Peter, *Industrieller Friede?* (1976, p. 89).

71. Viteles (1923, p. 213); Hoff (1978, p. 186).

72. Brady (1933, pp. 333–335); Stollberg (1981, pp. 89–90); Hoff (1978, p. 177). See also the more measured endorsement of Woldt, "Die Stellung der Gewerkschaften zum Problem der Fließarbeit," published in *Gewerkschafts-Archiv* in 1926, as reproduced in Hinrichs and Peter (1976, pp. 264–268).

73. Tarnow, "Warum arm sein?" published in *Gewerkschaften und Wirtschaft* in 1928. Quoted in Hinrichs and Peter (1976, pp. 78, 88). See also *ZfB* 4(1927):274–275.

74. Published in *Correspondenzblatt*. Quoted in Stollberg (1981, p. 88).

75. Quoted in Stollberg (1981, p. 90). A few German communists also subscribed to the idea of scientific management being a preparation for communist society. See Stollberg (1981, p. 106).

ism, craftsmanship, and group production—frequently sponsored by
the Christian unions—were summarily dismissed as "romantic de-
tours."[76] Some leaders went even further in their arguments, suggesting that the engineering profession, a quite conservative body,
was also helping out in the long march towards Socialism. In 1927
Ludwig Preller, a social democrat in the regional government of Sax-
ony, stated that

> one can only be grateful to the Association of German Engineers for
> having, perhaps unconsciously, facilitated the recognition of this social-
> ist development with their contributions to the topic of assembly-line
> work. Theirs is the striving for helping to convert assembly-line into
> planned economy. The socialists' task will then be to transform that as
> yet capitalist planned economy into a socialist communal economy.[77]

Some leaders of the Free Unions aired the negative consequences
of industrial rationalization. They mentioned deskilling (especially of
female workers), work intensification, monotony, and labor redun-
dancy.[78] Others, like Eggert, pointed out the negative macroeconomic
effects deriving from increased industrial production in conjunction
with layoffs and steady or rising prices.[79] But many of these writers
thought that the negative aspects of rationalization could be avoided
if economic democracy and joint decision making were strengthened,
and reeducation efforts increased.[80] In the midst of the world economic depression, some union leaders would argue that "had the
German economy not followed the path of rationalization, the crisis
today would not be smaller but more acute."[81] Only the communist

76. Hoff (1978, p. 190); Ebbinghaus (1984, pp. 187–188). See also Seidel, "Psychotechnik und Werkzufriedenheit," published in *Die Gesellschaft* in 1926, as reproduced in Hinrichs and Peter (1976, pp. 246–249).

77. Preller, "Fließarbeit und Planwirtschaft," published in the *Sozialistischen Monatshefte* in 1927. Reproduced in Hinrichs and Peter (1976, p. 241).

78. Hoff (1978, pp. 178, 185). See also the blistering critique of the Bedaux
System by Kaiser, "Methoden kapitalistischer Rationalisierung: Das Bedaux-System,"
published in *Die Internationale* in 1930. Reproduced in Hinrichs and Peter (1976, pp.
276–284).

79. See *ZfB* 4(1927):384–385. Eggert did not criticize rationalization as such,
rather, he proposed that the state force producers to cut prices once rationalization
increased the productivity of their plants. See also Hoff (1978, pp. 180–181); and
Rubinstein, "Die kapitalistische Rationalisierung," published in *Unter dem Banner des
Marxismus* in 1929. Reproduced in Hinrichs and Peter (1976, pp. 285–298).

80. Hoff (1978, pp. 173–174, 179, 182, 191–192); Stollberg (1981, pp.
91–102).

81. Fritz Naphtah, as quoted in Hinrichs and Peter (1976, p. 97).

and anarcho-syndicalist leaderships, who gained in proportional share of total union membership after 1924 at the expense of the Free Unions, continued pointing to the negative aspects: work intensification, isolation of workers and limitation of their collective power, and the profit motive implicit in all rationalization efforts. The contrast with the Soviet communists' honeymoon with scientific management could not be sharper.[82]

The State Provides Institutional Support. The German state was not merely a role model for industry to imitate. Engineers, industrialists, and especially labor leaders collaborated to mobilize vast amounts of state resources to promote scientific management and industrial rationalization under the framework of corporatism. It has been noted above that many of the promoters of scientific management in Germany enjoyed a huge stock of political capital. At the end of World War I there was no organization of note, public or private, specifically devoted to the advancement of scientific management in any country of the world except for the New York–based Taylor Society, founded in 1911. The only two countries that created such an organization before 1923 were France and Germany. The German organization, the *Reichskuratorium für Wirtschaftlichkeit* (National Board of Efficiency), best known by the acronym RKW, was to become the model for similar organizations in other countries.

The immediate antecedent of the RKW was the Section on Labor Science created in 1920 by Reichsminister for Labor Alexander Schlicke to stimulate industrial rationalization. Schlicke had been president of the Federation of Metal Workers for many years before entering the government. A year later, in 1921, a group of employers, officials and engineers approached the Reichsminister for the Economy, Robert Schmidt (another union leader), to found a permanent institute dedicated to the promotion of rationalization in industry. The outcome was the RKW, an autonomous, semi-official entity mostly financed by the state.[83]

---

82. Stollberg (1981, pp. 105–108, 190–192); Hinrichs and Peter (1976, pp. 79–83, 98–101); Hoffmann (1985, pp. 50–65). Demar, "Die Rationalisierung der Produktion und die politische Arbeit im Betrieb," published in *Die Kommunistische Internationale* in 1927. Reproduced in Hinrichs and Peter (1976, pp. 976–982). See also Rocker's 1927 book, *Die Rationalisierung der Wirtschaft und die Arbeiterklasse* (1980, pp. 45–51, 69–84).

83. During 1925–31 an average of 96 percent of the RKW's expenditures were covered by state contributions. The proportion of public funds dropped to 32 percent in 1931–33. See RKW, *Jahresbericht 1932–33* (1933, p. 14). See also Büttner, *Das*

Among the businessmen involved in the founding of the RKW was Carl Friedrich von Siemens, Werner Siemens's third son and president of the 60,000-worker Siemens industrial group of companies after the death of his two elder brothers. Siemens was elected to the German parliament in 1920 as a member of the Democratic Party (the one to which Rathenau and Max Weber belonged), and he served until 1924. When the RKW was founded, he became its first president. Like Rathenau, Siemens believed in corporatist solutions to politics and in the organization of the economy "from above."[84] As president of the RKW, Siemens brought in some of his collaborators. The most noted was Carl Köttgen, a doctor in engineering familiar with British and American industry, who later became president of the engineering association (VDI) and the RKW itself.[85] During the Siemens-Köttgen years, especially in 1925–31, the RKW was to become a large and effective organization with a full-time staff of 50, a staggering number of committees (over 200 in the early 1930s), with as many as 4,000 active committee members, and a newsletter (*RKW-Nachrichten*) that sold about 12,000 copies even during the gloomy year of 1932. In all, over 2 million copies of different rationalization brochures were distributed in a single year. The RKW administered 80,000 psychological tests annually.[86]

The problem the RKW was meant to solve was clear from the beginning. As Siemens declared in 1925, "All Germans agree that our present production is too small and therefore too expensive." One way of improving the situation, he maintained, was to realize the possibility of transferring and adapting American ideas to Germany.[87]

Rationalisierungs-Kuratorium der deutschen Wirtschaft (1973, pp. 7–28); Stollberg (1981, p. 123). The title of Büttner's book refers to the new denomination of the RKW when it was reactivated in 1950. Nonetheless, the old RKW acronym survived.

84. Goetzeler and Schoen, *Wilhelm und Carl Friedrich von Siemens* (1986, pp. 68, 78–79).

85. On his trips to the United States, see the review of his book, *Das wirtschaftliche Amerika* (Berlin, 1925) in *ZfB* 2(1925):299–300.

86. See RKW, *Jahresbericht 1928* (1929, pp. 3, 6); *ZfB* 3(1926):141; Kieser, ed. (1993, p. 102). The success of the RKW accounts for the comparatively low number of German companies that were members of the International Management Institute of the International Labour Office during its few years of existence (1927–32). France, Great Britain and Italy had more members than Germany, while Czechoslovakia and Switzerland, despite the smaller size of their economies, had about the same number of members as Germany. See IMI, *Annual Reports* for the years 1929, 1930, 1931, and 1932.

87. Büttner (1973, pp. 12–13); Locke (1984, pp. 273–275). Fear of American competition was widespread in the 1920s. See Levy's 1935 book, *Industrial Germany* (1966, p. 211).

Unions also took part in the organization. The Christian and Free Unions had had representatives on the governing body of the RKW since 1925, although regular collaboration started only somewhat later.[88] In 1930 the RKW published a massive 1,234-page volume summarizing its activities to date, the *Handbuch der Rationalisierung* (*Handbook of Rationalization*), of which two editions were printed within months. A third edition was published in 1933.[89]

Despite the importance of the RKW, it did not stand alone as an organizational tool to promote the adoption of scientific management. There were special institutions similar to the RKW for agriculture, building and housing (architect Walter Gropius served as its vice-president), and standardization of norms. The German Normalization Committee (*Deutscher Normenausschuß*) was the central standardization agency, with which architects Behrens and Muthesius collaborated. Founded in 1926, it continued the efforts of the wartime Normalization Committee on Machine-Building. The *Deutsche Industrie-Normen* or DIN (German Industrial Norms) came out of the activities of these two organizations, and became the industrial and measurement standards in most continental European countries. Another organization of importance was the National Committee for Work Time Determination (*Reichsausschuß für Arbeitszeitermittlung*, or REFA). It was created at the initiative of employers and engineers in the metal sector. During its first ten years of existence, 1924–33, the REFA trained over 10,000 time-and-motion engineers, known as *REFA-Männer,* a word that can be found in German dictionaries even today. Its director, Friedrich-Ludwig Meyenberg, edited several REFA books which sold in excess of 100,000 copies. Other leading engineers, consultants, and authors at REFA included Kurt Hegner and Waldemar Hellmich.[90] The RKW created a Committee on Time-and-Motion Study in 1935.[91] Another organization was the Kaiser Wilhelm Institute for Work Physiology, which could count on the support of the unions.[92] In fact, the chairman of the Free Unions,

88. Stollberg (1981, pp. 123–124).

89. Reuter, ed. (1930). See also *ZfB* 5(1928):796.

90. Stollberg (1981, pp. 52–53); Urwick, *The Golden Book of Management* (1956, pp. 184–187, 216–219, 229–231). For the application of time-and-motion studies in plants producing single products or small batches, see the review of Hans Kummer's book, *Zeitstudien bei Einzelfertigung* (Berlin, 1926), in *ZfB* 4(1927):721–723.

91. See *ZfB* 20(1950):51–53.

92. In fact, the "science of work" (*Arbeitswissenschaft*) had its origins in the mid-19th century. See Rabinbach, *The Human Motor* (1990, pp. 189–195). See also Weber, "Zur Psychophysik der industriellen Arbeit" (1908–1909).

Theodor Leipart, was on the institute's board of directors. Interestingly, the only aspect of the institute's work that the unions did not like was its excessively "scientific" and unrealistic experiments taking place in laboratories rather than in real-life factories.[93]

THE THEORETICAL IMPACT OF SCIENTIFIC MANAGEMENT IN GERMAN BUSINESS CIRCLES

In Germany, an unlikely coalition of engineers, elite intellectuals and artists, labor unionists, and a few leading managers proposed to adopt scientific management as a solution to organizational problems perceived to be caused by increasing international pressures and changing economic structures of firms. The question to be addressed now refers to whether the new paradigm was successful in German managerial circles or not. There is a wealth of evidence indicating that German employers and managers embraced scientific management as a way to deal with organizational complexity and cut costs.[94] A systematic examination of the pieces on organizational matters published in the *Zeitschrift für Betriebswirtschaft* (*Journal of Business Administration*, hereafter abbreviated as *ZfB*) since early 1924 will help to assess the degree of success of different organizational paradigms in Germany throughout the twentieth century as organizational ideologies and techniques. *ZfB* is one of the three major journals of business administration that have lasted from the 1920s until the 1970s. Unlike the other two journals—which focused on accounting, finance, and marketing—the *ZfB* contained many articles on business organization.[95] Articles and lengthy review essays published in this journal were analyzed following the rules specified in Appendix A.

As shown in panel A of Table 3.1, thirty-two articles or lengthy review essays dealt with organizational issues in the 1924–42 period. The authors of scientific management articles highlighted different techniques such as the separation of conception and execution, division of labor, and specialization; time-and-motion studies and job

93. Brady (1933, pp. 330–331).

94. For a summary, see Hoffmann (1985, pp. 37, 66–84).

95. The others are the *Zeitschrift für Handelswissenschaftliche Forschung* and the *Zeitschrift für Handelswissenschaft und Handelspraxis*, followed after World War II by *Schmalenbachs Zeitschrift für Betriebswirtschaftliche Forschung* and *Betriebswirtschaftliche Forschung und Praxis*. See Locke (1984, pp. 222–223). On the impact and prestige of German management journals, see Jäger, *Unterschiede zwischen der deutschen und amerikanischen Organisationsforschung* (1989). On the rise of German management education since the 1890s to the 1920s, see Lindenfeld, "The professionalization of applied economics" (1990).

TABLE 3.1 Results of the content analysis of the articles and lengthy book reviews published in the *Zeitschrift für Betriebswirtschaft*, 1924–1942, by paradigm (SM: scientific management; HR: human relations; SA: structural analysis; NC: not classifiable)

A. Number of articles mentioning each of the content categories (see Appendix A) and themes (32 articles examined)

Content Categories	SM	HR	SA
Perceived problem	6	4	0
Form of solution	1	0	1
View of conflict	0	1	3
View of workers	2	3	0
Fascination with	6	6	0
Methodology	10	0	0
Selection of workers	2	0	0
Distribution of tasks	15	0	1
Authority structures	2	3	2
Process of work	10	1	0
Preferred rewards	7	1	0
Economic incentives	5	0	0

B. Number of articles (N) and themes classified by paradigm

	SM				HR				SA				NC
		Themes				Themes				Themes			
Year Period	N	Mean	Min	Max	N	Mean	Min	Max	N	Mean	Min	Max	N
1924–26	6	3.8	2	6	2	4.0	3	5	0	—	—	—	2
1927–29	5	2.8	2	4	1	4.0	4	4	0	—	—	—	0
1930–32	6	3.3	2	5	1	3.0	3	3	1	3.0	3	3	0
1933–35	2	2.0	2	2	0	—	—	—	0	—	—	—	2
1936–38	2	2.5	1	4	0	—	—	—	0	—	—	—	1
1939–42	0	—	—	—	1	2.0	2	2	0	—	—	—	0
All years	21	3.1	1	6	5	3.4	2	5	1	3.0	3	3	5
Pages	120	5.7	1	18	41	8.2	2	16	11	11	11	11	30

Sources: The articles included in the analysis are the following:

SM: *ZfB* 1:87–90, 196–198, 334–342, 387–390; 3:631–633, 887–889; 4:497–506, 721–723; 5: 24–32, 309–312; 6:158–159; 7:66–69; 8:303–305, 547–550, 712–720, 766–778; 9:541–559; 10:53–57; 12:15–33; 15:92–97, 204–209.

HR: *ZfB* 2:201–204; 3:115–131; 4:797–799; 9:605–617; 18:163–171.

SA: *ZfB* 9:422–433.

NC: *ZfB* 2:73–81; 3:791–794; 10:235–240, 658–670; 13:214–216.

analysis; and standardization, work simplification, mechanization, and assembly-line work. As in the United States, few articles presented a comprehensive view of the ideology of scientific management. Only the ideological theme of the fascination with machinery, technology, mass production, and the factory aesthetic surfaced in a substantial number of articles (one-third of those written from a scientific management perspective), a finding consistent with the importance of the modernist mentality in Germany.

Panel B of Table 3.1 presents the results of the classification of the pieces into one of the paradigms. Twenty-one pieces (three in four) were classified as scientific management. Five pieces figure under the human relations category, and just one was a structural analysis piece. The average piece cited 3.1 themes in the case of scientific management (with a maximum of 6), and 3.4 in the case of human relations (a maximum of 5). In general, therefore, only a few different themes tended to appear together in the same piece. Scientific management pieces clearly predominate up to 1932, but there is no dominant paradigm thereafter. No scientific management piece was published in *ZfB* after 1939. Not surprisingly, the five articles or reviews focusing on Fordism were published before 1928, when Ford's troubles began.

Of the twenty pieces for which information on the author was available, fourteen were written by persons with university degrees in business administration, and only four were written by engineers. The two remaining authors were a navy officer and a doctor in law (the author of the only article classified as structural analysis). None of the authors could be identified as a union leader. While only a few of the organizational articles published in the *ZfB* during the 1924–42 period were written by engineers or persons with technical qualifications, the engineer was often presented as *the* person who could solve Germany's productivity problems.

Whenever a book reviewed in the *ZfB* suggested that there might be reasons for Germany not to imitate American scientific management, the reviewer would attack the author's argument simply by saying that the book lacked scientific value.[96] Also, the editors and reviewers for the *ZfB* seemed to be interested in undermining any social democratic or conservative dreams of a corporatist and Taylorized economy à la Rathenau or à la Moellendorff. In fact, neither Rathenau nor Moellendorff were ever cited. Books advancing these

96. *ZfB* 5(1928):632–634.

ideas were severely criticized by the reviewers for being "uncritical," "non-scientific," or "socialist."[97] Likewise, when a book linked the success of Fordism to the existence of a Socialist economy and government, in what became known as "white socialism," or when Fordism was presented as an alternative to revolutionary Marxism (as in Jakob Walcher's 1926 book, *Ford or Marx*), the reviewer would dismiss it as "socialist propaganda."[98]

THE PRACTICAL ADOPTION OF SCIENTIFIC MANAGEMENT TECHNIQUES

The first successful attempts at introducing selected scientific management techniques took place in firms such as Robert Bosch, AEG, Siemens, Krupp, and Loewe shortly before or during World War I. In 1914–15 Frank Gilbreth was hired as a consultant by the Auer Electric Company in Berlin. With the chemical and electromechanical sectors booming, scientific management became a very relevant set of techniques, given that those two industries relied on unskilled workers to a much greater extent than the traditional industrial sectors. The case of AEG is perhaps the best to illustrate the extensive implementation of scientific management techniques such as standardization, time-and-motion studies, and the assembly line in a company whose management strongly advocated technocratic solutions, collaboration with the state and the labor unions, and a modernist approach to the design of products and production processes.[99]

The practical implementation of scientific management techniques in Germany during the 1920s was extensive: product and process standardization, job analysis and simplification, time-and-motion studies, speed-ups, and various piecework schemes (including the differential rate). The efforts were especially intense and fruitful in the iron and steel, machine-building, electrotechnical, and automotive industries. Vereinigte Stahlwerke (the second largest steel combine in the world, with 200,000 employees) created a research center on the psycho-physiology of "heavy work," which also engaged in time-and-motion training. Building materials, paper, cigarettes, and footwear

97. *ZfB* 2(1925):401. The author of the book, a militant Socialist, was then the emeritus president of the Viennese Research Society for Scientific Management. See also the review in *ZfB* 4(1927):718–721.

98. Bönig, "Technik und Rationalisierung in Deutschland zur Zeit der Weimarer Republik" (1980, pp. 406–407); *ZfB* 4(1927):718–721.

99. Homburg (1978) and (1984, pp. 107–108); Stollberg (1981, pp. 31–42); Ebbinghaus (1984, pp. 179–181). Details and references to AEG's extensive programs were discussed in the early sections of this chapter.

were also "rationalized." In the cardinal coal-mining industry, job-analysis techniques and standardization were used to mechanize extraction, transportation, and sorting. In 1929 about 80 percent of all coal production was mechanized, up from just 2 percent before World War I. Students of the period have pointed out, though, that by the 1930s much remained to be done in the scientific management of mining operations.[100] Many firms implemented the assembly line for the first time in the mid-1920s. The pioneers were Opel in 1923, AEG and Ford Germany in 1924, and Siemens shortly afterwards.[101] The Bedaux System was first implemented in 1926, and by 1931, Continental, several companies in the machine-tools industry, and seven large steel firms were using it.[102]

The new management methods were also applied in the service sector. Scientific management techniques facilitated the successful merger of Germany's separate railway administrations into the Reichsbahn, the largest railway company in the world and easily Europe's largest organization (713,000 employees). Standardization, simplification, and scientific personnel selection were used with much success at the massive Reichspost, which in 1926 employed 356,000 workers. Except for textiles, no branch of German industry escaped rationalization and scientific management.[103] Most of the case studies in industry and in the service sector point out that the engineers played a dominant role in the introduction of the new techniques, with state institutions and labor unions collaborating quite assiduously and effectively.

THE DISTINCTIVENESS OF GERMAN SCIENTIFIC MANAGEMENT

The general argument of this section has been that changes in economic structures, growing international pressures, and mounting labor unrest rendered early German entrepreneurial ideologies obsolete. Bureaucratic ideology was implemented to do away with labor unrest, but the former two problems persisted or worsened. Scientific management was then proposed as a solution to those two challenges by such varied actors as engineers, intellectual and artistic elites, the labor unions, and political leaders within a framework of corporatism. Such

100. Enquete-Ausschuß, *Untersuchung der Erzeugungs- und Absatzbedingungen der deutschen Wirtschaft* (1931, pp. 80–81); Brady (1933, pp. 79–82, 118–121, 154–156, 163–164, 186–190, 263–271, 288, 290); Hoffmann (1985, pp. 188–199).

101. Trieba and Mentrup (1983, p. 108); Homburg (1984, pp. 107–108).

102. Hinrichs and Peter (1976, p. 81); Hachtmann, *Industriearbeit im "Dritten Reich"* (1989, p. 364, n. 45); Brady (1933, pp. 163–164).

103. Brady (1933, pp. 252–263, 288, 290); Burchardt (1977, p. 85).

a mixture of institutional factors was quite different from the situation in the United States. The role played by artistic elites, labor unions, and the state in the 1920s has no parallel in democratic countries during this period. Managerial elites accepted the solution and applied scientific management techniques in piecemeal fashion throughout German industrial and service sectors. The fact that the labor unions collaborated in the implementation of scientific management and modern assembly-line techniques under a corporatist scheme guaranteed the continued importance of the German tradition of *Handwerk* and meant that "the integrity of the plant community was preserved." Moreover, the proportion of skilled workers in total industrial employment remained roughly unaltered between 1900 and 1930 at 49 percent, in spite of the extensive implementation of scientific management and Fordism.[104]

Labor Unrest and Organizational Ideas During the Nazi Period

The management ideas proposed in Germany during the 1933–45 period did not form a coherent body, nor did they significantly influence developments thereafter. The study of this period is nonetheless important because it exemplifies how totalitarian regimes may find it difficult to make labor "totally" subservient to their designs. Most interestingly, the Nazi regime did not formally discard the use of "foreign" methods (as happened in Japan at the same time), nor did it try to conceal the true origins of some of the most widely used organizational techniques, such as the assembly line. Hitler himself was quoted as having said in early 1942 (i.e. after Pearl Harbor) that the "founders of American technology" were "almost distinct Swabian-Germanic human beings."[105] This section will show that the Nazi totalitarian regime in fact explored ways to manage workers that diverged from the experiments of the Soviet Union or its satellite states.[106]

Initially, the Nazi regime preferred to justify its economic policies by reference to idealist rather than openly materialist principles. Thus, patriotic-populist productivism was reinforced with a rhetorical em-

104. Piore and Sabel, *The Second Industrial Divide* (1984, p. 146); Lee (1978, pp. 447, 454); Kieser, ed. (1993, pp. 84–85).
105. Hachtmann (1989, pp. 75, 77–81).
106. Bendix, *Work and Authority in Industry* (1974, pp. 202–211, 341–433). See also section K of the Bibliography.

phasis on communication, cooperation, and leadership. The relatively neutral terms of *Belegschaft* (personnel) and *Unternehmer* (employer) were changed to the ideologically loaded *Gefolgschaft* (retinue) and *Betriebsführer* (business firm leader), respectively, as a result of the implementation of the *Führerprinzip*. The new terminology became quasi-mandatory after the passing of the National Labor Order Act in January, 1934.[107] Language aside, this legislation also granted employers the prerogative to determine working time, pauses, wages, behavior in the firm, and sanctions. The Weimar codetermination works councils were abolished. The new worker councils (*Vertrauensräte*) could play only a secondary role in decision making.[108]

The Nazi regime proposed to apply scientific management in a way consistent with the ideology of maximum productivity "for the German people." The institute in charge of time-and-motion studies (REFA) increased its activities considerably (70,000 efficiency engineers took part in REFA-sponsored courses in 1936–44, versus no more than 10,000 throughout the 1920s). But group wage incentives rather than individual ones were emphasized. The terms *performance community* (*Leistungsgemeinschaft*), and *strengthening of comradeship and community* (*Kameradschafts- und Gemeinschaftsstärkung*) became legal tender in an ideological attempt to make time-and-motion studies and small-group activities compatible with each other.[109]

The management proposals of the *Deutsche Arbeitsfront* (DAF)— the vertical employer-worker unions created in 1933 after certain hesitation on the part of the Nazi leadership—also echoed the guidelines of Nazi managerial thought. In the late 1930s the DAF could count on a revenue twice as large as that of the Nazi party.[110] Given the regime's determination to raise productivity and its preference for idealist solutions, the DAF's ideological campaign took shape promptly. It was in the attempt to legitimate total managerial authority and scientific management techniques that welfare schemes and participatory programs were initially introduced. Hence, a mixed or hybrid pattern emerged. The most important agency was initially created in mid-1933, the *Nach der Arbeit* (NdA, After Work) office,

107. Crone, *Das Gesetz zur Ordnung der nationalen Arbeit* (1934, §1 and §2, p. 137); *ZfB* 18(1941):163–171; Hartmann, *Authority and Organization in German Management* (1959, pp. 82–84).

108. Schumann (1958, pp. 121, 125–126); Mason, "Labour in the Third Reich, 1933–1939" (1966, pp. 114–118).

109. Hachtmann (1989, pp. 175–180, 185–186).

110. Mason (1966, p. 120); Schumann (1958, pp. 49–94).

which followed the Italian example of the *Dopolavoro* programs in name, substance, and scale.[111] The NdA was renamed in November, 1933, as National-Socialist Community "Strength through Joy" (*NS-Gemeinschaft "Kraft durch Freude"* or KdF). The KdF received special attention from the DAF and Nazi party leaderships, and also a large budget to organize education, entertainment, travel, and sports programs aimed at workers of all industries. The agency served the propaganda goals of the regime both at home and abroad, and its recreational programs were specifically and consciously designed, in the words of one of its leaders, to "overhaul" workers so as to "increase the performance of the German people in all areas of activity," just as "one must overhaul car engines after a certain number of kilometers."[112] A special office, the National Agency "Beauty of Work" (*Reichsamt "Schönheit der Arbeit"*), was created within the KdF to promote both scientific and communitarian improvements in industry. By 1940 this agency had helped redecorate about 26,000 workshops, and build 24,000 washing and changing rooms, 18,000 canteens, 17,000 gardens, and 3,000 sports grounds in factories. Although the primary goals of the KdF were to enhance industrial efficiency and publicize the regime abroad, its programs certainly helped to improve the living and working conditions of German workers in the midst of a huge armaments and capital-goods production program.[113]

The DAF's indoctrination program could also count on the experience and organizational capabilities of the German Institute for Technical Work Education (DINTA). DINTA had been originally created in 1925 at the initiative of Albert Vögler, the general director of Vereinigte Stahlwerke, a Nazi, and one of the staunchest supporters of the Anti-Bolshevist Liga. In its first years of existence, DINTA launched a "Struggle for the Soul of Our Workers." Such was the title of a book by the organization's first managing director. Its early slogan was, "One State, One Reich, One People, One Spirit." Many employers were enthusiastic, and by 1930 three hundred German and Austrian firms were collaborating with DINTA.[114] The DINTA

111. See the enthusiastic account by an Italian observer, Santoro, *Quatre années d'Allemagne d'Hitler vues par un étranger* (1938, pp. 136–139). On the *cultura dopolavoristica*, see De Grazia, *The Culture of Consent* (1981).

112. Quoted in Schumann (1958, p. 142). See, in particular, pp. 138–145.

113. Mason (1966, p. 120); *ZfB* 13(1936):203–204, 243–245.

114. Hinrichs and Peter (1976, pp. 70–74). On employers' enthusiasm about DINTA, see *ZfB* 8(1931):47–51.

approach to labor indoctrination included a careful selection of young workers and engineers for its four-year programs, which were run in "military fashion," and emphasized a "higher view of life" cultivating the virtues of hard work, ambition, and family life. Non-unionization was greatly encouraged, and, as a result, the Free Unions refused to collaborate. In 1933 DINTA's organizational apparatus was absorbed by the DAF.[115]

The early idealistic emphasis on cooperation, participation, and harmonious human relationships at work would soon become a necessity rather than an ideological preference. The implementation of the ambitious Four Year Plan after September, 1936, caused considerable strain in the labor market. According to the plan's director, Hermann Goering, employer competition for skilled workers by means of higher wages was having

> a most deleterious effect on the worker's sense of belonging to his firm, and on labor morale. The high and unregulated turnover of labor causes unrest in the workshops. In many cases workers leave their jobs without giving notice, thereby breaking their contracts; or alternatively, they force their employers to dismiss them by behaving in an ill-disciplined way.[116]

Goering's approach to the problem between late 1936 and mid-1938 was to improve working conditions, welfare schemes, and training programs while carefully avoiding the establishment of administrative controls, which became finally inevitable in June, 1938. Even with administrative and coercive controls in place, and the increasing militarization of industry after 1939, Nazi control over German labor was far from "total."[117]

Organizationally speaking, the regime's crumbling control over workers meant that the ideological campaign based on human relations approaches and appeals to patriotism would have to be strengthened. Management intellectuals of this period (e.g. Karl Arnhold and Walter Thoms) tried to address the pressing issue of reestablishing order in the factory. Their books developed the concepts of "working community," patriotic productivism, and "leadership" with racist overtones. In 1941 one of the DAF's leaders, Josef Mand, wrote that

115. Brady (1933, pp. 82, 331 n. 19, 332 n. 24, 353); Gillingham, "The 'deproletarianization' of German society" (1986, p. 424). Union leaders strongly criticized DINTA. See, for instance, Fricke, "Die Rechtfertigung des DINTA," published in *Die Arbeit* in 1928, as reproduced in Hinrichs and Peter (1976, pp. 252–263).

116. Quoted from a 1936 memorandum in Mason (1966, p. 128).

117. Mason (1966, pp. 131–141); Gillingham (1986, pp. 426–429).

"the organization of personnel must arrange human collective life in the industrial firm so that working life—like the articulation of the people that it is—sets free the strengths of the race as the creative organizer of work achieving maximum performance." Technical factors (room conditions, tools, flows of materials) were also presented as important in the quest for higher productivity; the only restriction was that "for the working person the machine must be a work aide, not a work dictator."[118] The National Committee for Productivity Increase—another Nazi creature, but located within the RKW—published a series of brief books on management after 1938. A Siemens engineer, Erich Kupke, contributed to the series with a booklet entitled *Everybody Thinks Together!*, which sold 25,000 copies in four editions. The slogan "Tidiness, Order, Security" was suggested, but some of the posters reproduced in the book also praised the stopwatch and being on time. Employee participation was encouraged through suggestion boxes, like the ones installed at AEG and Siemens with great success.[119]

The beginning of the war made propaganda at work more stringent,[120] while the incorporation of women in the labor force posed a new challenge. Some experts suggested the use of small work groups, but also of scientific methods.[121] The reliance on human relations only appeared to fade away towards the end of the war. Industrial rationalization was intensified—with excellent productivity results—after architect Albert Speer (the former chief of the "Beauty of Work" agency) was appointed Minister of Armaments in 1942.[122] In his memoirs, Speer acknowledged Rathenau's contributions to wartime economic rationalization and pointed out that his predecessor in the ministry had profited from the advice of a former Rathenau

118. *ZfB* 18(1941):163–171. Quotations appear on pp. 165 and 169.

119. Kupke, *Jeder denkt mit!* (1941), first published in 1939; Pflaume, *Die Umschulung im Eisen und Metall verarbeitenden Industrie* (1939).

120. See Hauskern et al., *Mitarbeit der Gefolgschaft* (1942).

121. Pflaume, *Frauen im Industriebetrieb* (1943, pp. 20–22, 82–84). There is ample evidence indicating that scientific management was a usual way of organizing unskilled and women workers during the war. See Hachtmann (1989, p. 76). Female employment increased by 500,000 during the war, mostly in semi-skilled occupations. Women were discriminated against in apprenticeship programs. See Gillingham (1986, p. 428).

122. Kennedy, *The Rise and Fall of the Great Powers* (1987, pp. 353–357); Mason (1966, p. 120); Zilbert, *Albert Speer and the Nazi Ministry of Arms* (1981, pp. 34–35). Zilbert observes that Speer's job was facilitated by the fact that many small workshops had flexible technologies that could be converted to war production at a very low cost (1981, pp. 36–37).

aide.[123] Managerial writings tended to concentrate more on the scientific management component of the Nazi ideological hybrid. In a booklet written in 1942 but not published until 1944, another engineer called for the "total rationalization of industrial firms," including aspects such as plant layout, production flows, assembly lines, ergonomics, time-and-motion studies, division of labor, and job analysis. Productivist propaganda and participation in the firm were relegated to the background.[124]

The Irrelevance of the Human Relations Approach in the Postwar Context

Scientific management dominated the debate about organizational paradigms in Germany during the 1920s and again in 1945–55. The Nazi regime looked for a combination of scientific management techniques with some ideas about the "community" and "leadership." This line of reasoning was discontinued after 1945. Bureaucratization of industry slowed down as a result of the war and its aftermath.[125] The most significant development, however, was the reconstruction of the West German economy after wartime destruction, and the loss in territory, industrial facilities, and natural resources due to the rearrangement of borders in Eastern Europe. Undoubtedly, industrial investment in new plants and equipment also propitiated scientific management. Thus, neither the changes in economic structures nor international pressures challenged the received paradigm.

The fact that scientific management was not challenged during the immediate postwar period does not eliminate the possibility that some groups promoted new organizational paradigms, especially those successful in other countries. Human relations was the organizational paradigm that ideologically predominated in the two countries that served as models for the creation of the new Federal Republic of Germany: Britain and the United States. Thus, it becomes essential

123. Speer, *Inside the Third Reich* (1970, p. 208). Speer is not very specific about the kinds of techniques or organizational ideas that he introduced in order to raise arms production. On Speer and the other Nazi architects, see Lane (1968, pp. 147–216).

124. Schleip, *Totale Rationalisierung des Industriebetriebes* (1944, p. 88). There were some earlier attempts at "total rationalization," like the proposals to economize on clerical work by means of simplifying written German. For example, in a brief article published in *ZfB* 17(1940):44, Dr. P. Linser suggested eliminating capital letters and certain "unnecessary" combinations of consonants. Another bizarre rationalization attempt involved the reform of the Gregorian calendar. An RKW-sponsored committee was created in 1930 to discuss the issue. See RKW, *Jahresbericht 1930* (1931, pp. 78–79).

125. See Figure B.1 in Appendix B.

to study whether previous or existing industrial experiences and mentalities could possibly provide a foundation for human relations approaches, regardless of the continued applicability of scientific management. In Germany, social Catholicism provided such a foundation, although the successful corporatist model of industrial relations made the human relations approach redundant.

GERMAN ATTEMPTS TO INTRODUCE HUMAN RELATIONS: WELFARE CAPITALISM, SOCIAL CATHOLICISM, AND THE CHRISTIAN UNIONS

As Bendix pointed out, the origins of human relations ideology must be looked for in, among other areas, industrial partnership experiments implemented by employers with workers' collaboration or consent. Welfare capitalism, as an idea linked to that of partnership, meant that not everything was discipline and obedience but that "a notion of community between the leader and the lead" also existed.[126] Industrial welfare practices initiated by early entrepreneurs and aimed at keeping skilled workers appeared first. The paternalistic "industrial partnership" of medium-sized and big industrialists proliferated after German unification. Social welfare measures were made compulsory by state legislation, starting in the 1890s.[127] But the idea of cooperation between employers and workers for the benefit of the people involved, and not merely as a way of increasing profits, gained support in Germany thanks to the rise of social Catholicism. The Catholic workers' movement began during the 1860s in local clubs organized by priests and supported by employers in certain areas of Western Europe. The clubs offered educational, recreational, and religious activities, but there was little concern with labor conditions. Slowly, though progressively, labor conditions became a topic for discussion.[128]

Such was the preoccupation with the subject in Germany as well as in other European countries that Pope Leo XIII grasped the opportunity to rail against both Liberalism and Socialism, and propose the Christian "third way" in the famous 1891 encyclical, "On the Conditions of Workers" (best known as *Rerum Novarum*). The social doctrine of the Catholic Church was to have momentous implications

---

126. Hartmann (1959, p. 81).

127. Kocka (1971, pp. 139–140), (1973, pp. 170, 173–174); McCreary (1968, p. 43); Lee (1978, pp. 461–462); McCreary (1968); Goetzeler and Schoen, *Wilhelm und Carl Friedrich von Siemens* (1986, pp. 69, 72–75, 93–94); Flora and Alber, "Modernization, democratization, and the development of welfare states in Western Europe" (1981, p. 59); Schumpeter (1976, pp. 341–342).

128. Slomp (1990, p. 38).

for the future viability of the human relations paradigm in predominantly Catholic countries such as Spain.[129] After condemning the "miserable and wretched conditions" affecting workers in the industrial world, the Pope made a reference to the "inhumanity of employers." But the core of the encyclical was devoted to a defense of private property and the family, and to a blistering attack on socialism, Socialist unions, and their leaders. With some reticence, the encyclical asked the state to legislate against inhuman conditions in industry, and to do so in a typical corporatist fashion. It also emphasized that "where men know they are working on what belongs to them, they work with far greater eagerness and diligence." The most crucial paragraph stated that Christian workers faced a choice between joining unions in which "there is a danger to religion," and forming "their own associations," which should be founded and run according to Catholic doctrine.[130]

The German Center Party and the Catholic Circles took up the suggestion to create Christian unions after 1895, although at first they failed to exert enough influence to remove the ban on political association that impeded the creation of a Christian union movement. This was finally possible four years later, when the government realized that Christian unions would perhaps help to counterbalance the strength of the socialists. The membership of the Christian unions grew steadily, though not very rapidly, until the 1910s, when it reached 350,000 members. They also benefited from the 1918–22 union boom, surpassing the mark of 1.5 million members but still dwarfed by the Free Unions. The Christian unions and the Catholic writers not only supported the codetermination movement during the Weimar Republic but also enlarged its ideological scope along lines quite different from social democratic ideas. The idea of codetermination was linked to the worker's "human personality," "creative" potential, and "sense of belonging." Most importantly, the idea of "work groups" was discussed by Christian (and also by anarchist) thinkers as an alternative to Taylorized production.[131]

The fortieth anniversary of *Rerum Novarum* was celebrated during

---

129. On the German background, see Alexander, "Church and society in Germany" (1953).

130. Leo XIII, "On the conditions of workers" (1943, §5, §6, §18–23, §48, §51, §66, §74).

131. Stollberg (1981, pp. 128, 130–132); Stegmann, *Der soziale Katholizismus und die Mitbestimmung in Deutschland* (1974, pp. 150–157); Moses (1982, p. 134–135, 511–512); Bowen (1947, pp. 75–118).

the pontificate of Pius XI with a new encyclical. Drafted by Oswald von Nell-Breuning and other German Jesuits, "Forty Years After on Reconstructing Social Order" (*Quadragesimo Anno*) represented a more direct attack on economic (and political) liberalism.[132] At the same time, the old condemnation of socialism was repeated. The 1931 encyclical was much more explicit as to employer-worker cooperation than that of 1891. There was an advocation of "partnership-contracts," so that workers could "become sharers in ownership or management or participate in some fashion in the profits received." There were also direct references to the social, self-realization, and satisfaction needs of the worker.[133]

German Christian doctrine—combining paternalism, realism, personalism, and natural law—played a key role in advancing ideas about an organic community, solidarity, the humanization of work, personal dignity, and subsidiarity (i.e. that decisions should be made at the lowest possible level).[134] It should be no surprise, then, to find that the six most important German scholars writing on the human dimension of industrial work after World War II were all Catholics: Wilhelm Kalveram, Guido Fischer, August Marx (a Jesuit priest), Arthur Mayer, Peter Hofstätter, and Oswald von Nell-Breuning. All of the leading scientific management experts of the Weimar period were Protestants, with the exception of Walther Rathenau (who was Jewish), and Friedrich von Gottl-Ottlilienfeld (Catholic). Gottl-Ottlilienfeld had some typically Catholic reservations about Taylorism, for he distinguished between *Taylorismus* (Taylorism) and *Taylorei,* a term conveying the negative effects of scientific management on the workers.[135] German social Catholicism helped to absorb American human relations ideas and blend them with a Catholic approach to the social problems of the working human being. German human relations theorists drawing on Catholic sources referred to the "perverse" effects of scientific management but, unlike those in the United States, they rarely leveled the charge that scientific management "jeopardized" previous achievements of society.[136]

132. Pius XI, "Forty years after on the reconstruction of social order" (1943, §46). Nell-Breuning admitted being the main author of the encyclical much later. See Stegmann (1974, p. 168 n. 58).

133. Pius XI (1943, §65, §118).

134. For other German Christian authors, see Alexander (1953, pp. 508–530); Kolbinger, ed., *Betrieb und Gesellschaft* (1966).

135. See Giesel (1963, pp. 25–76); Hinrichs and Peter (1976, pp. 64–66).

136. For a discussion of reactionary arguments, see Hirschman, *The Rhetoric of Reaction* (1991).

INSTITUTIONAL FACTORS IMPEDING THE ADOPTION
OF HUMAN RELATIONS

The Position of the Unions.   Social Catholicism created at best a "minority" mentality, not one shared by all German intellectuals or the entire working or employer classes. Besides, the Catholic management intellectuals did not enjoy much political or scientific prestige within Germany.[137] As in Britain and the United States, the postwar years witnessed various attempts to improve the situation of workers. Although the American High Commission in Germany, and also the French occupation authorities, had promoted human relations approaches to work organization since 1946, union leaders depicted human relations as a "superficial method" that failed to address the "real" problem.[138] Although no systematic evidence exists as to union opposition to the human relations approach, it is clear that neither workers nor unions took any steps to promote it. Moreover, union leaders continued defending scientific management as a way to increase the welfare of the working class.[139]

Codetermination and Works Councils as Solutions to Industrial Relations.   Part of the inadequacy and irrelevance of human relations theory in the German situation can be attributed to the existence of a firm political will to solve industrial relations problems by means of codetermination and works councils. Despite the liberal democratic character of the new Federal Republic, economic and labor issues were to be handled within the corporatist framework of the so-called *soziale Marktwirtschaft* (social market-economy). In contrast to the United States, where joint management-labor committees were established in the 1920s at the initiative of employers,[140] in Germany worker committees were first encouraged by state legislation dating back to 1891. As in the United States, the committees would have authority over shop floor matters and welfare provisions. Almost thirty years later, the Weimar constitution and a subsequent 1920

137. Kaste, *Arbeitgeber und Humanisierung der Arbeit* (1981, pp. 31–32). On the limited relevance of the religious cleavage, see Linz, "Cleavage and consensus in West German politics" (1967).

138. Hartmann (1959, pp. 84–95); Carew, *Labour under the Marshall Plan* (1987, pp. 163–164, 217–223).

139. Wirtschaftswissenschaftliches Institut der Gewerkschaften (Britische Zone), *Gewerkschaften und Arbeitsstudien* (1948); Wirtschaftswissenschaftliches Institut der Gewerkschaften, *Rationalisierung und Arbeitnehmerschaft* (1950, pp. 40–41).

140. See Bendix (1974, pp. 281–285).

codetermination law were to initiate a qualitatively different phase. Works councils were to be organized at the plant, regional, and national levels. The social democrats had in mind the joint management of the industrial enterprise by employers and workers, but their plan achieved comparatively little practical realization despite the passage of additional legislation throughout the early 1920s.[141]

After the interim period of 1945–49, the Christian democratic federal government was pressed by steel and coal workers to pass the 1951 codetermination law, which mandated worker representation on the supervisory boards (with five positions out of eleven) and managing boards (with the labor director) of all companies in those two industries; however, a rise in employer self-confidence and changes in the Christian democratic attitude towards labor and capitalism prevented codetermination from being legally adopted in other industries. After a major political struggle, a Works Councils Law was passed in 1952 that required all firms with five or more employees to have a works council that would meet with management to negotiate grievances, wages, working conditions, plant rules, hiring or firing groups of workers, major organizational changes in the plant, and welfare schemes. The codetermination and management-labor cooperation schemes satisfied the Christian wing in the new, unified Federation of German Unions (*Deutscher Gewerkschaftsbund*, DGB) more than it did the dominant social democratic wing. Codetermination and works councils were often seen by social democrats as an alternative to nationalization. During the 1950s German workers lost an annual average of 0.04 days per worker due to industrial conflict, compared to a staggering 0.55 for the United States and 0.13 for Britain. Clearly, the legal establishment and successful practical functioning of codetermination and works councils, with the resulting industrial peace, discouraged more debate about foreign models of management-worker cooperation such as human relations.[142]

The Role of the State. Given the German experience with scientific management, another factor that could have favored the success of

141. Thimm, *The False Promise of Codetermination* (1980, p. 18).

142. Sturmthal, *Workers Councils* (1964, pp. 53–85); Lawrence, *Managers and Management in West Germany* (1980, pp. 42–50); Berghahn and Karsten, *Industrial Relations in West Germany* (1987, pp. 104–129, 167–191); Sturmthal, *Comparative Labor Movements* (1972, p. 94). See also the comparative statistics in Appendix B. On the restoration of economic interest groups in West Germany after 1945, see Kocka, "1945: Neubeginn oder Restauration?" (1979).

human relations thought was the institutional support of a strong government or semi-official entity. The organization that had promoted scientific management so forcefully, the RKW, was not dismantled but rather resurrected in 1950 under a new name that preserved the RKW acronym. The institute for time-and-motion study (REFA) also continued its activities after the war.[143] Moreover, the RKW became the German Productivity Center, as required by the Marshall Plan and its management agencies, the Organization for European Economic Cooperation (OEEC, 1948), and the European Productivity Agency (EPA, 1953). As in the 1920s, scientific management techniques were on the agenda. Economy Minister, later Federal Chancellor, Ludwig Erhard (of *Wirtschaftswunder* fame) was one of the staunchest defenders of rationalization as a way to boost productivity and living standards.[144] The RKW was not completely oblivious to human relations. In 1952 it introduced a kind of human relations program under the slogan *Sinnvoller arbeiten—zufrieden leben* (working meaningfully—living satisfied).[145] An RKW discussion group called *Mensch und Arbeit* (The Human Being and Work) addressed aspects such as business leadership and communication, and advocated the study of worker attitudes and opinions.[146] But the emphasis seemed to be placed on the "humanization" of rationalized industrial production rather than on the radically new characterization of employers and workers that human relations postulates. Just two of the eighty-one reports published in the RKW Foreign Service Series in 1951–58 dealt with human relations issues.[147]

The Belated Consolidation of the Social Sciences. Although social Catholicism became a vigorous movement in Germany, it influenced only a few sociologists and business administrators. After 1925, the

143. The first two postwar presidents of RKW (1950–1963) also came from the Siemens enterprises. See Freitag, "Das Haus Siemens und das RKW" (1963).

144. Büttner (1973, pp. 30–76); *Deutscher Betriebswirtschafter-Tag* 6(1953) and 7(1954). As late as 1960, EPA thought that scientific management should be promoted in German engineering schools. See Fehlauer, ed., *Die arbeitswissenschaftliche Ausbildung von Ingenieuren in europäischen Ländern* (1962, pp. 9–10, 61–72).

145. *ZfB* 21(1951):504–508; 22(1952):115–116.

146. A volume with the discussions was published in 1958. See *ZfB* 30(1960):129.

147. The first of these reports pointed out that human relations was an ill-defined concept. See Bramesfeld et al., *Human Relations in Industry. Die menschliche Beziehungen in der Industrie* (1956, pp. 13, 98, 100–101). The second report was more optimistic, but lacked specific recommendations. See Bornemann et al., *Gruppenarbeit und Produktivität* (1958, pp. 104–109). This report received a favorable review in *ZfB* 30 (1960):581.

science of German business administration was dominated by figures such as Eugen Schmalenbach (an accounting theorist), Heinrich Nicklisch (a business economist), and Fritz Schmidt (also a business economist).[148] In the area of organization, the teachings of these three professors were more consistent with scientific management or with Fayol's administrative approach than with human relations.[149] In 1950, sociologist and human relations theorist Wilhelm Hasenack accused both Schmalenbach and Schmidt of dealing with objective, technical, and financial factors only, thus making it impossible to address the question of human work in the business firm. Clearly, Catholic management thinkers like Kalveram, Fischer, Marx, Mayer, and Nell-Breuning were in the minority and could not exert enough influence.[150]

The sociological profession was in no way prepared or willing to promote human relations either. An Institute for the Sociology of the Business Firm (*Betriebssoziologie*) was founded in 1928 at the Berlin Higher Technical School to study "the human side of the production process." Goetz Briefs, one of the institute's directors, was heavily influenced by Catholicism,[151] but the institute's research and publications were primarily devoted to historical and theoretical rather than managerial aspects, emphasizing social policy and reform. Moreover, its activities had to be scaled down after 1934, and it was officially terminated in 1938. According to one of the researchers at the institute, this meant that industrial sociology virtually disappeared from the German scene until the early 1950s.[152] In the mid-1930s the whole of German sociology experienced years of political and racial persecution. By 1938 around two-thirds of all German sociologists had been expelled from their academic positions or forced into exile.[153]

148. See: Locke (1984, pp. 199–241); Bellinger, *Geschichte der Betriebswirtschaftslehre* (1967, pp. 56–62); Forrester, *Schmalenbach and After* (1977).

149. See, for example, Schmidt's articles in the *ZfB* 8(1931):766–778; 12(1935): 15–33. It should be carefully noted, however, that both Wilhelm Kalveram and Guido Fischer had been students of Schmidt in Frankfurt.

150. *ZfB* 20(1950):592–595; Locke, *Management and Higher Education Since 1940* (1989, p. 137).

151. Schuster, *Industrie und Sozialwissenschaften* (1987, p. 359). See also the series editors' introduction to Geck, *Die sozialen Arbeitsverhältnisse im Wandel der Zeit* (1931, p. iii).

152. Geck, "Zur Entstehungsgeschichte der Betriebssoziologie" (1951, pp. 112–116).

153. Lepsius, "Sociology in the interwar period" (1987, p. 47).

After the war German sociology *in* Germany had to virtually start all over again. Some representatives of the "older" postwar generation were instrumental in the introduction of "American" empirical sociology. The Office of the Military Government, U.S., helped in the endeavor with its encouragement of opinion surveys in the fields of industrial relations, politics, and market research, sometimes with the support of the unions.[154] Cologne Professor Leopold von Wiese shared some interests with American human relations theorists, as is evident in his theory of interpersonal relations (*Beziehungslehre*), but he was about to retire at the end of the war.[155] René König, apart from being a noted Durkheim commentator and later founder and president of the International Sociological Association, was interested in survey methods and sociometry, but most of his applied research was in the fields of the family and ethnology, not work or industry.[156] König also helped to introduce structural-functional theory.[157]

It is fair to say that German sociology has always been heavily reliant on "conflict-oriented" traditions dating back to the work of Hegel and Marx, and reinforced by Weber and Michels, both of whom pioneered modern structural-organizational analysis. Simmel, Mannheim, the Frankfurt School, and, to some extent, Tönnies also belong to this tradition.[158] Thus, there is a contrast between a German sociology largely concerned with exploring the socio-political order from an institutional, historical, and conflict-oriented perspective, and a more diverse American sociology that produced influential human relations theorists like Homans or W. F. Whyte.[159] Some leading German sociologists criticized human relations explicitly. Writing and

154. Weyer, *Westdeutsche Soziologie 1945–1960* (1984, pp. 316–319, 321).

155. Lepsius, "Die Entwicklung der Soziologie nach dem Zweiten Weltkrieg 1945 bis 1967" (1979, pp. 29–30), and (1987, p. 40).

156. Years later, König showed his frustration about the reception of American informal group theory in Germany as a theory of small groups, which he thought distorted the original theory as stated by Roethlisberger. König was especially critical of Geck's reviews of French and American human relations books in the *Kölner Zeitschrift für Soziologie* 1(1948–49), pp. 483–486, and 2(1949–50), pp. 139–142, 289–299. See König, "Die informellen Gruppen im Industriebetrieb" (1961, pp. 62–63).

157. Lepsius (1979, pp. 36–37). For a sample of König and colleagues' reception of American social psychological and group theory, see König, Atteslander, Treinen, and Stieber, "Betriebssoziologische Mikroanalyse" (1956). See also Scherke, *Die Arbeitsgruppe im Betrieb* (1956).

158. Collins, *Three Sociological Traditions* (1985, pp. 47–56, 94–101); Freund, "German sociology in the time of Max Weber" (1978). See also Alexander, "The Parsons revival in German sociology" (1984, p. 396).

159. Lepsius, *Strukturen und Wandlungen im Industriebetrieb* (1960, pp. 9–11).

publishing in England, Germany, and the United States, Ralf Dahrendorf attacked human relations for "psychologizing" structural conflicts in the business firm.[160] In the very few instances that Catholic authors publishing in the management journals such as the *ZfB* cited or quoted German sociologists, they had to criticize the conflict tradition (in particular, Dahrendorf), and argue for the possibility of avoiding conflict and promoting efficiency through social harmony.[161]

THE LIMITED IMPACT OF HUMAN RELATIONS IN GERMANY

Four interrelated phenomena were taking place in Germany at about the time human relations proposals were being made: (1) the continued applicability of scientific management due to postwar changes in economic structures and in international pressures, including a slowdown in the bureaucratization process due to World War II and reconstruction; (2) the lack of interest on the side of the dominant unions, the state, and the established professions; (3) the relative underdevelopment of the social sciences; and (4) a wave of "technical optimism" supporting the view that the negative effects of mechanization and automation could be overcome simply by the rationalization of the economic, technical, and social conditions of work without subscribing to the human relations revolution.[162] The question to be examined now is whether the minority influence of Catholic social doctrine sufficed to make human relations the dominant voice in management circles during the 1950s.

Management intellectuals who were not Catholic paid little attention to the new paradigm. Handbooks of business administration published in the 1950s and early 1960s with contributions by management theorists and practitioners devoted much more attention to scientific management topics than to human relations ones.[163] Human relations found few friends at the Federal Union of German Employer Associations (BDA), in sharp contrast with the AMA and the NAM in the United States. The official journal of the BDA, *Der Arbeitgeber*

160. Dahrendorf, *Sozialstruktur des Betriebes* (1959b, p. 86). See also Dahrendorf's criticism of Mayo in *Class and Class Conflict in Industrial Society* (1959a, pp. 111–114), originally published in German in 1957, and the critique of the Hawthorne experiments in another Dahrendorf book later edited by Wolfram Burisch, *Industrie- und Betriebssoziologie* (1969, pp. 48–56).

161. *ZfB* 38(1968):379–382.

162. Kaste (1981, pp. 46–58); Fürstenberg, "Industrial sociology" (1990). See also Popitz et al., *Das Gesellschaftsbild des Arbeiters* (1957).

163. See the four-volume dictionary edited by Seischab and Schwantag, *Handwörterbuch der Betriebswirtschaft* (1956–1962).

(*The Employer*), discussed topics such as collective bargaining, codetermination, social policy, and labor law at length. Human relations themes were entirely absent, while several issues of the journal featured special sections on scientific management as late as the 1970s. The annual reports of the Federation of German Industry (BDI) show a similar picture.[164] The Federation of Catholic Entrepreneurs (BKU) or the proponents of social Catholic doctrine failed to convince enough managers of the relevance of the human relations approach. Human relations enjoyed little space in the pages of the management journal *ZfB*, and even fewer articles were published in the other two leading management journals.[165] The only postwar three-year period in which human relations articles predominate numerically is between 1953 and 1955 (see Panel B of Table 3.2). In contrast to the American or Spanish cases, however, few of those articles were published by practicing managers. In 1950–52 scientific management articles were the most numerous, and after 1959 structural analysis articles clearly take the lead, with the exception of the anomalous 1962–64 period. Panel A of Table 3.2 shows that the most frequent human relations themes appearing in the *ZfB* journal were the perceived problem (monotony, conflict, absenteeism, turnover), the fascination with communal life and social groups, and the importance of leadership, participation, and communication. There was an emphasis on the perverse effects of the technical rationalization of work, but, unlike in the United States, Britain, and Spain, arguments using the jeopardy thesis against scientific management appeared rarely. *Techniques* and *methodologies* (job enlargement or enrichment, teamwork activities, surveys and questionnaires), moreover, were only discussed in a few articles.[166]

The practical rejection of human relations in Germany during the 1950s and 1960s was almost total. There is no evidence of German firms implementing human relations techniques during the 1950s and 1960s. A few human relations associations were created but never attracted much attention.[167] As shown by several surveys conducted

164. See *Der Arbeitgeber* 18(1966), 19(1967):540–592, 26(1974):331–345; Bundesverband der deutschen Industrie, *Jahresbericht* 1951–52:25–27, 1959–60:55, 72–73.

165. See *Schmalenbachs Zeitschrift für Betriebswirtschaftliche Forschung*, and *Betriebswirtschaftliche Forschung und Praxis*.

166. One of these techniques, job rotation, had been discussed in the interwar period. See Krause, "Leistungssteigerung durch Arbeitswechsel" (1933).

167. The Stuttgart Group Training-Within-Industry for the Advancement of Work Relations in Business originated at the human relations training courses sponsored by

in the early 1950s, workers were not interested in better human relations at work, but in better pay and other material improvements. Employers generally acted upon workers' opinions, rejecting what they thought was an "American cultural import" anyway.[168]

Economic Changes and the Rise of Structural Analysis

The bureaucratic habits and ideas became a source of *ideological* inspiration for German industrialists and trade unionists after 1870. The preoccupation with American economic success between 1900 and 1929 directed most of the attention to scientific workshop techniques and assembly-line work, with a new outburst after the war until the early 1950s. The creation of wider market areas in continental Europe after 1957, the increasing diversification of West Germany's largest companies, and the stability of the collective bargaining industrial relations system shifted the focus of attention away from tasks, individuals, and groups towards the structure of complex organizations. American and British structural-organizational sociology was embraced by the younger generation of German sociologists in the 1960s (those born after 1925), who reintroduced Weber into German sociology. All these factors contributed to making structural analysis the most prominent organizational theory of the 1960s and early 1970s in Germany.

FACTORS FAVORING A STRUCTURAL APPROACH
TO ORGANIZING

Economic Developments and Structural Changes. Economic developments partly account for the end of scientific management's overwhelming dominance of organizational debates in Germany. The internationalization and diversification of the country's economic structure and of its major corporations became the new dominant challenge. A different organizational theory was needed to address

---

U.S. military authorities. See *ZfB* 21(1951):507. Other groups were the Study Circle "New Business Firm," located in Düsseldorf and formed by engineers, university professors, and executives (see *ZfB* 25(1955):251–252); and the Study Group for the Advancement of Partnership in the Economy, Bad Soden, which had over 100 members. See *ZfB* 26(1956):251–253.

168. Kaste (1981, pp. 27–29, 31, 39–40); Institut für Sozialforschung, *Betriebsklima* (1955); Friedeburg, *Soziologie des Betriebsklimas* (1963); Lepsius (1960, pp. 29–42); Berghahn, *The Americanization of West German Industry 1945–1973* (1986, pp. 250–253); Hartmann (1963, pp. 168–173) and (1959, p. 86); Lawrence (1980, pp. 101–102).

TABLE 3.2   Results of the content analysis of the articles and lengthy book reviews published in the *Zeitschrift für Betriebswirtschaft*, 1950–1970, by paradigm (SM: scientific management; HR: human relations; SA: structural analysis; NC: not classifiable)

A. Number of articles mentioning each of the content categories (see Appendix A) and themes (56 articles examined)

Content Categories	SM	HR	SA
Perceived problem	3	11	9
Form of solution	2	0	8
View of conflict	1	7	5
View of workers	3	7	4
Fascination with	5	12	2
Methodology	14	1	3
Selection of workers	2	0	0
Distribution of tasks	8	6	12
Authority structures	2	13	17
Process of work	6	5	10
Preferred rewards	16	5	0
Economic incentives	12	1	0

B. Number of articles (N) and themes classified by paradigm

Year Period	SM	Themes			HR	Themes			SA	Themes			NC
	N	Mean	Min	Max	N	Mean	Min	Max	N	Mean	Min	Max	N
1950–52	11	4.8	2	8	5	4.0	3	5	1	2.0	2	2	1
1953–55	1	3.0	3	3	4	4.2	4	5	2	4.0	3	5	0
1956–58	0	—	—	—	1	5.0	5	5	1	3.0	3	3	2
1959–61	2	3.0	2	4	2	6.5	5	8	6	2.8	1	4	0
1962–64	1	3.0	3	3	0	—	—	—	0	—	—	—	0
1965–67	1	3.0	3	3	0	—	—	—	3	3.7	2	6	1
1968–70	0	—	—	—	2	3.5	3	4	7	3.6	2	7	2
All years	16	4.2	2	8	14	4.4	3	8	20	3.3	1	7	6
Pages	140	8.8	2	24	127	9.1	2	19	292	14.6	3	27	58

Sources: The articles included in the analysis are the following:

SM: *ZfB* 20:105–116, 212–220, 243–246, 518–523, 637–646; 21:35–43, 269–293, 603–610; 22: 80–92, 541–550, 586–594; 23:450–452; 31:641–654, 655–665; 33:509–518; 35:370–376.

HR: *ZfB* 20:173–177, 257–266, 746–748, 21:257–268; 22:253–264; 23:648–655, 689–697; 24:43–52; 25:65–80; 26:669–678; 31:577–596, 721–732; 38:379–382, 621–632.

SA: *ZfB* 20:733–743; 23:667–675; 24:416–425; 27:193–198; 29:18–28; 30:153–158, 263–273; 31: 30–43, 272–277, 750–759; 35:663–683; 36:271–288; 37:373–394; 38:149–176, 409–432; 39:1–22, 101–128; 40:1–16, 725–746, 817–832.

NC: *ZfB* 21:611–619; 27:276–292; 28:90–97; 36:260–267; 40:27–36, 359–374.

the new situation. The West German economy had successfully rebuilt itself by the mid-1950s after an impressive economic "miracle" (*Wirtschaftswunder*). Prewar industrial and energy-production levels were surpassed no later than 1958, despite the loss in territory, population, industrial base, and mineral deposits to the German Democratic Republic and other East European countries. Throughout the 1950s the West German economy grew at a faster rate than any other major economy in the world except for that of Japan. The major industries—chemicals, electrotechnical, metal, automobile, machinery—consolidated their competitive positions in the German and world markets. American-imposed decartelization of German industry proceeded in such a way that international competitive capabilities were enhanced rather than reduced. Moreover, the Federation of German Industry (BDI) successfully lobbied for a relatively benign 1957 legislation. The only lasting effect of U.S.-sponsored antitrust en- forcement was the breakup of I-G Farben into Bayer, Hoechst, and BASF. After 1966, mergers remained a common phenomenon in German industry. Neither did the new legislation stop the trend towards industrial concentration or affect the old pattern of business groups organized around the major banks.[169] After a slowdown in the 1940s due to the war and its aftermath, the process of industrial bureaucratization accelerated again in the 1950s and 1960s, though not reaching the record highs of Britain and the United States. Furthermore, the largest 200 West German industrial corporations were much more diversified along different product lines in 1953 than in 1929, and the process continued throughout the rest of the 1950s and especially during the 1960s.[170] Unlike most other major countries during the 1955–70 period, West Germany saw an increase in the relative shares of *both* industrial (from 47 to 49 percent) and services employment (from 35 to 42 percent), clearly at the expense of agricultural employment.[171] The relevance of structural theories of organization increases with the product diversification of industrial firms and

169. Between 1954 and 1960 the eight-firm concentration ratio rose in most industries: by 18.9 percent points in oil (to a 1960 level of 91.5 percent), 8.4 in the car industry (67.0), 7.4 in mining (42.0), 6.2 in steel (57.8), and 3.1 in chemicals (40.6). It only decreased in rubber, precision mechanics and optics, foundries, and plastics. See Berghahn and Karsten (1987, pp. 193–194).

170. Chandler (1990, pp. 696–721); Kocka, "The rise of the modern industrial enterprise in Germany," in Chandler and Daems, eds. (1980, pp. 80, 104); Dyas and Thanheiser, *The Emerging European Enterprise* (1976, pp. 29, 64, 288–289). See also the comparative statistics in Appendix B; and Pross (1965, pp. 106–120).

171. See the comparative statistics in Appendix B.

the growth of the service sector (adding to the variety of organizational technologies, goals, and clienteles).

New International Opportunities. The largest German firms had traditionally been deeply involved in world trade and foreign direct investment in manufacturing and distribution. In 1957 West Germany together with France formed the core of the European Economic Community (EEC). The West German economy rapidly became more international thereafter, growing much more interconnected with those of Great Britain, Italy, the United States, and, above all, France. In 1950 German exports and imports represented only 13 percent of the country's GDP. By 1960 the proportion had more than doubled, reaching 41 percent in 1970, compared to only 13 percent for the United States. Only Great Britain relied on world trade to a greater extent than Germany. West Germany's share of world trade doubled over the same period, while German direct foreign investment abroad trebled during the 1960s, reaching by 1970 a proportion of GDP similar to the one for the United States. In 1967 the stock of German direct investment abroad represented 16 percent of GDP, more than twice the proportion for the United States, and five times the British proportion. In turn, the presence of American multinationals in Germany also increased during the 1960s, making it easier to imitate American organizational patterns.[172] By any measure, the late 1950s and 1960s represented a time of international opportunities and expansion for German firms. The new organizational challenges that emerged as a result of internationalization required a more structural approach to organizing, and the greater international connectedness of the German economy favored the adoption of foreign ideas such as American structural analysis.

Continued Stability of Industrial Relations. Apart from operating in bigger economic spaces and producing a wider variety of products, West German companies faced a relatively high unionization proportion (about 40 percent of the gainfully employed population) but little industrial unrest. The 1949 Industrial Agreement Act was based on the principle of collective agreement (*Tarifvertrag*) not on contractual freedom. An effective hierarchy of labor courts was created to resolve labor disputes, and the quasi-corporatist relationship among

172. UNCTC, *Salient Features and Trends in Foreign Direct Investment* (1983); Franko, *The European Multinationals* (1976, pp. 12–13); Chandler (1990, p. 159); see also the comparative statistics in Appendix B.

the state, the employer associations, and the labor unions also promoted stability.[173] Since the 1950s more than 90 percent of all work contracts had become covered by collective agreements, up from no more than 5 percent before 1914 and about 40 percent during the 1920s. The typical collective agreement was signed between a union and an employers' federation covering many plants in a large territory, and normally included a "no-strike" clause. As in many other countries, wage increases were primarily linked to sectorial productivity and not to individual or group performance. Although the role of the unions and of collective bargaining was somewhat reduced as a result of the actions of the works councils—which frequently improved wages and conditions set in regional or national collective agreements—most members of the councils were union members. The general stabilizing effects of collective bargaining probably account for much of the extraordinarily good record in working hours lost due to industrial conflict until the early 1970s. During the 1960s the average West German worker lost 0.01 days per year due to industrial conflict, compared to the 0.38 days of the average American worker and the 0.14 days of the average British worker. This was despite the massive arrival of Southern European and Turkish guest workers in the 1960s, who represented 8.5 percent of the labor force by 1970.[174] The extremely low rates of industrial conflict resulting from the successful functioning of the sector-wide collective bargaining system and firm-level works councils solved many of the problems that the human relations paradigm meant to deal with as an ideology and as a set of techniques. As German companies became more international, bureaucratic, and diverse, and the industrial relations system more formal and stable, managers looked for theories of organization that could deal with the new dominant technical problems: how to organize different product lines within the same corporation, how to adapt the organization to its environment, how to organize R&D, manufacturing, and sales on a world scale, and how to manage and promote change in complexly bureaucratized structures.

The Rise of Structural Sociology and Behavioral Science. The professionals who first showed an interest in meeting these new challenges in

173. Weber, *Unternehmerverbände zwischen Markt, Staat, und Gewerkschaften* (1987).

174. Berghahn and Karsten (1987, pp. 75–103); Lee (1978, p. 475); Sturmthal (1972, pp. 67–68, 75–76, 150, 159–164); Slomp (1990, pp. 132–135, 139); Vogl, *German Business After the Economic Miracle* (1973, pp. 71–107); Statistisches Bunde-

Germany were the sociologists. The "younger" generation of German academic sociologists became the channel for the transfer of Anglo-Saxon structural-organizational analysis precisely at the moment when Weber began, at last, to exert an impact on German sociology.[175] At the same time, sociology experienced years of growth at German universities.[176] The central figures of German organizational sociology since the late 1950s had been Dahrendorf, Mayntz, and Luhmann, although none of them wrote exclusively on organization theory. Ralf Dahrendorf was the initiator of German structural, conflict-oriented organizational sociology in the late 1950s, with his studies on industrial sociology, the social structure of the business firm, and the larger issues of class and class conflict as emerging from authority relations in the workplace.[177]

Renate Mayntz was perhaps the academic sociologist whose influence was most strongly felt in management education and industrial circles. Her first work on organization theory was published in German as *The Social Organization of the Industrial Firm* (1958), in which she discussed the formal aspects of organization (hierarchy, offices, domination, autonomy, line-and-staff structures, communication lines), paying attention to the functions of formal structure. She also discussed the factors that influence formal organization (technology, economic system, social structure, legal environment). She argued that whether the firm makes "needles, canned meat, Diesel engines or fighter aircraft" should have an impact on the formalized structure, but failed to theorize relevant dimensions of product or object vari-

---

samt, *Bevölkerung und Wirtschaft 1872–1972* (1972, p. 148); see also the comparative statistics in Appendix B.

175. The crucial point was reached in 1964 when the German Sociologists' Day celebrated the 100th anniversary of Weber's birth. See Lepsius (1987, p. 39; 1979, pp. 42, 51).

176. The first chair of sociology had been established only after World War I. Forty years after, in 1960, there were 35 professors and 50 assistant positions specifically devoted to the teaching of sociology at German universities. The number of professors rose rapidly to reach 190 by 1971, and 279 by 1974. The number of assistant positions rose even more steeply to 450 in 1971, and 551 in 1974. The number of sociology students trebled between 1963–64 and 1970–71 to a total of 5,593. Moreover, sociology students represented 1.6 percent of all university students in 1970–71, up from just 0.7 percent in 1963–64. See Hardin, *The Professionalization of Sociology* (1977, pp. 51, 57, 65).

177. Dahrendorf (1959a, 1959b), and Burisch (1969). Another student of class conflict and its roots in the workplace was Hans Paul Bahrdt. See his *Industriebürokratie* (1958), which draws on Marx's, Dahrendorf's, and C. Wright Mills's theories of the white-collar worker.

ability. Then Mayntz introduced informal organization in her analysis, only to get a more complete picture of reality, not to claim that nurturing informal groups would increase industrial performance. In fact, she framed the discussion in terms of informal power, informal leadership, status, uses, and institutions, not in terms of harmony, equilibrium, managerial leadership, and community.[178]

Mayntz's most influential book was *Sociology of Organization* (1963), which had sold over 50,000 copies by the time of its ninth reprint in 1977. Danish, Dutch, and Spanish translations of the book were published within five years of the first edition. The book is a relentless defense of a structural, conflict-oriented sociological model of organizations. *Sociology of Organization* starts with references to the ubiquity of complex organizations in modern society and an account of Weberian organizational sociology in terms of power, domination, and authority. Organizational structure, process, and relationship with the environment are the variables she takes into account. All the important ideas of a structural and contingency approach to organizing are discussed: the need to match the structure with the environment, the absence of a "one best way" to organize, the use of typologies to decide how to organize, the idea that conflict is structural and may help to attain a better environmental match, centralization and decentralization as policy variables, formalization and structuralization of control mechanisms and communication channels, the recruitment of personnel (taking into account formal qualifications), and the various ways to reward people in organizations (prestige, influence, power, status, salary, job security). Moreover, Mayntz criticized on empirical grounds the argument of human relations theorists that worker satisfaction necessarily leads to increased production.[179]

Finally, Niklas Luhmann made an important contribution to organization theory with his 1964 book, *Functions and Consequences of Formal Organization,* now in its third edition.[180] For Luhmann, formalization in organizations serves two functions: the differentiation of expectations, which is necessary for the regulation of the relationship between the individual and the organization; and the differentia-

178. Mayntz, *Die soziale Organisation des Industriebetriebes* (1958, pp. 14–40, 59–62, 78–86).

179. Mayntz, *Soziologie der Organisation* (1963, pp. 7–18, 23, 32, 45–46, 55–57, 75–77, 81–89, 101, 112–116, 120–125, 128–129, 147–148).

180. Luhmann, *Funktionen und Folgen formaler Organisation* [1964] (1976). For a bibliography of his works up to 1980, see Luhmann, *The Differentiation of Society* (1982, pp. 435–438).

tion of systems, which helps to configure subsystems and structures.[181] Although Luhmann does not regard conflict as the central
organizational process and pays a great deal of attention to topics
such as informal behavior, presentation of the self, and individual
motivation, his approach, combining systemic and functionalist theories, becomes a "functional structuralist" one that has been used by
many other German structural theorists of organizations. Luhmann
has also done theoretical work aimed at criticizing and elaborating
Lawrence and Lorsch's contingency framework of analysis.[182]

Dahrendorf, Mayntz, and Luhmann received part of their training
or spent extensive periods of time at Anglo-Saxon institutions of
higher learning, and thus had first-hand contact with the new trends
in organizational analysis. As had happened in the 1920s with scientific management, books written by successful American business
practitioners appeared promptly. Most of Peter Drucker's books were
translated (but not *Concept of the Corporation*). The most widely publicized one was *Practice of Management,* originally published in 1954,
with seven German editions between 1956 and 1970. Drucker, well-
acquainted with European developments, explicitly wrote in this book
that part of the productivity differential between the two sides of the
Atlantic was due to the "lower proportion of managers and techni-
cians and the poor organization structure of European industry."[183]
Ernest Dale's *Great Organizers* appeared in 1960, and Alfred Sloan's
My Years with General Motors was translated only two years after the
original American edition of 1963 and reprinted twice in less than
two years. Also important was Mayntz's compilation of some twenty
German, English, and, above all, American contributions to structural
organization theory, which appeared in 1968 as *Bureaucratic Organization.*[184]

Behavioral science also developed in Germany during the 1950s
and 1960s. The Institute for Industrial Research at the Free University of Berlin, directed by Erich Kosiol, trained many of the future
professors specializing in organization theory and decision-making

181. Luhmann (1976, pp. 59–88). See also Schluchter's review of Luhmann's
book in "Modes of authority and democratic control" (1987, pp. 307–311).
182. Luhmann, "A general theory of organized social systems" (1976), and "Organisationstheorie" (1981); Meja, Misgeld, and Stehr, "The social and intellectual organization of German sociology since 1945" (1987, p. 7). See also the conceptualization
by Sommer, *Die Bedeutung interpersonaler Beziehungen für die Organisation der Unternehmung* (1968); Kieser, ed., *Organisationstheoretische Ansätze* (1981, pp. 76–93).
183. Drucker, *The Practice of Management* (1954, p. 42).
184. Mayntz, ed., *Bürokratische Organisation* (1968).

from a behavioral point of view, such as Erwin Grochla and Knut Bleicher. Kosiol himself contributed to organization theory with his task and functional analysis, building on the writings of Fayol. The institute had the support of firms such as AEG, Electrolux, IBM Deutschland, Siemens, and Telefunken. An Institute for Business Organization and Automation (BIFOA) was created in 1964 at the University of Cologne, which was in touch with American researchers in the area of behavioral decision making.[185] It should be pointed out that the success of German structural thinking in organization theory and managerial thought was restricted to the realm of the theoretical and conceptual. The ZfB did not publish a single original article reporting on empirical studies of organizations from the structural point of view. This contrasts with the bulk of the scientific management articles published until the mid-1950s, which contained extensive empirical or historical data. At best, the results of American structural studies were commented on. Neither did sociologists engage in major empirical studies of organizations.[186]

The Negligible Role of the State.   There is very little evidence showing that state institutions like the RKW favored in any significant way the structural approach to organizational analysis. The RKW did not engage directly in any extensive project of structural comparative analysis of German industrial organizations, nor did it provide funds for that purpose. Agencies like a National Science Foundation (which provided funds for some of the first structural investigations in the United States) or the Ministry of Technology (which played a similar role in England) were lacking in Germany. Wealthy, research-oriented, American-style business schools do not exist in West Germany.[187] Sociologist Rainer Lepsius criticized the human relations

185. Kosiol, *Institut für Industrieforschung 1948–1958* (1959); Bleicher, *Zentralisation und Dezentralisation von Aufgaben in der Organisation der Unternehmungen* (1966); Grochla and Szyperski, eds., *Information Systems and Organizational Structure* (1975); Wunderer, "Leadership" (1990).

186. Three exceptional empirical structural analysis studies are Lukatis, *Organisationsstrukturen und Führungsstile in Wirtschaftsunternehmen* (1972); Wilpert, *Führung in deutschen Unternehmen* (1977); and Kieser in *Schmalenbachs Zeitschrift für Betriebswirtschaftliche Forschung* 26(9)(1974):569–590.

187. There are a number of tiny research institutes or training centers, both public and private, that, to my knowledge, did not engage in or provide funds for large-scale structural analysis research projects. See the survey by Fiedler-Winter, *Die Management-Schulen* (1973, pp. 59–194).

emphasis, small-group research, and leadership models in an RKW publication series, proposing instead a structural approach.[188]

THE THEORETICAL IMPACT OF STRUCTURAL ANALYSIS IN MANAGEMENT CIRCLES

The increasing economic scale and scope of West German companies and the availability of structural theories of organization had an impact on managerial thought. The annual reports of the Federation of German Industry (BDI) show the increasing attention paid to the problem of adapting organizational structures to new conditions (rising complexity, market growth and integration in Europe, technological change, etc.) since the mid-1960s.[189] At the annual meetings of the German Society for Business Administration, attended by the country's most prominent business and political leaders, the organizational sessions included topics such as decentralization, divisionalization, and matrix structures. Top managers from firms such as AEG-Telefunken, Brown Boveri & Cie., Siemens & Halske, and Deutsche Philips discussed contingency theory in the context of the growing diversification and internationalization of German business.[190]

The influence of structural analysis among German management intellectuals (including both academics and practitioners) can be measured using the number of times that the world's leading international authors were mentioned in the German handbooks of management published during the 1960s and 1970s. The 7,000-page, four-volume, state-of-the-art *Dictionary of Business Administration,* published between 1956 and 1962, contained almost no references to either human relations or structural analysis authors, but considerable attention was given to scientific management. In contrast, the 1969 edition of the *Dictionary of Organization* contained an average of 8.5 mentions of the leading scientific management authors, an average of 15.6 mentions of the human relations authors, and an average of 18.8 mentions of the structural analysis authors. In the 1976 edition of the massive *Dictionary of Business Administration,* much more attention was devoted to organizational authors than in the previous edition of 1956–1962, and structural analysis authors received again more

188. Lepsius (1960, pp. 14, 15, 28, 29, 41, 49–51, 71–74).

189. See Bundesverband der deutschen Industrie (BDI), *Jahresbericht* 1962–63: 83–85, 1966:107, 1966–67:99–100, 1967–68:112–113, 1968–69:151.

190. See the proceedings of the *Deutscher Betriebswirtschafter-Tag:* 9(1956):57–62; 12(1959):104–117; 19(1966):367–374; 24(1971) I:53–68, II:9–21; 25(1972): 64–84.

mentions than either scientific management or human relations authors.[191] Already in 1961, the pages of a state-of-the-art, edited book on business organization was dominated by leading academics, managers, and consultants who concentrated on problems related to the organizational structure and offered structural solutions.[192] In the RKW-sponsored volume, *Handbook for the Organization Manager* (1968), the contributing engineers, business economists, and executives dealt extensively with structural problems and approaches to organizational management.[193] The annual meeting of the German Institute of Auditors in 1969 devoted one of its six working sessions to the problem of the structural organization of large corporations in terms of their functional departments, product lines, and market areas.[194] The impact of the sociological theory of organization and of modern behavioral management theory was apparent in the contributions of the German management intellectuals to these volumes and to conferences on business organization. Some consultants, like Heinrich B. Acker, sold several editions of their books on organizational analysis. Acker proposed a rudimentary contingency approach based on the number of exceptions or types of objects to be handled in the production process.[195]

Panel B of Table 3.2 shows that structural analysis articles became dominant in the *ZfB* journal since 1959. Only one article using a structural analysis approach had been published before the war. Half of the structural analysis articles of the postwar period identified a mismatch between the organization's technology or environment and its structure as the problem for analysis, and this recognition was coupled with the identification of a contingency approach as the way

191. The average numbers of citations were calculated for the 8 leading scientific management authors, 11 human relations authors, and 20 structural analysis authors included in Figure 1.1. See Seischab and Schwantag, eds., *Handwörterbuch der Betriebswirtschaft* (1956–1962, pp. 6809–6983); Grochla, ed., *Handwörterbuch der Organisation* (1969, pp. 1849–1886); Grochla and Wittmann, eds., *Handwörterbuch der Betriebswirtschaft* (1976, pp. 4878–5010). See also Schneider, *Geschichte betriebswirtschaftlicher Theorie* (1981, pp. 206–215).

192. Schnaufer and Agthe, *Organisation* (1961).

193. Degelmann, ed., *Organisationsleiter-Handbuch* (1968). On structural analysis, see pp. 86–115, 134–223, 278–300, 323–358, 900–930, 1385–1418; on human relations, see pp. 224–238, 857–883; and on scientific management, see pp. 422–492, 512–542, 543–571, 600–632.

194. Institut der Wirtschaftsprüfer, *Unternehmensführung und Unternehmensberatung* (1969, pp. 43–54, 125–130).

195. Acker, *Organisationsanalyse* (1966, pp. 51–77). See also his articles in *ZfB* 23(1953):667–675, and 24(1954):416–425.

to solve organizational problems (see Table 3.2).[196] Only three articles, however, clearly referred to the creation of typologies of organizations as the way to solve the contingency challenge. The majority of articles elaborated on the need to differentiate and integrate functions or activities in order to achieve organizational success. Almost all of the articles discussed centralization and decentralization as policy variables, as well as the usefulness of line-and-staff structures. Surprisingly, no article proposed to select workers according to formal qualifications, or suggested the use of bureaucratic rewards (careers, prestige, status, power) or seniority-based wages. Panel B of Table 3.2 also shows that the average structural analysis article published in ZfB touched on fewer themes than the average scientific management or human relations article.

The influence of German sociologists like Dahrendorf, Mayntz, and Luhmann was clear in many articles. One-third of the structural analysis articles cited at least one of their works and commented extensively on the views presented in them.[197] Structural organizational sociology was not the only theoretical tradition informing these pieces. The other major line of reasoning followed the Carnegie school of Simon, Cyert, and March, and later developments associated with behavioral decision-making models, game theory, and information microeconomics. This was especially true of articles written by authors with training in business economics.[198]

THE PRACTICAL IMPLEMENTATION OF STRUCTURAL IDEAS

There is ample evidence that German industrial and service firms engaged in major structural reorganizations during the 1960s. Nearly 400 firms implemented the Harzburg system of structural decentralization and integration. This model—a product of the research and consulting work done by Reinhard Höhn at the Academy for Management Cadres at Bad Harzburg—was aimed at relieving top management from all decisions that could possibly be made at a lower organizational level. It was based on clear specifications of competencies and responsibilities, top-bottom controls, coordination of infor-

196. The most interesting discussions of the contingency approach were ZfB 20(1950):733–743, and 30(1960):263–273.

197. See ZfB 35(1965):663–683; 36(1966):271–288; 37(1967):567–592; 38(1968):149–176, 409–432; 39(1969):1–22; 40(1970):1–16.

198. ZfB 38(1968):149–176, 409–432; 38(1968):149–176, 409–432, 39 (1969):1–22. Mayntz has also contributed to decision-making problems. See her "Conceptual models of organizational decision-making and their application to the policy process" (1976).

mation flows, and manipulation of structural components to maximize organizational performance. Firms such as Bayer, Hoechst,
Opel, BMW, Volkswagen, Continental, AEG, Krupp, and the Kars-
tadt and Kaufhof department stores implemented the Harzburg
system.[199]

The multidivisional form of organization, with all its associated
ideas about decentralization and control, and the differential organization according to technological and environmental contingencies,
were adopted by 50 of the 100 top German industrial firms by 1970,
up from a mere 16 percent in 1960. Among those firms with diversified product strategies, the proportion of multidivisionalization increased from 33 percent in 1960 to 89 percent in 1970. Famous
German firms with a multidivisional structure in 1970 included
Krupp, Mannesmann, Continental, Bosch, Hoechst, Bayer, BASF,
Siemens, AEG-Telefunken, Opel (General Motors), Ford Germany,
and Esso. Firms under family control (e.g. Brinkmann, Reemtsma,
Grundig) or heavily influenced by minority shareholders (e.g. Osram,
Volkswagen, Daimler-Benz, BMW) did not diversify and, accordingly, did not adopt the multidivisional structure. In 1970 German
levels of diversification and multidivisionalization were somewhat
lower than in the United States and Britain, about as high as in
France, and much higher than in Italy or Spain.[200] The important
fact, however, is that multidivisionalization increased steeply during
the 1960s, with most firms finally adopting the multidivisional structure after 1967. As opposed to both U.S. and British companies,
diversified German firms took a long time to implement the multidivisional structure. In the case of 14 of the top 40 firms that made the
transition after 1950, less than 10 years elapsed between diversification and adoption of the multidivisional structure. For 7 other firms,
the lag was between 10 and 20 years, and the lag was more than
20 years for 19 firms. The McKinsey consulting firm helped several
German firms in their reorganization, but its role was much more
limited than in Britain. Comparative studies have found that German
multinational firms increased operational decentralization and subsidiary autonomy during the 1960s and 1970s, approaching the levels

---

199. Kaste (1981, pp. 64–68); Berghahn (1986, pp. 256–257); Zepf, *Kooperativer
Führungsstil und Organisation* (1972, pp. 154–158); Kieser, ed. (1981, pp. 76–93).
See also Höhn, ed., *Das Harzburger Modell in der Praxis* (1967), *Verwaltung Heute*
(1970), *Die Stellvertretung im Betrieb* (1971).

200. See the comparative statistics in Appendix B; Franko, "The move toward a
multidivisional structure in European organizations" (1974).

of U.S. firms. The adoption of the Harzburg system, the multidivisional form, and decentralized international structures by so many German firms during the 1960s reveals the growing use of the structural analysis approach.[201]

Many German firms made the transition to the multidivisional form by themselves. After spending most of the 1950s rebuilding itself from World War II destruction, expropriation, and chaos, AEG diversified into electronics, data processing, office machinery, records, and tapes, in part through acquisitions of companies. The close personal contacts of top AEG managers with General Electric of the United States guided their reorganization of the firm along multidivisional lines in the 1950s. As was typical of firms in the chemical and electromechanical industries, AEG created several divisions, with a single member of the executive board (*Vorstand*) or a group of them overseeing one or more divisions. The lowest level of profit responsibility was generally two or three levels down from the executive board. A second reorganization took place at AEG in 1966–67 as part of the merger with Telefunken, also a multidivisional firm.[202]

A COMPARISON OF HUMAN RELATIONS AND STRUCTURAL
ANALYSIS IN GERMANY

Most German advocates of the human relations approach to organizing shared a view of work and industry that was rooted in a "minority" mentality, following the social doctrine of the Catholic Church, but neither contextual factors during the late 1940s and 1950s (reconstruction of the economy, success of codetermination and works councils) nor other relevant actors (unions, sociological and business administration professions, the state) favored the adoption of the human relations paradigm. As a result, management circles did not pay much attention to it. The contrast with the United States is clear. On the contrary, contextual changes taking place during the late 1950s and throughout the 1960s, such as product diversification, expansion of service employment, continued bureaucratization, growing importance of international trade, expansion of market areas, and consolidation of a formal collective-bargaining system, demanded a more struc-

---

201. Dyas and Thanheiser (1976, pp. 63–151); Chandler (1990, pp. 617–621); Negandhi, "Role and structure of German multinationals" (1986). Dyas and Thanheiser discuss in their book many interesting details of the organizational transition in several of the largest firms.

202. Dyas and Thanheiser (1976, pp. 54, 93–94, 121, 125); Chandler (1990, pp. 538–550).

tural approach to organizing. These conditions coincided with the growing interest in structural analysis in the German sociological profession. In contrast to their support for scientific management, state agencies like the RKW showed a negligible interest in promoting structural analysis. German management circles, nevertheless, proved receptive to the newly proposed paradigm. The relative similarity of the American and German situations after 1960 contrasts with the sharply different impact of human relations, which largely has to do with the crucial difference between the successful corporatist model of industrial relations in Germany and the inherently adversarial pattern of labor relations in the United States. The case of Spain, discussed in the next chapter, provides a polar contrast with the German experience in terms of the degree of socio-economic development, nature of the organizational problems, configuration of institutional factors, and pattern of resulting organizational change, in spite of the fact that corporatism characterizes both societies.

FOUR

Spain

Eclecticism, Human Relations, and Managerial Authoritarianism in a Less-Developed Country

Despite Spain's low degree of economic development until the 1960s, its entrepreneurial and managerial elites had to engage in fierce ideological debates due to the persistent problem of labor unrest. This factor alone guaranteed the occurrence of lively organizational debates. Had it not been for labor unrest, scientific management would have passed unnoticed before 1939. During the interwar period, management intellectuals proposed an eclectic mixture of ideas drawn from vocational guidance, scientific management, and industrial psychology to cope with working-class protest. Scientific management was only ideologically successful and widely implemented in practice during the unusual circumstances of the period of international isolation and economic self-sufficiency (1939–52). Social Catholicism, liberal thought, and the influence of academic sociology and psychology played a fundamental role in the reception and adoption of human relations ideas after 1953. As in Germany, the state was a key actor, though not only for the application of scientific management but also for the success of human relations. Finally, structural analysis could not address the continuing problem of labor unrest, and was not adequate given the low levels of bureaucratization, diversification, and service-sector employment. In contrast to its reception in Germany and the United States, structural analysis did not find any supporters before the 1980s.

The Eclecticism of the Pre-1939 Period

Spanish employers faced a recurrent problem of labor unrest in 1900–36 while the country's economy remained underdeveloped. The lack of support from professional groups or the state that might have promoted the implementation of scientific management, coupled with the early influence of vocational guidance and social Catholicism, produced the appearance of an "eclecticism of methods," an uneasy mixture of elements drawn from such diverse traditions as vocational guidance, scientific management, and industrial psychology. While the rebelliousness of labor presented a problem that might have favored the adoption of scientific management ideology and techniques, other conditions (economic backwardness, scarcity of engineers, pusillanimous state action) prevented the implementation of that organizational paradigm.

LABOR UNREST AS THE DOMINANT
ORGANIZATIONAL ISSUE

The social and political structures of Spain underwent deep changes between 1900 and 1975, but the most essential economic feature remained unchanged until at least 1950: the country's economy continued to be at the mercy of the performance of the agricultural sector. Despite the efforts to pursue an English-style model of industrialization in the nineteenth century, roughly two-thirds of Spain's labor force was accounted for by agriculture in 1900. A mountainous country with relatively little tillable land and high rates of population growth, Spain lacked capital and an internal market for industrial goods. Nevertheless, industry developed in a few enclaves: large iron and steel plants in the northern regions of Asturias and the Basque country, metal-working industries in the latter two areas and in Catalonia, coal mining in Asturias, and a relatively highly mechanized textile industry in Catalonia. Spain also had a relatively large network of modern (if poorly planned and deplorably run) railways that fell short of articulating a national market for goods and labor. The "failure" of the Spanish industrialization drive throughout the nineteenth century is reflected in the occupational structure of the country by 1900. Industrial prices remained well above those of the international competition, even after accounting for transportation and other distribution costs. Spanish industry fell victim to the everlasting problems with the state budget deficit, the failed waves of Prussian-style agrarian reform, the speculative nature of many investments (both national and foreign), the stubbornness of exploiting uneconomical energy resources (coal), the building of an inadequate and expensive railway infrastructure, the isolation of the country from foreign competition, the high illiteracy rate among the working class, the scarcity of entrepreneurial initiatives, and the lack of technical knowledge. Given the incapacity of industrial producers to compete internationally, the limited size of the Spanish market only exacerbated their problems. Spain's agriculture (except in the export-oriented Levant) remained subsistence-oriented rather than market-oriented, and was subject to recurrent crises that, in turn, affected industry severely.[1]

On top of these economic factors was the always problematic political situation and the challenge to the central state posed by the labor class in the industrial enclaves as well as by the conservative nationalist movements in the Basque country and Catalonia. Sociologist Juan Linz has observed a "recurrent pattern" in contemporary Spanish history of "short periods of high revolutionary enthusiasm carried by the hopes of broad segments of the citizenry, activation of radical masses pushed by poverty, withdrawal of the moderate reformist element, defeat of the forces of change by the intervention of the army, establishment of a conservative government, and a relatively prolonged period of peace and prosperity—without, however, arriving at a solution of basic underlying problems or creating fully legitimate institutions."[2] The Restoration of 1876–1923, a liberal-oligarchic constitutional monarchy, represented one such long period of peace and relative prosperity, except for important crises during the 1900s and after 1918. The loss of Cuba, Puerto Rico, and the Philippines in 1898 had ambivalent effects. The repatriation of colonial capitals helped the creation of powerful banks linked to industrial interests, but with the colonies went the protected overseas markets that were so lucrative to certain industrial sectors like the Catalan textile industry.

According to political economist Francisco Bernis, the business establishment at the turn of the century included bankers and industrialists of ancient Semitic origin, *indianos* (or *nouveaux riches* returning from the colonies), competent managers working for foreign subsidiaries, some wealthy landowners, Jesuit priests (especially in hydroelectric power firms), and certain politicians sitting on the boards of major oligopolistic firms.[3] This financial and industrial oligarchy was quite effective in organizing powerful lobbies to obtain favorable tariff protection and labor legislation. Their ideology of economic nationalism and staunch resistance to granting workers or their organizations any concessions was reflected in the legislation of the time.

1. Nadal, *El fracaso de la revolución industrial en España* (1975, pp. 39–53, 62–86, 122–154, 226–245); Tamames, *The Spanish Economy* (1986, pp. 85–86); Tuñón de Lara, "Progreso técnico y conciencia social, 1898–1936" (1984, pp. 19–21).

2. Linz, "Early state-building and late peripheral nationalisms against the state: The case of Spain" (1973a, p. 56).

3. See Roldán, García Delgado, and Muñoz, *La consolidación del capitalismo en España* (1973, vol. 1, pp. 26–27).

They believed in their superior spirit, traditional authority, and the legitimacy of their business successes, which justified their rule and control over manual workers.[4]

A renewed wave of industrialization took place after the outbreak of the war in 1914, when Spanish firms benefited from the country's neutrality.[5] By 1930, however, after the war and mid-1920s booms were over, agricultural jobs still represented 46 percent of the workforce. The Great Depression and the Civil War of 1936–39 caused a recession in the industrialization process. By 1950 agriculture still occupied half of the active population. During the period of (definitive) industrialization in 1953–1969, Spain finally approached the occupational structures of comparable countries like France and Italy.[6]

The series of partially successful, but never decisive, attempts at industrialization stretching over the 120 years between 1830 and 1950 leaves the impression of an ever-industrializing country with chronic and everlasting problems of social dislocation and labor unrest. Despite this long, agonizing process of industrialization, it is important to bear in mind that since the 1890s Spain has had an important modern urban social structure, sizeable professional and bureaucratic middle classes, and a relatively large industrial proletariat concentrated in Catalonia, the Basque country, Asturias, and, since the 1950s, in the Madrid area.[7] Thus, factors such as the geographical concentration of industry, the growth and radicalization of the industrial proletariat, and the large urban component in the social structure point to the potential relevance of issues relating to the labor problem and the organization of work.

The history of the Spanish labor movement until 1939 is one of recurrent cycles of mobilization, unionization, strikes (often linked to political goals), repression, and recovery of unions. The labor cycle appears to follow political events and to be constrained by economic downturns, although at some points it also affected the evolution of national politics and the economy. The right of association was initially acknowledged in 1869, although ambiguous legislation allowed for the discretionary repression of labor organizations. Adverse economic conditions (unemployment) and police or military force held

4. Montoya Melgar, *Ideología y lenguaje en las primeras leyes laborales de España* (1975, pp. 73–77).
5. Roldán, García Delgado, and Muñoz (1973, vol. 1, pp. 34–42, 53–68).
6. Tamames (1986, p. 14).
7. The classic study on the different "Spains" is Linz and De Miguel, "Within-nation differences and comparisons: The eight Spains" (1966b).

the unions in check. As in other industrial countries like Germany and the United States, employers would ask local police and army commanders to crush strikes. Under such circumstances, industrial conflict before, during, and after the Restoration period often became class warfare. After 1868, Anarchism and Anarcho-Syndicalism developed in the south and along the Mediterranean periphery, thanks to the strength of federal republicanism in those areas. Anarchist unions often engaged in indiscriminate violence. Their 1881 umbrella organization was severely repressed, disappearing by 1888. Anarchist unions remained small for the next two decades. The more tolerant liberal government in 1887 allowed for the creation of the Socialist Workers' Party (PSOE) that year, and of the Socialist General Workers' Union (UGT) the year after, which achieved membership growth in Madrid, Asturias, and the Basque country, but not in Catalonia. In 1900 unionization stood at only 5 percent of the industrial workforce.[8]

THE FIRST ORGANIZATIONAL DEBATES: LABOR UNREST IN CATALONIA

As the country's most dynamic region from economic, political, cultural, and social standpoints, Catalonia inaugurated the debate over the labor problem and the organization of work. Labor unrest became in Catalonia, even more so than in the rest of Spain, the problem posed by a militant proletariat threatening the bourgeois order. The Catalonia of the early 1900s was a region with a powerful industrial bourgeoisie controlling family interests in the textile and light manufacturing industries. Politically speaking, the bourgeoisie nurtured "Catalanist," regionalist, and autonomist sentiments, and was quite conservative. As regards economic policy, it was in favor of continued trade tariff protection, and organized itself into a most effective lobby, the Promotion of National Labor (*Fomento del Trabajo Nacional,* FTN). Apart from the consumer-oriented textile industry, other capital goods industries developed in the 1900s and 1910s, including large firms such as La Maquinista Terrestre y Marítima (transportation equipment, machine tools), Nueva Vulcano (metals), and several chemical companies. Hispano-Suiza, a subsidiary of a French company, was the only manufacturer and repairer of auto engines with workshops in Barcelona and Guadalajara, near Madrid.[9]

At the turn of the century Catalonia had a sizeable lower middle

8. Martin, *The Agony of Modernization* (1990, pp. 75–125, 237–262).
9. Tuñón de Lara (1984, pp. 24, 35, 37).

class and a growing working class. Barcelona had over half a million inhabitants, slightly less than Madrid, but that did not take into account the 300,000 or so living in the large industrial towns surrounding the city. In 1905 the industrial proletariat in Barcelona numbered perhaps 150,000, and as many as 250,000 in the industrial belt as a whole.[10] Until the 1890s Catalan labor followed patterns of association and unionization similar to its counterparts in the rest of Spain. But the regionalist sentiment and the centralist practices of the Socialist party led Catalan workers to reject the Socialist union (UGT) and pursue the anarchist path.[11]

The labor problem and the organization of work were to become crucial issues towards the late 1900s. After a series of ups and downs in the economic conditions that affected the power of the labor unions, a coalition of mainly nonpolitical and anarchist elements with some Socialist ones created a united union in Barcelona in 1907. The following two years proved to be especially hard for the working class, with staggering unemployment and prices. In 1909 the escalation of the war in the Rif area of the Spanish Protectorate in northern Morocco set in motion a chain of events that culminated in the Tragic Week of Barcelona. The Madrid government had decided to mobilize working-class reservists in order to cope with the guerrilla warfare against the regular army, and a large contingent was called from Catalonia, Valencia, and Aragón to be embarked at the Barcelona harbor. Public opinion was in a pacifist and isolationist mood after the colonial disaster of 1898. After the unions called for a general stoppage, violent incidents, barricades, and anticlerical assaults proliferated. The popular rebellion was crushed by the army, resulting in over 110 deaths, four workers executed, and the pedagogue and anarchist intellectual Francesc Ferrer i Guardia tried and executed.[12]

The events of 1909 certainly made an impression on the Catalan industrial bourgeoisie. In addition, the various anarchist unions and groups united their dispersed forces in 1910 under the flag of the National Confederation of Labor (CNT), which by 1919 had become the largest union at the national level. It seemed clear to the Catalan bourgeoisie that some kind of action was needed to ameliorate the labor problem. The first was of course to continue using sheer force. The employer organization FTN was particularly keen in pursuing a

10. Tuñón de Lara, *El movimiento obrero en la historia de España* (1972, pp. 371–454).

11. Martin (1990, pp. 91–92, 103–105).

12. Martin (1990, pp. 127–145); Tuñón de Lara (1972, pp. 371–454).

hard line. The second path was recourse to interlocutors between the employers and the workers, experts in vocational guidance and work organization. The goal was to "rationalize" the labor market, overcome the old antagonisms, create a "healthy" labor class, and advance in the common task of social progress. The creation of the Social Museum (*Museo Social*) by the provincial government of Barcelona in 1908 was the first institutional step in this direction. It was aimed at "the improvement of the moral and material situation of the popular classes," advising workers, and gathering relevant information.[13] In 1912 a quite effective Employment Bureau (*Bolsa de Trabajo*) was added because of the rising unemployment. A crucial institution was the Training Secretariat (*Secretariado del Aprendizaje*), founded in 1914 to improve the matching of work aspirants to jobs by means of the examination of their mental and physical aptitudes. The Training Secretariat enjoyed the political backing of the *Mancomunitat* (the autonomous administration of the four Catalan provinces, created in 1914), but it lacked adequate resources.[14]

It was against this background of mounting labor problems and emerging vocational guidance efforts that the first Spanish reactions to scientific management took place in Catalonia. Spanish translations of Taylor's *The Art of Cutting Metals* and *Shop Management* were published in Barcelona in 1912 and 1914, respectively. Münsterberg's *Psychology and Industrial Efficiency* was published in Madrid in 1914. The reception of Taylor's ideas in Catalonia was not unanimous at first. Santiago Valentí Camp, a Socialist and republican sociologist and politician, published a lengthy essay in 1914 in the influential Catalan cultural magazine *Estudio* (*Study*) proclaiming the adequacy of Taylor's method and pointing out that his recommendations were "worthy of esteem and praise." Valentí Camp asked the Spanish worker to take Taylorism as "the principle of a successive liberation, which will improve his living conditions considerably." He also declared that "the increase in production raises social wealth and that is good for both capitalists and workers."[15]

Valentí Camp's remarks about Taylorism were not echoed by anyone else in such positive terms. In fact, with a few exceptions, the

13. Estivill and Tomàs, "Orientación profesional en Cataluña: 1907–1917" (1978, p. 45).

14. Tomàs and Estivill, "Apuntes para una historia de la organización del trabajo en España, 1900–1936" (1979, pp. 21–25).

15. Valentí Camp, "Indagaciones y lecturas: La dirección científica del trabajo humano." (1914, pp. 243, 247, 253, 248).

early reaction to Taylorism by Spanish intellectuals and employers would have more in common with the position taken by Cipriano Montolíu in the same magazine in 1915, and published separately as a book one year afterwards. Montolíu was a jurist working for the Social Museum, a prominent personality in the Catalan regionalist milieu, and founder of the civic society Garden City in 1912. He mounted a devastating attack on Taylor's method of work organization. In his view, Taylorism could not deliver what it promised. The method capitalized on the advantages deriving from "firing workers, cutting wages, and other customary coercive means," while it disdained the possibility of "sharing profits equitably." According to Montolíu, Taylor also proposed to deprive the worker of "all personal initiative . . . , subjecting him or her to the higher precision allowed by the stopwatch and the slide rule," a process which might ultimately "destroy the human being as a personality, as a free individual and as a rational and sensitive person." In sum, the application of the Taylor system would "ominously reveal the great harms and dangers behind some of the methods that [Taylor] so eagerly recommends."[16]

The position of Montolíu anticipated the reticence with which scientific management was to be received by employers in Catalonia and the rest of Spain before the Civil War of 1936–39. For Spanish industry, unlike that of many other countries, including Germany, Britain, France, and the United States, the effects of World War I were not conducive to the application of scientific management principles. Between 1915 and 1917, Spanish (particularly Catalan) industrialists amassed stupendous fortunes as suppliers of manufactured goods to the allied powers. It was not until 1917 that the end of the European conflict, the rising cost of living, and the growth in union affiliation reminded enriched employers of the difficulties lying ahead. In 1919 a strike at a large electrical power company in Barcelona (La Canadiense) quickly escalated to a general strike. Anarchist terrorist violence was met by regionalist-backed police and army troops, who waged vicious war against the anarchist CNT leaders and organization.

Given the intensification of the labor problem, the employers and the autonomous government of the Mancomunitat renewed their efforts to improve work organization. In 1917 the Training Secretariat was transformed into the more effective Institute of Vocational Guidance (*Institut d'Orientació Professional,* IOP). The institute comprised

16. Montolíu, *El sistema de Taylor y su crítica* (1916, pp. 9, 20, 46).

three sections: statistical, anthropometric, and psychometric. It was staffed by prominent economists, pedagogues, physicians, and psychiatrists of moderate regionalist convictions, including José María Tallada, José Ruiz Castella, Luis Trías de Bes, Cipriano Montolíu, and Emilio Mira y López. They all believed that science could help to solve the problems of labor unrest and social dislocation. The parallel with the American Progressives is apparent.

Despite the use of the phrase *scientific organization of work* in many of the studies sponsored by the institute, its activities were more concerned with industrial psychology (as conceived by Münsterberg), physiology of work and fatigue studies, vocational guidance, and worker training than with Taylor's more revolutionary and complex system of scientific management.[17] The experiments under way in several small Catalan firms at the time seem to confirm the fact that innovations in work organization were aimed at introducing group incentives, profit-sharing, welfare schemes, and worker participation so as to "perfect production and achieve social peace."[18] The institute was especially active in its task of gathering psycho-physiological data on apprentices and job applicants, and in selecting the most adequate workers for the job openings available.[19] After the 1923 military coup, the powers of the Mancomunitat were curtailed, and the regional government was finally dissolved in 1926. As a result, the institute's activities were drastically reduced. The period of Catalan leadership in the debate over work organization in Spain came to an abrupt end.

ECLECTICISM AND CONTINUED LABOR UNREST DURING THE 1920s AND 1930s

It is crucial to introduce the concept of *eclecticism* of organizational methods in order to understand the attempts of Spanish employers and managers to solve the labor problem under the Dictatorship of

---

17. In this respect see the Institute's journal, *Anals de l'Institut d'Orientació Professional* 1(1920) (1): 7–19, 20–23; (2) 4–11, 16–25; 2(1921) (1): 7–20, 21–25, 52–63. See also Mira y López, *Manual de orientación profesional* (1959).

18. *Anals de l'Institut d'Orientació Professional* 1(1920), No. 2:64–69; 2(1921), No. 2:79–82. My interpretation of the reports in *Anals* is different than the one given by Tomàs and Estivill (1979, p. 29), who claim that it was the Taylor System that was being introduced. Even in the case of the Elizalde auto-repair shop (where time-and-motion studies were being conducted at the time, but only on holidays) workers were encouraged to participate in the reorganization process, and there were no engineers involved.

19. Tomàs and Estivill (1979, p. 26).

the 1920s as well as the democratic Republic of the 1930s. The elements of eclecticism first appeared during the 1910s and early 1920s in Catalonia. During the late 1920s and 1930s, Spanish organizational experts continued to draw on selective elements (goals and techniques) from almost every available theory (vocational guidance, industrial psychology, psychometrics, physiology, scientific management) in order to assert managerial authority in the face of labor unrest. The goal was to achieve industrial peace, not to increase productivity. The approach was distinctively humanist and social-reformist, focusing on the upgrading of worker skills. In general, the drive to introduce selective elements of scientific management was no more than an attempt to become "scientific" in outlook. Mass-production principles were rejected in favor of a craft-based conception of work. The final result was a confusion of heterogenous, and certainly incompatible, goals and techniques that would hamper the theoretical and practical development of scientific management in Spain.

Certain political and economic events promoted the rise of an eclectic approach to organization. Characteristically, the Dictatorship of Miguel Primo de Rivera, captain general of the Catalonia military region, started in 1923 with a coup instigated by Catalan employers demanding a hard-line approach to the labor problem. Primo de Rivera's creed was one of authoritarianism, love of order, technocratic modernization of the economy, increased intervention in the labor arena, and collaboration with the (by anarchist standards) moderate UGT Socialist labor union. The anarchist CNT remained disorganized, divided, confused, and bitterly repressed throughout the 1920s. Meanwhile UGT's nationwide membership stagnated, despite its enormous growth in the Valencian region. On the whole, strike activity and working days lost dropped substantially.[20] The dictator's economic policy was aimed at the modernization of the country's infrastructure (railways, roads, electric power, oil refining and distribution), and the protection of industrial interests. A new trade tariff was passed in 1922 (the famous *Arancel de Cambó*), and then raised in 1926–28. The second industrial revolution finally came to Spain: telephone (Standard Eléctrica, an ITT subsidiary), home appliances and electrical machinery (with investments by AEG, Siemens, and General Electric), aircraft construction, and the auto parts industry (Pirelli and others).[21] The 1920s also witnessed a steady process of

20. Martin (1990, pp. 263–270).
21. Velarde Fuertes, *Política económica de la Dictadura* (1973, pp. 45–135); Tuñón de Lara (1984, pp. 61–63); Martin (1990, pp. 276–279).

industrial concentration and increasing establishment size in most sectors—iron and steel, shipbuilding, machinery, consumer goods, chemicals, and electric power—although no single firm employed more than 5,000 workers.[22]

The economic policy of the Dictatorship was by no means restricted to protectionism and public works. The other major component was its regulatory interventionism in the labor arena within an enhanced framework of corporatism. In 1926, a civilian labor minister heavily influenced by the social doctrine of the Catholic Church, Eduardo Aunós, introduced the first Spanish Labor Code (mostly a compilation of previous legislation), thus reinforcing the interventionism of the state. Furthermore, he designed and legislated a National Corporatist Organization, also of social Catholic inspiration and Italian influence, but lacking the unitary labor union organization of the fascist corporatist model of Italy, and later of Portugal or Austria. Aunós's corporatism was social rather than state corporatism; it aimed at articulating *existing* organized interests rather than creating a completely new structure. He believed in craftsmanship, harmony, and industrial arbitration. The corporatist legislation of 1926 included a thorough regulation of the long-standing *comités paritarios* (joint management-worker committees), which were not very effective due to their quite limited functions and the lack of trade-union freedom.[23]

The interventionism of the state was not a new phenomenon. Social legislation regulating working conditions started in the 1870s, when the ideology of the *Lumpenproletariat*—the unjust misery of the working classes—first gained wide support among the governing class.[24] The first information-gathering institution, the Commission for Social Reforms, was created in 1883. The Institute for Social Reforms (1903) accelerated legislative action, while the creation of the Labor Inspection Body (1906) provided the means, if insufficient,

---

22. Soto Carmona, *El trabajo industrial en la España contemporánea, 1874–1936* (1989, pp. 111–144). For a historical account of the major firms in the various industrial and service sectors throughout the twentieth century, see Voltes Bou, *Historia de la empresa española* (1979), and Roldán, García Delgado, and Muñoz (1973, vol. 2).

23. Aunós Pérez, *La organización corporativa del trabajo* (n.d., pp. 14–15, 18–20); Ben-Ami, *Fascism from Above* (1938, p. 209); Linz, "A century of politics and interests in Spain" (1981, pp. 378, 380–381); Martin (1990, pp. 270–276); Soto Carmona (1989, pp. 403–404, 414–415); Montoya Melgar (1975, pp. 58–62). On paper, of course, the *comités paritarios* were one of the central institutions of the National Corporatist Organization. See Ministro de Trabajo, Comercio e Industria, "Real Decreto-Ley de 26 de Noviembre de Organización Corporativa Nacional" (1926, pp. 402–405), and "Real Decreto de 30 de Julio de nueva redacción del artículo 17 del Real Decreto-Ley de 26 de Noviembre de 1926 de Organización Corporativa Nacional" (1928).

24. Montoya Melgar (1975, pp. 13–40).

to make employers comply. Another important event was the creation of the National Institute for Social Security (1908), which coordinated a series of regulations on working conditions, as well as health, old age, and life insurance schemes. The legislative work of the 1920s Dictatorship consolidated an interventionist, corporatist, and paternalistic model of labor relations in which free collective bargaining was not feasible.[25]

In 1924 and again in 1928 the Dictatorship reformed and placed vocational training under a centralized and state-controlled scheme similar to the one introduced by Germany in the 1930s, and radically different from the Brazilian model of private initiative. The former Institute for Vocational Guidance (IOP) in Barcelona, as well as the more recent one created in Madrid in the 1920s, became the major research and teaching institutions under the new system. The legislation presented industrial psychology and scientific management as the most important techniques to improve vocational training, perfect worker selection, and increase productivity. On paper, the eclecticism could not be greater: scientific management was to be combined with upgrading the skills of the worker.[26]

By 1930 the successes of the Dictatorship had become disasters: incapacity to create a new political class, charges of corruption, mismanagement of the currency, economic downturn, and withdrawal of army and Socialist support. After the resignation of the dictator, popular clamor and the results of local elections in 1931 sufficed to oust the discredited monarch, and a Republic was proclaimed. The Great Depression was shallower in Spain than in Germany or the United States. Nonetheless, business profits plunged, and unemployment more than doubled. A leftist Republican-Socialist coalition was in power until 1934, which allowed for the control of the labor ministry by the Socialists. Unionization immediately jumped to 46 percent of the non-agricultural workforce, up from a mere 13 percent in 1920. The Socialists introduced modern collective bargaining and codetermination institutions following the Weimar example. But the hegemonic control of the Socialist UGT—with the anarchist CNT remaining on the margins and occasionally participating in local re-

25. Martín Valverde, "La formación del Derecho del Trabajo en España" (1987, pp. xv–xxix, xlviii–lxxvii, c–cxiv); Soto Carmona (1989, pp. 256–286); García Fernández, *La formación del Derecho del Trabajo* (1984, pp. 237–249).

26. Ministro de Trabajo y Previsión, "Estatuto de formación profesional" (1928, pp. 99–112); Soto Carmona (1989, pp. 225–238); Tomàs and Estivill (1979, pp. 32–39); Mallart, "Cincuentenario del originariamente llamado Instituto de Orientación y Selección Profesional" (1974).

volts—undermined the role of collective bargaining and perverted the function of the joint employer-worker committees, especially after 1933. For their part, the employers created new representative organizations following a corporatist model, so as to lobby the government for tariff protection as well as state credits and contracts. The old cycles of mobilization, unionization, strikes, violence, and repression came back, becoming particularly evident with the repression during and after the failed two-week revolution during October 1934, in the northern coal-mining and steel region of Asturias, which claimed 1,500 lives.[27]

FACTORS PREVENTING THE ADOPTION OF SCIENTIFIC MANAGEMENT

Backwardness of the Industrial Structure. In contrast to the situation in Germany, the authority of Spanish employers in the workplace came under attack for reasons other than the staggering complexity of operations, long-term increases in the bureaucratization of manufacturing firms, or the increasing size of industrial establishments. From the technical point of view, the limited complexity of most production establishments in Spain meant that old-fashioned, unsystematic organizational practices were still effective. As a whole, the country's economic structure was so backward that firm size or bureaucratization had not reached critical levels during the 1920s or 1930s. For example, industrial bureaucratization in Spain was some thirty or forty years behind in terms of the American, British, or German levels.[28] Rather, employers' troubles with their workers derived from the combination of a backward, inefficient, and agrarian-based economy with radicalized and quite powerful labor organizations.

Isolation from the International Environment. In Spain, international economic pressures had very little impact on the behavior of employers and workers. The Spanish economy of the 1920s and 1930s was both backward *and* isolated from the international economy. Although Spanish firms depended on imports of expensive raw material and capital goods, international pressures by no means induced employers to cut costs. Overall, the dependence on world trade was relatively low. Exports and imports represented only 8 percent of the

---

27. Linz (1981, pp. 382–386); Martin (1990, pp. 297–310); Soto Carmona (1989, pp. 399–415).
28. See the comparative statistics in Appendix B.

national product in 1920, and 18 percent in 1929, compared to 33 percent in Germany and 48 percent in Britain.[29] Cartelization and state regulation of consumer prices provided for frequent price increases that rendered efficiency-boosting programs unnecessary from the point of view of the managers and shareholders. If Spanish employers did not feel any international economic pressures, neither did they think of themselves as being involved in any major international political or military contest. A feeling of national pessimism followed the 1898 colonial disaster that placed the country in an isolationist mood. Spain became a second-rank power, remaining neutral during World War I. In brief, international economic, political, diplomatic, or military pressures played virtually no role. Spanish management intellectuals and practitioners were rightly concerned with labor turmoil as the dominant challenge facing them.

Labor's Opposition to Scientific Management. The political and economic rebelliousness of labor was, then, the problem that Spanish employers had to deal with. Managerial authority came under attack repeatedly, both within firms and at the local, regional, and national levels. Spanish labor unions were successful in challenging traditional managerial authority and the legitimacy of the political system despite the frequent periods of acute labor repression. The cycles of labor-organization expansion, crisis, and repression show that the long-term problems of the organization of work and of maintaining managerial authority were never solved permanently. In this sense, Spanish labor forced employers to experiment with innovative organizational ideas.

But, unlike those in Germany, labor organizations never disclosed any intentions of promoting the point of view that increased production through scientific management could improve the welfare of the working class. Enrique Santiago, a member of the national commission of the Socialist union, UGT, aired his distrust of employers and engineers in 1929. He portrayed quite accurately the dominant type of Spanish industrialism as

a bunch of machines laid out capriciously, without organic plan; a bunch of bosses and aspiring bosses [*jefecillos*], ignorant enough so that they cannot tell the good from the bad; anybody makes a good boss, insofar as he is "tough" with workers, and it matters little that profits be low or null in appearance. Then the state's subsidy will be

29. See, again, the comparative statistics in Appendix B.

greater and the banks will be able to better control industry and commerce.[30]

Throughout the 1923–24 period the Socialist UGT remained the largest and best organized labor union. It seems clear from Santiago's writings that organized labor in Spain did not follow the German example with regard to industrial rationalization, although it favored collaboration with the authoritarian regime of the 1920s. During the Civil War, Communist, anarchist, and Socialist labor unions embarked on the collectivization of the economy, moving further away from any technocratic organizational ideas such as scientific management.[31]

Scarcity of Engineers. In contrast to the German, French, and American cases, no large engineering establishment was available in Spain in the 1920s that could have taken on the task of promoting scientific management. In 1900 Spain had 3.4 engineers per 1,000 industrial workers, compared to 5.8 in the United States or 4.4 in Germany. But while the American ratio increased to 10.5 by 1920, the Spanish ratio sank to 2.7. Clearly, the increase in engineering graduates was outpaced by the increase in industrial employment. Engineering education was designed after the French elitist model. The graduating classes remained small until the mid-1920s in spite of the educational reforms in the 1900s. Scientific management was not taught at engineering schools until late in 1928, and then only nominally, with no additional organizational or financial resources.[32] In 1929–30 Spain had 5.6 engineers per 1,000 workers versus 15.1 in the United States and 11.0 in Germany.[33] In addition, Spanish industry and engineers were highly dependent on technology transfers from other countries. Few innovative applications, either technical or organizational, were initiated or developed in Spain. Frequently, foreign patents helped

30. From *Boletín de la Unión General de Trabajadores de España* 1(3) (August 1929):3. Santiago also supported state-controlled worker training. See 2(21) (September 1930):1–3. Another article against rationalization appeared in the same journal, 3(25) (January 1931):29–37. The UGT's journal included uncritical references to industrial rationalization in the following issues: 1(4) (April 1929):10–11; 1(7) (July 1929):39; 1(9) (September 1929):1–10. These should not be taken, however, as support for Taylorism. See also Soto Carmona (1989, p. 240).

31. On this topic, see Martin (1990, pp. 386–394); Dolgoff, ed., *The Anarchist Collectives* (1974); Voltes Bou (1979, pp. 465–477).

32. Ministro de Economía Nacional, "Estatuto sobre formación técnica de ingenieros industriales y de investigación" (1928, p. 118).

33. See the comparative statistics in Appendix B.

to create profitable monopolies that discouraged further technical or efficiency improvements.[34] Finally, the official and voluntary engineering associations lacked the prestige and power of their American, German, or French counterparts, and never engaged in a program to promote the managerial role that engineers could play in industry. Moreover, engineers paid little attention to scientific management developments in other countries. The leading engineering journal in Spain published only eight brief notes on scientific management in the almost 1,300 weekly issues published between 1910 and 1936.[35]

Dominant Antimodernist Mentality. Modernism helped to promote the spread of scientific management in the United States and Germany. Spain (Catalonia in particular) did harbor a modernistic arts and crafts movement similar to the English and German ones of the turn of the century. This movement had its architectural expression in the works of the Catalan modernists. But, unlike that in Germany, and in certain respects similar to that in England, Catalan and Spanish modernism was displaced in the 1910s by an extremely revivalist, nostalgic, classicist, Brunellesquian, and baroquely monumentalist movement—*Noucentisme.*[36] This step backward occurred precisely when scientific management became available as a tool claiming to have an answer to the labor problem. As a result, no modernist mentality was present in Spain or in Catalonia during the late 1910s and the 1920s that could induce managerial elites to embrace scientific management. In this respect, the Spanish case clearly departs from the German one, where the Artistic Workshops, the experiments at the AEG company, and the Bauhaus school provided a sound justification for the implementation of scientific management and Fordism. Spanish literature of the turn of the century adopted an anti-industrialist character.[37]

34. Tuñón de Lara (1984). It is interesting to note that leading intellectual and higher-education figures of the pre-1936 period like Miguel de Unamuno collaborated to reinforce the traditional Spanish disdain towards the applied sciences. See, in particular, Unamuno, "Doctores en industrias" (1968, p. 693), and his famous 1906 letter to Ortega y Gasset in Robles, ed., *Epistolario completo Ortega-Unamuno* (1987, p. 42): "That they [the Europeans] invent things? Let them invent! The electric bulb illuminates here as well as where it was invented."

35. See *Revista Minera, Metalúrgica y de Ingeniería* 59(1918):150, 253–254, 525–528, 541–542; 70(1919):94–96, 390; 71(1920):211–213; 77(1926):33–37.

36. Bohigas, *Reseña y catálogo de la arquitectura modernista* (1973, p. 245); Sánchez, ed., *Barcelone 1888–1929* (1992).

37. Litvak, *A Dream of Arcadia* (1975).

The *Modernisme català* of 1888–1914 (i.e. between the dates of the Barcelona Universal Exhibition and the creation of the autonomous Mancomunitat government) was a result of the growth of industry, machinery, and the industrial proletariat in Catalonia. The movement's program included various components: an eclectic Gothic revival, a strong arts and crafts influence, decorative arts elements, a rational mechanicistic ideology, and a bent towards social revisionism. In fact, the anti-Taylorite Cipriano Montolíu, a devout student of Ruskin's social philosophy, theorized against the practical-utilitarian component of Catalan *Modernisme,* and in favor of its utopian exaltation of nature.[38] Catalan *Modernisme* (with Antoni Gaudí as its leading figure) was based on the experience of local metal manufacturers and engineers, as well as on the Mediterranean tradition of building with brick. As in Germany, it pursued a "total work of art" by means of integrating architecture, ornamentation, and interior design.[39] In 1903 or 1906 German architect Walter Gropius visited Josep Puig i Cadafalch (also an architect and president of the Mancomunitat in 1917–24), and was impressed by Catalan industrial design. But the Catalan modernist workshops, unlike their German counterparts, did not abandon craftsmanship principles in favor of mass production.[40]

Catalan and Spanish modernism did produce a handful of important industrial buildings as well as hospitals, health-care centers, and wine-production complexes.[41] Industrial architecture was taught at the Barcelona School of Industrial Engineering.[42] After World War I, however, Catalan and Spanish industrial architecture received only limited influence from the new rationalism of Behrens, Gropius, and Le Corbusier, as is evident in one of the period's best buildings, Antonio Puig i Gairalt's Myrurgia Cosmetics factory (1928–1930).[43] In fact, the stabilization of Catalan conservative nationalism with the creation of the Mancomunitat autonomous government in 1914 marked the decline in modernism in Catalonia, and, as a consequence,

38. Freixa, *El modernismo en España* (1986, pp. 38–39).

39. Bohigas (1973, pp. 62, 96–102, 107, 252, 254).

40. Mackay, *Modern Architecture in Barcelona 1854–1939* (1985, pp. 32, 34); Jardí, *Puig i Cadafalch* (1975).

41. Villalón and Plasencia, "La estela de Gaudí" (1992).

42. Freixa (1986, p. 75).

43. Mackay (1985, pp. 58–59); Cardellach i Avilés, "La enseñanza de la construcción en las escuelas de ingenieros" (1909–1910), *Las formas artísticas en la arquitectura técnica* (1916). For the new rationalism in Spanish architecture during the 1950s and 1960s, see Frampton, *Martorell, Bohigas, Mackay* (1985).

in the rest of Spain.[44] Reportedly, the only joint application of scientific management and modernistic or avant-garde architectural principles in Spain throughout the 1910s and 1920s took place at the experimental urban project of the Ciudad Lineal (Linear City) in Madrid under the direction of its founder and mastermind, Arturo Soria. According to one Taylorite, scientific management techniques were implemented at the tramway workshops of the Ciudad Lineal as well as at those of two other Spanish cities.[45] In the leading Spanish intellectual magazine of the 1920s and the 1930s, *Revista de Occidente* (*Review of the Western World*), the debate over machine-age modernism by no means reached the climax of the German discussion.[46] As a whole, avant-garde modernism in Spain failed to create the kind of intellectual atmosphere that played such an important role in the propagation of scientific management in Germany.

Lack of State Support. Also in sharp contrast with the German case, the Spanish state did little to promote scientific management and industrial rationalization during the 1920s and 1930s, concentrating its efforts in vocational training within the overall corporatist approach to social problems. A private National Committee for Scientific Organization of Labor (*Comité Nacional de Organización Científica del Trabajo*, CNOCT) was created in 1928, lacking both moral and financial support from the government. It was awarded "national interest" status only in 1935, one year before its activities were discontinued because of the Civil War. The CNOCT was only fully backed up by the Catalan employer association FTN and several engineering associations. Under these material circumstances, it could only organize a few lectures and publish a journal. The only palpable effect of state intervention consisted of a reinforcement of the trend towards organizational eclecticism. The state bureaucracy and the political elite regarded corporatism and social reformism as the only ways to address

44. Bohigas (1973, p. 245); Freixa (1986, p. 107).
45. Gual Villalbí, *Principios y aplicaciones de la organización científica del trabajo* (1929, pp. 11–12); Soria y Mata, *Conferencia dada en el Ateneo Científico y Literario de Madrid* (1894), *Buen negocio* (1907). See also Tomàs and Estivill (1979, p. 32); García Hernández and Calvo Barrios, *Arturo Soria: Un urbanismo olvidado* (1981); Collins and Flores, *Arturo Soria y la Ciudad Lineal* (1968).
46. Only a handful of articles in *Revista de Occidente,* including one by Le Corbusier, furthered modernist points of view: 20(1928):157–193; 32(1931):308–313; 37(1932):348–352; 50(1935):1–55, 308–317. But there were also strongly antimodernist articles: 35(1932):1–42, 121–166, 241–277. See also the famous essay by José Ortega y Gasset, *La deshumanización del arte* (1991), first published in 1925.

the labor problem. As a result, any private initiatives such as the CNOCT were clearly to be subordinated to the higher goals of professional and vocational education, and the upgrading of worker skills.[47] Not surprisingly, the president of the CNOCT, General José Marvá y Mayer, served for many years as president of the social-reformist National Institute for Social Security (INP) and as a high-ranking official at the Labor Ministry. His leadership was nonetheless pusillanimous—he was an octogenarian when the CNOCT was created. The state's actions were also conducive to an eclecticism of methods rather than to scientific management, despite the frequent use of the phrase *scientific organization of labor.*[48]

THE THEORETICAL FAILURE OF SCIENTIFIC MANAGEMENT

The challenge of labor unrest did not coincide with a combination of institutional factors that could promote the acceptance and implementation of scientific management ideas and techniques. The study of organizational ideology and practice in pre-1939 Spain is a complex endeavor. It is useful to distinguish three groups of management intellectuals and organizational experts: convinced Taylorites, eclectic Taylorites, and eclectic Taylorites-in-transition. Only three management intellectuals can be labeled as convinced Taylorites. Leonardo Leprévost, a chemical engineer and lecturer at the Barcelona School of Industrial Engineering, worked for a steel company in the 1910s when he started studying and applying scientific management techniques. He was utterly convinced of the need to increase production, and attempted to implement scientific methods despite the frequent "bloody outrages" (in reference to anarchist violence). He defended Taylor's ideas, methods, and findings as "irrefutable." Moreover, he was explicitly against the vocational training of workers, arguing that scientific management could eliminate the need for skilled labor. He also criticized the charge by Catalan industrial psychologists that Taylorism sacrificed quality for quantity.[49] The second unreserved Taylorite was Emilio D'Ocón Cortés, an industrial engineer, who, after proposing the United States as an example to imitate, advocated for the "great role" that the state must assume in the application of Tay-

47. Ministro de Trabajo y Previsión (1928, p. 112).
48. On the CNOCT, see Tomàs and Estivill (1979, pp. 39–43).
49. Leprévost, *Economía industrial y administración de talleres* (1933, pp. 47–49, 258, 264–265). The book was first published in 1928. The author's only departure from Taylorism is his quite favorable assessment of profit sharing (1933, p. 207), which he based on Ford's programs.

lorism.[50] The third convinced Taylorite, Pedro Gual Villalbí, was the most important because of his strong political connections. An economist by training and secretary of the powerful Catalan employer lobby FTN, Gual Villalbí pursued a distinguished political career both before and after the Civil War that eventually catapulted him to the cabinet. He was one of the most important members of the CNOCT organization, taught production management at schools of commerce, and defended Taylor's viewpoints vigorously.[51]

The group of eclectic Taylorites was far more numerous. The paramount example is CNOCT's president, General José Marvá y Mayer, for whom Taylorism could be successfully implemented in Spain only if workers were allowed more discretion and it were introduced after considerable vocational training had taken place.[52] César de Madariaga y Rojo—a mining engineer, director of the world's largest quicksilver mining complex at Almadén, professor of engineering, and the most active member of the CNOCT—was another of the proponents of scientific management with "a human concern."[53] Javier Ruiz Almansa, a statistician by training, was the eclectic Taylorite who came closest to a human relations approach when he discussed the "sociological doctrine of human groups," the "moral factors behind productivity," and the firm as a "hierarchical system led by a boss" who must show a capacity for self-control. But he defended Taylorite principles as well.[54] José María Tallada—a lawyer, industrial engineer, and manager of several service-sector companies—was one of the few Catalan organizational experts who participated in the three most important institutions: the Barcelona Social Museum, the Catalan Institute for Vocational Guidance, and the CNOCT. He was convinced of the "neutral position" of the engineer in industrial society, and his "moral

50. See D'Ocón Cortés, *Organización científica del trabajo y racionalización de la producción* (1927, pp. 176–181).

51. Gual Villalbí (1929, pp. 347–369).

52. Marvá y Mayer, *Organización científica del trabajo antes y después de la guerra actual* (1917, pp. 43–53).

53. Madariaga y Rojo, *Organización científica del trabajo.* Vol. 1. *Las ideas* (ca. 1930, pp. 26–27, 89). See also his articles in *Revista de Organización Científica* (hereafter abbreviated as *ROC*): 2(1931):388–409; 3(1933):537–558; 4(1935):649–673. The author exiled himself in Latin America after 1939. He published a second book, *Iniciación al estudio del factor humano en la actividad económica* (1953), in which he still appears as an eclectic Taylorist.

54. Ruiz Almansa, *Manual práctico de organización científica del trabajo* (1929, pp. 22, 24, 72–73, 95–96, 99). See also his articles in *ROC*: 1(2) (1928):19–29; 2(1931): 483–505.

responsibility" to help solve the emerging problems of industrialism.[55] Other lesser figures of this group of eclectic Taylorites included Ramón Blanco y Pérez del Camino, Domingo Sert (the president of the employer organization FTN), and Pedro Pi y Suñer (a Republican politician).

Finally, the group of eclectic Taylorites-in-transition is by no means a residual category. It includes the management intellectuals who were eclectic Taylorites before 1939, and then unequivocally became human relations proponents after the war. The most important exponent of this group was José Mallart, a pedagogue and industrial psychologist, who published several important books and articles drawing on both scientific management and human relations.[56] Another figure in this group is Antidio Layret Foix, an industrial engineer of the large La Maquinista machine-tool and transportation-equipment company in Barcelona.[57] Both Mallart and Layret Foix became important human relations proponents during the 1950s and 1960s.

The results from a content analysis of the CNOCT's official journal, the *Revista de Organización Científica (ROC, Journal of Scientific Organization)*, are quite puzzling. (The analysis follows the guidelines specified in Appendix A.) Although most articles have been classified as scientific management, their authors also published human relations articles in the same journal (and sometimes within the same year), or wrote entire books in which they presented human relations views (e.g. Mallart). This was not true of the authors of German scientific management articles in this period, and thus the idea of the triumph of organizational eclecticism is further reinforced (see Table 4.1).

THE LIMITED IMPLEMENTATION OF SCIENTIFIC MANAGEMENT TECHNIQUES

All available studies on the practical implementation of scientific management in Spain before the Civil War agree that only a few isolated

55. Tallada, *L'organització científica de la indústria* (1922, pp. 21–23, 96–98), "El ingeniero social" (1912). His only article in *ROC*, however, was purely Taylorite: 2(1931):3–5.

56. Mallart, *El factor humano en la organización del trabajo* (1922, pp. 5–6, 8, 30–31, 31); *La organización científica del trabajo doméstico* (1933); *Organización científica del trabajo agrícola* (1934). See also his articles in *ROC:* 1(1) (1928):39–43; 1(2) (1928): 8–18; 1(4–5) (1929):7–10, 28–33, 39–45; 1(6) (1929):3–8; 2(1930):113–138, 156–162; 3(1933):573–577; 4(1934):1–47, 140–147; 4(1935):433–438. Also important are the articles by Genoveva Palacios, who married Mallart in the 1930s: 1(3) (1929):33–38; 1(4–5) (1929):46–55; 1(6) (1929):23–25.

57. See his two articles in *ROC:* 2(1931):506–514; 3(1932):16–20.

TABLE 4.1 Results of the content analysis of the articles and lengthy book reviews published in the *Revista de Organización Científica* (*ROC*), 1928–1936, by paradigm (SM: scientific management; HR: human relations; SA: structural analysis; NC: not classifiable)

A. Number of articles mentioning each of the content categories (see Appendix A) and themes (21 articles examined)

Content Categories	SM	HR	SA
Perceived problem	13	3	0
Form of solution	2	0	0
View of conflict	0	3	0
View of workers	0	1	0
Fascination with	2	0	0
Methodology	12	0	0
Selection of workers	7	0	0
Distribution of tasks	6	0	0
Authority structures	2	1	0
Process of work	5	0	0
Preferred rewards	4	2	0
Economic incentives	4	0	1

B. Number of articles (*N*) and themes classified by paradigm

	SM				HR				SA				NC
		Themes				Themes				Themes			
Year Period	*N*	Mean	Min	Max	*N*	Mean	Min	Max	*N*	Mean	Min	Max	*N*
1928–30	8	2.9	1	5	2	3.0	2	4	0	—	—	—	0
1931–33	5	3.4	2	5	1	2.0	2	2	0	—	—	—	0
1934–36	3	5.0	4	6	0	—	—	—	0	—	—	—	2
All years	16	3.4	1	6	3	2.7	2	4	0	—	—	—	2
Pages	275	17.2	2	71	18	6.0	4	6	0	—	—	—	12

Sources: The articles included in the analysis are the following:

SM: *ROC* 1(1):9–20, 39–43; 1(2):8–18; 1(3):33–38; 1(6):3–8, 23–25; 2:3–5, 113–138, 276–279, 388–409, 483–505, 506–514; 3:537–558; 4:1–47, 649–673; 5:1–72.

HR: *ROC* 1(4–5):39–45; 2:156–162; 3:16–20.

NC: *ROC* 4:140–147; 4:433–438.

experiences took place, as with the handful of small Barcelona firms and the experiments at the Ciudad Lineal in Madrid during the late 1910s described above. At the state-run armaments factory in Trubia, Asturias, the "Taylor method" was reportedly introduced with excellent results. In fact, managers there only experimented with various piecework methods.[58] Only 7 firms (mostly in the metal sector) out

58. See the report in the daily *El Sol* by Moreno Caracciolo, "El método Taylor en la fábrica de Trubia" (1919).

of the 125 surveyed in 1962 had introduced time-and-motion study in the 1920s, and only 3 more did so during the 1930s. In contrast, 10 firms introduced that technique during the 1940s, and 97 during the 1950s.[59] According to two prominent postwar management experts, scientific management was implemented comprehensively only in 3 firms: La Maquinista (mechanical equipment), Perfumerías Gal (consumer goods), and Standard Eléctrica (telephone equipment). These were among the most advanced, forward-looking, and bureaucratized firms in the country.[60] As José Mallart concluded, scientific management in Spain before 1939 was a "theoretical rather than a practical" movement.[61] The contrast with American and German developments could not be sharper, not only in the application of scientific management techniques but also, and most important, in the introduction of Fordist mass-production systems.

The case of Spain before 1939 shows remarkable differences from the German case. With no generalized changes in the economic structure of the country and its industrial firms, and no intention of competing on the international market, Spanish employers and managers concentrated their attention on the problem of labor turmoil. Radical and politicized labor unions posed threats that invited old-fashioned approaches (repression) rather than the detached, scientific solutions offered by Taylorism, although the Taylorite line was also pursued, with little success. During the Second Republic (1931–36), employers became again more worried about working-class mobilization and resorted to organized lobbying rather than to improved organization of work.[62] The absence of state support, the relative scarcity of engineers and limited influence of their professional associations, and the lack of an elite modernist mentality that might have favored the adoption of Taylorism led to the ideological and technical failure of scientific management in Spain before 1939. Excluding the particular case of the Soviet Union, Germany and Spain during the 1920s and early 1930s represent two extreme cases in the sense that all factors conducive to the success of scientific management were present in Germany but absent in Spain.

59. Pintado Fe and Torres Márquez, *Las técnicas de medida y retribución del trabajo en las empresas españolas* (1965, p. 22); Vegara, *La organización científica del trabajo. ¿Ciencia o ideología?* (1971, pp. 42–44).

60. Author's interviews with Fermín de la Sierra (May 31, 1989) and Alberto Pintado Fe (June 1, 1989), both conducted in Madrid.

61. Mallart, *Organización científica del trabajo* (1942, p. 76).

62. See Cabrera, *La patronal ante la II República* (1983).

Changing International, Economic, and Labor Problems During the Franco Regime, 1939–1975

The Civil War of 1936–39 ended with the victory of the nationalist front lead by General Francisco Franco. Under the new authoritarian regime, employers and managers faced a shifting combination of problems that required different organizational approaches. The Spanish economy underwent two distinct phases. During the first phase of international isolation and economic self-sufficiency, the labor problem was kept under control by means of sheer repression. Employers dealt with the scarcities resulting from economic isolation by implementing scientific management techniques so as to reduce waste and raise productivity. During the second phase of economic liberalization and indicative planning after 1953, the labor problem became pressing again, while international isolation was broken, and the economy became fully industrialized. Spanish employers and managers resorted then to human relations as the major source of ideological inspiration.

INTERNATIONAL AND LABOR PROBLEMS DURING THE YEARS OF ISOLATION, 1939–1952

Spain's economy underwent a long period of stagnation from the end of the Civil War in 1939 until the early 1950s. Production levels plummeted below those for 1929, not so much because of the destruction of industrial facilities and infrastructure during the war (which was fairly limited) but because of the disorganization of management and labor and the international economic and political blockade imposed on the country. Germanophile and protofascist at first, the Franco regime modified its stand towards the belligerents in World War II several times in order to maximize its chances of survival. As it became obvious that the allies would ultimately prevail, trade with the axis powers was drastically curtailed. The United States ignored and isolated Spain until the early 1950s, excluding her from the Marshall Plan. Britain and France followed a more realistic policy, establishing limited trade relations. General Charles de Gaulle was quoted as saying, in reference to Spain's most important source of hard currency, that "there is no such a thing as a fascist orange."[63] Bad crops, recurrent inflationary crises, high trade tariffs, and the

---

63. I am grateful to Professor Fernando Guirao of Yale University for this quotation.

resolve of the regime to achieve economic self-sufficiency were the main characteristics of the "years of hunger." State-administered import-substitution industrialization was the way chosen to achieve growth. But during the 1940s Spain's domestic product (calculated at factor costs) grew at an annual rate of only 1.3 percent. In 1940, 51 percent of the labor force was in agriculture, up from 46 percent in 1930. The share of agricultural employment would not again fall below 1930 levels until the mid-1950s.[64]

The authoritarian regime of Franco devoted much attention to the problem of labor unrest. In fact, most of the opposition to the 1936 army coup leading to the initial impasse and the Civil War had come from the working class. A new institutional framework was designed, including a single party (*Movimiento Nacional*), and a single, vertical union (*Organización Sindical*). The Falangist ideology of the regime's party and union conceived "a corporative system to integrate the defeated working class, disciplining it and at the same time giving it more symbolic than real participation in the new state," which was to be run by the army and the higher civil servants representing middle-class conservative values as well as business and landed interest groups.[65] The 1938 Labor Act (*Fuero del Trabajo*) sanctioned administrative controls of wages and working conditions, state paternalism, and the employers' right to control in the firm. Free unions were banned, and repression of left-wing union leaders became rampant. Execution, imprisonment, or exile was the outcome for perhaps one in every ten of the 3 million militant union members of 1939. The strategy proved successful for the regime: only a few, scattered (illegal) strikes took place until the early 1950s.[66] Spanish employers and managers were certainly not facing a labor unrest problem in the 1940s, thanks to the corporatist framework put in place by the new regime and the effectiveness of repression. Labor protest and sabotage were kept at historical lows. The problems encountered by employers and managers had more to do with international political and economic isolation, i.e. improving the employment of vital resources

64. Payne, *The Franco Regime 1936–1975* (1987, pp. 266–396); González, *La economía política del Franquismo* (1979, pp. 36, 115); Tamames (1986, p. 14).

65. Linz (1981, p. 387). See also, Linz, "An authoritarian regime: Spain" (1964), and "From Falange to Movimiento-Organización" (1970); De Miguel, *Sociología del Franquismo* (1975).

66. Amsden, *Collective Bargaining and Class Conflict in Spain* (1972, pp. 42–43, 78–81); Maravall, *Dictatorship and Political Dissent* (1978, pp. 66–70); Fishman, *Working-Class Organization and the Return of Democracy in Spain* (1990, pp. 88–89).

(raw materials, capital, labor), and difficulties in introducing new machinery, equipment, and technology.

Industrial Growth and Structural Changes. One of the most important pillars for the policy of economic self-sufficiency, and later for the implementation of scientific management, was the National Institute for Industry (*Instituto Nacional de Industria,* INI), a state-owned holding company. It was created in 1941 to increase production, reduce monopoly practices, and achieve national self-sufficiency in certain basic industrial sectors such as iron, steel, refined oil, chemicals, fertilizers, gas and electricity, shipbuilding, aircraft building, and armaments. It succeeded in increasing production but ran just short of achieving self-sufficiency, and certainly failed to reduce monopoly practices. The INI was extremely successful in introducing modern mass-production and continuous-flow techniques in a variety of industrial sectors with the creation of several automotive, chemical, and petrochemical companies, sometimes with limited foreign technology and capital.[67] At first industrial and service employment growth remained sluggish, and the bureaucratization of industry stayed comparatively low, but there were indications that industrial growth was picking up. The number of administrative employees per production worker in manufacturing industries in 1950 was less than half the number for the United States, Britain, or Germany. But the relevant comparison is that the Spanish bureaucratization ratio stood in 1950 at roughly the same level as that of Germany during the early 1920s or the United States during the 1910s, precisely when scientific management started to gain acceptance there. Moreover, bureaucratization and firm complexity were growing rapidly in most industrial sectors. Spanish industrial firms in the 1940s and 1950s were on average only somewhat smaller than in Japan, Italy, Britain, or France, although there were fewer firms with more than 1,000 workers. Industrial and service employment also advanced relative to agriculture.[68] The growing size, complexity, and bureaucratization of industrial firms was creating new technical challenges, as management intellectuals of the period were quick to point out. Numerous scien-

---

67. Tamames (1986, pp. 92–93, 129–130); Schwartz and González, *Una historia del Instituto Nacional de Industria* (1978, pp. 48–75).

68. See the comparative data in De Miguel and Linz, "Características estructurales de las empresas españolas" (1964b, p. 11). See also the comparative statistics in Appendix B.

tific management techniques were implemented to cope with the situation.

ENGINEERS, MILITARY OFFICERS, AND THE SUCCESS OF SCIENTIFIC MANAGEMENT

Apart from the industrial growth, structural changes in firms, and international isolation, the 1940s and early 1950s brought an increasing influence of engineers in economic policy-making and in managerial circles. INI's leadership fell victim to an engineering mentality that put technical effectiveness over any other consideration like profitability or social cost. Another form of their mental servitude was the obsessive emphasis on economies of scale and administrative centralization.[69] Moreover, many of the INI engineers were army or navy engineers, with an added authoritarian mentality and useful political connections in the higher spheres of the regime. The paramount figure was navy officer and engineer Juan Antonio Suanzes, longtime manager at several navy shipyards, minister of industry twice (1938–39, and 1945–51), and first president of the INI (1941–63). Suanzes was born in the same town as Franco, and had a longstanding friendship with him. An extreme nationalist, Suanzes was obsessed with Spain's industrial independence, the development of national economic forces, the need to put an end to the export of Spanish raw materials to other countries, and the lack of entrepreneurial initiatives. Suanzes was against private business interest groups, but often played into their hands. He hoped to be able to help Spain become a leading industrial power organized after corporatist principles, and to liberate Spaniards from their "inferiority complex."[70] The centrality of Suanzes to the success of scientific management during the 1940s and 1950s lies in his productivist ideology as head of the INI, and in his leading role in the foundation of the National Institute for the Rationalization of Work (*Instituto Nacional de Racionalización del Trabajo*, INRT). The use of the term *rationalization* owed much to German influence. In fact, the introduction of scientific management in Spain after the Civil War followed in part the Weimar Republic's corporatist solution to economic development, organizational innovation, and labor policy, although it occurred in the absence of a free labor movement.

69. Schwartz and González (1978, pp. 26–29, 34); Moya, *El poder económico en España 1939–1970* (1975, pp. 208–217).
70. Suanzes, *Ocho discursos* (1963, pp. 116, 127–128); Schwartz and González (1978, pp. 16–21); De Miguel (1975, pp. 52–54).

The INRT was created in 1946 to promote the implementation of scientific management, standardization and normalization, and industrial psychology. Unlike the institutions created in Spain during the 1910s and 1920s, the INRT was to be endowed with enough resources to achieve its goals. Its first president was Aureo Fernández Avila, a doctor in naval engineering, member of the board of directors of the INI, and vice-president of several large, state-owned shipbuilding, steel, and automotive companies.[71] Fermín de la Sierra, an industrial engineer, was named director of the scientific management department.[72] The INRT quickly became an active and influential organization, comparable to the German RKW. Numerous groups of industrial engineers, often with top management experience, collaborated with the INRT, and published articles or books in which they theorized about scientific management, proposed how to implement it, and described their own experiences.[73] A somewhat smaller group of army and navy engineers was also active in the INRT.[74]

71. See his articles in the INRT's journal *Racionalización:* 1(1948):129–132; 3(1950):81–92.

72. See *Racionalización* 1(1948):33–38. See also De la Sierra's articles in *Racionalización:* 2(1949):209–224; 4(1951):1–14.

73. The most outstanding Taylorite industrial engineers were [with their articles indicated in brackets]: Antonio Aceña, of the state-owned railway system RENFE [*Racionalización* 4(1951):161–166]; José Antonio de Artigas, also a member of the Francoist *Cortes* [*Racionalización* 1(1948):3–6]; Ciriaco Catalina, of Marconi Española [*Racionalización* 11(1958):393–400]; Franciso Donis Ortiz [*Racionalización* 9(1956): 481–488; 10(1957):10–16, 104–111, 203–210, 299–304, 392–397, 509–514]; José Echaide [*Racionalización* 4(1951):15–19]; Pío González Alvarez, of RENFE [*Racionalización* 9(1956):389–395; 13(1960):265–282]; Eduardo Labrandero, of RENFE [*Racionalización* 2(1949):353–371]; Baltasar Márquez [*Racionalización* 3(1950):13–18]; Emilio Peñas Penela [15(1962):647–654]; Víctor Rubio de Arriba ["Organización y productividad" (1950); *Racionalización* 2(1949):65–76]; Ernesto Ruiz Palá, of Hispano-Olivetti [*Racionalización* 8(1955):197–205]; José Sacristán Castelló, time-and-motion chief engineer at Standard Eléctrica [*Racionalización* 5(1952):489–502]; Félix San José, of the large construction company Agromán [*Racionalización* 5(1952):97–103]; Carlos Velasco Miguel, of Standard Eléctrica [*Aumento de productividad mediante el establecimiento de grupos de trabajo progresivo* (n.d.)]; Manuel Villar Lopesinos, of RENFE [*Racionalización* 3(1950):305–322]. Also Taylorite was Ricardo Ibarrola Monasterio, the director of the National Institute for Industrial Psychology [*Racionalización* 3(1950):1–12; 9(1956):106–112]. See also Rius Sintes, *Organización industrial* (1940).

74. The most outstanding Taylorite army and navy engineers were [with their articles indicated in brackets]: Antonio González de Guzmán [*Racionalización* 1(1948): 72–80; 8(1955):397–405]; Franciso Lucini Bayod [*Racionalización* 5(1952):9–15; 6(1953):328–338]; Florentino Moreno Ultra [*Racionalización* 4(1951):321–343; *Problemas y experiencias de organización científica en construcción naval* (n.d.); *Organización de los talleres de herreros de rivera de un astillero* (n.d.)].

Thus, engineers became very engaged in the management of industrial firms.[75] Finally, scientific management also had adepts among economists. Professor José Castañeda, one of the leading academic economists of the 1940s and 1950s, taught scientific management at the Madrid School of Industrial Engineers.[76] In the early 1970s the teaching of scientific management was still being justified because "it requires less training and intelligence" on the side of the worker.[77] Pedro Gual Villalbí, the old Taylorite of the pre-1939 period, continued doing behind-the-scene lobbying in favor of scientific management as secretary general of the Catalan employer association FTN, member and president of the National Economic Council, and minister without portfolio in several of Franco's governments (1957–65).[78]

The results from a content analysis of the official journal of the INRT (*Racionalización*)—the only widely-circulated management journal during this period—document the theoretical success of scientific management, especially after the late 1940s, although human relations articles were also frequent (see panel B of Table 4.2). Panel A of the table shows that there was an emphasis on techniques (time-and-motion study, specialization, division of labor, work simplification and standardization, wage systems, piecework), but not on the ideological component of the paradigm. This finding is consistent with the mix of organizational problems of the time, which had much to do with international isolation and low productivity, and little with labor unrest. Except for one of the authors, there was no evidence of a modernist fascination with machinery, technology, factory aesthetic, and mass production, in sharp contrast with German scientific managers.

THE ADOPTION OF SCIENTIFIC MANAGEMENT TECHNIQUES

During the 1940s and 1950s many Spanish firms implemented scientific management techniques in their workshops, and introduced mass-production systems. Half of the 40 companies surveyed by the

75. See De Miguel and Linz, "Nivel de estudios del empresariado español" (1964a, pp. 262, 264, 275).

76. Castañeda, *Apuntes de organización de empresas industriales* (1959, pp. 10–12, 14–22, 166–177, 236–310). See also his article in *Racionalización* 10(1957): 497–508.

77. Alcain and Lacalle, "La organización científica del trabajo" (1971, p. 68 n. 15).

78. Gual Villalbí, *Política de la producción* (1948, pp. 411–419). See also De Miguel (1975, pp. 169–171).

TABLE 4.2 Results of the content analysis of the articles and lengthy book reviews published in *Racionalización*, 1948–71, by paradigm (SM: scientific management; HR: human relations; SA: structural analysis; NC: not classifiable)

A. Number of articles mentioning each of the content categories (see Appendix A) and themes (88 articles examined)

Content Categories	SM	HR	SA
Perceived problem	20	20	2
Form of solution	6	0	3
View of conflict	3	14	1
View of workers	6	16	0
Fascination with	1	19	1
Methodology	31	6	1
Selection of workers	8	4	0
Distribution of tasks	20	1	2
Authority structures	1	31	5
Process of work	15	4	4
Preferred rewards	19	10	3
Economic incentives	18	2	0

B. Number of articles (N) and themes classified by paradigm

	SM				HR				SA				NC
		Themes				Themes				Themes			
Year Period	N	Mean	Min	Max	N	Mean	Min	Max	N	Mean	Min	Max	N
1948–50	9	3.7	1	7	3	2.7	2	4	0	—	—	—	1
1951–53	8	4.8	1	8	7	4.6	2	6	0	—	—	—	1
1954–56	7	4.1	2	7	9	3.0	1	4	0	—	—	—	1
1957–59	8	2.8	1	4	3	2.0	2	2	0	—	—	—	0
1960–62	3	2.7	2	3	2	3.0	3	3	3	3.7	3	5	4
1963–65	2	2.5	2	3	2	4.0	3	5	0	—	—	—	0
1966–68	3	4.3	3	7	4	3.8	3	4	0	—	—	—	0
1969–71	0	—	—	—	6	2.8	1	5	0	—	—	—	2
All years	40	3.7	1	8	36	3.3	1	6	3	3.7	3	5	9
Pages	356	8.9	4	22	225	6.2	2	15	17	5.7	4	8	65

Sources: The articles included in the analysis are the following:

SM: *Racionalización* 1:129–132; 2:65–76, 209–224, 273–282, 353–371; 3:1–12, 13–18, 243–247, 305–322; 4:1–14, 15–19, 161–166, 321–343; 5:9–15, 97–103, 489–502; 6:328–338; 7:386–394; 8:197–205, 397–405, 490–499; 9:1–7, 106–112, 389–395, 481–488; 10:10–16, 104–111, 203–210, 299–304, 392–397, 497–508, 509–514; 11:393–400; 13:265–282; 15:257–262, 647–654; 18:401–406, 519–525; 19:118–124; 21:230–243, 372–382.

HR: *Racionalización* 1:81–84; 3:93–97, 385–394; 4:167–178, 179–183; 5:305–310, 404–413; 6:1–11, 321–327, 417–420; 7:97–103, 283–288; 8:193–196; 9:8–23, 193–199, 289–300, 301–306, 396–402, 489–497; 11:9–13, 137–142; 12:143–146; 14:138–145, 265–272; 16:133–143; 18:289–297; 19:273–279, 280–288, 366–372; 21:83–89; 22:209–214; 24(4):12–19, (5):13–19, 20–23, (10):41–44, (12):17–19.

SA: *Racionalización* 13:641–649; 15:385–390, 522–526.

NC: *Racioalización* 1:7–15; 6:81–88; 8:297–306; 14:257–264, 391–394, 524–533, 654–660; 15:9–14, 391–396; 22:21–31, 295–298.

INRT in 1949 used time-and-motion studies and other scientific management techniques.[79] Four-fifths of the 125 industrial companies surveyed in 1962 had introduced time-and-motion studies for the first time during the 1950s.[80] The companies that implemented scientific management most comprehensively were the new firms created with foreign capital and technology that could benefit from the momentum of industrial growth created by the state-sponsored import-substitution policies and investments. Marconi Española and Standard Eléctrica (telephone and communications equipment), Hispano-Olivetti (typewriters, office equipment), and SEAT (a mixed public-private auto maker).[81] Also, new or totally revamped state-owned companies (the automotive company ENASA, the state railway system RENFE, and several navy shipyards, army arsenals, and other state-owned shipbuilding companies) were in the vanguard of the implementation of scientific management. Equally important and widespread were the activities of new consulting and engineering firms, of which Bedaux Española (created in 1940, and restructured in 1953) was the most important.[82] The Bedaux engineers successfully introduced new work arrangements and incentive systems based on time-and-motion studies at the Duro-Felguera metals company in the northern region of Asturias in 1953. The workers resisted the plan and staged a strike. The swift mediation of the Ministry of Labor created adequate conditions for the in-house engineers and the Bedaux consultants to proceed with the implementation.[83]

The theoretical and practical success of scientific management in Spain during the 1940s and early 1950s came about as a result of a situation quite different from the one prevalent in the 1920s and 1930s. The economic structure of the economy, and of industrial firms, had changed considerably. Spanish manufacturing firms around 1950 had degrees of bureaucratization similar to those of German

79. *Racionalización,* "La organización científica en la industria española" (1949).

80. Pintado Fe and Torres Márquez (1965, p. 22); Vegara (1971, pp. 42–44).

81. On SEAT, see the report by Pablo A. Vidal y Rius, a production engineer, in ASP, *Problemas de personal* (1960, pp. 72–88).

82. Egurbide, "El 'consulting' en España" (1976); Molero, "Las empresas de ingeniería" (1979). On Charles Bedaux's interview with General Franco in 1940, see Christy, *The Price of Power* (1984, pp. 207, 210–211).

83. There were, of course, other episodes of labor resistance like the one at the Duro-Felguera metals company in Asturias in 1953. In this case, Fermín de la Sierra of the INRT was immediately proposed by the Ministry of Labor to intermediate in the dispute, which was resolved rather quickly. Author's interviews with Fermín de la Sierra (May 31, 1989) and Alberto Pintado Fe (June 1, 1989).

and American firms back in the 1920s, that is, precisely when scientific management was adopted there. The country's political and economic isolation produced considerable problems. The policy of economic self-sufficiency used scientific management to ameliorate the situation. Worker power and unrest was at an all-time low. Accordingly, any worker opposition to scientific management could be easily overcome.[84] Numerous groups of industrial and military engineers were available to suggest applications and guide the implementation. State financial and moral support was also plentiful. The only condition that did not directly invite Taylorization was the absence of a modernist elite mentality.

ECONOMIC GROWTH, RENEWED LABOR PROBLEMS, AND HUMAN RELATIONS, 1953–1973

After the mid-1950s new economic and political developments would set different conditions for the debate about the organization of work. The 1950s were the decade of Spain's readmittance into the Western world, and of the liberalization of the economy. First, the United States approved foreign economic aid to Spain for 1952, and then signed a tremendously important treaty of friendship and cooperation (both military and economic) in 1953. Second, two years later, Spain joined the United Nations. Third, after 1957 a new economic team in the cabinet introduced various fiscal and monetary measures aimed at liberalizing the economy, allowing Spain to become a member of the International Monetary Fund and the Organization for European Economic Cooperation. These actions culminated in 1959 with a very successful economic stabilization program. Between 1954 and 1959 Spain's economic growth reached an annual cumulative rate of 3.8 percent.[85] After a brief recession following stabilization in 1959, several crucial economic forces had been set into motion: foreign investment provided for badly needed capital and technology; the labor surplus of perhaps 2 million workers (over 20 percent of the labor force) migrated mainly to Western Europe, thus helping to alleviate social tensions, and contributing to capital formation and to the balance of payments with their considerable money remittances; the tourism industry flourished; and renewed access to internationally cheap credit, energy, and raw materials helped to make many Spanish industrial products competitive. The only setback was the denial of

84. Consider the episode at Duro-Felguera in 1953 described in note 83.
85. González (1979, pp. 126, 130); De Miguel (1975, pp. 63–67, 223–226, 331–337); Payne (1987, pp. 450–493).

European Economic Community membership in 1962, which pleased certain protectionist industrial interests. After 1964, French-style indicative development plans were introduced to stimulate growth and improve social standards of living.[86] Although the plans did not achieve their goals of comprehensive *social* development or the reduction of regional and class-related differences, the economy grew at an average annual cumulative rate of 7.5 percent in 1963–69.[87] Industrial and service employment at last increased substantially, at the expense of agriculture. By 1970, over one-third of the labor force was employed in industry, and nearly two-fifths in the service sector, leaving only 27 percent in agriculture. Spain had finally joined the club of the industrialized countries.

Structural and Economic Changes. Abundant foreign investment and rapid economic growth resulted in the consolidation of modern mass-production and continuous-flow industries. In fact, several new export-oriented foreign firms established production facilities in the automotive, chemical, electromechanical, and consumer goods sectors. Manufacturing firms became more bureaucratized, shifting from 9.5 administrative per 100 production employees in 1950 to 15.3 in 1970. Salaried managers were becoming more numerous than entrepreneurs in Spanish firms, especially in the larger ones, and managers' educational levels were rising. The size of top management teams increased rapidly during this period. Although these changes were important, it is significant to note that bureaucratization levels in Spain were about half those in the United States, Germany, or Britain. This enormous difference had implications for the capacity of firms to implement advanced organizational techniques, as will be discussed below.[88]

86. García Delgado, "Crecimiento y cambio industrial en España 1960–1980." (1980, pp. 15–16, 18). On foreign investments, see Muñoz, Roldán, and Serrano, *La internacionalización del capital en España* (1978); Martínez González-Tablas, *Capitalismo extranjero en España* (1979).

87. See the two influential sociological reports by the Fundación Foessa, ed., *Informe sociológico sobre la situación social de España 1966* (1966), and *Informe sociológico sobre la situación social de España 1970* (1970).

88. This can be inferred from a 1959–60 cross-sectional survey of Spanish business stratified by region and firm size conducted by Linz and De Miguel. The cross-sectional differences observed by age of the entrepreneurs, heirs, and managers of the firms, as well as between more- and less-developed regions and by firm size, allow for the rough inference of longitudinal trends. See Linz and De Miguel, "Fundadores, herederos y directores en las empresas españolas" (1963–1964, vol. 21, pp. 17, 19; vol. 22, pp. 16, 24–28), and "El prestigio de las profesiones en el mundo empresarial" (1963b);

New Outburst of Labor Unrest.   Economic growth and bureaucratization, as well as stabilization, relative liberalization, and international opening of the Franco regime brought about a reawakening of the labor problem. One important difference with the past was that sheer repression could no longer be used without jeopardizing the regime's delicate international position. The government committed itself to introduce labor reforms after joining the International Labor Organization in 1951. New legislation on joint worker-management committees (*jurados de empresa*) was passed in 1947 and 1953, and a framework for collective bargaining was introduced in 1958. Reformers tried hard to keep up with the waves of strikes that took place in 1953, 1956, 1962, and 1969,[89] but the *jurados* were assigned collective agreement functions, thus minimizing the role of free bargaining, and maximizing the effect of employers' clauses about productivity. Moreover, the number of workers covered by collective agreements remained low until 1968. Collective agreements were not reported to eliminate conflict from the workplace.[90] The joint vertical labor-management unions were challenged by new unions such as CCOO (*Comisiones Obreras,* controlled by the Communist Party), and USO (*Unión Sindical Obrera,* created by ex-Socialist and Christian unionists). They pursued a strategy of infiltration of the official unions that was particularly successful in the new big firms of the Madrid industrial belt: Perkins Ibérica (a subsidiary of International Harvester), Standard Eléctrica, Marconi Española, Siemens, and the truck maker ENASA. Meanwhile, the Socialist UGT maintained a much-criticized position of boycott of the regime. In the 1960s economic strikes were made legal. Official statistics underestimated the extent of labor conflict, which was rampant though intermittent. In early 1969, mounting labor protests required the declaration of a nationwide state of exception, resulting in arrests of clandestine union leaders. This grave episode showed once more that the problem of labor unrest, coupled with changes in the structure of the economy and the firm, had again become pressing for Spanish employers and managers.[91]

De Miguel and Linz (1964a, pp. 262, 264, 278), (1964b, pp. 199, 289–296); Payno, *Los gerentes españoles* (1973). See also the comparative statistics in Appendix B.

89. Maravall (1978, p. 24); De Miguel and Linz, "Bureaucratisation et pouvoir discrétionnaire dans les entreprises industrielles espagnoles" (1964c).

90. See the report by the Catholic employers' association ASE (Acción Social Empresarial), *Valoración empresarial de los resultados de los convenios colectivos 1958–1970* (1972, p. 98).

91. Amsden (1972, pp. 61–62, 68–78, 87–162); Maravall (1978, pp. 27–29, 72–73, 74–76), and *El desarrollo económico y la clase obrera* (1970); Linz (1981, pp.

THE HUMAN RELATIONS SOLUTION TO LABOR UNREST: FAVORABLE FACTORS

Starting in the late 1950s, Spanish employers, managers, and organizational experts embraced the propositions of the human relations school. The growing stratum of middle managers, as well as the growing educational and managerial sophistication of the increasingly numerous salaried top directors, produced a new sensitivity to the problems and feelings of the worker.[92] Given that, politically speaking, employers and their interest organizations had to keep a low profile throughout the Franco decades (the official vertical unions were supposed to represent their interests), it is not surprising that they tried an uncontroversial ideological approach to the labor problem such as human relations.[93] The human relations approach also received support from several key Catholic and liberal intellectuals. Moreover, most of Spain's prominent sociologists and psychologists aligned themselves with the human relations school, as did the leaders of the Falangist offical unions. Finally, several of the organizations created by the state to improve organizational methods became quickly dominated by experts favoring the human relations paradigm.

Social Catholicism. The first key factor in the theoretical success of the ideology of human relations in Spain had to do with the mentality of the business elite. Traditionally, Spain's elites had been greatly influenced by Catholicism and certain conservative strains of liberal-humanist thought. The Catholic and liberal thought traditions converged on the issue of industrial relations to support the human relations approach. The social doctrine of the Roman Catholic Church became the dominant component in the mentality of much of the upper class during the Restoration period. The social Catholic movement failed, however, to organize a powerful Christian political party and effective Catholic trade unions following the German or Belgian

---

389–391); Tezanos, "Los conflictos laborales en España" (1974, p. 103); Fishman (1990, pp. 121–127); Macrométrica, *Cifras de la España económica* (1978, p. 108). See also Witney, *Labor Policy and Practices in Spain* (1965); Almendros Morcillo et al., *El sindicalismo de clase en España 1939–1977* (1978); Linz, "Opposition in and under an authoritarian regime: The case of Spain" (1973b).

92. Bendix, *Work and Authority in Industry* (1974, pp. 212–216, 319–340); De Miguel and Linz (1964b, p. 99).

93. Linz (1981, p. 388); Linz and De Miguel, *Los empresarios ante el poder público* (1966a).

examples.[94] Although some Catholic assessments of Taylorism were not negative,[95] early Catholic writers concerned with social issues (Severino Aznar, Pedro Sangro y Ros de Olano, Juan Zaragüeta), and regenerationist intellectuals (Montolíu, Posada) distanced themselves from scientific management by developing the concepts of "just wage" (performance-based but sufficient to meet family needs), "worker dignity," "vocational education," and work "as generator of human relations or a consequence of them."[96] Their activities at the Institute for Social Reform and at the National Institute for Social Security were, as mentioned above, conducive to the deflection of Taylorism and the appearance of an eclecticism of organizational methods both in Catalonia and in Spain as a whole.

As in Germany, Spanish Catholic theologians of the 1940s and 1950s received human relations theory, reinterpreted it according to Catholic social doctrine, and recommended its application in industrial settings. Catholicism was especially influential among top managers, given their elitist social extraction and the fact that many of them attended the elite Catholic management schools. The most influential Catholic management intellectuals were bishops or Jesuit priests. Martín Brugarola, a Jesuit priest and advisor of the official vertical unions, emphasized the "good" aspects of human relations theory, but thought Christian management should go beyond the merely instrumental and "positivistic" pursuit of higher productivity to promote true worker participation, responsibility, and social and human training. Despite this position, the ultimate authority of the employer was not to be challenged.[97] Another leading proponent of human relations was the powerful bishop Casimiro Morcillo of Bilbao in the Basque country, later archbishop, and member of the corporatist Cortes (a parliament of sorts), the Kingdom's Council, and the Regency

94. Tusell, *Historia de la democracia cristiana en España* (1986, vol. 1, pp. 31–43, 69–86).

95. See the chronicle in the social Catholic journal, *Paz Social*, "El 'Taylorismo' o sistema Taylor" (1913). This piece is also a sample of "organizational eclecticism" because the author(s) thought that Taylorism could lead to profit sharing.

96. See Sangro y Ros de Olano, *Sistemas de retribución del trabajo* (1910, p. 7); Aznar, *Remuneración del trabajo* (1935); Zaragüeta, *La vocación profesional* (1927); Montolíu (1916); Posada, *La organización científica del trabajo* (1929, pp. 26, 28–29).

97. In fact, Brugarola was echoing the criticisms by Pope Pius XII. See Brugarola, *La cristianización de las empresas* (1945a), *La dignidad del trabajo* (1945b), *Relaciones humanas y reforma de la empresa* (1957, pp. 8, 97–98, 121–122, 137–149, 175–191, 209–213), *Para ti, dirigente de empresa* (1971, pp. 20, 45, 54–58, 82–87, 88–93), and *Para ti, trabajador* (1972, pp. 20–21).

Council. He also mentioned the limitations of the human relations approach, but thought it a step in the right direction.[98] Bishop Rafael González Moralejo of Valencia, a theologian and economist by training, was pleased with the "rectification" of economic science by the human relations approach.[99] The Jesuit priest Mariano Sánchez Gil, a management educator, emphasized the need to apply human relations to both workers and managers.[100] Later theorists, like Fernando Guerrero Martínez and Jesuit priest Pedro Uriarte insisted again on the compatibility of human relations ideas with the Catholic social doctrine.[101]

The only important Spanish Catholic ideology of the time that was not explicitly conducive to a human relations approach was that of the Opus Dei, although there was nothing in it that would hinder the development of human relations either. The management school created by the Opus Dei in Barcelona in 1958 (IESE) offered training in human relations as well as in other modern American management methods, but no leading manager known to belong to the Opus Dei endorsed the human relations approach specifically.[102]

Most important were the research and educational organizations created under Catholic influence, at which human relations flourished. Of particular relevance was the association Employers' Social Action (*Acción Social Patronal,* ASP), later renamed as Entrepreneurial Social Action (*Acción Social Empresarial,* ASE), with branch offices in many Spanish provinces. ASP and ASE, mostly active in the late 1950s and throughout the 1960s, organized lectures and seminars on human relations and social policy in the firm, favoring the implementation of such human relations techniques as suggestion boxes, in-depth

98. Morcillo, *Cristo en la fábrica* (1956, pp. 167–171).

99. González Moralejo, "Prólogo" (1965). This is the foreword to the Spanish edition of *Human Relations in Modern Business,* an edited volume with the views of several American business managers. See also his contribution, "La empresa en el pensamiento teológico y en la doctrina pontificia," to the edited volume IEP, ed., *La empresa* (1962, pp. 25–26, 31, 32, 35–36, 40).

100. Sánchez Gil, *Deontología de ingenieros y directivos de empresa* (1960, pp. 230–237, 283–297).

101. Guerrero Martínez, "La reforma de la empresa" (1967), and "Participación activa de los trabajadores en la empresa" (1963); Uriarte, *El hombre en los sistemas económicos* (1969, pp. 34–49, 366–367).

102. Some aspects of the Opus Dei credo are consistent with human relations. See maxims nos. 15, 19, 343, 357, 373, and 457 in the book of Opus Dei founder Escrivá de Balaguer, *Camino* (1990). See also Moncada, *El Opus Dei, una interpretación* (1974, pp. 27–31); Moya (1975, pp. 171–180, 240–243); Casanova, *The Opus Dei Ethic and the Modernization of Spain* (1983, pp. 371–391).

interviews, work-satisfaction surveys, attitude and personality-based worker selection, and communication groups. Their activities were perhaps the most important channel for the diffusion of human relations ideas among practicing Spanish managers.[103] Also important were the *Instituto Social León XIII* of the Pontifical University (where Brugarola and González Moralejo taught),[104] and the Jesuit-run elite undergraduate and graduate management schools of the *Universidad Comercial de Deusto* in the Basque country (where Uriarte taught), and ICADE in Madrid (where Sánchez Gil was director of graduate programs). In fact, Luis Chalbaud, one of the founders and first director of the *Comercial* (1916), had been active in the Christian workers' associations and circles during the 1910s, and favored focusing management education efforts on training students in how to handle human relationships with subordinates and collaborators.[105] The journal of the graduates' association of the *Comercial* published several articles during the 1947–75 period on organizational analysis, most of them using a human relations approach.[106]

Liberal-Humanist Thought. In Spain, as opposed to Germany, the Catholic influence was not the only intellectual heritage that favored a human relations approach to organizing. Spanish liberal-humanist thought provided an equally powerful justification for the adoption of human relations. The dominant figure of liberal thought from the 1920s to the 1950s, recognized as such both in Spain and in the rest of Europe, was José Ortega y Gasset. His influence on Spanish human relations management intellectuals was extensive. Ortega himself once

103. ASP, *IV Congreso Luso-Español de Patronos Católicos* (1959), *Problemas de personal* (1960), *La comunicación en la empresa* (1962a, pp. 52–69, 72–86), *VIII Asamblea Nacional* (1962b), *Puntos de partida para los estudios sobre el perfeccionamiento de la empresa* (1963), *El empresario cristiano ante las circunstancias actuales* (1964), *Participación activa del personal en la empresa* (1966); ASE, *Por un mayor sentido comunitario de la empresa* (1967, pp. 15, 29–31), *La participación en la empresa* (1969), *Previsión, reclutamiento y selección de personal* (1970). In 1957, ASP published the Spanish edition of the American edited volume, *Human Relations in Modern Business*. See the third edition: ASP, *Relaciones humanas en la Empresa moderna* (1965).

104. Instituto Social León XIII, ed., *Comentarios a la Mater et Magistra* (1963).

105. Chalbaud, *Discurso leído en la solemne apertura de los estudios en la Universidad Comercial de Deusto* (1916, p. 12). See also Tusell (1986, vol. 1, p. 85).

106. See *Boletín de Estudios Económicos* 38(1956):29–47; 40(1957):3–13; 43(1958):3–12; 53(1961):263–278, 279–310; 64(1965):59–124, 189–205, 207–228; 81(1970):663–690; 94(1975):325–336. Only two literature reviews touched on Taylorism, the principles of organization, and certain structural ideas: 53(1961): 367–420 and 84(1971):981–1004.

declared at a 1954 meeting organized by the British Institute of Management that the human relations approach to management was "most praiseworthy." For him, the business executive should be a manager of human resources rather than a manipulator of technical variables.[107] Ortega's crucial influence derives from his position on progress, modernity, and technology as presented in his famous essay, *The Revolt of the Masses*.[108] Ortega was worried about Western decadence, and the alienation of the mass-person.[109] He was unambiguously against "modernism," and "modern culture," though in favor of modernization and economic advance. For him, the problem with modern culture was its "technicalism," which he carefully set apart from the venerable pursuits of pure science. In general, he showed his distaste for applied science (engineering, technology), but a devotion to theoretical science (physics).[110] This position alone helped to justify and reinforce the traditional disdain of Spanish intellectuals towards applied engineering, and any other associated knowledge like scientific management. But Ortega's influence on Spanish human relations theorists was not merely negative but also constructive. He clearly believed in the moral superiority of a ruling class of enlightened "gentlemen," the "select minority."[111]

During the 1950s and 1960s, Ortega's ideas became a major way to conceptualize the consequences of industrialism for the worker, using reactionary arguments of the "perversity" and "jeopardy" type.[112] The influence of Ortega is clear in the two most important Spanish human relations management intellectuals, Roberto Cuñat and Ramón de Lucas Ortueta.[113] Antidio Layret Foix—an eclectic

107. Ortega y Gasset, "Una vista sobre la situación del gerente o 'manager' en la sociedad actual" (1983, p. 28).

108. Ortega y Gasset, *La rebelión de las masas* (1986), originally published in the Madrid daily *El Sol* in 1929. For the convenience of the reader, page references will be provided for both the 1986 edition in Spanish, and the first English edition, *The Revolt of the Masses* (1932). Literal quotations have been transcribed from the English edition.

109. Ortega y Gasset (1986, pp. 68, 91, 99), (1932, pp. 14–15, 44, 55).

110. Ortega y Gasset (1986, pp. 82, 118–119, 120, 123, 139), (1932, pp. 32, 81–82, 83–84, 86–87, 108). Ortega insisted again on this theme in his 1933 lectures, *Meditación de la técnica* (1989, pp. 15, 40). See also Bell's discussion of Ortega's antimodernism in *The End of Ideology* (1988, p. 23).

111. Ortega y Gasset (1986, pp. 67, 155), (1932, pp. 13, 128). See again Bell (1988, p. 23).

112. Hirschman, *The Rhetoric of Reaction* (1991).

113. Cuñat, *Productividad y mando de hombres en la empresa española* (1958, p. 272); De Lucas Ortueta, *Técnicas de dirección de personal* (1961, p. 200), and *Manual de personal* (1974, p. 383).

Taylorite in the 1920s and now a human relations theorist—also cited Ortega, and appeared convinced that "the process of 'massification' can produce the slow death of an organization."[114] Even Taylorite engineer José Antonio de Artigas argued that technology should be "rehumanized," and that there would be "Spanish effectiveness" (a favorite catchphrase at the time) in the attainment of such a goal.[115] And for José Rubí Maroto, a political scientist working for the INRT, industrialization made the human being feel "devoured by the mass."[116] All these management intellectuals used concepts developed by Ortega to legitimize the use of a human relations approach.

The Support of Academic Sociologists and Psychologists. One of the most interesting aspects of the adoption of human relations in Spain was the enormous extent to which a relatively large group of academics in the various social sciences facilitated the reception of American ideas and then diffused them through their teaching and consulting work. The case of the sociological profession is especially striking. Postwar Spanish sociology received a variety of intellectual traditions: social Catholic reformism (Jaime Balmes, Severino Aznar), Krausist regeneracionism (Adolfo González Posada), and liberal-humanist thought (Unamuno, Ortega y Gasset). All these traditions converged to produce a state of mind favorable to human relations, as is evident in most of the writings by the leading sociologists of the late 1940s and 1950s who had an interest in industrial relations: Enrique Gómez Arboleya, Salustiano del Campo, and Bernardino Herrero Nieto.[117]

The influence of American, French, and Belgian (note the Catholic connection) human relations ideas in Spanish sociology is evident from a content analysis of the leading journal in the discipline. In the 1943–70 period no articles or book reviews on scientific management

114. In *Racionalización* 4(1951):172.
115. In *Racionalización* 1(1948):6. See also the book by Aunós Pérez, *Técnica y espiritualidad* (1962, pp. 16, 50, 112).
116. In *Racionalización* 19(1966):276.
117. Gómez Arboleya, "Teoría del grupo social" (1954); Del Campo, "Grupos pequeños y organización informal en la industria" (1958). Herrero Nieto published several articles in *Racionalización*: 9(1956):8–23, 193–199, 301–306, 396–402; and in *Revista Internacional de Sociología*: 11(1953):305–333. Del Campo (1958, p. 157) was somewhat eclectic in that he recommended drawing from both scientific management and human relations. For the sociological profession, see De Miguel and Moyer, "Sociology in Spain" (1979, pp. 28–58, 106–109); Gómez Arboleya, "Sociology in Spain," in Giner and Moreno, eds., *Sociology in Spain* (1990, pp. 17–53); Giner, "Spanish sociology under Franco," in Giner and Moreno, eds. (1990, pp. 55–72); CECA, ed., *Sociología española de los años setenta* (1971, pp. 22–23).

or structural analysis were published, but some thirty human relations pieces appeared.[118] Spanish social and industrial psychology were also dominated by human relations approaches. The most important psychologists of the 1950s and 1960s wrote on the social-psychological aspects related to human relations at work, and engaged in consulting activities for the government or for private firms: José Luis Pinillos, Mariano Yela, Miguel Siguán, and Máximo Fernández Hernández.[119] Other academic social scientists also participated in the reception of foreign influences and in the elaboration of human relations themes: ethnologist Claudio Esteva Fabregat; jurists Pablo Lucas Verdú, Manuel Alonso Olea, and Alfredo Montoya Melgar; economist José María Fernández Pirla; and engineer José de Orbaneja.[120] The case of Spain during the 1950s exemplifies how two different generation units—the engineers and army officers, on the one hand, and the theologians, sociologists, and psychologists, on the other—adopted radically different views on the organization of work. The first generation unit was responsible for the spread of scientific management

118. See *Revista Internacional de Sociología:* 9(1951):571–573; 11(1953):305–333; 13(1955):15–41, 43–56, 71–296; 14(1956):19–33, 165–167; 15(1957):551–554, 554–555, 593–618; 16(1958):5–38, 168–170; 17(1959):692–693, 694–696, 697–698; 19(1961):147–149, 337–354, 449–452, 452–454; 20(1962):25–31, 456–459, 466–467, 611–612; 22(1964):333–347, 489–503; 24(1966):202–204; 25(1967):202–203; 28(1970):131–132.

119. Pinillos, "Organización y conducta" (1959), "Exploración de la personalidad y aspectos motivacionales," in ASP, ed. (1960, pp. 29–53), and *Las ciencias humanas y la organización industrial* (1969); Yela, "Psicología del trabajo" (1967, pp. 591–592, 616–618), *Personalidad y eficacia* (1974, pp. 12–13), "Epílogo," in AEDJP, *La humanización del trabajo en Europa* (1979, pp. 241–250), and in *Racionalización:* 6(1953):417–420; Siguán, *Relaciones humanas en la administración pública* (1958), *Problemas humanos del trabajo industrial* (1963), and in *Revista Internacional de Sociología:* 15(1957):593–618, 16(1958):5–38; Fernández Hernández, *Psicología del trabajo* (1970), and in the journal *Jornal* 47(1955):8.

120. Esteva Fabregat, "El factor humano en la producción industrial" (1957), "La máquina y la deshumanización del trabajo" (1960), "Las relaciones humanas en el marco del trabajo y el sindicalismo," in *Jornal:* 81(1960):318–323, and *Antropología industrial* (1973); Lucas Verdú, in *Revista Internacional de Sociología:* 13(1955):15–41, 14(1956):19–33; Alonso Olea, "La empresa desde el punto de vista social," in IEP, ed. (1962, p. 68), and "Prólogo del traductor" (1958, pp. 10–11); Montoya Melgar, *El poder de dirección del empresario* (1965, pp. 102–119); Fernández Pirla, "La empresa desde el punto de vista económico," in IEP, ed. (1962, pp. 59–60); De Orbaneja y Aragón, *Nuevas bases de las relaciones humanas en la empresa* (n.d.), and in *Racionalización:* 7(1954):97–103. It is not unusual to find engineers who liked human relations, given the insistence of certain influential authors on the need for the engineer to become more than a mere "technician." See Hevia Cangas, *El ingeniero en la empresa* (1962, pp. 9–33, 53–54, 191).

techniques, while the second did its best to promote the human relations approach.

Academic social scientists with a taste for human relations created or came to dominate several influential research organizations. Especially important were the Institute for Political Studies (IEP), with which Gómez Arboleya, Del Campo, Alonso Olea, and Fernández Pirla collaborated; the Sociology Institute Balmes, in which an Industrial Sociology Department was created under Herrero Nieto's direction; the noted Social Institute León XIII, where Del Campo studied, did research, and taught; the industrial section of the School of Psychology and Psychotechnique at the University of Madrid (1956), where Professors Pinillos, Yela, and Siguán trained many experts in personnel management; and the experimental laboratory at the Higher Council for Scientific Research (CSIC), where Siguán did some research. Managers and consultants concerned with human relations were often invited to colloquia at these institutions.[121]

The Support of the Official Vertical Unions. The Falangist-oriented official vertical unions also supported the application of human relations techniques. They approached labor relations from a hierarchical, corporatist, paternalistic, and communitarian viewpoint.[122] Fernando Herrero Tejedor, one of the leading figures of the single-party *Movimiento Nacional* since the late 1950s and a prominent personality in the Franco regime, described the Falangist inclination to conceive of the business firm as a community and to "humanize technology" following Falange's social-justice, organicist, Christian, anti-individualist, anticapitalist, and paternalistic creed. He also called for more worker participation.[123] Between 1953 and 1961 the official journal of the vertical unions published several articles explicitly favoring human relations over scientific management. Ortega's theme of rehumanizing technology emerged repeatedly.[124] Martín Bruga-

121. See IEP, ed. (1962); Instituto Balmes de Sociología, *El elemento humano en la empresa* (1958).

122. The impact of Falangist ideology on labor law was clear since 1938. See Sempere Navarro, *Nacionalsindicalismo y relación de trabajo* (1982); Rodríguez Piñero, "Un modelo democrático de relaciones laborales" (1978).

123. Herrero Tejedor, "La doctrina del Movimiento Nacional sobre la empresa." In IEP, ed. (1962, p. 339).

124. See *Jornal: Organo de Difusión Sindicalista* 19(1953):7; 26(1954):4–5; 30(1954):1; 32(1954):1–2; 47(1955):8; 76(1959):362–372, 397–398; 81(1960): 318–323, 324–326; 86(1961):15–20, 36–43; 92(1961):866–874. Only two articles presented scientific management ideas without criticizing them: 12(1953):7; 30(1954):1.

rola, one of the major Catholic human relations theorists, served for many years as an advisor to the vertical unions on the subject of social policy in the firm. The official youth organization, the seedbed of many Falangist union leaders and enterprise managers, removed all "fascist accoutrements" from its training guides in favor of Kurt Lewin's ideas about group climate and leadership.[125] Other later books published by the single-party organization unambiguously defended the human relations approach, presenting ideas about the human group, the informal versus the formal, the relationship between satisfaction and productivity, and team spirit.[126]

The Support of the State for Human Relations. During the 1940s and most of the 1950s, the state promoted the spread of scientific management through the National Institute for Work Rationalization (INRT), as well as through the direct intervention in the economy by the INI holding company, but a crucial event took place in 1952 when the Ministry of Industry created the National Commission for Industrial Productivity (CNPI). This organization administered American technical aid and promoted productivity as required by the European Productivity Agency, surviving into the period of indicative planning during the 1960s.[127] As part of the same productivity program, a School of Industrial Organization (*Escuela de Organización Industrial*, EOI) was created in 1955 to train managerial cadres. The EOI offered courses in both production management and human relations.[128] Although the CNPI did teaching, training, and research on scientific management, it quickly devoted most of its activities touching on business organization to human relations.[129] Several of

125. Linz (1964, p. 310), (1970, p. 167). The official youth organization was called *Organización Juvenil Española* (OJE), formerly *Frente de Juventudes* (Youth Front). Cuñat, one of the most important human relations managers, was a leader at the *Frente* for ten years. See Cuñat (1958, pp. 10–11).

126. Lafourcade, *El factor humano en la empresa* (1965, pp. 96–100); Vicesecretaría General del Movimiento, *Crecimiento económico y política social* (1967, pp. 40–49). See also De Pedro y San Gil, *Relaciones humanas y técnicas de promoción de grupo* (1967).

127. Gil Peláez, "Los EE.UU en el movimiento español de la productividad" (1967). Even the technocrats in charge of indicative economic planning showed a concern with work satisfaction. See Comisaría del Plan de Desarrollo, *Factores humanos y sociales* (1967, pp. 194–198).

128. See *Racionalización:* 10(1957):30–32.

129. On scientific management, see CNPI, *Mejora de métodos de trabajo* (1960a), *Salarios, tiempos de trabajo e incentivos* (1960b), *Técnica y aplicación del cronometraje* (1962). On human relations, see Buesa and Molero, "Cambio técnico y procesos de trabajo" (1982, pp. 255–261); Barril Dosset, "Justificación de las relaciones humanas

the academic sociologists and psychologists (Del Campo, Pinillos, Siguán) collaborated with the CNPI, and two technical missions of Spanish managers traveled to the United States to acquire on-site knowledge of the application of human relations techniques.[130] The subordination of the initially Taylorite INRT to the CNPI meant that this organization too was now more inclined to support human relations.[131]

THE THEORETICAL IMPACT OF HUMAN RELATIONS IN MANAGEMENT CIRCLES

In the late 1950s a group of leading managers paved the way for the resounding theoretical success of human relations ideology and techniques among the Spanish managerial elite. The opinion leaders included Roberto Cuñat, Ramón de Lucas Ortueta, José Manuel González Páramo, and in the late 1960s, Eduardo Matute Butragueño. Cuñat, who was a doctor in economics and had been a leader at the official youth organization for ten years, served as personnel manager at Standard Eléctrica (ITT),[132] later becoming director of the TEA organizational consulting firm and a part-time teacher at the University of Madrid School of Economics and Business Management. He published several influential books in which he related his attempts to increase productivity and improve the social climate of the firm with human relations techniques such as personality-based worker selection, organization of work groups, company newspapers, suggestion boxes, and attitude surveys.[133] Cuñat argued that in order to rule the firm, one needs to combine ideology and techniques:

---

en la empresa" (1963). Sociologists Juan Linz and Amando de Miguel, at times associated with the EOI, conducted an important research project on the elite of Spanish entrepreneurs and managers with financial support from the CNPI. See Linz and De Miguel (1966).

130. See CNPI, *Relaciones humanas* (1959a), *Relaciones humanas: Memoria* (1961), and *Dirección de personal* (1959c).

131. José Mallart, who subscribed to organizational eclecticism in the 1920s and 1930s, worked at the INRT, becoming a true human relations expert. See Mallart, *Técnicas de dirección, administración y de oficina* (1959), *Psicosociología del desarrollo industrial* (1960), and *Psicología industrial y organizacional* (1981); see also Mallart and García Villegas, *La satisfacción en el trabajo como factor de productividad* (1951).

132. Standard Eléctrica, a subsidiary of ITT, was created in the 1920s to supply and operate the telephone system monopoly. In 1945, with the creation of the National Telephone Company of Spain (CTNE), Standard Eléctrica managed to obtain the monopoly of telephone equipment production for twenty more years.

133. Cuñat (1958, pp. 9–11, 29, 52, 62–79, 90–94, 192–212, 215, 226, 250, 272–275), and *Problemas humanos de la moderna organización del trabajo en la industria*

If intelligent rule in modern industry is inconceivable without a doctrine—for us the social doctrine of the Catholic Church—and if it has to be integrated within a science such as sociology, it must be taught to present and future managers in the form of techniques, which in many cases will not only entail a qualitative but also a quantitative assessment of the individual and collective reactions of workers.[134]

Ramón de Lucas Ortueta was a lawyer and doctor in industrial engineering in charge of mass production at Marconi Española (a major telecommunications equipment company), where he first introduced human relations techniques in 1955. He was the author of several widely read books, and also taught at the EOI management school, and at the Madrid School of Social Work.[135] González Páramo, a doctor in law and sociologist, was a manager or member of the board of directors of several companies, including hydroelectic ones, in which he implemented human relations techniques to improve worker participation.[136] Finally, Matute Butragueño was a lawyer, doctor in economics, and industrial psychologist who worked for the large petrochemical company CEPSA as personnel manager. In his capacity of part-time professor at the Madrid-based Jesuit ICADE and ICAI management and engineering schools, he taught human relations to a whole generation of elite Spanish managers.[137]

These management intellectuals welcomed Ortega's ideas as well as the social Catholic intellectual heritage, used sociological and psychological concepts (citing the major Spanish and foreign academic works), expounded the need to implement human relations tech-

---

(n.d., pp. 1, 6, 12, 15, 19). See also Cuñat et al., *Cómo funcionan los servicios de personal en las empresas españolas* (1963), and *Políticas de personal en las empresas españolas* (1965). See also his articles in *Racionalización:* 4(1951):179–183; 5(1952):404–413; 6(1953):1–11; 7(1954):283–288; 8(1955):193–196.

134. Cuñat (1958, p. 52).

135. De Lucas Ortueta (1961, pp. 15–16, 18–23, 190–197, 200–232), (1974, pp. 61–83, 365–419), *Organización científica de las empresas* (1963a, pp. 525–566). He also included uncritical discussions of scientific management in his books: (1963a, pp. 274–276, 385–457), and *Valoración de tareas y estructura de salarios* (1963b).

136. See his articles in *Racionalización:* 12(1959):143–146; 14(1961):138–145, 265–272. See also González Páramo, *La empresa y la política social* (1966). He taught part-time at the University of Madrid School of Economics, and at the Social Institute León XIII.

137. See Matute Butragueño's textbooks, *Apuntes de política de personal* (1967, pp. 45–56, 71–75, 83–90), *Política de personal* (1970), and *La dirección de personal en la empresa española* (1974, pp. 56–58, 126–127, 139–141, 204–209, 221–222). See also Feu Gutiérrez, Macías Martínez, and Matute Butragueño, *Psicología general e industrial* (1970).

niques, and benefited from the state's support for human relations programs.[138] It is no coincidence that these human relations management intellectuals worked for firms in the electrical and petrochemical industries headquartered in Madrid. It was precisely in these sectors and in the Madrid area where bureaucratization was highest. Also, illegal worker unionization was more widespread in the Madrid area than anywhere else in Spain, and it was particularly important at Standard Eléctrica and Marconi Española. Moreover, managers in highly bureaucratized firms tended to have less traditionalist views about labor problems, payment schemes, and productivity.[139]

Although it is hard to overestimate the importance of this group of four management intellectuals as practitioners, writers of influential books, consultants, and part-time teachers, they were not the only Spanish managers who embraced human relations as an ideology. The list of practicing managers who appeared to be convinced by the utility of the human relations approach is long. They created a quite influential elite organization, the Association for the Advancement of Management (*Asociación para el Progreso de la Dirección,* APD, directed by sociologist Herrero Nieto), and worked for the most important firms in a representative cross-section of the country's core industrial and service sectors: food and beverages, machinery, construction, steel, metals, electrical equipment, hydroelectrical, department stores, transportation, banking, and public utilities.[140]

The content analysis of the INRT's official journal (*Racionaliza-*

138. Manager Cuñat and psychology Professor Yela collaborated at Standard Eléctrica, and psychologist Fernández Hernández was director of the Department of Industrial Psychology and Sociology at the TEA consulting firm. See Yela (1974, pp. 6–7).

139. See Amsden (1972, p. 100); De Miguel and Linz (1964b, pp. 101–104), and "Los problemas de la retribución y el rendimiento vistos por los empresarios españoles" (1963); Linz and De Miguel, "El empresario español ante los problemas laborales" (1963a).

140. A partial list of firms includes Ebro Cía. de Azúcares y Alcoholes, Altos Hornos de Vizcaya, Hispanoil, Máquinas de Coser Alfa, Talleres Guerin, Echevarría, Vías y Construcciones, Agromán, Conductores Metálicos y Eléctricos, Guiral Industrias Eléctricas, Hidruña, Iberduero, Unión Eléctrica, Empresa Nacional de Electricidad, Frutera de Navegación, Iberia, Industrias Subsidiarias de Aviación, Banesto, Telefónica, Galerías Preciados, and Almacenes Tobaris. See Garrigues Walker et al., *La participación de los trabajadores en los consejos de administración* (1965); ASP (1961); CNPI (1959a, 1959c, 1961); APD, *Problemas actuales del director de personal* (1970); Travesi, ed., *La empresa española* (1969); Cuñat et al. (1963, 1965); Arana Gondra, ed., *Criterios sobre alta dirección de empresa* (1972, pp. 17–126); San Juan Rubio, "La descentralización en la dirección de la empresa" (1959). See also the applications of human relations to public administration by Carrasco Belinchón, *Manual de organización y métodos* (1966, pp. 343–373), and *Técnica y humanismo en la gestión local* (1969).

ción), shows the theoretical success of *both* scientific management and human relations in the postwar period, underscoring the partial over-lap of two generation units. Human relations articles appeared partic-ularly frequently in the 1951–56 and 1966–71 periods (see panel B of Table 4.2). In contrast to the scientific management pieces, human relations articles referred frequently to ideological issues (view of in-dustrial conflict and of workers, fascination with communal and group life). But only two sets of human relations techniques (down-playing hierarchy, and emphasizing leadership, communication and participation) were mentioned repeatedly. Little was written about how to organize small-group activities, group wage incentives, or about job enlargement, enrichment, or rotation (see panel A of Table 4.2). The theoretical aspects of human relations ideology appealed to Spanish managers to a greater extent than its associated practical techniques.

LIMITED PRACTICAL IMPLEMENTATION OF HUMAN RELATIONS TECHNIQUES

It seems that in Spain human relations was primarily an ideology and a language to address labor problems. Actual implementation of techniques only took place at a few of the largest, most highly bureaucratized, and most progressive firms, such as Standard Eléctrica and Marconi Española.[141] Surveys of large industrial firms conducted in the early 1980s concluded that human relations techniques and departments were only operating in a few firms, mostly very large and highly bureaucratized, and frequently foreign-owned (automo-tive, chemical, electrotechnical, and soft-drinks firms).[142] This evi-dence—together with the interest of many Spanish managers in the human relations approach—suggest that the main impediment to the implementation of human relations techniques by Spanish firms was their lack of resources due to their low degree of bureaucratization. It is unclear whether influential consulting firms such as TEA or the seminars at the National Commission for Industrial Productivity (CNPI) were successful in convincing managers to implement human relations, or if the graduates of the Jesuit-run elite business schools in Madrid, Barcelona, Bilbao, San Sebastián, Alicante, and Córdoba implemented the human relations techniques they were taught.[143] De-

141. Buesa and Molero (1982, p. 263).
142. Bueno Campos, ed., *La empresa española* (1987, p. 332); Castillo and Prieto, *Condiciones de trabajo* (1983, pp. 87–95).
143. At the Universidad Comercial de Deusto, both scientific management and human relations were taught as part of the curriculum. See Colinas Aguirrebengoa,

spite the fairly limited practical impact of the human relations paradigm, it is important to understand that in Spain social Catholicism and human relations had a quite important effect that often goes unnoticed. The writings by Spanish employers reveal how the social Catholic and human relations influence made them more sensitive towards labor problems and more responsible towards workers. Those are no small achievements in a country in which many managers of large firms seemed to have a short-term, instrumental conception of the enterprise. Above all, the human relations approach—with its implicit communitarianism and paternalism—was consistent with the dominant corporatist pattern of politics in Spain. In a way, employers and managers were merely adapting to the political institutions first created during the late nineteenth century, and later vigorously reinforced and expanded by the dictatorships of Primo de Rivera during the 1920s and of Franco after the Civil War.

WHAT EVER HAPPENED TO STRUCTURAL ANALYSIS?

The absence of structural analysis from the organizational debates in Spain until well into the 1980s was complete, both in theory and in practice. To begin with, the problem of labor unrest had not been handled during the 1960s in the way that it was successfully solved in the United States or in Germany. True collective bargaining or participation were impossible, given the absence of free labor unions. The proportion of workers covered by collective agreements never surpassed the ceiling of 40 percent, and it fluctuated considerably throughout the 1960s and early 1970s.[144] Dismissals of workers, as well as young engineers in managerial positions, and other preemptive disciplinary practices were used repeatedly to assert managerial authority.[145] The official figures for working days lost due to industrial conflict are misleading, and cannot be compared with those of democratic countries. Unemployment remained comparatively low during the 1960s and early 1970s, but at the cost of international out-migration and underemployment. Neither were economic changes conducive to structural approaches to organizing. Spanish industrial firms had not reached by 1970 the degree of industrial bureaucratization or product diversification of American or German firms back in

---

Historia de la Universidad Comercial de Deusto (1966, pp. 166–185). For the other schools see Martín de Nicolás Cabo, *La formación universitaria para la empresa* (1969, pp. 133–164); Frederick and Haberstroh, *Management Education in Spain* (1969).

144. Macrométrica (1978, p. 108).

145. Grupo de Trabajo para el Estudio de los Nuevos Problemas de la Ingeniería, *La crisis de los ingenieros españoles* (1975, pp. 178–181, 197).

1950.[146] The largest firms in Spain remained small and nationally oriented, with little foreign investments. In 1975 there were no Spanish industrial firms among the world's or Europe's 100 largest.[147] Also, the service sector in Spain remained comparatively small. With the labor unrest problem unsolved and structural-economic variables not reaching critical levels, structural analysis could not be in high demand. The only factor that demanded a structural approach was the increasing interconnection of the Spanish economy with those of the countries in its most immediate environment, especially after the favorable 1970 preferential trade agreement with the European Economic Community.[148]

The absence of support for the structural analysis approach from the professions (no interested sociologists or management theorists), the state (no research institutions), and the labor unions (indifference) was complete.[149] Leading international consulting companies such as McKinsey or Arthur D. Little were either absent or not very influential. As a result, not a single leading manager advocated a structural approach to organizational problems consciously and comprehensively. There are traces of structural analysis in some of the books or journals that have been mentioned above: line-and-staff organization, departmentalization à la Fayol, interdepartmental conflict, divisionalization as a solution to product diversification, and so on.[150] The manager who presented these rudimentary structural ideas most cogently was Ramón Arana Gondra, an industrial engineer, economist, senior manager at the large truck builder ENASA in Madrid, and former personnel manager at the construction and sanitation parts company

146. There are no data available on product diversification of Spanish firms, but the fact that, in contrast to most other Western countries, banks control vast industrial and service-sector groups has meant over the years that diversification was achieved by means of financial control (holdings, direct participation, interlocking directorates, etc.) rather than by intra-firm related or unrelated combinations of product lines. For data on Spanish banks' industrial groups and interlocking directorates, see Tamames, *La oligarquía financiera en España* (1977, p. 145); Muñoz, Roldán, and Serrano (1978, pp. 295–338); Rivases, *Los banqueros del PSOE* (1988).

147. Tamames, ed., *Anuario económico y social de España 1977* (1977, pp. 533–535).

148. See the comparative statistics in Appendix B.

149. In fact there was a reaction against American empirical sociology, with Marxism and the Frankfurt School gaining ground among Spanish sociologists in the late 1960s and 1970s.

150. See the following: De Lucas Ortueta (1967, pp. 110–118, 136–139, 157–166); González Páramo (1966, pp. 252–255), and in *Boletín de Estudios Económicos* 84(1971):981–1004; Donís Ortiz in *Racionalización:* 13(1960):641–649, 14(1961): 257–264, 391–394, and 15(1962):9–14, 391–306, 522–526.

Uralita.[151] The National Commission for Industrial Productivity (CNPI) published only one study on structural analysis.[152] The theoretical impact of structural analysis until the 1980s was therefore very limited (see panel B of Table 4.2). By the early 1980s very few large industrial firms had developed decentralized, divisionalized, or matrix structures. In fact, the managerial elite of Spanish industry seemed to be increasingly concerned with the economic crisis, the mounting labor problems, and the new rules of industrial behavior resulting from constitutional democratic reform. Although structural problems such as interdepartmental conflicts were present in half of the firms surveyed at the time, little was detected in terms of attempts at structural reorganization.[153] But the situation of the 1980s lies beyond the scope of this comparative study.

A NOTE ON THE AUTHORITARIAN MENTALITY OF SPANISH MANAGERS

One major mental component that runs across many Spanish management writings is what might be called *basic authoritarianism*: the idea that industrial life takes place in a hierarchical and ordered system ruled by a boss who "always knows more and better."[154] This mental attitude no doubt was reinforced by the long tradition of non-democratic political rule and of corporatism. Managerial authoritarianism is also present in many other societies, of course, including the United States and Britain, but Spanish managers were unique in that many of them tended to make their authoritarian mentality explicit and actually celebrate it. The concept of basic authoritarianism is useful because it helps to label a group of distinguished Spanish managers that would otherwise prove to be not classifiable. It also helps in understanding the ideology of certain scientific management and human relations management intellectuals.

The quintessential example of Spanish managerial authoritarianism is Gabriel Barceló Matutano, a doctor in civil engineering who did some graduate work at Grenoble and Oxford. His distinguished ca-

---

151. Arana Gondra, *El trabajo personal del director de empresa* (1963, pp. 123–158), *La estructura de la empresa española* (1965a, pp. 79–131, 145–147), *La estrategia del director de empresa* (1965b, p. 7), and *La estrategia del director de empresa* (1965c).

152. CNPI, *Curso de organización general de empresa* (1959b).

153. See the results reported by Bueno Campos, ed. (1987, pp. 331–333); De la Sierra et al., *Los directores de grandes empresas españolas ante el cambio social* (1981, pp. 156–157, 221–224, 228–229).

154. Linz (1964) and De Miguel (1975, p. 245) apply this concept to Spanish political life under Franco.

reer tells us much about the origins of his authoritarian mentality. After working in several public works and railway projects in Spanish-occupied Morocco, he became a senior engineer at the state-owned conglomerate Empresa Nacional Calvo-Sotelo, one of Franco's industrial flagships. He later served as general director and member of the board of directors of several hydroelectric companies. It was during his tenure as president of the Association for the Advancement of Management (APD) in the early 1970s that Barceló Matutano published several important books on managerial leadership. His style is eclectic, charismatic, paternalistic, and somewhat old-fashioned. The bottom line is an authoritarian approach to management. To begin with, he prefers the term *boss* (*jefe*) over *manager,* and the verb *rule* (*mandar*) over *manage.* For him, "the best way of directing and ruling is soft in form but forceful in content. *Fortiter in re, suaviter in modo.*" The boss "must not hesitate," and should "rule with unwavering firmness and true certainty of being obeyed."[155] The boss is presented as a human being characterized by personal strength, will, self-control, justice, tolerance, moderation, prudence, faith in the mission, gaiety and good humor, enthusiasm, and sense of time which typically result in "emotional stability." It so happens that being a boss is like fulfilling a moral mission. Ruling and directing are presented as ways of serving others because for the "collectivity the lack of authority is more harmful than its excess, and it is a great disgrace for leaders to be afraid to talk and act as leaders." Like most human relations managers, Barceló Matutano strongly believed in the moral superiority of those who rule.[156]

Other prominent Spanish managers of the 1960s and 1970s (e.g. José María Aguirre Gonzalo, Eduardo Barreiros, Antonio Barrera de Irimo, José María de Oriol y Urquijo) were not so stringent in their remarks about managerial leadership as Barceló Matutano, but showed a distinct taste for authoritarianism and only a mild inclination to accept human relations concepts.[157] It is hard, however, to find examples of authoritarian writings by managers who were members of the Opus Dei, despite the fact that *Camino*—the sect's spiritual

155. Barceló Matutano, *El dirigente del futuro* (1976, p. 40).

156. Barceló Matutano (1976, pp. 71–83, 137, 195–213), and *El oficio de mandar* (1975, pp. 42, 103–105, 113). He also included some isolated ideas of structural analysis in his books: (1975, pp. 75–79) and (1976, pp. 139–156).

157. See Oriol y Urquijo, "La empresa industrial," in IEP, ed. (1962, pp. 291–292); Hevia Cangas (1962, p. 19); see also the interviews of Travesi, ed. (1969) with Aguirre Gonzalo, Barreiros, Barrera de Irimo, and Boada.

guide—contains so many references to basic authoritarianism.[158] In sum, the concept of managerial authoritarianism helps to describe the mentality of a group of top Spanish managers who are hard to classify. The concept is also useful to complete the characterization of some noted scientific managers (Fernández Avila, Suanzes, Gual Villalbí) and human relations proponents (Cuñat) who presented certain ideas about managerial leadership that shared much with Barceló Matutano's approach.

SPANISH ORGANIZATIONAL DEBATES IN HISTORICAL
PERSPECTIVE

In pre-1939 Spain the organization of industrial work would not have generated any debate at all had it not been for the acute and recurrent problem of labor unrest. But the backwardness of the country's economic structure, the scarcity of engineers, the absence of a modernist mentality, and the pusillanimous role of the state prevented the adoption of scientific management. The corporatist framework of politics and the early impact of social Catholicism were more consistent with vocational guidance approaches. After the Civil War, scientific management was accepted as common practice in response to international isolation and the need to improve industrial management practices in the new large-scale enterprises, while the problem of labor unrest was temporarily solved. Corporatist economic and organizational policies contributed to the adoption of scientific management techniques and to the imitation of German "industrial rationalization." After the mid-1950s, working-class protest came back. The Catholic and liberal traditions, as well as academic social scientists, paved the way for the adoption of human relations ideology. The influence of Catholicism among the business elite was clear in the 1950s and 1960s, and is still a dominant force among that elite group today.[159] But human relations techniques were not implemented in Spain except in a handful of large and sophisticated firms. Structural analysis was not debated in the 1960s or 1970s because of the low levels of international integration, diversification, and bureau-

158. Escrivá de Balaguer (1990, maxims nos. 394, 457, 592, 614–629, 639, 832, 952, and 954).
159. See the survey data on religiosity and the Church's influence among elite managers and professionals in González Blasco and González-Anleo, *Religión y sociedad en la España de los 90* (1992, p. 31); Lozano and Bendala, "Los españoles más influyentes" (1992, p. 20).

cratization of Spanish firms, and because of the continuing primacy of the labor unrest problem.

The case of Spain exemplifies how debates about the organization of work can become heated and important in a relatively underdeveloped country. It also shows that professional groups (engineers, sociologists, psychologists) and elite mentalities (social Catholicism, liberal thought) have a tremendous impact on the kind of organizational theory that dominates the debates among management intellectuals. The Spanish experience bears little resemblance to developments in either the United States or Germany because of the effect of the characteristic traditional-humanist mode of thought. Striking similarities emerge, however, when comparing Spain with Great Britain, the subject of the next chapter.

FIVE

Great Britain
Industrial Retardation, Religious-Humanist Ideals, and the Rise of Social Science

The case of Great Britain raises some puzzling questions about ideological and organizational change. Why did British business elites reject scientific management in the face of the country's relative industrial decline? Why did a genuinely British version of human relations emerge as early as the 1910s, impregnating the thought of leading employers, managers, and government officials during the next four decades? What accounted for the widespread use of structural theories of organization that began in the late 1950s? These are the three basic questions addressed in this chapter. Several features of the British historical experience are discussed as potential explanations: the pioneering of the industrial revolution; the taste for practical invention, and the disdain for science-based technology; the fragmented yet powerful pattern of craft-based trades unionism; the unbroken political and social traditions; the pervasiveness of a social-reformist philosophy drawing from both Christian and Socialist sources; the slow but steady rise of social-science theorizing; and the relentless growth of the large and bureaucratized enterprise.

Scientific Management: A Chilly Reception

British managers and firms failed to see in scientific management a solution to their organizational problems. This development should be studied against the background of a country that pioneered an entrepreneurial ideology as well as a series of key labor-management and organizational techniques. Given this rich heritage and the premise that British industrialists were facing formidable problems at the turn of the century, which were the institutional factors that thwarted the adoption of scientific management?

ENTREPRENEURIAL IDEOLOGIES AND ORGANIZATIONAL THOUGHT DURING THE FIRST INDUSTRIAL REVOLUTION

In the process of becoming the champion of the industrial revolution, Britain made several crucial contributions to entrepreneurial ideology as well as to organizational thought and practice. The early British entrepreneurs formulated an ideology and individualism, laissez-faire, and self-dependence of labor in an attempt to consolidate their position vis-à-vis the aristocracy and to create a plentiful supply of docile industrial workers. The shift from the traditional "theory of the dependence" (J. S. Mill's phrase) of labor on the upper class to the ideology of self-dependence facilitated the justification of wage employment and, in general, of the adaptation of the worker to factory conditions and life in the city. Leading intellectuals such as Edmund Burke and Thomas Malthus lent a hand in the elaboration of this new ideology in the late eighteenth and early nineteenth centuries. In the 1840s the success of the Anti–Corn Law alliance between industrial workers and industrialists against the landed aristocracy consolidated a new balance of forces until the rise of trades unionism towards the end of the century.[1]

Britain also pioneered modern organization and management techniques. British political economists were perhaps the first modern thinkers to consider the problem of the efficient management of labor. Adam Smith discussed the causes and consequences of the division of labor in the first three chapters of the *Wealth of Nations* (1776). The immense potential increase in output that resulted from the division of labor was by no means first observed by him. Previous thinkers like Petty, Mandeville, Harris, and Turgot had referred to it in passing. Smith illustrated his point with the famous pin-making example. He explained that in some factories the work of making pins was divided into eighteen separate operations to be performed by ten different persons. Without division of labor, output used to be less than one pin per workman and day; now it could be as high as 4,800 pins per workman and day. Smith enumerated three different reasons for this phenomenal productivity boost: the increase of dexterity or proficiency in each workman; the saving of the time lost in passing from one operation to another; and the greater possibility of inventing and applying special-purpose machinery to facilitate and abridge work tasks.[2]

Building on Smith's ideas, political economist Charles Babbage

---

1. Bendix, *Work and Authority in Industry* (1974, pp. 38–108); Thompson, "Time, work-discipline, and industrial capitalism" (1967). The earliest instance of management thought in Britain are perhaps the twenty-eight rules of administration enunciated by Canterbury Bishop Grosseteste in 1240 or 1241. See Keil, "Advice to the magnates" (1965).

2. Smith, *Wealth of Nations* (1976, pp. 13–36).

proposed a refined analysis of the division of labor. Babbage's contributions to organizational thought are all included in his treatise, *On the Economy of Machinery and Manufactures* (1832). This book was a commercial success, with four editions between June 1832 and January 1835 selling over 10,000 copies before the end of 1836.[3] Babbage dealt with the effects and advantages of the use of tools and machines in manufacturing. The single most important chapter of the book is the one on the division of labor, in which Babbage concisely formulated the crucial principle that

> the master manufacturer, by dividing the work to be executed into different processes, each requiring different degrees of skill or of force, can purchase exactly that precise quantity of both which is necessary for each process; whereas, if the whole work were executed by one workman, that person must possess sufficient skill to perform the most difficult, and sufficient strength to execute the most laborious, of the operations into which the art is divided.[4]

Thus, while Smith pointed out only the *technical* advantages of the division of labor (economizing on the quantity of labor), Babbage extended the analysis to the *economic* aspects (economizing on the wage rate to be paid to the worker). Using a numerical illustration of the pin-making process, he showed that, without applying his principle, making each of the pins would cost as much as "three times and three-quarters" more.[5]

In addition, Babbage launched the fields of time-and-motion study and operations research. He was interested in human fatigue and in job evaluation, and was the first to develop *ad hoc* questionnaires to collect data. He argued that fatigue could be reduced if work and rest times were adequately combined, thus anticipating Bedaux's analysis. As regards operations research, Babbage explained the importance of the careful scheduling of the flows of raw materials, and of the duration of different manufacturing operations. A firm believer in the identity of interests between capital and labor, he showed his concern for the fact that many workers failed to see the advantages of machinery and rational organization. Babbage argued that, in the short term, the introduction of machinery would reduce employment, but that, given competitive markets, the increased demand for products re-

3. However, economic historian Eric Hobsbawm has claimed that contemporary English industrialists dismissed scientists like Babbage as "unpractical eccentrics." Hobsbawm, *Industry and Empire* (1969, p. 122).

4. Babbage, *On the Economy of Machinery and Manufactures* (1835, pp. 175–176).

5. Babbage (1835, pp. 184–186).

sulting from lower costs would require additional workers in the longer run. Being aware of the fact that many innovations in machinery or organization had been originated by workers themselves, Babbage proposed a scheme of worker remuneration in which a substantial part of wages should be tied to the plant's profitability. However, he failed to suggest a rule for dividing profits between capitalists and workers.[6]

The leading managers of the first industrial revolution introduced methods of standardization, accounting, advanced division of labor, work study, and payment by results. Mathew Boulton and James Watt, Jr., directors of the Soho Engineering Foundry near Birmingham, are generally considered to be the first systematic managers.[7] On the eve of the formulation of the scientific management paradigm in America, British engineers and efficiency experts were developing ideas about premium systems (James Rowan), production and cost control, managerial planning, and organizational structure (Joseph Slater Lewis).[8]

CONDITIONS DEMANDING NEW ORGANIZATIONAL IDEAS

During the first three decades of the twentieth century, British managers seemed to turn their backs on their history of organizational and managerial achievements. As part of that process, they rejected American scientific management, a paradigm in part consistent with the British heritage of managerial knowledge. These developments seem bewildering because of the country's relative industrial decline and the threat of foreign economic competition, the growth of large enterprises, and the trades unions' challenges to managerial authority, factors which promoted the adoption of scientific management in other countries. Scientific management as formulated in America had organizational answers to those three problems in its promise to reduce waste and costs, eliminate output restriction by workers, alleviate tensions between workers and managers, and enhance direct managerial control. But British employers and managers decided to reject scientific management solutions or were forced to do so by other circum-

6. Babbage (1835, pp. 30–37, 250–259, 334–341); Berg, "Babbage, Charles" (1987); Moseley, *Irascible Genius: The Life of Charles Babbage* (1964).

7. Urwick, *The Golden Book of Management* (1956, pp. 1–9); Pollard, *The Genesis of Modern Management* (1965, pp. 251–272).

8. Lewis, *The Commercial Organisation of Factories* (1896); Urwick, *The Development of Scientific Management in Great Britain* (1938, pp. 24–28) and (1956, pp. 36–39, 44–47); Urwick and Brech, *The Making of Scientific Managment*. Vol. 2. *Management in British Industry* (1946, pp. 72–87).

stances. Before explaining the institutional factors that prevented the success of scientific management in interwar Britain, we shall dwell upon the specific nature of the economic and organizational problems facing British firms.

Industrial Retardation and Foreign Competition. Britain emerged from the Victorian era as the world's leading industrial and trading nation. During most of the nineteenth century Britain dominated world commerce and consolidated a leading position in textiles, iron, steel, coal, shipbuilding, machinery, and engineering. A country of comparatively unbroken political and social traditions, Britain championed pragmatism, laissez-faire economics, and the ideology of free trade. Yet these apparent strengths turned into disadvantages with the emergence of the United States and Germany as competitors on the world market. The fact that the firms in the industries of the First Industrial Revolution remained profitable eliminated incentives for investment in the new, scientific-technological industries such as chemicals, electrical technology, and motor vehicles.[9] Late industrializers such as Germany and the United States were not facing such liabilities. As a result of the importance of the low-growth, older industries, the British economy merely crept, while those of Germany and the United States expanded rapidly.

Relative economic retardation was particularly problematic in Britain because of her dependence on foreign trade. The limited size of the home market coupled with a reliance on raw materials from overseas made the British economy vulnerable to international competition. British foreign trade represented over 40 percent of the national product during the first three decades of the century, while in the United States it accounted for no more than 12 percent. Moreover, the British share of total world trade gradually halved from a high of one-fifth in 1920 to just one-tenth by 1929.[10] Increased competition on the world market posed a problem for British industry.

In addition to the lack of investments in the new industrial sectors and the deteriorating position in the world market, no coherent industrial policy was articulated by the state. British industry reverted to its old laissez-faire ways after the period of state intervention during World War I that effectively boosted war production.[11] Britain was in fact an island of laissez-faire in a sea of protectionism. The successes

9. Chandler, *Scale and Scope* (1990, pp. 284–285).
10. See the comparative statistics in Appendix B.
11. Chandler (1990, pp. 295–296).

of foreign competitors, coupled with the mistakes of British manufacturers, created the additional problem of the balance of payments, while the government's stubborn attachment to the gold standard artificially taxed British products. During the 1920s the British economy went through a series of ups and downs, but on the whole the growth gap relative to Germany and the United States widened.[12]

Were British employers and managers aware of the country's (and their own) decline? Back in 1919, historian L. J. Williams argues, "the economic legacy was better described as vaguely disquieting rather than alarming."[13] The pages of the leading management journals (*System, Business, Unity, Journal of Industrial Administration*) devoted scant attention to the problems of national economic decline or foreign competition, in sharp contrast with German journals.[14] British industrialists were receiving contradictory signals because their country remained a leader in several industries, and it emerged victorious from the war. Another feasible explanation for the seemingly incomprehensible complacency of British industrialists lies in the pace and nature of changes taking place inside British firms.

Changes in the Structure of Firms.   British industrial firms underwent a process of growth and bureaucratization similar to the one that American and German firms were experiencing at the turn of the century. The big difference was, again, that the largest British firms were concentrated in the old, low-growth sectors, while the largest American and German firms were more evenly distributed across old and new sectors. Despite bureaucratization, however, the unique feature of British firms was the persistence of personal, frequently family, control. While professional managers were displacing founders and heirs from the top American and German industrial corporations, British firms became even more dominated by family interests during the 1920s (in 1930 roughly 70 percent of the top 200 firms had at least one family board member as opposed to 55 percent in 1919). As business historian Alfred Chandler has argued, personally managed and family-controlled firms tend to be biased against growth. The

12. Williams, *Britain and the World Economy, 1919–1970* (1971); Pollard, *The Development of the British Economy 1914–1967* (1969); Hobsbawm (1969, pp. 179–193).

13. Williams (1971, p. 15). Contrast this appreciation with Hobsbawm's statement (1969, p. 207): "The Victorian economy of Britain crashed in ruins between the two world wars."

14. See a few exceptions: *System* 30(1916):417–424, 35(1919):95–100, 41(1922):270–271, 44(1923):317–320.

overriding concern, it seems, was to maintain control rather than to increase market share or exports. But the financial control of the enterprise was by no means the only aspect of authority that British industrialists had to deal with.[15]

Patterns of Shop-Floor Control and Labor Unrest. British industrialists became genuinely concerned with the problem of labor control and unrest starting in the 1890s. During the great Victorian boom of 1850–75, employers followed a strategy of intensive use of labor with low fixed investments. Given high profitability, they readily accepted a delegated craft control of production on the shop floor. They lost control over the distribution of tasks, the pace of work, apprenticeship programs, and wage structures. A distinctive pattern of working-class organization developed in the late Victorian period with a core of occupation-based, cross-industry trades unions. Trades unions organized along occupational lines, as opposed to on an industry-wide basis, created the need to protect manual skills when new technologies rendered them obsolete. New unskilled unions appeared at the turn of the century, but they joined forces with the craft unions, using the Labour Party as their political platform. The free educational system was a key factor behind the growing cohesion of the British working class.[16]

Unlike their socialist counterparts in southern Europe, the British trades unions constituted a moderate movement committed to parliamentary democracy and to plant-level collective bargaining. They generally rejected corporatist arrangements except during wartime. Union membership soared during the years before World War I, a period of declining real wages, while a series of fierce legal and political battles were fought to keep trades unionism legal. By 1913 roughly 20 percent of all British workers were union members, compared to only 7 percent in the United States and 10 percent in Germany. The war put many Labour Party leaders in posts of responsibility, but the revolutionary events in Russia and the slump that followed the cessation of hostilities renewed the problem of labor unrest. By

---

15. Hannah, "Visible and invisible hands in Great Britain," in Chandler and Daems, eds., *Managerial Hierarchies* (1980, pp. 53–55); Chandler (1990, pp. 240–242, 292); Payne, "Industrial entrepreneurship and management in Great Britain" (1978, pp. 204–207); Briggs, "Industrial relations in Great Britain," in Flanders and Clegg, *The System of Industrial Relations in Great Britain* (1964, pp. 34–35); see also the comparative statistics in Appendix B.

16. Smelser, *Social Paralysis and Social Change* (1991).

1920 almost 40 percent of all British workers were union members. The 1920s were bleak years for the working class and the unions, with industrial unemployment remaining above 10 percent and a declining membership base. Nonetheless, British workers were losing twice and even three times more working days due to industrial conflict than their counterparts in Germany, Sweden, Italy, and France. The unions staged a general strike in 1926 which, despite its disruptiveness, failed to achieve the goal of strengthening union power and certainly had no major political consequences.[17]

British employers and managers did see in labor unrest a problem they had to reckon with. The pages of the leading management journals are filled with articles, statements, and notes on the problems of labor unrest, the practice of *ca' canny* (go slow), and other challenges to managerial authority. The industrialists and managers who published their thoughts in these journals presented industrial unrest as the "dominant" problem facing them.[18] In 1916 leading employers, and a few union leaders, created the National Alliance of Employers and Employed to obtain industrial peace and avert class war. Other employer associations promoted the introduction of welfare programs, and even the state—so reluctant to articulate an industrial policy—intervened with social legislation (the 1911 National Insurance Act).

Unlike those in the United States and Germany, British employers and managers were facing the three problems of relative decline and aggressive foreign competition, growing complexity of the enterprise, and mounting labor unrest all at once. Scientific management had answers to all three of those problems, as is exemplified by the response of American employers to complexity and labor unrest and by the way German industrialists addressed complexity and foreign competition. The following section introduces the institutional factors that rendered scientific management an unlikely solution in the British situation.

17. Lazonick, *Competitive Advantage on the Shop Floor* (1990, pp. 182–196, 215–217); Littler, "Deskilling and changing structures of control" (1982b, pp. 123–131); Pelling, *A History of British Trade Unionism* (1976, pp. 85–87, 109–111, 149–182); Pollard (1969, pp. 28–34); *Unity* (October 1926):83; see also the comparative statistics in Appendix B.

18. See, in particular, *System* 33(1918):289, 35(1919):95–100, 119–123, 36(1919):75–79, 173–176, 293–299, 300–302, 44(1923):77–80, 50(1926):5–7, 52(1927):269–271, 306; *Journal of Industrial Administration* 1(1921):5–9; *Unity* (September 1926):70–72, (January 1927):135–136, (May 1930):66–68, (January 1931):194–220, 231–236, (August-September 1933):122–123, (January 1937): 217–224. See also Child, *British Management Thought* (1969, pp. 44–83).

INSTITUTIONAL FACTORS AGAINST THE ADOPTION OF
SCIENTIFIC MANAGEMENT

Four major institutional factors prevented the use of scientific management ideology and techniques to solve the various problems confronting British industry from the 1910s to the 1930s: (1) the scarcity of engineers and their unwillingness to act as advocates of Taylorism, (2) the cultural conservatism and antimodernism of the country's intellectual and business elites, (3) the lack of state support, and (4) the opposition from the trades unions. The sharp contrast with the German situation and the striking similarities with relatively backward Spain will become apparent.

Scarcity and Unwillingness of Engineers. At the turn of the century, Britain could count on between 1.8 and 2.9 qualified engineers per 1,000 workers active in industry, depending on the source. The highest of those two ratios was only half the one for the United States, Germany, or France. Even backward Spain had more qualified engineers relative to industrial employment. Although Britain caught up with those other countries during the years before World War I, the quality of engineering education was in doubt.[19] A country of practical inventors and craftsmen, Britain had long neglected technical education. In an 1869 report, J. Scott Russel concluded that "as a rule, technical education does not exist." Universities failed to include science and technology in their curricula, while employers neglected the role of engineering and science in industry. In fact, British firms have traditionally admitted few engineers to the ranks of upper management. Given the absence of university programs in engineering, the professional associations were the only institutions that could test the competence of aspiring engineers. Various engineering associations appeared, but they did not introduce written examinations for entry until 1897 in the case of the Institution of Civil Engineers and 1912 in the case of the Institution of Mechanical Engineers, which, despite having been founded in 1847, was not awarded a Royal Charter until as late as 1930. In Britain, in contrast to Germany and France, engineering remained a low-prestige profession attracting mediocre students.[20]

19. Ahlström, *Engineers and Industrial Growth* (1982, pp. 13–14); Buchanan, *The Engineers* (1989, p. 233).
20. Ahlström (1982, pp. 79–93); Wiener, *English Culture and the Decline of the Industrial Spirit 1850–1980* (1985, p. 141); Dore, *British Factory, Japanese Factory* (1973, pp. 46–48); Glover and Kelly, *Engineers in Britain* (1987, pp. 99–115, 184–

Contrary to the enthusiastic reception given to American scientific management ideas by the German engineering profession, British engineers reacted with reticence and even open animosity. Only one of the three leading British engineering journals recorded the publication of Frederick Taylor's 1895 paper on piece-rate systems. His treatise titled *Shop Management* (1903) was not discussed by any of the four leading engineering journals published at the time. A handful of technical and trade journals commented on *The Principles of Scientific Management* (1911), but critically rather than admiringly.[21] A leader in *The Engineer* in 1911 explained the basic charge against scientific management, one that would recur in the future:

> We do not hesitate to say that Taylorism is inhuman. As far as possible it dehumanizes the man, for it endeavors to remove the only distinction that makes him better than a machine—his intelligence."[22]

The theme of scientific management as "a too rigorous systematization of method to the exlusion of all other considerations" appeared repeatedly during the early 1910s. True to their traditions, British engineers thought that commonsense approaches to management were sufficient; there was no need for an increased use of science or method. Moreover, they attacked the "scientistic" pretentiousness of Taylorism, thus undermining its most important claim to authority and to superior organizational practice:

> It is the ordinary doctrine of works that better methods must be adopted as soon as they present themselves. It is scientific, of course, but to call it scientific is like speaking of the common pump as a philosophical instrument.[23]

Moreover, *The Engineer* warned against the high administrative and supervisory costs associated with the Taylor system, and placed the burden of proof on the Taylorites: "We have yet to learn that British works managed on American lines have paid higher dividends than British works managed on British lines."[24] Only in the midst of World War I did the president of the Institution of Mechanical Engineers regret that "except in a few cases, workshop organization here

---

189); Buchanan (1989, pp. 106–122); Donnelly, "Science, technology and industrial work in Britain, 1860–1930" (1991); Locke, *The End of the Practical Man* (1984).

21. Levine, *Industrial Retardation in Britain 1880–1914* (1967, pp. 61–62).
22. Quoted in Levine (1967, p. 63).
23. Quoted from *The Engineer* (1913) in Levine (1967, p. 64).
24. Published in 1913. Quoted by Littler (1982, pp. 95–96).

has not received the attention given it in America or Germany."[25] But the wartime production drive, far from facilitating the adoption of scientific management ideas, further pushed British management thought and practice toward the problem of the dehumanization of industrial work. During the Great Slump (as the Great Depression was known in Britain) engineers blamed mechanization for growing unemployment, suggesting that mechanical advances were evolving much quicker than human and social relationships.[26] The Institute of Estimators, Planning, and Time Study Engineers (the first association for work study) was created as late as 1941. The contrast with German developments could not be sharper.

Elite Mentalities: Cultural Conservatism and Failed Modernism. During the decades preceding the formulation of the scientific management paradigm, the British business elite harbored a mentality of cultural conservatism that included several influences: a social philosophy grounded on naturalistic and organicist concepts, the ideals of handwork and craftsmanship, a social-reformist attitude, ruralism, nostalgia, and revivalism. This mentality was strikingly similar to the one developing in Spain at roughly the same time, but completely opposed to the dominant modernist-technocratic mentality in Germany and the United States. Closely intertwined with the aristocracy, most of the British business elite of company directors shared a common education at public schools and Oxbridge that emphasized the classics to the virtual exclusion of scientific, technical, and commercial subjects.[27] There was a hostility to "money-grubbing" and "acquisitive capitalist society," perceptible even in the writings by the leading economists such as John Stuart Mill, Alfred Marshall, and John Maynard Keynes. The elite of company directors and administrators thought of their function in society as something "higher" and more "genteel" than American "business management." Foreign ways of doing business were customarily dismissed for not being inspired in the values of "gentlemanliness," "humanity," "honor," and "craftsmanship."[28]

25. Quoted in Levine (1967, p. 60).

26. See *Industry Illustrated* 1(2)(1933):xv–xvi.

27. This was not so in the late medieval and early modern periods, as documented by Richardson, "Business training in medieval Oxford" (1941).

28. Wiener (1985, pp. 17–24, 90–94, 131, 140–144); Chandler (1990, pp. 292–293); Whitley, "The city and industry," and Stanworth and Giddens, "An economic elite," in Stanworth and Giddens, eds., *Elites and Power in British Society* (1974, pp.

British intellectuals and artists reinforced those beliefs. Instead of becoming a source of inspiration, the machine and the mechanic were seen as unnatural and inorganic. In fact, the leading Victorian social thinkers such as Thomas Carlyle, Charles Dickens, John Ruskin, and Herbert George Wells found it hard to come to terms with the machine age. As historian Herbert Sussman has put it, in Britain

> the opposition to mechanized production, the celebration of hand labor, the aesthetic distaste for the machine are but expressions of the deeper conflict between rationalism and intuitionism, between scientific and organic modes of thought.[29]

The close relationship between modernist art and industry that favored the adoption of scientific management in countries such as Germany and Italy did not develop in Britain. The 1851 Universal Exhibition at the massive Crystal Palace in Hyde Park, London, had been a demonstration of British industrial might and material advance. It was the *last* important world exhibition in Britain. The long Victorian period of political stability and economic expansion no doubt created the kind of complacency and aversion to change that would prove fatal to the development of the avante-garde movement in Britain. Moreover, the very philosophical foundations of the English Arts and Crafts movement were not conducive to new forms of mass manufacturing, for it favored "the production of unique specimens of artistic workmanship." The impact of the movement on industry was limited. The leader of the Arts and Crafts, William Morris, was himself a typical product of the Victorian era, with his disdain for technological progress. A craftsman, Morris vehemently railed against the principle of the division of labor and declared that mechanized work implied grave psychological hazards and was inherently oppressive. Similar points of view were expounded by the leading British architect of the time, Charles Rennie Mackintosh. It is ironic that the German pioneers of industrial design traveled to England in the early 1900s to learn about the Arts and Crafts, only to abandon the principles of individual work and craftsmanship so as to embrace rationalized methods of production.[30]

65–101); Coleman, "Gentlemen and players" (1973); Dubin, "Management in Britain" (1970); Wilkinson, *Gentlemanly Power* (1964).

29. Sussman, *Victorians and the Machine* (1968, p. 233).

30. Sussman (1968, pp. 104–134); Read, *Art and Industry* (1954, pp. 79–80, 219–225); Banham, *Theory and Design in the First Machine Age* (1980, pp. 44–45); Cooper ed., *Mackintosh Architecture* (1977); Pevsner, *An Enquiry into Industrial Art in England* (1937, pp. 136, 154–169, 179, 206–207).

The lack of collaboration between industry and the design community curtailed export-boosting efforts aimed at regaining economic dominance during the late 1910s and the 1920s. The Design and Industries Association was created in 1915, followed by the inception in 1920 of the British Institute of Industrial Art, amidst the indifference of manufacturers. A decade later, the Gorell Report (1931) commissioned by the British Board of Trade openly recognized the exhaustion of industrial art in Britain. In 1934 the board decided to create a Council for Art and Industry, which also failed to gain continued support from industry or from the state. A similar fate was met by English architecture, civil engineering, and housing design, which turned classical and revivalist after the early achievements of the Crystal Palace and the massive Firth of Forth Bridge. The failure of the British modernist movement not only removed the possibility of justifying the implementation of scientific management; in addition, no sustained efforts to standardize components, products, tools, and machinery were made.[31]

The decisively antimodernist stand of the British intelligentsia had direct consequences for their assessment of production and industry. Aldous Huxley in his 1932 book *Brave New World,* English-born Charles Chaplin in his 1936 movie *Modern Times,* and George Orwell in his 1946 article "James Burnham and the Managerial Revolution," or in his 1949 novel *Nineteen Eighty-Four,* satirized scientific methods of mass production and raised fears about the rise of bureaucratic managers in business and about the "massification" of society in a manner reminiscent of the writings of Spain's José Ortega y Gasset.[32]

British managers failed to grasp the significance of modern design for industry. Sir Ernest Lever (Lord Leverhulme), director of several important companies, argued against process simplification and product standardization because consumer tastes and the size of the market in Britain were so different from those in the United States.[33] During the 1930s, *Industry Illustrated* published one article on the need to promote industrial design, written by J. Craven Pritchard, sometime chairman of the Design and Industries Association. The editors explicitly criticized William Morris in 1934 for not realizing the new

31. Stewart, *Design and British Industry* (1987, pp. 39–73); Read (1954, pp. 222–234).

32. Huxley, *Brave New World* (1989, pp. 3, 52–55); Orwell, "James Burnham and the Managerial Revolution." (1968), and *Nineteen Eighty-Four* (1949).

33. See *System* 41(1922):270–271, 54(1928):333–334; *Business* 55(1929): 91–92, 113.

artistic opportunities created by mechanization. As part of their over-riding concern with the social situation of workers, however, the editors argued that rather than an engineer, "an architect is what a businessman must eminently be. He must prevent those personal maladjustments in industry." He must be "an architect of wealth and welfare," avoiding the "ugly, dull and irksome" tasks that make the worker's "soul ugly and [make] the temper and tone of his whole community ugly too." In 1946 the same editors quoted Morris to attack scientific management and praise the human relations ap-proach.[34] Consistent with their thought, the leading human relations proponents of the interwar period argued that utilitarian design of the modernist type was plain ugly.[35] They quoted Morris once again to criticize the "unpraised, unrewarded, monotonous drudgery which most [working] men are condemned to."[36] Clearly, the dominant British mentality could tolerate neither the ideology of scientific man-agement nor its social, aesthetic, and intellectual agenda.

Lack of Support from the State. As in Spain during the 1920s, state initiatives in the labor arena proved counter-productive for the adop-tion of scientific management in Britain. On the one hand, the state engaged in the promotion of social welfare programs and mechanisms of worker-management cooperation (Whitley councils), which were conducive to a human relations point of view. On the other, the state financed several important programs of industrial research during and after World War I that eventually departed from scientific manage-ment and actually evolved into a human relations approach to organi-zation. The 1917 report by the Health of Munition Workers Commit-tee, *Industrial Efficiency and Fatigue,* criticized economic incentives, pointing out that they were not the only motivator. In its research, the committee shifted its emphasis from physiological to psychologi-cal and social variables. Research by the Ministry of Reconstruction also underlined the importance of the human element. In 1923 the Industrial Fatigue Research Board, which continued the activities of the committee throughout the 1920s, issued a report on *Time and Motion Study* in which Taylor and Gilbreth were criticized for their speedup bias. Thus, a state-supported agency like the German Na-tional Board of Efficiency (RKW) was entirely lacking.[37] Only the

---

34. See *Industry Illustrated* 2(3)(1934):24–25, 2(8)(1934):13, 2(9)(1934):13, 14(3)(1946):11; *British Management Review* 3(1938):5–27.

35. C. H. Northcott, in *Industry Illustrated* 1(4)(1933):xx.

36. Morris, as quoted by Wallas, *The Great Society* (1914, p. 326).

37. Thomas, *The British Philosophy of Administration* (1978, pp. 13–17, 171–185); Child (1969, pp. 83–84); Urwick and Brech (1946, p. 191).

Balfour Committee of 1927 called attention to industrial efficiency as practiced in the United States, but business opinion leaders recommended prudence and emphasized the need to preserve the "mental equilibrium" of British management.[38]

The Opposition of Organized Labor. The trades union movement not only created a problem for British industrialists, but it also opposed both the ideology and the implementation of the techniques of scientific management. Trades unionists criticized the lack of any indication in the writings of the scientific managers as to how the increased surplus was to be divided. In addition, the perverse effects of scientific management (monotony, extreme subdivision of labor, automatism, speedups) were pointed out. In 1909 the Trades Unions Congress (TUC) appointed a subcommittee to investigate scientific management. Its conclusions were that scientific management threatened collective bargaining and trades unionism, promoted selfishness among workers, and was a cause of unemployment.[39]

National controversies over unemployment, incentive schemes, and trades union protest erupted in the early 1920s, as reflected in the pages of the London daily *Times*.[40] The ideological attack on scientific management frequently used the distinctiveness of the British character and way of life as an argument against the transfer of American management techniques, in contrast with the position taken by the German Free Unions during the 1920s. The following statement by Sir Ben Turner, sometime chairman of the Labour Party and of the TUC, and a delegate to America for the TUC in 1910, was published in 1927 while he was chairman of the TUC General Council:

> America is pointed out as a sample country where harder work brings progressively higher wages. I should not like our country to be Americanised. There "Money is the god" of most people. They seem to be no more happy than our people are. . . . I want gentleness of life more than the gold rush life. I believe it is more desirable to have less Americanism and more Humanism than I read about by the American intensive system of money-making.[41]

As late as 1929 the trades unions were still discussing whether to

38. See *System* 51(1927):142, 229–231, 274.
39. Brown, *Sabotage* (1977, pp. 151–152); Urwick and Brech (1946, p. 89). See also the opposition of trades unionist G. D. H. Cole in *The Sociological Review* 7(2) (April 1914):117–125.
40. See *System* 44(1923):165–167, 49(1926):9–11.
41. *Unity* (March 1927):166.

favor industrial rationalization measures, pointing out that they would only support them if rationalization were to be orchestrated by the state in consultation with the unions.[42] On the shop floor, British workers fought the introduction of scientific management techniques such as piecework schemes, time and motion studies, managerial planning, and the Bedaux System. For example, national union leaders thought the Bedaux scheme was "intensive scientific slavery . . . an inhuman system of speed-up that sought to turn people into machines," plant-level unionists argued that it was "a damnable pernicious system," and women workers cried, "We're going to be like slaves."[43]

THE THEORETICAL REJECTION OF SCIENTIFIC MANAGEMENT IN INTERWAR BRITAIN

Given the lack of favorable institutional factors, it should be no surprise to find few leading British employers, managers, or intellectuals defending the application of scientific management. Many were interested in the new paradigm, but with major reservations. Industrialist and Cornell-trained engineer Charles G. Renold had introduced time-and-motion studies in his firm in the early 1910s. He cautioned against Taylor's excessively mechanistic approach in his 1922 essay on scientific management in the *Encyclopaedia Britannica*.[44] The president of the British Chamber of Shipping, Sir William Seager, noted the "obstinate and destructive prejudice" against scientific management among British managers.[45] Edward Cadbury, director of several mass-media and food-processing firms, emphasized the perverse effects of Taylorism on the worker. Federick Taylor himself responded by saying that Cadbury was not competent to judge.[46]

Among the leading intellectuals, only Professor Sidney Webb, a Fabian Socialist and admirer of the Soviet Union, thought that scientific management under workers' control was good. But Professor

---

42. See the article by Herbert H. Elvin, of the TUC General Council, in *Unity* (December 1929):483–485.

43. Downs, "Industrial decline, rationalization and equal pay" (1990, pp. 59, 60, 72); Brown (1977, pp. 148–151); Pollard (1969, pp. 81–82). Downs (1990, pp. 47–48) explains that only a few union leaders (e.g., Ernest Bevin) favored industrial rationalization, but that the rank-and-file almost always opposed it.

44. Renold, "Scientific management" (1922, p. 380).

45. See *Business* 61(1932):9–10.

46. Cadbury, "Some principles of industrial organization: The case for and against scientific management" *The Sociological Review* 7(2) (April 1914):99–117. For the reactions of several managers to Cadbury's article, including Taylor's, see pp. 117–125.

Graham Wallas, author of one of the Fabian essays, charged scientific management with the problems of monotony at work. For liberal sociologist J. A. Hobson, "it seems evident that scientific management involves a loss or injury to the workers." Economist Sir William Ashley raised similar criticisms. The editors of the Socialist *The New Statesman* criticized scientific management for its high costs of implementation and deskilling effects on craftsmen, adding that the method was not as neutral and "scientific" as claimed.[47]

The British management intellectuals of the 1920s also criticized Taylorism, even though many of them were connected to the reformist Liberal Party, the parallel of the American Progressives. John Lee, director of several telecommunications companies, was perhaps the leading management intellectual of this period. He argued that the separation of conception from execution wasted the experience, initiative, and creativity of the worker, and that "human nature is too complex for the crude Scientific Management." He nonetheless expressed the hope that scientific management would reduce waste without causing more than "transitory social strain."[48] Oliver Sheldon, a manager at Rowntree & Co., attacked Taylorism for its lack of concern with the human element and rejected the application of time-and-motion study as suggested by American scientific managers, because people could not be treated as machines. Sheldon noted the "chilly reception" that British managers offered to scientific management.[49] Lyndall Urwick, a writer and consultant on organization who became director of the League of Nations' International Management Institute in Geneva, was a keen supporter of a scientific approach to management. But his concept of economic rationalization neglected the issue of shop organization along scientific management lines, and he eventually became a supporter of the human relations approach.[50] Lee, Sheldon, and Urwick saw in scientific management, however, a

47. Webb, *The Works Manager To-Day* (1979, pp. 11, 133–140), originally published in 1918; Wallas (1914, pp. 327–339); Hobson, *Work and Wealth* (1914, pp. 202–227), "Scientific management" *The Sociological Review* 6(3) (July 1913):197–212; *New Statesman*, "Scientific management" (1916); Ashley, *Scientific Management and the Engineering Situation* (1922, p. 25).

48. Lee, *Management* (1921, pp. 65–66, 70), and *An Introduction to Industrial Administration* (1925, pp. 132–133). Lee was the editor of the *Dictionary of Industrial Administration* (1928), in which several entries were devoted to scientific management (pp. 509–512, 715–717, 760–768).

49. Sheldon, "The art of management from a British point of view" (1923, p. 209); *The Philosophy of Management* (1924, pp. 229–231).

50. Urwick, *The Meaning of Rationalisation* (1929).

way of professionalizing a British management beset by the evils of nepotism and unsystematic thought. Other top managers saw only the negative aspects. At a dinner of the Royal Society, Sir F. Gowland Hopkins argued that scientific managers should address the "social dislocations" brought about by mechanization and rationalization.[51] Even the chairman of Ford Motor in Britain, Sir Percival Perry, declared that "men are more important than machines." Most British employers found Ford's wage policy "promiscuous."[52]

A content analysis of the articles published in the leading British management journals between 1913 and 1939 reveals the slight attention devoted to scientific management by British management intellectuals. The publication of *The Principles of Scientific Management* in 1911 did not produce a wave of articles on the subject. Scientific management articles were only published in relatively great numbers starting in 1916 and until 1921 as part of the rationalization drive during World War I (but one-third of the authors were American efficiency experts). During the mid-1930s a new burst of scientific management articles appeared (see panel B of Table 5.1). (Journal articles were coded according to the rules explained in Appendix A.) The ideological themes of scientific management were rarely discussed. Only the perceived problem (waste, output restriction, arbitrariness), the methodology of time-and-motion study, and the separation of conception from execution were mentioned frequently (see panel A of Table 5.1). In general, the managers and consultants publishing from the 1910s to the 1930s were interested in labor-saving machinery, technical improvements, and commonsense approaches to organization. The whole ideological approach and a large part of the technical approach of scientific management to organization was rejected in theory. Most management intellectuals, however, accepted the need to develop a scientific body of managerial knowledge that could provide a basis for the professionalization of British management.[53]

THE LIMITED PRACTICAL IMPLEMENTATION OF SCIENTIFIC MANAGEMENT

During the interwar period scientific management and mass-production techniques were not widely adopted in Britain. Techniques such as job analysis and time-and-motion study "spread un-

51. *Industry Illustrated* 1(12)(1933):1.
52. *Business* 60(1931):205, 236–237; Downs (1990, p. 47).
53. Child (1969, pp. 38–39); Urwick (1938, pp. 78–80).

TABLE 5.1 Results of the content analysis of the articles published in *System, Business,* and *Industry Illustrated,* 1913–1939, by paradigm (SM: scientific management; HR: human relations; SA: structural analysis; NC: not classifiable)

A. Number of articles mentioning each of the content categories (see Appendix A) and themes (72 articles examined)

Content Categories	SM	HR	SA
Perceived problem	43	16	3
Form of solution	3	0	2
View of conflict	2	2	0
View of workers	0	8	1
Fascination with	1	4	0
Methodology	35	1	0
Selection of workers	3	3	1
Distribution of tasks	21	3	3
Authority structures	5	10	3
Process of work	18	4	2
Preferred rewards	13	6	1
Economic incentives	14	0	0

B. Number of articles (*N*) and themes classified by paradigm

Year Period	SM				HR				SA				NC
	N	Mean	Min	Max	*N*	Mean	Min	Max	*N*	Mean	Min	Max	*N*
		Themes				Themes				Themes			
1913–15	3	2.0	2	2	0	—	—	—	0	—	—	—	1
1916–18	9	3.1	2	5	2	2.5	2	3	0	—	—	—	1
1919–21	8	3.1	2	4	1	3.0	3	3	0	—	—	—	2
1922–24	1	3.0	3	3	1	3.0	3	3	0	—	—	—	0
1925–27	5	2.8	2	4	0	—	—	—	0	—	—	—	0
1928–30	0	—	—	—	2	3.0	3	3	0	—	—	—	1
1931–33	7	3.7	2	6	5	2.8	2	4	2	3.0	3	3	0
1934–36	11	3.5	2	5	2	4.0	4	4	1	2.0	2	2	0
1937–39	2	4.5	4	5	3	3.3	3	4	0	—	—	—	2
All years	46	3.3	2	6	16	3.1	2	4	3	2.7	2	3	7
Pages	165	3.6	1	8	44	2.8	1	7	10	3.3	3	4	31

Note: Title of the journal varied as follows: *System* (1913–28), *Business* (1929–32), *Industry Illustrated* (1933–39).

Sources: The articles included in the analysis are the following:

SM: *System* 25:189–192, 475–480; 26:188–192; 29:89–97, 331–333; 30:114–119, 220–226, 271–276; 33:344–348; 34:227–234, 303–309; 35:129–133, 274–278; 36:254–255; 38:47–48, 430–431, 438–439; 39:177–178, 522–523; 40:406–408; 44:28–30; 48:69–70, 49:14–16; 50:105–107, 113–115; 51:75–77. *Business* 61(3):23, 4:15–16; 62(1):7–8. *Industry Illustrated* 1(1):10–12, 39–41, (6):41–44, 46–50; 2(3):24–25, (4):41–45, (5):23–25, (6):30–32, (11):27–31; 3(2):37, (11):11–13, (12):30–32; 4(1):14–17, (11):16–17, (12):20–22; 5(3):23–24; 6(1):27–28.

HR: *System* 33:319–322; 34:193–196; 36:101–104; 41:91–93. *Business* 56:72; 58:333–335; 61(4):26; 62(8):10. *Industry Illustrated* 1(5):xiii–xiv, (6):xxiii–xxvii; 3(10):34–39; 4(5):10–11; 6(1):24, (3):11–12, (9):11–12.

SA: *Business* 62(8):7–9. *Industry Illustrated* 1(2):xvii–xviii; 3(12):21–24.

NC: *System* 28:163–172; 30:417–424; 36:160–161; 39:71–72; 41:187–189; 54:320. *Business* 61(5):9–10. *Industry Illustrated* 3(8):43–45; 4(2):14–17, (6):10–13; 6(5):12–14, (11):37–39; 7(11):11–13.

evenly," while "traditional patterns of foremanship survived on a large scale."[54] Some students of this period have documented that British managers thought that Fordist principles were at odds with the prevailing craft system. British firms did not start implementing Fordist techniques until the very late 1920s. Moving assembly lines did not proliferate until the late 1930s. In the auto industry, not even the Ford Motor Company was able to reproduce the Detroit system in its British plants at Trafford Park and Dagenham. William Morris failed to introduce the Fordist powered assembly line or the minute division of labor at his Oxford Motor Company until the mid-1930s. He referred to his earlier, unsuccessful attempts as "*mess* production." Herbert Austin's introduction of the assembly line in the late 1920s without shifting from piecework to standard hour rates resulted in workers "pick[ing] the bodies up . . . and jump[ing] the pegs [to move the cars along faster than the assembly line]."[55]

As in the United States, scientific management began to spread as a result of consulting activities of several groups of neo-Taylorites, but only in the late 1930s. The most important one was Bedaux, whose British activities date back to the mid-1920s. In fact, the Bedaux System (including time-setting techniques and an incentive scheme) was only adopted widely in the United States and Britain. Bedaux began to be successful in Britain towards the late 1930s and early 1940s. In the early years of the Great Slump, the Bedaux engineers met with strong resistance from both workers and supervisors. Several week-long and a few month-long strikes were staged by workers to fight the introduction of the Bedaux System. The most controversial strikes took place during the early 1930s at the Richard Johnson and Nephew metals works in Manchester, the Wolsey Hosiery Company in Leicester, the Lucas aircraft factory in Birmingham, and the Rover car works in Coventry. In these cases, the Bedaux System was either totally abandoned or implemented with fundamental modifications. The TUC issued a heavily critical report and initiated legal action against the Bedaux consulting organization.[56]

---

54. Hill, *Competition and Control at Work* (1981, pp. 31–34); Lewchuck, *American Technology and the British Vehicle Industry* (1987, pp. 89–95); Clark, *Anglo-American Innovation* (1987, pp. 329–332).

55. Lewchuk, "Fordism and British motor car employers 1896–1932" (1983), and (1987, pp. 152–184); Downs (1990, p. 48 n. 6); Womack, Jones, and Roos, *The Machine that Changed the World* (1991, pp. 228–234); Tolliday, "Management and labour in Britain 1896–1939." (1987).

56. Littler, *The Development of the Labour Process in Capitalist Societies* (1982a, pp. 105, 117–145); Downs (1990); Brown (1977, pp. 231–249); *Unity* (March 1932): 24–25, (May 1932):65.

The case of Rover illustrates the reasons why scientific management techniques were not easily adopted in Britain before World War II. In the early 1930s, the managers at Rover decided to shift from an emphasis on small-batch production and high-quality cars to a strategy of long production runs of standardized cars. As a way of implementing such a change, they planned to accelerate the transition from an evolving craft-based system to Fordist mass production. Such an organizational change required cost cutting, productivity increases, changes in the prevailing patterns of division of labor, and more direct managerial control. The managers found in the Bedaux System the necessary inspiration and techniques. Employers in the area used to stratify their use of labor on the basis of age, skill level, and gender. Trades unions were also stratified by skill and segregated by gender. Given that the male workers were organized into unions, the management decided to try the Bedaux System with the female workers in the trimming department first, who were laboring under a fairly popular piecework scheme. When the first 8 affected women refused to accept the changes, they were summarily fired, with the result that the entire department of 150 women went on strike. Next, the management asked the male trimmers in another department to take over for the women. When they refused, and after receiving a firing threat, they too joined the striking women. The skilled and unionized male workers realized that management's true intention was to implement the Bedaux System throughout the works and not just in the female shops. National trades union leaders (Ernest Bevin) attempted to settle the dispute by giving Rover managers the right to introduce the Bedaux System in exchange for a higher minimum wage and the closing of the existing gender-based wage gap. But all workers at Rover resisted fiercely until the management withdrew the proposal. Interestingly, other employers in the area ostracized the Rover managers because of their intention to compromise with the trades unions, and their willingness to eliminate wage differentials by gender, a move that was at odds with the traditional structure of the local labor market. The local business association effectively put pressure on Rover to abandon the plan. In the end, the old division of labor and piecework schemes remained in place. The Rover case, of course, illustrates the inertia and aversion to change so characteristic of the British employer class of the time.[57]

57. This sketch of the Rover case is based on the excellent article by Downs (1990).

THE ADOPTION OF SCIENTIFIC MANAGEMENT AFTER WORLD WAR II

Scientific management techniques, including the Bedaux System, were widely adopted in Britain *after* World War II. Two institutional factors had changed when compared to the interwar situation. First, the Anglo-American Council on Productivity (AACP), and later the British Productivity Center (BPC), were created in combination with the Marshall Plan agencies to promote the adoption of advanced American management techniques, including scientific management and mass production. The state had finally joined in to accelerate organizational change in Britain so as to arrest the country's relative decline. *We Too Can Prosper* was the title of a famous AACP-sponsored report published in 1953 that recommended the adoption of the American system of manufacturing. The second relevant change in the institutional situation was that the TUC modified its attitude towards scientific management in 1950, arguing that "unions should seek to cooperate in the application of 'scientific management' which, even if not an exact science, can make a valuable contribution to increasing productivity in industry." In fact, the unions continued their policy of active collaboration until the late 1950s, even under a conservative government. Last, but not least, in a tight labor market workers were more willing to accept piecework and time studies because employers had to raise the rates in order to keep the best performers. Firms like ICI started to use time studies intensively only in the early 1950s.[58]

The parallel evolution of organizational ideologies and practices in Britain and Spain during the interwar period is rather striking, given the marked differences in economic development. Scientific management failed as an ideology and as a set of techniques in both countries between the World Wars, in contrast with the developments in the United States and Germany. To be sure, Britain and Spain differed in terms of the dominant organizational problems. In Spain firms were not nearly as big, complex, and bureaucratized as in Britain,

---

58. Carew, *Labour Under the Marshall Plan* (1987, pp. 133–157, 168–169, 201–211); Brown (1977, pp. 297, 314); Hutton, *We Too Can Prosper* (1953): TUC, *Trade Unions and Productivity* (1950, pp. 59–60); BIM, *The Application of Modern Management Techniques in the Smaller Enterprise* (1954); Bornstein and Gourevitch, "Unions in a declining economy" (1984); Clark (1987, pp. 329–332); *Industry Illustrated* 16(2)(1948):20–21. Another interesting, though not significant, change was the new favorable attitude towards industrial design that developed within the Federation of British Industries. See FBI, *Annual Report* for the years 1946 through 1964.

and foreign competition did not pose a similar threat because of the protectionist policies that sealed the Spanish market from the outer world. But labor unrest was a problem in both societies. The institutional factors affecting organizational change were also similar in both cases. Britain and Spain had comparatively few engineers, culturally conservative intellectual and business elites, no state agencies engaged in the promotion of new techniques, and militant unions opposing changes in patterns of shop-floor organization. In these four respects, the contrast with Weimar Germany could not be clearer. Scientific management techniques were widely adopted in Britain and Spain only during the 1940s and 1950s, when state agencies started promoting them in response to growing international pressures, and when opposition from the unions turned into collaboration. As will become evident in the following section, the success of the human relations ideology in Britain during the late 1940s and throughout the 1950s owed much to the same institutional factors present in Spain during roughly the same period, with the significant difference that human relations techniques were adopted in Britain but not in Spain.

The British Human Relations Movement

In Britain human relations provided a solution to the unique organizational problems facing the country and was consistent with the mentality shared by a majority of employers and managers. The growth and originality of British social-science research and consulting on human relations, the support of state agencies, and the collaboration of the trades unions and the Labour Party facilitated the adoption of the paradigm by managers as well as the adoption of its most important techniques. The acceptance of human relations ideology in Britain resulted from the same institutional factors as in Spain. The difference in degrees of adoption of human relations techniques is only explicable by reference to the much lower levels of bureaucratization and sophistication of Spanish firms.

THE NEW ORGANIZATIONAL PROBLEMS OF THE 1940s AND 1950s

The Great Slump of the 1930s was shallower in Britain than in the United States and Germany. The ensuing recovery was comparatively more robust, with the new industries faring relatively well (electric, motor vehicles, aircraft, rayon). After World War II, British industry recovered quickly, taking over many European markets thanks to the temporary weakness of Germany. Keynesian macroeconomic policies and the creation of a powerful sector of state-owned enterprises (coal, railways, gas, electricity) contributed to "managed" growth.[59] But British industrialists would soon be facing problems that required ideological and organizational action.

The Threat of Industrial Conflict and the Problem of Output Restriction. The nightmare of labor unrest facing British employers throughout the 1910s and 1920s subsided during the 1930s and after World War II. The average British worker lost only 0.15 days of work each year during the 1930s, drastically down from 1.80 days per annum during the previous decade. High unemployment and the subsequent weakening of the trades unions obviously helped reduce industrial conflict, as did the widespread introduction of welfare measures. During the late 1940s, industrial conflict remained low, but union membership started to rise again, surpassing the record high of 1929. With the Labour government creating one of the most extensive welfare states in the world, British workers and their trades unions saw many of their dreams come true. Also, industrial arbitration and collective bargaining seemed to work effectively. But the nationalization measures and the growth of trades-union power created a wave of criticism of private management in the press. As sociologist John Child argues, British managers had to regain and maintain their legitimacy.[60] By and large, industrial peace continued until 1955, despite the conservative victory in the general election of 1951. But the new 1955 election produced a wave of industrial conflict that reminded British employers and managers that industrial harmony could be a transitory state. Overall, industrial conflict levels in Britain (0.13 annual days lost per worker during the 1950s) remained much lower than in the United States (0.55) but higher than in Germany (0.04). Nevertheless, bad years such as 1957, 1959, and 1962, when conflict levels were between three and four times higher than average, reminded British employers and managers of the threat of reverting to the old situation of acute labor unrest.[61]

Furthermore, output restriction by workers continued being a common practice after World War II. Some witty politicians and popular writers referred to it as "modern Luddism." As late as 1964

59. Williams (1971); Pollard (1969, pp. 376–391).

60. Child (1969, pp. 111–112).

61. Pelling (1976); Pollard (1969, pp. 392–394); see also the comparative statistics in Appendix B.

the topic still aroused passions when the American consultant William Allen published a famous article in *The Sunday Times:* "Half time Britain on half pay," followed by a television series, "Half Time Britain." Output restriction was amenable to both scientific management and human relations techniques. Scientific management proponents readily argued that their approach could solve the problem. In the case of human relations, though, a paradox emerged: reasserting managerial control was, in principle, at odds with the emphasis on participation and communication.[62]

Further Changes in the Structure of Firms. The bureaucratization of British industrial firms continued unabated during the late 1940s and throughout the 1950s, following a trend similar to the one observed for American firms. The Great Slump and World War II represented a backlash to the service sector, but after the late 1940s it expanded again.[63] The increasing bureaucratization of the population of British organizations during these years created problems amenable to, and the conditions necessary for, the implementation of human relations techniques.

International Competitive Pressures. The British economy expanded quite steadily after World War II, but its growth rate (an annual 2.3% during the 1950s) lagged behind those for Germany (7.1%) and the United States (3.0%). In addition, the economy became more dependent on foreign markets at the same time that its share of world trade shrank still further.[64] Productivity studies showed that American workers were on average three times as productive as British ones. It was suggested that the productivity gap had to do with differences not only in capital intensity but also in management skills, implementation of scientific management, and techniques to improve the "atmosphere" in the factory.[65] Once again, industrial retardation created the kind of international pressures that proved favorable for the introduction of innovative organizational methods such as scientific management and mass-production technologies, and perhaps the human relations techniques designed to increase productivity. On the whole,

62. Brown (1977, pp. 297–298, 300–303).
63. See the comparative statistics in Appendix B, and Florence, *The Logic of British and American Industry* (1953).
64. See, again, the comparative statistics in Appendix B.
65. Rostas, *Comparative Productivity in British and American Industry* (1948, pp. 27–49, 64–66).

however, mounting international competitive pressures worked against the introduction of human relations.

INSTITUTIONAL FACTORS FAVORING THE HUMAN RELATIONS APPROACH

British employers and managers faced a unique mix of organizational problems during the late 1940s and 1950s. The threat, if not the actual occurrence, of industrial conflict, the persistence of output restriction, and the increasing bureaucratization of the enterprise called for ideological *and* technical solutions emphasizing the human aspect of work. International competitive pressures, however, required technical cost reductions, scientific management techniques, and investments in new technologies. The institutional factors accounting for the adoption of scientific management techniques during the postwar period were outlined above. This section discusses the elite mentalities, professional knowledge bases, state intervention programs, and trades-unions responses that created a favorable setting for the adoption of human relations ideology and techniques in Britain.

Elite Mentalities: Betterment, Fabianism, Humanism, Evolutionary New Thought, Religious Motives.   As in the case of Spain, an elite mentality facilitated the adoption of the human relations approach to organization in Britain. The industrial betterment movement, Fabian socialism, humanist thought, an evolutionary version of New Thought, and several Christian movements (among them, Quakerism and the Moot) shared a concern with the social conditions of workers in an industrial society. As in the United States and Spain, scientific management was attacked because of its perverse effects on the worker and the threat to undermine society's previous achievements.

Industrial betterment in Britain only gained momentum as a movement after 1913. Although the origins of welfare-based personnel management are to be found in nineteenth-century utopians such as Robert Owen, modern British betterment was largely religiously inspired. A handful of firms had introduced betterment programs, social work, and vocational guidance in factories. Increasing industrial unrest, unemployment, and poverty during the early twentieth century intensified the efforts at industrial betterment. With the help of welfare pioneers such as Benjamin Seebohm Rowntree (a Quaker and confectionery manufacturer) and Edward Cadbury (also a Quaker and chocolate manufacturer), an Institute of Personnel Management was founded in 1913 under the direction of Mary Wood, formerly a welfare manager at the Rowntree works. In fact, many of the founding members, presidents, and secretaries of these institutions were women. The welfare movement became coordinated after 1919 by the Industrial Welfare Society, led by the Reverend Robert Hyde. One prominent member of the welfare movement was Sir William Mather, chairman of Mather and Platt, one of the largest British machinery firms, and a liberal member of Parliament.[66]

These managers organized regular conferences, conducted studies on poverty and working conditions, and emphasized the need to reestablish harmony between managers and workers. Their paternalism was obvious: they knew better what the worker needed, how much of it, and when. They implicitly criticized scientific management. For example, Rowntree wrote in 1920 that "not only technical skill and a highly developed power of organization and administration [was needed], but insight, leadership, a profound sense of justice, and broad human sympathy with the whole body of workers." Rowntree was quite advanced for his time, for he advocated higher wages, shorter hours, profit sharing, joint control of working conditions, allocation of tasks, and piece rates. His overriding concern was, however, the problem of industrial strife. All his ideas were aimed at removing the "legitimate causes of labor unrest," although he and the other betterment leaders acknowledged the legitimacy of the trades unions.[67] But industrial betterment proponents readily argued that business efficiency would benefit from the welfare of employees.[68] Edward Cadbury was perhaps the most advanced betterment employer. He conducted several studies on the social conditions of workers in the sweating trades (subcontractors) and of women workers in general. Cadbury anticipated many key human relations techniques even before World War I, proposing and actually implementing the selection of employees based on their attitudes, feelings, character, and potential of loyalty, using suggestion schemes, and publishing company magazines.[69]

66. Niven, *Personnel Management 1913–63* (1967); Merkle, *Management and Ideology* (1980, pp. 218–225); Child (1969, pp. 35–41); Urwick (1956, pp. 5–9, 155–160); Urwick and Brech (1946, pp. 58–70, 193–207); Briggs, *Social Thought and Social Action* (1961). See also Rodgers, "Employers' organizations, unemployment and social politics in Britain during the inter-war period" (1988).

67. Rowntree, *The Way to Industrial Peace and the Problem of Unemployment* (1914), "Social obligations of industry to labour" (1920, p. 21), *The Human Factor in Business* (1921a), *The Human Needs of Labour* (1921b), *Industrial Unrest* (1922); Watson, *The Personnel Managers* (1977, p. 42).

68. Child (1969, p. 37).

69. Cadbury and Shann, *Sweating* (1908); Cadbury, Matheson and Shann, *Women's Work and Wages* (1906); Cadbury, *Experiments in Industrial Organization* (1912, pp. 1–10, 68–91, 212–220, 241).

During the 1920s British managers and industrialists, particularly those affiliated with the National Alliance of Employers and Employed, emphasized the themes of "pulling together," "industrial harmony," "conciliatory attitudes," "humane management," "worker participation," and "co-partnership."[70] The Marquis of Londonderry went as far as arguing that

> the further we move towards materialism, the quicker does this country go [to] its doom; but the more we march towards idealism, with an understanding of human nature and the rights that every individual is entitled to, the more will we progress and maintain our position as the foremost nation in the world.[71]

Managers urged employers and engineers to "develop a community of interest," and recognize the human qualities, capacities, and aspirations of workers.[72] Thus, the analysis of the human situation of workers in industry by the betterment pioneers anticipated many human relations themes and set the stage for the success of that paradigm of organization.

Fabian socialism and humanist thought were two other British cultural components that helped to create a mentality favorable to the human relations paradigm. Intellectuals from both traditions feared the concentration of power as a result of the growth of capitalist firms and of the state, and readily criticized scientific management (e.g., Graham Wallas). The new Fabians of the post–World War II era saw in human cooperation the "predominant force" of the socialist conception of society, and urged the "restoration of a feeling of participation and common purpose among the workers which is missing from capitalist industrial society."[73] Humanist thought was a major influence in the conceptualizations of the industrial betterment pioneers and would later underlie most of the writings of the opinion leaders in the field of human relations at work. Sociologist J. A. Hobson took a typically humanist approach to the subject of routine work, which, "destitute of noble purpose, demoralizes and denationalizes the workers, and, through its reactions upon individual and social

70. See *Unity* (February 1923):2, (April 1926):3, (August 1926):54, 56–57; (September 1926):70–72, April (1930):58–59.

71. *Unity* (April 1926):11.

72. See *Journal of Industrial Administration* 1(2)(1921):51–56, (March 1921): 67–77.

73. Albu, "The organization of industry" (1952); Cripps, *Towards Christian Democracy* (1945, pp. 47–57); Cooke, *The Life of Richard Stafford Cripps* (1957).

character, constitutes the heaviest drag upon the car of human progress."[74]

Before becoming Prime Minister, Harold Macmillan served as director of the Institute of Industrial Administration and Minister in several departments. He argued that the worker was discontent not only because of low wages but also because of the "more remote feeling of being little better than a cog in the industrial machine." For him, "the improvement of the machine and the development of mass production methods have made labor *dull*." Because of rampant deskilling, Macmillan stated that "the industrial system must be 'humanized'."[75] Europe's leading humanist intellectual, José Ortega y Gasset, was also influential in Britain, though not to the extent that he was in Spain. Ortega's impact was clear in the works by some of the leading British human relations writers of the postwar period. The British Institute of Management even invited Ortega to address its 1953 annual gathering at Torquay.[76]

Another mentality that facilitated the development of the human relations approach in Britain was an evolutionary version of New Thought. The British New Thought movement had its origins in Christian Science. A Higher Thought Centre was created in Nottingham in 1906, and the New Thought Alliance in London in 1914. The most important exponent of the blend of Social Darwinism and New Thought was Herbert N. Casson, a management educator well acquainted with the American situation and a best-selling author on both sides of the Atlantic during the 1920s. Like William Graham Sumner, Casson was not opposed to trades unions; in fact, he argued that they promoted progress.[77] His "formula for progress" was the following:

> In the Evolution of the human race upwards, all progress depends upon the production of a comparatively small number of improved individuals, who are superior to the mass in knowledge, skill or charac-

74. Hobson, *The Industrial System* (1909, pp. 310–311). Hobson was heavily criticized by Lenin because of his pusillanimous attack on imperialism.

75. Macmillan, *Reconstruction* (1934, pp. 119–120).

76. See, among others, Urwick, *The Pattern of Management* (1956, pp. 9, 23); *The Manager* 27(1959):32–36, 347; Schuster, *Christianity and Human Relations in Industry* (1951, p. 123); Wood, *E. F. Schumacher* (1984, pp. 41, 211–214).

77. Dresser, *A History of the New Thought Movement* (1919, pp. 258–268); Casson, *Common Sense on the Labor Question* (1903), *How to Keep Your Money and Make It Earn More* (1923), *Tips on Leadership* (1927).

ter, and who, by reason of their superior powers, render a new service to the mass of people among whom they live.[78]

Primarily worried about industrial strife, Casson departed from Social Darwinism to embrace betterment programs and propose a human relations approach: "Treat [workers] as people, that is the keynote of good management. Why do workers strike? Is it not, in most cases, to prove that they are people and not things?" Casson emphasized the importance of dealing with the human element in the industrial firm by strengthening "company feeling, team play and cooperation." He also proposed industrial betterment measures, suggestion systems, company magazines, and workers' committees. Casson asked managers not only to buy the time and labor of the worker but also his or her heart and soul.[79]

As in Spain, the most important elite mentality for the adoption of human relations in Britain had to do with religion. But Britain was a predominantly Anglican country, with a Catholic minority that has traditionally had little influence in the business world. Only a few business leaders appeared to be influenced by the social doctrine of the Roman Catholic Church. The most prominent one was Sir Josiah Stamp, whose distinguished professional career included serving as chairman of a railway company, Director of the Bank of England, vice president of the National Institute of Industrial Psychology, director of Nobel Industries and Imperial Chemical Industries (ICI), and chairman of the London School of Economics. Stamp regarded happiness as an essential part of a Christian order in the workplace. He emphasized individual freedom, initiative, and self-respect, as well as the pride of craftsmanship and of belonging to an organization.[80] After World War II, the Catholic Social Guild, Oxford, contributed to the diffusion of social-science research on human relations, using the Catholic social doctrine as a justification for the implementation of human relations techniques.[81] The founder of the Anglo-American

78. Casson, *Creative Thinkers* (1929, p. 11). Another proponent of evolutionary New Thought is the Viscount Slim. See *The Manager* 30(1962)(1):37–41.

79. Casson in *System* 34(1918):193–196, 36(1919):101–104, 220; Casson (1929, pp. 195–199); Child (1969, pp. 58, 75).

80. Stamp, *The Christian Ethic as an Economic Factor* (1926), *Motive and Method in a Christian Order* (1936, pp. 56–58), *The Science of Social Adjustment* (1937, pp. 18–21), *Christianity and Economics* (1938, pp. 116–117, 126–127).

81. See Fogarty, *Human Relations in Industry* (1954), *Personality and Group Relations in Industry* (1956), *Programme for Social Action* (1957, pp. 8–9, 65–99); Clump, *The Social Teaching of Pope Pius XII: 1956* (1958, pp. 51–85). Fogarty was a Professor

Council on Productivity, President of the Fabian Society, and Chancellor of the Exchequer Sir Stafford Cripps justified a human relations approach by reference to Christian social ideals, as did telephone-company executive John Lee.[82] Aldous Huxley, who had ridiculed Henry Ford in his novel, *Brave New World* (1932), collaborated with the Catholic-influenced Centre d'Études des Problèmes Humains, one of the leading human relations institutions in France during the 1950s.[83]

The most influential religious groups in the British movement toward the human relations approach were the Quakers and the Moot. Quakerism, an intensely Puritan secular ethic that originated in England and America during the mid-seventeenth century, was linked to humanist ideas. The British Quaker families controlled businesses in many sectors, including banking (Lloyds, Barclays), breweries, watchmaking, accounting (Price, Waterhouse & Co.), printing, confectionery (Cadbury, Rowntree), and newspaper publishing. By 1909 the Society of Friends had 19,000 members in Britain. The Quakers criticized war and exploitation, and were against the laissez-faire approach to labor management. They valued handwork, emphasized the "common will" and cooperation, and entertained egalitarian ideals. British Quaker employers were also among the most committed to social and industrial reform, including works councils. Annual conferences of Quaker employers were held between 1918 and 1948, with Rowntree playing a leading role. Many of the scientific management critics (Sheldon, Wood) and of the early human relations writers (Northcott, Urwick, Watts) worked for Quaker firms or were Quakers themselves.[84]

The other major religious influence came from the Moot, a group of intellectuals created by Anglican social reformer J. H. Oldham in 1938 to discuss issues of democracy and industrial relations first raised

---

of Industrial Relations at University College, Cardiff, and member of the National Executive Committee of the Catholic Social Guild. Clump was a Jesuit priest at the Indian Jesuit Institute of Social Order.

82. Cripps (1945, pp. 47–57); Lee, *The Social Implications of Christianity* (1922), *Industrial Organisation* (1923), *The Principles of Industrial Welfare* (1924). See also the article by the Bishop of Coventry in *The Manager* 25(1957):951–955.

83. Boltanski, "Visions of American management in postwar France" (1990, p. 360); Huxley (1989, pp. 3, 15, 52).

84. Child, "Quaker employers and industrial relations" (1964); Emden, *Quakers in Commerce* (1939). A later organizational thinker with a Quaker background was British-born economist Kenneth E. Boulding. See his *The Organizational Revolution* (1953).

at the international conference of the Universal Christian Council of Life and Work (1937).[85] The Moot brought together leading intellectuals such as T. S. Eliot, John Middleton Murry, Christopher Dawson, Sir Fred Clarke and, of course, Karl Mannheim. The democratic ideas of the Moot represented a reaction against totalitarianism, the uprooting of communal groups, the repression of the individual, and "mechanized barbarism." They aimed at promoting the development of the human personality by social reform, and spreading democratic ideals throughout society, including the industrial firm. Their ultimate goal was to save the democracies of the West through the basic principles of Christianity. The Moot became very influential throughout the 1940s.[86] Although the group's meetings were discontinued after Mannheim's death in 1947, the intellectual impact on some of the leading British human relations writers was clear, particularly on those also influenced by the Quaker ethic. The ideal of democracy in the workplace was a central theme in many British human relations writings.[87]

The Rise of Social-Science Theorizing and the Formulation of the Paradigm. Several of the elite mentalities that favored a human relations approach to organization in Britain waned after 1948. Industrial betterment was eclipsed by the rise of the welfare state. The Quaker employers' conferences and the Moot were disbanded in the late 1940s. Only humanist Socialism, Fabianism, and humanist thought remained important. Nevertheless, the impact of all those mentalities on the formulation of a British human relations paradigm was extensive and enduring. Moreover, their banner was carried by a long wave of social-science theorizing about human relationships at work that originated during World War I and reached a climax during the 1950s and early 1960s.

The first British social-science research on industrial work dates back to the Health of Munition Workers Committee (1915–17), whose approach was at first scientific-psychological but quickly started taking into account psychological and social aspects as monotony and fatigue became the dominant topics. The research of the committee

85. The word *moot* means something debatable, not decided, doubtful. *To moot* is to speak, to debate, to argue, to plead, to discuss, particularly an imaginary law case, as in the Inns of Court.

86. Loader, *The Intellectual Development of Karl Mannheim* (1985, pp. 149–162).

87. Northcott, *Personnel Management* (1945, pp. 178, 182); Urwick, *Leadership in the Twentieth Century* (1957, pp. 48–49); Child (1969, pp. 122, 124–130).

was heavily influenced by Rowntree during his tenure as director of the Ministry of Defence's Welfare Department. The emphasis on fatigue research was confirmed by the creation of the Industrial Fatigue Research Board (IFRB, 1918–28) and later the Industrial Health Research Board (IHRB), concerned with vocational guidance, work satisfaction, and repetition and variety at work.[88] The most important research institution of the 1920s was the semi-public National Institute of Industrial Psychology (NIIP), created in 1921 with the support of several industrialists, including Rowntree and Cadbury. Directed by psychology Professor Charles S. Myers, the NIIP continued conducting studies of monotony and fatigue but expanded its scope to topics such as emotions, stress, creative expression, self-respect, social groups, and leadership styles in actual industrial settings. Elton Mayo relied extensively on IFRB's research for his *Human Problems of an Industrial Civilization,* and published articles in the Journal of the NIIP.[89]

During the interwar period British social scientists criticized scientific management for its "perverse" effects. For Myers, under scientific management, "mechanically formulated by the engineer, . . . the mental factors of personality, sentiment and sympathy are sacrificed to purely physical considerations." Rather, the managers should encourage "workers to take an intelligent interest in the factory as a whole," and take into account their "natural instincts and emotions." For physiology Professor E. P. Cathcart, late chairman of IHRB, work groups, emotions, and the "group-mind" had to do with fatigue and waste as much as mechanical factors (Mayo also cited his research). Oxford physiologist H. M. Vernon rejected many aspects of scientific management, arguing instead for welfare measures and changes in tasks so as to reduce fatigue and monotony. Stanley Wyatt, of the Medical Research Council, underlined the importance of worker satisfaction and psychological adaptation as determinants of productivity.[90] Other social scientists such as Sir William Ashley, Graham

88. The chairman of the IHRB, Sir Arnold Wilson, Member of Parliament, was a defender of state industrial betterment. See Wilson and Levy, *Industrial Assurance* (1937), *Workmen's Compensation* (1939).

89. Thomas (1978, pp. 171–185); Urwick and Brech (1946, pp. 193–207); Welch and Myers, *Ten Years of Industrial Psychology* (1932); Myers, *Industrial Psychology in Great Britain* (1933); Mayo, *The Human Problems of an Industrial Civilization* (1933, pp. 1–54).

90. Myers, *Present-Day Applications of Psychology* (1918, pp. 7–19), *Mind and Work* (1920, pp. 23–24, 144, 168), *Industrial Psychology* (1926, pp. 26–28, 30, 33, 42), *A Psychologist's Point of View* (1933, pp. 45–61, 133–145, 146–161), *Business Rationalisa-*

Wallas, and J. A. Hobson also advanced important ideas about cooperation, work groups, community feelings, monotony, personal initiative and responsibility, and participation.[91] The important trend in all these authors was the growing interest in explaining variations in output in terms of a series of social-psychological variables (adaptation, emotions, feelings, sentiments, group dynamics, morale, satisfaction, stress, neurosis) as well as technical ones (hours of work, multiple shifts, work spells, rest periods, lost time, sickness, factory conditions).

The leading postwar social-science institution was the Tavistock Institute of Human Relations. It was created in 1946 with a grant from the Rockefeller Foundation to promote research and consulting in the areas of "the family, the factory and the rural community" as previously conducted by the Tavistock Clinic (1920). In 1947 the Tavistock Institute teamed up with the Research Center for Group Dynamics (first at MIT and then at the University of Michigan) to publish *Human Relations*, the leading journal in the field of organizations for almost two decades. Tavistock Publications was created also in 1947 to publicize the growing research output of the institute. Funding came from private sources as well as from the government's Industrial Productivity Committee and the Department of Scientific and Industrial Research. The institute did regular consulting work for such large firms as Glacier Metal, Lever Brothers, Unilever, and Vauxhall Motors.[92]

The Tavistock Institute hosted two important research programs: the Glacier Project and the comparative study of mining methods,

---

tion (1932, pp. 15, 26–53, 67), "Aspects of modern psychology," in Myers, Freeman, and Viteles, *Modern Psychology* (1941, pp. 1–22); Cathcart, *The Human Factor in Industry* (1928); Vernon, *Industrial Fatigue and Efficiency* (1921, pp. 5–7, 82–84, 138), *The Health and Efficiency of Munition Workers* (1940); Wyatt, *A Study of Variations in Output* (1944, pp. 15–16). For other criticisms of scientific management by members of the NIIP, see *Unity* (July 1928):217–218, (September 1928):242–243. See also *British Management Review* 2(1937):89–93; *Industry Illustrated* 1938(1):24. Other members of the NIIP or the IHRB used a scientific management approach: *Industry Illustrated* 1933(6):41–44, 46–50, 1934(4):41–45, 1935(2):37.

91. Ashley (1922); Wallas (1914), *Our Social Heritage* (1921, pp. 54–76), *Social Judgment* (1935); Hobson (1909, pp. 302–324), (1914, pp. 44–59), *Incentives in the New Industrial Order* (1922).

92. Trist and Murray, "Historical overview: The foundation and development of the Tavistock Institute" (1990); TIHR, *Development and Work: 1946–1950* (1950), *Report for the Four Years October, 1962 to September, 1960* (1960), *Report for the Year October, 1961 to September, 1962* (1962), *Report for the Year October, 1963 to September, 1964* (1964); Brown, "Research and consultancy in industrial enterprises" (1967).

which gave birth to the socio-technical systems approach. Elliott Jaques was the principal investigator at the Glacier Metal Co., a 3,600-worker light engineering factory in London. A psychologist, physician and qualified psychoanalyst, Jaques also completed the Ph.D. program in social relations at Harvard. The research team at Glacier was interested in studying the psychological and social factors behind group life, morale, productivity, stress, and attitudes towards work. They used the clinical method extensively. The findings emphasized the need for managers to deal with the complexities of human motivation and group interactions.[93]

The second major Tavistock project had to do with the impact of changing technological conditions on social relations at work. Psychologist Eric L. Trist was the principal investigator at one mine of the National Coal Board where the use of face conveyors facilitated the introduction of the longwall method of coal-getting. Trist was interested in studying how such a technological change affected task allocation among workers, the structure and self-regulation of work groups, and the work culture (i.e. workers' group affiliations and feelings). His conclusions were that managers needed to balance the requirements stemming from the new technology and the social structure of occupational roles in order to achieve optimal results, that people were a resource to be developed, and that workers should be assigned multiple, broad skills. This approach was termed *socio-technical systems,* a label that deservedly became famous. A. K. Rice (like Trist, part of the Glacier research team) arrived at similar conclusions in his research at a textile mill in India. The appearance of the socio-technical systems approach was consistent with the postwar adoption of mass-production technologies and scientific management techniques throughout British industry, and with the need to redesign work relationships to minimize the perverse effects of industrial rationalization.[94] The approach had a direct and widespread impact on the world-famous Swedish organizational initiatives of the late 1960s and early 1970s on the humanization of work.[95]

There were other social scientists not affiliated with the Tavistock

93. Jaques, *The Changing Culture of a Factory* (1951), *Measurement of Responsibility* (1956), *Work, Creativity, and Social Justice* (1970); Brown and Jaques, *Glacier Project Papers* (1965).

94. Trist and Bamforth, "Some social and psychological consequences of the long-wall method of coal-getting" (1951); Trist et al., *Organizational Choice* (1963); Rice, *Productivity and Social Organisation* (1958), *Learning for Leadership* (1965).

95. See Cole, *Strategies for Learning* (1989, pp. 89–92).

Institute who engaged in human relations research during the 1950s
and published it in the major sociology journals or in *Human Relations*. Academics such as J. A. C. Brown, R. F. Tredgold, R. J. Hacon,
and John Munro Fraser organized courses and seminars on human
relations at work and prosposed techniques such as group discussions,
role-playing, clinical counseling, and Training within Industry.
Brown wrote a very influential book, *The Social Psychology of Industry*,
introducing Moreno's sociometry as a human relations technique.[96]
Another popular book was Gordon Rattray Taylor's *Are Workers Human?* (1950), which introduced the non-specialized reader to the human relations approach to industrial conflict.[97] The research and consulting work of the Tavistock Institute and of other social scientists
helped to formulate a genuinely British brand of human relations
that developed somewhat independently from the American human
relations school and made original contributions such as the socio-
technical systems approach. Again, the contrast with Germany was
clear, and the similarities with Spain striking, although the Spanish
human relations school was not nearly so innovative as the British.

Support from the State. In Britain the human relations approach to
organization benefited from state institutional and financial support.
The early investigations of industrial psychology were initiated by the
Ministry of Munitions, and the major research institutes of the 1920s
and 1930s, such as the Industrial Fatigue Research Board, the Industrial Health Research Board, and the National Institute of Industrial
Psychology (NIIP), all received public funding. During World War
II the Tavistock Clinic became engaged in research on the selection
of army personnel. In 1941 the Report of His Majesty's Chief Inspec-
tor of Factories, Ernest Bevin (a lifelong trades unionist, supporter
of industrial rationalization, and later Minister of Labour), emphasized the "mental and psychological make-up" of workers. After the
war a number of state agencies funded research at the universities and
the Tavistock Institute, and established permanent research centers
on industry. The Human Factors Panel of the Industrial Productivity
Committee (1947–50), was chaired by human relations proponent

96. See Brown, *The Social Psychology of Industry* (1954); *British Journal of Sociology*
(December 1951):354–359, (March 1959):38–44; *The Sociological Review* (November
1962):313–327; *The Manager* 25(1957):119–121; and a great number of articles in
the journal *Human Relations*. Child (1969, pp. 115; Tredgold, *Human Relations in
Modern Industry* (1963), originally published in 1949; Hacon, *Conflict and Human
Relations Training* (1965); Fraser, *Human Relations in a Fully Employed Democracy*
(1960), *Industrial Psychology* (1962); Deverell, *Personnel Management* (1968).
97. Taylor, *Are Workers Human?* (1950).

George Schuster, who consulted regularly with Elton Mayo and urged more academic research on human relations. In 1952 the Ministry of Labour convened a national conference on human relations in industry, and in 1960 the Ministry of Education issued a circular emphasizing the need to cover sociological and pychological topics in the management curriculum. The Committees on Human Relations in Industry and Individual Efficiency in Industry (1953–57) of the Department of Scientific and Industrial Research and the Medical Research Council (MRC) also supported research at the Tavistock Institute with Conditional Aid funds. The Human Science Committee continued funding research at several institutions well into the 1960s.

Altogether, state agencies funded over 30 research groups, creating the most extensive network of social-science research centers on human relations of any European country. The major lines of research included: (1) "human response systems," i.e. research on the design of tasks and adaptation of the workers to the machine carried out at several university psychology departments, the MRC's Applied Psychology Unit, and the NIIP; (2) work satisfaction, absenteeism, turnover, and monotony at the Tavistock Institute, NIIP, and the MRC's Industrial Psychology Research Group; (3) small-group dynamics; and (4) supervision at Tavistock Institute and NIIP. The Anglo-American Council on Productivity (1948–52), created by Fabian Society member Sir Stafford Cripps, supported research and industrial applications on the "physical conditions and psychological attitudes which are affecting productivity." Finally, Training within Industry (TWI) came to Britain from America via the Ministry of Labour. In no other European country were state agencies so involved in funding and legitimizing human relations research and techniques. Moreover, British human relations research institutes benefited to a greater extent from American Conditional Aid through the European Productivity Agency than did their counterparts in other European countries, perhaps because of the more congenial British attitude towards the human relations approach.[98]

The Position of the Trades Unions.   Unlike those in Germany and the United States, the British trades unions, as well as the Labour Party,

---

98. Emery, "Applied social science in British industry," in EPA, *Social Research and Industry in Europe* (1960, pp. 81–90); *Industry Illustrated* 12(3)(1944):19; AACP, *Report of the First Session* (1948, p. 3), *Final Report of the Council* (1952); Carew (1987, pp. 186, 197–200); McGivering, Matthews, and Scott, *Management in Britain* (1960, pp. 112–113).

supported the human relations approach. Austen Albu, a manager and member of the Labour Party and the Fabian Society, praised the Hawthorne experiments and celebrated that "science is beginning to catch up with common sense." Of course Albu and other intellectuals raised the issue of the manipulative potential of human relations techniques, but, as John Child has documented, "by the 1950s some Labour Party intellectuals appeared ready to accept the spirit of Mayo's thesis to a remarkable degree." Members of the TUC General Council would recommend Mayo's books, emphasizing the need to improve communication and cooperation in the business firm, and suggesting that excessive technical progress disrupted social relationships and work groups in the factory. The TUC was sympathetic to the funding of human relations research because it liked its social-science approach to the study of the worker and of work groups.[99]

THE THEORETICAL ADOPTION OF THE HUMAN RELATIONS PARADIGM

Given all the favorable institutional factors it should be no surprise to find British employers and managers endorsing human relations ideology and techniques. There was a core of human relations thinking in industry before the pardigm as such was formulated in the United States. This group included John Lee and Oliver Sheldon, whose criticisms of scientific management were discussed in a previous section. These management intellectuals were aware of the research by the industrial psychologists and further theorized about the importance of human relationships at work.[100]

The reception of Elton Mayo's ideas in British business circles was overtly enthusiastic mainly because they reinforced the conventional wisdom among British managers that the human, social, and cooperative aspects of work should take precedence over the technical. The editors of *Industry Illustrated* put it nicely in 1933 on the occasion of the publication of *The Human Problems of an Industrial Civilization:*

> Dr. Mayo might perhaps take comfort from the fact that industrial executives at any rate, as revealed in the columns of this journal, are far more interested in the human than in the technological issues of their responsibilities.[101]

99. Child (1969, pp. 135–136); *The Manager* 23(1955):1037–1040; Carew (1987, pp. 186, 197–200).

100. Lee (1921, pp. 60–61); Sheldon (1924).

101. *Industry Illustrated* 1(12)(1933):1. See also the favorable review by C. H. Northcott in *Industry Illustrated* 2(8)(1934):63.

In another editorial, scientists and engineers were blamed for having created human and social problems in industry that changed for the worse "the most important single factor in production," that is, workers' attitudes towards work and their supervisors.[102]

The Mayoistic approach was adopted fairly quickly. In 1944 a manager at Austin Motor announced that "we are undoubtedly entering the sociological era of industry."[103] Sir Frederick Hooper, managing director of the Schweppes Group, used the cricket and football team as a metaphor of what the business firm should be like.[104] Lloyd Roberts, president of the Institute of Labour (later Personnel) Management, spoke in 1943 to an audience of foremen using yet another metaphor, "A Happy Ship." *Labour Management* reported:

> [Roberts] said that the old conception in industry was based on the amount of money to be made out of it, and he suggested that the proper outlook was how much happiness sprang from it; happiness resulting from the efficiency of its human relations and bred of a sense of security and self-respect in all the members of a team.

Roberts thought the manager should develop among workers a "feeling of working with the firm instead of for it . . . , make men's jobs interesting to them . . . , [and] ensure the right emotional reactions on the part of those he controls."[105] In addition Oliver Lyttleton, the Minister of Production, presented himself as a keen supporter of suggestion schemes.[106]

Human relations themes came up even more frequently once the difficulties of war were over. Mayo himself addressed the 1947 annual meeting of the Institute of Personnel Management. "Industry is a living organism, one and indivisible," stated Sir Frederick Bain, deputy chairman of Imperial Chemical Industries (ICI) and president of the Federation of British Industries.[107] When four leading executives met in 1953 to discuss whether British management had a philosophy, they readily argued that it was the concern for human relations that inspired their approach to management.[108] In 1959 managers

102. *Industry Illustrated* 3(10)(1935):9.

103. *Industry Illustrated* 12(11)(1944):27. On Austin Motor, see also Bramley, *The Voice of the Factory* (1944).

104. Child (1969, p. 124). See also Hooper, *Management in the Public Services* (1948).

105. Child (1969, p. 121); Roberts, *The Human Problems of Management* (1944, pp. 8, 19–20).

106. *Industry Illustrated* 13(2)(1945):22.

107. *Industry Illustrated* 17(5)(1949):223.

108. *The Manager* 21(1953):531–536.

from eighty-two top firms ranked several topics in terms of their importance to them as follows: attitudes and satisfactions, relations and communication, wages and salary, personnel organization, discipline, and physical conditions and work methods.[109] In 1960 Lord Baillieu, president of the British Institute of Management (BIM) and chairman of Dunlop Rubber, set the priorities for the year ahead as being the management of relationships among people, human relations, and harmony in the factory. Even as late as 1971, the director general of the BIM, John Marsh, emphasized the problems derived from the "impersonality of the organizational machine."[110]

The consensus about the positive effect of sound human relations upon productivity and efficiency emerged in the mid-1940s and remained virtually unchanged until well into the 1950s. The following two statements, taken from the writings of two leading managers, Lloyd Roberts and Lord Piercy, were made fifteen years apart from each other:

> Men are human beings with conscious- and sub-conscious interests, attachments and loyalties of their own—all of which, however seemingly irrelevant, will always express themselves sooner or later in terms of output.[111]

> To be efficient, so runs the *newer* thinking, the industrial enterprise must constitute a social group; a social group which is harmonious, confident in its leadership, aware of and interested in the common aim of the undertaking.[112]

Managers explictly adopting a human relations approach worked for firms such as Beyer Peacock Group, British Thomson-Houston, Philips Electrical, Imperial Chemical Industries, Steel Company of Wales, Rowntree, Schweppes, Stewarts & Lloyds, J. Sainsbury, Lloyds Bank, Harrods, The Electricity Council, British Electricity Board, and the National Coal Board.[113] Prominent politicians also endorsed human relations. Sir George Schuster, engaged in economic

109. Emery, "Applied social science in British industry," in EPA (1960, p. 90). The survey was conducted by the NIIP.

110. *The Manager* 28(1960):34–36; *Management Today* 39(9)(1971):126.

111. Anonymous, quoted by Roberts (1944, p. 20).

112. Lord Piercy in *The Manager* 27(1959):252. Emphasis added.

113. See *Industry Illustrated* 11(8)(1943):22–23; *The Manager* 21(1953):330–334, 531–536, 22(1954):364–367, 23(1955):1037–1040, 28(1960):37–44, 29(1961):519–522, 555; *Management Today* 39(9)(1971):89–91, 138; *British Management Review* 1(1936):82–98; Lawe, *Staff Management* (1944); Child (1969, p. 121).

planning and industrial relations policy-making, criticized the manipulative potential of Mayo's methods, but nonetheless endorsed human relations and justified its implementation by reference to Christian values. A similar approach was characteristic of Sir Stafford Cripps, who served as Minister during and after World War II. He declared that "the problem of human relationships is the most vital and important part of industrial efficiency."[114]

The management associations became quickly dominated by the human relations approach at the same time that their memberships soared. The Institute of Industrial Administration had 2,500 members when it merged with the British Institute of Management (BIM) in 1951, up from 500 in 1939. The BIM reached a membership of 19,000 by 1968. Membership in the Institute of Personnel Management grew from 800 in 1939 to 5,700 in 1963. The *British Management Review* and *Personnel Management* became vehicles for the adoption of human relations ideology and techniques. Headed by A. P. Young, the Institution of Works Managers (5,200 members in 1963), was on the leading edge of the implementation of American management techniques, including scientific management and human relations.[115]

A small number of more reflective practicing managers further elaborated the human relations paradigm, discussing in depth its ideological and technical approach to organization, and incorporating the latest social-science research from both sides of the Atlantic. The most prominent was Clarence H. Northcott, the labor manager at the Quaker firm of Rowntree. He was born in Australia (like Mayo), received his Ph.D. from Columbia, and worked at the National Industrial Conference Board in Boston, Massachusetts, before moving to York. He wrote several important books in which the influence of Mayo, Roethlisberger, Whitehead, Quakerism, and the Moot are apparent. In *Personnel Management* (1945), Northcott discussed human relations techniques such as interviews, job rotation, discussion groups, and suggestion systems. His ideological approach to management and organization, based on Christian values and human rela-

114. Schuster (1951), *Industry Illustrated* 15(7)(1947):25–27, 38; Cripps (1945, p. 48).

115. Child (1969, pp. 113–114; Marks, *Politics and Personnel Management* (1978, pp. 118–125); Balchin, *The Worker in Modern Industry* (1954); Young, *American Management Techniques and Practices and Their Bearing on Productivity in British Industry* (1949, pp. 35, 66–70). See also Young's article in *British Management Review* 4(1)(1939–43):14–22. He justified human relations with Christian values.

tions, was developed in *Christian Principles in Industry* (1958) as well as in his many articles published in the leading management journals.[116]

Lyndall Urwick was perhaps the most influential human relations management intellectual and consultant. Urwick worked for Rowntree after World War I and since 1934 had directed his own consulting firm. He also served as president of the BIM (1947–52). He published several books on human relations themes, and a staggering number of articles in the leading management journals, including several describing in painstaking detail the methods and the findings of the Hawthorne experiments. He also helped publicize the works of Mary Parker Follett and the research of the British social-science institutes. No other British management intellectual did more than Urwick to diffuse the ideas and techniques of human relations in Britain both as a writer and a consultant.[117] Another management consultant, James J. Gillespie developed a Mayoistic critique of scientific management and developed the concepts of work group, integrative and democratic leadership, social codes in the factory, and the "job whole." He also used Moreno's sociometry. Like Urwick, Gillespie was influenced by Christian values.[118]

Another original thinker was German-born Ernst F. Schumacher, who served as top economist and head of planning at the National Coal Board (NCB) in 1950. Influenced by socialist ideals, Ortega's *Revolt of the Masses,* the British wave of human relations, and the Buddhist concept of work as a good in itself, Schumacher advocated a "human" approach to organization, including smaller establishments and group production. In 1966 he left the NCB to develop the concept of "intermediate technology" as a central tool in relieving mass poverty in developing countries, culminating his efforts in a landmark book, *Small Is Beautiful* (1973).[119]

116. Northcott, *Personnel Management* (1945, pp. 59–64, 221–222, 230–267, 294–296), *Christian Principles in Industry* (1958, pp. 36–44, 49–53, 62–63). See also Northcott, "Principles and practice of industrial relations" (1928). See also his articles: *Industry Illustrated* 1(5)(1933):xiii–xiv, 2(3)(1934):48–51; *British Management Review* 1(1939–43):114–124.

117. Urwick, *Management of Tomorrow* (1933, pp. 147–158), *The Pattern of Management* (1956), *Leadership in the Twentieth Century* (1957). See also *The Manager* 22(1954):445–448. The series of twelve articles on the Hawthorne experiments was published in *Industry Illustrated* 12(1944) and 13(1945). See also *Journal of the British Institute of Management* 1(1957):240–251.

118. Gillespie, *The Principles of Rational Industrial Management* (1938), *Free Expression in Society* (1948), *Dynamic Motion and Time Study* (1951).

119. Wood (1984, pp. 41, 211–214, 235, 243, 268–270); Schumacher, *Small Is Beautiful* (1975).

In general, British managers combined the ideas coming from the United States (Mayo, Whitehead, Roethlisberger, Follett) with those of the British human relations school. Their humanist mentality, frequently combined with Christian values, also contributed to their view on organization. John Child has argued that the resulting synthesis included several assumptions and normative prescriptions: the firm as an organic unity; the worker as a "whole person"; management's responsibility to lead; the need to improve downward communications; the convenience of improving participation; and the thesis that higher productivity resulted from worker satisfaction and happiness.[120]

The human relations approach to organizing was frequently discussed in the management journals during the late 1940s and 1950s. Scientific management articles were still being published due to the renewed emphasis on the implementation of rationalization techniques as part of the postwar productivity effort (see panel B of Table 5.2). Both the ideological and technical aspects of the human relations paradigm received attention (see panel A of Table 5.2). The contents of the articles made the association between human relations and industrial conflict quite clear. The threat of industrial conflict during the late 1940s and 1950s was behind the wave of human relations articles. When conflict rates dropped in the 1960s, so did the number of human relations articles, but with the rise in industrial strife starting in the late 1960s, the human relations approach came back to the management journals (panel B of Table 5.2). This evidence shows the responsiveness of British management intellectuals to the problems they perceived as affecting industry and society.

PRACTICAL IMPLEMENTATION OF HUMAN RELATIONS TECHNIQUES BY FIRMS

Human relations succeeded in the United States, Spain, and Britain as an ideology of management during the 1950s. Business opinion leaders clearly advocated the implementation of the major human relations techniques in the United States and Britain. In Spain few management intellectuals discussed the techniques, while most Spanish firms failed to actually implement them because of the lack of the necessary organizational sophistication and staff. Developments in British firms were more similar to those in the United States. To begin with, a relatively high proportion (12 percent) of British com-

---

120. Child (1969, pp. 117–130). On the reception of Whitehead's and Roethlisberger's books, see Brown (1977, p. 247); *Industry Illustrated* 6(3)(1938):11–12, 11(2)(1943):14–16.

pany directors of industrial and service firms using a variety of technologies had backgrounds in human relations or personnel, compared to 19 percent with backgrounds in finance, 17 percent in production or research and development, and 14 percent in sales (for 25 percent the background was administration in general).[121]

The most important human relations techniques were widely adopted in Britain. Attitude surveys were first conducted in the 1930s by the National Institute of Industrial Psychology, acting as a consultant for several firms. Ashridge Management College, one of the leading business schools of the postwar period, conducted a great number of surveys in large British and international companies.[122] Organizational development techniques (i.e. the analysis of employee identities, conflicts, emotions and attachments, and of the ways to change them) was introduced from the United States by several consulting companies. Clients included Esso Petroleum and Imperial Chemical Industries (ICI). Job enrichment was a technique regularly used at

121. Betts, "Characteristics of British company directors" (1967; p. 79). Data based on a survey among 266 directors of 83 firms in radio and TV receivers, food processing, industrial plastics, retailing, and construction. In studies of the departmental background of American executives, personnel is not even a category. See Fligstein, "The intraorganizational power struggle" (1987).

122. Davey, Gill, and McDonnell, *Attitude Surveys in Industry* (1970).

TABLE 5.2   Results of the content analysis of the articles published in *Industry Illustrated, The Manager,* and *Management Today,* 1944–1973, by paradigm (SM: scientific management; HR: human relations; SA: structural analysis; NC: not classifiable)

A. Number of articles mentioning each of the content categories (see Appendix A) and themes (35 articles examined)

Content Categories	SM	HR	SA
Perceived problem	19	65	22
Form of solution	1	0	8
View of conflict	1	12	4
View of workers	1	38	1
Fascination with	1	27	0
Methodology	24	29	2
Selection of workers	21	6	0
Distribution of tasks	4	6	7
Authority structures	1	48	20
Process of work	8	13	18
Preferred rewards	8	12	1
Economic incentives	7	4	0

(Continued)

TABLE 5.2 *(Continued)*

B. Number of articles (N) and themes classified by paradigm

Year Period	SM N	Themes Mean	Min	Max	HR N	Themes Mean	Min	Max	SA N	Themes Mean	Min	Max	NC N
1944–46	0	—	—	—	23	3.5	1	5	0	—	—	—	0
1947–49	3	3.0	2	4	5	2.8	2	3	0	—	—	—	1
1950–52	3	3.0	2	4	2	2.0	2	2	1	2.0	2	2	4
1953–55	7	2.3	1	4	11	3.0	2	4	2	2.0	1	3	1
1956–58	4	2.2	2	3	6	2.8	2	4	2	2.5	2	3	2
1959–61	2	2.5	2	3	9	2.9	1	5	1	3.0	3	3	3
1962–64	1	3.0	3	3	3	2.7	2	3	3	3.3	3	4	2
1965–67	1	3.0	3	3	1	3.0	3	3	8	3.9	3	6	1
1968–70	0	—	—	—	4	4.8	4	6	3	3.0	3	3	1
1971–73	0	—	—	—	10	3.2	1	5	2	4.0	4	4	3
All years	21	2.6	1	4	74	3.2	1	6	22	3.0	1	6	18
Pages	84	4.0	1	14	320	4.3	2	8	97	4.4	2	7	65

Note: Title of the journal varied as follows: *Industry Illustrated* (1944–50), *The Manager* (1950–68), *Management Today* (1968–73).

Sources: The articles included in the analysis are the following:

SM: *Industry Illustrated* 15(10):26–27, 16(2):16–18, 26–28. *The Manager* 19:131, 195–196; 20:532–534; 21:86–88; 22:179–182, 291–304, 369–375, 653–657; 23:91–94, 281–283, 335–336; 24:141–145, 374–379; 25:453–455; 26:355–358; 27:413–415; 28:126–127; 31(5):50–52; 33(3):56–58.

HR: *Industry Illustrated* 12(2):17–18, (3):12–19, (11):12–16, 26–27, (12):12–16; 13(1):12–17, (2):12–16, 22–28, (3):12–18, 45–46, (4):12–16, (7):12–18, (8):12–15, (9):12–19, (10):14–19; 14(1):12–16, (2):12–15, (3):12–15, (5):12–17, (6):23–31, (7):12–17, (9):12–15; 15(3):29–30, (7):25–27, 28–30; 16(1):16–18, (9):22–24. *The Manager* 19:31–32, 681–684; 21:152–156; 22:305–308, 364–367, 445–448, 649–652, 728–731; 23:183–184, 583–585, 651–654; 24:58–62; 25:119–121, 630–632; 26:108–110, 111–113, 518–520; 27:32–36, 250–253, 331–335; 28:37–44, 275–276, 435–439; 29:289–293, 519–522, 691–693; 30(1):37–41, 12:42–44; 32(4):51–52; 35(5):35–44. *Management Today* 36(6):88–91; 37(2):74–77, (9):82–85; 38(5):82–85; 39(3):58–67, (4):90–93, (9):89–91; 40(1):50–53, 63–65, (5):35, (10):101–106, 119–128; 41(1):87–90, (5):85–89.

SA: *The Manager* 20:467–469; 22:316–319; 23:331–334; 25:269–272; 29:612–614; 32(7):15–21, (8):37–38, (11):31–35; 33(2):32–34, (8):28–33, (12):28–31, 37–38; 34(5):98–103; 35(8):64–69, (9):84–87, 98–101. *Management Today* 36(4):104–107, (10):86–93; 36(4):104–107, (10):86–93; 38(5):106–109; 39(3):86–93; 41(5):70–79.

NC: *Industry Illustrated* 17(5):229–230. *The Manager* 18:14–17, 17–18, 274–276; 20:150–152; 22:29–33, 291–297; 25:55–56, 394–398; 27:618–621; 28:103–109; 29:201–207; 31(6):55–58, 59–61; 33(11):35–36. *Management Today* 36(2):84–87; 39(9):66–69; 40(5):105–108; 41(4):87–89.

ICI and other large firms. T-groups and group-relations training were widely used by the 1960s, with the British Institute of Management (BIM), the Tavistock Institute, and some university social-science departments playing a key role in the organization of seminars for managers. Suggestion schemes had been implemented by a few British firms since the turn of the century but, as in the United States, they were widely adopted only in the 1950s with the help of the British Institute of Management, the British Productivity Council, and the Industrial Society (formerly the Industrial Welfare Society). A variety of human relations techniques were also implemented at hospitals of the National Health Service and at mining operations of the National Coal Board with excellent productivity results.[123]

The adoption of human relations techniques was greatly facilitated by the consulting companies, which acted as intermediaries between the producers of managerial knowledge and those applying it. Bedaux was the leading firm during the 1930s and 1940s, concentrating on scientific management techniques, but consulting firms using a human relations approach became dominant in the 1950s: Associated Industrial Consultants, PA (Personnel Administration) Management Consultants, MSL-Mackenzie Davey, William Schlackman Ltd., and, the most influential of all, Urwick, Orr and Associates, founded by Lyndall Urwick and Leslie Orr (previously at Bedaux). The National Institute of Industrial Psychology and the Tavistock Institute were also involved in consulting work with the major British firms. Social scientists such as Elliott Jaques did extensive private consulting, and Eric Trist was a permanent consultant for such major firms as Unilever, Shell, Philips Electrical, ICI, and Avon Rubber.[124]

The case of the Rowntree cocoa works in York illustrates the use of human relations ideology and techniques to preempt industrial conflict and reinforce the community of the plant. Building on the Quaker ethic as well as on a long tradition of industrial welfare programs and social-science research, the Rowntree managers were perhaps the most advanced of their time in Britain. The powerful personnel department at Rowntree used techniques such as interviews, discussion groups, suggestion systems, job rotation, and work groups throughout the 1940s and 1950s. Urwick acted as a consultant for Rowntree when those human relations techniques were being implemented.[125]

The cases of Shell and ICI exemplify the adoption of human rela-

---

123. Clark (1987, p. 336); Paul and Robertson, *Job Enrichment and Employee Motivation* (1970, pp. 20–83); Smith, "The T-group in industry" (1964); Trist and Sofer, *Group Relations Training: A Pilot Experiment* (1957); BIM, *Group Relations Training* (1960), *Suggestion Schemes* (1959); BPC, *Suggestion Schemes* (1957); Industrial Society, *Successful Suggestion Schemes* (1966), *Suggestion Scheme Statistics* (1965); Jago, *Suggestion Schemes* (1979, p. 1); Clewer, *The Human Implications of Work Study* (1955); Dore, *British Factory, Japanese Factory* (1973, p. 360).

124. See *Management Today* 39(6)(1971):88–93.

125. See Northcott (1945); Child (1964).

tions ideology and techniques by most of the largest British firms in the 1950s and early 1960s in response to growing organizational complexity and latent labor problems. Techniques such as attitude surveys, organizational development, job enrichment, and T-groups were used for many years at both firms. Shell created a Social Sciences Application Division, in conjunction with the Tavistock Institute, that regularly conducted morale surveys and applied other human relations techniques. Both firms hired leading academics as consultants, including Edgar Schein of MIT and Eric Trist. It should be noted, however, that both Shell and ICI were simultaneously implementing scientific management techniques for the first time in the early 1950s to meet the challenges of mounting international competition.[126]

The adoption of human relations ideology and techniques by British managers and firms has stirred some controversy over their actual contribution to organizational effectiveness and efficiency. Critics of human relations among British managers of the 1940s and 1950s argued that business was supposed to produce goods and services not "better men and women." In their view, fulfilling wider social responsibilities should not interfere with efficient production. Human relations seems to ask the manager to promote the self-actualization of people through work. Although higher productivity is a stated goal of human relations proponents, the emphasis on self-actualization, provided it is not merely rhetorical, could be detrimental to business performance and ultimately lead to suboptimal productivity. Historian Martin Wiener has argued in a recent best-selling book that the adoption of human relations exacerbated the relative industrial decline of Britain.[127] Unfortunately, there are no empirical studies investigating the effects of human relations ideology and techniques on the long-term productivity of British firms. It is possible, though, to examine some indirect evidence. One study of the departmental background of British company directors and the profitability of their firms provides contradictory evidence. Less-profitable firms tended to have higher proportions of directors with a human relations or personnel department background in the plastics and construction sectors, but the reverse was true for electrical appliances, food, and retailing.[128] The evidence presented in this study relating to the largest firms in the United States, Britain, and Spain that implemented hu-

126. Davey, Gill, and McDonnell (1970); Paul and Robertson (1970, pp. 20–83).
127. Child (1969, pp. 151–153); Wiener (1985, p. 144).
128. Betts (1967, p. 84).

man relations suggests that the ideology of human relations was used to come to terms with pressing problems such as labor unrest and output restriction. The firms that implemented human relations techniques in the United States and Great Britain were quite profitable indeed, and remained so.

One final observation about the relationship between worker participation schemes and the human relations paradigm is necessary. Harvie Ramsay has argued that participation schemes in Britain tended to appear cyclically whenever employers were experiencing some kind of threat to their "sacrosanct authority" such as trades-union pressure, tight labor markets resulting in high strike levels, large-scale political mobilization of the working class, or war. The five waves of participatory schemes between the mid-nineteenth century and the early 1960s (first and second profit-sharing waves, Whitley councils, first joint consultation wave, Joint Production Committees, and second joint consultation wave) seem to fit his model quite well. Ramsay further argues that the human relations approach was the ideological justification for the second wave of joint consultation schemes in the 1950s. "The 'natural solidarity' of work groups was to be channelled, as it had been in the [Joint Production Committees], to the benefit of all through joint consultation, led, of course, by those best suited and most responsibly minded—management." This wave of joint consultation started after World War II under the auspices of the Ministry of Labour, eventually affecting three out of every four firms.[129] The comparison with Germany is instructive. In Germany codetermination and works councils legislation made the human relations approach redundant. In Britain, however, joint consultation was in part a result of the human relations movement, which survived the short lives of most of the joint consultation schemes.

In Britain the human relations paradigm succeeded as an ideology of management under institutional conditions quite similar to the ones prevailing in Spain, despite the sharp difference in economic development and the absence of a corporatist framework. Perhaps the most crucial similarity had to do with the often religiously inspired, traditional humanist mode of thought that characterized business elites in both societies. Although rates of labor unrest were lower than in Spain and the United States, the threat of conflict was there, and output restriction remained a rampant practice. What made the

---

129. Ramsay, "Cycles of control" (1977, pp. 491–492); Child (1969, pp. 146–148). Two surveys on the spread of joint consultation were conducted, one by the NIIP (751 firms) and the other by a group of researchers (598 firms). The results were very similar.

human relations paradigm so attractive was, as Geoff Brown has argued, that it provided "a scientifically validated demonstration of the best ideas and practices already espoused by the advanced guard of British management thinkers."[130] As in Spain, those ideas and practices had originated in the traditional-humanist mentality. The human relations wave of theorizing, research, and consulting in Britain, however, had one major effect that was absent in Spain: it facilitated the adoption of the most important techniques associated with the paradigm by business firms, which in Britain were more bureaucratized and sophisticated than in Spain and hence had the panoply of white-collar expertise necessary to implement the techniques.

The Rise of Structural Analysis

British economic and business structures started undergoing important changes during the 1950s. The bureaucratization, internationalization, and diversification of all sorts of organizations, public and private, coupled with the rise of the service sector and the stabilization of industrial relations during the 1960s, produced a situation similar to the one prevalent in the United States and Germany. The formulation of a new approach to organization incorporating a contingency logic, together with the support of state agencies, facilitated the adoption of structural ideas by the leading management intellectuals as well as by industrial and public-sector firms.

NEW ORGANIZATIONAL PROBLEMS DURING THE LATE 1950s AND 1960s

The British economic scene did not change much during the 1960s from the situation in the 1950s. Keynesian stabilization policies, direct state intervention in the economy, and state welfare programs produced a period of full employment and favored a slow development of the internal mass-consumption market. The expansion in motor vehicles, electrical goods, oil refining, and chemicals barely compensated the decline in sectors such as textiles and shipbuilding. As a result the economy grew at a modest annual cumulative rate of 2.7 percent over the 1960s.[131] But there were important changes in the complexity, scale, and diversification of firms, their international presence, and the nature of industrial relations that created new organizational problems and opportunities.

130. Brown (1977, p. 247).
131. Pollard (1969, pp. 415–431); Hobsbawm (1969, pp. 249–272).

Complexity, Scale and Diversification of Firms. British firms had been growing in size, complexity, bureaucratization, and diversification since the turn of the century, but during the 1950s and 1960s those trends accelerated considerably, surpassing the levels reached in most other countries, including the United States. By the late 1960s Britain had more industrial firms with over 40,000 employees than either the United States or Germany, and the average number of workers per manufacturing plant was also higher. The 100 largest British manufacturing corporations accounted for 27 percent of total output in 1930, 30 percent in 1960, and 40 percent in 1970. The trend towards greater industrial concentration was more pronounced than in the United States, and in part resulted from the merger wave that followed the introduction of anticartel legislation in 1956. Public-sector organizations such as the National Coal Board or the Transport Board employed over 750,000 workers each, compared to General Motors' 250,000. Manufacturing firms were becoming more and more bureaucratized, from 21.3 administrative per 100 production employees in 1950 to 27.1 in 1960 and 36.4 in 1970, well ahead of the average for American firms (30.3 in 1970). British firms also were the most highly diversified ones, second only to American corporations. Only 28 of the 100 largest industrial firms pursued diversified product strategies back in 1950, versus 50 in 1960 and 62 in 1970. The British service sector (private and public) also expanded considerably during the 1950s and 1960s, representing 53 percent of all jobs by 1970. Again, Britain was second only to the United States in terms of the expansion of service organizations. By the mid-1960s Britain had a sizeable population of large, bureaucratized, and diversified firms operating in several countries, such as Unilever, Dunlop Rubber, Imperial Chemical Industries (ICI), Associated British Foods, Cadbury/Schweppes, Rio Tinto Zinc, Babcock and Wilcox, Hawker Siddeley, and Vickers, and a host of large, undiversified firms such as British American Tobacco, Imperial Tobacco, British Petroleum, Esso Petroleum, Royal Dutch/Shell, British Aircraft, British Leyland, and Rolls-Royce. Affiliates of foreign multinationals in sectors such as electrical, motor vehicles, and chemicals could be added to those lists.[132] The staggering degrees of bureaucratization and diversification of firms, and the growth of the service sector, introduced diffi-

132. Hannah, *The Rise of the Corporate Economy* (1983, pp. 70–89, 123–142), "Visible and invisible hands in Great Britain," in Chandler and Daems, eds. (1980, p. 67); Prais, *The Evolution of Giant Firms in Britain* (1976); Davenport-Hines and Jones, eds., *Enterprise, Management and Innovation in British Business 1914–1980* (1988).

culties in the management of large organizations operating in different markets, using different technologies, and serving diverse clienteles.

New International Opportunities. British firms also benefited in the late 1950s and 1960s from the expansion of world markets. In 1950 imports and exports accounted for 34 percent of the British national product, increasing to 36 percent in 1960 and to 43 percent in 1970, a proportion slightly above the one for West Germany and more than three times greater than the one for the United States. Although Britain did not join the European Economic Community until 1973, an expanding world economy offered multiple opportunities, and British multinational corporations were competing successfully in a variety of markets. Over three out of every four foreign subsidiaries owned by large British firms in 1971 had been created after 1955. British foreign direct investment was about 1 percent of the country's GDP throughout the 1960s, considerably more than that of Germany and the United States. By 1967 the stock of British direct investment abroad represented 15.6 percent of the GDP, compared to only 7.1 percent for the United States and 2.4 percent for Germany. This strategy of internationalization paid off: in 1971 Britain enjoyed a positive balance in royalties and fees representing 0.04 percent of the GDP, while Germany and Spain suffered from deficits.[133] As in the case of growing size, bureaucratization, and diversification, the internationalization of British firms required organizational action to manage product development, manufacturing, and marketing on a world scale.

Stabilization of Industrial Relations. The escalating structural problems facing British firms appeared at a time when the threat of industrial conflict began to fade away, and the system of industrial relations became more stable than in the late 1940s and 1950s. Over all, slightly fewer working days were lost due to industrial conflict during the 1960s than during the previous decade. The number of strikes remained almost unchanged, while their average length went down, and the number of workers involved per strike doubled. The peak industrial conflict between 1957 and 1959 was followed by a steady decline until 1970. During the 1960s employers and managers ap-

---

133. UNCTC, *Salient Features and Trends in Foreign Direct Investment* (1983, pp. 34–35); Whitley, Thomas, and Marceau, *Masters of Business?* (1981, pp. 12–13); see also the comparative statistics in Appendix B.

peared to be much less concerned about conflict than in the previous decade. Collective bargaining functioned comparatively well, with collective agreements covering over three-fourths of all workers. In the mid-1960s when informal agreements at the workplace level seemed to go beyond the formal system of industry-wide bargaining, and international competitiveness pressures did not allow for "free" wage increases, an innovative "productivity bargaining" system was introduced that covered 54 percent of all industrial workers in 1967–69.[134]

INSTITUTIONAL FACTORS FAVORING A STRUCTURAL APPROACH

By the early 1960s Britain had a core of large firms that ranked among the most bureaucratic and diversified in the world. These corporations found themselves operating under diverse technological conditions and competing in the world market with their German and American counterparts. They all were facing similar problems. Moreover, the service sector (including government agencies) was expanding quickly, adding technological diversity to the population of organizations. As in the German and American situations, the problem of industrial relations was handled with a variety of industry-wide collective bargaining mechanisms supplemented with informal workplace negotiations. In the United States and Germany such organizational problems and opportunities were met by a structural approach to organizing. The same institutional factors present in those two countries also favored the adoption and implementation of structural analysis by British managers and firms. In addition, structural analysis in Britain benefited from state support.

The Rise of Structural Social Science. Starting in the late 1950s several groups of British social scientists began doing research on the structure of organizations and their relation to technology and environment. Joan Woodward's research on organizational technology and structure, Tom Burns's on mechanistic and organismic structures, and the Aston Programme anticipated many of the findings of the American strategy-and-structure, technological, and organization-and-

---

134. Clegg, *Trade Unionism Under Collective Bargaining* (1976, p. 69); Lazonick (1990, pp. 204–209); Ramsay (1977, pp. 493–494); Flanders, "Collective Bargaining," in Flanders and Clegg, eds. (1964, pp. 274, 286); Liesner, ed., *Economic Statistics 1900–1983* (1985, p. 26).

environment schools. In fact, the British studies figure prominently in the major American surveys of the organizations literature.[135]

The most important structural theorist and consultant was sociologist Joan Woodward. She was educated at Oxford in politics, philosophy, economics, and social and public administration, serving as senior labor manager of the Royal Ordnance Factory at Bridgwater during the war. Her first research in the early 1950s at the Department of Social Science, University of Liverpool, had to do with industrial relations, attitudes and conflict in the docks and in retailing, but did not use the human relations approach then dominant in Britain.[136] Woodward directed the Human Relations Research Unit of the South Essex Technical College between 1953 and 1957. It was during this period that she did the pathbreaking research for *Management and Technology* (1958), concluding that there was no "one best way to organize," that the most successful industrial firms she studied adapted their organizational structure (in terms of administrative intensity, specialization, and flexibility) to the nature of their technology (unit, mass, or process). This booklet was the first concise statement of a contingency theory of organization.[137] After five years at Oxford, in 1961 Woodward moved to the Industrial Sociology Research Unit at Imperial College, London, where she became a professor in 1969. During this period she refined the technological contingency theory in *Industrial Organization* (1965).[138] Throughout her career, Woodward did consulting work for private firms as well as for the Post Office, the Department of Employment, and several hospitals. The impact of Woodward's research was far-reaching. It set the agenda for future organizational research on both sides of the Atlantic and shaped the outcome of ongoing research.

A second important research project was undertaken by sociologist Tom Burns at the Social Sciences Research Centre of the University of Edinburgh. He studied several Scottish and English electronics firms as well as a rayon mill. Burns presented his classic distinction between "mechanistic" and "organismic" systems in *The Management of Innovation* (1961), co-authored with psychologist G. M. Stalker.

135. Perrow, *Complex Organizations* (1986, pp. 142–144); Scott, *Organizations* (1987, pp. 104, 211–213, 224–225, 232–238, 241–244).

136. Woodward, *The Dock Worker* (1956), *The Saleswoman* (1960). See also her later collaborative study on democracy and participation: Flanders, Pomeranz, and Woodward, *Experiment in Industrial Democracy* (1968).

137. Woodward, *Management and Technology* (1958).

138. Woodward, *Industrial Organization* (1980).

Mechanistic structures were adequate under stable and certain conditions, whereas organismic structures worked best under uncertain and unstable conditions.[139] David Silverman, a sociologist at the University of London, refined the insights of both Woodward and Burns, developing elaborate typologies of organizations and conceptualizing conflict as a structural phenomenon.[140] Other sociologists also published research on organizations using a structural approach.[141]

The most extensive research project on the structure of organizations was initiated in 1961 at the Industrial Administration Research Unit of the University of Aston in Birmingham (then called the Birmingham College of Advanced Technology). The Aston Programme research team, directed by psychologist Derek S. Pugh, included psychologist Graham Harding, sociologists Robert Hinings and John Child, and former personnel manager David Hickson. The original idea was to make systematic comparisons across organizations. The research design maximized the variety of types of organizations (from prisons to industrial firms) and environments (from most stable to most rapidly changing). One key goal in the research was to develop precise measures of the relevant organizational variables. The results of this research—including a characterization of the relevant dimensions of technology, the management of interdepartmental conflict, organizational contexts, a taxonomy of structures, and the relationship between strategy and structure—first appeared in a series of articles published in *Administrative Science Quarterly* starting in 1963. The more detailed accounts of the research appeared as a three-volume set in the mid-1970s.[142] Pugh and Child were influential among the British business elite being trained at new institutions such as the London Business School during the early 1970s.[143]

The greatest popularizer of structural ideas in Britain was Rose-

---

139. Burns and Stalker, *The Management of Innovation* (1961). See also his later edited book on several aspects of modern organizations, *Industrial Man* (1969).

140. Silverman, *The Theory of Organisations* (1971).

141. See *The Sociological Review* 14(1)(March 1966):29–38, 17(1)(March 1969): 67–86; *British Journal of Sociology* 20(3)(September 1969):277–294; *The Manager* 33(12)(1965):28–31.

142. Pugh et al., "A conceptual scheme for organizational analysis." (1963), "The context of organization structures" (1969a), "An empirical taxonomy of structures of work organizations" (1969b); Walton et al., "The management of interdepartmental conflict" (1969); Child, "Organizational structure, environment and performance" (1972); Pugh and Hickson, *Organizational Structure in Its Context: The Aston Programme I* (1976); Pugh and Hinings, *Organizational Structure: Extensions and Replications. The Aston Programme II* (1976); Pugh and Payne, *Organizational Structure in Its Context: The Aston Programme III* (1977).

143. Barnes, *Managerial Catalyst* (1989).

mary Stewart, director of the Acton Society Trust (a management think tank), and later a teacher at the London School of Economics and the Oxford Centre for Management Studies (Templeton College). She published two textbooks in which the central topics were the organizational structure, technology, goals, differentiation and integration of functions, and decentralization.[144]

The major implication of this wave of structural research was that it shifted the level of analysis. Woodward's and Burns's criticism of scientific management and human relations was implicit, in that either approach missed the point that different technological or environmental conditions required different patterns of organization.[145] Even within the ranks of human relations research, certain ideas emerged that advanced a structural way of reasoning, such as Trist's sociotechnical systems. The Tavistock Institute itself published structural research. As in the United States and Germany during roughly the same period, the structural critics of human relations questioned the validity and universality of the findings as well as the possibility that higher satisfaction resulted from higher productivity and not the other way around.[146]

Support from the State. As had been the case with human relations research, the state itself and state agencies in charge of industrial research facilitated the creation of knowledge about the structure of organizations. The state also promoted the use of the structural approach by public-sector companies such as the National Coal Board, National Health Service, Post Office, and the Electricity Board. Cyril N. Parkinson's article and book on the needless proliferation of government bureaucracy certainly made an impact on the public and on policymakers, focusing their attention on the opportunities to improve the organization of public services.[147] The Department of Scientific and Industrial Research (and its successor, the Social Sciences Research Council) funded Woodward's industrial research at South East Essex and Imperial Colleges, Burns's electronics firms project at the University of Edinburgh (complemented with funds from the Ministry of Supply), as well as the Aston Programme. Woodward's early research also received support from the Medical Research Coun-

144. Stewart, *The Reality of Management* (1963), *The Reality of Organizations* (1970). See also in *The Manager* 29(1961):612–614.

145. For other social-science critiques of human relations see *The Sociological Review* 14(1) (March 1960):39–52.

146. Child (1969, pp. 170–173).

147. *The Economist*, "Parkinson's Law" (1955); Parkinson, *Parkinson's Law and Other Studies on Administration* (1957).

cil and the Conditional Aid scheme between the United States and Britain.

The Position of the Trades Unions. As in Germany and the United States, British trades-union leaders remained silent about structural analysis research and practice. Structural reorganizations of the major British firms were discussed by managers in the management journals, but no reference was made to either opposition or support from the unions. There is no evidence showing that workers or their unions opposed any of the reorganizations planned for public- or private-sector firms.

THE THEORETICAL ADOPTION OF STRUCTURAL ANALYSIS

As in America and Germany, British management intellectuals started to think in structural terms during the interwar period. The earliest structural thinker was Edward T. Elbourne, a mechanical engineer by training, manager, consultant, and founder of the Institute of Industrial Administration (1920). His *Factory Administration and Accounts* (1914) sold over 10,000 copies during the war. He discussed departmentalization, staff organization, organizational structures, and production routines. Lyndall Urwick, also a human relations proponent, contributed to the early trend of structural thought with the flawed "principles" approach. In a later book, *Fundamentals of Industrial Administration* (1934), Elbourne subscribed to Urwick's principles of administration (e.g. specialization, coordination, unity of command, span of control). Sir Alfred Mond, the chairman of Imperial Chemical Industries, was a staunch advocate for amalgamations and for a more structural approach to organizational problems.[148]

Interest in the principles of organization grew after World War II. The *British Management Review* devoted an entire issue in 1948 to the principles of administration, with articles by academics, consultants, managers, and government officials. Edward F. L. Brech, a management consultant at Urwick, Orr, suggested that the principles could not

148. Elbourne, *Factory Administration and Accounts* (1914, pp. 27–43), *The Management Problem* (1919), *Fundamentals of Industrial Administration* (1934); Child (1969, p. 88). See also his article in the *Journal of Industrial Administration* 1 (October 1921):171–182. Urwick, "Organization as a technical problem" (1937), originally published in 1933, *The Elements of Administration* (1944). See his articles in *Industry Illustrated* 3(12)(1935):21–24; *The Manager* 25(1957):114–118. Other managers using a structural approach published in: *Journal of Industrial Administration* 1(5)(1921): 131–139, 1(10)(1921):163–188, 1(11)(1921):203–207, 2(10)(1922):3–8; *Industry Illustrated* 1(2)(1933):xvii–xviii, xxiv, 3(12)(1935):21–24; *British Management Review* 1(3)(1936):25–33, 2(4)(1937):5–23, 4(3)(1939–43):136–139.

be applied uncritically to all sorts of organizations. Industrialist Sir Charles Renold discussed the "federal structure," a kind of divisional organization. Tavistock Institute's A. T. M. Wilson, later appointed worldwide social-science adviser of Unilever, argued that work relationships and satisfaction had to do with the structure of tasks.[149]

But British managers and consultants alone would not have elaborated and implemented the crucial idea of contingency without the influence of the wave of structural social-science theorizing and consulting starting in the late 1950s. In 1965 Joan Woodward wrote: "The emotion aroused [by her 1958 book, *Management and Technology*] was due to the suggestion that the failure was not human but circumstantial, the underlying assumption being that the principles of management theory were adequate only within a very limited area of technology." Woodward's technological contingency theory had a tremendous impact among those teaching management subjects, and also at the human relations stronghold of the British Institute of Management, which had all too willingly accepted the orthodoxy of the principles of administration.[150] The leading consultants, such as Urwick, accepted the new paradigm. Managers from a variety of firms explicitly adopted a structural approach in their writings and statements about organization, including British Petroleum, Imperial Chemical Industries, Imperial Tobacco Group, Shell, and other smaller manufacturing firms.[151] Certain practicing managers helped to further elaborate the paradigm. Sir Geoffrey Vickers, of the National Coal Board, was interested in the organizational setting of decision making following the tradition of Barnard, Simon, and Wildavsky. Wilfred Brown, chairman and managing director of Glacier Metal (where Jaques did his research), departed from human relations with his "task" approach (a kind of technological contingency theory), and was also interested in decision-making processes. He argued that "effective organization is a function of the work to be done and the resources and techniques available to do it."[152]

149. *British Management Review* 7(3)(1948); Brech, *Organisation* (1957); Brech, ed., *The Principles and Practice of Management* (1963, p. 43); Renold, *The Organisational Structure of Large Undertakings* (1948–49), *The Nature of Management* (1949); Child (1969, p. 184).

150. Woodward (1965, pp. 245–246).

151. See *The Manager* 32(7)(1964):15–21, 32(11)(1964):31–35, 34(5)(1966): 98–103; *Management Today* 39(3)(1971):86–93, 138, 142.

152. Vickers, *The Art of Judgment* (1965), *Towards a Sociology of Management* (1967), *Value Systems and Social Process* (1968), *Making Institutions Work* (1973); Brown, *Exploration in Management* (1960, p. 18); *Organization* (1971).

The theoretical success of structural analysis in Britain can be more systematically assessed by examining the articles published in *Management Today* (*The Manager* before 1968), which, with the *Financial Times*, was the most widely read publication among British managers.[153] The structural approach to organizing came to dominate the debates in the mid-1960s. Throughout the postwar period up to 1973, more structural analysis than scientific management pieces were published (see panel B of Table 5.2). The ideological themes of structural analysis came up rarely, as had been the case in the United States and Germany. However, the notion that the problem lay in a mismatch between the organizational technology or environment and the organizational structure, the various authority structures to cope with that problem, and the contingency approach were frequently discussed by the management intellectuals (see panel A of Table 5.2).

THE PRACTICAL IMPLEMENTATION OF STRUCTURAL IDEAS

Structural reorganizations are the only readily available quantitative indicators for the implementation of structural ideas about organization. Only a handful of the 100 largest British industrial corporations had divisional structures in 1950. By 1970, however, 70 of them were divisionalized (73 in the United States). The British case is peculiar because in 1970 there were more divisionalized than fully diversified corporations among the 100 largest (70 versus 62).[154] This phenomenon suggests the extent to which British companies were eager to imitate a foreign form of organization perceived as successful even when it did not fit their particular situation. Over two-thirds of the divisional corporations had used the consulting services of McKinsey. The massive establishment of manufacturing operations on British soil by American companies during the 1950s and 1960s also accounted for part of the transfer of new structural forms. The process of diversification and divisionalization was accompanied by a growth in "general management" courses at management schools in response to the growing need for managers who knew how to handle specialists.[155]

153. Huczynski, *Management Gurus* (1993, p. 287).
154. See the comparative statistics in Appendix B.
155. Dyas and Thanheiser, *The Emerging European Enterprise* (1976, p. 29); Channon, *The Strategy and Structure of British Enterprise* (1973); Chandler (1990, pp. 158, 615, 618–619); Hannah, "Visible and invisible hands in Great Britain," in Chandler and Daems, eds. (1980, p. 57); Hannah (1983); Clark (1987, pp. 338–340); Whitley, Thomas, and Marceau (1981, p. 20); Gunz, "Generalists, specialists, and the reproduction of managerial structures" (1980).

The forces driving the process of structural reorganization can be better understood by looking at company experiences such as those of Shell and ICI. In the late 1950s Shell was facing serious organizational problems deriving from its diversification into petrochemicals and from its joint activities with Royal Dutch Petroleum, with which it had been amalgamated back in 1907. McKinsey was first asked to reorganize Shell's operations in Venezuela. When this experiment was crowned with success, the McKinseys moved into the central offices in London. ICI was facing similar problems in the 1950s as a result of its diversification into heavy organic chemicals, paints, pharmaceuticals, and fibers. In addition, the firm was engaging in a major process of internationalization. Traditionally run by scientists, ICI appointed a former civil servant, Paul Chambers, as chairman in 1960. He asked McKinsey in 1962 to take a look at the firm's organization. By the late 1960s both Shell and ICI had full-fledged multidivisional structures in place, which allowed them to pursue more ambitious, but eventually problematic, diversification strategies into areas largely unrelated to their core businesses.[156]

Public-sector organizations also implemented structural ideas. British Railways introduced structural decentralization of operational decision making and centralization of control starting in the late 1950s. McKinsey advised the British Broadcasting Corporation (BBC) on structural restructuring. The National Coal Board (NCB) called in a manager from ICI, a multidivisional company, to recommend changes in the organizational structure. The Fleck Report (1957) on the NCB dealt almost exclusively with its organizational structure. The Herbert Report (1956) on Electricity Supply discussed decentralization, staffs, and the possibility of creating area divisions. The British railway system also hired structural experts to reorganize its operations. The Post Office engaged in structural reorganizations during this period under the guidance of McKinsey.[157] At the massive National Health Service, the years between 1950 and 1970 represented a period of "technocratic change," with the introduction of program-evaluation techniques, accounting procedures, and "a machinery of administration." The construction of new District General Hospitals after 1962 proceeded with a rationalistic organizational logic in mind, but the overall web of hospitals and services became harder to coordi-

156. Channon (1973, pp. 115–116, 141–144); *Management Today* 41(5)(1973): 70–79.

157. Parker, "Can British management close the gap?" (1967). McKinsey's reorganization of the Post Office was apparently controversial.

nate, and costs soared. McKinsey consultants were hired to devise a fix, which was implemented after 1974 with the introduction of Area Boards and a streamlined managerial structure under the classic structuralist slogan, "Maximum delegation downward, maximum accountability upward."[158] Structural analysis had much more of an impact on the organization of public-sector agencies in Britain than in either the United States or Germany, partially because state research agancies in Britain were much more committed to the development of the structural approach than they were in the other two countries.

THE BRITISH CASE IN HISTORICAL AND COMPARATIVE PERSPECTIVE

The evolution of British managerial ideologies and organizational practices during the first half of this century resembles the Spanish experience in intriguing ways. The business elite rejected scientific management during the interwar period in both countries for quite similar reasons (lack of engineering input, antimodernism, unintended consequences of state intervention in the economy, and opposition from the trades unions). Also, a similar configuration of institutional factors accounts for the success of human relations ideology in both countries (social-science theorizing and consulting, religious-humanist ideals, active state support, and trades-union collaboration). The only (but significant) discrepancy was the failure of human relations techniques in Spain, owing to the limited bureaucratization and sophistication of firms. Nonetheless, given the differences in economic development and in structure of the business sectors in both countries, the agreement in terms of institutional conditions and ideological outcomes is all the more remarkable. Interestingly, the British case differs sharply from the German one in terms of organizational problems and institutional conditions, as well as in terms of the degrees of adoption of scientific management between the world wars, and of human relations after 1945. The case of the United States approximates the German one in relation to the adoption of scientific management techniques during the interwar period, and the British one with regard to the adoption of human relations ideology and techniques after 1945. One important difference between Britain and the United States was that in Britain scientific management techniques were extensively implemented for the first time after World War II, resulting in some overlap with the success of human relations

---

158. Jervis, *Bosses in British Business* (1974, pp. 115–117); Brech (1957, pp. 397–412); Klein, *The Politics of the National Health Service* (1989, pp. 62–99).

ideology and the introduction of the techniques associated with the paradigm. This peculiarity of the British case had implications for the kind of dominant human relations theory, which—as is evident in Trist's socio-technical systems—took into consideration the efforts at rationalization and the need to humanize work simultaneously and within a unified framework.

The story of structural analysis seems radically different. Starting in the late 1950s the British situation converged considerably with the one prevalent in Germany and the United States. Changes in the business and government sectors, internationalization, and stabilization of industrial relations opened the road to the adoption of structural ideas and forms. The contrast with relatively underdeveloped Spain during the 1960s and even the 1970s became apparent. Perhaps the best way to summarize the overall British pattern is the one proposed by John Child. In Britain, he argues, the management movement often found itself in a "defensive position," caught up between a glorious industrial past and an ambiguous present beset by declining competitiveness and labor troubles.[159] This contrasts with the more successful dynamism of managerial capitalism in the United States and Germany, but resembles the "low-profile" behavior of Spanish employers and managers during the Franco decades. Again, Spanish and British managers shared a traditional-humanist mode of thought that had direct implications for their organizational tastes. Even when British management practice approximated the American and German pattern during the 1960s (largely by imitation), the improvements in terms of productivity and competitiveness did not follow suit.

159. Child (1969, p. 112).

SIX

Comparing Patterns of Adoption

The preceding four chapters have documented historical patterns of organizational change in the United States, Germany, Spain, and Great Britain as a result of the selective adoption of the three major paradigms of organization. Organizational change was evaluated at the theoretical level, looking at the extent to which management intellectuals discussed and accepted the ideology and/or the techniques of each paradigm. This empirical assessment was complemented with relevant information on the implementation of organizational techniques by firms and with case studies at the firm level in each of the countries. A historical interpretation of observed change based on certain limited pairwise comparisons was made along the way. This chapter compares the organizational problems, institutional factors, and outcomes for all four countries simultaneously and in a systematic way. The goal is to draw some theoretically meaningful causal conclusions about the ways in which organizational change takes place that could be applicable beyond the four countries included in this study.

The historical evidence presented in previous chapters was organized around the perceived organizational problems facing the employer and managerial class during different time periods, as well as around institutional factors favoring or impeding the adoption of particular organizational paradigms as solutions to those problems. The three variables accounting for organizational problems (structural changes, international pressures or opportunities, labor unrest) together with the four institutional factors (business-elite mentalities, professions, role of the state, and workers' responses) configure the *conditions* under which a particular *outcome* (i.e. degree of adoption of a paradigm) is observed to occur. It is important to note that countries differ not only in terms of the sequence of organizational outcomes, but also in terms of the process of organizational change itself. Different configurations of problems and institutional factors have operated to produce the observed patterns of change.

THE ADOPTION OF SCIENTIFIC MANAGEMENT

The adoption of the scientific management paradigm took place in response to different problematic conditions in each of the countries studied, and was fueled by different configurations of institutional factors. As a consequence, different patterns of organizational change can be identified. The information contained in each of the country chapters is summarized in Table 6.1 (at the risk of oversimplification). One result common to all four countries studied was that the ideology of scientific management was not widely accepted, as shown by the content analysis of articles and books written by management intellectuals. The ideological themes typical of the scientific management approach appeared rarely. By contrast, the techniques associated with the paradigm were frequently discussed and generally accepted by the management intellectuals in the United States and Germany. The actual implementation of the techniques of scientific management was extensive in the United States and Germany during the interwar period, and in Spain and Britain starting in the mid-1940s. From the point of view of the dominant organizational problems, the cases of the United States and Great Britain during the interwar period were similar, in that changes in the structure of firms (growing size and complexity, bureaucratization) took place in the midst of labor unrest but *without* the presence of international pressures. (Remember that the content analysis of management journals confirmed the conclusions by economic historians that the British business elite failed to perceive the danger of international competition and Britain's decline.) Even though workers and their unions were opposed, scientific management techniques and Fordism were adopted in the United States because two crucial institutional factors were present, namely, the increasing influence of engineers, and a favorable mentality among the business elite and the public (Progressivism, modernism, mass consumption/production culture). Neither of those two factors were present in Britain between the world wars. In fact, evidence at the firm level, as in the case of Rover and its surrounding business community, indicate that aversion to change on the part of British employers and stiff resistance from workers account for the divergent patterns of organizational change up to 1940 in the United States and Britain, the two liberal-democratic societies in this study.

Bringing the German case into the analysis changes the basic parameters of the comparison. The organizational problems facing German business during the interwar period were different from those in the two Anglo-Saxon countries, in that structural changes in firms coincided with international competitive pressures but low rates of labor unrest. Bureaucratic ideology and practices drawn from the experience of the German army and state were effective in addressing increasing size and complexity and, in part, labor unrest. The reform-

TABLE 6.1 The adoption of scientific management (SM) in comparative perspective

Variables	United States	Germany	Spain	Great Britain
Problem for Analysis				
Degree of adoption of SM	High (1920–39) as technique; low as ideology	High (1920–33) as technique; low as ideology	Low (1920–36) [high (1939–53) as technique]	Low (1914–39) [high (1939–50) as technique]
Explanatory Factors				
1. Structural changes	Rise of large business firms; growing complexity; bureaucratization	Increasing firm size, complexity, and bureaucratization	Economic backwardness; small size, low degree of bureaucratization of firms [structural change 1939–60]	Increasing firm size, complexity, and bureaucratization
2. International pressures or opportunities	Weak, except during WWI; economy not dependent on world trade	Late industrializer; dependence on exports and imports; political isolation; USA as threat	Protectionism, but with access to foreign capital and technology [isolation, 1939–53]	Free-trade ideology; still dominant in world trade [competitive pressures in 1939–53]
3. Industrial relations system, and labor unrest problem	Powerful unions; adversarial pattern of industrial relations; high rates of conflict	Labor unrest prevented by bureaucratic controls and corporatism; reformist labor unions	Virulent labor unrest; repressed but powerful labor unions [labor unrest solved, 1939–55]	High rates of labor unrest; craft-based trades unionism with delegated shop-floor control [less unrest 1945–53]
4. Business-elite mentalities	Progressivism; efficiency craze; technocratic modernism; mass production/consumption culture	Dominant modernistic mentality: Deutsche Werkstätten, AEG's programs, Bauhaus	No modernistic elite mentality; early impact of social Catholicism and of traditional humanism	Elite antimodernism; early impact of industrial betterment and religious values
5. Professions	Efficiency experts; emergent engineering profession; powerful associations (ASME)	Numerous engineers; engineers occupy key positions in industry; powerful organizations (VDI, REFA)	Few engineers, no strong professional associations [engineers more numerous and powerful after 1939]	Few qualified engineers, no strong professional associations; engineers reject SM [still no technocracy after 1945]
6. Role of the state	Weak: initiative left to the private sector	Strong: National Board of Efficiency (RKW), German Normalization Committee, REFA	Weak: no official entity; corporatism promotes vocational guidance [strong role after 1939: INRT, INI]	Weak: No official entity; state research condemns SM and praises human relations [strong role after 1945: AACP, BPC]
7. Workers' response	Shop-floor resistance to SM	Unions promote SM	Unions oppose SM [unions neutralized after 1939]	Trades unions oppose SM [support after 1945]

ist behavior of the dominant Free Unions during the Wilhelmine decades indicated the extent to which bureaucratic controls helped appease a militant working class. The international competitive pressures building up at the turn of the century required new approaches to organization. The political isolation and economic crises leading to and following World War I set the stage for the adoption of scientific management during the democratic Weimar Republic of the 1920s. The corporatist pattern was reinforced by the war, and the counter-revolutionary measures adopted during its immediate aftermath were in large measure also conducive to a consolidation of corporatist controls over the economy and the labor arena. The corporatist solution gave the labor unions a role to play in economic and social policy-making.

The German version of scientific management, "industrial rationalization," was a reflection of this mixed public-private, orchestrated, and corporatist organization of the economy. During the Weimar Republic union leaders occupied key governmental positions, accepted industrial rationalization programs, and actively collaborated with management. As in the United States, German business elites embraced the techniques of scientific management and actually succeeded in implementing them in practice. But the German pattern of organizational change during the interwar period was unique, because in the midst of economic difficulty a national alliance was forged to overcome the situation, with industrialists, avant-garde artists, engineers, the state, and the labor unions all supporting the adoption of scientific management. The role of the state and the labor unions was very prominent, even pivotal. Arguably, given that international pressures were the driving problem, it was almost necessary for the state and the unions to promote or support organizational change directly. The German case is also unique because of the impact of avant-garde modernism and its ideas about standardization. The case of AEG illustrated the interplay of the various institutional factors behind the adoption of scientific management in Germany. Broadly speaking, the German business elite did not wholeheartedly adopt the ideology of scientific management, except for the belief in the need to use science to reduce waste. Most important, German top managers did not use scientific management to destroy the unions. The content analysis of the managerial writings of the period suggests that they were primarily interested in the organizational techniques. Managers collaborated with the unions to implement industrial rationalization. German industrial firms and public organizations like the Reichspost and the Reichsbahn implemented scientific management techniques extensively. But this implementation did not deskill workers, as was often the case in the United States. In fact, the old tradition of *Hand-werk* survived intact, and industrial firms, both large and small, continued taking advantage of the rich skills of German workers.

The case of Spain during the interwar period exemplifies how labor unrest alone (without structural changes at the firm level or international pressures) may prompt some management intellectuals to propose the introduction of scientific management. In contrast to the events in Germany, the corporatist pattern of politics in Spain did not entirely succeed in integrating the labor unions into the political and economic mainstream. The adoption of the major ideological and technical postulates of scientific management in prewar Spain was hampered by the absence of a favorable mentality, the small size of the engineering establishment, the lack of state support, and the opposition from the unions. The degree of Spain's economic development clearly sets her apart from the other three countries in this study. It is instructive, however, to observe that the Spanish attempts to introduce scientific management before the Civil War failed not because organizational problems were not pressing (labor unrest in particular), but because the engines of organizational change had not yet been started. A comparison of Britain and Spain is illuminating in this respect despite the sharp difference in economic development. The overall situation in both countries changed drastically during the 1940s. Spanish firms experienced structural changes similar in nature and in degree to the ones that had taken place in American and German industry during the first two decades of the century. International pressures tightened in both cases, although they had quite different origins. British firms found it harder to compete in the world market, while the Spanish economy was isolated from world trade. Thus, structural changes and international pressures prompted the adoption of scientific management techniques in both countries during the 1940s and 1950s. Institutional factors such as state support, and collaboration (or at least lack of opposition) from the unions facilitated their adoption. Additionally, engineers became more influential (both in the polity and in the economy) and numerically important in Spain precisely during this period. The influence of engineers became apparent in the Duro-Felguera case study, where worker opposition to the Bedaux System was overcome with the mediation of the Ministry of Labor. One final similarity between Spain and Britain is the early impact of the traditional-humanist mode of thought in both societies, often following Christian or Catholic ethics. This characteristic mode of thought contributed to delaying and shaping the adoption of scientific management.

The comparison of the adoption of scientific management in the four societies yields two major processes of organizational change defined in terms of institutional configurations. In the United States, engineers met the crucial challenges of growing size and complexity, and of labor unrest, resulting in the acceptance of scientific management techniques by the management intellectuals, and their implementation by firms. The techniques were adopted in the face of union opposition. In Germany, in contrast, a coalition of engineers, state officials, and labor unions responded to growing structural problems and international pressures between the world wars, and in Britain and Spain this occurred after 1940, also with the outcomes of theoretical acceptance and practical implementation of scientific management techniques. In no situation did scientific management ideology succeed completely over a significant period of time. Management intellectuals and practitioners were mostly interested in the techniques, although they drew selectively from the ideology to support their arguments.

The sample of countries and situations used for the analysis of scientific management includes cases with extreme combinations of explanatory conditions (interwar Germany, interwar Spain, interwar Britain) as well as intermediate ones (interwar United States, postwar Britain, postwar Spain). Introducing other cases would only add detail within the same range of variation for the seven explanatory conditions. Even the case of the Soviet Union during the interwar period is remarkably similar to the German one, with structural changes, international pressures, favorable modernist mentality, important engineering influence, vigorous state action, tacit collaboration (or perhaps co-optation) of workers and their unions, and widespread adoption of scientific management techniques. Soviet versions of scientific management were transferred to East Germany during the late 1940s, to China during the 1950s, and to Cuba during the 1970s. Modernism, the influence of technocratic elites, and the state were crucial in the French and Italian adoption of scientific management, while state actions in response to international pressures played a key role in interwar Japan, in the absence of a well-organized engineering profession. In the Netherlands and Switzerland, professional groups were most important. The case of Brazil during the 1930s and 1940s approximates that of Spain during the 1940s. Scientific management techniques were adopted during an import-substitution industrialization drive orchestrated by engineering elites and the corporatist state that successfully industrialized the country. Argentina under the regime of General Perón provides a contrast, in that the corporatist state was not able to surmount labor opposition to scientific management.[1] Reviewing other important countries thus indicates that most of the variation in terms of explanatory conditions and combinations of them is already captured by the sample of countries included in this study. Therefore, it is safe to argue that the patterns of organizational change resulting from the adoption of scientific management in the United States, Germany, Spain, and Great Britain illustrate a wide range of historical experiences.

THE ADOPTION OF HUMAN RELATIONS

The adoption of the human relations paradigm in the two decades following World War II took place in a dual context of further changes in the structure of firms, and of growing industrial conflict (see Table 6.2). Human relations ideology was widely adopted by management intellectuals and practitioners in the United States, Spain, and Britain as a response to labor turmoil, but human relations techniques were only widely discussed by American and British management intellectuals, not by Spanish ones. The rise of social-science theorizing and consulting was the most important institutional factor, with business-elite mentalities, the state, and the unions playing a key supportive role in Spain and Britain but not in the United States. In Germany, the situation of industrial peace made the human relations approach appear redundant, in spite of the efforts of a small group of Catholic management intellectuals. But why were human relations techniques adopted by the major American and British firms but not by their Spanish counterparts? This question becomes intriguing when one realizes that other favorable institutional factors were present in Spain but not, for example, in the United States, such as the Catholic mentality, the support from the state, and the collaboration of the officialist labor unions. Moreover, the corporatist framework was well established in Spain and was consistent with the communitarianism and paternalism of the human relations approach. The answer seems to lie in the smaller size and bureaucratization of Spanish firms when compared to those in the United States and Britain. Clearly, Spanish firms lacked the resources and the staff to implement human relations techniques. The fact that the few Spanish firms that actually implemented the techniques were highly bureaucratized and large (e.g. Standard Eléctrica, Marconi Española) lends additional support to this explanation.

After World War II organizational outcomes in Britain began to

1. On the adoption of scientific management in these countries, see sections G through L in the Bibliography.

TABLE 6.2 The adoption of human relations (HR) in comparative perspective

Variables	United States	Germany	Spain	Great Britain
Problem for Analysis				
Degree of adoption of HR	High (1945–55) as ideology and technique	Low (1945–55) as ideology and technique	High (1954–70) as ideology; low as technique	High (1950–70) as ideology and technique
Explanatory Factors				
1. Structural changes	Continued bureaucratization; economic affluence	WWII slows down bureaucratization; strong recovery from war and destruction	Bureaucratization and size starting to increase but only in two sectors (electrotechnical, petrochemicals)	Bureaucratization and size grow at increasing rates
2. International pressures or opportunities	Weak: firms grow, thanks to internal market; cold war and Red scare not very relevant	Strong: reconstruction; technical readjustment of West German economy	Weak: liberalization; new economic and trade opportunities	Increasingly strong: growth lag, productivity gap, need to compete on world market
3. Industrial relations system, and labor unrest problem	Great strike wave of 1946; highest industrial conflict among rich countries	Formal collective bargaining system; works councils; codetermination law; industrial peace	Labor unrest re-emerges; failure of collective bargaining and of codetermination system	Output restriction; threat of labor unrest; occasional outbursts of conflict
4. Business-elite mentalities	Weak humanist and Christian mentality	Weak minority mentality; paternalistic industrial welfarism, and social Catholicism	Social Catholicism; humanist-liberal thought (Ortega); organizations of Catholic employers (ASP, ASE)	Industrial betterment, Quakerism, the Moot, Fabianism, humanist-liberal thought
5. Professions	Academic sociologists and psychologists promote HR theories, do consulting	Few interested sociologists, social psychologists, or business theorists	Academic sociologists and psychologists embrace HR; influential research and consulting organizations	Social scientists formulate a British HR paradigm (Tavistock) and do consulting
6. Role of the state	State played no role	Weak: RKW still promotes rationalization and SM	Strong: INRT and National Commission for Industrial Productivity (CNPI)	Strong: funding for research and direct intervention
7. Workers' response	Ambiguous	Unions reject HR	Official unions favor HR	Trades unions favor HR

converge with those in the United States. The adoption of scientific management techniques during the 1940s and early 1950s, the adoption of human relations ideology and techniques during the 1950s and early 1960s, and then the adoption of structural analysis techniques testify to the increasing parallelism in organizational outcomes between the two Anglo-Saxon societies. The cases of ICI and Shell illustrated the new willingness of British managers to implement innovative organizational paradigms after World War II. The experience of those two British firms with human relations differed little from that of IBM in the United States, but the overall process of organizational change was different in the two countries. Unlike those in the United States, British state agencies and trades unions collaborated with social-science academics and consultants to make human relations a successful paradigm in theory and in practice. Moreover, as in Spain, a variety of mentalities (Christian values, Fabianism, liberal humanism) contributed to making the business elite more prone to accepting human relations postulates. The case of Rowntree exemplified the impact of managerial mentalities on the adoption of human relations. These differences between Britain and the United States in terms of the process of organizational change were not without implications. The most important was at the ideological level, for British conceptualizations of human relationships at work emphasized the issue of democracy in the workplace and often lacked the essentially manipulative component of the American ideology. Moreover, the fact that scientific management techniques were implemented during roughly the same period as human relations ones contributed to the formulation of a peculiarly British version of organization theory, the "socio-technical systems" approach, which combined elements drawn from both paradigms.

Germany was no haven for the human relations paradigm for a variety of fundamental reasons. First and foremost, labor unrest was not a problem. Second, there were institutional mechanisms that addressed the other problems that human relations was supposed to deal with. Labor problems were kept to a minimum, thanks to the effective codetermination, works councils, and collective bargaining systems put in place during the early 1950s, which built on a long tradition of corporatism. Third, bureaucratization slowed down as a result of the postwar reorganization of enterprises, thus making it harder for firms to devote resources to the implementation of human relations techniques. Fourth, the very need to reorganize production called for scientific management techniques, which were widely used during the immediate postwar years. The most interesting aspects of the failure of the human relations paradigm in Germany refer to the crucial lack of a social-science profession and to the significant religious cleavage. The absence of a well-organized and influential social-science community in the 1940s and 1950s made it hard to develop and adopt the paradigm of human relations. The contrast with Britain and the United States is clear in this respect. The attempts by German Catholic management intellectuals to introduce human relations theory did not succeed. Developments in Catholic Spain during the same period underscore the historical significance of religion, a variable often neglected in studies of organizational change.

The available information on the adoption of human relations in other countries helps to extrapolate the findings of this study beyond its four-country scope. In the Soviet Union, American ideas about human relations were offered a dramatically different reception from the one met by scientific management. Soviet management intellectuals criticized human relations for employing manipulative techniques at the service of monopoly capitalism. Given that labor unrest posed no real threat to the authority of the economic and party hierarchies, and that the social sciences could exert little influence, it should be no surprise to find very little adoption of human relations in the Soviet Union or its satellite states after World War II.[2] In France, a school of human relations at work developed after World War II under Jean Coutrot, Georges Friedmann, and others, in part as a reaction to scientific management. Recent research has shown that industrial conflict and the need to create a new managerial elite untainted by Vichy collaborationism interacted with the rise of state planning agencies and state-owned firms as well as with "economic humanism" and the Catholic mentality to produce the acceptance of the basic human relations postulates by the emerging postwar French business elite. The French pattern of adopting human relations ideology looks quite similar to the Spanish one except for the effect of the official vertical unions and the pervasive influence of managerial authoritarianism in Spain. As in Spain, there is no evidence indicating that French firms implemented human relations techniques to the extent that their American and British counterparts did.[3]

2. See, for example, Bogomólova, *La doctrina de las "relaciones humanas"* (1977). This is a Spanish translation published in Cuba. See also Bendix, *Work and Authority in Industry* (1974, pp. 341–433).

3. Boltanski, "Visions of American management in postwar France" (1990) and *Les cadres* (1982, pp. 155–236); Maier, "Postscript: Ideologies of industrial management since the Depression" (1987, pp. 53–63); Friedmann, *Industrial Society* (1977), originally published in 1947, and *The Anatomy of Work* (1964), originally published in 1956.

THE ADOPTION OF STRUCTURAL ANALYSIS

The acceptance of structural analysis techniques and organizational forms by management intellectuals and their implementation by firms seem to have followed a relatively simple pattern during the 1960s and early 1970s (see Table 6.3). Firms in the United States (e.g. IBM), Germany (e.g. AEG), and Britain (e.g. ICI and Shell) were highly bureaucratized, implemented diversification policies, took advantage of new international opportunities, and did not have to deal with the problem of labor unrest, given the relatively smooth functioning of the mechanisms of collective bargaining. Social-science research and consulting in those three countries, and the support or direct intervention of state agencies in the British public sector, facilitated the adoption of the paradigm. Again, despite the convergence in outcomes, the process of change was different. The fact that state agencies intervened in the British case had implications for the nature and the extent of the adoption of structural analysis techniques. The process of change in Britain was much more mimetic than in either the United States or Germany, and it affected public-sector organizations to a much greater extent (e.g. National Coal Board, Post Office, and National Health Service). The situation in Spain was quite different from the ones prevailing in the other three countries, because firms were structurally less complex and operated only within the country's borders. Most important, labor unrest remained the dominant problem facing employers and managers; hence the continued validity of human relations ideology until well into the 1970s.

Future research ought to find contrast cases to see if the simple pattern of adoption of structural analysis in the United States, Germany, and Britain is universal. Available evidence from the French, Italian, and Japanese cases adds some interest to the comparison of patterns of adoption of structural analysis. For example, the largest Italian manufacturing firms were comparable in size, bureaucratization, and diversification to their British or French counterparts, and yet they did not adopt the multidivisional structure to nearly the same extent. Perhaps the lack of social-science research and consulting or problematic industrial relations diverted managerial attention to other areas. Neither did Japanese top manufacturing firms adopt the multidivisional structure to the same extent that the British did, despite the fact that the degrees of diversification of the largest British and Japanese firms were almost equal. In Japan, of course, the configuration of major firms into powerful intermarket or independent business groups offers an interorganizational arrangement that in part elimi-

TABLE 6.3 The adoption of structural analysis (SA) in comparative perspective

Variables	United States	Germany	Spain	Great Britain
Problem for Analysis				
Degree of adoption of SA	High (1960–75) as technique	High (1960–75) as technique	Low (1960–75)	High (1960–75) as technique
Explanatory Factors				
1. Structural changes	High levels of bureaucratization and diversification; rise of the service sector	Increasing levels of bureaucratization and diversification; growth of the service sector	Comparatively low levels of bureaucratization, diversification; small service sector	British firms among largest, most bureaucratized, and diversified in the world; growth of the service sector
2. International pressures or opportunities	Saturation of domestic markets; new market opportunities abroad; multinationalization of firms	Increasing dependence on foreign trade; larger market areas (EEC); multinationalization of firms	Rapid economic growth, but not a member of EEC; no multinationals	Economic growth, internationalization of firms, new trade opportunities
3. Industrial relations system, and labor unrest problem	Rise of collective bargaining; industrial conflict reduced	Consolidation of formal collective bargaining and codetermination; industrial peace	Labor unrest problem worsens; illegal unions repressed; instabiliry	Stabilization of industrial relations; conflict levels drop
4. Business-elite mentalities	Not relevant	Not relevant	Not relevant	Not relevant
5. Professions	Social scientists formulate contingency theory and do consulting	Sociologists and management theorists promote SA	No sociologists or management theorists promote SA; disdain for structural approach	Social scientists formulate contingency theories of organization and do consulting
6. Role of the state	Weak	Weak: RKW provides no funds	No support from state educational or research institutions	Strong state support for research, and direct intervention in public-sector firms
7. Workers' response	Not relevant	Not relevant	Not relevant	Not relevant

nates the need for the muldivisional form.[4] Most interestingly, during the 1970s, precisely when Japanese companies began outstripping their Western competitors, several of Japan's largest companies moved back to a functional structure. Meanwhile, 13 of the top 100 American manufacturing corporations made the transition to the multidivisional form. This pattern suggests no relationship whatsoever between the problem of international competitiveness and the adoption of the multidivisional form.[5]

AN OVERVIEW OF PATTERNS OF ADOPTION

Organizational change is a complex phenomenon. This study has reduced that complexity by focusing only on change resulting from the impact of the major models of organization. The mechanisms of change and its consequences vary greatly across societies. From a social-systems point of view, the mechanisms regulating organizational change describe the dynamics of the system, while the consequences of change describe the system outcomes. Both aspects are important for the study of organization from a cross-national perspective. This study has documented that organizational outcomes were different in the four countries examined in terms of both the paradigms that were adopted and the timing of the adoption. The comparative information summarized in this chapter at the risk of oversimplifying the richness of detail contained in the country chapters allows us to reach several important conclusions for the dynamics of organizational change.

First, structural changes seem to be a necessary, but not sufficient, condition for the adoption of the technical components of organizational paradigms. The adoption of paradigms in all four countries always took place in the presence of structural changes. It seems that in order for organizational techniques to be adopted in practice, a certain level of firm size, complexity, bureaucratization, and sophistication is required. This finding is doubly significant. On the one hand, it lends support to the arguments of a large body of organizational

---

4. See Orrù, Biggart, and Hamilton, "Organizational isomorphism in East Asia," in Walter W. Powell and Paul J. DiMaggio, eds., *The New Institutionalism in Organizational Analysis* (1991, pp. 361–389); Gerlach, *Alliance Capitalism* (1992); Whitley, *Business Systems in East Asia* (1992).

5. Dyas and Thanheiser, *The Emerging European Enterprise* (1976, p. 29); Franko, "The move toward a multidivisional structure in European organizations" (1974); Suzuki, "The strategy and structure of top 100 Japanese industrial enterprises 1950–1970" (1980); Kono, *Strategy and Structure of Japanese Enterprises* (1984); Fligstein, *The Transformation of Corporate Control* (1990, p. 336).

studies emphasizing that new organizational tools are developed as a response to increasingly complex managerial tasks and are only feasible precisely in complex organizational settings. On the other hand, however, the fact that structural changes do not suffice to produce change, but need to interact with other problems or institutional factors, underscores the importance of studying the institutional context of organizational change.

The second finding has to do with the interaction between favorable state action and worker collaboration. The adoption of scientific management in Germany, Britain, and Spain, and of human relations in Britain followed this pattern of change. Only the adoption of paradigms in the United States and the adoption of structural analysis in general deviates from this pattern. Except in the case of human relations in Britain, the combination of state action and worker collaboration is typical of countries where international opportunities or pressures invite the adoption of the paradigm in question. This finding is consistent with the expectation that problems or opportunities resulting from the international environment generally require the collaboration of the state and the labor unions if they are to be dealt with decisively and effectively.

The third finding has to do with the role played by professional groups. Many previous studies have underlined the relevance of professional groups such as engineers or the social scientists for the adoption of scientific management and human relations. Given the cases and historical periods considered in this study, it is possible to conclude that professional groups alone—without active state support, favorable elite mentalities, or worker collaboration—can achieve the adoption of the techniques of a paradigm if all three organizational problems or opportunities are present. This situation is the one found in the adoption of human relations in the United States and of structural analysis in both the United States and Germany. Professionals may, by their own actions, generate enough momentum to make an organizational paradigm successful if there happens to be an embarrassment of organizational problems or opportunities to deal with. But new knowledge developed, elaborated, and spread by professional groups is not always necessary to produce the technical adoption of a paradigm. For example, in the case of the adoption of scientific management techniques in Great Britain after World War II, the engineering profession did not play an important role as such. The adoption of scientific management in Britain was facilitated by the collaboration of state agencies and of the trades unions.

Lastly, favorable elite mentalities are a *crucial* part of the configuration of institutional factors producing the adoption of a paradigm only if industrial unrest is a problem. The adoption of scientific management techniques in the United States and of human relations ideology in Britain and Spain illustrate this pattern. This finding is theoretically appealing because it highlights the fact that elite mentalities are more relevant and powerful when labor unrest is present than when the problem lies in structural changes or international pressures. Although they stem from different intellectual traditions and propose different solutions to industrial conflict, both technocratic modernism and Christian humanism had a negative view of conflict and believed in the potential cooperation between workers and employers. It is important to realize that the case of interwar Germany is unique because of the interaction of all four institutional factors, including a favorable modernist mentality. From a purely comparative perspective, however, what sets Germany apart is really the interaction between the state and the labor unions, and not the role played by the engineering profession and the modernist mentality, which were also present in the United States.

To summarize, structural changes such as growing size, complexity, and bureaucratization seem to be crucially necessary for the adoption of new organizational paradigms. In fact, this study deals with how managers and workers have come to terms with the increasing impact of economic competition, wage dependency, and factory bureaucracy in industrial societies. No other explanatory condition aside from structural change was "necessary" for the adoption of new paradigms. Professional groups were dispensable if labor unions and the state could collaborate. That kind of collaboration was found to be necessary only when the international environment was part of the problem. Business-elite mentalities alone produced organizational change only when industrial conflict was a perceived problem.

The goal of the comparisons in this chapter has been to identify and explain differences in institutional configurations, organizational outcomes, and patterns of change that can be extended to other cases. A formal deduction of the conclusions reached here appears in Appendix D. The concluding chapter discusses the same evidence from a different perspective. It raises several larger questions, such as the correlation among theoretical discussions, managerial ideologies, and organizational practice; the contributions to social theory; the recurrence of managerial and organizational knowledge over time; the recent surge of organizational eclecticism; the implications for management research and education; the link between organizational behavior and religion; and the issue of managerial ideologies and the political order.

SEVEN

A Historical and Comparative Perspective on *Homo Hierarchicus*

The rise of *Homo hierarchicus* at the turn of the century with the generalization of wage dependency and factory bureaucracy created new organizational realities. Bureaucratization, coupled with other changes in the domestic and international environments of firms and, in some countries, with persistent labor unrest, brought about new organizational problems that stimulated the ideological and organizational imagination of managers. Different configurations of organizational problems, managerial perceptions of them, and institutional factors affected the ways in which organizational change took place in different societies. The history of organizational change is in fact an account of how employers, managers, workers, professionals, state officials, and intellectuals have come to terms with the reality of *Homo hierarchicus* in different historical and national contexts.

This study builds on the classic research by Reinhard Bendix, *Work and Authority in Industry* (1956). It is an extension of his work because new cases have been taken into consideration, and the analysis has been carried up to the mid-1970s. While Bendix focused on managerial ideologies, however, this book addresses the distinction between *organizational* ideologies and techniques, both at the theoretical and the practical levels. In particular, the correlation between theoretical discussion of techniques and their actual implementation by firms has been assessed in each country. The geopolitical position of countries in the world has been considered systematically. The effects of differences in development and relative rates of growth have also been taken into account. The role of the professions has been expanded and studied in comparative terms. Elite mentalities as sources of organizational ideas have been used to understand cross-national variations in the adoption of paradigms. Finally, organizational problems, institutional factors, and outcomes have been systematically compared. There are several selected themes, implications, and contributions of this study that go beyond the attempt in the previous chapter to identify, understand, and explain comparative patterns of adoption.

CONTRIBUTIONS TO SOCIAL THEORY

As a study in comparative social change, this book has something to offer not only to the fields of organizational analysis and management but also to social theory. A theory of social action has been articulated as part of the study's framework of analysis. Structural conditions have been conceptualized as presenting social actors with certain opportunities or problems that invite or require action. Often, those opportunities or problems have to do with power differentials or changes in power relationships. A variety of institutional factors have been proposed as affecting the perception of problems and the choices about paths of action, including elite mentalities, professional groups, state activities, and workers' responses.[1]

Organizational models, as institutionalized ways of analyzing problems and devising solutions, are used by managers and firms in different countries to achieve goals rather than define the goals themselves. This study has highlighted the importance of cognition—how actors find out what is going on that affects them. Organizational ideology serves not only as a justification of authority but also as a cognitive tool to frame problems in such a way that the mass of often ambiguous or contradictory worldly experience can be interpreted.[2] For example, human relations ideology helped British employers and managers focus on labor problems both during the interwar period and in the years after World War II. As mentioned in the chapter on Britain, the situation was confusing because the country still enjoyed a prominent position as a world power, but there were disquieting trends of labor conflict and relative industrial retardation. Human relations, and its associated mentalities, helped British managers sort out that complex reality, characterize the problem, and devise a solution. This finding is consistent with the phenomenological tradition in sociology and organization theory, which now provides the microfoundation for the new institutionalism in organizational analysis. The central idea here is that managers and employers use ideologies not only to legitimate actions but also to make sense out of worldly experience.[3]

1. DiMaggio and Powell, "The Iron Cage." (1983); Powell and DiMaggio, eds., *The New Institutionalism in Organizational Analysis* (1991, pp. 1–38); Swidler, "Culture in action" (1986).

2. Swidler (1986); DiMaggio and Powell, "Introduction," in Powell and DiMaggio, eds. (1991, p. 9).

3. Collins, *Three Sociological Traditions* (1985, pp. 180–227); Berger and Luckmann, *The Social Construction of Reality* (1967); DiMaggio and Powell, "Introduction," in Powell and DiMaggio, eds. (1991, pp. 19–22).

One important aspect of the present study has been the distinction between ideology and techniques. In some cases, organizational models have succeeded as ideologies but not as techniques (e.g. human relations in Spain), or vice versa (scientific management in the United States and Germany). It is important to emphasize that the contrast should be drawn between ideology and techniques, *not* between ideology and practice. When employers and managers mount ideological campaigns to enlist the cooperation of their subordinates, they are performing a typical managerial task and thus engaging in managerial practice. Ideologies are also *practical* aids for managers because of their cognitive potential. Another relevant contrast is the one between the theoretical discussion of ideologies and techniques by the management intellectuals and the actual implementation of organizational techniques by firms. In this respect the interesting problem is to see whether the ideological and technical approach that is preached in theory by the management intellectuals gets translated into actual practice in organizations. For example, German human relations proponents recommended the practical adoption of human relations ideology and techniques, but their proposals fell on deaf ears. Spanish human relations proponents were more effective than their German counterparts in that they succeeded in spreading the ideology of human relations among the country's business elite. A few German and Spanish management intellectuals even discussed the techniques at length, but most firms did not implement them. By contrast, British and American human relations proponents preached both the ideology and the techniques, and a large proportion of firms actually implemented the techniques.

The theoretical discussion of organizational techniques by the management intellectuals usually precedes, or at least goes hand in hand with, their implementation by firms. The cases of scientific management in the United States and Germany, and of human relations in the United States and Britain support that hypothesis. But it is not so clear from the evidence presented in this book that the implementation of techniques has to be preceded by the widespread adoption of the ideology consistent with them. Consider the case of scientific management in the United States and Germany between the world wars. In both cases scientific management failed as an organizational ideology, but the techniques associated with the paradigm were both accepted by the management intellectuals and implemented widely by firms. Generally, the ideological and technical components of the paradigm reinforce each other, but the absence of either does not seem to prevent the adoption of the other.

The historical evolution of organizational ideologies can be described in terms of a series of reactions against previous approaches. Scientific management in part represented a reaction against traditional managerial practices and an emerging welfare capitalism. Structural analysis exploited the limitations of the "one best way" approach to organizing implicit in the other two paradigms. The rise of the human relations paradigm is perhaps the best example of ideological reaction. Management intellectuals following a human relations approach in the United States, Spain, and Britain used two basic types of reactionary arguments against scientific management—the *perversity* and *jeopardy* theses, to use Hirschman's terms.[4] The charge of perversity consisted of accusing scientific management of actually decreasing productivity because of the monotony, demoralization, and alienation brought about by scientifically engineered jobs. The indictment of jeopardy had to do with the "ills of industrialism": the social dislocation resulting from the threats that scientific management posed to established institutions and ways of life, such as interpersonal cooperation, sense of belonging, the community, and so on. German human relations theorists relied heavily on the perversity thesis to the exclusion of jeopardy arguments. It is interesting that Hirschman's futility thesis was almost never used in any of the four countries, suggesting that there was little disagreement about the tremendous impact of scientific management.

Structural and institutional macrovariables have occupied a central place as explanations of observed patterns of organizational change at the ideological and technical levels. There are two major reasons for adopting a macro view in this study. First, as Bendix argued in his classic book, comparative breadth is only attainable at the expense of depth of analysis. Second, broad, sweeping changes such as the ones that constitute the subject matter of this study only become apparent when taking into account long periods of time. Variables such as bureaucratization, diversification, international pressures, labor unrest, the professions, and the state all operate at a macroscopic level of analysis. Yet the dependent variable in this study is defined at the level of individual managers and firms. This creates a micro-macro tension and the need for a link between levels of analysis.[5] The focus on macro variables over extended periods of time requires a constant shifting of levels of analysis in order to show how individuals and firms embedded in a particular set of structural and institutional cir-

4. Hirschman, *The Rhetoric of Reaction* (1991).
5. Alexander and Giesen, "From reduction to linkage," in Alexander et al., eds., *The Micro-Macro Link* (1987, pp. 1–42).

cumstances make interpretations and purposefully act. The country has been used as the basic unit of comparative analysis for making cross-national comparisons. Geopolitical variables have been related to the political and economic pressures or opportunities faced by different countries during different time periods. This book has also looked for the macro-micro link with the analysis of the biographical backgrounds, mentalities, and motives of individual managers and management intellectuals. In addition, the strategies and organizational practices of firms and other organizations have been explored and related to the macrovariables in the organizational case studies contemplated for each country.

The distinction between mentality and ideology has been constantly used throughout this study to explore the effects of mentalities (i.e. sets of unreflective assumptions, mental dispositions, modes of thought, intellectual legacies) on the propensity of managers to accept certain ideologies over others.[6] The cases of Germany, Britain, and Spain have been particularly rich in terms of the interaction between mentalities and organizational ideologies. One important finding of this study has been the crucial relevance of elite mentalities whenever labor unrest was a problem confronting employers and managers. Technocratic modernism and Christian humanism (including the social doctrine of the Catholic Church) embraced the possibility of organizing workers and employers so as to avoid conflict.

This study has found professional groups (engineers, psychologists, sociologists, management theorists) to be quite important for the adoption of the three paradigms of organization. In all four countries professionals played key roles as theorists, researchers, translators, popularizers, educators, and consultants. Their access to top managerial positions also facilitated the spread of particular paradigms. The question remains, however, whether professionals were (1) merely proposing organizational solutions to deal with real problems, (2) primarily advancing their own goals as an elite group, or (3) out of self-interest, creating new organizational problems themselves with their insights and research. In other words, were professionals servants of power, technocrats, or witty sellers of specialized knowledge attempting to create a monopoly market for their services?[7] There is evidence in this study to support each of those three

6. Geiger, "Mentalität und Ideologie," in *Die soziale Schichtung des Deutschen Volkes* (1932, pp. 77–79).

7. Brint, "Rethinking the policy influence of experts" (1990); Freidson, *Professional Powers* (1986); Larson, *The Rise of Professionalism* (1977).

views. Managers used professionals and their knowledge to advance business goals such as efficiency, profits, and control over workers, as in the case of human relations experts in the United States, Spain, and Great Britain. But professionals also behaved as relatively autonomous technocrats, and they sometimes clashed with management, as in the case of engineers in the United States. Finally, professionals all too frequently created consulting firms and educational institutions that catered to a market for specialized management services.

What these perspectives miss, however, is the crucial fact that engineers, psychologists, sociologists, and management theorists were competing with each other for the attention of such relevant actors as employers, managers, union leaders, state officials, and other elites. The mentalities, training, approaches, and solutions of each professional group were different, and so were their institutional bases of support. Hence the importance of studying professional groups from a *systemic* and *ecological* viewpoint.[8] In all four countries professional groups were found to compete for management's and labor's attention, state resources, and educational and research assets. The changing influence of different professional groups over time helped to explain differences in the adoption of organizational paradigms.

At any rate, two interesting differences in the behavior of professionals were found by country. First, professionals in innovator countries (e.g. human relations proponents in the United States and Great Britain) behaved as monopoly-builders, whereas professionals in imitator countries (e.g. human relations proponents in Spain) behaved more as servants of power, that is, as intermediaries between managers in their own country and managers and theorists in another country. Second, professionals involved in the early stages of the adoption of a paradigm tended to be more like monopoly-builders or like technocrats than like servants of power. They were trying to convince or force managers and other elite groups to adopt the paradigm. Once paradigms became institutionalized, however, professionals working within the paradigmatic tradition steered toward behaving like servants of power.

DOES THE HISTORY OF ORGANIZATIONAL PARADIGMS FOLLOW AN OSCILLATING PATH?

This research has addressed the process of organizational change as it derives from the adoption of the three major paradigms, or models,

8. Abbott, *The System of Professions* (1988).

of organization. It could be argued that the term *paradigm* is just an elegant word for what in fact are mere managerial fads promoted by self-interested professional groups. But why then did workers in different countries respond in a variety of ways (opposition, collaboration, indifference) to the implementation of supposedly capricious and ephemeral fads? And why did firms invest so much money and effort in implementing organizational techniques? Managers, union leaders, workers, and government officials took scientific management, human relations, and structural analysis seriously, even with passion. This suggests that, far from being a fad, the adoption of a model or paradigm raised critical issues of (and had direct consequences for) control, efficiency, profits, growth, wages, quality of working life, and power relationships in the firm and society. Most of the time professional groups were providing interpretations for and solutions to *real* problems.

Fads or not, the twentieth-century history of organizational paradigms suggests a cyclical path in which theories and conceptions oscillate between rational and natural approaches. Several students of management theory and practice have pointed out this pattern in the United States. There seems to be an unresolved tension between rational and natural approaches, mechanistic and organic solidarity, and individualism and communalism that has haunted employers and managers in their attempt to establish and maintain authority and control in the workplace; hence the observed American twentieth-century pattern of oscillation from rational (scientific management), to natural (human relations), to rational (structural analysis), and to natural (organizational culture) solutions.[9]

9. See, for example, Kanter, *The Change Masters* (1984, pp. 44–47); Pascale, *Managing on the Edge* (1990, pp. 16–23); Huczynski, *Management Gurus* (1993, pp. 276–296); Scott, *Organizations* (1987, pp. 20–24); Barley and Kunda, "Design and devotion" (1992). I disagree with Barley and Kunda's tenet that scientific management and systems rationalism triumphed as ideologies of management in the United States. I argue, however, that they were adopted as practical techniques. I also reject Barley and Kunda's conclusions as to the effects of cycles of labor unrest on the adoption of rational versus natural approaches. Contrary to their conclusions, I have documented that American managers used human relations in the 1940s and 1950s to deal with labor unrest precisely when the economy was expanding. In contrast to their analysis, what really matters is not when the paradigm is formulated (their "surge" phase) but rather when it is adopted by managers and firms. As the best study of Hawthorne has concluded, the Bell System was responding to "labor unrest inside the companies and external political and social pressures" when it decided to begin the experiments. See Gillespie, *Manufacturing Knowledge* (1991, p. 17). On the issue of individualism and commitment in the United States, see Bellah et al., *Habits of the Heart* (1986).

While the pendulum metaphor seems to work well for the United States, this study shows that it fails to account for the historical sequences observed in Germany, Spain, or Britain. In Germany the dominant modernist mood among the business elite facilitated the adoption of rational approaches and undermined natural theories such as human relations. Thus, the German experience shows no oscillating pattern. By constrast, the marked antimodernist stand of the business elite in Britain and Spain delayed and deflected the adoption of scientific management solutions, and certainly facilitated the acceptance of human relations. As a result, the sequence and timing of paradigms was different in the four countries. A comparative look at the question of oscillation, then, reveals the intrinsic limitation of drawing conclusions from a single empirical case. The argument against cycles is also supported by the conceptualization in Chapter 1 of structural analysis as a paradigm that subsumes scientific management and human relations as special cases.

The cyclical or pendulum metaphor is appealing, though, because it emphasizes that organizational paradigms and managerial practice are not like good wine—they do not necessarily improve with time. This is a very important idea, given the tendency among Marxist sociologists (Braverman, Burawoy), radical political economists (Edwards), and business historians (Chandler) alike to conceive of the history of organizational paradigms as a continuous march towards greater managerial sophistication and capitalist success.[10] Again, a cross-national, comparative lens helps in qualifying the strong statements made by these authors. Instead of using a "theory of stages," with each higher stage preserving the achievements of the lower stages, this study has been inspired by a "theory of alternatives," and an explicit rejection of evolutionism, in line with Max Weber.[11] The best reviews of the organizations literature tend to support the thesis that managerial and organizational knowledge does not necessarily get better with time, but their implicit argument is based on a different perspective, one emphasizing the permanently revolutionary state of organizational analysis as a science, populated by a multiplicity of theories that hardly complement each other.[12]

Another attractive feature of the cyclical analogy is that it seems

---

10. Braverman, *Labor and Monopoly Capital* (1974); Burawoy, "The anthropology of industrial work" (1979b); Edwards, *Contested Terrain* (1979); Chandler, *The Visible Hand* (1977).

11. Schluchter, *The Rise of Western Rationalism* (1981, pp. 1–2).

12. Perrow, *Complex Organizations* (1986); Scott, *Organizations* (1987).

to explain certain current developments. A new paradigm of "organizational culture" has emerged and received widespread attention in North America and Europe during the 1980s. Proponents of the organizational culture approach are openly critical of the rational solutions proposed by structural analysis. Like the human relations theorists, they use Hirschman's jeopardy and perversity theses to make reactionary arguments against previous paradigms of organization, which are blamed for the decline in American and European productivity. Although William Ouchi's best-selling book, *Theory Z* (1981), is supposed to deal with how to transfer the seemingly superior Japanese management techniques to America, many parts of it could have been written by Elton Mayo a long time ago:

> As a nation, we have developed a sense of the value of technology and of a scientific approach to it, but we have meanwhile taken people for granted.
>
> In American life, intimacy has traditionally been found in the family, the club, the neighborhood, the lifelong friendship, and the church. Yet all of these traditional sources of intimacy, or primary contact with others, are threatened by our present form of industrial life.
>
> The notion that productivity may be dependent upon trust, subtlety, and intimacy, for example, probably seems strange to most people.[13]

The human relations theorists and managers of mid-century would feel quite at home with the preceding statements. Like Voltaire, Ouchi is a master at the old tactic of praising a foreign way of doing things to scourge one's compatriots and advance one's favorite position on a particular issue. The famous 1979 NBC documentary, *If Japan Can, Why Can't We?*, became a landmark of this tradition.

In Search of Excellence, Corporate Cultures, and *The Art of Japanese Management* were other popular management texts of the 1980s that used an essentially Mayoistic approach to organization. Together with Ouchi's, these books sold in excess of 1.5 million copies during the 1980s in the United States alone. These authors conceive of organizational cultures as "systems of informal rules," and a "strong culture" is thought to enable "people to feel better about what they do, so they are more likely to work harder." The business firm is seen as a community, almost to the exclusion of all other possible group memberships that workers may have. The buzzwords of the organizational culture paradigm include *sense of belonging, integrative leadership, organizational climate, involvement, participation, loyalty, commitment,*

13. Ouchi, *Theory Z* (1981, pp. 4, 8–9, 10).

harmony, interdependence, cohesiveness, and team spirit. Human relations techniques such as interviews, social observation, group dynamics, and morale surveys are proposed to diagnose the problem and foster an atmosphere of cooperation in the workplace. The echoes of the human relations paradigm could not resonate louder. The overall tone is strongly paternalistic.[14]

Current changes in world economic leadership seem to call into question the choice of paradigms analyzed in the present study. The argument can be made that scientific management, human relations, and structural analysis largely originated in the United States. As a result, any comparative study focusing on these eminently American paradigms is bound to miss important cross-national variations. There are two reasons why this comparative study of the three major paradigms makes sense. First, there were quite independent sources of organizational thought in Germany, Great Britain, and elsewhere that contributed to the formulation of the three paradigms. It is simply not true that all the research and theorizing on organizational paradigms has been conducted by Americans or in the United States. An effort has been made in this study to document the importance of the German industrial rationalization movement, and the British human relations and structural analysis schools, which in many respects were ahead of American ideas and actually influenced them. Even in Spain, the Catholic-influenced management intellectuals developed some original ideas. Second, the United States happened to be the leading economic power during the historical period covered in this study, and this had implications for the adoption of organizational ideas. The economic, political, and military power of the United States meant that managers and professionals in other countries tried to emulate American organizational practices. The United States was the "reference society." The debates about organization in Germany, Great Britain, and Spain tended to be dominated by what was going on in the United States. This, of course, does not necessarily mean that all American organizational paradigms were accepted by managers and firms in other countries, as this book has repeatedly shown.

There is one last aspect of the cyclical analogy that deserves comment. The concatenation of cycles in organizational thought and practice seems to support Immanuel Kant's conception of history as a

14. Peters and Waterman, *In Search of Excellence* (1982, pp. 4–6, 99); Deal and Kennedy, *Corporate Cultures* (1982, pp. 5, 8–19, 22, 129–139); Pascale and Athos, *The Art of Japanese Management* (1981, pp. 49–52, 86, 125–129); *Business Week,* "Corporate culture" (1980); Uttal, "The corporate culture vultures" (1983).

sequence of discrete periods, each shaped by a single dominant idea or conception. However, a fair part of the evidence presented in this study is inconsistent with the notion of periodically dominant paradigms. In fact, mutually contradictory paradigms or conceptions have been used in the same country at the same time by the same firms. For example, American and German employers and managers implemented both scientific management and welfare capitalism between the world wars. British and Spanish employers and managers used scientific management techniques and human relations ideology during the years immediately after World War II. British employers during the 1960s implemented structural analysis techniques while they were still using scientific management and human relations. It is true that the theoretical discussions within the business elite tended to be dominated by only one paradigm during a particular period. In the murky world of ideological and technical practice, however, the most adequate metaphor seems to be one of layers or sediments of different organizational paradigms, not one of periodically dominant paradigms that totally replace old approaches and, in turn, disappear completely with the success of the next paradigm.

CURRENT TRENDS

Managers tend to adopt ideas and techniques selectively from a variety of places and traditions. There seems to be a growing consensus today that managers and firms should master a combination of ideas and techniques selectively drawn from the three basic models or paradigms of organizational management. The rationalism and technocratism of scientific management have endured as an approach to cost-cutting and production optimization. Leadership style and employee involvement are now being used not only to boost productivity but also to improve quality standards and foster innovation. And large corporations still need fair doses of structural analysis to find organizational arrangements that promote innovation and adaptability to change. Thus, selective elements from the three basic paradigms have become part of a core of conventional organizational wisdom that newly proposed paradigms seem to take for granted.

Lean production and Total Quality Management (TQM) are the two increasingly dominant organizational approaches of the 1990s. Management intellectuals and practitioners are paying an enormous amount of attention to them. The success of these two paradigms tends to undermine the thesis that organizational theory and practice keep on oscillating between rational and natural approaches, because they combine elements from both. Lean production, originally pioneered at Toyota Motor in Japan, is becoming the most generally accepted way of organizing a design-production-distribution system. TQM is the newest trend in the quality-enhancement movement.

The lean-production paradigm mounts a blistering attack on both Fordist mass production and structural analysis à la Sloan, which are presented as outgrowths of mass production and scientific management. Isolated attempts to humanize work are also criticized for being uncompetitive and self-defeating, even romantic. The major point made by the lean-production proponents is that insights drawn from scientific management, human relations, and structural analysis need to be combined in the way that the Japanese lean manufacturers pioneered back in the 1950s and have been refining ever since. Although lean production applies to R&D, supply, and distribution as well as to manufacturing, the organization of production is the central part of the system, and everything else follows from it. Multiple, small-lot production is favored over long, high-volume runs. The contribution of scientific management to lean production is clear: time-and-motion studies and improved accounting methods are used to eliminate waste and unnecessary worker movements, and to reduce changeover times. The goal is to arrive at the "one best way" of organizing manufacturing so that production costs are minimized, inventories and cycle times drastically reduced, labor productivity boosted, and quality standards raised. Just-in-time, low-cost, high-quality, lean production is the end result. One major departure from Fordism and scientific management is the substitution of a "pull" system of assembly-line feeding for the inefficient "push" system characteristic of mass production.

Lean production also uses human relations insights and techniques. Teamwork is as important a principle in the organization of production as scientific task engineering. Over two-thirds of the work force in many of the model lean firms are organized into teams in order to facilitate communication and cooperation. The employment system is also characterized by job security, training in a wide variety of skills, frequent job rotation, a reduced number of job classes, low specialization, and informal cooperation among workers in different teams or units. A suggestion system guarantees constant feedback to and from R&D, suppliers, and distributors, as well as to and from other areas of production. Higher quality and lower cost are expected to result from lower absenteeism and turnover, and increased job satisfaction. The firm is explicity conceived as a community, with employees being trained in firm-specific but broad skills. Worker happiness is presented as a result of the challenges, demands for improvement, and intrinsic satisfaction characteristic of the job.

Finally, the lean-production approach incorporates certain structural analysis concerns. The environment of the organization is scanned in order to make changes in product R&D, the employment system, and the structure of the organization. The issues of decentralization, control, horizontal communication, division of labor between headquarters and subsidiaries, and organizational adaptation to environmental change are prominent. Issues of multinational organizational structure and coordination of global activities are raised to a level of importance not seen since the heyday of structural analysis in the 1960s.

Like scientific management and human relations, lean production incorporates a powerful ideology that is fundamentally visionary. A better world is promised for everyone involved: the consumer gets low prices, variety, and quality; the worker can enjoy job security, satisfaction, challenging tasks, and even higher wages; the engineer can stretch her imagination to develop new designs and production processes; the manager can enjoy the challenges of being responsive to the customer and playing the global competitive game; and the economy benefits from inflation-busting cost reductions and from the counter-cyclical mechanism built into the zero-inventory system. The Massachusetts Institute of Technology authors of the best-selling book on automobile manufacturing, *The Machine that Changed the World,* put it concisely in 1990 after five years of extensive and fruitful research on the nature and potential of lean production:

> Our conclusion is simple: Lean production is a superior way for humans to make things. It provides better products in wider variety at lower cost. Equally important, it provides more challenging and fulfilling work for employees at every level, from the factory to headquarters. It follows that the whole world should adopt lean production, and as quickly as possible.

The authors firmly believe that "lean production will supplant both mass production and the remaining outposts of craft production in all areas of industrial endeavor to become the standard global production system of the twenty-first century." The book finishes in a triumphant tone: "That world will be a very different, and a much better, place."[15]

15. Womack, Jones, and Roos, *The Machine that Changed the World* (1991, pp. 48–137, 192–222, 225, 250, 251, 278). See Cusumano, *The Japanese Automobile Industry* (1985, pp. 73–185, 262–319), for a different account of the rise of the lean-production system in Japan emphasizing government protectionism and union busting as additional explanations for the success of the system. Consider also the case of the General Motors-Toyota joint venture in California: Adler, "Time-and-motion regained" (1993). Other important sources include Dohse et al., "From 'Fordism' to

Total Quality Management (TQM) is also an eclectic approach. The Japanese Quality Control Circle (QCC) movement emerged in part from certain group-dynamics experiments conducted in the early postwar period in the tradition of Kurt Lewin. Matsushita pioneered QCCs in the early 1960s, adding a strong production-management component. Other Japanese companies used QCCs to boost morale and to shift from an inspection-oriented approach to quality control to one emphasizing prevention and employee involvement. The early Japanese movement was influenced by the key human relations scholars in the United States.[16] W. Edwards Deming, perhaps the leading figure of the quality movement, did much consulting work for Japanese companies in the 1950s and 1960s after having been at the Hawthorne Works of Western Electric in the 1930s. In the 1980s he became famous for helping Ford implement its successful quality-control system. Not surprisingly, Deming endorsed the classic human relations findings, and was heavily influenced by the work of Herzberg, Maslow, and his MIT colleague Douglas McGregor.[17] On top of the core human relations techniques, TQM includes many scientific management as well as a few structural analysis aspects. Companies now using TQM identify low productivity, low or changing product quality, high employee absenteeism and turnover, fear and morale problems, and bureaucratic paralysis as the leading organizational problems. The proposed solution is typically eclectic, for it combines improved process management, human relations techniques, and structural organizational fixes. Employees and managers are trained in statistical control, production management, and detailed job-analysis techniques in order to help them apprehend the basics of efficiency and quality in product design, manufacturing, distribution, and sales. Participatory schemes, attitude surveys, teamwork, and transformational leadership techniques are implemented to make employees and managers more motivated, collaborative, innovative, and responsive. Finally, flatter organizational structures, federations of companies, and divisional autonomy are proposed to uproot perverse bureaucratic habits and structures. TQM is eclectic insofar as techniques are concerned. As an ideology, however, it leans towards the familiar

'Toyotism'?" (1985); Kenney and Florida, *Beyond Mass Production* (1993); Kamata, *Japan in the Passing Lane* (1982).

16. Cole, *Strategies for Learning* (1989, pp. 79–104).

17. Waring, *Taylorism Transformed* (1991, p. 131); Blumberg, *Industrial Democracy* (1973, pp. 77–78, 244 n. 7); Cusumano (1985, pp. 320–373); Gabor, *The Man Who Discovered Quality* (1990, pp. 40–42); Deming, *Out of the Crisis* (1986).

human relations approach. Its rhetoric of "total customer satisfaction" gives the firm a moral mission. It also assigns management a leading role, with the old proposal of upgrading employees from mere subordinates to partners in a team. In addition, TQM underscores cherished values such as personal improvement, growth, and perfection.[18]

If empirically true, the surge of organizational eclecticism during the 1990s lends support to the main thesis of this book: that the history of organizational analysis can be interpreted in terms of the three basic paradigms of scientific management, human relations, and structural analysis. The forces underlying the rise of *Homo hierarchicus* since the late nineteenth century—factory bureaucracy and wage dependency—initiated a long process of rationalization. In the course of the twentieth century, attempts at rationalization of organizational ideologies and techniques have yielded the three broad approaches discussed in this book. The contribution of this comparative and historical study has been to point out cross-national variations and to use them as a way to understand outcomes and patterns of change.

The postmodern and feminist critiques have recently challenged the received stock of rationalized organizational ideologies and techniques discussed in this book. Postmodern theorists propose that management has been invariably "modernist," rational, and technical, while feminism has questioned the assumptions and achievements of bureaucratic organization. Both groups of critics reject the cultural and gender biases as well as the deterministic character inherent in scientific management, human relations, and structural analysis. They also discard the principles of hierarchical division of labor and of differentiation-and-integration for being counter-productive or even oppressive.[19] They charge those two essentially modernist principles both with the performance problems of present organizations and with the inequality and discrimination generated by the concentration of power within and around "modern" organizations. When it comes to describing the organization of the future, both approaches strike similar chords. The "postmodern" and the "feminist" organization is small, informal, flexible, flat, decentralized or polycentralized, democratic, participative, networked, and based on a culture of trust. Both perspectives argue in favor of organizational designs that allow em-

18. The discussion on TQM draws on the author's experience at IBM over a five-day period in the summer of 1992, and on several press reports. See also *Business Week*, "Quality" (1992).

19. Note the use of Hirschman's (1991) reactionary theses of perversity and jeopardy.

powered employees to derive nonmaterial satisfactions from work, to self-actualize, and to fulfill spiritual needs. Although the revivalist tone is apparent in these descriptions, postmodernism and feminism do offer refreshing and distinctive ways of studying organizations as arenas in which meaning and power are generated and transacted, and as outcomes of particular institutional patterns. Like the flexible-specialization school of Michael Piore and Charles Sabel or the new non-hierarchical electronic organizations based on the coordination capabilities of networked computers, postmodernism and feminism offer alternatives to *Homo hierarchicus*. If a new, non-eclectic organizational paradigm with implications for managerial practice emerges in the near future, it is most likely to be heavily influenced by these schools of thought.[20]

ORGANIZATIONAL BEHAVIOR AND RELIGION

The link between organizational behavior and religion has been all too frequently relegated to the background or totally ignored in studies of management and organization. Even research dealing with organizational culture has neglected the influence of religion, although comparative studies of organizations have found religion to be an extremely relevant variable. Hofstede argued in his classic study of work cultures that cross-national differences in perceptions of power distance, uncertainty avoidance, and individualism were in part the result of different religious backgrounds. Dore found that the Mencian form of Confucianism in Japan and the Christian ethic in Britain were at the root of the dramatically different patterns of industrial and employment relations as well as organizational behavior of managers, supervisors, and workers in the factories he analyzed. Dore even argued that the concept of original virtue in Confucianism was consistent with the assumptions of McGregor's Theory Y, while the concept of original sin in Christianity was akin to the assumptions of Theory X.[21]

Religious differences have been used throughout this study to understand the adoption of scientific management and human relations as paradigms of organization by the management intellectuals. Previ-

20. Clegg, *Modern Organizations* (1990, pp. 17–18, 176–207); Ferguson, *The Feminist Case Against Bureaucracy* (1984, pp. 69, 205–207); Piore and Sabel, *The Second Industrial Divide* (1984); Malone and Rockart, "Computers, networks and the corporation" (1991).

21. Hofstede, *Culture's Consequences* (1980, pp. 21, 131–133, 181–187, 236–238, 293–296); Dore, *British Factory, Japanese Factory* (1973, pp. 234, 277, 401–402, 408).

ous research has found that management intellectuals influenced by Confucianism or Buddhism generally endorsed the idea that there are intrinsic satisfactions to be derived from work, while Christian management intellectuals underscored the extrinsic rewards. Both Confucianism and Buddhism help to define the business firm as a community. In contrast, Christianity places the emphasis on individual effort. In principle, then, the Christian ethic seems to be more consistent with scientific management than with human relations.

This book, however, has presented systematic evidence that Catholicism and Protestantism have different effects on the kind of organizational paradigm that is adopted. Catholicism has generally emphasized the community, self-actualization, paternalism, and organicism, while Protestantism has emphasized individualism, instrumentalism, independence, and contractualism. In Germany, Protestant management intellectuals generally supported the scientific management paradigm, while Catholic ones took sides with the human relations school. In Spain, the dominant Catholic background played a key role in the reception, adoption, and adaptation to local conditions of American ideas about human relations at work. In Britain, Christian humanist ideals similar to those proposed by the Roman Catholic Church prompted management intellectuals to accept human relations. In the United States, religion did not play a role either in the formulation or in the widespread adoption of the human relations paradigm. This finding proves once more that there were several alternative paths or patterns of change to a similar final result. Except for the case of the United States, the evidence in this book confirms the crucial importance of religion in the study of organizational behavior and the significant difference between Protestant and Catholic approaches to economic and organizational life.[22]

IMPLICATIONS FOR MANAGEMENT RESEARCH AND EDUCATION

The field of management research and education is in the midst of a process of internationalization. As countries other than the United States design and successfully implement their own distinctive approaches to organization, research and teaching in management needs to catch up with developments in the real world. This book shows

22. For the classic analysis of these differences, see Weber, *The Protestant Ethic and the Spirit of Capitalism* (1958). The issue of whether capitalism and Catholicism are compatible with each other continues to generate heated arguments, particularly after the publication of the papal encyclical, *Centesimus Annus* in 1991. See Novak, *The Catholic Ethic and the Spirit of Capitalism* (1993); Neuhaus, *Doing Well and Doing Good* (1992).

that cross-national comparisons have always been relevant—that national circumstances affect the applicability of different models of management. The contribution of this book to the current debate over internationalization of the curriculum at the top management schools is that configurations of institutional factors at the country level of analysis directly affect the management of organizations as well as competition among firms. Accordingly, research and teaching in organizational behavior and in international management would be enriched by a careful and systematic consideration of the cross-national dimension.

Organizational behavior is too often taught in an institutional vacuum. Different approaches to organization should not only be evaluated on the basis of their intrinsic quality as scientific theories or the support they receive from empirical evidence drawn from one country only. They should also be assessed in the context in which they originated and developed with attention to the historical and institutional circumstances that shaped their acceptance or rejection by such relevant actors as employers, managers, workers, professionals, academics, and politicians. Courses in organizational behavior ought to address the extent to which different national economic institutions, religious backgrounds, or industrial relations systems affect the applicability of the various approaches that are currently being taught. Finally, the organizational behavior curriculum should recognize that organizational paradigms include an ideology in addition to a set of techniques. Organizational ideologies should be presented not only as justifications of managerial authority but also as cognitive tools for managers.

The field of international management can benefit from the insights of comparative social science and organizational research when tackling the difficult issues of managing across national borders. The management of cross-cultural teams within multinational corporations and of cross-border strategic alliances or projects should again take into account that national institutional contexts differ and that those differences are reflected in the behavior of people and organizations. Finally, the evidence contained in this book speaks to the problem of cross-national economic and organizational emulation, which has become perhaps the single most important issue in international management today. A detailed study of national configurations of institutional factors is the best way to understand if, when, and how organizational techniques can be transferred across national borders.[23]

23. See Arias and Guillén, "The transfer of organizational techniques across borders" (1993).

Current developments such as the economic integration of the European countries and the fall of Communism offer exciting "research laboratories" for studying the evolution of organizational ideologies and techniques. In both situations, the fundamental change has to do with the transformation of business elites. In Europe, the creation of a coherent trading bloc and the relatively free expansion of truly "transnational" firms is bound to generate an increasingly numerous and powerful European business elite separate from the traditional "local" elites defined at the country level of analysis. One would expect the European elite to be held together by a modernist mentality rather than one based on religion, humanism, or other country-specific mentalities. Accordingly, one might anticipate a revival of the scientific management and structural analysis approaches among the members of the emerging European business elite. The competitive challenge posed by East Asian firms and the need to readapt organizational structures to new, larger economic spaces also point in the direction of a renewed emphasis on the technical and structural aspects of organization.

The fall of Communism has meant the breakdown of a distinct system of authority and management characterized by the uneasy combination of two interlocking hierarchies: the party and the central planning system.[24] It is premature to advance future trends even in countries like China, where the transition has been more gradual. It seems clear, however, that the once-preponderant emphasis on scientific management solutions is bound to fade away. The dismantling of the commanded economies and firms, and the arrival of foreign investors to Eastern Europe and the Special Economic Zones in mainland China create new opportunities for studying the transfer of organizational models across national boundaries. The key to understanding future patterns in the evolution of organizational models in post-Communist societies, however, lies in the transformation of the economic elite and in the nature of the emerging elite of employers and managers.

MANAGEMENT INTELLECTUALS AND THE POLITICAL ORDER

The authority of the employer became effectively dissociated from that of the government after the contractual right to property was established by the philosophers of the Enlightenment and later protected by legislation. As a result, ideologies of management took a life of their own. Ideologies emphasizing self-dependence, character,

---

24. For a description, see Bendix, *Work and Authority in Industry* (1974, pp. 341–433) and the references in section K of the Bibliography.

or constancy flourished in Britain, the United States, Germany, and Spain during the early period of entrepreneurial industrialization. The appearance of *Homo hierarchicus* complicated matters immensely. Changing trends in industrial development, international competition, and labor relations prompted a variety of responses. Several isomorphic institutional forces such as international competition, shared mentalities, professional groups, and state actions guaranteed that management intellectuals in different societies actually considered similar versions of the three basic paradigms of scientific management, human relations, and structural analysis. Theoretical acceptance and implementation of the paradigms, of course, differed greatly by country.

The fact that the same organizational paradigms have historically appealed to people of widely different political persuasions enhances the cognitive value of organizational ideologies and the technical usefulness of the paradigms, regardless of their underlying political and social philosophy. For example, scientific management appealed to Communists in the USSR (Lenin, Trotsky), Fascists in Italy (Mussolini, Marinetti), Progressives in the United States (Brandeis, Hoover), reactionary chauvinists in France (Clemenceau), liberal engineers in prewar Spain (Soria), authoritarian engineers in postwar Spain (Suanzes, Fernández Avila), and conservatives (Rathenau, Siemens), avant-garde artists (Behrens, Gropius, Wagner), and social democrats and labor unionists (Bauer, Schlicke) in Weimar Germany, as well as Nazi technocrats (Speer). Human relations engaged liberal executives in the United States (Johnson, Watson), Fabians in Britain (Wallas, Albu, Cripps), liberal journalist-managers (the Servan-Schreiber brothers) and technocratic socialists (Delors) in France, Catholic and Quaker management intellectuals in Britain, Germany, and Spain, and liberal thinkers (Ortega y Gasset) as well as authoritarian political leaders (Herrero Tejedor) in Spain. For all those people, organizational ideologies were cognitive *tools* rather than mere expressions of a (nonexistent) common political orientation.

The apparent lack of correlation between political regime and acceptance of different organizational paradigms should not lead one to the conclusion that management intellectuals are irresponsive to, or can abstract themselves from, the political order prevailing in their society. On the contrary, this study helps us to understand how the dominant pattern of politics had direct consequences for the ways in which ideological and organizational problems appeared and were addressed by the management intellectuals. The relationship between the political order and the adoption of different approaches to organization during the twentieth century is complex, even if totalitarian political regimes are excluded from the analysis. The choice of countries for intensive comparative research was made with the intention of providing some insights into the relationship between political patterns and organizational ideologies. The evidence contained in the country chapters points to an interaction between the dominant pattern of politics (liberal democracy versus corporatism), and the characteristic mode of thought (modernist-technocratic versus traditional-humanist) to produce the four situations illustrated by the case studies:

Characteristic Mode of Thought	Dominant Pattern of Politics	
	Liberal Democracy	Corporatism
Modernist-technocratic	United States	Germany
Traditional-humanist	Great Britain	Spain

In the United States we find a liberal-democratic political pattern with a characteristic modernist-technocratic mode of thought in the government and business bureaucracies, the engineering profession, and even within the unusually sophisticated and empirically oriented social-science research and consulting community. Labor problems could not be handled as they were in Germany, through corporatist intermediation. As a result, management intellectuals adopted scientific management and human relations as they sought to come to terms with the problems of organizational complexity and labor turmoil, even with the opposition of the labor unions. An early adoption of structural analysis followed as organizational complexity, diversification, and international opportunities demanded a new approach.

In Germany, the dominant corporatist pattern of politics (fundamentally unchanged, if not reinforced, from the Weimar Republic to the Federal Republic) interacted with the modernist-technocratic mode of thought in the state and business bureaucracies, as well as in the engineering profession and labor unions, to produce an early adoption of scientific management in response to rising organizational complexities and international pressures. The German version of scientific management—commonly referred to as *industrial rationalization*—included an implementation of the basic scientific management techniques, the reorganization of entire industrial sectors and distribution channels, and the coordination of the economy by means of corporatist institutions. The corporatist framework of codetermination and works councils created after World War II in the

Federal Republic channeled industrial disputes successfully during the 1950s and 1960s, thus rendering the human relations paradigm irrelevant. The characteristic technocratic approach yielded an early adoption of structural analysis in both the United States and Germany at a time when industrial relations were quite peaceful and stable.

In Great Britain and in Spain the traditional-humanist mode of thought contributed to postponing the adoption of scientific management. Traditional-humanist approaches to labor management and organization had originated in elite mentalities emphasizing the community, the integration of the worker, and the avoidance of conflict. Various Christian ethics, the social doctrine of the Roman Catholic Church, liberal and conservative reformism, humanist thought, even Fabian and academic Socialism contributed to creating the traditional-humanist mode of thought so typical of the elite managers in Britain and Spain during much of the twentieth century. Corporatism in Spain provided the framework for the adoption of scientific management after the Civil War. State agencies intervened in the economy indirectly by promoting organizational change or directly, given the huge public investments in basic industrial sectors. The engineering profession could at last exert an enormous influence, thanks to the role given to professional groups in Franco's corporatist regime and economic institutions. The pattern and the outcome of the adoption of scientific management in postwar Spain had much to do with the German model of industrial rationalization. The one missing factor in Spain was the modernist intellectual agenda of the German scientific managers, a finding consistent with the importance of traditional-humanist thought even among Spanish engineers and technocrats. Reforms of labor market legislation—often inspired by paternalistic notions—and the creation of official vertical unions representing both workers and employers contained labor unrest during the 1940s. The outburst of industrial turmoil during the late 1950s and 1960s set the stage for the adoption of human relations ideology. In Britain, the rise of state interventionism after World War II facilitated a belated adoption of scientific management in spite of the lack of a technocracy. As in the United States, liberal-democratic Great Britain embraced human relations, but British employers and managers, like their Spanish counterparts, believed in human relations theory as a result of their mentality of traditional humanism. In the United States, however, mentalities played almost no role. It was the decisively technocratic and empirical approach of the social sciences of human relations that convinced American management intellectuals.

The interaction between politics and mode of thought also influenced arguments raised against scientific management by the human relations theorists. One would expect a dominant modernist-technocratic mode of thought to limit the occurrence of reactionary ideological arguments against scientific management or, at least, to reduce the recourse to "jeopardy" arguments. The reason is that both modernism and technocratism reject negative views of progress, or the notion that *Homo hierarchicus* has traded off some past achievements for attaining a higher level of consumption. Management intellectuals in Britain and Spain criticized scientific management both because of its perverse effects and because it jeopardized previous societal achievements or ways of life. This finding is consistent with the dominant traditional-humanist mentality. German human relations theorists did use the perversity thesis but not the jeopardy argument, a finding again consistent with the expected effect of the dominant modernist-technocratic mode of thought in that society. The hypothesis is not confirmed by the fact that American management intellectuals, like their British and Spanish counterparts, used both kinds of arguments. At this point the corporatist pattern in Germany and the liberal-democratic tradition in the United States become relevant. In spite of the widespread adoption of scientific management in Germany, human relations theorists did not find it necessary to criticize scientific management for jeopardizing previous achievements or ways of life, given that the corporatist institutions guaranteed some basic social rights and provisions, kept social dislocation to a minimum, and in fact facilitated the preservation and enhancement of workers' skills. Those mechanisms were not available in the United States, and as a result management intellectuals found it necessary to attack scientific management on the basis of its effects on previous achievements.

Institutional factors affect the ideological and technical choices made by management intellectuals and firms when confronted with organizational problems. Political patterns tend to have more complex effects than the seven institutional factors contemplated in this research because they affect both the problem and the choice of solution. The comparative study of the effect of politics on organizational issues was the central theme in the classic research by Reinhard Bendix. He pursued a clear-cut contrast between Anglo-Saxon and Russian/Soviet civilizations at a time when world economic, military, and political supremacy was at stake. In the United States and Britain political life was deeply rooted in the liberal-democratic tradition, while the Russian/Soviet political pattern had shifted from tsarist autocracy to Communist totalitarianism. Bendix demonstrated that politics had profound implications for how entrepreneurs and managers addressed the issue of authority. The present study has explored a less stark distinction, one drawn between liberal-democratic and corporatist societies, that also had consequences for the ways in which the few managed the many in organizations. The effects of political patterns on organizations are complex and contingent upon the characteristic mode of thought among the management intellectuals. It seems possible to conclude that *the dominant pattern of politics sets limits to the repertoire of organizational approaches that are either possible or necessary, while the characteristic mode of thought affects the choice of alternatives.*

Employers and managers constitute a social group that collectively faces challenges related to the definition of organizational problems, the maintenance of authority, and the management of organizations. Dealing with organizational complexity, creating and motivating a productive work force, and competing in the international arena are problems that continuously affect managers, firms, industrial sectors, and countries. Over time, there has been a tendency towards the institutionalization of management as an abstract endeavor. This trend, coupled with the rise of standard patterns of professionalism, has produced an underlying managerialist theory and ideology that plays a key role in understanding the adoption of new paradigms across industries and countries. Genuinely new paradigms such as flexible specialization or non-hierarchical electronic organization will be adopted to the extent that they are consistent with that abstract managerialist ideology.

The successful operation of the firm under capitalism and democratic government derives in large measure from the way in which the social group of economic directors understands its function, and by the adequacy of its technical knowledge and training to the demands of the situation. Our continuous search for economic advance and social fairness will certainly be facilitated by a deeper understanding of organizational ideologies and techniques, including their feasibility under different societal, cultural, and economic conditions. This comparative study of different models of management has attempted to show that organizational change in different societies results from a variety of configurations of institutional factors, in spite of the pervasiveness of economic competition, wage dependency, and factory bureaucracy.

APPENDIX A

Content Analysis of Journal Articles

Part of the empirical evidence presented on the theoretical acceptance of organizational paradigms rests on a content analysis of articles published in management journals. The articles have been primarily used as "direct indicators," and only secondarily as testimonies, social bookkeeping, or correlates of events.[1] The goal of the content analysis was twofold: (1) to have an indication of the frequency with which ideological and technical themes appear over time; and (2) to classify articles as scientific management, human relations, or structural analysis pieces. Content analysis is a technique for making valid inferences about "the sender(s) of [the] message, the message itself, or the audience of the message." Table A.1 lists the content categories used to identify the different key recording units (themes) corresponding to each of the three paradigms.[2] This table is a simplified summary of the general characteristics, ideological features, and techniques of the three paradigms (see Table 1.1). The content analysis of the journals was conducted by the author. It involved: (1) reading the articles on organization for each of the journals selected for analysis; (2) recording the content categories and themes observed to appear; and (3) assigning articles to one of the three paradigms. Articles that were not classifiable were left in a residual category. This content analysis allowed the author to minimize his subjective judgment and to systematize data collection, so that the same content categories were investigated for each paradigm. Previous content analyses of management publications have used computer-generated counts of key terms or phrases, but for this analysis all articles were actually read by the author.

1. Dibble, "Four types of inference from documents to events" (1963).
2. R. P. Weber, *Basic Content Analysis* (1985, pp. 9, 56–57).

305

TABLE A.1 Simplified list of key recording units (i.e. themes) for analyzing journal articles

Content categories	Themes Corresponding to Each of the Paradigms		
	Scientific Management	Human Relations	Structural Analysis
Perceived problem	Soldiering, waste, disorder; management's arbitrariness and greed, lack of control	Monotony of work, conflict, unrest, absenteeism, turnover, low morale	Organizational structure-technology-environment mismatch
General form of solution	Normative: one best way	Normative: one best way	Contingency approach
View of industrial conflict	Avoidable: more surplus benefits both workers and management	Avoidable: cooperation is in the nature of man; firm as social system	It is structurally shaped, and is not necessarily bad; it generates change
View of workers, and way of dealing with them	Driven by self-interest; need to be told what to do and supervised	Driven by psychosocial norms, needs, emotions; need to be lead	Behave according to their structural situation
Fascination with	Machinery, technology, factory aesthetic, mass production	Communal life, human interaction in social groups	Ubiquity and complexity of organizations in modern society
Methodology	Time-and-motion study, job analysis	Surveys, interviews, discussion groups	Comparative study of cases, typologies of organizations
Selection of workers	On-site, scientific psycho-physiological testing and evaluation	On-site selection based on social affinity, attitudes, personality	Formal qualifications
Distribution of tasks	Conception and execution of tasks separated; division of labor; specialization	Job enlargement, enrichment, rotation	Differentiation and integration of functions
Authority structures	Simple managerial hierarchy, unity of command	Downplays hierarchy, emphasizes leadership, communication, and participation; suggestion systems	Complex hierarchy; line-and-staff structures; centralization and decentralization as policy variables
Organization of the process of work	Work simplification, standardization, assembly-line work	Small-group activities; teamwork	Departmentalization, divisionalization, matrix structures, profit centers
Preferred rewards	Wages, bonuses	Stability, security, work satisfaction, recognition	Prestige, status, power, promotion, salaries
Preferred economic incentives	Performance-based or piecework wages	Group wage incentives	Seniority-based salaries

APPENDIX B

Comparative Statistics

This appendix presents a number of useful comparative statistics on the United States, Germany, Great Britain, and Spain. Table B.1 presents level indicators for several crucial years over the twentieth century, including the ratio of administrative to production employees in industry, total and employed population, industrial and services employment, proportion of union membership, coverage of collective agreements, importance of exports and imports, share of world trade, flow of foreign investment, number of foreign subsidiaries, proportion of diversified and multidivisional firms, and number of qualified engineers. Table B.2 presents period indicators on GDP growth rates, unemployment, and working days lost due to industrial conflict. Figure B.1 shows the evolution of the ratio of administrative to production employees in industry over the twentieth century.

The following are the sources for Tables B.1 and B.2, and Figure B.1:

For several countries: Ahlström (1982, pp. 14, 107–108); Banks (1971, pp. 171–206); Bendix (1974, p. 214); Dyas and Thanheiser (1976, pp. 29, 64–65); Flora et al., eds. (1983); Liesner, ed. (1985), (1989); Mitchell (1980); Franko (1976, p. 12); OECD, *Balance of Payments of OECD Countries 1960–1977* (Paris: OECD, 1979), pp. 14–15, 30–31, 46–47, 150–151.

United States: Fligstein (1990, p. 336); Melman (1951, pp. 62–93); U.S. Bureau of the Census, *Historical Statistics of the United States: Colonial Times to 1970. Part 1* (Washington, D.C.: U.S. Bureau of the Census, 1975), *Census of Population: 1950.* Vol. 2. *Characteristics of the Population. Part 1: United States Summary* (Washington, D.C.: U.S. Bureau of the Census, 1953), pp. 290–291, *Census of Population: 1960.* Vol. 1. *Characteristics of the Population. Part 1: United States Summary* (Washington, D.C.: U.S. Bureau of the Census, 1963), pp. 557–558, *Census of Population: 1970.* Vol. 1. *Characteristics of the Population. Part 1: United States Summary. Section 2* (Washington, D.C.: U.S. Government Printing Office, 1973), p. 788; U.S. Department of Labor, *Handbook of Labor Statistics 1974* (Washington, D.C.: U.S. Government Printing Office, 1974), p. 396.

TABLE B.1 Comparative level indicators for the United States (USA), Germany (GER), Great Britain (GBR), and Spain (SPA), 1900–1970

Indicator	1900				1913				1920				1929			
	USA	GER	GBR	SPA	USA	GER	GBR	SPA	USA	GER	GBR	SPA	USA	GER	GBR	SPA
Ratio of administrative to production employees in industry (%)[a]	8.1	6.0	...	...	13.0	9.0	10.2	...	15.6	10.7	12.0	...	17.9	13.0	13.6	...
Total population (millions)	76.1	56.0	41.2	18.6	97.2	67.0	45.6	20.3	106.5	...	43.7	21.3	121.8	64.7	45.7	23.5
Employed population (millions)[b]	27.0	25.0	18.0	6.6[c]	37.0	30.0	20.3	7.5[c]	39.2	31.0	20.3	7.5[c]	47.6	32.0	19.5	8.3[c]
Industrial employment (%)[b]	24.3	38.6	43.7	16.0[c]	29.4	40.5	44.0	17.6[c]	32.3	41.0	48.4	21.9[c]	29.2	40.8	44.9	26.5[c]
Services employment (%)[b]	31.5	25.1	43.2	17.8[c]	37.9	25.9	44.1	19.0[c]	39.5	27.3	42.7	20.8[c]	44.7	29.8	47.3	28.0[c]
As a percent of total employment:																
Union membership	3.2	3.5	11.2	5.0	7.3	10.3	20.4	...	12.9	30.0	38.7	13.0	7.2	17.9	24.9	...
Collective agreements	...	...	...	...	...	5.2	11.8[d]	...	...	...	...	...	...	38.4	...	...
Exports + Imports (% of GDP)	12.0	32.0	39.0	...	11.0	39.8	47.9	21.5	15.2	33.8	43.6	8.0	9.4	...	47.8	18.4
Share of world trade (%)	11.7	12.5	20.9	1.5	11.3	13.8	15.9	1.2	17.3	2.4	20.6	0.6	10.9	6.1	10.8	1.1
Foreign investment (% of GDP)	...	...	...	...	...	...	...	...	...	...	...	...	...	...	...	...
No. of foreign subsidiaries	...	...	...	...	...	...	...	...	11	...	...	...	15	...	...	...
Diversified firms (%)[e]	...	...	...	...	...	...	...	...	0	...	...	...	2	...	...	...
Multidivisional firms (%)[e]	...	...	...	...	...	...	...	...	0	...	...	...	13	...	...	...
Multidivisional/diversified (%)[e]	...	...	...	...	...	...	...	...	...	...	...	...	...	...	...	...
Engineers per 1,000 employed in industry[f]	5.8	4.4	2.9	3.4	8.5	5.4	4.5	...	10.5	...	...	2.7	15.1	11.0	...	5.6

(Continued to page 309)

Indicator	1950				1960				1970			
	USA	GER	GBR	SPA	USA	GER	GBR	SPA	USA	GER	GBR	SPA
Ratio of administrative to production employees in industry (%)[a]	23.6	15.5	21.3	9.5	28.9	20.6	27.1	...	30.3	...	36.4	15.3
Total population (millions)	152.3	47.8	50.6	28.0	180.7	55.4	52.4	30.4	205.1	60.6	55.4	34.0
Employed population (millions)[b]	58.9	20.4	23.3	10.4c	65.8	26.0	24.2	12.1	78.7	26.2	24.8	12.9
Industrial employment (%)[b]	32.9	44.7	51.6	26.6c	30.8	48.4	48.4	30.2	28.2	48.6	44.9	35.9
Services employment (%)[b]	54.4	33.1	44.5	25.9c	59.5	38.3	48.2	29.2	66.8	42.5	53.0	37.3
As a percent of total employment:												
Union membership	24.3	26.7	39.7	...	25.9	24.5	40.6	...	24.6	25.6	...	...
Collective agreements	...	90.0	70.4	0.0	73.0g	...	...	3.0	65.0g	...	...	32.0
Exports + Imports (% of GDP)	7.7	13.1	33.8	...	9.4	28.5	36.1	14.0	12.6	40.8	43.0	22.0
Share of world trade (%)	18.3	4.5	12.6	0.7	14.8	9.0	9.5	0.6	...	...	...	...
Foreign investment (% of GDP)	...	...	...	...	0.6	0.2	1.0	0.0	0.8	0.7	1.1	0.0
No. of foreign subsidiaries[h]	...	...	...	...	...	...	...	...	4,246	792	2,269	...
Diversified firms (%)[e]	38	39	28	...	60	49	50	...	76	56	62	...
Multidivisional firms (%)[e]	20	5	6	...	52	16	24	...	73	50	70	...
Multidivisional/diversified (%)[e]	53	13	21	...	87	33	48	...	96	89	113	...
Engineers per 1,000 employed in industry[f]	27.7	19.7	...	...	43.2	...	...	...	55.3	...	...	...

Notes: Ellipsis points indicate data not available. Germany stands for the Reich before 1945, and the Federal Republic after 1949.

[a] Industry includes manufacturing only; the figures for administrative employees exclude owners and top executives; some ratios calculated by linear interpolation when exact year not available.

[b] Same as above, for Germany only.

[c] Based on active population.

[d] 1910.

[e] Based on the 84 largest English, 100 largest German, and 100 largest U.S. industrial firms. U.S. data refer to 1919, 1929, 1948, 1959, and 1969.

[f] For Spain, figures are estimates.

[g] Plant workers in industrial and service firms in metropolitan areas only. Data are for 1960–61 and 1971–72.

[h] For U.S. data, refer to 1968; for Germany and Britain, to 1971.

TABLE B.2 Comparative period indicators for the United States (USA), Germany (GER), Great Britain (GBR), and Spain (SPA), (means for the years indicated)

Indicator	1900–13				1920–29				1950–59				1960–69			
	USA	GER	GBR	SPA	USA	GER	GBR	SPA	USA	GER	GBR	SPA	USA	GER	GBR	SPA
GDP cumulative growth rate (%)	3.7	2.7	1.4	1.7[a]	3.6	4.2[b]	1.4	1.6	3.0	7.1	2.3	3.8[c]	4.0	4.1	2.7	7.5
Unemployment (percent of labor force, mean of annual ratios)	4.7	2.5	4.4	...	4.7	8.2	7.7	...	4.5	6.0	1.7	...	4.8	1.0	2.0	1.4
Working days lost per employed worker (mean of annual ratios)	...	.30	.40	...	...	.48	1.80	...	.55	.04	.13	...	.38	.01	.14	.02[d]

Notes: Ellipsis points indicate data not available. Germany stands for the Reich before 1945, and the Federal Republic after 1949.

[a] 1906–13 only.

[b] 1925–29 only.

[c] 1954–59 only.

[d] Legal strikes in 1963–69 only.

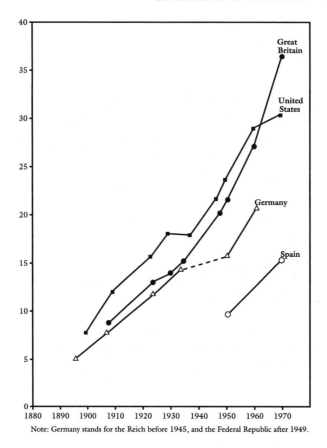

Note: Germany stands for the Reich before 1945, and the Federal Republic after 1949.

Figure B.1. Ratios of administrative to production employees in industry (per 100).

Germany: Bendix (1974, p. 225); Berghahn and Karsten (1987, pp. 147, 226, 236); Enquete-Ausschuß, *Untersuchung der Erzeugungs- und Absatzbedingungen der deutschen Wirtschaft* (Berlin: Mittler & Sohn, 1931), pp. 72–73; Jarausch (1990, p. 237); Statistischen Reichsamt, *Statistik des Deutschen Reichs*, vol. 466 (Berlin: Paul Schmidt, 1937), pp. 194–196; Statistisches Bendesamt, *Bevölkerung und Kultur. Volks- und Berufszählung von 6. Juni 1961. Heft 13: Erwerbspersonen in beruflicher Gliederung* (Stuttgart: W. Kohlhammer, 1968), p. 46, *Bevölkerung und Wirtschaft 1872–1972* (Wiesbaden: Statistisches Bundesamt, 1972), p. 142; Markovits (1968, p. 451).

Great Britain: Central Statistical Office, *Annual Abstract of Statistics No. 88 1938–1950* (London: HMSO, 1952), p. 130; *Annual Abstract of Statistics 1963* (London: HMSO, 1963), p. 127; *Annual Abstract of Statistics No. 101 1964* (London: HMSO, 1964), p. 133; Mitchell (1962); Mitchell and Jones (1971); Buchanan (1989, p. 233); Melman (1956, p. 73); Flanders, "Collective bargaining," in Flanders and Cleff, eds. (1964, pp. 274–286).

Spain: Almarcha et al., eds. (1975); Banco de Bilbao, *Renta nacional de España y su distribución provincial 1955–1975* (Bilbao: Banco de Bilbao, 1978), pp. 29–31, 116–172; Consejo de Economía Nacional, *La renta nacional de España 1940–1964* (Madrid: Consejo de Economía Nacional, 1965), pp. 158, 164, 366; Dirección General de Estadística, *Censo de población de 1930: Resúmenes generales* (Madrid, n.d.), p. 8; Instituto Geográfico y Estadístico, *Censo de la población de España 1900, Tomo IV* (Madrid, 1907), p. 214; Instituto Nacional de Estadística, *Censo de la población de España 1950* (Madrid: INE, n.d.), pp. 588–590; *Censo de la población de España 1970,* vol. 3 (Madrid: INE, 1974), p. 53; Macrométrica (1978, p. 35); Martin (1990, p. 249); Servicio General de Estadística *Censo de población de 1920. Tomo V: Resultados de la clasificación de los habitantes de España por su profesión* (Madrid, 1929), p. 424; Tamames (1986, p.14); Tamames, ed. (1977, p. 366).

APPENDIX C

The Adoption of Scientific Management and Human Relations Techniques in the United States: Industry-Level Comparisons, 1935–46

This appendix explores the historical adoption across American industrial and service sectors of selected scientific management and human relations techniques, focusing on the long-term, strategic actions of workers and employers. Over the four decades following the end of World War I, American employers pursued the centralization of personnel administration through the creation of personnel departments, while organized labor's strategy was aimed at forcing employers to sign union contracts. Other variables included in the analysis are technology and the manufacturing/service dichotomy. The data used in the multivariate analysis come from surveys conducted by the National Industrial Conference Board for the years 1935, 1939, and 1946. The analysis that follows is limited because: (1) the indicators used capture only a small portion of what scientific management and human relations represent as paradigms of organization; and (2) the data are only available at the industry level. Therefore, the results reported in this appendix should be taken with a healthy dose of caution.

The implementation of scientific management techniques such as time-and-motion study are hypothesized to depend on the strategies pursued by employers and workers. The creation of a personnel department is expected to have a positive effect on the application of scientific management techniques. The introduction of bureaucratized promotion, rating, seniority, and welfare schemes associated with personnel departments allowed employers to justify the continued application of techniques such as time-and-motion study. The positive or negative sign of the effect of union contracts is open to contradictory expectations. On one hand, a negative effect is hypothesized if the existence of union contracts is taken as evidence of the strength of labor unions *and* labor unions are assumed to oppose the implementation of scientific management. On the other, a positive effect of union contracts must be expected if the agreement granted the employer the prerogative to organize production and design working conditions in exchange for higher guaranteed wages, fringe benefits, seniority rights, and other welfare schemes.

313

The implementation of human relations techniques such as suggestion systems, employee magazines, and morale surveys are also hypothesized to depend on the strategies of employers and workers. The creation of personnel departments provided the expertise necessary for implementing human relations solutions to labor problems. A positive effect is therefore expected. Given organized labor's contempt for human relations postulates, the existence of a powerful union in the workplace and the signing of a union contract with the employer should indicate the difficulty of implementing human relations techniques. Alternatively, an employer facing a powerful union and being forced to sign a union contract might be tempted to use human relations techniques to better understand its employees and supervisors or in a blunt attempt to undermine union strength. Theoretically speaking, both negative and positive effects of union contracts on the implementation of human relations techniques are possible.

The nature of the work being done in the firm has an influence on the way labor problems arise and on the ways in which management deals with them. Service-sector firms, by the nature of their operations, are less likely to be able to implement scientific management techniques than manufacturing firms. Of course, certain kinds of repetitive service-sector tasks, such as handling documents, records, pieces of mail, and merchandise, are amenable to scientific management principles and techniques. But those kinds of operations account for a limited proportion of the work done at service-sector firms. Regardless of the efficiencies accruing from the implementation of scientific management techniques, it is conceivable that service firms whose outputs are hard to measure would use scientific management to justify their operating procedures, as predicted by neoinstitutional theories of organizations.[1]

Mass-production and assembly-manufacturing firms are more likely to apply scientific management techniques directly than others employing more traditional technologies. Mass-production techniques were developed mostly in new industries (e.g. automobiles, electrical manufacturing, rubber and rubber products). Continuous-flow industries such as chemicals and petroleum may also apply scientific management principles to increase efficiency both in the core

---

1. DiMaggio and Powell, "The Iron Cage" (1983); Meyer and Rowan, "Institutionalized organizations: Formal structure as myth and ceremony" (1977); Tolbert and Zucker, "Institutional sources of change in the formal structure of organizations" (1983).

process technology and in the peripheral workshops that support the production process and guarantee its uninterrupted operation. Mass-production, assembly, and continuous-flow firms face analyzable production problems as well as minimal operational exceptions, and tend to emphasize quantity and stability. As a result, they can plan in advance, formalize, and centralize decision making.[2] The traditional industrial sectors (food, leather, machinery, metals, paper, printing, glass, textiles) developed along craft-based lines or failed to invest in mass-production techniques to the extent that the industries of the second industrial revolution did. In addition to being affected by low technology, firms in older industries tend to resist change and succumb to inertia to a greater extent than those in new industries.[3] In sum, firms in the new mass-production, assembly, and continuous-flow industries are hypothesized to implement scientific management techniques to a greater extent than firms in any other manufacturing sector.

Service firms and manufacturing firms in the mass-production, assembly, and continuous-flow sectors are more likely to implement human relations techniques for other reasons. First, service firms or manufacturing firms with mass-production, assembly or continuous-flow technologies generally have more highly educated and progressive managerial cadres. Second, the numerical predominance of white-collar workers in service firms has frequently been related to the primacy of social over technical workplace problems. Moreover, the problems of monotony, absenteeism, turnover, and low morale resulting from the scientific rationalization of the production process are normally more severe in mass-production firms than in the craft-based or more traditional sectors. In brief, human relations techniques are hypothesized to be more likely in service-sector firms in general and in manufacturing firms with mass-production, assembly, or continuous-flow technologies.

The data come from several U.S. national surveys on personnel practices and industrial relations in industrial and service sectors conducted by the New York–based National Industrial Conference Board in 1935, 1939, and 1946.[4] All the information was originally collected at the firm level. Unfortunately, the NICB published the

---

2. Perrow, "A framework for comparative organizational analysis" (1967); Woodward, *Management and Technology* (1958).

3. Stinchcombe, "Social structure and organizations" (1965); Hannan and Freeman, *Organizational Ecology* (1989).

4. NICB (1936), (1940), (1947).

data in cross-tab form by firm size (number of employees) and, with some exceptions, by sector. When compared to other studies covering the same time period, the NICB surveys provide the least biased and most comprehensive information in terms of geographical scope and industrial coverage.[5] The 1935 sample covers 2,452 firms (15 percent service firms) employing 4.5 million workers. This represents about 15.5 percent of the total number of workers in the industries included in the survey. The 1939 data set includes 2,700 firms (18 percent service) with 5 million workers. The 1946 sample is composed of 3,498 firms (13 percent service) with an unknown number of workers. These industry-level data (including both industrial and service sectors) were used to conduct multivariate regression analyses of the prevalence of scientific management and human relations techniques. A pooled cross-sectional and time-series data set of eighteen manufacturing and service sectors for the years 1935, 1939, and 1946 was used in the analysis. Pooling was deemed necessary to increase the efficiency of the ordinary least squares (OLS) estimates. A set of two dummy variables for the years 1939 and 1946 was introduced in every regression equation estimated by the OLS method in order to control for pooling. The simplifying assumption is that all time-related differences are captured by the constant term, while the slope coefficients for the independent variables are common to all units and points in time.[6]

The eighteen industrial and service sectors used in the multivariate analysis included five service sectors (banking; insurance; gas and electricity; transportation and communication; and mercantile, wholesale and retail) and five industrial sectors coded as having mass-production, assembly, or continuous-flow technologies (automobiles, chemicals, electrical manufacturing and equipment, rubber, and petroleum). Sample statistics for the pooled sample (1935, 1939, and 1946) appear in Table C.1.

Table C.2 reports the regression results for the adoption of time study. Clearly, service-sector firms in the sample found it hard to implement time study before 1946 or did not try at all. Based on the sample included in the analysis, model A predicts a negative percentage of service firms with time study in 1935. Adding personnel department as a regressor increases the explanatory power of the model (see model B), and also wipes out the 1946 time effect. As hypothe-

5. Baron et al., "Mission control?" (1988, p. 501). Other surveys include Parks (1935, 1936), FMM (1946a, 1946b), Peirce School (1935), Wallace (1952).

6. Johnston, *Econometric Methods* (1984, pp. 396–407).

TABLE C.1   Pooled sample statistics on the adoption of scientific management and human relations by American firms in eighteen industrial and service sectors in 1935, 1939, and 1946 (n = 54)

Variable	Name	Mean	Std Dev	Min	Max
Percent applying time study	TIMESTUD	32.03	25.18	2.5	83.1
Percent with suggestion system	SUGGEST	27.78	9.04	13.3	55.0
Percent with employee magazine	MAGAZINE	24.29	15.53	4.5	67.0
Percent with personnel department	PERSDEPT	48.11	18.06	16.0	77.2
Percent with union contract	UNIONCON	43.51	31.69	1.6	96.3
Service sector = 1	SERVICE	0.28	0.45	0.0	1.0
MAC technology = 1	MACTECH	0.28	0.45	0.0	1.0

Notes: The eighteen industrial and service sectors included are automobiles; chemicals; electrical manufacturing and equipment; food; leather; machines and machine tools; metals and metal products; paper; printing; rubber; stone, clay, and glass; textiles; petroleum; banking; insurance; gas, electricity, public utilities; transportation and communication; mercantile, wholesale, and retail.

MACTECH stands for "mass-production, assembly, or continuous-flow technology." The following industries were coded as MACTECH: automobiles; chemicals; electrical manufacturing and equipment; rubber; petroleum.

sized, technology has a large impact on the proportion of firms using time study (models C and E), but if personnel department is included in the equation, the significant effect of manufacturing technology vanishes (models D and F). (The sample correlation of personnel department and technology is 0.27.) Finally, the proportion of firms having signed a union contract is not significant in any of the models, suggesting perhaps that as the proportion of union contracts increases, the two interpretations of its expected effect cancel each other out.[7]

The regression results for the adoption of certain human relations techniques are reported in Table C.3. Service-sector firms are no more likely than industrial firms to have introduced suggestion systems (model A), but when the proportion of firms with a personnel department is entered in the equation, then being in the service sector has a negative effect. As expected, the effect of a personnel department is positive (models B, D, and F). The effect of technology is also positive but, as with time study, it vanishes if the proportion of personnel

7. The proportion of union contracts was used in models with fewer independent variables than the ones reported in table C.2, but the results were insignificant. The proportion of firms with a union contract also failed to reach significance when entered in the equation as a lagged regressor. In the lagged case, of course, the pooled sample was smaller because only the 1939 and 1946 data could be used for the dependent variable.

TABLE C.2 OLS regression estimates for the adoption of time study by American firms. Pooled sample of eighteen industrial and service sectors in 1935, 1939, and 1946 ($n = 54$)

Variables	A	B	C	D	E	F
SERVICE	-34.340***	-45.553***	-29.607***	-41.922***	-30.243***	-41.972***
	(-5.835)	(-7.444)	(-5.131)	(-5.810)	(-5.051)	(-5.736)
MACTECH			16.193***	6.048	16.245***	6.105
			(2.807)	(0.903)	(2.792)	(0.897)
PERSDEPT		0.736***		0.612**		0.610**
		(3.792)		(2.608)		(2.539)
UNIONCON		0.002			-0.059	-0.010
		(0.015)			(-0.448)	(-0.080)
YEAR1939	12.339*	12.747*	12.339**	12.723**	14.044*	13.013*
	(1.911)	(1.872)	(2.038)	(2.222)	(1.953)	(1.906)
YEAR1946	13.761**	-3.493	13.761**	-0.509	17.273*	0.160
	(2.131)	(-0.323)	(2.273)	(-0.064)	(1.739)	(0.014)
Constant	32.867***	6.120	27.054***	8.459	28.028***	8.714
	(6.778)	(0.701)	(5.415)	(0.989)	(5.108)	(0.946)
Model's F score	13.182***	12.805***	13.215***	13.185***	10.440***	10.761***
R-square	44.16	57.15	51.90	57.87	52.10	57.87

Note: Student's t in parentheses beneath regression coefficient. Definitions of variables are given in Table C.1.

*$0.05 \leq p < 0.10$.

**$0.01 \leq p < 0.05$.

***$p < 0.01$.

departments is controlled for (models C and E versus models D and F). Again, the proportion of firms with a union contract does not have any significant effect. Curiously enough, the prevalence of suggestion systems in the firms in the sample tends to decline after 1939 when one controls for the proportion of firms with personnel department (models B, D, and F).

Service-sector firms are more likely to publish an employee magazine than industrial firms (see lower panel of Table C.3). As expected, the proportion of personnel departments and of union contracts have positive effects (model B). Technology also has the expected positive effect (models C and E), but when the proportion of personnel departments is controlled for, neither of the two variables reaches significance levels (models D and F). Finally, the proportion of union contracts exerts the expected positive effect in two of the three models where it was included as a regressor.

One of the most important techniques of human relations is the morale survey. Unfortunately, no data where collected by the NICB on the prevalence of morale surveys until 1946, and even then the information is available at the industry level only for that year. Regression models similar to the ones reported in Tables C.2 or C.3 (but without the year dummies) where run on the 1946 data by sector ($n = 26$) with the proportion of firms using morale surveys as the dependent variable. None of the regressors reached significance at the 0.10 level (the results are available from the author upon request). The highest proportions of firms conducting morale surveys in 1946 were in aircraft (23%), wholesale and retail (22%), glass (18%), communications and broadcasting (15%), paints, pigments and varnishes (13%), and public utilities (12%). The service/manufacturing or new/old technology dichotomies are therefore not helpful in understanding the high prevalence of morale surveys in those industries.

The multivariate analysis of the information contained in the NICB surveys provides some new insights into the study of the adoption and prevalence of organizational techniques across American industrial and service sectors. First, the employers' strategy of comprehensive personnel administration in the face of labor unrest and mounting challenges to managerial authority was associated with the implementation of scientific management and human relations techniques. In the case of scientific management, the empirical findings confirm that employers were able to trade in welfare schemes and stable, long-term employment for control over the organization of production. As regards human relations, personnel departments provided an adequate institutional framework for social scientists to apply their theories and

TABLE C.3 OLS regression estimates for the adoption of suggestion systems and employee magazines by American firms. Pooled sample of eighteen industrial and service sectors in 1935, 1939, and 1946 ($n = 54$)

Variables	A	B	C	D	E	F
			SUGGEST			
SERVICE	−1.788	−6.915**	0.861	−5.193	1.449	−4.795
	(−0.636)	(−2.501)	(0.322)	(−1.569)	(0.526)	(−1.459)
MACTECH			9.061***	4.074	9.013***	3.615
			(3.393)	(1.326)	(3.368)	(1.182)
PERSDEPT		0.399***		0.301***		0.324***
		(4.553)		(2.796)		(3.009)
UNIONCON		0.087			0.054	0.080
		(1.549)			(0.901)	(1.422)
YEAR1939	1.350	−0.933	1.350	1.539	−0.227	−0.776
	(0.438)	(−0.303)	(0.482)	(0.586)	(−0.069)	(−0.253)
YEAR1946	0.350	−14.170***	0.350	−6.664*	−2.897	−12.007**
	(0.114)	(−2.900)	(0.125)	(−1.835)	(−0.634)	(−2.309)
Constant	27.708***	11.736***	24.455***	15.315***	23.554***	13.273***
	(11.968)	(2.975)	(10.575)	(3.905)	(9.333)	(3.207)
Model's F score	0.204	4.534***	3.063**	4.354***	2.603**	4.043***
R-square	1.21	32.08	20.00	31.20	21.33	34.04

(Continued to page 321)

			MAGAZINE			
SERVICE	18.957***	15.623***	21.352***	17.046***	22.825***	17.824***
	(4.813)	(3.631)	(5.348)	(3.247)	(5.630)	(3.458)
MACTECH			8.195**	4.648	8.076**	3.752
			(2.053)	(0.953)	(2.050)	(0.782)
PERSDEPT		0.337**		0.214		0.260
		(2.474)		(1.254)		(1.537)
UNIONCON		0.164*			0.136	0.156*
		(1.871)			(1.533)	(1.771)
YEAR1939	2.939	−1.612	2.939	3.073	−1.009	−1.449
	(0.680)	(−0.337)	(0.702)	(0.738)	(−0.207)	(−0.301)
YEAR1946	7.311*	−10.361	7.311*	2.321	−0.819	−8.116
	(1.692)	(−1.363)	(1.745)	(0.403)	(−0.122)	(−0.995)
Constant	15.606***	0.578	12.664***	6.162	10.408***	2.173
	(4.808)	(0.094)	(3.663)	(0.990)	(2.802)	(0.335)
Model's F score	8.688***	7.648***	7.988***	6.779***	7.036***	6.424***
R-square	34.27	44.34	39.47	41.39	42.30	45.06

Note: Student's t in parentheses beneath regression coefficient. Definitions of variables are given in Table C.1.

*$0.05 \leq p < 0.10$.

**$0.01 \leq p < 0.05$.

***$p < 0.01$.

programs. Second, the existence of union contracts has mixed effects on the adoption of the scientific management and human relations techniques, which cancel each other out. An alternative interpretation is, of course, that union contracts (and the implicit union power) are not relevant at all, a tenet that is hard to support given the historical evidence available.[8]

Third, service-sector firms did not engage in the implementation of scientific management techniques in an attempt to gain legitimacy. The results can be better understood if one accepts that service-sector tasks are not as amenable to scientific management as those of manufacturing industries. On the contrary, service-sector firms were more likely to have employee magazines. No differences were observed for suggestion systems. These results, then, partially confirm the tenet that dominantly white-collar organizations are likely to be more concerned with the social than with the technical aspects of work. Finally, industries in which mass-production, assembly, and continuous-flow technologies predominate have a higher prevalence of both scientific management and human relations techniques. These results may be interpreted as evidence for the postulates of the technological school of organizational thought. Alternatively, one might consider the explanation that mass-production, assembly, and continuous-flow technologies are characteristic of new, second-generation industrial firms (as opposed to the traditional industries dating back to the first industrial revolution).

8. Bendix, *Work and Authority in Industry* (1974); Baritz, *The Servants of Power* (1960).

APPENDIX D

A Systematic Comparison of Conditions and Outcomes of Adoption

The purpose of this appendix is to formalize the comparative analysis of the configurations of factors underlying the adoption of organizational paradigms in the four countries. As discussed in Chapter 6, a systematic comparison of cases reveals interesting and unexpected insights at the cost of simplifying the rich historical information contained in the country chapters. The analysis relies on the Boolean method recently proposed by sociologist Charles Ragin.[1] The dependent variables will be dichotomous *categorical* (whether the degrees of adoption of a paradigm's ideology and techniques were comparatively high or low in each country). The explanatory conditions are also dichotomous. Other techniques of analysis, purely parametric ones in particular, are not feasible, given that there are seven explanatory variables and a limited number of cases.[2] Boolean analysis, as a non-parametric qualitative method of analysis, surmounts all the technical problems associated with the above combination of requirements, provided that one is willing to accept the limitation that all variables, both the dependent and the independent, should be treated as or converted into binary (i.e. dichotomous) variables.[3] The goals in using a Boolean methodology are to assess the "limits and boundaries" of each explanatory condition and to see how they interact in configurations, not to determine which one does a better job of ex-

---

1. Ragin, *The Comparative Method* (1987).

2. Quantitative parametric or semi-parametric techniques developed for the analysis of dependent categorical variables include logistic regression, probit, proportional hazards, and log-linear models. Small sample size either makes the estimation of these models impossible or renders all statistical inferences imprecise. See Aldrich and Nelson, *Linear Probability, Logit, and Probit Models* (1984); Hanushek and Jackson, *Statistical Methods for Social Scientists* (1977, pp. 187–205); Tuma and Hannan, *Social Dynamics* (1984, pp. 116–264); Fienberg, *The Analysis of Cross-Classified Categorical Data* (1980, pp. 40–41). On the relevance of sample size for selecting an appropriate research methodology, see Ragin (1987, pp. 49–50, 55, 57, 69, 161–162).

3. This limitation is not especially serious. First, most comparative analyses dichotomize variables (e.g. low-high, present-absent, large-small, etc.). Second, polytomous categorical or even interval variables can always be expressed in terms of a set of dichotomous variables with no (or minimal) loss of information.

plaining the variation observed.[4] The approach is case-oriented; it attempts to understand each case individually because of its "intrinsic value," and to analyze all cases simultaneously as "wholes."[5]

Boolean analysis begins by constructing a "truth table."[6] In this table each row represents one of the possible combinations of the two values that explanatory conditions may take. The number of explanatory conditions in this study is seven. The truth table would potentially have $2^7 = 128$ rows (i.e. all the possible combinations of 0's and 1's) and seven columns. Each of the cases needs to be allocated to one and only one of the rows on the basis of the historical evidence from the country chapters. An eighth column is used to code the dependent variable, that is, whether the degree of adoption of the organizational paradigm was high or low. The information contained in the truth table can now be used in direct fashion to write a "primitive Boolean expression" for the dependent variable that assumes maximum complexity of explanatory conditions and interactions among them. This primitive expression is then subjected to an algorithm, a set of rules. The logic is to reduce or minimize the complexity of the theoretical scheme (the maximum of 128 possible combinations of causal factors that may produce a high degree of adoption of the organizational paradigm). The algorithm involves two steps: Boolean minimization (resulting in a partially reduced expression), and Boolean implication (resulting in a logically minimal expression). The logically minimal expression shows the simplest set of combinations of values in the explanatory conditions that produce a high degree of adoption of an organizational paradigm. In other words, the necessary and/or sufficient conditions for success of the organizational paradigm under study can be identified with rigor despite the complexity of the initial conceptual scheme involving a maximum of 128 possible comparisons. Finally, this analysis of necessary and sufficient conditions may be used to create a typology of patterns of adoption and of organizational change.

4. Ragin (1987, p. 169). Thus the methodological approach differs radically from the one taken in recent studies on the bureaucratization process and on the diffusion of organizational structures or control mechanisms, including Tolbert and Zucker, "Institutional sources of change in the formal structure of organizations" (1983), who use a proportional hazards regression model, and Fligstein, "The spread of the multidivisional form among large firms, 1919–1979" (1985) and "The intraorganizational power struggle" (1987), who estimates logistic regression models.

5. Ragin (1987, pp. 54–55).

6. The method and the algorithm are described by Ragin (1987, pp. 85–124). There is a personal computer package available: Drass, *QCA 2.02: Qualitative Comparative Analysis* (1988). All the analyses that follow were conducted using this package.

The algorithm for working out the model proposed will not be used for its own sake but only insofar as it forces one to state assumptions, hypotheses, and definitions of variables in an explicit way. The algorithm also sets quite clearly the standards and rules for drawing inferences, sorting out similar cases, and deriving conclusions.[7] In other words, the method will be used first to organize the data, and then as a guide to obtain rigorous conclusions as to the different configurations of explanatory conditions that produce the adoption of the organizational paradigms.

The seven explanatory conditions may take one of two values. A value of 1 was assigned if, and only if, the condition was favorable to the adoption of the paradigm. A value of 0 was assigned if, and only if, the condition was not favorable to the adoption of the paradigm. It is important to note that the same condition may be coded differently depending on the organizational paradigm under consideration. For example, a high level of industrial conflict is assumed to be favorable to the adoption of human relations (there is an organizational problem that needs that approach), but unfavorable to the adoption of structural analysis (industrial peace would be the favorable condition). In a country with a high level of industrial conflict, the condition of industrial relations would be coded 1 for human relations but 0 for structural analysis. A systematic comparative analysis by paradigm follows, with a final section comparing organizational problems and institutional factors across paradigms.

THE ADOPTION OF SCIENTIFIC MANAGEMENT

As documented in Chapters 2–5, and summarized in Table 6.1, scientific management never succeeded as a comprehensive organizational ideology in any of the six situations studied (interwar United States, interwar Germany, interwar Spain, postwar Spain, interwar Britain, and postwar Britain). Nevertheless, the techniques of scientific management were accepted by the management intellectuals and implemented by firms in the United States and Germany between the world wars, and in Britain and Spain during the 1940s and early 1950s. We can summarize the observed patterns of adoption by specifying whether each of the explanatory conditions (i.e. the three organizational problems and the four institutional factors) favored (denoted by 1) or impeded (denoted by 0) the adoption of the paradigm. The resulting truth table for the adoption (1) or nonadoption (0) of scientific management techniques in the six situations of Table 6.1 follows:

7. Ragin (1987, pp. 111–112).

Country and Period	STRUC	WORLD	INREL	MENTA	PROFS	STATE	WORKE	OUTCOME
USA (1920–39)	1	0	1	1	1	0	0	1
GER (1920–33)	1	1	0	1	1	1	1	1
SPA (1920–36)	0	0	1	0	0	0	0	0
SPA (1939–53)	1	1	0	0	1	1	1	1
GBR (1914–39)	1	0	1	0	0	0	0	0
GBR (1939–50)	1	1	0	0	0	1	1	1

The seven explanatory variables are structural changes (STRUC), international pressures (WORLD), industrial relations system (INREL), elite mentalities (MENTA), role of the professions (PROFS), role of the state (STATE), and workers' responses (WORKE). The truth table is a codified summary of what we know about the adoption of scientific management techniques in the cases under scrutiny. The information in this table can be used to write an expression that describes the four cases for which the outcome was the acceptance and implementation of scientific management techniques (OUTCOME = 1) in terms of the combination of explanatory conditions that produced that outcome. The presence of a favorable condition is denoted in the expression by caps (e.g. WORLD), while its absence is indicated by lowercase (e.g. world). This is called a primitive Boolean expression:

```
SMT = STRUC world    INREL MENTA PROFS state   worke
    + STRUC WORLD inrel    MENTA PROFS STATE WORKE
    + STRUC WORLD inrel    menta PROFS STATE WORKE
    + STRUC WORLD inrel    menta profs STATE WORKE   [D.1]
```

SMT stands for a high degree of adoption of scientific management techniques. In a Boolean expression multiplication means "intersection" (or simultaneity) of conditions, while addition (denoted by the + sign) means "or." In words, given the sample of six countries and periods, there is a high degree of adoption of scientific management techniques if any of the four configurations of intersecting conditions stated in expression [D.1] occurs.

Expression [D.1] describes an exceedingly complex set of conditions. The goal is to simplify this expression to the greatest extent possible by eliminating redundancies and commonalties in the observed patterns of organizational change. The Boolean approach allows us to reduce the complexity by discarding conditions and configurations of conditions that, from a comparative perspective, are not crucial for explaining the observed outcome. Under the assumption that combinations of the seven explanatory conditions other than those in the table are instances of a low degree of adoption or nonadoption (i.e. OUTCOME = 0),[8] the logically minimal Boolean expression for a high degree of adoption of scientific management techniques (SMT) is

SMT = STRUC world INREL MENTA PROFS state worke
  + STRUC WORLD inrel menta STATE WORKE
  + STRUC WORLD inrel PROFS STATE WORKE   [D.2]

Expression [D.2] suggests that, given the sample of countries and time periods, there are three configurations of conditions under which scientific management techniques achieve a high degree of adoption. Understanding the implications of the three patterns is easier when distinguishing between the combinations of organizational problems and institutional factors.

Two different combinations of organizational problems appear in expression [D.2]. In the first situation, or line, in the expression the problem is the intersection (or coincidence) of structural changes, weak international pressures, and labor unrest (interwar United States). The second (postwar Britain) and third (interwar Germany and postwar Spain) situations, however, present a problem resulting from structural changes and strong international pressures but with labor peace. This result confirms the intuitive analysis in Chapter 6. Management intellectuals and firms basically perceived two different types of organizational problems that would be amenable to scientific management techniques. The two patterns make a great deal of sense because they emphasize the cross-cutting pressures to which employers and managers were exposed. It was not simply structural changes in firms (increasing size and complexity, bureaucratization) that required new organizational approaches. Structural changes interacted with either labor turmoil or international competitive pressures to create a problematic situation that rendered old organizational ideas and techniques inadequate and prompted the implementation of a new approach.

This detailed comparative analysis also allows us to identify necessary and/or sufficient conditions for the adoption of paradigms. On the basis of this sample, and assuming that other combinations of conditions are instances of a low degree of adoption, structural change

---

8. A more simplifying assumption would be to use combinations other than those in the sample as evidence of high degree of diffusion (i.e. OUTCOME = 1) for the Boolean minimization but *not* for the implication process. The reason for not making this looser assumption is that, given the great number of other combinations among seven explanatory conditions and the relatively small sample sizes, the results would be distorted enormously. See Ragin (1987, pp. 109–111).

(STRUC) is the only necessary (but *not* sufficient) explanatory condition. Structural change is a necessary condition because STRUC is the only variable that appears in each of the three additive terms (lines) of expression [D.2] either as a present condition (in caps) *or* as an absent condition (in lowercase). (Note that a combination of caps and lowercase is not indicative of necessary status.) However, STRUC is not a sufficient condition, because other conditions must be met in order to produce the outcome of high degree of adoption. Interestingly, the importance of the role of a professional group (in this case, engineers) is not a necessary condition. This result is conditioned by the inclusion of the case of postwar Britain, where the adoption of scientific management techniques took place in the absence of a strong, numerous, and influential engineering profession. Still, the evidence presented in the country chapters has documented the enormous importance of the engineering profession in the United States, Germany, and Spain for the adoption of scientific management techniques in each of the cases.

Two most general patterns also emerge in terms of configurations of institutional factors behind the adoption of scientific management techniques. In the case of the interwar United States (with problems of structural changes and labor unrest), strong professional input coupled with a favorable set of mentalities, even with weak state effects and opposition from labor, sufficed for the adoption of scientific management techniques. However, when the organizational problem was a combination of structural changes and international pressures but no labor unrest, the favorable institutional factors were either state action and labor-union collaboration (as in postwar Britain) or the professions, state action, and labor-union collaboration (as in interwar Germany and postwar Spain). Interestingly, in Germany between the world wars and in Spain during the early Franco period, labor-union collaboration facilitated the adoption of scientific management techniques precisely during a period of relative industrial peace. This systematic comparative analysis brings to the fore another unexpected result referring to the role of the modernist elite mentality in Weimar Germany. As explained in Chapter 3, modernism united government officials, engineers, artists, business elites, and labor-union leaders under the banner of scientific management and industrial rationalization in an effort to cope with the problems deriving from complex structural changes in firms and mounting international pressures. The case of interwar Germany, however, corresponds to the last term of expression [D.2], in which the modernist elite mentality is not present. This means that it was not a crucial condition for the adoption of scientific management techniques from a *comparative* point of view.

THE ADOPTION OF HUMAN RELATIONS

As noted in the country chapters, the ideology and the techniques of human relations were unevenly adopted by country. In the United States and Britain the paradigm succeeded both as an ideology and as a set of techniques, while in Germany it failed on both counts. In Spain, however, the ideology of human relations was adopted, but only a few management intellectuals discussed the techniques, and firms rarely implemented them. Therefore, the comparative analysis will be conducted separately for ideology and techniques. The following truth table summarizes the conditions behind the adoption of human relations *ideology* in the four countries after World War II:

Country and Period	STRUC	WORLD	INREL	MENTA	PROFS	STATE	WORKE	OUTCOME
USA (1945–55)	1	1	1	0	1	0	0	1
GER (1945–55)	0	0	0	0	0	0	0	0
SPA (1954–70)	0	1	1	1	1	1	1	1
GBR (1950–60)	1	0	1	1	1	1	1	1

Under the assumption that combinations of the seven explanatory conditions other than those in the truth table are instances of a low degree of adoption (i.e. OUTCOME = 0), the logically minimal Boolean expression for a high degree of adoption of human relations ideology (HRI) is

HRI = STRUC WORLD INREL menta   PROFS state   worke
    + STRUC world   INREL MENTA PROFS STATE WORKE
    + struc   WORLD INREL MENTA PROFS STATE WORKE   [D.3]

This logically minimal expression is the same as the primitive expression directly drawn from the truth table. In other words, the Boolean minimization and implication procedures have not been useful at all. There are two necessary but not sufficient conditions: presence of labor unrest (INREL = 1) and presence of relevant professional groups (PROFS = 1), a finding consistent with the initial hypothesis about the conditions favoring a human relations approach. Before going any further into the patterns of change in expression [D.3], it is useful to write the truth table for the adoption of human relations *techniques*:

Country and Period	STRUC	WORLD	INREL	MENTA	PROFS	STATE	WORKE	OUTCOME
USA (1945–55)	1	1	1	0	1	0	0	1
GER (1945–55)	0	0	0	0	0	0	0	0
SPA (1954–70)	0	1	1	1	1	1	1	0
GBR (1950–60)	1	0	1	1	1	1	1	1

Note that the values for the explanatory conditions are the same as in the table for the adoption of human relations ideology. Under the assumption that combinations of the seven explanatory conditions other than those in the truth table are instances of a low degree of adoption (i.e. OUTCOME = 0), the logically minimal expression is again the same as the primitive expression:

HRT = STRUC WORLD INREL menta   PROFS state   worke
   + STRUC world   INREL MENTA PROFS STATE WORKE [D.4]

In the adoption of human relations techniques, there are three necessary conditions: the two pointed out for the ideology (labor unrest and professions), and, in addition, structural changes in firms (STRUC). This result is very important. It confirms the intuitive explanation for the failure of human relations techniques to be widely implemented by firms in Spain in spite of the fact that the overwhelming majority of management intellectuals adopted the ideology of human relations. In other words, the systematic comparative analysis singles out the relatively smaller size and lower bureaucratization of firms in Spain as an explanation for the non-implementation of human relations techniques there. The lack of white-collar expertise and of the necessary scale of operation prevented Spanish firms from using human relations techniques. Only a few firms with such resources adopted the techniques.

The analysis of necessary conditions for the adoption of the human relations paradigm yields other interesting results. It is significant to note that, from a comparative perspective, the effects of elite mentalities, the state, and collaboration of workers are not crucial for understanding the cross-national patterns of adoption. This obviously contradicts the importance attributed in the country chapters to those three factors in the adoption of human relations in Britain and Spain. The fact that in the United States they played no role explains why they do not appear to be necessary factors from a comparative perspective. There are, however, two crucial similarities among the three cases that underscore the existence of a core and common mechanism in the adoption of human relations ideology in the United States, Britain, and Spain. Both the presence of industrial conflict and the theoretical and consulting work of social-science professionals are necessary conditions for the adoption of not only the ideology but also the techniques of human relations.

Those similarities should not lead one to the conclusion that there is just one pattern of organizational change related to the human relations paradigm. The two additive terms in expression [D.4] represent quite different situations in two important respects. While both agree in the presence of structural changes and industrial conflict, in the first term there are international opportunities (a factor favoring human relations), while in the second there are international pressures. In the presence of structural changes, industrial conflict, and international threats (as in postwar Britain), the success of human relations techniques required the presence of all four favorable institutional factors: mentality, professions, state action, and union collaboration. In the case of the United States, the absence of international threats made it possible to adopt human relations without the help of favorable mentalities, state actions, and union collaboration.

THE ADOPTION OF STRUCTURAL ANALYSIS

The international adoption of the structural analysis paradigm offers less of comparative interest than the adoption of the other two paradigms. As explained in the country chapters, there were no relevant mentalities or workers' responses that favored or opposed the adoption of the paradigm. Therefore, the MENTA and WORKE variables have been coded as "don't care terms," denoted by a dash (—). The Boolean method will handle these variables as if they did not exist. The truth table for the adoption of structural analysis techniques follows:

Country and Period	STRUC	WORLD	INREL	MENTA	PROFS	STATE	WORKE	OUTCOME
USA (1960–75)	1	1	1	—	1	0	—	1
GER (1960–75)	1	1	1	—	1	0	—	1
SPA (1960–75)	0	0	0	—	0	0	—	0
GBR (1960–75)	1	1	1	—	1	1	—	1

Under the assumption that combinations of the seven explanatory conditions other than those in the truth table are instances of a low degree of adoption (i.e. OUTCOME = 0), the logically minimal expression for a high degree of adoption of structural analysis techniques (SAT) is

SAT = STRUC WORLD INREL PROFS   [D.5]

This result was expected, given the simple pattern in the truth table. In the United States, Germany, and Britain during the late 1950s and 1960s, structural analysis techniques provided a solution to the problems posed by increasing structural changes (bureaucratization, diversification, growth of service employment) and the internationalization of firms, coupled with the opportunity deriving from the stabilization of industrial relations. The presence of groups of professional social scientists who engaged in research and consulting work was also required to produce the outcome of adoption.

ORGANIZATIONAL PROBLEMS AND INSTITUTIONAL FACTORS COMPARED ACROSS PARADIGMS

Given that all explanatory conditions were coded as 1 if favorable for the adoption of the paradigm and as 0 otherwise, it becomes possible to pool the three samples for the adoption of the techniques associated with the three paradigms. The goal is to generate insights into the comparative adoption of organizational paradigms in general. The combined truth table for the adoption of the techniques of any one of the three paradigms follows:

Country and Period	STRUC	WORLD	INREL	MENTA	PROFS	STATE	WORKE	OUTCOME
USA (1920–39), SMT	1	0	1	1	1	0	0	1
GER (1920–33), SMT	1	1	0	1	1	1	1	1
SPA (1920–36), SMT	0	0	1	0	0	0	0	0
SPA (1939–53), SMT	1	1	0	0	1	1	1	1
GBR (1914–39), SMT	1	0	1	0	0	0	0	0
GBR (1939–50), SMT	1	1	0	0	0	1	1	1
USA (1945–55), HRT	1	1	1	0	1	0	0	1
GER (1945–55), HRT	0	0	0	0	0	0	0	0
SPA (1954–70), HRT	0	1	1	1	1	1	1	0
GBR (1950–60), HRT	1	0	1	1	1	1	1	1
USA (1960–75), SAT	1	1	1	—	1	0	—	1
GER (1960–75), SAT	1	1	1	—	1	0	—	1
SPA (1960–75), SAT	0	0	0	—	0	0	—	0
GBR (1960–75), SAT	1	1	1	—	1	1	—	1

Under the familiar assumption that configurations of the seven explanatory conditions other than those in the truth table are instances of a low degree of adoption (i.e. OUTCOME = 0), the logically minimal Boolean expression for a high degree of adoption of the techniques of any one paradigm (PAR) is

PAR = STRUC INREL   MENTA PROFS state   worke
    + STRUC WORLD inrel   menta   STATE   WORKE
    + STRUC INREL   MENTA PROFS STATE   WORKE
    + STRUC WORLD PROFS   STATE WORKE
    + STRUC WORLD INREL   PROFS   [D.6]

This logically minimal expression represents a substantial reduction in empirical complexity. There are several important findings in expression [D.6] that an intuitive analysis could not yield. First, the only necessary, though not sufficient, condition is the presence of structural changes. It seems that in order for organizational techniques to be adopted in practice, a certain level of firm size, complexity, bureaucratization, and sophistication is required.

Second, new knowledge developed and diffused by professional groups is not universally necessary to produce organizational change. This comparative analysis suggests what other agents may be behind change in response to perceived organizational problems. If professions are not crucial for the adoption, then, among other conditions, state action and worker collaboration are necessary (see the second line in expression [D.6], and contrast it with the other four lines). This was, for example, the case of the adoption of scientific management techniques in Great Britain after World War II, which stands in sharp contrast with the pivotal role played by the engineering profession in the United States, Germany, and Spain.

The third finding also has to do with the interaction between favorable state action and worker collaboration. That interaction appears in three of the additive terms, which describe the adoption of scientific management in Germany, Britain, and Spain, and of human relations in the latter two countries. Only the adoption of paradigms in the United States and the adoption of structural analysis in general deviate from this pattern. Except in the case of human relations in Britain, the intersection of state action and worker collaboration is typical of countries where international opportunities or pressures favor the adoption of the paradigm in question.

Fourth, the last and simplest additive term in expression [D.6] indicates that the presence of professions is only sufficient to produce the adoption of the paradigm in question if, and only if, it intersects with the presence of all three organizational problems or opportunities. This situation is the one found in the adoption of human relations in the United States and of structural analysis in both the United States and Germany.

Fifth, favorable elite mentalities are only found in configurations of factors leading to the adoption of a paradigm if they intersect with industrial unrest (first and third additive terms in expression [D.6]). Moreover, as the second additive term shows, it is precisely in the explicit absence of industrial conflict that elite mentalities are explicitly *not* important for the adoption of the paradigm. The historical situations for which the intersection of industrial unrest and favorable elite mentalities was active are the adoption of scientific management techniques in the United States, and of human relations techniques in Britain.

The third additive line in expression [D.6] singles out two interesting historical situations in the adoption of human relations. Both in Britain (1950–60) and in Spain (1954–70), industrial conflict (or the threat of conflict) and output restriction on the shop floor represented problems that management had to deal with in some way or another. When human relations was used as a solution, however, the trades unions in Britain and the officialist vertical unions in Spain collaborated in the ideological campaign and even promoted the practical implementation of techniques. This paradoxical behavior invites speculation about the oligarchic tendencies of British trades unions and the lack of representativeness of the officialist vertical unions in Spain.

BIBLIOGRAPHY

This bibliography is organized under the following headings:

A. Theory and Methods (p. 335)

Countries Included in the Study

B. Comparative Analyses of Several Countries (p. 342)

C. United States (p. 349)

D. Germany (p. 363)

E. Spain (p. 375)

F. Great Britain (p. 386)

Other Countries

G. Brazil (p. 397)

H. France (p. 398)

I. Italy (p. 399)

J. Japan (p. 401)

K. Soviet Union (p. 403)

L. Other Countries (p. 405)

A. THEORY AND METHODS

Abbott, Andrew. 1983. "Sequences of social events: Concepts and methods for the analysis of order in social processes." *Historical Methods* 16(4) (Fall):129–147.

———. 1984. "Event sequence and event duration: Colligation and measurement." *Historical Methods* 17(4) (Fall):192–204.

———. 1988. *The System of Professions: An Essay on the Division of Expert Labor.* Chicago: University of Chicago Press.

Albrow, Martin. 1980. "The dialectic of science and values in the study of organizations." In Graeme Salaman and Kenneth Thompson, eds., *Control and Ideology in Organizations.* Cambridge, Massachusetts: MIT Press, pp. 278–296.

Aldrich, John H., and Forrest D. Nelson. 1984. *Linear Probability, Logit, and Probit Models.* Sage University Paper series on Quantitative Applications in the Social Sciences No. 07-045. Beverly Hills, California: Sage.

Alexander, Jeffrey C., and Bernhard Giesen. 1987. "From reduction to linkage: The long view of the micro-macro debate." In Jeffrey C. Alexander, Bernhard Giesen, Richard Münch, and Neil J. Smelser, eds., *The Micro-Macro Link.* Berkeley: University of California Press, pp. 1–42.

Arias, María Eugenia, and Mauro F. Guillén. 1993. "The transfer of organizational techniques across borders: Combining neoinstitutional and comparative perspectives." Working paper. Fontainebleau, France: INSEAD.

Avineri, Shlomo. 1968. *The Social & Political Thought of Karl Marx*. Cambridge: Cambridge University Press.

Barley, Stephen R., and Gideon Kunda. 1992. "Design and devotion: Surges of rational and normative ideologies of control in managerial discourse." *Administrative Science Quarterly* 37(3) (September):363–399.

Barley, Stephen R., Gordon W. Meyer, and Debra C. Gash. 1988. "Cultures of culture: Academics, practitioners, and the pragmatics of normative control." *Administrative Science Quarterly* 33(1) (March):24–60.

Bell, Daniel. [1960] 1988. *The End of Ideology: On the Exhaustion of Political Ideas in the Fifties*. Cambridge, Massachusetts: Harvard University Press.

———. 1973. *The Coming of Post-Industrial Society: A Venture in Social Forecasting*. New York: Basic.

———. [1976] 1978. *The Cultural Contradictions of Capitalism*. New York: Basic.

Bendix, Reinhard. [1956] 1974. *Work and Authority in Industry: Ideologies of Management in the Course of Industrialization*. With a new Introduction and Conclusion. Berkeley: University of California Press.

———. [1960] 1977. *Max Weber: An Intellectual Portrait*. Berkeley: University of California Press.

Berger, Peter L., and Thomas Luckmann. [1966] 1987. *The Social Construction of Reality: A Treatise in the Sociology of Knowledge*. New York: Anchor.

Blaug, Mark. 1975. "Kuhn versus Lakatos, or paradigms versus research programmes in the history of economics." *History of Political Economy* 7(4) (Winter):399–433.

Bourdieu, Pierre. [1972] 1977. *Outline of a Theory of Practice*. Cambridge: Cambridge University Press.

———. [1984] 1988. *Homo Academicus*. Stanford, California: Stanford University Press.

Braverman, Harry. 1974. *Labor and Monopoly Capital: The Degradation of Work in the Twentieth Century*. New York: Monthly Review Press.

Brint, Steven. 1990. "Rethinking the policy influence of experts: From general characterizations to analysis of variation." *Sociological Forum* 5(3): 361–385.

Burawoy, Michael. 1979a. *Manufacturing Consent: Changes in the Labor Process under Monopoly Capitalism*. Chicago: The University of Chicago Press.

———. 1979b. "The anthropology of industrial work." *Annual Review of Anthropology* 8:231–266.

———. 1983. "Between the labor process and the state: The changing face of factory regimes under advanced capitalism." *American Sociological Review* 48(5) (October):587–605.

———. 1985. *The Politcs of Production: Factory Regimes Under Capitalism and Socialism*. London: Verso.

Burrell, Gibson, and Gareth Morgan. [1979] 1985. *Sociological Paradigms and Organisational Analysis: Elements of the Sociology of Corporate Life*. Hants, England: Gower.

Carruthers, Bruce G., and Wendy Nelson Espeland. 1991. "Accounting for rationality: Double-entry bookkeeping and the rhetoric of economic rationality." *American Journal of Sociology* 97(1) (July):31–69.

Casson, Mark. 1982. *The Entrepreneur: An Economic Theory*. Totowa, New Jersey: Barnes & Noble.

Child, John. [1976] 1984. *Organization: A Guide to Problems and Practice*. 2d ed. London: Paul Chapman.

———. 1981. "Culture, contingency and capitalism in the cross-national study of organizations." *Research in Organizational Behavior* 3:303–356.

Clawson, Dan. 1980. *Bureaucracy and the Labor Process: The Transformation of U.S. Industry, 1860–1920*. New York: Monthly Review Press.

Clegg, Stewart R. 1990. *Modern Organizations: Organization Studies in the Postmodern World*. London: Sage Publications.

Cohen, Michael D., James G. March, and Johan P. Olsen. 1972. "A garbage can model of organizational choice." *Administrative Science Quarterly* 17(1) (March):1–25.

Collins, Randall. 1985. *Three Sociological Traditions*. New York: Oxford University Press.

Crane, Diana. 1972. *Invisible Colleges: Diffusion of Knowledge in Scientific Communities*. Chicago: University of Chicago Press.

Crozier, Michel. [1963] 1964. *The Bureaucratic Phenomenon*. Chicago: University of Chicago Press.

Dahl, Robert A. 1971. *Polyarchy: Participation and Opposition*. New Haven, Connecticut: Yale University Press.

Dibble, Vernon K. 1963. "Four types of inference from documents to events." *History and Theory* 3(2):203–221.

DiMaggio, Paul J. 1979. "Review essay: On Pierre Bourdieu." *American Journal of Sociology* 84(6) (May):1460–1474.

———. 1983. "State expansion and organizational fields." In Richard H. Hall and Robert E. Quinn, eds., *Organizational Theory and Public Policy*. Beverly Hills, California: Sage, pp. 147–161.

———. 1988. "Interest and agency in institutional theory." In Lynne G. Zucker, ed., *Institutional Patterns and Organizations: Culture and Environment*. Cambridge, Massachusetts: Ballinger, pp. 3–21.

DiMaggio, Paul J., and Walter W. Powell. 1983. "The Iron Cage revisited: Institutional isomorphism and collective rationality in organizational fields." *American Sociological Review* 48(2) (April):147–160.

Drass, Kriss A. 1988. *QCA 2.02: Qualitative Comparative Analysis*. Dallas, Texas: Department of Sociology, Southern Methodist University.

Du Boff, Richard B., and Edward S. Herman. 1980. "Alfred Chandler's new business history: A review." *Politics and Society* 10(1):87–110.

Edwards, Richard. 1979. *Contested Terrain: The Transformation of Work in the Twentieth Century*. New York: Basic.

Erikson, Kai T. 1970. "Sociology and the historical perspective." *American Sociologist* 5(4) (November):331–338.

Erikson, Kai, and Steven Peter Vallas, eds. 1990. *The Nature of Work: Sociological Perspectives.* New Haven, Connecticut: Yale University Press.

Etzioni, Amitai. 1964. *Modern Organizations.* Englewood Cliffs, New Jersey: Prentice-Hall.

Evans, Peter B., Dietrich Rueschemeyer, and Theda Skocpol, eds. 1985. *Bringing the State Back In.* Cambridge: Cambridge University Press.

Ferguson, Kathy E. 1984. *The Feminist Case Against Bureaucracy.* Philadelphia: Temple University Press.

Fienberg, Stephen E. [1977] 1980. *The Analysis of Cross-Classified Categorical Data.* 2d ed. Cambridge, Massachusetts: The MIT Press.

Foucault, Michel. [1969] 1980. *The Archaeology of Knowledge.* New York: Harper Torchbooks.

Freidson, Eliot. 1986. *Professional Powers: A Study of the Institutionalization of Formal Knowledge.* Chicago: University of Chicago Press.

Geertz, Clifford. 1973. *The Interpretation of Cultures: Selected Essays.* New York: Basic.

Geiger, Theodor. 1932. *Die soziale Schichtung des deutschen Volkes: Soziographischer Versuch auf Statistischer Grundlage.* Stuttgart: Ferdinand Enke.

Gerschenkron, Alexander. 1962. *Economic Backwardness in Historical Perspective: A Book of Essays.* Cambridge, Massachusetts: The Belknap Press of Harvard University Press.

Giddens, Anthony. 1979. *Central Problems in Social Theory.* London: Macmillan.

———. 1982. *Profiles and Critiques in Social Theory.* Berkeley: University of California Press.

———. 1984. *The Constitution of Society.* Berkeley: University of California Press.

Giedion, Siegfried. [1948] 1969. *Mechanization Takes Command: A Contribution to Anonymous History.* New York: W. W. Norton.

Goldman, Paul, and Donald R. Van Houten. 1977. "Managerial strategies and the worker: A Marxist analysis of bureaucracy." *Sociological Quarterly* 18 (Winter):108–125.

Habermas, Jürgen. [1968] 1971. "Technology and science as 'ideology.'" In *Toward a Rational Society: Student Protest, Science, and Politics.* London: Heinemann, pp. 81–122.

———. [1981] 1984. *The Theory of Communicative Action.* Vol. 1. *Reason and the Rationalization of Society.* Boston: Beacon.

———. [1981] 1987. *The Theory of Communicative Action.* Vol. 2. *Lifeworld and System: A Critique of Functionalist Reason.* Boston: Beacon.

Hall, Peter A. 1989. "Conclusion: The politics of Keynesian ideas." In Peter A. Hall, ed., *The Political Power of Economic Ideas: Keynesianism across Nations.* Princeton, New Jersey: Princeton University Press, pp. 361–391.

Hannan, Michael T., and John Freeman. 1989. *Organizational Ecology.* Cambridge, Massachusetts: Harvard University Press.

Hanushek, Eric A., and John E. Jackson. 1977. *Statistical Methods for Social Scientists*. Orlando, Florida: Academic.

Hechter, Michael. 1987. *Principles of Group Solidarity*. Berkeley: University of California Press.

Hirschman, Albert O. 1982. "Rival interpretations of market society: Civilizing, destructive, or feeble?" *Journal of Economic Literature* 20 (December): 1463–1484.

———. 1989. "How the Keynesian revolution was exported from the United States, and other comments." In Peter A. Hall, ed., *The Political Power of Economic Ideas: Keynesianism across Nations*. Princeton, New Jersey: Princeton University Press, pp. 347–359.

———. 1991. *The Rhetoric of Reaction: Perversity, Futility, Jeopardy*. Cambridge, Massachusetts: Harvard University Press.

Huczynski, Andrzej A. 1993. *Management Gurus: What Makes Them and How to Become One*. London: Routledge.

Jepperson, Ronald L., and John W. Meyer. 1991. "The public order and the construction of formal organizations." In Walter W. Powell and Paul J. DiMaggio, eds., *The New Institutionalism in Organizational Analysis*. Chicago: University of Chicago Press, pp. 204–231.

Johnston, J. 1984. *Econometric Methods*. 3d ed. New York: McGraw-Hill.

Kalleberg, Arthur L. 1966. "The logic of comparison: A methodological note on the comparative study of political systems." *World Politics* 19(1) (October):67–82.

Kamenka, Eugene. 1989. *Bureaucracy*. Oxford: Basil Blackwell.

Kuhn, Thomas S. [1962] 1970. *The Structure of Scientific Revolutions*. 2d ed., enlarged. Chicago: University of Chicago Press.

Larson, M. S. 1977. *The Rise of Professionalism*. Berkeley: University of California Press.

Laslett, Barbara. 1991. "Biography as historical sociology: The case of William Fielding Ogburn." *Theory and Society* 20:511–538.

Lenin, Vladimir I. [1916] 1939. *Imperialism: The Highest Stage of Capitalism*. New York: International Publishers.

Linz, Juan J. 1975. "Totalitarian and authoritarian regimes." In Fred I. Greenstein and Nelson W. Polsby, eds., *Handbook of Political Science*. Vol. 3. *Macropolitical Theory*. Reading, Massachusetts: Addison-Wesley, pp. 175–411.

———. 1978. *The Breakdown of Democratic Regimes: Crisis, Breakdown, and Reequilibration*. Baltimore, Maryland: The Johns Hopkins University Press.

Malone, Thomas W., and John F. Rockart. 1991. "Computers, networks and the corporation." *Scientific American* 254(3) (September):92–99.

Mannheim, Karl. [1927] 1952. "The problem of generations." In Paul Kecskemeti, ed., *Essays on the Sociology of Knowledge*. London: Routledge & Kegan Paul, pp. 276–322.

———. 1936. *Ideology and Utopia: An Introduction to the Sociology of Knowledge*. New York: Harvest.

Martins, Herminio. 1972. "The Kuhnian 'revolution' and its implications for sociology." In T. J. Nossiter, A. H. Hanson, and S. Rokkan, eds., *Imagination and Precision in the Social Sciences*. London: Faber & Faber, pp. 13–58.

Marx, Karl. [1845–1846] 1972. "The German ideology: Part I." In Robert C. Tucker, ed., *The Marx-Engels Reader*. New York: W. W. Norton, pp. 110–164.

———. [1867, 1885, 1894] 1967. *Capital: A Critique of Political Economy*. 3 vols. Edited by Friedrich Engels. New York: International Publishers.

Merton, Robert K. 1973. *The Sociology of Science: Theoretical and Empirical Investigations*. Edited and with an introduction by Norman W. Storer. Chicago: University of Chicago Press.

Meyer, John W., and Brian Rowan. 1977. "Institutionalized organizations: Formal structure as myth and ceremony." *American Journal of Sociology* 83(2) (September):340–363.

Mill, John Stuart. 1845. "The claims of labour." *Edinburgh Review* 81(164): 498–525.

———. [1881] 1950. "Of the four methods of experimental inquiry." In *Philosophy of Scientific Method*. Edited, with an introduction by Ernest Nagel. New York: Hafner, 211–233.

Olson, Mancur. 1965. *The Logic of Collective Action: Public Goods and the Theory of Groups*. Cambridge, Massachusetts: Harvard University Press.

———. 1982. *The Rise and Decline of Nations: Economic Growth, Stagflation, and Social Rigidities*. New Haven, Connecticut: Yale University Press.

Parsons, Talcott. [1951] 1964. *The Social System*. New York: Free Press.

Pérez-Díaz, Víctor M. 1978. *State, Bureaucracy and Civil Society: A Critical Discussion of the Political Theory of Karl Marx*. Atlantic Highlands, New Jersey: Humanities Press.

Perrow, Charles. [1972] 1986. *Complex Organizations: A Critical Essay*. 3d ed. New York: Random House.

———. 1991. "A society of organizations." *Theory and Society* 20(6) (December):725–762.

Powell, Walter W., and Paul J. DiMaggio, eds. 1991. *The New Institutionalism in Organizational Analysis*. Chicago: University of Chicago Press.

Ragin, Charles C. 1987. *The Comparative Method: Moving Beyond Qualitative and Quantitative Strategies*. Berkeley: University of California Press.

Ricoeur, Paul. 1986. *Lectures on Ideology and Utopia*. Edited by George H. Taylor. New York: Columbia University Press.

Roth, Guenther, and Wolfgang Schluchter. 1979. *Max Weber's Vision of History*. Berkeley: University of California Press.

Rueschemeyer, Dietrich. 1986. *Power and the Division of Labour*. Cambridge: Polity.

Sabel, Charles F. 1982. *Work and Politics: The Division of Labor in Industry*. Cambridge: Cambridge University Press.

Schein, Edgar H. [1965] 1988. *Organizational Psychology*. 3d ed. Englewood Cliffs, New Jersey: Prentice-Hall.

Schluchter, Wolfgang. [1979] 1981. *The Rise of Western Rationalism*. Trans. with an introduction by Guenther Roth. Berkeley: University of California Press.

Schmitter, Philippe C. 1974. "Still the century of corporatism?" In Frederick B. Pike and Thomas Stritch, eds., *The New Corporatism: Social-Political Structures in the Iberian World*. Notre Dame, Indiana: University of Notre Dame Press, pp. 85–131.

Schmitter, Philippe C., and Gerhard Lehmbruch, eds. 1979. *Trends Toward Corporatist Intermediation* Beverly Hills, California: Sage.

Schumpeter, Joseph A. [1934] 1949. *The Theory of Economic Development: An Inquiry into Profits, Capital, Credit, Interest, and the Business Cycle*. Trans. by Redvers Opie. Cambridge, Massachusetts: Harvard University Press.

———. [1942] 1976. *Capitalism, Socialism and Democracy*. With a new introduction by Tom Bottomore. New York: Harper Torchbooks.

Scott, W. Richard. [1981] 1987. *Organizations: Rational, Natural, and Open Systems*. 2d ed. Englewood Cliffs, New Jersey: Prentice-Hall.

Skocpol, Theda. 1979. *States and Social Revolutions: A Comparative Analysis of France, Russia, and China*. New York: Cambridge University Press.

Skocpol, Theda, ed. 1984. *Vision and Method in Historical Sociology*. New York: Cambridge University Press.

Smelser, Neil J. 1976. *Comparative Methods in the Social Sciences*. Englewood Cliffs, New Jersey: Prentice-Hall.

Stark, David. 1980. "Class struggle and the transformation of the labor process: A relational approach." *Theory and Society* 9(1) (January):29–88.

Stinchcombe, Arthur L. 1965. "Social structure and organizations." In James G. March, ed., *Handbook of Organizations*. Chicago: Rand McNally, pp. 142–193.

———. [1968] 1987. *Constructing Social Theories*. Chicago: University of Chicago Press.

———. 1978. *Theoretical Methods in Social History*. New York: Academic.

———. 1990. *Information and Organizations*. Berkeley: University of California Press.

Swidler, Ann. 1973. "The concept of rationality in the work of Max Weber." *Sociological Inquiry* 43(1):35–42.

———. 1986. "Culture in action: Symbols and strategies." *American Sociological Review* 51(2) (April):273–286.

Tafuri, Manfredo. [1973] 1976. *Architecture and Utopia: Design and Capitalist Development*. Cambridge, Massachusetts: MIT Press.

Tilly, Charles. 1984. *Big Structures, Large Processes, Huge Comparisons*. New York: Russell Sage Foundation.

Tolbert, Pamela S., and Lynne G. Zucker. 1983. "Institutional sources of change in the formal structure of organizations: The diffusion of civil service reform, 1880–1935." *Administrative Science Quarterly* 28(1) (March):22–39.

Tuma, Nancy Brandon, and Michael T. Hannan. 1984. *Social Dynamics: Models and Methods:* Orlando, Florida: Academic.

Useem, Michael. 1984. *The Inner Circle: Large Corporations and the Rise of Business Political Activity in the U.S. and U.K.* New York: Oxford University Press.

Wallerstein, Immanuel. 1974, 1980, 1988. *The Modern World-System.* 3 vols. New York: Academic Press.

Walton, John. 1973. "Standarized case comparison: Observations on method in comparative sociology." In Michael Armer and Allen D. Grimshaw, eds., *Comparative Social Research: Methodological Problems and Strategies.* New York: John Wiley & Sons, pp. 173–191.

Weber, Max. [1904] 1958. *The Protestant Ethic and the Spirit of Capitalism.* New York: Charles Scribner's Sons.

———. [1922] 1978. *Economy and Society: An Outline of Interpretive Sociology.* 2 vols. Edited by Guenther Roth and Claus Wittich. Berkeley: University of California Press.

Weber, Robert Philip. 1985. *Basic Content Analysis.* Sage University Paper series on Quantitative Applications in the Social Sciences No. 07-049. Beverly Hills, California: Sage.

Wilensky, Harold L. 1964. "The professionalization of everyone?" *American Journal of Sociology* 70(2) (September):137–158.

Wrong, Dennis H. 1961. "The oversocialized conception of man in modern sociology." *American Sociological Review* 26(2) (April):183–193.

———. [1979] 1988. *Power: Its Forms, Bases, and Uses.* With a new preface. Chicago: University of Chicago Press.

B. COMPARATIVE ANALYSES OF SEVERAL COUNTRIES

A. B. Osigweh, Yg., ed. 1989. *Organizational Science Abroad: Constraints and Perspectives.* New York: Plenum.

AEDJP (Asociación Española de Directores y Jefes de Personal). 1979. *La humanización del trabajo en Europa.* Madrid: Ibérico Europea.

Ahlström, Göran. 1982. *Engineers and Industrial Growth: Higher Technical Education and the Engineering Profession During the Nineteenth and Early Twentieth Centuries: France, Germany, Sweden, and England.* London: Croom Helm.

Alcock, Antony. 1971. *History of the International Labour Organisation.* London: Macmillan.

Alvarez Alvarez, José Luis. 1991. *The International Diffusion and Institutionalization of the New Entrepreneurship Movement: A Study in the Sociology of Organizational Knowledge.* Doctoral dissertation. Cambridge, Massachusetts: Committee of Business Studies of Harvard University.

Banham, Reyner. [1960] 1980. *Theory and Design in the First Machine Age.* 2d ed. Cambridge, Massachusetts: MIT Press.

Banks, Arthur S. 1971. *Cross-Polity Time-Series Data.* Cambridge, Massachusetts: MIT Press.

Benevolo, Leonardo. [1966] 1977. *History of Modern Architecture.* 2 vols. Cambridge, Massachusetts: MIT Press.

Brossard, Michel, and Marc Maurice. 1976. "Is there a universal model of organization structure?" *Internatioal Studies of Management and Organization* 6(3) (Fall):11–45.

Byrt, William. 1989. *Management Education: An International Survey*. New York: Routledge.

Carew, Anthony. 1987. *Labour under the Marshall Plan: The Politics of Productivity and the Marketing of Management Science*. Detroit: Wayne State University Press.

Chandler, Alfred D., Jr. 1990. *Scale and Scope: The Dynamics of Industrial Capitalism*. With the assistance of Takashi Hikino. Cambridge, Massachusetts: The Belknap Press of Harvard University Press.

Chandler, Alfred D., Jr., and Herman Daems, eds. 1980. *Managerial Hierarchies: Comparative Perspectives on the Rise of the Modern Industrial Enterprise*. Cambridge, Massachusetts: Harvard University Press.

Child, John, Michael Fores, Ian Glover, and Peter Lawrence. 1983. "A price to pay? Professionalism and work organization in Britain and West Germany." *Sociology* 17(1) (February):63–78.

Chipp, Herschel B., ed. 1968. *Theories of Modern Art: A Source Book by Artists and Critics*. Berkeley: University of California Press.

Clark, Peter A. 1987. *Anglo-American Innovation*. Berlin and New York: Walter de Gruyter.

Clegg, Hugh Armstrong. 1976. *Trade Unionism under Collective Bargaining: A Theory Based on Comparisons of Six Countries*. Oxford: Basil Blackwell.

Clutterbuck, David, and Stuart Crainer. 1990. *Makers of Management: Men & Women Who Changed the Business World*. London: Macmillan.

Cole, Robert E. 1979. *Work, Mobility, and Participation: A Comparative Study of American and Japanese Industry*. Berkeley: University of California Press.

———. 1985. "The macropolitics of organizational change: A comparative analysis of the spread of small-group activities." *Administrative Science Quarterly* 30(4) (December):560–585.

———. 1989. *Strategies for Learning: Small-Group Activities in American, Japanese, and Swedish Industry*. Berkeley: University of California Press.

Conrads, Ulrich, ed. [1964] 1970. *Programs and Manifestoes on 20th-Century Architecture*. Cambridge, Massachusetts: MIT Press.

De Bettignies, H.-C., and P. Lee Evans. 1977. "The cultural dimension of top executives' careers: A comparative analysis." In Theodore D. Weinshall, eds., *Culture and Management: Selected Readings*. Harmondsworth, Middlesex: Penguin, pp. 277–292.

Devinat, Paul. 1927. *Scientific Management in Europe*. International Labour Office Studies and Reports, Series B, No. 17. Geneva: International Labour Office.

DeVos, Ton. 1981. *U.S. Multinationals and Worker Participation in Management: The American Experience in the European Community*. Westport, Connecticut: Quorum.

Dore, Ronald. 1973. *British Factory, Japanese Factory: The Origins of National Diversity in Industrial Relations*. Berkeley: University of California Press.

Dresser, Horatio Willis. 1919. *A History of the New Thought Movement.* New York: Crowell.

Dunlop, John T., and Walter Galenson, eds. 1978. *Labor in the Twentieth Century.* New York: Academic.

Dyas, Gareth P., and Heinz T. Thanheiser. 1976. *The Emerging European Enterprise: Strategy and Structure in French and German Industry.* Boulder, Colorado: Westview.

Ebbinghaus, Angelika. 1984. *Arbeiter und Arbeitswissenschaft: Zur Entstehung der "Wissenschaftlichen Betriebsführung."* Opladen: Westdeutscher Verlag.

Elger, Tony, and Bill Schwarz. 1980. "Monopoly capitalism and the impact of Taylorism: Notes on Lenin, Gramsci, Braverman and Sohn-Rethel." In T. Nichols, ed., *Capital and Labour: A Marxist Primer.* London: Fontana, pp. 358–369.

EPA (European Productivity Agency). 1955. *Specialized Training in the Field of Work Study.* Paris: EPA.

———. 1956. *Human Relations in Industry.* Rome Conference. Paris: EPA.

———. 1960. *Social Research and Industry in Europe.* Paris: EPA.

Fehlauer, Rudolph, ed. 1962. *Die arbeitswissenschaftliche Ausbildung von Ingenieuren in europäischen Ländern.* Report of the European Productivity Agency. RKW Auslandsdienst Reports Series No. A23. Berlin: Beuth-Vertrieb.

Flora, Peter, and Jens Alber. 1981. "Modernization, democratization, and the development of welfare states in Western Europe." In Peter Flora and Arnold J. Heidenheimer, eds., *The Development of Welfare States in Western Europe.* New Brunswick, New Jersey: Transaction, pp. 37–80.

Flora, Peter, et al., eds. 1983. *State, Economy, and Society in Western Europe 1815–1975: A Data Handbook in Two Volumes.* Frankfurt: Campus; London: Macmillan; and Chicago: St. James Press.

Form, William H. 1969. "Occupational and social integration of automobile workers in four countries: A comparative study." *International Journal of Comparative Sociology* 10(1–2) (March and June):95–116.

Franko, Lawrence G. 1974. "The move toward a multidivisional structure in European organizations." *Administrative Science Quarterly* 19(4) (December):493–506.

———. 1976. *The European Multinationals: A Renewed Challenge to American and British Big Business.* Stamford, Connecticut: Greylock.

Fridenson, Patrick. 1978. "The coming of the assembly line to Europe." In Wolfgang Krohn, Edwin T. Layton, and Peter Weingart, eds., *The Dynamics of Science and Technology,* Vol. 2. *Sociology of the Sciences.* Boston: D. Reidel, pp. 159–175.

Glaser, William A. 1971. "Cross-national comparisons of the factory." *Journal of Comparative Administration* 3(1) (May):83–117.

Golomstock, Igor. 1990. *Totalitarian Art in the Soviet Union, the Third Reich, Fascist Italy and the People's Republic of China.* New York: Iconeditions, HarperCollins.

González, Richard F., and Claude McMillan, Jr. 1961. "The universality of

American management philosophy." *Journal of the Academy of Management* 4(1) (April):33–41.

Gospel, Howard F., and Craig R. Littler, eds. 1983. *Managerial Strategies and Industrial Relations: An Historical and Comparative Study*. London: Heinemann.

Granick, David. 1972. *Managerial Comparisons of Four Developed Countries: France, Britain, United States, Russia*. Cambridge, Massachusetts: MIT Press.

Haire, Mason, Edwin E. Ghiselli, and Lyman W. Porter. 1966. *Managerial Thinking: An International Study*. New York: John Wiley & Sons.

Handy, Charles, Colin Gordon, Ian Gow, and Collin Randlesome. 1988. *Making Managers*. London: Pitman.

Hannah, Leslie, ed. 1976. *Management Strategy and Business Development: An Historical and Comparative Study*. London: Macmillan.

Harbison, Frederick, and Charles A. Myers. 1959. *Management in the Industrial World: An International Analysis*. New York: McGraw-Hill.

Hardin, Bert. 1977. *The Professionalization of Sociology: A Comparative Study Germany-USA*. Frankfurt and New York: Campus.

Hauser, Arnold. [1951] 1960. *The Social History of Art*. Vol. 4. *Naturalism, Impressionism, the Film Age*. New York: Vintage.

Haydu, Jeffrey. 1988. *Between Craft and Class: Skilled Workers and Factory Politics in the United States and Britain, 1890–1922*. Berkeley: University of California Press.

Hickson, David J., et al. 1974. "The culture-free context of organization structure: A tri-national comparison." *Sociology* 8(1) (January):59–80.

Hofstede, Geert. 1980. *Culture's Consequences: International Differences in Work-Related Values*. Newbury Park, California: Sage.

Hofstede, Geert, and M. S. Kassem, eds. 1976. *European Contributions to Organization Theory*. Assen, The Netherlands: Van Gorcum.

Horváth, Dezsö. 1981. "Bureaucratic structures in cross-national perspective: A study of British, Japanese, and Swedish Firms." In Günter Dlugos and Klaus Weiermair, eds., *Management Under Differing Value Systems: Political, Social, and Economical Perspectives in a Changing World*. Berlin: Walter de Gruyter, pp. 537–563.

ILO (International Labor Office). 1938. *Historical Survey of the Contribution of the International Labor Organization to the Study of Management*. Geneva: ILO.

————. 1973. *Resultat des activités de conseils, de promotion et de diffusion des techniques modernes de management*. Geneva: ILO.

IMI (International Management Institute). 1930–1933. *Annual Report*. Years 1929, 1930, 1931, and 1932. Geneva: IMI.

Inkson, J. H. K., et al. 1970. "A comparison of organization structure and managerial roles: Ohio, U.S.A., and the Midlands, England." *Journal of Management Studies* 7(3) (October):347–363.

Jacoby, Henry. [1969] 1973. *The Bureaucratization of the World*. Trans. by Eveline L. Kanes. Berkeley: University of California Press.

Kassalow, Everett M. 1969. *Trade Unions and Industrial Relations: An International Comparison*. New York: Random House.

Katznelson, Ira, and Aristide R. Zolberg, eds. 1986. *Working-Class Formation: Nineteenth-Century Patterns in Western Europe and the United States*. Princeton, New Jersey: Princeton University Press.

Knights, David, Hugh Willmott, and David Collinson, eds. 1985. *Job Redesign: Critical Perspectives on the Labour Process*. Aldershot, England: Gower.

Kogut, Bruce. 1991. "National organizing principles of work and the erstwhile dominance of the American multinational corporation." Working paper 91-14. Philadelphia: Reginald H. Jones Center for Management Policy Strategy and Organization, The Wharton School.

Kogut, Bruce, and David Parkinson. 1991. "The diffusion of American organizing principles to Europe." Working paper. Philadelphia: The Wharton School.

Kornhauser, Arthur W. 1930. "Industrial psychology in England, Germany, and the United States." *Personnel Journal* 8(6) (April):421–434.

Kujawa, Duane. 1980. *The Labour Relations of United States Multinationals Abroad: Comparative and Prospective Views*. International Institute for Labour Studies Research Series No. 60. Geneva: International Institute for Labour Studies.

Lammers, Cornelis J., and David J. Hickson. 1979. *Organizations Alike and Unlike: International and Inter-Institutional Studies in the Sociology of Organizations*. London: Routledge & Kegan Paul.

Lane, Christel. 1989. *Management and Labour in Europe: The Industrial Enterprise in Germany, Britain, and France*. Hants, England: Edward Elgar.

Lazonick, William. 1990. *Competitive Advantage on the Shop Floor*. Cambridge, Massachusetts: Harvard University Press.

Leavitt, Harold J. 1957. "On the export of American management education." *Journal of Business* 30(3):153–161.

Leo XIII, Pope. [1891] 1943. "On the conditions of workers (*Rerum Novarum*)." In *Two Basic Encyclicals*. Washington, D.C.: The Catholic University of America Press, pp. 2–81.

Liesner, Thelma, ed. 1985. *Economic Statistics 1900–1983*. New York: Facts On File Publications.

———. 1989. *One Hundred Years of Economic Statistics*. London: The Economist Publications.

Lipset, Seymour Martin, and Reinhard Bendix. [1959] 1967. *Social Mobility in Industrial Society*. Berkeley: University of California Press.

Littler, Craig R. 1982a. *The Development of the Labour Process in Capitalist Societies: A Comparative Study of the Transformation of Work Organization in Britain, Japan, and the USA*. London: Heinemann.

Locke, Robert R. 1984. *The End of the Practical Man: Entrepreneurship and Higher Education in Germany, France, and Great Britain, 1880–1940*. Greenwich, Connecticut: Jai Press.

———. 1989. *Management and Higher Education Since 1940: The Influence of America and Japan on West Germany, Great Britain, and France.* Cambridge: Cambridge University Press.

Maier, Charles S. 1970. "Between Taylorism and technocracy: European ideologies and the vision of industrial productivity in the 1920s." *Journal of Contemporary History* 5(2):27–61. Reprinted in *In Search of Stability: Explorations in Historical Political Economy.* Cambridge, England: Cambridge University Press, pp. 22–53.

————. 1987. "Postscript: Ideologies of industrial management since the Depression." In *In Search of Stability: Explorations in Historical Political Economy.* Cambridge: Cambridge University Press, pp. 53–69.

McLeod, Mary. 1983. "Architecture or revolution: Taylorism, technocracy, and social change." *Art Journal* 43(2) (Summer):132–147.

McMillan, Charles J. 1973. "The structure of work organization across societies." *Academy of Management Journal* 16(4) (December):555–569.

Maurice, Marc, Arndt Sorge, and Malcolm Warner. 1980. "Societal differences in organizing manufacturing units: A comparison of France, West Germany, and Great Britain." *Organization Studies* 1(1):59–86.

Meigniez, R. 1962. *Evaluation of Supervisory and Management Training Methods.* Paris: OECD.

Merkle, Judith A. 1980. *Management and Ideology: The Legacy of the International Scientific Management Movement.* Berkeley: University of California Press.

Mitchell, B. R. 1971. "Statistical Appendix, 1700–1914." *The Fontana Economic History of Europe.* Vol. 4. London: Collins.

————. 1980. *European Historical Statistics 1750–1975.* 2d ed., revised. New York: Facts on File.

Montmollin, Maurice de, and Olivier Pastré, eds. 1984. *Le Taylorisme: Actes du colloque international sur le taylorisme organisé par l'Université de Paris-XIII, 2–4 mai 1983.* Paris: Éditions la Découverte.

Moody, Joseph N., ed. 1953. *Church and Society: Catholic Social and Political Thought and Movements 1789–1950.* New York: Arts.

Mosson, Thomas M. 1965. *Management Education in Five European Countries.* London: Business Administration.

Nath, Raghu. 1968. "A methodological review of cross-cultural management research." *International Social Science Information* 20(1):35–62.

Nath, Raghu, ed. 1988. *Comparative Management: A Regional View.* Cambridge, Massachusetts: Ballinger.

Negandhi, Anant R. 1983. "Cross-cultural management research: Trend and future directions." *Journal of International Business Studies* 14(2) (Fall): 17–28.

Neuhaus, Richard John. 1992. *Doing Well and Doing Good: The Challenge to the Christian Capitalist.* New York: Doubleday.

Novak, Michael. 1993. *The Catholic Ethic and the Spirit of Capitalism.* New York: Free Press.

OECD (Organization for Economic Cooperation and Development). 1962.

Register of Research in the Human Sciences Applied to Problems of Work and Directory of Relevant Research Institutions. Paris: OECD.

———. 1963. *Problèmes et perspective de la formation et du perfectionnement à l'administration des entreprises*. Paris: OECD.

Pichierri, Angelo. 1978. "Diffusion and crisis of scientific management in European industry." In S. Giner and M. S. Archer, eds., *Contemporary Europe*. London: Routledge & Kegan Paul, pp. 55–73.

Piore, Michael J., and Charles F. Sabel. 1984. *The Second Industrial Divide: Possibilities for Prosperity*. New York: Basic.

Pius XI, Pope. [1931] 1943. "Forty years after on reconstructing social order (*Quadragesimo Anno*)." In *Two Basic Encyclicals*. Washington, D.C.: The Catholic University of America Press, pp. 82–195.

Poggioli, Renato. [1962] 1968. *The Theory of the Avant-Garde*. Cambridge, Massachusetts: The Belknap Press of Harvard University Press.

Pugh, D. S., D. J. Hickson, and C. R. Hinings. 1964. *Writers on Organizations: An Introduction*. London: Hutchinson.

———. [1964] 1971. *Writers on Organizations*. 2d ed. Harmondsworth, Middlesex: Penguin.

———. [1964] 1983. *Writers on Organizations*. 3d ed. Harmondsworth, Middlesex: Penguin.

Pugh, D. S., and D. J. Hickson. [1964] 1989. *Writers on Organizations*. 4th ed. London: Penguin.

Rabinbach, Anson. 1990. *The Human Motor: Energy, Fatigue, and the Origins of Modernity*. New York: Basic.

Rogers, Jane. 1988. *MBA: The Best Business Tool? A Guide to British and European Business Schools*. Special Report No. 1154. London: The Economist Publications.

Rokkan, Stein. 1970. *Citizens, Elections, Parties: Approaches to the Comparative Study of the Processes of Development*. Oslo: Universitetsforlaget.

Rybczynski, Witold. 1992. "Collapsing modernism." *The New York Review of Books* (February 13):12–15.

Schmidt, Herbert B. 1956. "Developing business leadership in Europe." *Business Horizons* (December):69–81.

Slomp, Hans. 1990. *Labor Relations in Europe: A History of Issues and Developments*. New York: Greenwood.

Sorge, Arndt, and Malcolm Warner. 1986. *Comparative Factory Organisation: An Anglo-German Comparison of Manufacturing, Management, and Manpower*. Aldershot, Hants, England: Gower.

Stopford, John M., and Louis T. Wells, Jr. 1972. *Managing the Multinational Enterprise: Organization of the Firm and Ownership of the Subsidiaries*. New York: Basic.

Sturmthal, Adolf. 1964. *Workers Councils: A Study of Workplace Organization on Both Sides of the Iron Curtain*. Cambridge, Massachusetts: Harvard University Press.

———. 1972. *Comparative Labor Movements: Ideological Roots and Institutional Development*. Belmont, California: Wadsworth.

Thimm, Alfred L. 1980. *The False Promise of Codetermination: The Changing Nature of European Workers' Participation*. Lexington, Massachusetts: Lexington Books.

UNCTC (United Nations Centre on Transnational Corporations). 1983. *Salient Features and Trends in Foreign Direct Investment*. New York: United Nations.

Urwick, Lyndall. 1956. *The Golden Book of Management: A Historical Record of the Life and Work of Seventy Pioneers*. London: Newman Neame.

Urwick, Lyndall, and E. F. L. Brech. 1945. *The Making of Scientific Management*. Vol. 1. *Thirteen Pioneers*. London: Management Publications Trust.

Viteles, Morris S. 1923. "Psychology in business—in England, France and Germany." *Annals of the American Academy of Political and Social Science* 110(199) (November):207–220.

Webber, Ross A., ed. 1969. *Culture and Management: Text and Readings in Comparative Management*. Homewood, Illinois: Irwin.

Whitley, Richard. 1992. *Business Systems in East Asia: Firms, Markets and Societies*. London: Sage.

Whitley, R., A. Thomas, and J. Marceau. 1981. *Masters of Business? Business Schools and Business Graduates in Britain and France*. London: Tavistock.

Womack, James P., Daniel T. Jones, and Daniel Roos. [1990] 1991. *The Machine That Changed the World: The Story of Lean Production*. New York: Harper Perennial.

Wood, Stephen, and John Kelly. [1982] 1988. "Taylorism, responsible autonomy and management strategy." In R. E. Pahl, ed., *On Work: Historical, Comparative & Theoretical Approaches*. Oxford: Basil Blackwell, pp. 175–189.

C. UNITED STATES

Adler, Paul S. 1993. "Time-and-motion regained." *Harvard Business Review* 71(1) (January):97–108.

Akin, William E. 1977. *Technocracy and the American Dream: The Technocrat Movement, 1900–1941*. Berkeley: University of California Press.

Allen, George Howard, ed. 1950. *Individual Initiative in Business*. Cambridge, Massachusetts: Harvard University Press.

Allen, Louis A. 1958. *Management and Organization*. New York: McGraw-Hill.

AMA (American Management Association). 1946. *Annual Report 1946*. New York: AMA.

———. 1948. *25 Years of Management Progress*. New York: AMA.

American Federationist. 1935. "A. F. L. report on the Bedaux system." *American Federationist* 42(9) (September):936–943.

Amon, Richard F., et al. 1958. *Management Consulting*. Cambridge, Massachusetts: Graduate School of Business Administration, Harvard University.

Appley, Lawrence A. [1956] 1963. *The Management Evolution*. New York: American Management Association.

Back, Kurt W. 1972. *Beyond Words: The Story of Sensitivity Training and the Encounter Movement*. New York: Russell Sage Foundation.

Banham, Reyner. 1986. *A Concrete Atlantis: U.S. Industrial Building and European Modern Architecture*. Cambridge, Massachusetts: MIT Press.

Banta, Martha. 1993. *Taylored Lives: Narrative Productions in the Age of Taylor, Veblen, and Ford*. Chicago: University of Chicago Press.

Barber, Bernard. 1970. "L. J. Henderson: An introduction." In *L. J. Henderson On the Social System*. Chicago: University of Chicago Press, pp. 1–53.

Baritz, Loren. 1960. *The Servants of Power: A History of the Use of Social Science in American Industry*. Middletown, Connecticut: Wesleyan University Press.

Barnard, Chester I. 1938. *The Functions of the Executive*. Cambridge, Massachusetts: Harvard University Press.

Baron, James N., Frank R. Dobbin, and P. Devereaux Jennings. 1986. "War and peace: The evolution of modern personnel administration in U. S. industry." *American Journal of Sociology* 92(2) (September):350–383.

Baron, James N., P. Devereaux Jennings, and Frank R. Dobbin. 1988. "Mission control? The development of personnel systems in U. S. industry." *American Sociological Review* 53(4) (August):497–514.

Bedaux, Charles E. 1917. *The Bedaux Efficiency Course for Industrial Application*. Grand Rapids, Michigan: The Bedaux Company.

Bedaux Company. 1942. *More Production, Better Morale: A Program for American Industry*. New York: The Bedaux Company.

Bellah, Robert N., Richard Madsen, William M. Sullivan, Ann Swidler, and Steven M. Tipton. [1985] 1986. *Habits of the Heart: Individualism and Commitment in American Life*. New York: Perennial Library.

Bendix, Reinhard, and Lloyd H. Fisher. 1949. "The perspectives of Elton Mayo." *Review of Economics and Statistics* 31(4) (November 1949): 312–319.

Berg, David N., ed. 1992. *Keeping the Faith: The Clinical Tradition in Organizational Behavior at Yale, 1962–1988*. Woodbridge, Connecticut: The Berg Group.

Biggers, John D., et al. 1949. *Human Relations in Modern Business: A Guide for Action Sponsored by American Business Leaders*. New York: Prentice-Hall.

Blake, Robert R., and Jane S. Mouton. 1964. *The Managerial Grid*. Houston: Gulf.

Blau, Peter M., and W. Richard Scott. 1962. *Formal Organizations: A Comparative Approach*. Scranton, Pennsylvania: Chandler Publishing.

Blau, Peter M., and Richard Schoenherr. 1971. *The Structure of Organizations*. New York: Basic.

Blumberg, Paul. [1968] 1973. *Industrial Democracy: The Sociology of Participation*. New York: Schocken.

Bornemann, A. 1957. "The development of economics and administration in the school of business." *Journal of Business* 30(1):131–140.

Brandes, Stuart D. [1970] 1976. *American Welfare Capitalism 1880–1940*. Chicago: University of Chicago Press.

Brody, David. 1980. *Workers in Industrial America: Essays on the Twentieth Century Struggle.* New York: Oxford University Press.

Bureau of Economic Analysis. 1972. *U. S. Direct Investments Abroad 1966. Part II: Investment Position, Financial and Operating Data. Group 2. Preliminary Report on Foreign Affiliates of U. S. Manufacturing Industries.* Springfield, Virginia: National Technical Information Service, U. S. Department of Commerce.

Burnham, James. 1941. *The Managerial Revolution: What Is Happening in the World.* New York: John Day.

Bursk, Edward C., ed. 1949. *Business and Religion: A New Depth Dimension in Management.* New York: Harper & Brothers.

————. 1950. *Human Relations for Management: The Newer Perspective.* New York: Harper & Brothers.

Bursk, Edward C., and Donald T. Clark. 1949. "Reading habits of business executives." *Harvard Business Review* 27(3) (May):330–345.

Business Week. 1980. "Corporate culture." *Business Week* (October 27): 148–160.

————. 1992. "Quality: The Key to Growth for Small Companies and for America." *Business Week* (November 30):66–75.

Callahan, Raymond E. 1962. *Education and the Cult of Efficiency: A Study of the Social Forces That Have Shaped the Administration of the Public Schools.* Chicago: University of Chicago Press.

Calvert, Monte A. 1967. *The Mechanical Engineer in America, 1830–1910: Professional Cultures in Conflict.* Baltimore: Johns Hopkins University Press.

Chandler, Alfred D., Jr. 1962. *Strategy and Structure: Chapters in the History of the American Industrial Enterprise.* Cambridge, Massachusetts: MIT Press.

————. 1977. *The Visible Hand: The Managerial Revolution in American Business.* Cambridge, Massachusetts: The Belknap Press of Harvard University Press.

Chase, Stuart. 1948. *The Proper Study of Mankind: An Inquiry into the Science of Human Relations.* New York: Harper & Brothers.

Chase, Stuart, Stanley H. Ruttenberg, Edwin G. Nourse, and William B. Given, Jr. 1950. *The Social Responsibility of Management.* New York: School of Commerce, Accounts, and Finance, New York University.

Cheit, E. F. 1985. "Business schools and their critics." *California Management Review* 27(3):43–62.

Christy, Jim. 1984. *The Price of Power: A Biography of Charles Eugène Bedaux.* Toronto: Doubleday.

Committee on Elimination of Waste in Industry. 1921. *Waste in Industry.* Washington, D. C.: Federation of American Engineering Societies.

Copeland, M. T. 1955. *And Mark an Era: The story of the Harvard Business School.* Boston: Little, Brown.

Cyert, Richard M., and James G. March. 1963. *A Behavioral Theory of the Firm.* Englewood Cliffs, New Jersey: Prentice-Hall.

Dahl, Robert A., Mason Haire, and Paul F. Lazarsfeld. 1959. *Social Science*

Research on Business: Product and Potential. New York: Columbia University Press.

Dale, Ernest. 1949. *Greater Productivity Through Labor-Management Cooperation: Analysis of Company and Union Experience.* New York: American Management Association.

———. [1952] 1959. *Planning and Developing the Company Organization Structure.* New York: American Management Association.

———. 1960. *The Great Organizers.* New York: McGraw-Hill.

———. 1965. *Management: Theory and Practice.* New York: McGraw-Hill.

———. 1967. *Organization.* New York: American Management Association.

Dale, Ernest, and L. C. Michelon. 1966. *Modern Management Methods.* Cleveland, Ohio: World Publishing.

Davis, Mike. 1975. "The stop watch and the wooden shoe: Scientific management and the Industrial Workers of the World." *Radical America* 8(6) (January–February):69–95.

Deal, Terrence E., and Allan A. Kennedy. 1982. *Corporate Cultures: The Rites and Rituals of Corporate Life.* Reading, Massachusetts: Addison-Wesley.

Deming, W. Edwards. [1982] 1986. *Out of the Crisis.* Cambridge, Massachusetts: MIT Center for Advanced Engineering Study.

Department of Commerce. 1971. *U. S. Direct Investments Abroad 1966. Part I: Balance of Payments Data.* Washington, D. C.: Government Printing Office.

Dertouzos, Michael L., Richard K. Lester, and Robert M. Solow. 1989. *Made In America: Regaining the Productive Edge.* Cambridge, Massachusetts: MIT Press.

Diemer, Hugo. 1904. "A bibliography of works management." *Engineering Magazine* 27(4) (July):626–642.

Dobb, Maurice. [1928] 1959. *Wages.* Rev. ed. Cambridge: Cambridge University Press.

Donald, W. J., ed. 1931. *Handbook of Business Administration.* New York: McGraw-Hill, for the American Management Association.

Donham, W. B. 1922. "Business teaching by the case system." *American Economic Review* 12(1):53–65.

Dos Passos, John. [1936] 1979. *The Big Money.* Third book of the trilogy *U.S.A.* New York: New American Library.

Drucker, Peter F. [1946] 1972. *Concept of the Corporation.* Rev. ed. New York: New American Library.

———. 1954. *The Practice of Management.* New York: Harper & Row.

Dubin, Robert, George C. Homans, Floyd C. Mann, and Delbert C. Miller. 1965. *Leadership and Productivity: Some Facts of Industrial Life.* San Francisco: Chandler.

Edwards, John R. 1912. "The fetishism of scientific management." *Journal of the American Society of Naval Engineers* 24(2) (May):355–416.

Emerson, Harrington. 1912. *The Twelve Principles of Efficiency.* New York: The Engineering Magazine.

Etzioni, Amitai, ed. 1961. *Complex Organizations: A Sociological Reader.* New York: Holt, Rinehart and Winston.

Ewen, Stuart. 1976. *Captains of Consciousness: Advertising and the Social Roots of the Consumer Culture*. New York: McGraw-Hill.

Fisher, Anne B. 1991. "Morale crisis." *Fortune* (November 18):70–80.

Fleming, Donald, and Bernard Bailyn. 1969. *The Intellectual Migration: Europe and America, 1930–1960*. Cambridge, Massachusetts: The Belknap Press of Harvard University Press.

Fligstein, Neil. 1985. "The spread of the multidivisional form among large firms, 1919–1979." *American Sociological Review* 50(3) (June):377–391.

———. 1987. "The intraorganizational power struggle: The rise of finance personnel to top leadership in large corporations, 1919–1979." *American Sociological Review* 52(1) (February):44–58.

———. 1990. *The Transformation of Corporate Control*. Cambridge, Massachusetts: Harvard University Press.

FMM (Factory Management and Maintenance). 1946a. "How management in 100 plants gets information to workers." *Factory Management and Maintenance* 104(7) (August):114–117.

———. 1946b. "Wage incentive practices in 65 plants." *Factory Management and Maintenance* 104(9) (September):126–128.

Follett, Mary Parker. 1918. *The New State: Group Organization, the Solution of Popular Government*. New York: Longmans, Green.

———. 1924. *Creative Experience*. New York: Longmans, Green.

———. 1942. *Dynamic Administration: The Collected Papers of Mary Parker Follett*. Edited by Henry C. Metcalf, and L. Urwick. New York: Harper & Brothers.

Ford, Henry. 1923. *My Life and Work*. With Samuel Crowther. Garden City, New York: Doubleday.

———. 1926. "Henry Ford expounds mass production." *The New York Times* (September 19), section 10, p. 1.

Fortune. 1953. "The Crown Princes of Business." *Fortune* 48 (October):150–153, 258–268.

Franke, Richard Herbert. 1979. "The Hawthorne experiments: Re-view." *American Sociological Review* 44:861–867.

———. 1980. "Worker productivity at Hawthorne (Reply to Schlaifer)." *American Sociological Review* 45:1006–1027.

Franke, Richard Herbert, and James D. Kaul. 1978. "The Hawthorne experiments: First statistical interpretation." *American Sociological Review* 43(5) (October):623–643.

Fromm, Erich. 1957. "Man is not a thing." *The Saturday Review* (March 16):9–11.

Gabor, Andrea. 1990. *The Man Who Discovered Quality: How W. Edwards Deming Brought the Quality Revolution to America*. New York: Times Books/Random House.

Gantt, Henry L. 1911. *Work, Wages, and Profits: Their Influence on the Cost of Living*. New York: The Engineering Magazine.

———. 1916. *Industrial Leadership*. Address delivered in the Page Lecture Series, 1915, Before the Senior Class of the Sheffield Scientific School, Yale University. New Haven, Connecticut: Yale University Press.

————. 1919. *Organizing for Work*. New York: Harcourt, Brace.

Garner, S. P. 1968. "Highlights in the development of cost accounting." In Michael Hatfield, ed., *Contemporary Studies in the Evolution of Accounting Thought*. Belmont, California: Stevenson, pp. 210–221.

George, Claude S., Jr. 1968. *The History of Management Thought*. Englewood Cliffs, New Jersey: Prentice-Hall.

Gilbreth, Frank B. 1909. *Bricklaying System*. New York: Myron C. Clark.

————. 1911. *Motion Study: A Method for Increasing the Efficiency of the Workman*. With an introduction by Robert Thurston Kent. New York: D. Van Nostrand.

————. 1912. *Primer of Scientific Management*. With an introduction by Louis D. Brandeis. New York: D. Van Nostrand.

Gilbreth, Frank B., and Lillian M. Gilbreth. 1917. *Applied Motion Study: A Collection of Papers on the Efficient Method to Industrial Preparedness*. New York: Sturgis & Walton.

————. 1918. *Fatigue Study: The Elimination of Humanity's Greatest Unnecessary Waste. A First Step in Motion Study*. New York: Sturgis & Walton.

Gilbreth, Lillian M. 1914. *The Psychology of Management: The Function of the Mind in Determining, Teaching and Installing Methods of Least Waste*. New York: Sturgis & Walton.

Gillespie, Richard. 1991. *Manufacturing Knowledge: A History of the Hawthorne Experiments*. Cambridge: Cambridge University Press.

Given, William B., Jr. 1949. *Bottom-Up Management: People Working Together*. New York: Harper & Brothers.

Glover, John Desmond, and Gerald A. Simon, eds. 1976. *Chief Executive's Handbook*. Homewood, Illinois: Dow Jones-Irwin.

Gordon, R. A., and J. E. Howell. 1959. *Higher Education for Business*. New York: Columbia University Press.

Gouldner, Alvin W. 1954. *Patterns of Industrial Bureaucracy*. New York: Free Press.

Griswold, Alfred Whitney. 1933. *The American Gospel of Success*. Unpublished Ph.D. diss. New Haven, Connecticut: Yale University Graduate School.

————. 1934a. "Three puritans on prosperity." *New England Quarterly* 7(3) (September):475–493.

————. 1934b. "New Thought: A cult of success." *American Journal of Sociology* 40(3) (November):309–318.

Gulick, Luther. 1937. "Notes on the theory of organization." In Luther Gulick and Lyndall Urwick, eds., *Papers on the Science of Administration*. New York: Institute of Public Administration, Columbia University, pp. 1–45.

Gutman, Herbert G. 1973. "Work, culture, and society in industrializing America, 1815–1919." *American Historical Review* 78 (June):531–588.

Haber, Samuel. 1964. *Efficiency and Uplift: Scientific Management in the Progressive Era 1890–1920*. Chicago: University of Chicago Press.

Haire, Mason, ed. 1962. *Organization Theory in Industrial Practice*. New York: John Wiley & Sons.

Hedrick, Joan D. 1982. *Solitary Comrade: Jack London and His Work*. Chapel Hill: The University of North Carolina Press.

Herzberg, Frederick. [1966] 1973. *Work and the Nature of Man*. New York: New American Library.

Herzberg, Frederick, B. Mausner, and B. Snyderman, 1959. *The Motivation to Work*. 2d ed. New York: John Wiley & Sons.

Homans, George Caspar. 1949. "Some corrections." *Review of Economics and Statistics* 31(4) (November 1949):319–321.

———. 1950. *The Human Group*. New York: Harcourt, Brace & World.

———. [1961] 1974. *Social Behavior: Its Elementary Forms*. New York: Harcourt Brace Jovanovich.

———. 1984. *Coming to My Senses: The Autobiography of a Sociologist*. New Brunswick, New Jersey: Transaction.

Hoslett, Schuyler Dean, ed. 1946. *Human Factors in Management*. Parkville, Missouri: Park College Press.

Hotchkiss, W. E. 1920. "The basic elements and their proper balance in the curriculum of a collegiate business school." *Journal of Political Economy* 28(2):89–112.

Hounshell, David A. 1984. *From the American System to Mass Production 1800–1932: The Development of Manufacturing Technology in the United States*. Baltimore: Johns Hopkins University Press.

Hoxie, Robert Franklin. 1915. *Scientific Management and Labor*. New York: D. Appleton.

Iron Age. 1946. "Executive poll shows human relations to be prime responsibility." *The Iron Age* 158 (September 19):153–154.

Jacoby, Sanford M. 1983. "Union-management cooperation in the United States: Lessons from the 1920s." *Industrial and Labor Relations Review* 37(1) (October):18–33.

———. 1985. *Employing Bureaucracy: Managers, Unions, and the Transformation of Work in American Industry, 1900–1945*. New York: Columbia University Press.

Jacoby, Sanford M., ed. 1991. *Masters to Managers: Historical and Comparative Perspectives on American Employers*. New York: Columbia University Press.

Jelinek, Mariann. 1980. "Toward systematic management: Alexander Hamilton Church." *Business History Review* 54(1) (Spring):63–79.

Jenks, Leland H. 1960. "Early phases of the management movement." *Administrative Science Quarterly* 5(3) (December):421–447.

Johnson, Robert Wood. 1947. *People Must Live and Work Together or Forfeit Freedom*. Garden City, New York: Doubleday.

———. 1949. *Robert Johnson Talks It Over*. New Brunswick, New Jersey: Johnson & Johnson.

Jones, Stephen R. G. 1990. "Worker interdependence and output: The Hawthorne studies reevaluated." *American Sociological Review* 55(2) (April): 176–190.

———. 1992. "Was there a Hawthorne effect?" *American Journal of Sociology* 98(3) (November):451–468.

Jordy, William H. [1982] 1986. *The Impact of European Modernism in the Mid-Twentieth Century*. Vol. 5 of *American Buildings and Their Architects*. New York: Oxford University Press.

Kahn, Robert L., and Elise Boulding, eds. 1964. *Power and Conflict in Organizations.* London: Tavistock.

Kakar, Sudhir. 1970. *Frederick Taylor: A Study in Personality and Innovation.* Cambridge, Massachusetts: MIT Press.

Kanter, Rosabeth Moss. [1983] 1984. *The Change Masters: Innovation & Entrepreneurship in the American Corporation.* New York: Touchstone.

Katz, Harry C., Thomas A. Kochan, and Kenneth R. Gobeille. 1983. "Industrial relations performance, economic performance, and QWL Programs: An interplant analysis." *Industrial and Labor Relations Review* 37(1) (October):3–17.

Koontz, H. 1961. "The management theory jungle." *Academy of Management Journal* 4(3):174–188.

———. 1980. "The management theory jungle revisited." *Academy of Management Review* 5(2):175–187.

Kornhauser, Arthur. 1946. "Are public opinion polls fair to organized labor?" *Public Opinion Quarterly* 10(4) (Winter):484–500.

———. 1949. "The contribution of psychology to industrial relations research." In Industrial Relations Research Association, *Proceedings of the First Annual Meeting,* Cleveland, Ohio, December 29–30, 1948, pp. 172–188.

Kornhauser, Arthur, Robert Dubin, and Arthur M. Ross, eds. 1954. *Industrial Conflict.* New York: McGraw-Hill.

Landsberger, Henry A. 1958. *Hawthorne Revisited.* Ithaca, New York: Cornell University Press.

Lane, Robert E. 1962. *Political Ideology: Why the American Common Man Believes What He Does.* New York: Free Press of Glencoe.

Lawrence, Paul R., and Jay W. Lorsch. [1967] 1969. *Organization and Environment: Managing Differentiation and Integration.* Homewood, Illinois: Richard D. Irwin.

Layton, Edwin T., Jr. 1971. *The Revolt of the Engineers: Social Responsibility and the American Engineering Profession.* Cleveland, Ohio: The Press of Case Western Reserve University.

———. 1975. "The diffusion of scientific management and mass production from the U. S. in the twentieth century." *Proceedings of the 14th International Congress on the History of Science.* Tokyo: Science Council of Japan, pp. 377–386.

Lazarsfeld, Paul F., William H. Sewell, and Harold L. Wilensky, eds. 1967. *The Uses of Sociology.* New York: Basic.

Lewis, Geoff. 1988. "Big changes at Big Blue." *Business Week* (February 15):92–98.

Likert, Rensis. 1961. *New Patterns of Management.* New York: McGraw-Hill.

Lipset, Seymour Martin, ed. 1986. *Unions in Transition: Entering the Second Century.* San Francisco: Institute for Contemporary Studies Press.

Litterer, Joseph A. 1961. "Systematic management: The search for order and integration." *Business History Review* 35(4) (Winter):461–476.

———. 1963. "Systematic management: Design for organizational recoupling in American manufacturing firms." *Business History Review* 37(4) (Winter):369–391.

Littler, Craig R. 1978. "Understanding Taylorism." *British Journal of Sociology* 29(2) (June):185–202.

Loewy, Raymond. 1979. *Industrial Design*. Woodstock, New York: Overlook.

Lorsch, Jay W., and Stephen A. Allen, III. 1973. *Managing Diversity and Interdependence: An Organizational Study of Multidivisional Firms*. Boston: Division of Research, Graduate School of Business Administration, Harvard University.

McCraw, Thomas K., ed. 1988. *The Essential Alfred Chandler: Essays Toward a Historical Theory of Big Business*. Boston: Harvard Business School Press.

McGregor, Douglas. 1960. *The Human Side of Enterprise*. New York: McGraw-Hill.

McKelvey, Jean Trepp. 1952. *AFL Attitudes toward Production 1900–1932*. Cornell Studies in Industrial and Labor Relations. Vol. 2. Ithaca, New York: Cornell University Press.

Mann, Roland, ed. 1971. *The Arts of Top Management: A McKinsey Anthology*. New York: McGraw-Hill.

March, James G., and Herbert A. Simon. 1958. *Organizations*. New York: John Wiley.

Marrow, Alfred J. 1969. *The Practical Theorist: The Life and Work of Kurt Lewin*. New York: Basic Books.

Marshall, L. C. 1917. "A balanced curriculum in business education." *Journal of Political Economy* 25(1):84–105.

Maslow, Abraham. 1954. *Motivation and Personality*. New York: Harper.

Mason, Ralph L. 1949. "Experiences with employee opinion surveys." *Advanced Management* 14(2) (September):98–100.

Maynard, H. B., ed. 1960. *Top Management Handbook*. New York: McGraw-Hill.

Mayo, Elton. 1933. *The Human Problems of an Industrial Civilization*. New York: Macmillan. There is a reprint edition (Salem, New Hampshire: Ayer, 1977).

———. 1945. *The Social Problems of an Industrial Civilization*. Boston: Division of Research, Graduate School of Business Administration, Harvard University. There is a reprint edition (Salem, New Hampshire: Ayer, 1988).

Meikle, Jeffrey L. 1979. *Twentieth Century Limited: Industrial Design in America, 1925–1939*. Philadelphia: Temple University Press.

Melman, Seymour. 1951. "The rise of administrative overhead in the manufacturing industries of the United States 1899–1947." *Oxford Economic Papers* 3(1) (February):62–93.

Mills, C. Wright. 1949. "The contribution of sociology to studies of industrial relations." In Industrial Relations Research Association, *Proceedings of the First Annual Meeting,* Cleveland, Ohio, December 29–30, 1948, pp. 199–222.

———. 1951. *White Collar: The American Middle Class*. New York: Oxford University Press.

———. 1956. *The Power Elite*. New York: Oxford University Press.

Milton, Charles R. 1970. *Ethics and Expediency in Personnel Management: A Critical History of Personnel Philosophy*. Columbia: University of South Carolina Press.

Miner, John B. 1965. *Studies in Management Education*. New York: Springer.

Montgomery, David. 1974. "The 'New Unionism' and the transformation of workers' consciousness in America, 1909–1922." *Journal of Social History* 7(4) (Summer):509–529.

———. 1979. *Workers' Control in America: Studies in the History of Work, Technology, and Labor Struggles*. Cambridge: Cambridge University Press.

———. 1987. *The Fall of the House of Labor: The Workplace, the State, and American Worker Activism, 1865–1925*. Cambridge: Cambridge University Press.

Mooney, James D. 1937. "The principles of organization." In Luther Gulick and Lyndall Urwick, eds., *Papers on the Science of Administration*. New York: Institute of Public Administration, Columbia University, pp. 89–98.

Mooney, James D., and Alan C. Reiley. 1939. *The Principles of Organization*. New York: Harper & Brothers.

Moore, Russell F. 1970. *AMA Management Handbook*. New York: American Management Association.

Morman, Edward T., ed. 1989. *Efficiency, Scientific Management, and Hospital Standardization: An Anthology of Sources*. New York: Garland.

Morrow, L. C. 1922. "The Bedaux principle of human power measurement." *American Machinist* 56(7) (February 16):241–245.

Mullins, Nicholas C. 1973. *Theories and Theory Groups in Contemporary American Sociology*. With the assistance of Carolyn J. Mullins. New York: Harper & Row.

Münsterberg, Hugo. 1913. *Psychology and Industrial Efficiency*. Boston: Houghton Mifflin.

Nadworny, Milton J. 1955. *Scientific Management and the Unions, 1900–1932: A Historical Analysis*. Cambridge, Massachusetts: Harvard University Press.

NAM (National Association of Manufacturers). 1946. *Human Relations and Efficient Production*. New York: NAM.

———. 1949. *Industry Believes*. 4th ed. New York: NAM.

Nelson, Daniel. 1974. "Scientific management, systematic management, and labor, 1880–1915." *Business History Review* 48(4) (Winter):479–500.

———. 1975. *Managers and Workers: Origins of the New Factory System in the United States 1880–1920*. Madison: University of Wisconsin Press.

———. 1980. *Frederick W. Taylor and the Rise of Scientific Management*. Madison: University of Wisconsin Press.

NICB (National Industrial Conference Board). 1928. *The Economic Status of the Wage Earner in New York and Other States*. New York: NICB.

———. 1929. *Industrial Relations Programs in Small Plants*. New York: NICB.

———. 1936. *What Employers Are Doing for Employees*. NICB Studies No. 221. New York: NICB.

———. 1940. *Personnel Activities in American Business*. Studies in Personnel Policy No. 20. New York: NICB.

———. 1944. *Company Organization Charts*. Studies in Personnel Policy No. 64. New York: NICB.

———. 1947. *Personnel Activities in American Business*. Studies in Personnel Policy No. 86. New York: NICB.

———. 1948. *Personnel Practices in Factory and Office*. Studies in Personnel Policy No. 88. New York: NICB.

———. 1951. *Experience with Employee Attitude Surveys*. Studies in Personnel Policy No. 115. New York: NICB.

———. 1954. *Personnel Practices in Factory and Office*. Studies in Personnel Policy No. 145. New York: NICB.

———. 1958. *Organization of Staff Functions*. Studies in Personnel Policy No. 165. New York: NICB.

———. 1959. *Charting the Company Organization Structure*. Studies in Personnel Policy No. 168. New York: NICB.

———. 1964. *Personnel Practices in Factory and Office: Manufacturing*. Personnel Policy Study No. 194. New York: NICB.

———. 1965a. *Top Management Organization in Divisionalized Companies*. Studies in Personnel Policy No. 195. New York: NICB.

———. 1965b. *Organization Structures of International Companies*. Studies in Personnel Policy No. 198. New York: NICB.

———. 1969. *Behavioral Science: Concepts and Management Applications*. Studies in Personnel Policy No. 216. New York: NICB.

Noble, David F. 1977. *America by Design: Science, Technology, and the Rise of Corporate Capitalism*. New York: Alfred A. Knopf.

Opulente, Blaise J., ed. 1960. *Thought Patterns: Toward a Philosophy of Business Education*. Jamaica, New York: St. John's University Press.

Osborn, Alex F. 1953. *Applied Imagination: Principles and Procedures of Creative Thinking*. New York: Charles Scribner's Sons.

Ouchi, William. 1981. *Theory Z: How American Business Can Meet the Japanese Challenge*. Reading, Massachusetts: Addison-Wesley.

Palmer, Donald A., P. Devereaux Jennings, and Xueguang Zhou. 1993. "Late adoption of the multidivisional form by large U.S. corporations: Institutional, political, and economic accounts." *Administrative Science Quarterly* 38(1) (March):100–131.

Parks, Donald S. 1935. "How trends personnel work?" *Factory Management and Maintenance* 93(5) (May):201.

———. 1936. "1936 personnel trends." *Factory Management and Maintenance* 94(12) (December):39.

Pascale, Richard Tanner. 1990. *Managing on the Edge: How the Smartest Companies Use Conflict to Stay Ahead*. New York: Simon and Schuster.

Pascale, Richard Tanner, and Anthony G. Athos. 1981. *The Art of Japanese Management: Applications for American Executives*. New York: Simon and Schuster.

Pearse, Robert F. 1974. *Manager to Manager: What Managers Think of Management Development*. New York: AMACOM.

———. 1977. *Manager to Manager II: What Managers Think of their Managerial Careers*. New York: AMACOM.

Peirce School. 1935. *Current Personnel Practices*. Philadelphia: Peirce School of Business Administration.

Perrow, Charles. 1967. "A framework for the comparative analysis of organizations." *American Sociological Review* 32(2) (April):194–208.

———. 1970. *Organizational Analysis: A Sociological View*. Belmont, California: Wadsworth.

Person, Harlow S. 1937. "The Bedaux System." *The New Republic* 93(1199) (November 24):71.

Peters, Thomas J., and Robert H. Waterman, Jr. 1982. *In Search of Excellence: Lessons from America's Best-Run Companies*. New York: Harper & Row.

Pierson, Frank C., et al. 1959. *The Education of American Businessmen: A Study of University-College Programs in Business Administration*. New York: McGraw-Hill.

Raff, Daniel M. 1988. "Wage determination theory and the Five-Dollar Day at Ford." *Journal of Economic History* 48(2) (June):387–399.

Redlich, F. 1957. "Academic education for business." *Business History Review* 31(1):35–91.

Rodgers, Daniel T. 1978. *The Work Ethic in Industrial America, 1850–1920*. Chicago: University of Chicago Press.

Roethlisberger, Fritz J. 1945. "The foreman: Master and victim of double talk." *Harvard Business Review* 23(3) (Spring):283–298.

———. 1977. *The Elusive Phenomena: An Autobiographical Account of My Work in the Field of Organizational Behavior at the Harvard Business School*. Edited by George F. F. Lombard. Boston: Division of Research, Graduate School of Business Administration, Harvard University.

Roethlisberger, F. J., and William J. Dickson. [1939] 1967. *Management and the Worker: An Account of a Research Program Conducted by the Western Electric Company, Hawthorne Works, Chicago*. Cambridge, Massachusetts: Harvard University Press.

Sass, Steven A. 1982. *The Pragmatic Imagination: A History of the Wharton School 1881–1981*. Philadelphia: University of Pennsylvania Press.

Schlaifer, Robert. 1980. "The relay assembly test room: An alternative statistical interpretation." *American Sociological Review* 45:995–1005.

Scott, William G. 1992. *Chester I. Barnard and the Guardians of the Managerial State*. Lawrence: University Press of Kansas.

Secrist, H. 1920. "Research in collegiate schools of business." *Journal of Political Economy* 28(5):353–374.

Selekman, Benjamin M. 1947. *Labor Relations and Human Relations*. New York: McGraw-Hill.

Shepard, Jean L. 1938. *Human Nature at Work*. New York: Harper & Brothers.

Silk, Leonard S. 1960. *The Education of Businessmen*. New York: Committee for Economic Development.

Simon, Herbert A. [1945] 1976. *Administrative Behavior: A Study of Decision-Making Processes in Administrative Organization*. 3d ed. New York: Free Press.

Sklar, Martin J. 1988. *The Corporate Reconstruction of American Capitalism, 1890–1916: The Market, the Law, and Politics*. Cambridge: Cambridge University Press.

Sloan, Alfred P. [1963] 1972. *My Years with General Motors*. Edited by John McDonald, with Catharine Stevens. Garden City, New York: Anchor.

Smith, Terry. 1993. *Making the Modern: Industry, Art, and Design in America*. Chicago: University of Chicago Press.

Spates, Thomas G. 1960. *Human Values Where People Work*. New York: Harper & Brothers.

———. 1965. *Man and Management*. New Haven, Connecticut: The Carl Purington Rollins Printing Office of the Yale University Press.

Special Task Force to the Secretary of Health, Education and Welfare. 1973. *Work in America*. (No publisher)

Steinmetz, George, and Erik Olin Wright. 1989. "The fall and rise of the Petty Bourgeoisie: Changing patterns of self-employment in the postwar United States." *American Journal of Sociology* 94(5) (March):973–1018.

Stowers, Harvey. 1946. *Management Can Be Human*. New York: McGraw-Hill.

Sullivan, Mark. 1932. *Our Times: The United States 1900–1925*. Vol. 4. *The War Begins 1909–1914*. New York: Scribner's.

Sumner, William Graham. [1883] 1974. *What Social Classes Owe to Each Other*. Caldwell, Idaho: Caxton.

Sutton, Francis X., Seymour E. Harris, Carl Kaysen, and James Tobin [1956] 1962. *The American Business Creed*. New York: Schocken.

Sward, Keith. [1948] 1972. *The Legend of Henry Ford*. New York: Atheneum.

Taylor, Frederick W. 1895. "A piece rate system: Being a step toward partial solution of the labor problem." *Transactions of the American Society of Mechanical Engineers* 16:856–883.

———. [1903] 1972a. *Shop Management*. With an introduction by Henry R. Towne. In *Scientific Management*. Westport, Connecticut: Greenwood.

———. [1911] 1967. *The Principles of Scientific Management*. New York: W. W. Norton.

———. [1912] 1972b. *Taylor's Testimony Before the Special House Committee*. In *Scientific Management*. Westport, Connecticut: Greenwood.

Teece, D. J., and S. G. Winter. 1984. "The limits of neoclassical theory in management education." *American Economic Review* 74(2):116–121.

Thompson, James D. 1967. *Organizations in Action: Social Science Bases of Administrative Theory*. New York: McGraw-Hill.

Time. 1942. "Bedaux reformed." *Time* 39(3) (January 19):69–70.

————. 1952. "Human relations: A new art brings a revolution to industry." *Time* 59(15) (April 14):96–97.

Tolan, Sandy. 1990. "The Border Boom: Hope and heartbreak." *New York Times Magazine* (July 1):16–21, 31, 40.

Towne, Henry R. 1886. "The engineer as an economist." *Transactions of the American Society of Mechanical Engineers* 7:428–432.

Trahair, Richard C. S. 1984. *The Humanist Temper: The Life and Work of Elton Mayo.* New Brunswick, New Jersey: Transaction.

Twentieth Century Fund. 1949. *Partners in Production.* New York: The Twentieth Century Fund.

UAW (United Auto Workers). 1949. "Deep therapy on the assembly line." *Ammunition* (April):47–51.

Urwick, L., and E. F. L. Brech. 1948. *The Making of Scientific Management.* Vol. 3. *The Hawthorne Investigations.* London: Management Publications Trust.

Uttal, Bro. 1983. "The corporate culture vultures." *Fortune* 108 (October 17):66–72.

Viteles, Morris S. 1932. *Industrial Psychology.* New York: W. W. Norton.

Vroom, Victor H. 1964. *Work and Motivation.* New York: John Wiley & Sons.

Wallace, R. F. 1952. "How are you doing personnel-wise?" *Factory Management and Maintenance* 110(8) (August):110–112.

Wardwell, Walter I. 1979. "Critique of a recent professional 'put-down' of the Hawthorne research." *American Sociological Review* 44:858–861.

Waring, Stephen P. 1991. *Taylorism Transformed: Scientific Management Theory since 1945.* Chapel Hill: The University of North Carolina Press.

Warner, W. Lloyd, and J. O. Low. 1947. *The Social System of the Modern Factory. The Strike: A Social Analysis.* Vol. 4 of the Yankee City Series. New Haven, Connecticut: Yale University Press.

Watson, Thomas J. 1954. *As a Man Thinks.* Armonk, New York: International Business Machines Corporation.

Watson, Thomas J., Jr. 1963. *A Business and Its Beliefs: The Ideas that Helped Build IBM.* New York: McGraw-Hill.

————. 1986. "Tom Watson looks at the past and future." *The Wall Street Journal* (April 7) Section 2, p. 26.

Watson, Thomas J., Jr., and Peter Petre. 1990. *Father, Son & Co.: My Life at IBM and Beyond.* New York: Bantam.

Whitehead, Thomas North. 1938. *The Industrial Worker: A Statistical Study of Human Relations in a Group of Manual Workers.* 2 vols. Cambridge, Massachusetts: Harvard University Press.

————. 1947. *Leadership in a Free Society: A Study in Human Relations Based on an Analysis of Present-Day Industrial Civilization.* Cambridge, Massachusetts: Harvard University Press.

Whitley, R. 1984a. "The development of management studies as a fragmented adhocracy." *Social Science Information* 23(4–5):775–818.

————. 1984b. "The scientific status of management research as a practically oriented social science." *Journal of Management Studies* 21(4):369–390.

Whyte, William Foote. 1951. *Pattern for Industrial Peace.* New York: Harper & Brothers.

————. 1953. *Leadership and Group Participation.* Bulletin 24 (May). Ithaca, New York: New York State School of Industrial and Labor Relations, Cornell University.

————. 1959. *Man and Organization: Three Problems in Human Relations in Industry.* Homewood, Illinois: Richard D. Irwin.

————. 1961. *Men at Work.* Homewood, Illinois: Dorsey and Richard D. Irwin.

————. 1969. *Organizational Behavior: Theory and Application.* Homewood, Illinois: Richard D. Irwin and Dorsey.

Whyte, William Foote, ed. 1946. *Industry and Society.* New York: McGraw-Hill.

Whyte, William H., Jr. 1956. *The Organization Man.* New York: Simon and Schuster.

Whyte, William H., Jr., and the editors of Fortune. [1950] 1952. *Is Anybody Listening?* New York: Simon and Schuster.

Wilson, Richard Guy, Dianne H. Pilgrim, and Dickran Tashjian. 1986. *The Machine Age in America 1918–1941.* New York: The Brooklyn Museum-Harry N. Abrams.

Wood, Stephen, and John Kelly. 1982. "Taylorism, Responsible Autonomy and Management Strategy." In Stephen Wood, ed., *The Degradation of Work? Skill, Deskilling and the Labour Process.* London: Hutchinson, pp. 74–89.

Yates, JoAnne. 1989. *Control through Communication: The Rise of System in American Management.* Baltimore: Johns Hopkins University Press.

Zieger, Robert H. 1986. *American Workers, American Unions, 1920–1985.* Baltimore: Johns Hopkins University Press.

D. GERMANY

Acker, Heinrich B. [1963] 1966. *Organisationsanalyse.* 2d, enlarged ed. Baden-Baden: Verlag für Unternehmensführung Dr. Max Gehlen.

Alexander, Edgar. 1953. "Church and society in Germany." In Joseph N. Moody, ed., *Church and Society: Catholic Social and Political Thought and Movements 1789–1950.* New York: Arts, pp. 325–583.

Alexander, Jeffrey C. 1984. "The Parsons revival in German sociology." In Randall Collins, eds., *Sociological Theory 1984.* San Francisco: Jossey-Bass, pp. 394–412.

Bahrdt, Hans Paul. 1958. *Industriebürokratie: Versuch einer Soziologie des industrialisierten Bürobetriebes und seiner Angestellten.* Stuttgart: Ferdinand Enke.

Barron, Stephanie, et al. 1991. *Degenerate Art: The Fate of the Avant-Garde in Nazi Germany.* New York: Harry N. Abrams.

Bauhaus-Archiv Museum. 1981. *Bauhaus Archiv-Museum. Sammlung Katalog.* Berlin: Bauhaus-Archiv Museum für Gestaltung.

Bayer, Herbert, Walter Gropius, and Ise Gropius. [1938] 1975. *Bauhaus 1919–1928.* New York: The Museum of Modern Art.

Behrens, Peter, and H. De Fries. 1918. *Vom sparsamen Bauen: Ein Beitrag zur Siedlungsfrage.* Foreword by Dr. Dernburg. Berlin: Verlag der Bauwelt.

Bellinger, Bernhard. 1967. *Geschichte der Betriebswirtschaftslehre.* Stuttgart: C. E. Poeschel.

Benz, Wolfgang, and Hermann Graml, eds. 1988. *Biographisches Lexikon zur Weimarer Republik.* Munich: Beck.

Berghahn, Volker R. 1986. *The Americanization of West German Industry 1945–1973.* Cambridge: Cambridge University Press.

Berghahn, Volker R., and Detlev Karsten. 1987. *Industrial Relations in Germany.* Oxford: Berg.

Blaich, Fritz. 1984. *Amerikanische Firmen in Deutschland 1890–1918.* Wiesbaden: Franz Steiner.

Bleicher, Knut. 1966. *Zentralisation und Dezentralisation von Aufgaben in der Organisation der Unternehmungen.* Berlin: Duncker & Humblot.

Bönig, Jürgen. 1980. "Technik und Rationalisierung in Deutschland zur Zeit der Weimarer Republik." In Ulrich Troitzsch and Gabriele Wohlauf, eds., *Technik-Geschichte: Historische Beiträge und neuere Ansätze.* Frankfurt: Suhrkamp, pp. 390–419.

Bornemann, Ernest, et al. 1958. *Gruppenarbeit und Produktivität: Bericht über eine Studienreise in USA.* RKW-Auslandsdienst Heft 72. Munich: Carl Hanser.

Bowen, Ralph H. 1947. *German Theories of the Corporative State, with Special Reference to the Period 1870–1919.* New York: Whittlesey House.

Brady, Robert A. 1932. "The meaning of rationalization: An analysis of the literature." *Quarterly Journal of Economics* 46(3) (May):526–540.

———. 1933. *The Rationalization Movement in German Industry: A Study in the Evolution of Economic Planning.* Berkeley: University of California Press.

Bramesfeld, Erwin, et al. 1956. *Human Relations in Industry: Die menschliche Beziehungen in der Industrie. Beobachtungen einer deutschen Studiengruppe in USA.* RKW-Auslandsdienst Heft 41. Munich: Carl Hanser.

Braun, Klaus. 1978. *Konservatismus und Gemeinwirtschaft: Eine Studie über Wichard von Moellendorff.* Duisburg: Walter Braun Verlag.

Brecht, Bertolt. 1976. *Bertolt Brecht Poems.* Edited by John Willett and Ralph Manheim with the cooperation of Erich Fried. London: Eyre Methuen.

Briefs, Goetz. 1931. "Betriebssoziologie." In Alfred Vierkandt, ed., *Handwörterbuch der Soziologie.* Stuttgart: Ferdinand Enke, pp. 31–52.

Buchhändler-Vereinigung. 1971. *Verzeichnis lieferbarer Bücher 1971–72.* Frankfurt: Buchhändler-Vereinigung.

Buddensieg, Tilmann, ed. [1979] 1984. *Industriekultur: Peter Behrens and the AEG, 1907–1914.* In collaboration with Henning Rogge. Trans. by Iain Boyd Whyte. Cambridge, Massachusetts: MIT Press.

Burchardt, Lothar. 1977. "Technischer Fortschritt und socialer Wandel: Das Beispiel der Taylorismus-Rezeption." In Wilhelm Treue, ed., *Deutsche Technikgeschichte: Vorträge vom 31, Historikertag am 24. September 1976 in Mannheim.* Göttingen: Vandenhoeck & Ruprecht, pp. 52–98.

Burisch, Wolfram. [1956] 1969. *Industrie- und Betriebssoziologie.* 5th ed., revised and expanded from the previous work by Ralf Dahrendorf. Berlin: Walter de Gruyter.

Büttner, Hans Wolfgang. 1973. *Das Rationalisierungs-Kuratorium der deutschen Wirtschaft.* Ämter und Organisationen der Bundesrepublik Deutschland Nr. 44. Düsseldorf: Droste.

Campbell, Joan. 1978. *The German Werkbund: The Politics of Reform in the Applied Arts.* Princeton: Princeton University Press.

Crone, Hans. 1934. *Das Gesetz zur Ordnung der nationalen Arbiet nebst Parallelvorschriften und das bisherige Recht: Systematische Darstellung.* Munich: J. Schweitzer Verlag (Arthur Sellier).

Dahrendorf, Ralf. [1957] 1959a. *Class and Class Conflict in Industrial Society.* Stanford, California: Stanford University Press.

———. 1959b. *Sozialstruktur des Betriebes—Betriebssoziologie.* Thirteenth reprint. Wiesbaden: Betriebswirtschaftlicher Verlag.

Darnton, Robert. 1991. "The Fall of the House of Art: Hitler's blitzkrieg against modern art." *The New Republic* (May 6):27–33.

Degelmann, Alfred, ed. 1968. *Organisationsleiter-Handbuch.* Published in cooperation with the Rationalisierungs-Kuratorium der deutschen Wirtschaft. Munich: Verlag Moderne Industrie.

Dolivo-Dobrowolsky, Michael von [1912] 1984. "Modern mass production in the electrical appliance factory of the AEG." In Tilmann Buddensieg, ed., *Industriekultur: Peter Behrens and the AEG, 1907–1914.* Cambridge, Massachusetts: MIT Press, pp. 256–261.

Droste, Magdalena. 1990. *Bauhaus 1919–1933.* Cologne: Benedikt Taschen.

Enquete-Ausschuß. 1931. *Untersuchung der Erzeugungs- und Absatzbedingungen der deutschen Wirtschaft.* Berlin: Mittler & Sohn.

Farmer, John David, and Geraldine Weiss. 1971. *Concepts of the Bauhaus: The Busch-Reisinger Museum Collection.* Cambridge, Massachusetts: The Busch-Reisinger Museum, Harvard University.

Feldman, Gerald D. 1981. "German Interest Group Alliances in War and Inflation, 1914–1923." In Suzanne Berger, ed., *Organizing Interests in Western Europe: Pluralism, Corporatism, and the Transformation of Politics.* Cambridge: Cambridge University Press, pp. 159–184.

Fiedler-Winter, Rosemarie. 1973. *Die Management-Schulen.* Düsseldorf: Econ Verlag.

Forrester, David A. R. 1977. *Schmalenbach and After: A Study of the Evolution of German Business Economics.* Glasgow: Strathclyde Convergencies.

Frankfurter Zeitung. 1927. *Wege zur Rationalisierung: Sonderabdruck aus der Frankfurter Zeitung.* Frankfurt: Druck der Frankfurter Societäts-Druckerei.

Freitag, Georg. 1963. "Das Haus Siemens und das RWK: Ein Beitrag zur Gründung und Entwicklung der deutschen Rationalisierungsbewegung." *Rationalisierung* 14(11):247–252.

Freund, Julien. 1978. "German Sociology in the Time of Max Weber." In Tom Bottomore and Robert Nisbet, eds., *A History of Sociological Analysis.* New York: Basic, pp. 149–186.

Friedeburg, Ludwig von. 1963. *Soziologie des Betriebsklimas: Studien zur Deutung empirischer Untersuchungen in industriellen Großbetrieben.* Frankfurt: Europäische Verlagsanstalt.

Fürstenberg, Friedrich. 1990. "Industrial Sociology." In Erwin Grochla and Eduard Gaugler, eds. *Handbook of German Business Management.* Stuttgart: C. E. Poeschel, vol. 1, pp. 1106–1118.

Geck, L. H. Adolf. 1931. *Die sozialen Arbeitsverhältnisse im Wandel der Zeit: Eine geschichtliche Einführung in die Betriebssoziologie.* Berlin: Julius Springer.

———. 1951. "Zur Entstehungsgeschichte der Betriebssoziologie." In Karl Gustav Specht, ed., *Soziologische Forschung in unserer Zeit: Ein Sammelwerk Leopold von Wiese zum 75. Geburtstag.* Cologne: Westdeutscher, pp. 107–122.

Geils, Peter, and Willi Gorzny. 1979. *Gesamtverzeichnis des deutschsprachigen Schrifttums (GV) 1700–1910.* Munich: K. G. Saur.

Giedion, Siegfried. [1954] 1992. *Walter Gropius.* New York: Dover.

Giesel, Hermann. 1963. *Der soziale Gehalt des Taylor-Systems: Eine Untersuchung des Taylor-Bildes in der Gegenwartsliteratur.* Ph.D. diss. Cologne: Faculty of Economic and Social Sciences of the University of Cologne.

Gillingham, John. 1986. "The 'deproletarianization' of German society: Vocational training in the Third Reich." *Journal of Social History* 19(3) (Spring):423–432.

Gispen, Kees. 1989. *New Profession, Old Order: Engineers and German Society, 1815–1914.* Cambridge: Cambridge University Press.

———. 1990. "Engineers in Wilhelmian Germany: Professionalization, Deprofessionalization, and the Development of Nonacademic Technical Education." In Geoffrey Cocks and Konrad H. Jarausch, eds., *German Professions, 1800–1950.* New York: Oxford University Press, pp. 104–122.

Goetzeler, Herbert, and Lothar Schoen. 1986. *Wilhelm und Carl Friedrich von Siemens: Die zweite Unternehmergeneration.* Wiesbaden: Franz Steiner.

Grochla, Erwin, ed. 1969. *Handwörterbuch der Organisation.* Stuttgart: C. E. Poeschel.

———. 1980. *Handwörterbuch der Organisation.* 2d ed. Stuttgart: C. E. Poeschel.

Grochla, Erwin, and Norbert Szyperski, eds. 1975. *Information Systems and Organizational Structure.* Berlin: Walter de Gruyter.

Grochla, Erwin, and Waldemar Wittmann, eds. 1976. *Handwörterbuch der Betriebswirtschaft.* 4th ed. 3 vols. Stuttgart: C. E. Poeschel.

Gropius, Walter. [1935?] 1956. *The New Architecture and the Bauhaus.* London: Faber and Faber.

Grün, Oskar. 1966. *Informale Erscheinungen in der Betriebsorganisation*. Berlin: Duncker & Humblot.

Hachtmann, Rüdiger. 1989. *Industriearbeit im "Dritten Reich": Untersuchungen zu den Lohn- und Arbeitsbedingungen in Deutschland 1933–1945*. Göttingen: Vandenhoeck & Ruprecht.

Hartmann, Heinz. 1959. *Authority and Organization in German Management*. Princeton, New Jersey: Princeton University Press.

————. 1963. *Amerikanische Firmen in Deutschland: Beobachtungen über Kontakte und Kontraste zwischen Industriegesellschaften*. Cologne and Opladen: Westdeutscher.

Hauskern, Dipl.-Volkswirt, et al. 1942. *Mitarbeit der Gefolgschaft*. Berlin, Wien, Leipzig: Otto Elsner.

Hays, K. Michael. 1992. *Modernism and the Posthumanist Subject: The Architecture of Hannes Meyer and Ludwig Hilberseimer*. Cambridge, Massachusetts: MIT Press.

Helfer, Christian. 1963. "Über militärische Einflüsse auf die industrielle Entwicklung in Deutschland." *Schmollers Jahrbuch* 83(5):597–609.

Hellige, Hans Dieter. 1968. "Wilhelm II. und Walther Rathenau: Ein Gespräch aus dem Jahre 1900." *Geschichte in Wissenschaft und Unterricht* 19(9) (September):538–544.

Herbert, Gilbert. 1984. *The Dream of the Factory-Made House: Walter Gropius and Konrad Wachsman*. Cambridge, Massachusetts: The MIT Press.

Herf, Jeffrey. 1984. *Reactionary Modernism: Technology, Culture, and Politics in Weimar and the Third Reich*. Cambridge, England: Cambridge University Press.

Hinrichs, Peter, and Lothar Peter. 1976. *Industrieller Friede? Arbeitswissenschaft, Rationalisierung und Arbeiterbewegung in der Weimarer Republik*. Cologne: Pahl-Rugenstein.

Hoff, Andreas. 1978. "Gewerkschaften und Rationalisierung: Ein Vergleich gewerkschaftlicher Argumentationsmuster Heute und vor fünfzig Jahren." *Mehrwert* 15–16:167–208.

Hoffmann, Rainer-W. 1985. *Wissenschaft und Arbeitskraft: Zur Geschichte der Arbeitsforschung in Deutschland*. Frankfurt: Campus.

Höhn, Reinhard. [1964] 1971. *Die Stellvertretung im Betrieb*. Bad Harzburg: Verlag für Wissenschaft, Wirtschaft und Technik.

————. 1970. *Verwaltung Heute: Autoritäre Führung oder modernes Management*. Bad Harzburg: Verlag für Wissenschaft, Wirtschaft und Technik.

Höhn, Reinhard, ed. 1967. *Das Harzburger Modell in der Praxis: Rundgespräch über die Erfahrungen mit dem neuen Führungsstil in der Wirtschaft*. Bad Harzburg: Verlag für Wissenschaft, Wirtschaft und Technik.

Holborn, Hajo. 1986. "The Prusso-German school: Moltke and the rise of the general staff." In Peter Paret, ed., *Makers of Modern Strategy: From Machiavelli to the Nuclear Age*. Princeton, New Jersey: Princeton University Press, pp. 281–295.

Homburg, Heidrum. 1978. "Anfänge des Taylorsystems in Deutschland vor dem Ersten Weltkrieg: Eine Problemskizze unter besonderer Berücksichtigung der Arbeitskämpfe bei Bosch 1913." *Geschichte und Gesellschaft* 4: 170–194.

———. 1984. "Le Taylorisme et la rationalisation de l'organisation du travail en Allemagne, 1918–1939." In Maurice de Montmollin, and Olivier Pastré, eds., *Le Taylorisme: Actes du colloque international sur le taylorisme organisé par l'Université de Paris-XIII, 2–4 mai 1983.* Paris: Éditions la Découverte, pp. 99–113.

Institut der Wirtschaftsprüfer. 1969. *Unternehmensführung und Unternehmensberatung.* Düsseldorf: Verlagsbuchhandlung des Instituts der Wirtschaftsprüfer.

Institut für Sozialforschung. 1955. *Betriebsklima: Eine industriesoziologische Untersuchung aus dem Ruhrgebiet.* Frankfurt: Europäische Verlagsanstalt.

Isaacs, Reginald. 1991. *Gropius: An Illustrated Biography of the Creator of the Bauhaus.* Boston: Bulfinch.

Jäger, Davor. 1989. *Unterschiede zwischen der deutschen und amerikanischen Organisationsforschung.* Munich: VVF.

Jarausch, Konrad H. 1990. *The Unfree Professions: German Lawyers, Teachers, and Engineers, 1900–1950.* New York: Oxford University Press.

Joll, James. 1960. "Walther Rathenau: Prophet without a Cause." In *Intellectuals in Politics: Three Biographical Essays.* London: Weidenfeld and Nicolson, pp. 59–129.

Junghanns, Kurt. 1982. *Der Deutsche Werkbund: Sein erstes Jahrzehnt.* Berlin: Henschelverlag.

Kaste, Hermann. 1981. *Arbeitgeber und Humanisierung der Arbeit: Eine exemplarische Analyse.* Opladen: Leske Verlag + Budrich.

Kellermann, Bernard. [1913] 1915. *The Tunnel.* New York: The Macaulay Co.

Kennedy, Paul. 1987. *The Rise and Fall of the Great Powers: Economic Change and Military Conflict from 1500 to 2000.* New York: Random House.

Kern, Hans, et al. 1942. *Mitarbeit der Gefolgschaft.*Vol. 4 of the Schriftenreihe des Reichsausschusses für Leistungssteigerung. Berlin, Wien, Leipzig: Otto Elsner.

Kessler, Count Harry. [1928] 1930. *Walther Rathenau: His Life and Work.* New York: Harcourt, Brace.

Kieser, Alfred, ed. 1981. *Organisationstheoretische Ansätze.* Munich: Vahlen.

———. 1993. *Organisationstheorien.* Stuttgart: Verlag W. Kohlhammer.

Kirsch, Karin. 1989. *The Weissenhofsiedlung: Experimental Housing Built for the Deutscher Werkbund, Stuttgart, 1927.* New York: Rizzoli.

Kocka, Jürgen. 1969. "Industrielles management: Konzeptionen und modelle in Deutschland vor 1914." *Vierteljahrschrift für Sozial- und Wirtschaftsgeschichte* 56(3) (October):322–372.

———. 1971. "Family and bureaucracy in German industrial management, 1850–1914: Siemens in comparative perspective." *Business History Review* 45(2) (Summer):133–156.

———. 1973. "Management und Angestellte im Unternehmen der Industriellen Revolution." In Rudolph Braun et al., eds., *Gesellschaft in der industriellen Revolution*. Cologne: Kiepenheuer & Witsch, pp. 162–201.

———. 1978. "Entrepreneurs and Managers in German Industrialization." In Peter Mathias and M. M. Postan, eds., *The Cambridge Economic History of Europe*. Vol. 3. *The Industrial Economies: Capital, Labour, and Enterprise. Part 1: Britain, France, Germany, and Scandinavia*. Cambridge: Cambridge University Press, pp. 492–589.

———. 1979. "1945: Neubeginn oder Restauration?" In Carola Stern and Heinrich August Winkler, eds., *Wendepunkte deutscher Geschichte 1848–1945*. Frankfurt: Fischer Taschenbuch Verlag, pp. 141–168.

Kolbinger, Josef, ed. 1966. *Betrieb und Gesellschaft: Soziale Betriebsführung*. Berlin: Duncker & Humblot.

König, René. 1961. "Die informellen Gruppen im Industriebetrieb." In Erich Schnaufer and Klaus Agthe, eds., *Organisation*. Berlin: Deutscher Betriebswirte-Verlag, pp. 55–118.

König, René, Peter Atteslander, Heiner Treinen, and Hans-Wolfgang Stieber. 1956. "Betriebssoziologische Mikroanalyse." *Kölner Zeitschrift für Soziologie und Sozialpsychologie* 8(1):46–91.

Kosiol, Erich. 1959. *Institut für Industrieforschung 1948–1958*. Berlin: Duncker & Humblot.

Krause, Erwin. 1933. "Leistungssteigerung durch Arbeitswechsel." *Industrielle Psychotechnik* 10(4) (April):97–106.

Kupke, Erich. 1941. *Jeder denkt mit! Innerbetrieblicher Erfahrungsaustausch und lebendige Mitarbeit der Gefolgschaft—Wege zur Leistungssteigerung in deutschen Betrieben*. Vol. 1 of the Schriftenreihe des Reichsausschusses für Leistungssteigerung. Berlin, Wien, Leipzig: Otto Elsner.

Lane, Barbara Miller. 1968. *Architecture and Politics in Germany, 1918–1945*. Cambridge, Massachusetts: Harvard University Press.

Lattmann, Charles. 1974. *Die Humanisierung der Arbeit und die Demokratisierung der Unternehmung: Ziele, Wege und Grenze*. Bern and Stuttgart: P. Haupt.

Lawrence, Peter A. 1980. *Managers and Management in West Germany*. New York: St. Martin's.

Lee, J. J. 1978. "Labour in German industrialization." In Peter Mathias and M. M. Postan, eds., *The Cambridge Economic History of Europe*. Vol. 7. *The Industrial Economies: Capital, Labour, and Enterprise. Part 1: Britain, France, Germany, and Scandinavia*. Cambridge: Cambridge University Press, pp. 442–491.

Lepsius, M. Rainer. 1960. *Strukturen und Wandlungen im Industriebetrieb: Industriesoziologische Forschung in Deutschland*. Munich: Carl Hanser.

———. 1979. "Die Entwicklung der Soziologie nach dem Zweiten Weltkrieg 1945 bis 1967." In Günther Lüschen, ed., *Deutsche Soziologie seit 1945: Entwicklungsrichtungen und Praxisbezug*. Opladen: Westdeutscher, pp. 27–70.

———. 1987. "Sociology in the Interwar Period: Trends in Development and Criteria for Evaluation." In Volker Meja, Dieter Misgeld, and Nico Stehr, eds., *Modern German Sociology*. New York: Columbia University Press, pp. 37–56.

Levy, Hermann. [1935] 1966. *Industrial Germany: A Study of Its Monopoly Organisations and Their Control by the State*. New York: Kelley.

Lindenfeld, David F. 1990. "The professionalization of applied economics: German counterparts to business administration." In Geoffrey Cocks and Konrad H. Jarausch, eds., *German Professions, 1800–1950*. New York: Oxford University Press, pp. 213–231.

Linz, Juan J. 1967. "Cleavage and consensus in West German politics: The early fifties." In Seymour M. Lipset and Stein Rokkan, eds., *Party Systems and Voter Alignments*. New York: Free Press, pp. 283–321.

Luhmann, Niklas. [1964] 1976. *Funktionen und Folgen formaler Organisation*. 3d ed. Berlin: Duncker & Humblot.

———. 1976. "A general theory of organized social systems." In Geert Hofstede and M. S. Kassem, eds., *European Contributions to Organization Theory*. Assen, The Netherlands: Van Gorcum, pp. 96–113.

———. 1981. "Organisationstheorie." In *Soziologische Aufklärung 3: Soziales System, Gesellschaft, Organisation*. Cologne: Westdeutscher, pp. 335–414.

———. 1982. *The Differentiation of Society*. Trans. by Stephen Holmes and Charles Larmore. New York: Columbia University Press.

Lukatis, Ingrid. 1972. *Organisationsstrukturen und Führungsstile in Wirtschaftsunternehmen*. Frankfurt: Akademische Verlagsanstalt.

McCreary, Eugene C. 1968. "Social welfare and business: The Krupp welfare program, 1860–1914." *Business History Review* 42(1) (Spring):24–49.

McClelland, Charles E. 1991. *The German Experience of Professionalization: Modern Learned Professions and Their Organizations from Early Nineteenth Century to the Hitler Era*. Cambridge: Cambridge University Press.

Markovits, Andrei S. 1986. *The Politics of the West German Trade Unions: Strategies of Class and Interest Representation in Growth and Crisis*. Cambridge: Cambridge University Press.

Mason, T. W. 1966. "Labour in the Third Reich, 1933–1939." *Past and Present* 33 (April):112–141.

Mayntz, Renate. 1958. *Die soziale Organisation des Industriebetriebes*. Stuttgart: Ferdinand Enke.

———. 1963. *Soziologie der Organisation*. Hamburg: Rowohlt.

———. 1976. "Conceptual models of organizational decision making and their application to the policy process." In Geert Hofstede and M. S. Kassem, eds., *European Contributions to Organization Theory*. Assen, The Netherlands: Van Gorcum, pp. 114–125.

Mayntz, Renate, ed. 1968. *Bürokratische Organisation*. Cologne: Kiepenheuer & Witsch.

Meja, Voker, Dieter Misgeld, and Nico Stehr. 1987. "The social and intellectual organization of German sociology since 1945." In Volker Meja, Dieter Misgeld, and Nico Stehr, eds., *Modern German Sociology*. New York: Columbia University Press, pp. 1–30.

Michels, Robert. [1911] 1962. *Political Parties: A Sociological Study of the Oligarchical Tendencies of Modern Democracy*. New York: Free Press.

Moellendorf, Wichard von. 1912. "Der Ingenieur." *Die Zukunft* 20(52) (September 28):425–432.

———. 1913. "Psychologie und Wirtschaftsleben." *Die neue Rundschau* 24(2) (February):258–262.

———. 1914a. "Germanische Lehren aus Amerika." *Die Zukunft* 86 (March):323–332.

———. 1914b. "Taylorismus und Antitaylorismus." *Die neue Rundschau* 26(3) (March):411–417.

Möller, Paul. 1903. "Eine Studienreise in den Vereinigten Staaten von Amerika." *Zeitschrift des Vereines deutscher Ingenieure* 47(27) (July 4):972–979; 47(28) (July 11):1008–1014.

Moses, John A. 1982. *Trade Unionism in Germany from Bismarck to Hitler 1869–1918*. 2 vols. London: George Prior.

Muszynski, Bernhard. 1975. *Wirtschaftliche Mitbestimmung zwischen Konflikt- und Harmoniekonzeptionen: Theoretische Voraussetzungen geschichtliche Grundlagen und Hauptprobleme der Mitbestimmungsdiskussion der BRD*. Meisenheim am Glan, West Germany: Verlag Anton Hain.

Negandhi, Anant R. 1986. "Role and Structure of German Multinationals: A Comparative Profile." In Klaus Macharzina and Wolfgang H. Staehle, eds., *European Approaches to International Management*. Berlin and New York: Walter de Gruyter, pp. 51–66.

Nerdinger, Winfried. 1985. "Walter Gropius—From Americanism to the New World." In *Walter Gropius*. Berlin: Gebrüder Mann Verlag, pp. 9–28.

Nerdinger, Winfried, ed. 1982. *Richard Riemerschmid, vom Jugendstil zum Werkbund: Werke und Dokumente*. Munich: Prestel.

———. 1990. *The Walter Gropius Archive*. 4 vols. New York, London, and Cambridge, Massachusetts: Garland and Harvard University Art Museums.

NICB. 1931. *Rationalization of German Industry*. New York: National Industrial Conference Board.

Nicklisch, Heinrich. 1926–1928. *Handwörterbuch der Betriebswirtschaft*. 5 vols. Stuttgart: C. E. Poeschel.

Oberschelp, Reinhard, ed. 1976. *Gesamtverzeichnis des deutschsprachigen Schrifttums (GV) 1911–1965*. Munich: Verlag Dokumentation.

Osswald, Richard. 1987. *Lebendige Arbeitswelt: Die Sozialgeschichte der Daimler-Benz AG von 1945 bis 1985*. Stuttgart: Deutsche Verlags-Anstalt.

Pentzlin, Kurt. 1963. *Meister der Rationalisierung*. Düsseldorf: Econ-Verlag.

Pflaume, Eberhard. 1939. *Die Umschulung in der Eisen und Metall verarbeitenden Industrie*. Vol. 2 of the Schriftenreihe des Reichsausschusses für Leistungssteigerung. Berlin, Wien, Leipzig: Otto Elsner.

———. 1943. *Frauen im Industriebetrieb: Einsatz, Schulung, Leistung*. Vol. 5 of the Schriftenreihe des Reichsausschusses für Leistungssteigerung. Berlin, Wien, Leipzig: Otto Elsner.

Popitz, Heinrich, Hans Paul Bahrdt, Ernst August Jüres, and Hanno Kesting. 1957. *Das Gesellschaftsbild des Arbeiters: Soziologische Untersuchungen in der Hüttenindustrie.* Tübingen: J. C. B. Mohr.

Pross, Helge. 1965. *Manager und Aktionäre in Deutschland: Untersuchungen zum Verhältnis von Eigentum und Verfügungsmacht.* Frankfurter Beiträge für Soziologie No. 15. Frankfurt: Europäische Verlagsanstalt.

Rathenau, Walther. [1909] 1918. "Massengüterbahnen." In *Gesammelte Schriften,* vol. 3. Berlin: S. Fischer Verlag, pp. 153–169.

———. [1917] 1918. *Von kommenden Dingen.* In *Gesammelte Schriften,* vol. 3. Berlin: S. Fischer Verlag, pp. 7–366.

———. 1918. *Die neue Wirtschaft.* Berlin: S. Fischer Verlag.

———. 1985. *Walther Rathenau: Industrialist, Banker, Intellectual, and Politician. Notes and Diaries 1907–1922.* Edited by Hartmut Pogge von Strandmann. Notes and Diaries trans. by Caroline Pinder-Cracraft, with Hilary and Harmut Pogge von Strandmann. Oxford: Clarendon Press.

Reuter, Fritz, ed. 1930. *Handbuch der Rationalisierung.* Berlin: Spaeth & Linde.

RFGWBW (Reichsforschunggesellschaft für Wirtschaftlichkeit im Bau- und Wohnungswesen). 1929. *Bericht über die Versuchssiedlung in Dessau.* Berlin: RFGWBW.

RKW (Reichskuratorium für Wirtschaftlichkeit). 1928–1933. *Jahresbericht.* Years 1927 through 1932–33. RKW-Veröffentlichungen Nos. 27, 46, 60, 75, 85, and 95. Berlin: Reichskuratorium für Wirtschaftlichkeit.

Rocker, Rudolf. 1980. *Die Rationalisierung der Wirtschaft und die Arbeiterklasse.* Frankfurt: Verlag Freie Gesellschaft.

Roth, Guenther. 1963. *The Social Democrats in Imperial Germany: A Study in Working-Class Isolation and National Integration.* With a preface by Reinhard Bendix. Totowa, New Jersey: Bedminster.

Santoro, Cesare. 1938. *Quatre années d'Allemagne d'Hitler vues par un étranger.* Berlin: Internationaler Verlag.

Scheidig, Walther. [1966] 1967. *Weimar Crafts of the Bauhaus 1919–1924: An Early Experiment in Industrial Design.* New York: Reinhold.

Scherke, Felix. 1956. *Die Arbeitsgruppe im Betrieb, ihre Untersuchung, Diagnostizierung und Behandlung.* Wiesbaden: Betriebswirtschaftlicher Verlag.

Schleip, Walter. 1944. *Totale Rationalisierung des Industriebetriebes.* Vol. 8 of the Schriftenreihe des Reichsausschusses für Leistungssteigerung. Berlin, Wien, Leipzig: Otto Elsner.

Schluchter, Wolfgang. 1972. *Aspekte bürokratischer Herrschaft: Studien zur Interpretation der fortschreitenden Industriegesellschaft.* Munich: List.

———. "Modes of authority and democratic control." In Volker Meja, Dieter Misgeld, and Nico Stehr, eds., *Modern German Sociology.* New York: Columbia University Press, pp. 291–323.

Schmied, Wieland, ed. 1978. *Neue Sachlichkeit and German Realism of the Twenties.* London: Art Council of Great Britain.

Schmiede, Rudi, and Edwin Schudlich. [1976] 1978. *Die Entwicklung der*

Leistungsentlohnung in Deutschland. 3d ed. Frankfurt and New York: Campus.

Schmoller, Gustav. 1892. "Ueber die Entwicklung des Grossbetriebes und die soziale Klassenbildung." *Preussische Jahrbücher* 69(4) (April):457–480.

Schnaufer, Erich, and Klaus Agthe, eds. 1961. *Organisation.* Berlin: Deutscher Betriebswirte-Verlag.

Schneider, Dieter. 1981. *Geschichte betriebswirtschaftlicher Theorie.* Munich: Oldenbourg.

Schönhoven, Klaus. 1980. *Expansion und Konzentration: Studien zur Entwicklung der Freien Gewerkschaften im Wilhelminischen Deutschland 1890 bis 1914.* Stuttgart: Klett-Cotta.

Schulin, Ernst. 1987. "Max Weber and Walther Rathenau." In Wolfgang J. Mommsen and Jürgen Osterhammel, eds., *Max Weber and his Contemporaries.* London: Allen & Unwin, pp. 311–322.

Schultze, Ernst. 1923. *Organisatoren und Wirtschaftsführer.* Leipzig: Borckhaus.

Schumann, Hans-Gerd. 1958. *Nationalsozialismus und Gewerkschaftsbewegung. Die Vernichtung der deutschen Gewerkschaften und der Aufbau der "Deutschen Arbeitsfront."* Hannover: Norddeutsche Verlagsanstalt O. Goedel.

Schuster, Helmuth. 1987. *Industrie und Sozialwissenschaften: Eine Praxisgeschichte der Arbeits- und Industrieforschung in Deutschland.* Opladen: Westdeutscher.

Seischab, Hans, and Karl Schwantag, eds. 1956–1962. *Handwörterbuch der Betriebswirtschaft.* 3d ed. 4 vols. Stuttgart: C. E. Poeschel.

Seubert, Rudolf. 1914. *Aus der Praxis des Taylor-Systems, mit eingehender Beschreibung seiner Anwendung bei der Tabor Manufacturing Company in Philadelphia.* Berlin: Julius Springer.

Sommer, Klaus. 1968. *Die Bedeutung interpersonaler Beziehungen für die Organisation der Unternehmung.* Berlin: Duncker & Humblot.

Speer, Albert. [1969] 1970. *Inside the Third Reich: Memoirs.* New York: Macmillan.

Spencer, Elaine Glovka. 1984. *Management and Labor in Imperial Germany: Ruhr Industrialists.* New Brunswick, New Jersey: Rutgers University Press.

Stark, Gary D. 1981. *Entrepreneurs of Ideology: Neoconservative Publishers in Germany, 1890–1933.* Chapel Hill: University of North Carolina Press.

Statistisches Bundesamt. 1972. *Bevölkerung und Wirtschaft 1872–1972.* Wiesbaden: Statistisches Bundesamt.

Stegmann, Franz Josef. 1974. *Der soziale Katholizismus und die Mitbestimmung in Deutschland: Vom Beginn der Industrialisierung bis zum Jahre 1933.* Munich: Verlag Ferdinand Schöningh.

Stollberg, Gunnar. 1981. *Die Rationalisierungsdebatte, 1908–1933: Freie Gewerkschaften zwischen Mitwirkung und Gegenwehr.* Frankfurt a. d. Main and New York: Campus Verlag.

Stolper, Gustav, Karl Häuser, and Knut Borchardt. 1967. *The German Economy 1870 to the Present*. New York: Harcourt, Brace & World.

Strandmann, Hartmut Pogge von. 1985. "Introduction: Walther Rathenau, a biographical sketch." In Walther Rathenau, *Walther Rathenau: Industrialist, Banker, Intellectual, and Politician. Notes and Diaries 1907–1922*. Oxford: Clarendon Press, pp. 1–26.

Trieba, Voker, and Ulrich Mentrup. 1983. *Entwicklung der Arbeitswissenschaft in Deutschland: Rationalisierungspolitik der deutschen Wirtschaft bis zum Faschismus*. Munich: Minerva-Publikation.

Veblen, Thorstein. [1915] 1939. *Imperial Germany and the Industrial Revolution*. New York: Viking.

Vogl, Frank. 1973. *German Business after the Economic Miracle*. London: Macmillan.

Weber, Hajo. 1987. *Unternehmerverbände zwischen Markt, Staat, und Gewerkschaften*. Frankfurt and New York: Campus.

Weber, Max. 1908–1909. "Zur Psychophysik der industriellen Arbeit." *Archiv für Sozialwissenschaft und Sozialpolitik* 27(1908):730–770; 28(1909): 219–277, 719–761; 29(1909):513–542.

Weyer, Johannes. 1984. *Westdeutsche Soziologie 1945–1960: Deutsche Kontinuitäten und nordamerikanischer Einfluß*. Berlin: Duncker & Humblot.

Whitford, Frank. 1984. *Bauhaus*. London: Thames and Hudson.

Wiedermann, Herbert. [1964] 1967. *Die Rationalisierung aus der Sicht des Arbeiters: Eine soziologische Untersuchung in der mechanischen Fertigung*. 2d ed., revised and expanded. Cologne: Westdeutscher.

Wilpert, Bernhard. 1977. *Führung in deutschen Unternehmen*. Berlin: Walter de Gruyter.

Wingler, Hans M. [1979] 1983. *The Bauhaus-Archiv Berlin: Museum of Design*. Braunschweig: Westermann.

Wingler, Hans M., ed. [1962] 1969. *The Bauhaus: Weimar, Dessau, Berlin, Chicago*. Cambridge, Massachusetts: MIT Press.

Wirtschaftswissenschaftliches Institut der Gewerkschaften (Britische Zone). 1948. *Gewerkschaften und Arbeitsstudien*. Cologne: Bund-Verlag.

Wirtschaftswissenschaftliches Institut der Gewerkschaften. 1950. *Rationalisierung und Arbeitnehmerschaft: Entwurf einer gewerkschaftlichen Stellungsnahme*. Cologne: Bund-Verlag.

Wunderer, Rolf. 1990. "Leadership." In Erwin Grochla and Eduard Gaugler, eds., *Handbook of German Business Management*. Stuttgart: C. E. Poeschel, vol. 2, pp. 1302–1315.

Zepf, Günter. 1972. *Kooperativer Führungsstil und Organisation*. Wiesbaden: Betriebswirtschaftlicher Verlag Dr. Th. Gabler.

Zilbert, Edward R. 1981. *Albert Speer and the Nazi Ministry of Arms: Economic Institutions and Industrial Production in the German War Economy*. London: Associated University Presses.

E. SPAIN

Alcain, Ramón, and Daniel Lacalle. 1971. "La organización científica del trabajo." *Cuadernos para el Diálogo*. Special issue 27 (October):63–69.

Almarcha, Amparo, et al. 1975. *Estadísticas básicas de España 1900–1970*. Madrid: Confederación Española de Cajas de Ahorro.

Almendros Morcillo, Fernando, Enrique Jiménez-Asenjo, Francisco Pérez Amorós, and Eduardo Rojo Torrecilla. 1978. *El sindicalismo de clase en España 1939–1977*. Barcelona: Península.

Alonso Olea, Manuel. 1958. "Prólogo der traductor." In Theodore Caplow, *Sociología del trabajo*. Madrid: Instituto de Estudios Políticos, pp. 7–14.

Alzugaray, Juan José. 1989. *Egregios ingenieros*. Madrid: Ediciones Encuentro.

Amsden, Jon. 1972. *Collective Bargaining and Class Conflict in Spain*. London: London School of Economics and Political Science.

APD. 1970. *Problemas actuales del director de personal*. Madrid: Asociación para el Progreso de la Dirección.

Arana Gondra, Ramón. 1963. *El trabajo personal del director de empresa*. Bilbao: Ediciones Deusto.

———. 1965a. *La estructura de la empresa española*. Madrid: Asociación para el Progreso de la Dirección.

———. 1965b. *La estrategia del director de empresa. Capítulo I: La estrategia de las comunicaciones*. Madrid: Varicop.

———. 1965c. *La estrategia del director de empresa: La estrategia en la asignación de responsabilidades*. Madrid: Varicop.

Arana Gondra, Ramón, ed. 1972. *Criterios sobre alta dirección de empresa*. Madrid: Asociación para el Progreso de la Dirección.

ASE (Acción Social Empresarial). 1967. *Por un mayor sentido comunitario de la empresa: Plan de trabajo 1967–68. Segunda parte: La empresa como comunidad de fines*. Madrid: Comisión Nacional de ASE.

———. 1969. *La participación en la empresa. Segunda y tercera parte: La empresa como escuela de participación y el dirigente de empresa ante el hecho de la participación*. Madrid: ASE.

———. 1970. *Previsión, reclutamiento y selección de personal*. Madrid: ASE.

———. 1972. *Valoración empresarial de los resultados de los convenios colectivos en España 1958–1970*. Madrid: Confederación Española de Cajas de Ahorro.

ASP (Acción Social Patronal). [1957] 1965. *Relaciones humanas en la Empresa moderna*. 3d ed. Madrid: ASP.

———. 1959. *IV Congreso Luso-Español de Patronos Católicos: Productividad y Consumo*. Barcelona: ASP-UCIDT.

———. 1960. *Problemas de personal: Selección profesional, primas colectivas, convenios colectivos*. Madrid: Comisión Nacional de ASP.

———. 1961. *La remuneración del trabajo*. Madrid: Comisión Nacional de ASP.

———. 1962a. *La comunicación en le empresa*. Madrid: ASP.

———. 1962b. *VIII Asamblea Nacional: El empresario ante la "Mater et Magistra."* Madrid: ASP.

―――. 1963. *Puntos de partida para los estudios sobre el perfeccionamiento de la empresa.* Madrid: ASP.

―――. 1964. *El empresario cristiano ante las circustancias actuales.* Madrid: ASP.

―――. 1966. *Participación activa del personal en la empresa.* Madrid: ASP.

Aunós Pérez, Eduardo. n.d. *La organización corporativa del trabajo.* Madrid: Publicaciones del Consejo Superior de Trabajo, Comercio e Industria.

―――. 1962. *Técnica y espiritualidid.* Madrid: Instituto Editorial Reus.

Aznar, Severino. 1935. *Remuneración del trabajo.* Madrid: Imprenta Sáez Hermanos.

Barceló Matutano, Gabriel. [1972] 1976. *El dirigente del futuro.* 4th ed. Madrid: Asociación para el Progreso de la Dirección.

―――. [1974] 1975. *El oficio de mandar.* 2d ed. Madrid: Asociación para el Progreso de la Dirección.

Barril Dosset, Rafael. 1963. "Justificación de las relaciones humanas en la empresa." *Productividad* 28 (July–August–September):10–17.

Ben-Ami, Schlomo. 1983. *Fascism from Above: The Dictatorship of Primo de Rivera in Spain 1923–1930.* Oxford: Clarendon Press.

Bohigas, Oriol. 1973. *Reseña y catálogo de la arquitectura modernista.* Barcelona: Lumen.

Brugarola, Martín. 1945a. *La cristianización de las empresas.* Madrid: Fax.

―――. 1945b. *La dignidad del trabajo.* Barcelona: Editorial Vicente Ferrer.

―――. 1957. *Relaciones humanas y reforma de la empresa.* Madrid: Euramérica.

―――. 1971. *Para ti, dirigente de empresa.* Madrid: Asesoría Eclesiástica Nacional de Sindicatos.

―――. 1972. *Para ti, trabajador.* Madrid: Asesoría Eclesiástica Nacional de Sindicatos.

Bueno Campos, Eduardo, ed. 1987. *La empresa española: Estructura y resultados.* Madrid: Instituto de Estudios Económicos.

Buesa, Mikel, and José Molero. 1982. "Cambio técnico y procesos de trabajo: Una aproximación al papel del Estado en la introducción de los métodos de la organización científica del trabajo en la economía española durante los años cincuenta." *Revista de Trabajo* 67–68:249–268.

Cabrera, Mercedes. 1983. *La patronal ante la II República: Organizaciones y estrategia 1931–1936.* Madrid: Siglo Veintiuno.

Cardellach i Avilés, Félix. 1909–1910. "La enseñanza de la construcción en las escuelas de ingenieros." *Anuario de la Universidad de Barcelona 1909 à 1910,* pp. 229–346.

―――. 1916. *Las formas artísticas en la arquitectura técnica.* Barcelona: Agustín Bosch.

Carrasco Belinchón, Julián. 1966. *Manual de organización y métodos. I: Funciones directivas.* Madrid: Instituto de Estudios de Administración Local.

―――. 1969. *Técnica y humanismo en la gestión local.* Málaga: Colegio Oficial de Secretarios, Interventores y Depositarios de Administración Local de la Provincia de Málaga.

Casanova, José V. 1983. *The Opus Dei Ethic and the Modernization of Spain.*

Ph.D. diss., New School for Social Research. Ann Arbor, Michigan: University Microfilms International.

Castañeda, José. 1959. *Apuntes de organización de empresas industriales.* Madrid: Litografía E. Nieto.

Castillo Alonso, Juan José. 1984. "Las 'neuvas formas de organización del trabajo.'" *Revista Española de Investigaciones Sociológicas* 26 (April–June): 201–212.

————. 1986. "El Taylorismo hoy: ¿Arqueología industrial?" *Arbor* 483 (March):9–40.

Castillo, Juan José, and Carlos Prieto. 1983. *Condiciones de trabajo: Hacia un enfoque renovador de la sociología del trabajo.* Madrid: Centro de Investigaciones Sociológicas.

CECA, ed. 1971. *Sociología española de los años setenta.* Madrid: Confederación Española de Cajas de Ahorros.

Chalbaud, Luis. 1916. *Discurso leído en la solemne apertura de los estudios en la Universidad Comercial de Deusto.* Bilbao: La Editorial Vizcaína.

CNPI (Comisión Nacional de Productividad Industrial). n.d. *Curso de relaciones humanas.* Madrid: CNPI.

————. 1959a. *Relaciones humanas.* Madrid: CNPI.

————. 1959b. *Curso de organización general de empresa.* Madrid: CNPI.

————. 1959c. *Dirección de personal: Memoria de un viaje a Estados Unidos.* Madrid: CNPI.

————. 1960a. *Mejora de métodos de trabajo.* Madrid: CNPI.

————. 1960b. *Salarios, tiempos de trabajo e incentivos.* Madrid: CNPI.

————. 1961. *Relaciones humanas: Memoria.* Madrid: CNPI.

————. 1962. *Técnica y apliación del cronometraje.* Madrid: CNPI.

Colinas Aguirrebengoa, Juan Antonio. 1966. *Historia de la Universidad Comercial de Deusto, 1916–1966.* Bilbao: Universidad Comercial de Deusto.

Collins, George R., and Carlos Flores. 1968. *Arturo Soria y la Ciudad Lineal.* Madrid: Revista de Occidente.

Comisaría del Plan de Desarrollo. 1967. *Factores humanos y sociales.* Madrid: Comisaría del Plan de Desarrollo Económico y Social de Presidencia del Gobierno.

Consejo de Economía Nacional. 1965. *La renta nacional de España 1940–1964.* Madrid: Consejo de Economía Nacional.

Cuñat Cosonís, Roberto. n.d. *Problemas humanos de la moderna organización del trabajo en la industria.* Reuniones técnicas de información sobre organización de la producción. Madrid: Instituto Nacional de Racionalización del Trabajo.

————. [1957] 1958. *Productividad y mando de hombres en la empresa española.* 2d ed. Madrid: Euramérica.

Cuñat Cosonís, Roberto, et al. 1963. *Cómo funcionan los servicios de personal en las empresas españolas: Prácticas y políticas.* 2d ed. Madrid: Asociación para el Progreso de la Dirección.

————. 1965. *Políticas de personal de las empresas españolas.* Madrid: Asociación para el Progreso de la Dirección.

De la Sierra, Fermín, Juan José Caballero, and Juan Pedro Pérez Escanilla.

1981. *Los directores de grandes empresas españolas ante el cambio social.* Madrid: Centro de Investigaciones Sociológicas.

De Lucas Ortueta, Ramón. [1960] 1974. *Manual de personal: Técnicas de dirección de personal.* 7th ed. Madrid: Index.

———. 1961. *Técnicas de dirección de personal.* 2d ed. Madrid: Cámara Oficial de la Industria de Madrid.

———. 1963a. *Organización científica de las empresas.* 4th ed. Madrid: (No publisher).

———. 1963b. *Valoración de tareas y estructura de salarios.* Madrid: Artes Gráficas y Ediciones.

———. 1967. *La dirección y la estructura de la empresa: Cómo organizar, cómo dirigir.* Madrid: Colección de Temas Empresariales.

De Miguel, Amando. 1975. *Sociología del Franquismo: Análisis ideológico de los ministros del régimen.* Barcelona: Euros.

De Miguel, Amando, and Juan J. Linz. 1963. "Los problemas de la retribución y el rendimiento, vistos por los empresarios españoles." *Revista de Trabajo* 1 (March):35–140.

———. 1964a. "Nivel de estudios del empresariado español." *Arbor* 57(219) (March):33–63.

———. 1964b. "Características estructurales de las empresas españolas: Tecnificación y burocracia." *Racionalización* 17(1) (January–February):1–11; 17(2) (March–April):97–104; 17(3) (May–June):193–208; 17(4) (July–August):289–296.

———. 1964c. "Bureaucratisation et pouvoir discrétionnaire dans les entreprises industrielles espagnoles." *Sociologie du Travail* 6(3) (July–September):258–278.

De Miguel, Jesús M., and Melissa G. Moyer. 1979. "Sociology in Spain." *Current Sociology* 27(1) (Spring):1–299.

De Orbaneja y Aragón, José. n.d. *Nuevas bases de las relaciones humanas en la empresa.* Reuniones técnicas de información sobre la organización científica del trabajo en la industria. Madrid: Instituto Nacional de Racionalización del Trabajo.

De Pedro y San Gil, Xavier. 1967. *Relaciones humanas y técnicas de promoción de grupo.* Zaragoza: Obra Sindical "Cooperación," Escuela de Gerentes Cooperativos.

Del Campo, Salustiano. 1958. "Grupos pequeños organización informal en la industria." *Revista de Estudios Políticos* 101 (September–October): 123–159.

Díaz Díaz, Gonzalo. 1980, 1983, 1988. *Hombres y documentos de la filosofía española.* 3 vols. Madrid: Consejo Superior de Investigaciones Científicas.

Díez Nicolás, Juan, Juan del Pino Artacho, and Rafael Gobernado Arribas. 1984. *Cincuenta años de sociología en España: Bibliografía de sociología en lengua castellana.* Málaga: Universidad de Málaga.

D'Ocón Cortés, Emilio. 1927. *Organización científica del trabajo y racionalización de la producción.* Toledo: F. Serrano.

Dolgoff, Sam, ed. 1974. *The Anarchist Collectives: Worker's Self-Management in the Spanish Revolution, 1936–1939.* Montreal: Black Rose.

Egurbide, Pedro. 1976. "El 'consulting' en España." *Información Comercial Española* 513 (May):133–137.

Escrivá de Balaguer, Josemaría. [1939] 1990. *Camino.* Madrid: Rialp.

Esteva Fabregat, Claudio. 1957. "El factor humano en la producción industrial." *Cuadernos de política social* 36:7–25.

———. 1960. "La máquina y la deshumanización del trabajo." *Cuadernos de política social* 47:43–77.

———. 1973. *Antropología industrial.* Barcelona: Planeta.

Estivill i Pascual, Jordi, and Josep R. Tomàs i Llacuna. 1978. "Orientación profesional en Cataluña." *Cuadernos de Pedagogía* 4(47) (November): 44–47.

Fernández Hernández, Máximo. 1970. *Psicología del trabajo: La adaptación del hombre a su tarea.* Madrid: Index.

Feu Gutiérrez, A. M., A. Macías Martínez, and E. Matute Butragueño. 1970. *Psicología general e industrial.* Madrid: ICAI-ICADE.

Fishman, Robert M. 1990. *Working-Class Organization and the Return to Democracy in Spain.* Ithaca, New York: Cornell University Press.

Frampton, Kenneth. [1984] 1985. *Martorell, Bohigas, Mackay: Trente ans d'architecture 1954–1984.* Paris: Electa Moniteur.

Frederick, W. C., and C. J. Haberstroh. 1969. *La enseñanza de dirección de empresas en España. Management Education in Spain.* Bilingual edition. Madrid: Moneda y Crédito.

Freixa, Mireia. 1986. *El Modernismo en España.* Madrid: Cátedra.

Fundación Foessa, ed. 1966. *Informe sociológico sobre la situación social de España 1966.* Madrid: Euramérica.

———. 1970. *Informe sociológico sobre la situación social de España 1970.* Madrid: Euramérica.

García Delgado, José Luis. 1980. "Crecimiento y cambio industrial en España, 1960–1980: Viejos y nuevos problemas." *Economía Industrial* 197 (May):13–24.

García Fernández, Manuel. 1984. *La formación del Derecho del Trabajo.* Palma de Mallorca: Facultad de Derecho de la Universidad de las Islas Baleares.

García Hernández, Ramón, and Jesús Calvo Barrios. 1981. *Arturo Soria: Un urbanismo olvidado.* Madrid: Junta Municipal del Distrito de Ciudad Lineal.

Garrigues Walker, Antonio, Francisco Lapiedra de Federico, Víctor Fernández González, and Isaac Borge Piñán. 1965. *La participación de los trabajadores en los consejos de administración.* Madrid: Asociación para el Progreso de la Dirección.

Gil Peláez, José. 1967. "Los EE. UU. en el movimiento español de la productividad." *Información Comercial Española* 409 (September):145–148.

Giner, Salvador, and Luis Moreno, eds. 1990. *Sociology in Spain.* Madrid: CSIC.

Gómez Arboleya, Enrique. 1954. "Teoría del grupo social." *Revista de Estudios Políticos* 76(July–August):3–33.

González, Manuel-Jesús. 1979. *La economía política del Franquismo, 1940–1970: Dirigismo, mercado y planificación.* Madrid: Tecnos.

González Blasco, Pedro, and Juan González-Anleo. 1992. *Religión y sociedad en la España de los 90*. Madrid: Ediciones SM.

González Moralejo, Rafael. [1957] 1965. "Prólogo." In *Relaciones humanas en la empresa moderna: Guía de actuación práctica patrocinada por dirigentes de empresa americanos*. 3d ed. Madrid: Acción Social Patronal, pp. ix–xxi.

González Páramo, José Manuel. 1966. *La empresa y la política social*. Tomo 1. *Análisis interdisciplinar del conflicto*. Madrid: Rialp.

Gracián, Baltasar. [1642] 1944. *Agudeza y arte de ingenio*. In *Obras completas*. Madrid: M. Aguilar, pp. 53–290.

Grupo de Trabajo para el Estudio de los Nuevos Problemas de la Ingeniería. 1975. *La crisis de los ingenieros españoles*. Madrid: Ayuso.

Gual Villalbí, Pedro. 1929. *Principios y aplicaciones de la organización científica del trabajo*. Barcelona: Editorial Juventud.

———. 1948. *Política de la producción*. Barcelona: Editorial Juventud.

Guerrero Martínez, Fernando. 1963. "Participación activa de los trabajadores en la empresa." In Instituto Social León XIII, *Comentarios a la Mater et Magistra*. Madrid: Biblioteca de Autores Cristianos, pp. 328–364.

———. 1967. "La reforma de la empresa." *Arbor* 68(263) (November): 159–197.

Hevia Cangas, Fernando. 1962. *El ingeniero en la empresa*. Madrid: Euramérica.

IEP. 1962. *La empresa*. Madrid: Instituto de Estudios Políticos.

Instituto Balmes de Sociología. 1958. *El elemento humano en la empresa*. Madrid: CSIC.

Instituto Social León XIII, ed. 1963. *Comentarios a la Mater et Magistra*. Madrid: Biblioteca de Autores Cristianos.

Jardí, Enric. 1975. *Puig i Cadafalch: Arquitecte, polític i historiador de l'art*. Mataró: Caixa d'Estalvis Laietana.

Lafourcade, Agustín. 1965. *El factor humano en la empresa*. Madrid: Ediciones del Movimiento.

Leprévost, Leonardo. [1928] 1933. *Economía industrial y organización de talleres*. 2d ed. Barcelona: Labor.

Linz, Juan J. 1964. "An Authoritarian Regime: Spain." In Erik Allardt, and Yrjö Littunen, eds., *Cleavages, Ideologies and Party Systems: Contributions to Comparative Political Sociology*. Helsinki: The Academic Bookstore, pp. 291–341.

———. 1970. "From Falange to Movimiento-Organización: The Spanish Single Party and the Franco Regime." In Samuel Huntington and Clement Moore, eds., *Authoritarian Politics in Modern Society: The Dynamics of Established One-Party Systems*. New York: Basic, pp. 128–203.

———. 1972. "Intellectual roles in sixteenth- and seventeenth-century Spain." *Daedalus* 101(2) (Summer):59–108.

———. 1973a. "Early State Building and Late Peripheral Nationalisms Against the State: The Case of Spain." In S. N. Eisenstadt and Stein Rokkan, eds., *Building States and Nations*. Vol. 2. *Analyses by Region*. Beverly Hills, California: Sage, pp. 32–116.

————. 1973b. "Opposition In and Under an Authoritarian Regime: The Case of Spain." In Robert A. Dahl, ed., *Regimes and Oppositions*. New Haven, Connecticut: Yale University Press, pp. 171–259.

————. 1981. "A Century of Politics and Interests in Spain." In Suzanne Berger, ed., *Organizing Interests in Western Europe: Pluralism, Corporatism, and the Transformation of Politics*. Cambridge: Cambridge University Press, pp. 365–415.

Linz, Juan J., and Amando de Miguel. 1963a. "El empresario español ante los problemas laborales." *Revista de Política Social* 60 (October–December):5–105.

————. 1963b. "El prestigio de las profesiones en el mundo empresarial." *Revista de Estudios Políticos* 128 (March–April):23–76, 129–130 (May–August):5–33.

————. 1963–1964. "Fundadores, herederos y directores en las empresas españolas." *Revista Internacional de Sociología* 21(81) (January–March 1963):5–38; 21(82) (April–June 1963):185–216; 22(85) (January–March 1964):5–28. Abridged English version: "Founders, heirs, and managers of Spanish firms." *International Studies of Management and Organization* 4(1–2) (Spring–Summer 1974):7–40.

————. 1966a. *Los empresarios ante el poder público: El liderazgo y los grupos de intereses en el empresariado español*. Madrid: Instituto de Estudios Políticos.

————. 1966b. "Within-Nation Differences and Comparisons: The Eight Spains." In Richard L. Merritt and Stein Rokkan, eds., *Comparing Nations: The Use of Quantitative Data in Cross-National Research*. New Haven, Connecticut: Yale University Press, pp. 267–319.

Litvak, Lily. 1975. *A Dream of Arcadia: Anti-Industrialism in Spanish Literature, 1895–1905*. Austin: University of Texas Press.

Lozano, Vicente, and Eduardo Bendala. 1992. "Los españoles más influyentes." *Actualidad Económica* (August 3):14–25.

Ludevid, Manuel. 1976. *Cuarenta años de sindicato vertical*. Barcelona: Laia.

Mackay, David. 1985. *Modern Architecture in Barcelona (1854–1939)*. Sheffield, England: The Anglo-Catalan Society.

Macrométrica. 1978. *Cifras de la España económica*. Madrid: Fondo Editorial, Standard Eléctrica.

Madariaga y Rojo, César de. ca. 1930. *Organización científica del trabajo*. Vol. 1. *Las ideas*. Madrid: Juan Ortiz.

————. 1953. *Iniciación al estudio del factor humano en la actividad económica: Elementos de psicoeconomía*. Madrid: Aguilar.

Mallart, José. 1922. *El factor humano en la organización del trabajo: Para los patronos, para los obreros, para los técnicos*. Porto: Artes & Letras.

————. 1933. *La organización científica del trabajo doméstico*. Segovia: Imprenta de Carlos Martín.

————. 1934. *Organización científica del trabajo agrícola*. Barcelona: Salvat.

————. 1942. *Organización científica del trabajo*. Barcelona: Labor.

————. 1959. *Técnicas de dirección, administración y de oficina*. Madrid: Asociación Iberoamericana para la Eficacia y la Satisfacción en el Trabajo.

———. 1960. *Psicosociología del desarrollo industrial*. Vol. 1. *Relaciones humanas*. Madrid: Cámara Oficial de la Industria de la Provincia de Madrid.

———. 1974. "Cincuentenario del originariamente llamado Instituto de Orientación y Selección Profesional." *Revista de Psicología General y Aplicada* 29(131) (November–December):931–942.

———. 1981. *Psicología industrial y organizacional*. Madrid: Asociación Iberoamericana para la Eficacia y la Satisfacción en el Trabajo.

Mallart, José, y Pilar García Villegas. 1951. *La satisfacción en el trabajo como factor de productividad: Encuesta con 1291 trabajadores*. Madrid: Asociación Iberoamericana para la Eficacia y la Satisfacción en el Trabajo.

Maravall, José María. 1970. *El desarrollo económico y la clase obrera: Un estudio sociológico de los conflictos obreros en España*. Barcelona: Ariel.

———. 1978. *Dictatorship and Political Dissent: Workers and Students in Franco's Spain*. London: Tavistock.

Martin, Benjamin. 1990. *The Agony of Modernization: Labor and Industrialization in Spain*. Ithaca, New York: ILR Press.

Martín de Nicolás Cabo, Juan. 1969. *La formación universitaria para la empresa*. Barcelona: Ariel.

Martín Valverde, Antonio. 1987. "La formación del Derecho del Trabajo en España." In *La legislación laboral histórica*. Madrid: Cortes Generales, 1987, pp. xv–cxiv.

Martínez, Robert Esteban. 1984. *Business Elites in Democratic Spain*. PhD diss. New Haven, Connecticut: Yale University Graduate School.

Martínez González-Tablas, Angel. 1979. *Capitalismo extranjero en España*. Madrid: Cupsa.

Marvá y Mayer, José. 1917. *Organización científica del trabajo antes y después de la guerra actual*. Lecture delivered at the Real Academia de Jurisprudencia y Legislación, Madrid, March 2 and 4. Madrid: Jaime Ratés.

Matute Butragueño, Eduardo. 1967. *Apuntes de política de personal*. Madrid: ICAI-ESDE.

———. 1970. *Política de personal*. Madrid: ICADE.

———. 1974. *La dirección de personal en la empresa española*. Madrid: Librería ICAI.

Ministro de Economía Nacional. 1928. "Estatuto sobre formación técnica de ingenieros industriales y de investigación." In *Enciclopedia Jurídica Española* (1928 Appendix, 2:113–119). Barcelona: Francisco Seix.

Ministro de Trabajo, Comercio e Industria. 1926. "Real Decreto-Ley de 26 de Noviembre de Organización Corporativa Nacional." In *Enciclopedia Jurídica Española* (1926 Appendix, 2:402–410). Barcelona: Francisco Seix.

———. 1928. "Real Decreto de 30 de Julio de nueva redacción del artículo 17 del Real Decreto-Ley de 26 de Noviembre de 1926 de Organización Corporativa Nacional." In *Enciclopedia Jurídica Española* (1928 Appendix, 2:587–590). Barcelona: Francisco Seix.

Ministro de Trabajo y Previsión. 1928. "Estatuto de formación profesional."

In *Enciclopedia Jurídica Española* (1928 Appendix, 2:93–113). Barcelona: Francisco Seix.

Mira y López, Emilio. [1947] 1959. *Manual de orientación profesional.* 5th ed. Buenos Aires: Kapelusz.

Molero, José. 1979. "Las empresas de ingeniería." *Información Comercial Española* 552 (August):59–71.

Moncada, Alberto. 1974. *El Opus Dei, una interpretación.* Madrid: Indice.

Montolíu, Cipriano. [1915] 1916. *El sistema de Taylor y su crítica.* Barcelona: Casa Editorial Estudio.

Montoro Romero, Ricardo. 1981. *La universidad en la España de Franco, 1939–1970: Un análisis sociológico.* Madrid: Centro de Investigaciones Sociológicas.

Montoya Melgar, Alfredo. 1965. *El poder de dirección del empresario.* Foreword by Manuel Alonso Olea. Madrid: Instituto de Estudios Políticos.

———. 1975. *Ideología y lenguaje en las primeras leyes laborales de España.* Madrid: Civitas.

Morcillo, Casimiro. 1956. *Cristo en la fábrica.* Madrid: Euramérica.

Moreno Caracciolo, M. 1919. "El método Taylor en la fábrica de Trubia." *El Sol* (July 25):12.

Moreno Ultra, Florentino. n. d. *Problemas y experiencias de organización científica en construcción naval.* Reuniones técnicas de información sobre productividad. Madrid: Instituto Nacional de Racionalización del Trabajo.

———. n. d. *Organización de los talleres de herreros de rivera de un astillero.* Reuniones técnicas de información sobre productividad. Madrid: Instituto Nacional de Racionalización del Trabajo.

Moya, Carlos. 1975. *El poder económico en España 1939–1970; Un análisis sociológico.* Madrid: Túcar.

Muñoz, Juan, Santiago Roldán, and Angel Serrano. 1978. *La internacionalización del capital en España 1959–1977.* Madrid: Edicusa.

Nadal, Jordi. 1975. *El fracaso de la revolución industrial en España, 1814–1913.* Barcelona: Ariel.

Ortega y Gasset, José. [1925] 1991. *La deshumanización del arte.* Madrid: Revista de Occidente en Alianza Editorial.

———. [1929] 1986. *La rebelión de las masas.* Madrid: Espasa-Calpe. English trans. *The Revolt of the Masses.* New York: W. W. Norton, 1932.

———. [1933] 1989. *Meditación de la técnica y otros ensayos sobre ciencia y filosofía.* Madrid: Revista de Occidente en Alianza Editorial.

———. [1954] 1983. "Una vista sobre la situación del gerente o 'manager' en la sociedad actual." In *El "manager" en la sociedad actual.* With an introduction by Julián Marías. Madrid: Asociación para el Progreso de la Dirección.

Payne, Stanley G. 1987. *The Franco Regime 1936–1975.* Madison: The University of Wisconsin Press.

Payno, Juan Antonio. 1973. *Los gerentes españoles: Su comportamiento en la dirección de las empresas.* Madrid: Moneda y Crédito.

Paz Social. 1913. "El 'Taylorismo' o sistema Taylor." *La Paz Social* 7(76) (June 1913):322–323.

Pérez Díaz, Víctor. 1987. *El retorno de la sociedad civil: Repuestas sociales a la transición, la crisis económica y los cambios culturales de España 1975–1985.* Madrid: Instituto de Estudios Económicos.

Pinilla de las Heras, Esteban. 1968. *Los empresarios y desarrollo capitalista: El caso catalán.* Barcelona: Península.

Pinillos, José Luis. 1959. "Organización y conducta." *Productividad* 11 (April–May–June):3–13.

———. 1969. *Las ciencias humanas y la organización industrial: Nuevos caminos.* Madrid: Instituto Superior de Dirección de Empresas.

Pintado Fe, Alberto, and Luis Torres Márquez. 1965. *Las técnicas de medida y retribución del trabajo en las empresas españolas.* Madrid: Escuela de Organización Industrial.

Posada, Adolfo. 1929. *La organización científica del trabajo.* Madrid: Minuesa de los Ríos.

Racionalización. 1949. "La Organización Científica en la industria española." *Racionalización* 2(2) (March–April):99–107.

Rius Sintes, Isidro. 1940. *Organización industrial.* Barcelona: Bosch.

Rivases, Jesús. 1988. *Los banqueros del PSOE.* Barcelona: Ediciones B.

Robles, Laureano, ed. 1987. *Epistolario completo Ortega-Unamuno.* Madrid: El Arquero.

Rodríguez Piñero, Miguel. 1978. "Un modelo democrático de relaciones laborales. " In José Cabrera Bazán et al., *Ideologías jurídicas y relaciones de trabajo.* Sevilla: Publicaciones de la Universidad de Sevilla, pp. 9–41.

Roldán, Santiago, José Luis García Delgado, and Juan Muñoz. 1973. *La consolidación del capitalismo en España,* 2 vols. Madrid: Confederación Española de Cajas de Ahorro.

Rubio de Arriba, Víctor. 1950. "Organización y productividad." *Arbor* 16(54) (June 1950):221–231.

Ruiz Almansa, Javier. 1929. *Manual práctico de organización científica del trabajo.* Barcelona: Editiorial Cultura.

San Juan Rubio, Serafín. 1959. "La descentralización en la dirección de la empresa." *Anales de Mecánica y Electricidad* 26(1) (January–February): 21–25.

Sánchez, Alejandro, ed. 1992. *Barcelone 1888–1929: Modernistes, anarchistes, noucentistes ou la création fiévreuse d'une nation catalane.* Paris: Autrement, Série Mémoires no. 16.

Sánchez Gil, Mariano. 1960. *Deontología de ingenieros y directivos de empresa.* Madrid: Aguilar.

Sánchez Rodrigo, Mariano. 1959. "La difusión de los principios y métodos de dirección de empresa." *Productividad* 10 (January–March):43–56.

Sangro y Ros de Olana, Pedro. 1910. *Sistemas de retribución del trabajo.* Madrid: Centro de Publicaciones Católicas.

Sastre García, Vicente José. 1976. "Las ciencias sociales en España." *Documentación Social* 24 (November).

Schwartz, Pedro, and Manuel-Jesús González. 1978. *Una historia del Instituto Nacional de Industria, 1941–1976*. Madrid: Tecnos.

Sempere Navarro, Antonio Vicente. 1982. *Nacionalsindicalismo y relación de trabajo*. Madrid: Akal.

Siguán, Miguel. 1958. *Relaciones humanas en la administración pública*. Madrid: Presidencia del Gobierno.

———. [1959] 1963. *Problemas humanos del trabajo industrial*. Madrid: Rialp.

Soria y Mata, Arturo. 1894. *Conferencia dada en el Ateneo Científico y Literario de Madrid* (May 14). Madrid: Sucesores de Rivadeneyra.

———. 1907. *Buen negocio*. Madrid: Compañía Madrileña de Urbanización.

Soto Carmona, Alvaro. 1989. *El trabajo industrial en la España contemporánea (1874–1936)*. Barcelona: Anthropos.

Suanzes, Juan Antonio. 1963. *Ocho discursos*. Madrid: Centro de Estudios Económicos y Sociales del Instituto Nacional de Industria.

Suárez Suárez, Andrés S. 1981. *Orden económico y libertad*. Madrid: Pirámide.

Tallada, Josep M. 1912. "El ingeniero social." *Boletín del Museo Social (Butlletí del Museu Social)* 3(14) (April):50–55.

———. 1922. *L'organització científica de la indústria*. Barcelona: Institut d'Orientació Professional.

Tamames, Ramón. 1977. *La oligarquía financiera en España*. Barcelona: Planeta.

———. 1986. *The Spanish Economy: An Introduction*. London: C. Hurst.

Tamames, Ramón, ed. 1977. *Anuario económico y social de España 1977*. Barcelona: Planeta.

Tezanos, José Félix. 1974. "Los conflictos laborales en España." *Revista Española de la Opinión Pública* 38 (October–December):93–110.

Tomàs, Josep R., and Jordi Estivill. 1979. "Apuntes para una historia de la organización del trabajo en España, 1900–1936." *Sociología del Trabajo* 1:17–43.

Travesi, Andrés, ed. 1969. *La empresa española*. Madrid: Asociación para el Progreso de la Dirección.

Tuñón de Lara, Manuel. 1972. *El movimiento obrero en la historia de España*. Madrid: Taurus.

———. 1984. "Progeso técnico y conciencia social, 1898–1936." In José Luis García Delgado, ed., *España, 1898–1936: Estructuras y cambio*. Madrid: Universidad Complutense, pp. 17–70.

Tusell, Javier. 1986. *Historia de la democracia cristiana en España*. 2 vols. Madrid: SARPE.

Unamuno, Miguel de. [1898] 1968. "Doctores en industrias." In *Obras completas*, vol. 3. Madrid: Escelicer, pp. 692–697.

Uriarte, Pedro. 1969. *El hombre en los sitemas económicos: Reflexión psicosociológica*. Bilbao: Mensajero.

Valentí Camp, Santiago. 1914. "Indagaciones y lecturas: La dirección científica del trabajo humano." *Estudio* 20 (August):232–253.

Vegara, José María. 1971. *La organización científica del trabajo: ¿Ciencia o ideología? Introducción crítica*. Barcelona: Fontanella.

Velarde Fuertes, Juan. 1973. *Política económica de la Dictadura*. Madrid: Guadiana.

Velasco Miguel, Carlos. n. d. *Aumento de productividad mediante el establecimiento de grupos de trabajo progresivo: Grupo de montaje progresivo del aparato telefónico*. Reuniones técnicas de información sobre productividad. Madrid: Instituto Nacional de Racionalización del Trabajo.

Vicesecretaría General del Movimiento. 1967. *Crecimiento económico y política social*. Madrid: Ediciones del Movimiento.

Villalón, Teclo, and Pedro Plasencia. 1992. "Le estela de Gaudí." *Sobremesa* 9(96) (October):55–65.

Voltes Bou, Pedro. 1979. *Historia de la empresa española: La evolución empresarial dentro de la economía española*. Barcelona: Editorial Hispano Europea.

Witney, Fred. 1965. *Labor Policy and Practices in Spain: A Study of Employer-Employee Relations under the Franco Regime*. New York: Praeger.

Yela, Mariano. 1967. "Psicología del trabajo." In David Katz, ed., *Manual de psicología*. Madrid: Ediciones Morata, pp. 565–620.

———. 1974. *Personalidad y eficacia: La dinámica de las actitudes en la empresa*. Barcelona: Cros.

Zaragüeta, Juan. 1927. *La vocación profesional*. San Sebastián: Nueva Editorial.

F. GREAT BRITAIN

AACP (Anglo-American Council on Productivity). 1948. *Report of the First Session*. London: AACP.

———. 1951. *Education for Management*. London: AACP.

———. 1952. *The Final Report*. London: AACP.

Albu, Austen. 1952. "The organization of industry." In R. H. S. Crossman, ed., *New Fabian Essays*. New York: Frederick A. Praeger, pp. 121–142.

Ashley, Sir William. 1922. *Scientific Management and the Engineering Situation*. Barnett House Papers No. 7. London: Oxford University Press.

Babbage, Charles. [1832] 1835. *On the Economy of Machinery and Manufactures*. 4th ed., enlarged. London: Charles Knight. (A recent reprint is New York: A. M. Kelley, 1971.)

Balchin, Nigel. 1954. *The Worker in Modern Industry*. London: Institute of Personnel Management.

Barnes, William. 1989. *Managerial Catalyst: The Story of the London Business School, 1964–1989*. London: Paul Chapman.

Berg, Maxine. 1987. "Babbage, Charles." In John Eatwell, Murray Milgate, and Peter Newman, eds., *The New Palgrave: A Dictionary of Economics*. London: Macmillan, vol. 1, pp. 166–167.

Betts, Roger. 1967. "Characteristics of British company directors." *Journal of Management Studies* 4(1) (February):71–88.

Beynon, Huw. 1973. *Working for Ford*. London: Allen Lane.

BIM (British Institute of Management). 1954. *The Application of Modern Management Techniques in the Smaller Enterprise*. London: BIM.

———. 1959. *Suggestion Schemes: Results from Two Companies*. London: BIM.

———. 1960. *Group Relations Training*. London: BIM.

Bornstein, Stephen, and Peter Gourevitch. 1984. "Unions in a declining economy: The case of the British TUC." In Peter Gourevitch et al., eds., *Unions and Economic Crisis: Britain, West Germany and Sweden*. London: George Allen & Unwin.

Boulding, Kenneth E. 1953. *The Organizational Revolution: A Study in the Ethics of Economic Organization*. New York: Harper & Brothers.

Bowie, James A. 1930. *Education for Business Management: The Case for the Further Development of Educational Facilities*. London: Oxford University Press.

BPC (British Productivity Council). 1957. *Suggestion Schemes*. London: The Council.

Bramley, James F. 1944. *The Voice of the Factory: A Manual of Work Relations*. Longbridge, Birmingham, England: Austin Motor Co., Ltd.

Brech, Edward Franz Leopold. 1957. *Organisation: The Framework of Management*. London: Longmans.

Brech, Edward Franz Leopold, ed. [1953] 1963. *The Principles and Practice of Management*. 2d ed. London: Longmans.

Briggs, Asa. 1961. *Social Thought and Social Action: A Study of the Work of Seebohm Rowntree 1871–1954*. London: Longmans.

Brown, Geoff. 1977. *Sabotage: A Study in Industrial Conflict*. Nottingham: Spokesman.

Brown, J. A. C. 1954. *The Social Psychology of Industry: Human Relations in the Factory*. Harmondsworth, Middlesex, England: Penguin.

Brown, Richard K. 1967. "Research and consultancy in industrial enterprises: A review of the contribution of the Tavistock Institute of Human Relations to the development of industrial sociology." *Sociology* 1(1) (January 1967):33–60.

Brown, Wilfred. 1960. *Exploration in Management*. New York: John Wiley & Sons.

———. 1971. *Organization*. London: Heinemann.

Brown, Wilfred, and Elliott Jacques. 1965. *Glacier Project Papers*. London: Heinemann.

Buchanan. R. A. 1989. *The Engineers: A History of the Engineering Profession in Britain, 1750–1914*. London: Jessica Kingsley.

Burns, Tom, ed. 1969. *Industrial Man: Selected Readings*. Harmondsworth, Middlesex, England: Penguin.

Burns, Tom, and G. M. Stalker. 1961. *The Management of Innovation*. London: Tavistock.

Cadbury, Edward. 1912. *Experiments in Industrial Organization*. London: Longmans, Green.

Cadbury, Edward, M. Cécile Matheson, and George Shann. 1906. *Women's Work and Wages: A Phase of Life in an Industrial City*. London: T. Fisher Unwin.

Cadbury, Edward, and George Shann. 1908. *Sweating*. Social Service Handbooks, No. 5. London: Headley Brothers.

Casson, Herbert N. 1903. *Common Sense on the Labor Question*. Booklet, not copyrighted.

————. 1923. *How to Keep Your Money and Make It Earn More.* New York: B. C. Forbes.

————. 1927. *Tips on Leadership: Life Stories of Twenty-Five Leaders.* New York: B. C. Forbes.

————. 1929. *Creative Thinkers: The Efficient Few Who Cause Progress and Prosperity. An Explanation of the Rise and Fall of Business Firms and Nations.* New York: B. C. Forbes.

Cathcart, Edward Provan. 1928. *The Human Factor in Industry.* London: Oxford University Press.

Channon, Derek F. 1973. *The Strategy and Structure of British Enterprise.* Boston: Division of Research, Graduate School of Business Administration, Harvard University.

Child, John. 1964. "Quaker employers and industrial relations." *Sociological Review* 12(3) (November):293–315.

————. 1969. *British Management Thought: A Critical Analysis.* London: George Allen & Unwin.

————. 1972. "Organizational structure, environment and performance: The role of strategic choice." *Sociology* 6(1) (January):1–22.

Clewer, Winston. 1955. *The Human Implications of Work Study.* London: Industrial Welfare Society.

Clump, Cyril C. 1958. *The Social Teaching of Pope Pius XII: 1956.* Oxford: Catholic Social Guild.

Coleman, D. C. 1973. "Gentlemen and players." *Economic History Review,* series 2, 26(1):92–116.

Cooke, Colin. 1957. *The Life of Richard Stafford Cripps.* London: Hodder & Stoughton.

Cooper, Jackie, ed. 1977. *Mackintosh Architecture: The Complete Buildings and Selected Projects.* London: Academy; and New York: St. Martin's.

Copeman, G. H. 1955. *Leaders of British Industry: A Study of the Careers of More Than a Thousand Public Company Directors.* London: Gee.

Cripps, Stafford. 1945. *Towards Christian Democracy.* London: George Allen & Unwin.

Davenport-Hines, R. P. T., and Geoffrey Jones, eds. 1988. *Enterprise, Management and Innovation in British Business 1914–80.* London: Frank Cass.

Davey, D. Mackenzie, D. Rockingham Gill, and P. McDonnell. 1970. *Attitude Surveys in Industry.* Information Report 3 (new series). London: Institute of Personnel Management.

Deverell, C. S. 1968. *Personnel Management: Human Relations in Industry.* London: Gee.

Donnelly, J. F. 1991. "Science, technology and industrial work in Britain, 1860–1930: Toward a new synthesis." *Social History* 16(2) (May): 191–201.

Downs, Laura Lee. 1990. "Industrial decline, rationalization and equal pay: The Bedaux strike at Rover automobile company." *Social History* 15(1) (January):45–73.

Dubin, Robert. 1970. "Management in Britain: Impressions of a visiting professor." *Journal of Management Studies* 7(2) (May):183–198.

The Economist. 1955. "Parkinson's Law." *The Economist* (November 19): 635–637.

Elbourne, Edward Tregaskiss. 1914. *Factory Administration and Accounts*. London: Longmans, Green.

———. 1919. *The Management Problem*. London: The Library Press.

———. 1934. *Fundamentals of Industrial Administration*. London: MacDonald & Evans.

Emden, Paul H. 1939. *Quakers in Commerce: A Record of Business Achievement*. London: Sampson Low, Martson.

FBI (Federation of British Industries). 1946–1964. *Annual Report*. Years 1946 through 1964. London: FBI.

Flanders, Allan, and H. A. Clegg, eds. 1964. *The System of Industrial Relations in Great Britain: Its History, Law and Institutions*. Oxford: Basil Blackwell.

Flanders, Allan, Ruth Pomeranz, and Joan Woodward. 1968. *Experiment in Industrial Democracy: A Study of the John Lewis Partnership*. London: Faber and Faber.

Florence, P. Sargant. 1953. *The Logic of British and American Industry: A Realistic Analysis of Economic Structure and Government*. London: Routledge & Kegan Paul.

Fogarty, Michael P. 1954. *Human Relations in Industry*. Oxford: Catholic Social Guild.

———. 1956. *Personality and Group Relations in Industry*. London: Longmans.

———. 1957. *Programme for Social Action*. Oxford: Catholic Social Guild.

Fraser, John Munro. 1960. *Human Relations in a Fully Employed Democracy*. London: Sir Isaac Pitman & Sons.

———. 1962. *Industrial Psychology*. Oxford: Pergamon.

Gillespie, James J. 1938. *The Principles of Rational Industrial Management*. London: Sir Isaac Pitman & Sons.

———. 1948. *Free Expression in Society: A Social-Psychological Study of Work and Leisure*. London: Pilot.

———. 1951. *Dynamic Motion and Time Study*. Brooklyn, New York: Chemical.

Glover, Ian A., and Michael P. Kelley. 1987. *Engineers in Britain: A Sociological Study of the Engineering Dimension*. London: Allen & Unwin.

Gunz, Hugh. 1980. "Generalists, specialists, and the reproduction of managerial structures." *International Journal of Management and Organization* 10(1–2) (Spring–Summer):137–164.

Hacon, R. J. 1965. *Conflict and Human Relations Training*. Oxford: Pergamon.

Handy, Charles B. [1976] 1985. *Understanding Organizations*. 3d ed. London: Penguin.

Hannah, Leslie. [1976] 1983. *The Rise of the Corporate Economy*. 2d ed. London: Methuen.

Hill, Stephen. 1981. *Competition and Control at Work: The New Industrial Sociology*. Cambridge, Massachusetts: MIT Press.

Hobsbawm, Eric J. [1968] 1969. *Industry and Empire: From 1750 to the Present Day*. Harmondsworth, Middlesex, England: Penguin.

Hobson, J. A. 1909. *The Industrial System: An Inquiry into Earned and Unearned Income*. London: Longmans, Green.

———. 1914. *Work and Wealth: A Human Valuation*. London: Macmillan.

———. 1922. *Incentives in the New Industrial Order*. London: Leonard Parsons.

Hooper, Sir Frederick C. 1948. *Management in the Public Services: A Portrait of the Public Administrator*. London: Institute of Public Administration.

Howarth, Thomas. [1952] 1977. *Charles Rennie Mackintosh and the Modern Movement*. 2d ed. London: Routledge.

Hutt, Allen. 1975. *British Trade Unionism: A Short History*. 6th ed., revised and enlarged. London: Lawrence & Wishart.

Hutton, Graham. 1953. *We Too Can Prosper: The Promise of Productivity*. London: George Allen & Unwin.

Huxley, Aldous. [1932] 1989. *Brave New World*. New York: Harper & Row.

Industrial Society. 1965. *Suggestion Scheme Statistics*. London: Industrial Society.

———. 1966. *Successful Suggestion Schemes*. London: Industrial Society.

IPM (Institute of Personnel Management). 1969. *Personnel Management: A Bibliography*. London: IPM.

Jago, Alison. 1979. *Suggestion Schemes*. IPM Information Report No. 27. London: Institute of Personnel Management.

Jaques, Elliott. 1951. *The Changing Culture of a Factory: A Study of Authority and Participation in an Industrial Setting*. London: Tavistock.

———. 1956. *Measurement of Responsibility: A Study of Work, Payment, and Individual Capacity*. Cambridge, Massachusetts: Harvard University Press.

———. 1970. *Work, Creativity, and Social Justice*. London: Heinemann.

Jeremy, David J., and Christine Shaw, eds., 1984–1986. *Dictionary of Business Biography: A Biographical Dictionary of Business Leaders Active in Britain in the Period 1860–1980*. 5 vols. London: Butterworths.

Jervis, F. G. J. 1974. *Bosses in British Business: Managers and Management from the Industrial Revolution to the Present Day*. London: Routledge & Kegan Paul.

Keil, I. 1965. "Advice to the magnates: Management education in the thirteenth century." *Bulletin of the Association of Teachers of Management* 17 (March):2–8.

Klein, Rudolf. [1983] 1989. *The Politics of the National Health Service*. 2d ed. London: Longman.

Lawe, F. W. 1944. *Staff Management*. London: Institute of Personnel Management.

Lee, John. 1921. *Management: A Study of Industrial Organisation.* London: Sir Isaac Pitman & Sons.

————. 1922. *The Social Implications of Christianity.* London: Student Christian Movement.

————. 1923. *Industrial Organisation: Developments and Prospects.* London: Sir Isaac Pitman & Sons.

————. 1924. *The Principles of Industrial Welfare.* London: Sir Isaac Pitman & Sons.

————. 1925. *An Introduction to Industrial Administration.* London: Sir Isaac Pitman & Sons.

————. 1937. "The Pros and Cons of Functionalization." In Luther Gulick and Lyndall Urwick, eds., *Papers on the Science of Administration.* New York: Institute of Public Administration, Columbia University, pp. 171–179.

Lee, John, ed. 1928. *Dictionary of Industrial Administration: A Comprehensive Encyclopaedia of the Organisation, Administration, and Management of Modern Industry.* 2 vols. London: Sir Isaac Pitman & Sons.

Levine, A. L. 1967. *Industrial Retardation in Britain 1880–1914.* New York: Basic.

Lewchuk, Wayne. 1983. "Fordism and the British motor car employers 1896–1932." In Howard F. Gospel, and Craig R. Littler, eds., *Managerial Strategies and Industrial Relations: An Historical and Comparative Study.* London: Heinemann, pp. 82–110.

————. 1987. *American Technology and the British Vehicle Industry.* Cambridge: Cambridge University Press.

Lewis, J. Slater. 1896. *The Commercial Organisation of Factories.* London: E. & F. N. Spon.

Littler, Craig. 1982b. "Deskilling and Changing Structures of Control." In Stephen Wood, ed., *The Degradation of Work? Skill, Deskilling and the Labour Process.* London: Hutchinson, pp. 122–145.

Loader, Colin. 1985. *The Intellectual Development of Karl Mannheim: Culture, Politics, and Planning.* Cambridge: Cambridge University Press.

McGivering, I. C., D. G. J. Matthews, and W. H. Scott. 1960. *Management in Britain: A General Characterisation.* Liverpool: Liverpool University Press.

Macmillan, Harold. 1934. *Reconstruction: A Plea for a National Policy.* London: Macmillan.

Marks, Winifred Rose. 1978. *Politics and Personnel Management: An Outline History, 1960–1976.* London: Institute of Personnel Management.

Melman, Seymour. 1956. *Dynamic Factors in Industrial Productivity.* Oxford: Basil Blackwell.

Mitchell, B. R. 1962. *Abstract of British Historical Statistics.* With the collaboration of Phyllis Deane. Cambridge: Cambridge University Press.

————. 1971. *Second Abstract of British Historical Statistics.* Cambridge: Cambridge University Press.

Moseley, Maboth. 1964. *Irascible Genius: The Life of Charles Babbage.* Chicago: Henry Regnery.

Myers, Charles S. 1918. *Present-Day Applications of Psychology.* London: Methuen.

———. 1920. *Mind and Work: The Psychological Factors in Industry and Commerce.* London: University of London Press.

———. 1926. *Industrial Psychology.* New York: The People's Institute.

———. [1926] 1933. *Industrial Psychology in Great Britain.* 2d ed. London: Jonathan Cape.

———. 1932. *Business Rationalisation: Its Dangers and Advantages Considered from the Psychological and Social Standpoints.* London: Sir Isaac Pitman & Sons.

———. 1933. *A Psychologist's Point of View: Twelve Semi-Popular Addresses on Various Subjects.* London: William Heinemann.

Myers, Charles S., Frank N. Freeman, and Morris S. Viteles. 1941. *Modern Psychology.* Philadelphia: University of Pennsylvania Press.

New Statesman. 1916. "Scientific management." *The New Statesman* 7(167) (June 17):259–260.

Niven, M. M. 1967. *Personnel Management 1913–63: The Growth of Personnel Management and the Development of the Institute.* London: Institute of Personnel Management.

Northcott, Clarence H. 1928. "Principles and practice of industrial relations." In Clarence H. Northcott et al., *Factory Organisation.* London: Sir Isaac Pitman & Sons, pp. 106–153.

———. 1945. *Personnel Management: Its Scope and Practice.* New York: Pitman Publishing.

———. 1958. *Christian Principles in Industry: Their Application in Practice.* London: Sir Isaac Pitman & Sons.

Orwell, George. [1946] 1968. "James Burnham and the managerial revolution." In *The Collected Essays, Journalism and Letters of George Orwell.* Vol. 4. *In Front of Your Nose, 1945–1950.* London: Secker & Warburg, pp. 160–181.

———. 1949. *Nineteen Eight-Four.* London: Secker & Warburg.

Parker, Hugh. 1967. "Can British management close the gap?" *McKinsey Quarterly* 4(1) (Summer):38–44.

Parkinson, C. Northcote. 1957. *Parkinson's Law and Other Studies in Administration.* Boston: Houghton Mifflin.

Paul, W. J., and K. B. Robertson. 1970. *Job Enrichment and Employee Motivation.* London: Gower.

Payne, Peter L. 1978. "Industrial entrepreneurship and management in Great Britain." In Peter Mathias and M. M. Postan, eds., *The Cambridge Economic History of Europe.* Vol. 7. *The Industrial Economies: Capital, Labour, and Enterprise. Part 1: Britain, France, Germany, and Scandinavia.* Cambridge: Cambridge University Press, pp. 180–230.

Pelling, Henry. [1963] 1976. *A History of British Trade Unionism.* 3d ed. London: Macmillan.

Pevsner, Nikolaus. 1937. *An Enquiry into Industrial Art in England.* Cambridge: Cambridge University Press.

Pollard, Sidney. [1962] 1969. *The Development of the British Economy 1914–1967.* 2d ed. New York: St. Martin's.

———. 1965. *The Genesis of Modern Management: A Study of the Industrial Revolution in Great Britain.* Cambridge, Massachusetts: Harvard University Press.

———. 1978. "Labour in Great Britain." In Peter Mathias and M. M. Postan, eds., *The Cambridge Economic History of Europe.* Vol. 7. *The Industrial Economies: Capital, Labour, and Enterprise. Part 1: Britain, France, Germany, and Scandinavia.* Cambridge: Cambridge University Press, pp. 97–179.

Prais, S. J. 1976. *The Evolution of Giant Firms in Britain: A Study of the Growth of Concentration in Manufacturing Industry in Britain 1909–70.* Cambridge: Cambridge University Press.

Pugh, D. S., and D. J. Hickson. 1976. *Organizational Structure in its Context: The Aston Programme I.* Westmead, Farnborough, Hants, England: Saxon House.

Pugh, D. S., and C. R. Hinings. 1976. *Organizational Structure: Extensions and Replications: The Aston Programme II.* Westmead, Farnborough, Hants, England: Saxon House.

Pugh, D. S., and R. L. Payne. 1977. *Organizational Structure in its Context: The Aston Programme III.* Westmead, Farnborough, Hants, England: Saxon House.

Pugh, D. S., et al. 1963. "A conceptual scheme for organizational analysis." *Administrative Science Quarterly* 8(3) (December):289–315.

———. 1968. "Dimensions of organizational structure." *Administrative Science Quarterly* 13(1) (June):63–105.

———. 1969a. "The context of organization structures." *Administrative Science Quarterly* 14(1) (March):91–114.

———. 1969b. "An empirical taxonomy of structures of work organizations." *Administrative Science Quarterly* 14(1) (March):115–126.

Ramsay, Harvie. 1977. "Cycles of control: Worker participation in sociological and historical perspective." *Sociology* 11(3) (September):481–506.

Read, Herbert. [1934] 1954. *Art and Industry: The Principles of Industrial Design.* New York: Horizon.

Renold, Charles G. 1922. "Scientific management." *The Encyclopaedia Britannica.* 12th ed., new volumes, vol. 32, pp. 378–381.

———. 1948–1949. "The organizational structure of large undertakings: Management problems." *Winter Proceedings* No. 3. London: British Institute of Management.

———. 1949. *The Nature of Management.* London: British Institute of Management.

Revans, R. W. 1965. *Science and the Manager.* London: MacDonald.

———. 1966. *The Theory of Practice in Management.* London: MacDonald.

Rice, A. K. 1958. *Productivity and Social Organization: The Ahmedabad Experiment*. London: Tavistock.

———. 1965. *Learning for Leadership: Interpersonal and Intergroup Relations*. London: Tavistock.

Richardson, H. G. 1941. "Business training in medieval Oxford." *American Historical Review* 46(4):259–280.

Roberts, R. Lloyd. 1944. *The Human Problems of Management*. London: Institute of Personnel Management.

Rodgers, Terence. 1988. "Employers' organizations, unemployment and social politics in Britain during the inter-war period." *Social History* 13(3) (October):315–341.

Rose, Harold. 1970. *Management Education in the 1970s: Growth and Issues*. London: Her Majesty's Stationery Office.

Rostas, L. 1948. *Comparative Productivity in British and American Industry*. Cambridge: Cambridge University Press.

Rowntree, B. Seebohm. 1914. *The Way to Industrial Peace and the Problem of Unemployment*. London: T. Fisher Unwin.

———. 1920. "Social obligations of industry to labour." In A. E. Berriman et al., eds., *Industrial Administration: A Series of Lectures*. Manchester: Manchester University Press, pp. 1–21.

———. 1921a. *The Human Factor in Business*. London: Longmans, Green.

———. 1921b. *The Human Needs of Labour*. London: Thomas Nelson & Sons.

———. 1922. *Industrial Unrest: A Way Out*. New York: George H. Doran.

Schumacher, Ernst F. [1973] 1975. *Small Is Beautiful: Economics as if People Mattered*. New York: Harper & Row.

Schuster, George. 1951. *Christianity and Human Relations in Industry*. London: Epworth.

Sheldon, Oliver. 1923. "The art of management from a British point of view." *Bulletin of the Taylor Society* 8(6) (December):209–214.

———. 1924. *The Philosophy of Management*. London: Sir Isaac Pitman & Sons.

———. 1928. "The organisation of business control." In Clarence H. Northcott et al., *Factory Organisation*. London: Sir Isaac Pitman & Sons, pp. 8–61.

Silverman, David. 1971. *The Theory of Organisations: A Sociological Framework*. New York: Basic.

Smelser, Neil J. 1991. *Social Paralysis and Social Change: British Working-Class Education in the Nineteenth Century*. Berkeley: University of California Press.

Smith, Adam. [1776] 1976. *An Inquiry into the Nature and Causes of the Wealth of Nations*. 2 vols. General editors, R. H. Campbell and A. S. Skinner; textual editor, W. B. Todd. Oxford: Clarendon Press.

Smith, Peter B. 1964. "The T-group in industry." *The New Society* 97(August 6):11–13.

Stamp, Sir Josiah. 1926. *The Christian Ethic as an Economic Factor*. London: Epworth.

———. 1936. *Motive and Method in a Christian Order*. New York: Abingdon.

———. 1937. *The Science of Social Adjustment*. London: Macmillan.

———. 1938. *Christianity and Economics*. New York: Macmillan.

Stanworth, Philip, and Anthony Giddens, eds. 1974. *Elites and Power in British Society*. Cambridge: Cambridge University Press.

Stewart, Richard. 1987. *Design and British Industry*. London: John Murray.

Stewart, Rosemary. 1963. *The Reality of Management*. London: Heinemann.

———. 1970. *The Reality of Organizations: A Guide for Managers and Students*. London: Macmillan.

Stigler, George J. 1951. "The division of labor is limited by the extent of the market." *Journal of Political Economy* 59(3) (June):185–193.

Sussman, Herbert L. 1968. *Victorians and the Machine: The Literary Response to Technology*. Cambridge, Massachusetts: Harvard University Press.

Taylor, Gordon Rattray. 1950. *Are Workers Human?* London: Falcon.

Thomas, A. B. 1980. "Management and education: Rationalization and re-production in British business." *International Studies of Management and Organization* 10(1–2):71–109.

Thomas, Rosamund M. 1978. *The British Philosophy of Administration: A Comparison of British and American Ideas 1900–1939*. London: Longman.

Thompson, E. P. 1967. "Time, work-discipline, and industrial capitalism." *Past and Present* 38 (December):56–97.

TIHR (Tavistock Institute of Human Relations). 1950. *Development and Work: 1946–1950*. London: TIHR.

———. 1960. *Report for the Four Years October, 1956 to September, 1960*. London: TIHR.

———. 1962. *Report for the Year October, 1961 to September, 1962*. London: TIHR.

———. 1964. *Report for the Year October, 1963 to September, 1964*. London: TIHR.

Tolliday, Steven. 1987. "Management and Labour in Britain 1896–1939." In Steven Tolliday and Jonathan Zeitlin, eds., *The Automobile Industry and Its Workers*. New York: St. Martin's Press, pp. 29–56.

Tredgold, R. F. [1949] 1963. *Human Relations in Modern Industry*. New York: International Universities Press.

Trist, Eric L., and K. W. Bamforth. 1951. "Some social and psychological consequences of the longwall method of coal-getting." *Human Relations* 4(1) (November):3–38.

Trist, Eric L., G. W. Higgin, H. Murray, and A. B. Pollock. 1963. *Organizational Choice: Capabilities of Groups at the Coal Face Under Changing Technologies*. London: Tavistock.

Trist, Eric L., and Hugh Murray, eds. 1990. "Historical overview: The foundation and development of the Tavistock Institute." In *The Social Engage-

ment of Social Science: A Tavistock Anthology. Vol. 1. *The Socio-Psychological Perspective.* Philadelphia: University of Pennsylvania Press, pp. 1–34.

Trist, Eric L., and C. Sofer. 1957. *Group Relations Training: A Pilot Experiment.* London: Tavistock.

TUC (Trades Union Congress). 1950. *Trade Unions and Productivity.* London: British Trades Union Congress.

Urwick, Lyndall. 1929. *The Meaning of Rationalisation.* London: Nisbet.

———. 1933. *Management of Tomorrow.* London: Nisbet.

———. 1937. "Organization as a technical problem." In Luther Gulick and Lyndall Urwick, eds., *Papers on the Science of Administration.* New York: Institute of Public Administration, Columbia University, pp. 47–88.

———. 1938. *The Development of Scientific Management in Great Britain.* London: Management Journals.

———. 1944. *The Elements of Administration.* New York and London: Harper & Brothers.

———. 1956. *The Pattern of Management.* Minneapolis: University of Minnesota Press.

———. 1957. *Leadership in the Twentieth Century.* New York: Pitman.

Urwick, L., and E. F. L. Brech. 1946. *The Making of Scientific Management.* Vol. 2. *Management in British Industry.* London: Management Publications Trust.

Vernon, H. M. 1921. *Industrial Fatigue and Efficiency.* London: George Routledge & Sons.

———. 1940. *The Health and Efficiency of Munition Workers.* London: Oxford University Press.

Vickers, Sir Geoffrey. 1965. *The Art of Judgment: A Study of Policy Making.* New York: Basic.

———. 1967. *Towards a Sociology of Management.* New York: Basic.

———. 1968. *Value Systems and Social Process.* New York: Basic.

———. 1973. *Making Institutions Work.* New York: John Wiley & Sons.

Wallas Graham. 1914. *The Great Society: A Psychological Analysis.* New York: Macmillan.

———. 1921. *Our Social Heritage.* New Haven, Connecticut: Yale University Press.

———. 1935. *Social Judgment.* New York: Harcourt, Brace.

Walton, R. E., et al. 1969. "The management of interdepartmental conflict: A model and review." *Administrative Science Quarterly* 14(1) (March): 73–84.

Watson, Tony J. 1977. *The Personnel Managers: A Study in the Sociology of Work and Employment.* London: Routledge & Kegan Paul.

Webb, Sidney. [1917] 1979. *The Works Manager To-Day: An Address Prepared for a Series of Private Gatherings of Works Managers.* In Alfred Chandler, ed., *Management Thought in Great Britain.* New York: Arno, vi + 157 pp.

Welch, Henry J., and Charles S. Myers. 1932. *Ten Years of Industrial Psychol-*

ogy: An Account of the First Decade of the National Institute of Industrial Psychology. London: Sir Isaac Pitman & Sons.

Whalley, Peter. 1990. "Markets, managers, and technical autonomy in British plants." In Sharon Zukin and Paul DiMaggio, eds., *Structures of Capital.* New York: Cambridge University Press, pp. 373–394.

Wiener, Martin J. [1981] 1985. *English Culture and the Decline of the Industrial Spirit 1850–1980.* London: Penguin.

Wilkinson, Rupert. 1964. *Gentlemanly Power: British Leadership and the Public School Tradition.* London: Oxford University Press.

Williams, L. J. 1971. *Britain and the World Economy, 1919–1970.* London: Fontana/Collins.

Wilson, Sir Arnold, and Hermann Levy. 1937. *Industrial Assurance: An Historical and Critical Study.* London: Oxford University Press.

———. 1939. *Workmen's Compensation.* 2 vols. London: Oxford University Press.

Wood, Barbara. 1984. *E. F. Schumacher: His Life and Thought.* New York: Harper & Row.

Wood, Stephen, ed. 1982. *The Degradation of Work? Skill, Deskilling, and the Labour Process.* London: Hutchinson.

Woodward, Joan. 1950. *Employment Relations in a Group of Hospitals.* London: The Institute of Hospital Administrators.

———. 1956. *The Dock Worker: An Analysis of Conditions of Employment in the Port of Manchester.* Liverpool: Liverpool University Press.

———. 1958. *Management and Technology.* London: Her Majesty's Stationery Office.

———. 1960. *The Saleswoman: A Study of Attitudes and Behaviour in Retail Distribution.* London: Pitman.

———. [1965] 1980. *Industrial Organization: Theory and Practice.* 2d ed. Oxford: Oxford University Press.

Woodward, Joan, ed. 1970. *Industrial Organization: Behavior and Control.* Oxford: Oxford University Press.

Wyatt, Stanley. 1944. *A Study of Variations in Output.* London: His Majesty's Stationery Office.

Young, A. P. 1949. *American Management Techniques and Practices and Their Bearing on Productivity in British Industry: A Survey.* London: Institution of Works Managers.

G. BRAZIL

Baer, Werner. 1989. *The Brazilian Economy: Growth and Development.* 3d ed., updated and enlarged. New York: Praeger.

Campa, José Manuel. 1990. "Exchange rates and economic recovery in the 1930s: An extension to Latin America." *Journal of Economic History* 10(3) (September):677–682.

Cordeiro, Laerte Leite. 1968. *Administração geral e relaçoes industriais na pequena empresa brasileira.* Rio de Janeiro: Fundação Getúlio Vargas.

Dean, Warren. 1969. *The Industrialization of São Paulo, 1880–1945.* Austin: University of Texas Press.

Erickson, Kenneth Paul. 1977. *The Brazilian Corporative State and Working-Class Politics.* Berkeley: University of California Press.

Guzzo Decca, Maria Auxiliadora. 1987. *A vida fora fábricas: Cotidiano operário em São Paulo, 1920–1934.* Rio de Janeiro: Paz e Terra.

Pinheiro, Paulo Sérgio de M. S., et al. 1979. *A classe operaria no Brasil: Documentos, 1889 a 1930.* Vol. 1. *O movimiento operário.* São Paulo: Editora Alfa Omega.

———. 1981. *A classe operaria no Brasil: Documentos, 1889 a 1930.* Vol. 2. *Condições de vida e de trabalho, relações com os empresários e o Estado.* São Paulo: Editora Brasiliense.

ROC. 1932. "Instituto de Organisação Racional do Trabalho de São Paulo." *Revista de Organisação Cientifica* 1(1) (January):35–38.

Saenz Leme, Marisa. 1978. *A ideologia dos industriais brasileiros, 1919–1945.* Petrópolis: Vozes.

Shapiro, Helen. 1989. "State intervention and industrialization: The origins of the Brazilian automotive industry." (Summary of Ph.D. diss.) *Journal of Economic History* 49(2) (June):448–450.

Skidmore, Thomas E., and Peter H. Smith. 1989. "Brazil: Development For Whom?" In *Modern Latin America.* New York: Oxford University Press, pp. 140–180.

Weinstein, Barbara. 1990. "The industrialists, the state, and the issues of worker training and social services in Brazil, 1930–1950." *Hispanic American Historical Review* 70(3) (August):379–404.

H. FRANCE

Boesiger, W., and H. Girsberger. 1967. *Le Corbusier 1910–65.* New York: Praeger.

Boltanski, Luc. 1982. *Les cadres: La formation d'un groupe social.* Paris: Les Éditions de Minuit.

———. 1990. "Visions of American management in postwar France." In Sharon Zukin and Paul DiMaggio, eds., *Structures of Capital.* New York: Cambridge University Press, pp. 343–372.

Brooks, H. Allen, ed. 1987. *Le Corbusier.* Princeton, New Jersey: Princeton University Press.

Confédération Générale du Travail. 1978. *Des manufactures à la crise du Taylorisme: Contribution à l'étude de la crise des conditions de travail.* Paris: Centre Confédéral d'Etudes Economiques et Sociales de la CGT.

Fohlen, Claude. 1970. "The Industrial Revolution in France, 1700–1914." *The Fontana Economic History of Europe.* Vol. 4. London: Collins.

———. 1973. "France, 1920–1970." *The Fontana Economic History of Europe.* Vol. 6. London: Collins.

———. 1978. "Entrepreneurship and management in France in the nineteenth century." In Peter Mathias and M. M. Postan, eds., *The Cambridge Economic History of Europe.* Vol. 7. *The Industrial Economies: Capital, La-*

bour, and Enterprise. Part 1: Britain, France, Germany, and Scandinavia. Cambridge: Cambridge University Press, pp. 347–381.

Friedmann, Georges. [1947] 1977. *Industrial Society: The Emergence of the Human Problems of Automation.* Edited with an introduction by Harold L. Sheppard. New York: Arno.

———. [1956] 1964. *The Anatomy of Work: Labor, Leisure and the Implications of Automation.* Trans. by Wyatt Rawson. New York: Free Press of Glencoe.

Green, Christopher. 1976. *Léger and the Avant-Garde.* New Haven, Connecticut: Yale University Press.

Humphreys, George C. 1986. *Taylorism in France 1904–1920: The Impact of Scientific Management on Factory Relations and Society.* New York: Garland.

IMI. 1930. *Le controle budgetaire des entreprises Hans Renold Limited.* Geneva: International Management Institute.

Le Corbusier (Charles Edouard Jeanneret). [1923] 1986. *Towards a New Architecture.* New York: Dover.

———. [1924] 1987. *The City of To-Morrow and Its Planning.* New York: Dover.

Lequin, Yves. 1978. "Labour in the French economy since the revolution." In Peter Mathias and M. M. Postan, eds., *The Cambridge Economic History of Europe.* Vol. 7. *The Industrial Economies: Capital, Labour, and Enterprise. Part 1: Britain, France, Germany, and Scandinavia.* Cambridge: Cambridge University Press, pp. 296–346.

Marc, Maurice. 1974. "Conditions de travail: Le taylorisme en question. Numéro special." *Sociologie du Travail* 16(4) (October–December).

Montmollin, Maurice de. 1981. *Le Taylorisme à visage humain.* Paris: Presses Universitaires de France.

Moss, Bernard H. 1976. *The Origins of the French Labor Movement, 1830–1914: The Socialism of Skilled Workers.* Berkeley: University of California Press.

Schmalenbach, Werner. 1985. *Fernand Léger.* Trans. by Robert Allen, with James Emmons. New York: Abrams.

Trepo, Georges. 1979. "Improvement of working conditions and job redesign in France." In C. Cooper and E. Mumford, eds., *The Quality of Working Life in Western and Eastern Europe.* London: Associated Press, pp. 159–179.

I. ITALY

Ammassari, Paolo. 1969. "The Italian blue-collar worker." *International Journal of Comparative Sociology* 10(1–2) (June):3–21.

Buselli, G., R. Finzi, and G. Predrocco. 1976. *Materiali per lo studio dell'organizzazione del lavoro durante il regime fascista.* Bologna: Cooperativa Libraria Universitaria Editrice.

Cafagna, Luciano. 1971. "The Industrial Revolution in Italy, 1830–1914." *The Fontana Economic History of Europe.* Vol. 4. London: Collins.

Cannistraro, Philip V., ed. 1982. *Historical Dictionary of Fascist Italy.* Westport, Connecticut: Greenwood Press.

Capecchi, Vittorio. 1989. "The informal economy and the development of flexible specialization in Emilia-Romagna." In Alejandro Portes, Manuel Castells, and Lauren A. Benton, eds., *The Informal Economy: Studies in Advanced and Less Developed Countries*. Baltimore, Maryland: The Johns Hopkins University Press, pp. 189–215.

Celant, Germano, and Ida Gianelli. 1990. *Memoria del futuro: Arte italiano desde las primeras vanguardias a la posguerra*. Milano and Madrid: Bompiani/Centro de Arte Reina Sofía.

Clark, M. 1977. *Antonio Gramsci and the Revolution that Failed*. New Haven, Connecticut: Yale University Press.

De Grazia, Victoria. 1981. *The Culture of Consent: Mass Organization of Leisure in Fascist Italy*. Cambridge: Cambridge University Press.

Derossi, Flavia. 1982. *The Technocratic Illusion: A Study of Managerial Power in Italy*. Armonk, New York: M. E. Sharpe.

Dubla, Ferdinando. 1986. *Gramsci e la fabbrica*. Manduria: Lacaita.

Ferraresi, Franco, and Giovanni Gasparini. 1976. "The present state of organizational sociology in Italy." In Geert Hofstede and M. S. Kassem, eds., *European Contributions to Organization Theory*. Assen, The Netherlands: Van Gorcum, pp. 208–230.

Gentile, Emilio. 1975. *Le origini dell' ideologia fascista*. Roma: Laterza.

Gramsci, Antonio. [1964] 1971. "Americanism and Fordism." In *Selections from the Prison Notebooks*. New York: International Publishers, pp. 279–322.

J. 1914. "Il sistema Taylor." *L'Economista* 41 (November 8):712–713.

Joll, James. 1960. "F. T. Marinetti: Futurism and Fascism." In *Intellectuals in Politics: Three Biographical Essays*. London: Weidenfeld and Nicolson, pp. 131–178.

Lyttelton, Adrian. 1976. "Italian Fascism." In Walter Laqueur, ed., *Fascism: A Reader's Guide*. Berkeley: University of California Press, pp. 125–150.

Marinetti, Fillipo Tommaso. [1909] 1983. *Manifesto of Futurism*. New Haven, Connecticut: Silliman College Press for the Yale Library Associates.

———. [1914] 1980. *Messagio*. Reprinted in Reyner Banham, *Theory and Design in the First Machine Age*. 2d ed. Cambridge, Massachusetts: MIT Press, pp. 128–130.

Milward, Alan S. 1976. "Fascism and the economy." In Walter Laqueur, ed., *Fascism: A Reader's Guide*. Berkeley: University of California Press, pp. 379–412.

Mortara, Vittorio. 1973. *L'analisi delle strutture organizzative*. Bologne: Il Mulino.

Olivetti, Adriano. [1928] 1976. "L'Organizzazione in una fabbrica italiana de macchine per scrivere." *L'Organizzazione Scientifica del Lavoro* 10:616–628. Reprinted in G. Buselli, R. Finzi, and G. Predrocco, eds., *Materiali per lo studio dell'organizzazione del lavoro durante il regime fascista*. Bologna: Cooperativa Libraria Universitaria Editrice, pp. 119–131.

Pedrocco, G. 1976. "Introduzione: L'Organizzazione scientifica del lavoro in Italia dal decollo industriale all Seconda Guerra Mondiale." In G. Buselli, R. Finzi, and G. Predrocco, eds., *Materiali per lo studio dell'organizzazione del lavoro durante il regime fascista*. Bologna: Cooperativa Libraria Universitaria Editrice, pp. 5–16.

Ricossa, Sergio. 1973. "Italy, 1920–1970." *The Fontana Economic History of Europe*. Vol. 6. London: Collins.

Rollier, Matteo. 1979. "Taylorism and the Italian Unions." In C. Cooper and E. Mumford, eds., *The Quality of Working Life in Western and Eastern Europe*. London: Associated Press, pp. 214–225.

Sapelli, Giulio. 1976. "Appunti per una storia dell'organizzazione scientifica del lavoro in Italia." *Quaderni di Sociologia* 25 (April–September): 154–171.

———. 1978. *Organizzazione lavoro e innovazione industriale nell'Italia tra le due guerre*. Torino: Rosenberg & Sellier.

Steri, Francesco. 1979. *Taylorismo e fascismo*. Roma: Editrice Sindacale Italiana.

Talamo, Magda. 1979. *I dirigenti idustriali in Italia: Autoritá, comando e responsabilitá sociali*. Torino: Einaudi.

Tessari, Roberto, ed. 1976. *Letteratura e industria*. Bologne: Zanichelli.

J. JAPAN

Azumi, Koya. 1969. *Higher Education and Business Recruitment in Japan*. New York: Teachers College Press.

Cusumano, Michael A. 1985. *The Japanese Automobile Industry: Technology and Management at Nissan and Toyota*. Cambridge, Massachusetts: The Council on East Asian Studies and Harvard University Press.

Dohse, Knuth, Ulrich Jürgens, and Thomas Malsch. 1985. "From 'Fordism' to 'Toyotism'? The social organization of the labor process in the Japanese automobile industry." *Politics & Society* 14(2):115–146.

Evans, Robert, Jr. 1970. "Evolution of the Japanese system of employer-employee relations, 1868–1945." *Business History Review* 44(1) (Spring): 110–125.

Friedman, David. 1988. *The Misunderstood Miracle: Industrial Development and Political Change in Japan*. Ithaca, New York: Cornell University Press.

Gerlach, Michael L. 1992. *Alliance Capitalism: The Social Organization of Japanese Business*. Berkeley: University of California Press.

Gordon, Andrew. 1985. *The Evolution of Labor Relations in Japan: Heavy Industry, 1853–1955*. Cambridge, Massachusetts: Council on East Asian Studies, Harvard University.

———. 1989. "Araki Tōichirō and the shaping of labor management." In Tsunehiko Yui and Keiichiro Nakagawa, eds., *Japanese Management in Historical Perpsective. The International Conference on Business History 15. Proceedings of the Fuji Conference*. Tokyo: University of Tokyo Press, pp. 173–191.

———. 1991. *Labor and Imperial Democracy in Prewar Japan*. Berkeley: University of California Press.

Hazama, Hiroshi (with Jacqueline Kaminski). 1979. "Japanese labor-management relations and Uno Riemon." *Journal of Japanese Studies* 5(1) (Winter):71–106.

Johnson, Chalmers. 1982. *MITI and the Japanese Miracle: The Growth of Industrial Policy, 1925–1975*. Stanford, California: Stanford University Press.

JPC (Japan Productivity Center). 1960. *Personnel Management Study in Japan, 1960*. Tokyo: JPC.

Kamata, Satoshi. [1973] 1982. *Japan in the Passing Lane: An Insider's Account of Life in a Japanese Auto Factory*. New York: Pantheon.

Kenney, Martin, and Richard Florida. 1993. *Beyond Mass Production: The Japanese System and Its Transfer to the U.S.* New York: Oxford University Press.

Kono, Toyohiro. 1984. *Strategy and Structure of Japanese Enterprises*. Armonk, New York: M. E. Sharpe.

Nakase, Toshikazu. 1979. "The introduction of Scientific Management in Japan and its characteristics—Case studies of companies in the Sumitomo Zaibatsu." In Keiichiro Nakagawa, ed., *The International Conference on Business History 4: Labor and Management. Proceedings of the Fourth Fuji Conference*. Tokyo: University of Tokyo Press, pp. 171–202.

NMAJ (National Management Association of Japan). 1935. *The Rationalization Movement in Japan*. Tokyo: NMAJ.

Noda, Nobuo. 1969. *How Japan Absorbed American Management Methods*. Tokyo: Asian Productivity Organization.

Okuda, Kenji. 1971a. "Managerial evolution in Japan. I: 1911–1925." *Management Japan* 5(3):13–19.

———. 1971b. "Managerial evolution in Japan. II: 1926–1945." *Management Japan* 5(4):16–23.

———. 1989. "Comment." In Tsunehiko Yui and Keiichiro Nakagawa, eds., *Japanese Management in Historical Perspective. The International Conference on Business History 15. Proceedings of the Fuji Conference*. Tokyo: University of Tokyo Press, pp. 192–196.

Sasaki, Satoshi. 1987. "Scientific management movement in pre-war Japan." *Japanese Yearbook on Business History* 4:50–76.

Suzuki, Y. 1980. "The strategy and structure of top 100 Japanese industrial enterprises 1950–1970." *Strategic Management Journal* 1(3) (July–September):265–291.

Taira, Koji. 1978. "Factory labour and the Industrial Revolution in Japan." In Peter Mathias and M. M. Postan, eds., *The Cambridge Economic History of Europe*. Vol. 7. *The Industrial Economies: Capital, Labour, and Enterprise. Part 2: The United States, Japan, and Russia*. Cambridge: Cambridge University Press, pp. 166–214.

Tsuchiya, Moriaki. 1979. "Comments." In Keiichiro Nakagawa, ed., *The International Conference on Business History 4: Labor and Management. Proceedings of the Fourth Fuji Conference*. Tokyo: University of Tokyo Press, pp. 203–205.

Westney, D. Eleanor. 1987. *Imitation and Innovation: The Transfer of Western*

Organizational Patterns to Meiji Japan. Cambridge, Massachusetts: Harvard University Press.

Yamamura, Kozo. 1978. "Entrepreneurship, ownership, and management in Japan." In Peter Mathias and M. M. Postan, eds., *The Cambridge Economic History of Europe.* Vol. 7. *The Industrial Economies: Capital, Labour, and Enterprise. Part 2: The United States, Japan, and Russia.* Cambridge: Cambridge University Press, pp. 215–264.

Yamazaki, Hiroaki. 1989. "The development of large enterprises in Japan: An analysis of the top 50 enterprises in the profit ranking table 1929–1984." *Japanese Yearbook on Business History* 5:12–55.

Yoshino, M. Y. 1968. *Japan's Managerial System: Tradition and Innovation.* Cambridge, Massachusetts: MIT Press.

Yui, Tsunehiko. 1989. "Development, organization, and business strategy of industrial enterprises in Japan 1915–1935." *Japanese Yearbook on Business History* 5:56–87.

K. SOVIET UNION

Andrews, Richard, and Milena Kalinovska, eds. 1990. *Art into Life: Russian Constructivism 1914–1932.* New York: Rizzoli.

Bailes, Kendall E. 1977. "Alexei Gastev and the Soviet controversy over Taylorism, 1918–24." *Soviet Studies* 29(3) (July):373–394.

Bann, Stephen, ed. 1974. *The Tradition of Constructivism.* New York: Viking.

Barron, Stephanie, and Maurice Tuchman, eds. 1980. *The Avant-Garde in Russia, 1910–1930: New Perspectives.* Los Angeles: The Los Angeles County Museum of Art.

Baumgarten, Franciska. 1924. *Arbeitswissenschaft und Psychotechnik in Russland.* Munich and Berlin: R. Oldenbourg.

Beissinger, Mark R. 1988. *Scientific Management, Socialist Discipline, and Soviet Power.* Cambridge, Massachusetts: Harvard University Press.

Berliner, Joseph S. 1988. *Soviet Industry from Stalin to Gorbachev: Essays on Management and Innovation.* Ithaca, New York: Cornell University Press.

Bhérer, Harold. 1982. *Management soviétique: Administration et planification.* Québec, Canada: Flemy-Presses de la Fondation Nationale des Sciences Politiques (Paris).

Bienstock, Gregory, Solomon M. Schwartz, and Aaron Yugow. 1944. *Management in Russian Industry and Agriculture.* London: Oxford University Press.

Bogomólova, N. 1977. *La doctrina de las "relaciones humanas": Arma ideológica de los monopolios.* Havana: Departamento de Orientación Revolucionaria del Comité Central del Partido Comunista de Cuba.

Bowlt, John E. [1976] 1988. *Russian Art of the Avant Garde.* New York: Thames and Hudson.

Bowra, Cecil Maurice. 1948. *A Second Book of Russian Verse.* London: Macmillan.

Brown, Geoff. 1977. "Stakhanovism or Socialism?" In *Sabotage: A Study in Industrial Conflict.* Nottingham: Spokesman, pp. 252–267.

Conyngham, William J. 1982. *The Modernization of Soviet Industrial Manage-*

ment: Socioeconomic Development and the Search for Viability. Cambridge: Cambridge University Press.

Crisp, Olga. 1978. "Labour and Industrialization in Russia." In Peter Mathias and M. M. Postan, eds., *The Cambridge Economic History of Europe.* Vol. 7. *The Industrial Economies: Capital, Labour, and Enterprise. Part 2: The United States. Japan, and Russia.* Cambridge: Cambridge University Press, pp. 308–415.

Dobb, Maurice. [1948] 1966. *Soviet Economic Development since 1917.* 6th ed. London: Routledge & Kegan Paul.

Ebbinghaus, Angelika. 1975. "Taylor in Russland." *Autonomie* 1:3–15.

Fülöp-Miller, René. 1965. *The Mind and Face of Bolshevism: An Examination of Cultural Life in Soviet Russia.* New York: Harper & Row.

Gloeckner, Eduard. 1981. *Der sowjetische Ingenieur in der industriellen Arbeitswelt.* Berlin: Osteuropa Institut.

Gvishiani, Jermen M., and Gavriil Kr. Popov. 1976. "Developments in the theory of management within the planned socialist economy." In Geert Hofstede and M. S. Kassem, eds., *European Contributions to Organization Theory.* Assen, The Netherlands: Van Gorcum, pp. 160–171.

Kahn, Selirn O. 1982. *Pioneers of Soviet Architecture.* New York: Rizzoli.

Kaser, M. C. 1978. "Russian entrepreneurship." In Peter Mathias and M. M. Postan, eds., *The Cambridge Economic History of Europe.* Vol. 7. *The Industrial Economies: Capital, Labour, and Enterprise. Part 2: The United States, Japan, and Russia.* Cambridge: Cambridge University Press, pp. 416–493.

Kopp, Anatole. 1985. *Constructivist Architecture in the USSR.* New York: St. Martin's.

Leites, Nathan. 1985. *Soviet Style in Management.* New York: Crane Russak.

Lenin, Vladimir I. 1971. *Selected Works.* New York: International Publishers.

Lieberstein, Samuel. 1975. "Technology, work, and sociology in the USSR: The NOT movement." *Technology and Culture* 16(1) (January):48–66.

Lorenz, Richard, ed. 1969. *Proletarische Kulturrevolution in Sowjetrußland (1917–1921): Dokumente des "Proletkult."* Munich: Deutscher Taschenbuch Verlag.

Marshall, Herbert, ed. 1942. *Mayakovsky and his Poetry.* London: Pilot.

Milner, Boris Zakharovich. 1986. *Design of Management Systems in USSR Industry: A Systems Approach.* Boston: Reidel.

Siebel, Werner. 1981. "Maschinenmensch und Zeitliga: Bemühungen Gastevs um die Industrialisierung von Lebens- und Arbeitsweisen nach der russischen Revolution." *Ästhetik und Kommunikation* 45–46:20–21.

Tatar, Melanie. 1979. *Wissenschaftliche Arbeitsorganisation: Arbeitswissenschaften und Arbeitsorganisation in der Sowjetunion 1921–1935.* Wiesbaden: Hanassowitz.

Thompson, James Clay. 1983. *Administrative Science & Politics in the USSR & the United States: Soviet Responses to American Management Techniques, 1917–Present.* New York: Praeger.

Traub, Rainer. 1978. "Lenin and Taylor: The fate of 'Scientific Management' in the (early) Soviet Union." *Telos* 37 (Fall):82–92.

Voloshin, A. 1950. *Kuznetsk Land*. Trans. by Rose Prokofieva. *Soviet Literature* 7 (1950):3–152.

L. OTHER COUNTRIES

Autorenkollektiv. 1974. *Intensivierung durch Rationalisierung: Erfahrungen und Probleme der Leitung in sozialistischen Betrieben und Kombinaten*. Berlin: Dietz.

Baylis, Thomas A. 1974. *The Technical Intelligentsia and the East German Elite: Legitimacy and Social Change in Mature Communism*. Berkeley: University of California Press.

Bloemen, Erik Sybrand Arnold. 1988. *Scientific Management in Nederland 1900–1930*. Amsterdam: NEHA.

Blom, Raimo, et al. 1991. "The economic system and the work situation: A comparison of Finland and Estonia." *International Sociology* 6(3) (September):343–360.

Deppe, Rainer, and Dietrich Hoss. 1980. *Sozialistische Rationalisierung: Leistungspolitik und Arbeitsgestaltung in der DDR*. Frankfurt a. d. Main and New York: Campus Verlag.

FORDC. 1965. *El trabajo en Cuba socialista*. Miami, Florida: Frente Obrero Revolucionario Democrático Cubano.

González Rodríguez, Lázaro. 1977. *La introducción de los principios básicos de la organización científica del trabajo en la economía cubana*. Havana: Editorial de Ciencias Sociales.

James, Daniel. 1981. "Rationalisation and working class response: The context and limits of factory floor activity in Argentina." *Journal of Latin American Studies* 13(2) (November):375–402.

Jaun, Rudolf. 1986. *Management und Arbeiterschaft: Verwissenschaftlichung, Amerikanisierung und Rationalisierung der Arbeitsverhaltnisse in der Schweiz, 1873–1959*. Zurich: Chronos.

Landsberger, Henry A., and Raúl Dastres. 1964. *La situación actual y el pensamiento del administrador de personal chileno: Un informe preliminar*. Santiago: Instituto de Organización y Administración de Empresas (INSORA) de la Universidad de Chile.

Piorkowsky, Michael-Burkhard. 1980. *Sozialistische Warenproduktion und Betriebswirtschaftslehre: Zur Entwicklung der Unternehmen und der Unternehmenstheorie im Sozialismus sowjetischen Typs*. Berlin: Duncker und Humblot.

INDEX

407